So Help Us, God

So Help Us, God

American Presidents and the Bible

Carl J. Richard

ROWMAN & LITTLEFIELD
Lanham • Boulder • New York • London

Rowman & Littlefield
Bloomsbury Publishing Inc, 1385 Broadway, New York, NY 10018, USA
Bloomsbury Publishing Plc, 50 Bedford Square, London, WC1B 3DP, UK
Bloomsbury Publishing Ireland, 29 Earlsfort Terrace, Dublin 2, D02 AY28, Ireland
www.rowman.com

Copyright © 2025 by The Rowman & Littlefield Publishing Group, Inc.

All rights reserved. No part of this publication may be: i) reproduced or transmitted in any form, electronic or mechanical, including photocopying, recording or by means of any information storage or retrieval system without prior permission in writing from the publishers; or ii) used or reproduced in any way for the training, development or operation of artificial intelligence (AI) technologies, including generative AI technologies. The rights holders expressly reserve this publication from the text and data mining exception as per Article 4(3) of the Digital Single Market Directive (EU) 2019/790.

British Library Cataloguing in Publication Information Available

Library of Congress Cataloging-in-Publication Data Available

ISBN 979-8-8818-0633-0 (cloth : alk. paper) | ISBN 979-8-8818-0634-7 (ebook)

For product safety related questions contact productsafety@bloomsbury.com.

∞™ The paper used in this publication meets the minimum requirements of American National Standard for Information Sciences—Permanence of Paper for Printed Library Materials, ANSI/NISO Z39.48-1992.

For Hansford Hair, a good man and a lifelong friend

Contents

	Preface	ix
	Introduction	xi
Chapter 1	Influences	1
Chapter 2	An Invaluable Guide	41
Chapter 3	Heroes and Villains	79
Chapter 4	Providence	101
Chapter 5	Prayer	129
Chapter 6	God-Given Rights and Equality	153
Chapter 7	Israels: Old, New, and Restored	177
Chapter 8	Faith, Morality, and the Survival of the Republic	213
Chapter 9	The Afterlife	245
Chapter 10	The Orthodox and the Unorthodox	259
Chapter 11	Human Nature and Balanced Government	289

Epilogue	305
Appendix I: Presidential Terms and Denominations	307
Appendix II: Cherished Scriptures	309
Notes	313
Index	387

Preface

Any volume that discusses the religious opinions of forty-five American presidents (Grover Cleveland is counted twice in the traditional numbering because his terms were nonconsecutive), whose lives spanned three centuries, cannot be comprehensive. This book can serve only as a starting point for the study of the presidents' relationship with the Bible.

In addition to discussing the presidents' use of the Bible in their political rhetoric, this book also examines the theological and moral principles they derived from Scripture. Focusing exclusively on the numerous verses the presidents cited and the various biblical figures to whom they alluded while neglecting to examine the ideas they derived from the Bible—ideas that were central to their worldviews and fundamental to the political systems they led—would leave a stunted and distorted impression of biblical influence.

Nearly all modern presidents, as well as some early ones, have employed speechwriters. Nevertheless, these presidents not only scrutinized and approved the addresses they delivered, but they often altered the wording to render them more compatible with their own beliefs and styles. For this reason, presidents' speeches generally comport well with their private letters and diary entries. Thus, in this volume, I have attributed statements made in presidential speeches to the presidents themselves.

I would like to thank Rowman & Littlefield Publishing Group for allowing me to reproduce from my previous book, *The Founders and the Bible* (2016), both the basic structure of this work and specific passages concerning the first five presidents, who were also founders. I would also like to express my deepest gratitude to two friends and admired colleagues who are experts in the field of American religious history, Daniel L. Dreisbach and Eran Shalev, for taking precious time from their busy schedules to critique the first draft of this manuscript. Their insights were invaluable. Additionally, I would like to thank my editor, Jon Sisk, for his unfailing enthusiasm and encouragement. As always, I would like to thank my precious wife, Debbie, my other half, for her unceasing prayers and support. As Proverbs 31:10–12 states regarding the good wife: "Her value is far above rubies. The heart of her husband safely trusts in her, so that he shall have great gain. She does him good and not harm all the days of her life."

Introduction

American presidents were raised in a biblical culture that pervaded their schools, homes, churches, and society. Until the mid-twentieth century, the curricula of most public schools included Bible reading. In the eighteenth and nineteenth centuries, most grammar schools and colleges even required the study of the New Testament in the original Greek.

Most presidents were profoundly influenced by devout parents and grandparents, who had inculcated biblical principles in the home, as well as by pious siblings and wives. A few were the sons of ministers; others, the brothers of clerics. Some were the sons of Sunday school teachers; others, their husbands. Some married pastors' daughters.

Most presidents attended church services throughout their lives, listening to sermons that quoted Scripture extensively. A few seriously considered entering the ministry. Several held church offices, such as elder, vestryman, warden, and trustee. A few even preached sermons. Several served as Sunday school teachers.

Religious revivals continually reenergized the biblical culture in which presidents were raised. These revivals led directly to the American Revolution, the Civil War, the Progressive Era, and the modern civil rights movement.

Given most presidents' immersion in Scripture as children, it is not surprising that many of them have considered the Bible an invaluable guide, an incomparable source of spiritual and moral wisdom. Several devoted the considerable time and effort required to read the Bible in other languages besides

English and the Greek they learned in school. Some, such as Abraham Lincoln, delivered speeches written in the style of the King James Bible, imbued them with biblical themes, and peppered them with scriptural quotations.

The fact that presidents have referred to biblical passages in private diaries and letters and that they have continued to refer to them long after their political careers ended testifies to the sincerity of their devotion to Scripture. Although socially and politically useful, most presidents' public references to the Bible were not mere formalities or exercises in political opportunism. In fact, many presidents took advantage of the greater leisure time afforded by retirement from political office to study the Bible. Furthermore, throughout their lives, many presidents have promoted the spread of biblical knowledge, not only in foreign nations via missionaries but among their own children and grandchildren and in American society generally, for they have deemed Christian faith crucial not only to the salvation of souls but also to fostering the morality that they have considered essential to the survival and success of the republic.

The Bible has furnished presidents a rich source from which to draw moral and political lessons, which they then applied to contemporary problems, both personal and political. Their political rhetoric has been suffused with biblical allusions intended to persuade their fellow citizens to pursue favored courses of action.

The Bible has facilitated communication by furnishing a common set of stories, knowledges, and ideas, a literature select enough to provide common ground yet rich enough to address a wide range of human problems from a variety of perspectives. Biblical stories and the lessons they impart have proved a vital source of unity in a nation whose people are separated from one another by vast stretches of terrain and are divided by an ever-increasing number of denominations. Scriptural references have also allowed presidents to impress audiences with their own piety and virtue and to appropriate the support of divine authority for their arguments and causes.

Furthermore, the Bible has supplied presidents with an invaluable resource in making sense of the confusing events of their day. Even those presidents who rejected fundamental biblical doctrines tended to view the Bible as a source of wisdom and to value the moral and political lessons they learned from its rich collection of stories.

Many presidents have turned to the vivid stories in the Bible for heroes who personify such virtues as charity, love, self-sacrifice, endurance, forgiveness, piety, righteousness, faith, humility, wisdom, courage, loyalty, truthfulness, and industriousness. Presidents have also derived from these stories a rich collection of villains who have served as equally useful object lessons in their political discourse, exemplifying such vices as cruelty, dishonesty, greed, selfishness, folly, infidelity, pride, envy, idolatry, lust, and hypocrisy.

In addition to heroes and villains, presidents have derived from the Bible the concept of an omniscient, omnipotent, caring God who not only created the universe but who also intervenes in it. Most have referred to this mysterious intervention as "Providence." A few presidents believed that God carries out his will through natural causes alone, but many have been willing to speak of miracles. Nearly all of the presidents who first served the nation as warriors, as well as those who served as wartime presidents, perceived God's hand not only in military victories but in defeat as well. Many believed that God preserved them on the battlefield. Several claimed that God led them to their spouses.

Presidents have found ways of reconciling their belief in Providence with the various misfortunes that befell them and their families, friends, and nation, sometimes attributing those hardships to divine judgment against sin and, at other times, emphasizing God's remarkable capacity to bring good out of evil. They have believed that hardships, such as wars, natural disasters, economic depressions, and the deaths of loved ones, teach wisdom, patience, and compassion, provide opportunities for generosity, and remind sufferers of the brevity of this life and the need to prepare for the eternal afterlife.

Presidents' supreme confidence in the wisdom and goodness of an omnipotent, interventionist God has been crucial to their successes. It has given them the fortitude to endure deaths and disasters with a sense of optimism and purpose. The assurance that their individual efforts on behalf of the nation would be blessed has given them the confidence to endure various trials.

An inevitable result of presidents' belief in a caring, intervening God of infinite power has been their confidence in the efficacy of prayer. Most have offered their own prayers and have been greatly encouraged by the knowledge that large numbers of Americans were praying for them. In fact, this confidence in the power of prayer has often led them to call for both public and private prayer on behalf of themselves and the nation.

While most presidents have believed that God is fully prepared to intervene in human affairs, they have also been convinced that, as the author and enforcer of natural rights, God is most eager to grant liberty to all people and to defend it. Both the belief in the existence of such rights and the belief that they are shared equally by all people is rooted in the narrative of the book of Genesis, which states that God created humans in his own image and, in the process, assigned to each individual a high value and dignity, and which asserts that all human beings derive from the same couple. Presidents' belief in equally held, God-given rights has been crucial, furnishing them the courage to struggle against both domestic and global opponents of these concepts, thus making possible their victories in the Civil War, the world wars, the Cold War, and civil rights contests. Like the Christian minister Martin Luther King Jr., these presidents have understood that the most effective means of undermining racial inequality was to highlight the stark contrast between the principles enshrined in a book that the vast majority of Americans regarded as the Word of God and the actual practices of American society and government.

Most presidents have also shared the conviction, reaching back to the very beginning of the nation, that the United States is a new Israel, a nation chosen by God to accomplish a sacred purpose. Just as God selected Israel as his chosen vessel to advance ethical monotheism, so he destined the United States to play the leading role in spreading freedom around the globe. He did this by erecting the nation as a republican city on a hill, a model of liberty that would also serve as a safe haven for the world's oppressed.

These presidents have believed that the United States' divine mission entails both blessings and responsibilities. Divine blessings have included its abundant natural resources, tremendous prosperity, an influx of hardworking immigrants, a highly improbable victory over the greatest power on earth in the Revolutionary War, a federal constitution of unparalleled excellence, the acquisition of new territories, and military victories in the War of 1812, the Mexican War, the Civil War, the Spanish-American War, the world wars, and the Cold War. This belief in a divine mission has given presidents a sense of identity and purpose and the courage to face the challenges of their time.

Since the early twentieth century, American presidents have supported the restoration and defense of the nation of Israel at least partly on biblical grounds, while, at the same time, retaining the traditional conception of the United States as a new Israel. American presidents have appeared to embrace the view that the United States and Israel are two different chosen nations with varying but interlocking missions and destinies.

Most presidents have also shared a belief in the excellence of Christian morality, especially its emphasis on humility, charity, and forgiveness, and in the necessity of faith and morality (defined largely in Judeo-Christian terms) to the survival and success of the republic. Not only have they considered piety essential to the nation's retention of God's favor, but they have also believed that popular virtue, which is vital to the survival and success of all republics, depends on a widespread belief in an omniscient God who rewards virtue and punishes vice. In short, presidents have contended that religious belief is essential in two ways: supernaturally, by securing for the nation the favor of an omniscient, interventionist God, and naturally, by inclining individuals toward the virtues necessary to society and against the vices that endanger it. Even those few presidents who stopped short of the contention that widespread faith in an omniscient, omnipotent, and intervening God is essential to the survival of the republican government argued that it is an invaluable aid to it. Like the other presidents, they claimed that such faith inhibits behavior that is harmful to society and produces a belief in the dignity and rights of all human beings that is the bedrock of democracy.

Most presidents have also derived from the Bible a belief in an afterlife characterized by rewards and punishments. This belief has comforted them in dealing with the deaths of loved ones and helped motivate their efforts and sacrifices on behalf of the nation. The biblical doctrine of the afterlife has provided presidents with priceless comfort. While the Protestant denominations of most presidents have interpreted the Bible to assert that salvation comes through faith alone, not good deeds, they have also taught that good deeds are the inevitable product of a sincere faith and earn their doers greater rewards in heaven than those received by the slothful. This belief has arguably been more responsible for the sacrifices made by American presidents on behalf of the nation than their ambition for fame. Thus, the Bible has served as a crucial unifying force that, in large part, has bridged the differences between presidents created by their rich variety of denominational affiliations, their diverse religious experiences, and their various geographical regions, political parties, and ideologies.

But, not surprisingly, the religious beliefs of American presidents have also differed in important respects. While most presidents have believed in the divine origin and authority of the Bible, in the divinity of Jesus, and in the New Testament doctrine that faith in Jesus is essential to salvation, six chief executives—John Adams, Thomas Jefferson, John Quincy Adams, Rutherford Hayes, William Howard Taft, and Richard Nixon—dissented from these orthodox views. Furthermore, several important presidents, including George Washington, the later James Madison, and James Monroe, left no record of their opinions concerning these matters.

Presidents have also disagreed concerning human nature. While most early presidents possessed a pessimistic view of human nature that accords with the biblical doctrine of original sin, most modern presidents have possessed a more optimistic outlook. A pessimistic conception of human nature encouraged the founders to resist British claims to unchecked power and led them to establish numerous checks and balances in their national and state constitutions. However, beginning in the Progressive Era, a more optimistic view of human nature has grown in popularity, a conception that has gone hand in hand with a loose interpretation of the Constitution, which has, in turn, permitted a dramatic increase in the power of the federal government. These presidents have revealed their reasoning through this question: If human nature is good, why not entrust the federal government with unchecked power to act on behalf of the majority?

In the following chapters, I discuss the educational system, familial influences, church experiences, and religious revivals that have immersed presidents in the Bible, their lifelong engagement with Scripture, their biblically infused political rhetoric, their powerful belief in a divine Providence that protects them and guides their nation, their resultant belief in the power of prayer, their belief in God-given rights and spiritual equality, their belief in a national mission to advance the cause of liberty across the globe, their belief in the excellence of Christian ethics and in the necessity of religion to the survival and success of republican government, their belief in an afterlife, their religious differences, the influence of the founding presidents' biblical conception of human nature on their establishment of constitutional checks and balances, and the effect of modern presidents' more optimistic outlook on their willingness to undermine these checks and balances.

CHAPTER 1

Influences

American presidents were raised in a biblical culture that pervaded their schools, homes, churches, and society. Until the mid-twentieth century, the curricula of most public schools included Bible reading. In the eighteenth and nineteenth centuries, most grammar schools and colleges even required the study of the New Testament in the original Greek. Most presidents were also influenced by devout parents and grandparents, who inculcated biblical principles in the home, as well as by pious siblings and wives. Most attended church services throughout their lives, listening to sermons that quoted Scripture extensively. This biblical culture was continually reenergized by the religious revivals that led directly to the American Revolution, the Civil War, the Progressive Era, and the modern civil rights movement.

School

The Bible provided not only one of the principal motives for the settlement of the American colonies but also the chief impetus for colonial education. Protestant theology inculcated a strong belief in the importance of literacy, teaching that salvation came solely through faith in Jesus, which, in turn, came primarily through reading Scripture. Thus, primers taught the skill of reading by employing biblical passages with which the learner was already familiar, having already heard them in church. Students then progressed to collections of psalms (Psalters) and then to the Bible itself, a traditional progression endorsed by John Locke in *Some Thoughts Concerning Education*.[1]

While primary schools taught both boys and girls to read the Bible, grammar schools, masculine institutions of secondary education, focused on the study of Greek and Latin. But even these schools required competence in Bible reading for admission, and Saturday afternoons were set aside for religious instruction. Some grammar schools required children to give an account of the Sunday sermon the following day. Each day typically began with the master leading his pupils in prayer and concluded with one of the older students reciting the Lord's Prayer in Latin, thus combining piety with linguistic instruction. At the Boston Latin School, students were required to translate "a Psalm or something divine" into Latin. Since most grammar school masters were recent college graduates who were preparing for a career in the ministry, they took the religious component of the grammar school curriculum seriously.[2]

Teachers at nearly all eighteenth- and nineteenth-century grammar schools and academies, as well as most private tutors, required their students to study the New Testament in the original Greek. James Madison's early training under Donald Robertson and Reverend Thomas Martin was so thorough that although he arrived at the College of New Jersey (now Princeton) in 1769 only two weeks before final examinations in the Greek New Testament and other subjects, he passed them all. In the 1780s John Quincy Adams translated the Greek New Testament every day as preparation for entrance into, first, the University of Leyden and, later, Harvard. In 1813 James K. Polk did the same at an academy operated by the Zion Presbyterian Church in Frierson, Tennessee.[3]

The public high schools and private preparatory schools established in the nineteenth and early twentieth centuries also included strong religious components, such as nonsectarian Bible reading. Groton Academy, the private boarding school that Franklin Roosevelt attended at the end of the nineteenth century, was founded and led by an Episcopalian minister named Endicott Peabody. A strict but caring man who enjoyed playing sports with the students, Peabody sought to cultivate in the boys "manly Christian character, having regard to moral and physical as well as intellectual development." Life at Groton centered around the chapel, with its regular morning and evening services. Roosevelt did well in the sacred studies part of the curriculum. He attended noncompulsory Lenten services and prayer meetings and helped teach a children's Sunday school class on campus. He later asked Peabody to preside at his wedding ceremony. Forty years after graduating from Groton, he wrote to Peabody, "I count it among the blessings of my life that it was given to me in formative years to have the privilege of your guiding hand." As late as the 1930s, Jimmy Carter and his fellow pupils read chapters from the Bible in their public school in Plains, Georgia.[4]

All but one of the American colleges established during the colonial period were denominational, and most college presidents and trustees were ministers. In 1636, only six years after landing in the wilderness in Massachusetts, the Puritans established Harvard College, the first institution of higher learning in the American colonies. Its principal purpose was to train ministers—not only in theology but also in logic, rhetoric, and science—although almost half of the graduates went into medicine, law, and other professions. The College of William and Mary (1693) was established for the training of Anglican ministers, and Yale College (1701) was formed for Connecticut Puritans who believed that Harvard had become too unorthodox. All three colleges required biblical orthodoxy of their faculty members and instituted strict rules of moral and religious conduct for students.[5]

As a result of the Great Awakening, Presbyterians established the College of New Jersey (renamed Princeton, 1746); Anglicans, King's College (Columbia, 1754); Baptists, the College of Rhode Island (Brown, 1764); members of the Dutch Reformed Church, Queen's College (Rutgers, 1766); and Congregationalists, Dartmouth College (originally for Native Americans, 1769). Only Benjamin Franklin's College of Philadelphia (the University of Pennsylvania, 1751) was officially nondenominational, though dominated by Anglicans and Presbyterians.[6]

College entrance requirements in the eighteenth and nineteenth centuries demanded the students be able to translate the Greek New Testament into English and read the Bible in both English and Greek. Until 1763 Greek reading at Harvard was confined almost exclusively to Homer and the New Testament. Even at Benjamin Franklin's nondenominational College of Philadelphia, the Bible was read in the institution's English school, and Franklin himself proposed that scriptural readings accompany the college's morning and evening prayers. In 1815 James K. Polk translated the Gospel of John as part of his entrance requirement at the University of North Carolina, whose president was a Presbyterian minister. Each student there was examined periodically on the Bible. In 1820 Franklin Pierce was required to demonstrate that he could translate the Greek New Testament in order to enter Bowdoin College. Bowdoin was typical in that it required attendance at two daily chapel services and Sunday-evening Bible recitations. Students could be admonished or even suspended for violating the Sabbath. From 1852 to 1853, James Garfield translated the apostle Paul's letter to the Romans into English at the Western Reserve Eclectic Institute, soon renamed Hiram College. In the 1870s Woodrow Wilson studied the Bible, including the Greek New Testament, at Davidson College in North Carolina. Students at nearly every American college were required to attend prayer sessions, as well as Sunday worship services. Senior theses often focused on religious subjects. Commencement ceremonies opened and closed with prayers.[7]

It was not until the post–Civil War era that bankers, merchants, and industrialists began to displace clergymen as college trustees. Even thereafter, institutions of higher learning, including the public ones, remained Christian in many respects, as college and university presidents went to great lengths to assure the public. As late as 1940, nearly half of all American colleges and universities continued to require student attendance at chapel services. In the 1950s public ceremonies at the University of California at Berkeley continued to feature prayers and hymns. The religious element at private colleges was even stronger. When Ronald Reagan attended Eureka College, a Disciples of Christ school in Illinois, in the 1930s, the college required students to prepare and recite a lesson from the Bible each week in order to propagate "the sublime morality of the Divine volume."[8]

While some college students, teenagers freed from parental supervision for the first time, were rowdy, others were sober and pious. While at Princeton, James Madison, who was the son of devout parents as well as the cousin of the first Episcopalian bishop in Virginia, chose to copy passages regarding the Gospels of Matthew and Luke and the Acts of the Apostles from William Burkitt's *Expository Notes* (1724), a commentary on the New Testament, into his commonplace book. (Students at nearly all American schools were required to keep commonplace books; these were notebooks in which they copied the passages from their studies that they found most interesting. Since the choice of what was copied was left to the individual student, these passages serve as intriguing windows into the young pupils' minds.) Madison had fallen under the sway of the president of the college, the Presbyterian minister John Witherspoon. Witherspoon served as Madison's personal tutor during his senior year and for the six months he remained following graduation to pursue further studies in the Hebrew language, ethics, and theology. Madison seriously considered a career in the ministry, calling divinity "the most sublime of all Sciences," and urged his friend William Bradford, who had decided against a ministerial career, to keep that option open later in life. Similarly, after leaving Western Reserve Eclectic Institute, James Garfield attended Williams College in Massachusetts, where he joined the Theological Society, helped conduct multidenominational campus revivals, and studied Hebrew, claiming he was "delighted with the noble language."[9]

Although Calvin Coolidge chafed under the Amherst requirement that students attend chapel exercises every weekday and for two services every Sunday, he later came to see great value in the practice. He wrote,

> If attendance on these religious services ever harmed any of the men of my time, I have never been informed of it. The good it did I believe was infinite.

Not the least it was the discipline that resulted from having constantly to give some thought to things that young men would often prefer not to consider. If we did not have the privilege of doing what we wanted to do, we had the much greater benefit of doing what we ought to do. It broke down our selfishness, it conquered our resistance, it supplanted impulse, and finally it enthroned reason.[10]

Coolidge was also profoundly inspired by a philosophy course taught by a devout Christian named Charles E. Garman. Coolidge later recalled,

He believed in the Bible and constantly quoted it to illustrate his position. He divested religion and science of any conflict with each other and showed that each rested on the common basis of our ability to know the truth. To Garman was given a power which took his class up into a high mountain of spiritual life and left them alone with God. In him was no pride of opinion, no atom of selfishness. He was a follower of the truth, a disciple of the Cross, who bore the infirmities of us all. . . . What he revealed to us of the nature of God and man will stand. Against it the gates of hell shall not prevail [Matthew 16:18].

Garman's use of the Socratic method, combined with his willingness to listen to students' arguments and to ask searching questions of all philosophies, including his own theology, inspired even unorthodox students, such as William James. Years after leaving Amherst, Coolidge kept *The Letters, Lectures, and Addresses of Charles E. Garman* on his nightstand.[11]

Some presidents were influenced by the piety of classmates; others, by revivals held at the university. While at Bowdoin, Franklin Pierce chose to be roommates with his new friend Zenas Caldwell. Pierce later recalled that Caldwell was "a man of well-considered and firmly established religious opinions . . . and one of the truest and most consistent followers of the Blessed Redeemer." He added, "While we occupied the same room, he was on his knees every night and I by his side praying for himself and me. He conquered me by his faith and Christian life." Benjamin Harrison was so affected by a revival conducted at Miami University of Ohio that he seriously considered entering the Presbyterian ministry. Although he chose law in the end, he emphasized the spiritual and moral obligations of attorneys in a speech to his fellow students: "Fellow Christians, if you adopt this Profession, let me effectively entreat you to remember that you are to do all to the glory of God."[12]

It is important to note that even denominational colleges admitted all qualified students, and religious instruction there, aside from the theology courses taken by future ministers of the denomination, was nonsectarian. By accepting students from all states and denominations and instructing them in a generalized Christianity that focused on nonsectarian Bible study, American colleges proved a crucial instrument in forging a shared sense of identity and purpose among future political leaders that was crucial to national unity.[13]

Home

Most American presidents received biblical training in the home as well as at school. Indeed, it was in the home that moral lessons derived from Scripture were not merely taught but lived. Pious grandparents, parents, siblings, and wives profoundly influenced presidents.

George Washington's wife, Martha, attended church services regularly and read her Bible daily, including her children and grandchildren in these devotions. On her deathbed in 1802, she talked to her children at length about "the Christian faith and its obligations."[14]

Abigail Adams, the wife of one president and the mother of another, was herself the daughter of a minister. Her belief in Providence sustained her during the many years in which her husband was away, serving his country as a congressman and a diplomat. She taught her eldest son, the future president John Quincy Adams, to recite the Lord's Prayer each morning before getting out of bed. After he departed for France with his father in 1778 at the age of eleven, she wrote to remind him, "Adhere to those religious Sentiments and principles which were early instilled in your mind and remember that you are accountable to your Maker for all your words and actions." After John Quincy barely survived another ocean voyage the following year, Abigail used the occasion to make a point, writing to her son:

> You have seen how inadequate the aid of Man would have been if the winds and seas had not been under the particular Being who stretched out the Heavens as a span [Isaiah 42:5], who holdeth the ocean in the hollow of his hand [Isaiah 40:12], and rideth upon the wings of the wind [2 Samuel 22:11]. . . . The only sure and prominent foundation of virtue is Religion. Let this important truth be engraven upon your Heart, and that the foundation of Religion is Belief in the one [and] only God and a just sense of [His] attributes as a Being infinitely wise, just, and good, to whom you owe the highest Reverence." [. . . This deity] superintends and governs all nature, even to clothing the lilies of the field [Matthew 6:28–30] . . . but more particularly regards man, whom he created in his own image and breathed life into an immortal spirit [Genesis 2:7] capable of a happiness beyond the grave, for the attainment of which he is bound to the performance of certain duties, which all tend to the happiness and welfare of society, and are comprised in one short sentence expressive of

universal benevolence, 'Thou shalt love thy Neighbor as thyself' [Leviticus 19:18; Matthew 19:19].

When Abigail's daughter passed away in 1813, she wrote, "My own loss is not to be estimated by words and can only be alleviated by the consoling belief that my Dear Child is partaking of the Life and immortality brought to Light by him who endured the cross and is gone before to a prepare a place for those who Love him and express his commandments." Although Abigail, like her husband, became a Unitarian in later years, she quoted Scriptures, contradicting the usual Deist practice of relying on reason alone, to justify her opposition to the doctrine of the Holy Trinity and continued to declare, in contradiction to Deist belief, that Jesus "shall come to Judge the World in righteousness, all power being given him by the Father." Whatever unorthodox opinions John Adams himself adopted, his closeness to so strong a Christian presence in his household and in the rearing of his children must partly account for his continual expressions of reverence for the Bible and his lifelong anger at anyone who publicly assaulted it.[15]

Abigail exerted an even greater influence on her eldest son, John Quincy. When she passed away in 1818, he wrote in his diary:

> She was more to me than a mother. . . . Oh, God! May I die the death of the righteous, and may my last end be like hers [Numbers 23:10]! . . . Never have I known another human being the perpetual object of whose life was so unremittingly to do good. It was a necessity of her nature. Yet so unostentatious, so unconscious even, of her own excellence that even the objects of her kindness often knew not whence it came. She had seen the world—its glories, without being dazzled; its vices and follies, without being infected by them. She had suffered often and severely from long and painful sickness, always with calmness and resignation. . . . Her price was indeed above rubies [Proverbs 31:10]."

Twenty-five years later, when John Quincy visited a school, someone read the June 1778 letter from his mother quoted above, which had since been published. John Quincy recorded in his diary, "I actually sobbed as he read, utterly unable to suppress my emotion. Oh, my mother! Is there anything on earth so affecting to me as thy name? So precious as thy instructions to my childhood, so dear as the memory of thy life? I answered I know not what."[16]

In addition to being taught prayers by his mother at a young age, which resulted in his reciting the Lord's Prayer for company before dinner, Thomas Jefferson also received tutelage from his elder sister, Jane, whom he loved deeply. Jane taught him to sing the Psalms, which may be why he always loved that book more than any other in the Old Testament.[17]

Andrew Jackson's mother, Elizabeth, and his wife, Rachel, were both devout Presbyterians. In fact, Elizabeth intended Andrew for the Presbyterian ministry. Although Andrew was not cut out for the clerical life, Elizabeth bequeathed him a strong religious streak, which was later reinforced by Rachel. In 1818 Rachel wrote to her nephew and ward, Andrew Jackson Donelson, who was just starting at West Point. Regarding her recently deceased brother, she quoted Job 1:21: "The Lord giveth, and the Lord taketh away. Blessed be the name of the Lord." She then urged Andrew, "Experience convinces me that pure and undefiled religion is the greatest treasure on earth and that all the amiable qualities hang on this. . . . It will be a lamp to his feet and a light to his pathway [Psalms 119:105]." Regarding "the crucified Redeemer," she wrote: "O that my friends would fly to his expanded arms, imbibe His spirit, emulate His example, and obey His commands. . . . Farewell, dear nephew. May this God who holds the destinies of all men in His hands order your destiny, happy in every sense of the word." The following year, she wrote to a friend who lost his wife and child in childbirth:

> My Friend, you have not to weep as those who have no hope [1 Thessalonians 4:13]. . . . Look forward to that happy period when we Shall meet all our Dear Friends in Heaven, where the parting sigh will no more be heard; all Tears will be wiped from our eyes [Revelation 7:17; 21:4]. But let us first Secure an interest in a Crucified Redeemer. . . . Put your trust in the Lord; he will never Desert nor forsake those that Choose him [Deuteronomy 31:6]. . . . May the God of all Comfort [2 Corinthians 1:3] Speak Peace to your Heart and say, "My grace is sufficient for thee [2 Corinthians 12:9]." Amen.

In 1828, overwhelmed with grief at the repeated slander of her as an adulteress, the most terrible accusation that could be brought against a pious woman of her day, by the followers of her husband's opponent in the presidential election, John Quincy Adams, Rachel responded by quoting scripture. Writing to a friend, she quoted Philippians 4:13: "I can do all things through Christ who strengthens me." She wrote regarding her slanderers:

> How many prayers have I offered up for their repentance. . . . They have offended God and man—inasmuch as "if you offend one of the Least of my little ones, you offend me" [a paraphrase of Matthew 18:6]. Now I leave them to themselves. I fear them not. I fear Him that can kill the Body and Cast the soul into Hellfire [Matthew 10:28]. O Eternity, awful is the name. . . . Let not your Heart be troubled [John 14:1]. I am on the rock of ages. In the world

I have tribulation [John 16:33]. Jesus says, "In me you shall have peace; my peace I give into you, not as the world gives [John 14:27]."

But the stress was detrimental to her health. She passed away between her husband's election and his inauguration. His epitaph for her included these lines: "Her piety went hand in hand with her benevolence, and she thanked her Creator for being permitted to do good. A being so gentle and so virtuous slander might wound but could not dishonor." He wrote to a friend, "Her virtues, her piety & Christianity have ensured her that future happiness which is promised to the disciples of Christ." In retirement he visited Rachel's grave alone every day, just before sunset.[18]

James K. Polk's mother, Jane, was another pious Presbyterian who took great pleasure in reading the Bible, especially the book of Psalms. She relied on her faith in times of trouble. When her husband died in 1828, she attempted to console her children by referring to divine sovereignty, writing, "Holy, Just, and true are thou, O God. It is thou that has a right to every Creature thou hast made." Polk later recalled, "I had a pious mother. She carefully instructed me in the principles of Christianity. The impressions thus made have never been erased. I always have and, I trust, always shall venerate the Sabbath."[19]

Polk's wife, Sarah, possessed similar beliefs and exerted a similar influence on him. Early in her husband's political career, she adopted the stratagem of discouraging her husband's political associates from attempting to consult with him on the Sabbath by appearing dressed, announcing that it was time to go to church, and dragging them along. After a few such occasions, James's impious associates made it a point to stay out of the Polks' parlor at church time. In Washington the Polks declined to receive even illustrious visitors on the Sabbath.[20]

James Buchanan's mother, Elizabeth, was equally devout. She was a modest and self-effacing woman who based her life on the Ten Commandments and the Sermon on the Mount. Her quiet faith impressed her eldest son. He later recalled, "She was a sincere and devout Christian from the time of my earliest recollection and had read much on the subject of theology; and what she read once she remembered forever." He added that she died "in the calm but firm assurance that she was going home to her Father and her God." He concluded, "Under Providence, I attribute any little distinction which I may have acquired in the world to the blessing which He conferred on me in granting me such a mother." His brother Edward was a Presbyterian minister.[21]

Ulysses Grant's mother, sister, and wife were all pious Methodists. Grant's parents, Jesse and Hannah, boarded various Methodist preachers at their home for more than forty years. It was Ulysses's job to care for these guests' horses. He remembered his mother as "a pure-minded, simple-hearted, earnest Methodist Christian," adding, "I owe . . . all that I am to her earnest, modest, and sincere piety." His sister married a Methodist preacher. His wife, Julia, was the granddaughter of John Wrenshall, an English preacher who helped establish Methodism in Pittsburgh.[22]

Rutherford Hayes's mother and wife were both devout Methodists. His mother, Sophia, often hosted visiting preachers and had long theological conversations with them. She organized the first Sunday school in her village and taught a Bible class. She was the treasurer of the Ladies Branch Bible Society, which met in her home. Not trusting her son to the local school until long after he was ready, she taught him to read and write using the *Dilworth Reader*, which was filled with religious aphorisms. She often spoke to him of God, salvation, and heaven and read to him from *Pilgrim's Progress*, which she claimed was the next best book to the Bible. Rutherford's wife, Lucy, attended the Wesleyan Female Seminary in Cincinnati, where she gave a commencement address called "The Influence of Christianity on National Prosperity." Her suitors included Methodist ministers who were attracted by her devotion to the faith. She exerted a powerful influence on her husband. As the First Lady, she banned alcohol at the White House, leading critics to dub her Lemonade Lucy. In 1877 she and Rutherford oversaw the baptism of two of their children, as well as a neighbor's child, in the Blue Room of the executive mansion. She later served as president of the Women's Home Missionary Society. After she passed away in 1889, her husband recalled,

> All humanity was dear to her, and beyond any person I ever saw she loved to make all happy, and was gifted with the faculty of doing it. She loved Christ and all good Christians. . . . She had friends she valued in every church, and of no church. . . . Her religion [focused on] treating all others according to the Golden Rule. . . . She was so modest about her own religious character that it would have shamed her to be spoken of as "saintly." . . . I never happened to know a person whose knowledge of the Bible was equal to hers.[23]

James Garfield's wife, Lucretia, was so pious that she rejected a previous suitor, a man she loved, because he did not share her faith. She wrote, "I will withhold my hand ever from the one I love should I be convinced that by bestowing it I should in any way lessen the little power I have of benefiting others, or cause myself to serve less faithfully my Savior. . . . I knew that

I could not lead the life I ought bound to one who was not [a Christian]." She had no such problem with Garfield. The couple's letters expressed a shared faith that was never more comforting than when their little daughter passed away in 1863. Lucretia wrote,

> I hope, dear Jamie, that you are trying to look up, through tears though it be, to our Savior's face and from His words of comfort gathering peace to your soul, and larger strength to do well the work of life. These words have been much in my heart today: "The Father chasteneth whom He loveth" [Hebrews 12:6], and the thought has come to me that not only has He honored us in giving us to keep a while a little nature so pure and noble but that He also loves us so well that He will make surer our clinging to Him by taking our cherished one to Himself, that where our treasure is, there may our hearts be also [Matthew 6:21].[24]

Grover Cleveland's father, Richard, was a Presbyterian pastor in Caldwell, New Jersey, as well as a district secretary of the Home Missionary Society. Richard named his son after Stephen Grover, his predecessor as pastor of the church. Grover Cleveland's brother, William, was also a minister, and his sister, Anna, had married one. Their father led family worship every evening. In 1888 Grover recalled that he had attended three services every Sunday as a boy. He also remembered "a kind and affectionate father, consecrated to the cause, and called to his rest and his reward in the midday of his usefulness" and "the prayers and pious love of a sainted mother, and a family circle hallowed and sanctified by the spirit of Presbyterianism." Two years later, he added, "I was reared and taught in the strictest school of Presbyterianism. I remember well the precepts and examples of my early days, and I acknowledge that to them I owe every faculty of usefulness I possess and every just apprehension of the duties and obligations of life."[25]

Benjamin Harrison's parents, John and Elizabeth, were also devout Presbyterians. Every Saturday afternoon at 4:00 p.m., the family assembled in the parlor and sang hymns until bedtime. Every day Benjamin heard his mother pray over him, "May God bless you and keep you continually under His protecting care."[26]

William McKinley's mother, Allison, and her sister volunteered their time to sweep, scrub, and paint their Methodist church in Niles, Ohio, regularly. They did "all but the preaching." Allison was also famed for tending to the sick, acting as a peacemaker, and boarding visiting preachers. When William became president, she prayed, "Oh God, keep him humble," and continued to express regret that he had not gone into the ministry, where he could have been more useful.[27]

Theodore Roosevelt's father and namesake generally deposited Teddy and his siblings at their Sunday school classes on the way to teaching his own. After church the senior Theodore then made the children read aloud their own synopses of the sermon. He spent Sunday evenings visiting the children who lived at the lodge of the Children's Aid Society, an organization he had helped establish that placed New York City orphans in country homes. He led his own children in Bible reading and prayer every morning. The junior Theodore called him "the best man I ever knew." After he passed away, Teddy wrote, "Nothing but my faith in the Lord Jesus Christ could have carried me through this, my terrible time of trial and sorrow."[28]

Woodrow Wilson was named for his maternal grandfather, Thomas Woodrow, a Scottish Presbyterian minister who had settled in Ohio. Woodrow's father, Joseph, was not only a minister but also a leader of the Presbyterian Church in the United States, the Southern Presbyterian denomination, for over thirty years. While in Wilmington, North Carolina, Woodrow helped his father edit the minutes of the denomination's General Assembly and manage the *North Carolina Presbyterian*. Woodrow idolized his father, frequently writing in his diary that his sermons were "excellent as usual." He later recalled that Joseph would lie on the couch by the fire on Sunday afternoons and added, "I would sit on the rug beside him, and we would have wonderful talks." In 1906 Woodrow declared, "I have had the unspeakable joy of having been born and bred in a minister's family." In his father's epitaph, he characterized him as "a thoughtful student of life and of God's purpose, a lover and servant of his fellow man, a man of God." He recalled, "I remember my father as essentially humble and devout before God. . . . A man who believed much more in the efficacy of Christian simple and pure living than in dogmatic advice or spiritual conversation—a robust Christian."[29]

In 1883 Wilson met his first wife, Ellen, the daughter of a pastor, at a service at her father's church. Their correspondence was always peppered with religious sentiment. Ellen paid for the biblical training of poor boys and girls in the Appalachian Mountains. After she passed away, Wilson approved the creation of the Ellen Wilson Fund for the Christian Education of Mountain Youth.[30]

Warren G. Harding's mother, Phoebe, was first a devout Methodist and then a devout Seventh Day Adventist who had the reputation of being the most knowledgeable woman concerning the Bible in her rural Ohio community. Thus, it is not surprising that she bequeathed Warren the middle name Gamaliel, the name of the famous rabbi who taught the apostle Paul and who argued against the persecution of Christians (Acts 5:34–39; 22:3). Harding's mother made sure that he and his brothers prayed and read the Bible, as well as various collections of Bible stories. His brother George was nicknamed "the Deacon" because of his piety. George even refused to allow his sons to travel to the arena in Chicago where their uncle was to be nominated for president because the nomination occurred on a Saturday, the Adventist Sabbath.[31]

Pious grandparents influenced Calvin Coolidge. He later recalled the death of his namesake and grandfather when he was just six years old: "During his last illness he would have me read to him the first chapter of the Gospel of John, which he had read to his grandfather. I could do very well until I came to the word 'comprehended,' with which I always had difficulty. On taking the oath as President in 1925, I placed my hand on that Book of the Bible in memory of my first reading it." Coolidge's Baptist grandmother, Sarah, acted as a Sunday school superintendent until Coolidge's father replaced her in that post. Coolidge later recalled, "She was a constant reader of the Bible and a devoted member of the church who daily sought for divine guidance in prayer. I stayed with her at the farm much of the time, and she had much to do with shaping the thought of my early years. She had a benign influence over all who came into contact with her. The Puritan severity of her convictions was tempered by the sweetness of a womanly charity. There were none whom she ever knew that had not in some way benefited by her kindness." Every day she read a chapter of the Bible to her grandson.[32]

Herbert Hoover descended from a long line of devout Quakers. His great-grandmother Rebecca, who lived to be ninety-five, served as the family's matriarch, monitoring the piety and morality of her progeny, since she considered herself responsible for their souls. In 1951, Hoover recalled regarding his Quaker upbringing, "The religious characteristics of the faith were literal belief in the Bible, great tolerance, and a conviction that spiritual inspiration sprang from the 'inward light' in each individual. . . . Individual Bible-reading was a part of the Quaker concept of education—and before I left Iowa I had read the Bible in daily stints from cover to cover. . . . Even the babies were present at the invariable family prayers and Bible readings every morning." Eight years later he wrote, "Under my austere Quaker upbringing, my book reading had been limited to the Bible, the encyclopedia, and a few novels which dealt with the sad results of Demon Rum and the final regeneration of the hero." After Hoover's mother, Huldah, was widowed and left to raise three children in poverty, she wrote, "We know not what is before us, but as children of the Lord, we can trust it *all* to Him who knows what is best [emphasis in original]." She was a popular preacher, invited to speak by many Quaker communities. She founded and was a leader in the Young People's Prayer Meeting before passing away of typhoid fever at thirty-five. Herbert kept on his wall the motto, God's promise, that his mother had given him, "I will never leave thee nor forsake thee [Hebrews 13:5]."[33]

Franklin Roosevelt's father, James, served as a vestryman and warden in St. James Church, an Episcopalian church in Hyde Park, New York. Reverend Pearsons Newton, a longtime rector of the church, later recalled of James that "as vestryman and warden[,] he served St. James parish with constant zeal . . . witnessing by his kindliness and charm of manner to the nobility and honor of his inner Christian character." Franklin followed in his father's footsteps, holding the same church offices.[34]

Harry Truman possessed devout grandfathers and parents and a pious wife. Truman later recalled that both grandfathers were devout Baptists, who were "good men, as good as they come." He added, "They had firm opinions about right and wrong, and they practiced what they preached and believed. Both of these men were trustful souls and never failed to help anyone around them who needed help. My father and mother were the same way. I never saw them turn a tramp away hungry, and we had many applications for food at the back door at the time I was growing up." Truman's wife, Bess, was so fastidious about church attendance and so insistent on her husband's appearance at Sunday service that he was able to take advantage of this trait during his retirement years. One weekend, after she had insisted that the former president mow the lawn, Truman, wishing to avoid the chore, began mowing it on a Sunday morning. Astonished, she called out, "What are you doing on Sunday?" He smiled and replied, "I'm doing what you asked me to." Truman relates, "Meanwhile, the neighbors continued to pass by the house. Their glances were not lost on Mrs. Truman. She never asked me to mow the lawn again."[35]

Dwight Eisenhower's grandfather Jacob was a preacher of the Brethren in Christ, more popularly known as the River Brethren. Regarding his grandparents' philosophy, Dwight later recalled, "The future life was of paramount importance. It was going home to glory. This life was only a preparation." Two of Eisenhower's uncles were also preachers. His uncle Abraham established an orphanage in Oklahoma, where he farmed to feed the children.[36]

Eisenhower's parents, David and Ida, were devout members of the Watchtower Society, a denomination that later became known as the Jehovah's Witnesses. Dwight recalled, "They believed the admonition 'The fear of God is the beginning of wisdom [Psalms 111:10].' [. . .] There was nothing sad about their religion. They believed in the Bible with happiness and contentment. They tried their best to instill the Bible, its doctrines, its beliefs, its convictions, in their sons. . . . They never stopped—they never had time—to hate or despise an enemy or those that used them spitefully. They accepted their trials and tribulations and met them with courage and with never a thought of failure." David studied the New Testament in the original Greek at Lane University in Lecompton, Kansas. Thereafter, he often read the Greek New Testament, not trusting translations. One night a week, the family gathered in the parlor to read the Bible. The boys took turns reading the passages, followed by a discussion to help them find meanings that might seem obscure. The Bible was Ida's "favorite reading." In fact, she once won a prize for memorizing 1,325 Bible verses. She prided herself on never having to look up a scriptural reference. She hosted Bible studies.[37]

Once, when Eisenhower was a boy, he was sent to his room after having a temper tantrum when his parents told him he was too young to go trick-or-treating. Shortly after, his mother entered his room and sat quietly for a while. Finally, she spoke. Eisenhower recalled, "As she often did, she drew on the Bible, paraphrasing it, I suppose. This time she said: 'He that conquereth his own soul is greater than he who taketh a city [Proverbs 16:32].'" Eisenhower continued, "I have always looked back on that conversation as one of the most valuable moments of my life." The legendary calmness and self-control he developed contributed to his appointment to the position of Allied Supreme Commander during World War II and to his success in that position and as president. He was able to take many cities as a general because he conquered his own soul as a boy.[38]

Despite Ida's pacifism, which was a prominent teaching of the Jehovah's Witnesses, she "refused to try to push her beliefs" on Dwight, who opted for a military career. Eisenhower recalled, "Her happy disposition came from the depth of her faith." He declared, "A deep, Bible-centered faith has colored my life since childhood. Devout parents, who loved the Bible as dearly as life itself, made sure of that."[39]

John F. Kennedy's mother, Rose, was a pious Catholic who attended Mass daily, sometimes twice a day. Every morning on her way home with the children from their daily walk, she brought them to St. Aidan's Church in Brookline, Massachusetts, because "I wanted them to understand that Church isn't just for Sundays and special times on the calendar but [that it] should be a part of life." She insisted on the recitation of grace before every meal and on nightly prayer. After her eldest son, Joseph Jr., died in World War II, her faith consoled her. She later recalled, "As soon as I fully accepted that God had his reasons for taking Joe, I began to recover. And my recovery was speeded up by all the wise and wonderful letters I received from various priests and nuns I had known over the years."[40]

A devout Baptist, Lyndon Johnson's mother, Rebekah, was the granddaughter of a minister who served as Sam Houston's pastor and as the president of Baylor University. Her father, Joseph Baines, was famous for his piety and integrity. His law partner claimed that Baines "was always more concerned about doing right and acting honorable than he was about the success of the suit." Rebekah recalled, "He taught me that 'a lie is an abomination unto the Lord.'" Rebekah often taught young Lyndon stories from the Bible. In 1964, after quoting Proverbs 22:6 ("Train up a child in the way he should go, and when he is old, he will not depart from it"), Lyndon recalled, "In my childhood, I . . . had the great blessing of a devout and faithful mother. . . . There was always prayer—aloud, proud, and unapologetic." He continued, "Throughout the long, busy, and sometimes hectic years since, observance of some of that training became irregular, especially the practice of returning thanks before each meal." But this changed after the assassination of Johnson's predecessor, John F. Kennedy, and his own unexpected ascension to the presidency in 1963: "In those first few dark days of November, when the pressures were the heaviest and the need of strength from Above the greatest, Lady Bird and I sat down together to eat a meal alone. No word or glance passed between us, but in some way we found ourselves bowing together, and I found myself speaking the words of grace that I had learned at my mother's knees so many years ago." In 1965 Johnson recalled that his mother, "with the Bible in her lap," often quoted Jesus in Luke 23:34: "Father, forgive them, for they know not what they do." Johnson frequently used the same expression.[41]

Gerald Ford's mother, Dorothy, was active in Grace Episcopal Church in Grand Rapids, Michigan, where she met her second husband, for whom Ford was renamed. Ford later recalled, "She was engaged in one church or civic activity after another. And when she wasn't attending meetings, she was busy baking bread or sewing clothes for needy families." She later died in church, just before a service, an end that Ford considered appropriate. He also remembered, "Our parents brought up my brothers and me in an atmosphere of personal prayer, belief in God and the Bible, and the Episcopalian denomination. This upbringing has been the anchor for my own religious development, which includes a dedication to the teachings of Jesus Christ." His stepfather, Gerald Ford Sr., whom he always considered his real father, was a vestryman and Sunday school teacher at the church. Ford's wife, Betty, also served as a Sunday school teacher for years. She read the Bible every morning before breakfast, her favorite verse being 1 Peter 5:7 ("Cast all your anxieties on God, for He cares about you"), and a prayer book every evening. She kept the Prayer of St. Francis in her bathroom so that it was the first and last thing she saw each day. When the president of the Jewish National Fund had a heart attack at a dinner, she rushed to the microphone and led a prayer for the dying rabbi.[42]

Jimmy Carter's father, mother, sister, and wife were all pious Christians. Regarding his father, Earl, who was a farmer, deacon, and Sunday school teacher, Carter later recalled, "A religious man, my daddy prayed for some dry weather but also for strength and courage to deal with whatever came. Although the weather did not always suit him, the most important part of his prayers was answered." Earl also had a habit of giving secretly to people in need. When Jimmy was four years old, his parents taught him his first Bible verse, 1 John 4:16: "God is love." He later remembered, "My first church was my family. I first heard the Bible read in my family. I first heard prayer in my family. I learned about God within the family." In 1980 he said, "When I make a sound judgment it's because I remember my upbringing, I remember the principles that I learned in Sunday school and church and listening to my daddy." He recalled that his sister, Ruth, who had become an evangelist in a charismatic church, "had a habit of praying as though she was talking to a friend about the constantly evolving events of her life." He added, "She always seemed to be aware of the presence of the Holy Spirit."[43]

Carter's wife, Rosalynn, regarding her own Methodist upbringing, recalled, "God was a real presence in my life, especially in those revival times. We were taught to love Him and felt very much the necessity and the desire to live the kind of life He would have us live, to love one another and be kind, to help those who needed help, and to be good." She later credited the scriptures she memorized and the hymns she sang as a girl with sustaining her during difficult times. She taught a Sunday school class after the Carters returned to Plains, Georgia, following Jimmy's service in the US Navy. In 1987 she wrote, "I had learned many years ago to release my problems to God, something I had to do often in all our political years when I was trying to do so many different things at once. 'Here it is, God. You take it. I can't handle it alone,' I would say. It helped me through the good times and the bad. I knew that God loved me. I had found God's love a shield around me that protected me in the midst of controversy or letdowns." In 1997 Jimmy wrote, "For the last twenty years, Rosalynn and I have read a portion of the Bible each night. When we're together, we alternate reading aloud, and when we're apart, we enjoy knowing that we are contemplating the same text. We have been through the entire Bible several times in Spanish, to practice our foreign language as we nurture ourselves spiritually." While president, he consulted his wife on nearly every decision, calling her "an extension of me." She even attended cabinet meetings. Yet she remained humble. In retirement she was a member of the team that cleaned the couple's church.[44]

Ronald Reagan's mother, Nelle, seldom missed services at the Disciples of Christ church in Dixon, Illinois, where she taught Sunday school. Her favorite scripture verse was 2 Chronicles 7:14: "If my people, who are called by my name, shall humble themselves and pray and seek my face and turn from their wicked ways, then will I hear from heaven and will forgive their sin and will heal their land." In 1983 Reagan recalled, "I have a very special old Bible. And alongside a verse in the Second Book of Chronicles there are some words, handwritten, very faded now. And, believe me, the person who wrote those words was an authority. Her name was Nelle Wilson Reagan. She was my mother. And she wrote about that verse, 'A most wonderful verse for the healing of the nations.'" In his Mother's Day address that year, Reagan said, "Now and then I find guidance and direction in the worn brown Bible I used to take the oath of office. It's been the Reagan family Bible, and like many of yours, has its flyleaf filled with important events, its margins scrawled with insights and passages underlined for emphasis. My mother, Nelle, made all those marks in that book. She used it to instruct her two young sons, and I look to it still." Five months later, he said, "Nelle Reagan, my mother, God rest her soul, had an unshakable faith in God's goodness. And, while I may not have realized it in my youth, I knew she planted that faith very deeply in me. She made the most difficult Christian message seem very easy. . . . Her way was forgiveness and goodness, and both began with love." In 1986 Reagan noted, "Prayer, of course, is deeply personal. Many of us have been taught to pray by people we love. In my case, it was my mother. I learned quite literally at her knee. My mother gave me a great deal, but nothing she gave me was more important than this special gift, the knowledge of the happiness and solace to be gained by talking to the Lord." In 1990 he wrote, "My mother—a small woman with auburn hair and a sense of optimism that ran as deep as the cosmos—told me that everything in life happened for a purpose. She said all things were part of God's Plan, even the most disheartening setbacks, and in the end, everything worked out for the best." Reagan was baptized in his mother's church at age twelve, and for the rest of his life, he followed her example of paying a tithe to the church. Even during the Great Depression, when her family had little, she brought hot meals to prisoners at the local jail and food to those who had nothing to eat. She often quoted the Bible at length to those who needed comfort and hope. After she moved to Hollywood in 1938 to be near her actor-son, she served in a prison ministry in Los Angeles. She brought her grandchildren, Maureen and Michael, to Sunday school. Ronald recalled, "She was the gentlest, the kindest woman that anyone ever knew."[45]

George H. W. Bush's mother, Dorothy, whom he called "one of God's most special people," was a Bible reader. In 1985 he wrote, "Her goodness, her kindness, her propensity to forgive, her love, all stem directly from her following the Bible and her faith in God. Mother is a Christian. Her light really does shine." Each morning she prayed with her husband, Prescott. When she could no longer see well enough to read in her women's Bible study group, she quoted the verses from memory. A daughter-in-law who belonged to the group said, "Those who heard her say, gently, 'The Lord is my shepherd [Psalms 23:1],' knew then that He truly was." George later recalled, "Mum was . . . a Christian that knew her Bible and was lifted by her faith. . . . She lived her faith—teaching not just family but so many friends too by her example, by the way she lived her own life." After Bush participated in a contentious television interview with Dan Rather in 1988, during which Bush got in a few zingers of his own, he received dozens of congratulatory calls—and one admonishing call from his mother. After he hung up the phone, Bush reported, "She said that just because that other man was rude was no excuse for me to be." Dorothy prayed with her young grandson, George W., when he slept at her house. In her final moments in 1992, she asked her son, who was then the president, to read to her from the Bible next to her bed. She had written her own eulogy eleven years earlier:

> This is a service of gratitude to God for the easiest life ever given to anyone to live on this earth and all because of LOVE. From my mother's knee I learned to know Jesus and that He would always be with me if at night in bed I would just tell Him any mean, selfish, even untrue things I had done during the day. He would lift them from my mind, and I would awake refreshed, and later along the way if there was a steep incline, He would take my hand and help me up the hill. How right she was.

Dorothy left instructions that attenders at her funeral should wear bright colors to signify their joy that she was now in heaven.[46]

Bush's wife, Barbara, the only woman besides Abigail Adams with the distinction of having been the wife of one president and the mother of another, was a devout Christian who served as a Sunday school teacher at First Presbyterian Church of Midland, Texas. Later, regarding the death of her three-year-old daughter, Robin, from leukemia, she recalled, "For one last time I combed her hair, and we held our precious little girl. I never felt the presence of God more strongly than at that moment." She knew that

Robin was in heaven. In 1994 Barbara wrote, "Religion has played such an important part in our lives. It's a very personal thing with us, but I know we could not have survived the difficult times without our faith and the support of our religious family. Whether we were worshipping in our enormous church in Houston, St. Martin's; our two tiny churches in Kennebunkport, First Congregational Church and St. Ann's; the tiny little chapel at Camp David; or St. John's Church, across from the White House, we always have felt part of a very special community." In her later years, though suffering from back pain, she continued to attend church regularly; she placed a prayer book between her lower spine and the back of the pew for support so she could make it through the service. In spite of her ailments, she spent countless hours stitching kneelers for the church. On her deathbed she told her son Jeb, "I believe in Jesus, and He is my savior. I don't want to leave your dad, but I know I will be in a beautiful place." She selected for her funeral John 6:38–40, in which Jesus declares, "I came down from heaven not to do my own will, but the will of Him who sent me. And this is the will of my Father who has sent, that I should lose nothing of all that He has given me, but should raise it up again on the last day. This is indeed the will of . . . Him who sent me, that all who see the Son and believe in Him may have eternal life, and I will raise them up on the last day."[47]

Presidents' family Bibles have served not only as sources of spiritual and moral edification but also as historical records of the births, baptisms, and marriages of family members, a function that has denoted its special status among all the books of the household. In 1929 Franklin Roosevelt took the oath of office as governor of New York on a Dutch family Bible that was nearly three centuries old. Four years later, he took the oath of office as president on it, with his hand placed on 1 Corinthians 13, the famous chapter about love. Dwight Eisenhower cherished the German Bible, translated by Martin Luther, which one of his ancestors had brought to America in 1741. He recalled that his parents kept it in the front room, that it featured "antique Fraktur type," and that it contained a record of the family's births, marriages, and deaths. When asked if he wished to retrieve some mementos from his childhood home before it was turned over to the Eisenhower Foundation, he considered several possibilities but declared, "Of course, my real choice would be the old family Bible."[48]

Church

In the eighteenth, nineteenth, and early twentieth centuries, speeches constituted one of the most popular forms of entertainment, and the sermon was one of the most common types of oratory. Churches served not only as places of worship but also as community centers, gathering places where news was exchanged, youthful friendships were started, and courtships began.[49]

Most presidents have attended church services regularly, where they have heard sermons filled with scriptural references. Considered in isolation, this regularity of church attendance does not provide evidence of belief, but it does suggest that sermons have constituted one source of the biblical knowledge presidents have often displayed in their private letters and public speeches.

A lifelong member of the same small church, George Washington was an Anglican/Episcopalian vestryman. Yet he took advantage of his time in Philadelphia during the American Revolution and at the Constitutional Convention to attend the services of other denominations. During the early portion of his presidency in New York, he mostly attended Anglican services, but he repeated his pattern of visiting the churches of other denominations when traveling. While visiting York, Pennsylvania, in 1791, he wrote in his diary, "There being no Episcopal Minister present in the place, I went to hear the morning Service performed in the Dutch Reformed Church—which, being in that language, not a word of which I understood, I was in no danger of becoming a proselyte to its religion by the eloquence of the Preacher."[50]

In 1811 John Adams noted, "I have been a church-going animal for seventy-six years, from the cradle." In fact, while serving in the Continental Congress, Adams attended services at many different churches in Philadelphia, a city famous for its large number of denominations. One day in 1774, he visited a Presbyterian church and enjoyed the sermon regarding the Lord's Supper, though he still thought his own "Congregational Way best." He attended a Mass at St. Mary's Church the same afternoon, where he "heard a good, short moral Essay upon the Duty of Parents to their Children, founded in Justice and Charity, to take care of their Interests, temporal and spiritual." In his retirement years in Quincy, Massachusetts, he attended Unitarian services twice every Sunday.[51]

Between 1767 and 1785, Thomas Jefferson was a vestryman at two different Anglican churches and a regular attender of their services. While vice president, he attended prayers every morning, as well as a course of sermons delivered by Thomas Clagger, the Senate chaplain. While president, Jefferson attended multidenominational services in the Hall of the House of Representatives regularly and even assisted in singing Psalms 100. After Jefferson retired, he worshipped regularly at multidenominational services conducted at the Albemarle County Courthouse in Virginia. He explained in 1822, "The court-house is the common temple one Sunday in the month to each [denomination]. Here Episcopalian and Presbyterian, Methodist and Baptist meet together, join in hymning their Maker, and listen with attention and devotion to each other's preachers." To a lover of tolerance like Jefferson, it was a beautiful sight.[52]

In 1806, as the first Boylston Professor of Rhetoric and Oratory at Harvard, a post he held while serving as a US senator, John Quincy Adams delivered a series of lectures on the art of rhetoric in which he emphasized the importance of preaching. Regarding the functions of the preacher, he declared, "As the ambassador for Christ (2 Corinthians 5:20), it is his great and awful duty to call sinners to repentance. His only weapon is the voice; and with this he is to appall the guilty and to reclaim the infidel; to rouse the indifferent and to shame the scorner. He is to inflame the lukewarm, to encourage the timid, and to cheer the desponding believer. He is to pour the healing balm of consolation into the bleeding heart of sorrow, and to sooth with celestial hope the very agonies of death."[53]

Adams was as regular a churchgoer as his father, and he was equally willing to attend the services of other denominations. At various times and in various countries, he attended Catholic Masses as well as Unitarian, Episcopalian, Presbyterian, and Methodist services. While serving as US minister to Russia, he attended Eastern Orthodox, Roman Catholic, and Anglican liturgies. He almost always jotted down in his diary the scriptural text on which each sermon was based and then critiqued the sermon. In 1820 he heard Edward Everett preach on 1 Corinthians 7:29: "Brethren, the time is short." Adams called it "the most splendid composition as a sermon that I ever heard delivered." He added, "It abounded in splendid imagery, in deep pathos, in cutting satire, in profound reflections of morals, in coruscations of wit, in thunderbolts of feeling." In 1824, during the election season that would carry him to the presidency, Adams heard a sermon on patience, based on Luke 21:19: "By your endurance you will gain your souls." Adams commented, "Self-control in trying seasons is the most necessary of all properties, and never was it more needed for me in the whole course of my life—perhaps never near so much."[54]

While living in Washington during the last decades of his life, Adams attended Episcopalian, Presbyterian, Unitarian, and other services. In 1826 he was overcome with emotion on returning to the church in Quincy, Massachusetts, "where the earliest devotions of my childhood were performed" in order to attend his father's funeral. As he sat in his father's pew, "I looked around the house with enquiring thoughts. Where were those whom [he] was then wont to meet in this house? The aged of that time, the pastor by whom I had been baptized, the deacons who sat before the communion-table, have all long since departed." Only those who had been children like himself remained, surrounded by the large families they had since spawned. The sermon in Revelation 2:10, "Be thou faithful unto death, and I will give thee a crown of life," was "intelligent and affecting." The following year, already aware of the difficulties involved in his reelection, he recorded the value he perceived in church attendance:

> Hope in the goodness of God, reliance upon His mercy in affliction, trust in Him to bring light out of darkness and good out of evil, are the comforts and promises which I desire from attendance on public worship. They help to sustain me in the troubles that are thickening upon me, and although every day adds to the gloom and threatening fury of the storm, and not a ray of light is discernible before me, yet do I gather strength and fortitude, and a vague and indefinite confidence of escaping, or passing unhurt through the furnace that awaits me, from the constant exhortations to trust in the Lord which abound in the Psalms, as well as in the selections of hymns at the churches where I attend.[55]

In 1836 Adams noted, "There is scarcely a Sunday passes over my head but, in attendance upon divine service, I hear something of which a pointed application to my own situation and circumstances occurs to my thoughts. It is often consolation, support, encouragement—sometimes warning and admonition, sometimes keen and trying remembrance of deep distress." In 1841 Adams wrote regarding a sermon by the Congregationalist Reverend Nathaniel Frothingham on Psalms 139:23 ("Search me, O God, and know my heart; try me, and know my thoughts"): "I think I never in my life heard a sermon of purer morality, of more elevated piety, of more affecting exhortation, of deeper impression. It was upon the duty of regulating, controlling, and directing the thoughts."[56]

In 1844 Adams was impressed by a sermon delivered by J. H. Hopkins, the Episcopalian bishop of Vermont. The sermon was on Hebrews 2:15: "And deliver them who through fear of death were all their lifetime subject to bondage." Adams recorded,

> The Bishop's discourse was on the fear of death inherent in the nature of man, on his subjection to bondage throughout life by that fear, and on redemption from that bondage by sincere faith in Christ the Redeemer—a close, compact argument, all flowing from and returning to the text—death, bondage, redemption. What intense feeling, what absorbing interest, what searching pathos, are interwoven with the solemn discussion of these topics! The Bishop seized upon them and familiarly handled them all—in composition of refined

and elegant simplicity, in a tone of delivery kind, affectionate, and deeply impressive. It is long since I have heard an appeal so eloquent to my own conscience; and when the enquiry came to every hearer, whether he could safely and confidently rely upon his own right to the blessing of the redemption from that bondage of the fear of death, my conscience smote me, and an involuntary tear stole down my cheek. I had never before, to my remembrance, heard the name of Bishop Hopkins. I shall remember him as long as any trace of memory remains upon my brain.

The same year Adams accepted the chairmanship of the National Lord's Day Convention, which urged the keeping of the Sabbath.[57]

Andrew Jackson attended a wide variety of church services—Baptist, Methodist, and Presbyterian—while a congressman in Washington. His friend John Eaton noted, "Every Sunday he takes himself to some one of the churches and returns again about 1 o'clock." While president, Jackson attended Presbyterian services most often but also attended Episcopalian services. In retirement he became a member of a Presbyterian church near the Hermitage and attended its services regularly for the rest of his life. He had delayed church membership while president because he did not wish it to be said that he was attempting to exploit religion for political purposes.[58]

A regular churchgoer, William Henry Harrison was one of the founders and vestrymen of Christ Church, an Episcopalian church in Cincinnati. While a congressman and during the brief period of his presidency, he occupied a pew in St. John's Episcopal Church in Washington.[59]

James K. Polk and his wife, Sarah, were regular attenders at a Presbyterian church in Columbia, Tennessee, in the 1820s and, later, at the First Presbyterian Church in Washington. Polk also managed to visit other denominations. In fact, he was deeply affected by a revival sermon preached by the Methodist Reverend John B. McFerrin in 1833. Twelve years later, on his fiftieth birthday, Polk took advantage of his wife's absence due to inclement weather to attend a service at Foundry Methodist Church. He noted in his diary, "Mrs. Polk being a member of the Presbyterian church, I generally attend that church with her, though my opinions and predilections are in favour of the Methodist Church." That day the preacher's text was Acts 17:31: "He hath appointed a day in which He will judge the world in righteousness by the man whom He hath ordained." Polk wrote, "It awakened the reflection that I had lived fifty years, and before fifty years more would expire, I would be sleeping with the generations which have gone before me. I thought of the vanity of this world's honours, how little they would profit me half a century hence, and that it was time for me to be 'putting my House in Order.'" Polk lived less than four more years. He also attended several multidenominational services in the Hall of the House of Representatives, as well as occasional Baptist, Congregationalist, and Lutheran services, and at least one Mass at St. Matthew's in Washington. At the dedication of a Baptist church, he "heard an excellent sermon from the text, 'For I am not ashamed of the Gospel of Christ [Romans 1:16].'" At a Methodist chapel, he heard "a most impressive sermon from the text 'The carnal mind is enmity against God [Romans 8:7].'"[60]

James Buchanan was a regular attender of Presbyterian services. Regarding his longtime pastor in Mercersburg, Pennsylvania, Reverend John King, an unpretentious and witty scholar, Buchanan wrote, "My memory loves to dwell upon that great and good man. . . . [He] had none of that gloomy bigotry which too often passes in these days for superior sanctity." In fact, Buchanan claimed that he had "never known any human being for which I felt greater reverence than Dr. King." Buchanan bequeathed a large sum of money to his church.[61]

Like John Quincy Adams, Buchanan attended other denominations' services while serving as a diplomat overseas. He was particularly fond of an Anglican chapel in St. Petersburg, writing in his diary in 1833, "I went to the English chapel and heard an excellent, animated, evangelical discourse." The text was 2 Peter 3:9, "on the longsuffering [nature] of God and the repentance to which this should naturally lead" sinners. Buchanan added, "I was struck by the solemnity of this little congregation in a strange land. May God be with them! It is the most impressive sermon I have heard since I left America." Two decades later, while serving as US minister to Britain, he attended both Anglican and Free Church of Scotland services, including an Anglican service at a church in the English countryside that predated the Norman invasion. Although his mind wandered during the "very poor" sermon delivered there, his thoughts were spiritual: "My thoughts ran upon the numerous successive generations of mortals which had worshipped in this church for nearly a thousand years & the fleeting nature of man. But the Lord endureth forever & is the stay of those who put their trust in him."[62]

Ulysses Grant was a frequent attender of Methodist services in Galena, Illinois. While president, he and his wife, Julia, regularly attended services at Metropolitan Methodist Church in Washington. The church's preacher, John P. Newman, who became a close friend of the Grants, later recalled, "Storm of no kind ever kept him away. He was the most attentive and appreciative listener I ever had. . . . He was president of our Board of Trustees and a liberal contributor."[63]

While president, Rutherford Hayes regularly attended services at Foundry Methodist Church in Washington with his wife, Lucy. After his presidential term was completed, Hayes became a trustee of the Methodist Episcopal Church of Fremont, Ohio, a church that was later renamed the Hayes Memorial Methodist Church in his honor.[64]

James Garfield was also a lifetime churchgoer. At the age of eighteen in 1850, he attended a series of revival meetings led by Disciples of Christ evangelist William Lillie. On March 4 Garfield wrote in his diary, "Today I was 'buried with Christ in Baptism and arose to walk [in] newness of life [Romans 6:4].'" Three days later, he wrote, "Bro. Lillie is powerfully wielding the sword of truth." In 1852 he took copious notes of sermons delivered by several different preachers at a camp meeting. In 1853 he referred to a sermon by Amos S. Hayden on Providence in connection with prayer as "one of the finest sermons that I ever heard—very logical and instructive and several times burningly eloquent." In 1862, heartbroken by the carnage of the Civil War, he wrote to his wife, Lucretia, from his army camp outside Corinth, Mississippi, on a Sunday: "I have never longed so much as now for a quiet day in Church and a good religious sermon from some good man." In 1866, after hearing a sermon by the famous preacher Henry Ward Beecher, Garfield wrote in his diary, "He spoke on Love, a very searching and powerfully analytic discourse. The secret of Beecher's great power is a finely disciplined metaphysical intellect united to a large and sympathetic heart and moved by earnest and honest conviction." The following year, he heard the famous preacher Charles Spurgeon deliver a sermon in a packed house at Metropolitan Tabernacle in London, which held seven thousand people. Overwhelmed first by the a cappella singing of thousands of voices in unison, Garfield then relished Spurgeon's sermon, which contrasted the responses of Job and the apostle Paul to suffering. Garfield noted,

> He evidently proceeds upon the assumption that the Bible, all the Bible, in its very words, phrases, and sentences is the word of God and that a microscopic examination of it will reveal ever opening beauties and blessings. All the while he impresses you with that, and also with the living fullness and abundance of his faith in the presence of God and the personal accountability of all men to Him. An unusual fullness of belief in these respects seems to me to lie at the foundation of his power. . . . Every good man ought to be thankful for what Spurgeon is doing. . . . I felt that Spurgeon had opened an asylum where the great untitled, poor and destitute of this great city come and find their sorrows met with sympathy, their lowliness and longings for a better life touched by a large heart and an undoubted faith.

In 1873 Garfield noted, "It is rare that I stay at home from church. . . . I think a man should maintain the habit [of churchgoing] partly for his own sake and partly for the sake of others." While in Washington, he regularly attended services at the Disciples of Christ's Vermont Avenue Church.[65]

Like Garfield, Grover Cleveland was an admirer of Reverend Henry Ward Beecher. After Beecher died in 1887, Cleveland wrote to his widow: "More than thirty years ago I repeatedly enjoyed the opportunity of hearing him in his own pulpit. His warm utterances and the earnest interest he displayed in the practical things related to useful living, the hopes he inspired, and the manner in which he relieved the precepts of Christianity from gloom and cheerlessness made me feel that, though a stranger, he was my friend. Many years afterward we came to know each other; and since that time my belief in his friendship, based upon acquaintance and personal conduct, has been to me a source of the greatest satisfaction." Seven years later, Cleveland recalled a sermon in which Beecher contrasted the miseries of a hedonistic lifestyle with the satisfactions, both temporal and eternal, "of those who love and serve God and labor for humanity." In 1903 Cleveland claimed that this sermon "remained fresh and bright in my mind during all the time that has since passed." He added, "In days of trial and troublous perplexity its remembrance has been an unfailing comfort, and in every time of depression and discouragement the lesson it taught has brought restoration of hope and confidence. I remember as if it were but yesterday the fervid eloquence of the great preacher. . . . What this sermon has been to me in all these years I alone know." While president, Cleveland regularly attended services at the First Presbyterian Church.[66]

Benjamin Harrison became a Presbyterian deacon at the age of twenty-four, in 1857, and an elder in the church before his twenty-eighth birthday, in 1861, a position he occupied until his death four decades later. While fighting in the Union Army in Tennessee in 1864, he wrote to his wife, Caroline: "This is a beautiful Sabbath, and my heart yearns to sit with you in the house of God at home, and to go with my dear little ones to the Sabbath school I love so much, but if it cannot be . . . I must endeavor to find such grace as God will afford me in my private meditations in my lonely cabin, or at a brief service in the open air." While president, Harrison regularly attended services at the Presbyterian Church of the Covenant.[67]

William McKinley learned Hebrew from Reverend W. F. Day, his Methodist pastor in Poland, Ohio. He later served as a trustee of a Methodist church in Canton, Ohio, for most of his life. Active in the church, he often hosted visiting ministers. While president, he attended First Methodist Church of Washington.[68]

Theodore Roosevelt was a regular churchgoer. In 1900 he wrote, "I belong to the Dutch Reformed Church, to which my fathers have always belonged. The church I go to here in Albany is the same that my predecessor as Governor, old Peter Stuyvesant, went to when Albany was called Fort Orange, and New York New Amsterdam, two centuries and a half ago." While in Washington, he attended services at Grace Reformed Church, a church that belonged to a denomination closely associated with the Dutch Reformed Church, while his wife and children attended Episcopalian services. Every Saturday he sent flowers from the White House greenhouses to adorn his church on Sundays. He was so zealous about church attendance that during the gas rationing of World War I, he walked the three miles from his home in Sagamore Hill to the local church and back again each Sunday, even after an operation made it difficult for him to walk. He had no need for the hymn book; he sang hymns from memory. In 1917 he urged,

> On Sunday go to church. Yes—I know all the excuses. I know that one can worship the Creator and dedicate oneself to good living in a grove of trees, or by a running brook, or in one's own house, just as well as in church. But I also know that as a matter of cold fact the average man does not thus worship or thus dedicate himself. If he stays away from church, he does not spend his time in good works or in lofty meditation. He looks over the colored supplement of the newspaper; he yawns; and he finally seeks relief from the mental vacuity of isolation by going where the combined mental vacuity of many partially relieves the mental vacuity of each particular individual.

Regarding the churchgoer, Roosevelt added, "Even if he does not hear a good sermon, the probabilities are that he will listen and take part in reading some beautiful passages from the Bible, and if he is not familiar with the Bible, he has suffered a loss which he had better make all possible haste to correct."[69]

Woodrow Wilson's enjoyment of sermons was not confined to his father's. In 1876 he wrote in his diary that at the First Presbyterian Church of Princeton, he'd "heard a most eloquent sermon from a Canadian minister" named William Stephenson. He added, "His theme was the suffering of Christ. I never heard a man who had such a wonderful command of words as this one—his flow of appropriate beautiful and picturesque words was simply overwhelming, almost making my head swim." In 1899 Wilson was enthralled by a service at St. Giles in Edinburgh. He wrote, "I can vouch for it, if this morning's sermon be a typical example, that the Gospel is preached to them [the Scots] with simplicity and honest force. The sermon seemed to me to strike home. Certainly, I felt the force of it myself."[70]

While president, Wilson attended services at Central Presbyterian Church in Washington. In 1913 he referred to it as "a dear old-fashioned church such as I used to go to when I was a boy, amidst a congregation of simple and genuine people." A month later, he elaborated "We are immensely pleased with our little church here. It is so simple and old-fashioned. And the people in it are so genuine and fundamentally self-respecting. We never have had there the sense of being stared at or made capital of for the benefit of the congregation." Regarding the increased security since the assassination of William McKinley twelve years earlier, Wilson lamented, "If only I could go without having a secret service man sit right behind me, and half a dozen secret service men wait about the church while I am in it! What fun it will be some day to escape from arrest." Three months later, at a ceremony celebrating the laying of the cornerstone of the church's new building, he declared, "Every place of worship is sanctified by the repeated self-discovery which comes to the human spirit. As congregations sit under the word of God and utter the praise of God, there must come to them visions of beauty not elsewhere disclosed. . . . There is revealed to man what it is his duty to be and do. Therefore, I, in looking forward to the privilege in worshipping in this place, shall look forward with the hope that there may be revealed to me, as to you, fresh comprehension of duty and of privilege." In 1919, while in Paris, Wilson seldom missed services, despite being extremely busy negotiating the Treaty of Versailles. On Saturday, May 17, at a meeting of the Council of Four, he moved that a meeting scheduled for the following day be canceled and "that we all go to church." The motion carried, and British Prime Minister David Lloyd George and his daughter accompanied Wilson and his wife to a service at the Scottish Presbyterian Church. Wilson regarded Reverend Hugh Black's sermon "on the Lessons of the War" as "one of the most impressive" he had ever heard. Four months later, a few days before he suffered a devastating stroke, Wilson waved off his personal physician's concerns about his fatigue so he could attend a service at St. Paul's Protestant Episcopal Cathedral in Los Angeles.[71]

Calvin Coolidge and his wife, Grace, regularly attended services at Edwards Congregational Church in Northampton, Massachusetts. They later became members of the First Congregational Church in Washington. Coolidge claimed that the sermons of this church's pastor, Reverend Jason Pierce, were "the best in Washington."[72]

Franklin Roosevelt enjoyed Episcopalian services in Hyde Park and in Washington, relishing the hymns and psalms, though it was difficult for him to maneuver his leg braces in the narrow pews. He also enjoyed attending Methodist Christmas services because he liked the denomination's spirited singing style. He once brought Winston Churchill, who was an Anglican, to such a service, where the British prime minister heard "O Little Town of Bethlehem" for the first time. Roosevelt scheduled a private religious service, either in the White House or at Christ Church, just before each of his four inaugurations.[73]

Harry Truman was a lifelong Baptist. In 1952 he wrote in his diary, "I've never been of the opinion that Almighty God cares for the building or the form that a believer approaches the Maker of Heaven and Earth. 'When two or more or gathered together [Matthew 18:20]' or when one asks for help from God, he'll get it just as surely as will panoplied occupants of any pulpit. Forms and ceremonies impress a lot of people, but I've never thought that the Almighty could be impressed by anything but the heart and soul of the individual. That's why I'm a Baptist, whose church authority starts from the bottom—not the top." Yet when Truman was a child, his mother had enrolled him in the nearest Sunday school, which was Presbyterian. It was there that he met a lovely Episcopalian girl named Elizabeth (Bess) Wallace, whom he would eventually marry.[74]

As a senator and as vice president, Truman attended services at the First Baptist Church of Washington most Sundays, sitting in a back pew to avoid creating a distraction. But when Truman assumed the presidency in 1945, he discovered what most other modern presidents have learned: it is virtually impossible for a president to avoid distracting fellow worshipers. Truman soon found himself attending services at the chapel of Walter Reed Hospital, where photographers were banned. The problem continued even in his retirement years: "I have found that I cannot appear regularly in church, either in Grandview or Independence, without feeling like a showpiece or someone on exhibit. So, I do not go as often as I would want to. People ought to go to church to worship God—not to see some mortal who is there."[75]

While in the army, Dwight Eisenhower attended the services of various denominations. For instance, while stationed at Camp Gaillard in the Panama Canal Zone in the 1920s, he and his wife, Mamie, attended interdenominational services conducted by the camp's chaplain, Father Aristides Simoni, an Italian priest who struggled futilely against the discordance created by Puerto Rican soldiers singing in Spanish while the other congregants sang in English. During the presidential election campaign of 1952, Eisenhower rejected the distasteful advice to join a denomination for political advantage; however, starting on the morning of his inauguration, he began attending Presbyterian services with Mamie, who had been a lifelong member of that denomination. Shortly thereafter, he experienced the same phenomenon that appalled Truman. When the Eisenhowers officially joined

Edward L. R. Elson's National Presbyterian Church, the reverend assured the president that "there would be the minimum of publicity," but he then proceeded to issue a press release about the president's decision to join his church. Furious, Eisenhower wrote in his diary, "Mamie and & I joined a Presbyterian Church. We were scarcely home before the fact was being publicized by the Pastor to the hilt. I had been promised by him that there was to be no publicity. I feel like changing at once to another church of the same denomination. I shall if he breaks out again!"[76]

As a boy, John F. Kennedy attended St. Francis Xavier Church in Brookline, Massachusetts. Although he was never the most devout Catholic, he found the church a place of solace. After the death of his brother Joe, he felt some comfort in kneeling beside his sister Kathleen in the familiar pew of their childhood church.[77]

Lyndon Johnson became a member of the Disciples of Christ Church at age fourteen, when he made a profession of faith and was baptized during a revival sponsored by the denomination. He later became a member of the denomination's National City Christian Church in Washington. But as vice president and president, he most often attended Episcopalian services with his wife, Lady Bird (Claudia), at St. Mark's Church. During Johnson's presidency, his daughter Lucy converted to Catholicism, after which he would sometimes attend Mass with her at the small, simple, and racially integrated St. Dominick's Church; Johnson also sought out local Catholic chapels for private prayer and meditation. On one particular Sunday in 1966, he attended both a Catholic Mass with Lucy and an Episcopalian service with his other daughter, Lynda Bird. He found it "a very encouraging sign" that both sermons revolved around the theme of "Love thy neighbor as thyself" (Leviticus 19:18; Matthew 19:19). While at his ranch in the latter part of his presidency and during his retirement years, he often attended Mass at St. Francis Xavier Catholic Church in Stonewall, Texas. Its pastor, Father Wunibald Schneider, became a close friend and spiritual advisor, so much so that Johnson intervened with Schneider's bishop to prevent the priest's transfer to another parish. Nevertheless, Johnson continued to attend Episcopalian services with his wife, as well as Disciples of Christ services.[78]

A lifelong Episcopalian, Gerald Ford attended Immanuel Church-on-the-Hill in Alexandria, Virginia, while a congressman. In addition to serving as an usher and lay reader at the church, he was also a member of a church committee that provided services to low-income families.[79]

Jimmy and Rosalynn Carter were members of a series of Baptist churches in Plains, Atlanta, and Washington. In retirement, the Carters became members of Maranatha Church, a small church in Plains, where they taught

Sunday school classes. Jimmy later wrote, "Having a church home has helped fulfill a need for stability and a sense of belonging for us." In 1997 he noted, "Many of us have gotten away from preparing ourselves for worship. Instead, we assess church services almost as if they were shows put on to entertain us. . . . What makes a successful worship service is not the beauty of the music or the eloquence of the preacher or even the friendliness of the greeting we receive. Instead, it's the presence of God in our hearts, and that depends on our attitude and what we are seeking. We need to be prepared mentally and spiritually to participate fully in worship."[80]

Since Ronald Reagan's father was an alcoholic, his pastor, Reverend Ben Cleaver of the First Christian Church of Dixon, Illinois, acted as a surrogate father for the youth, even teaching him how to drive. Reagan dated Cleaver's daughter Margaret for eight years. Reagan later recalled that he was "as close to being a 'minister's kid' as one can be without actually moving into the rectory." Unfortunately, as president, Reagan would discover, like many of his predecessors, that his attendance presented serious problems for his fellow worshippers. In fact, he became so concerned that he might be endangering them, given the threats against his life and terrorist bombings around the world, that he stopped attending services. Five months after John Hinckley's assassination attempt in 1981, Reagan wrote in his diary, "It bothers me not to be in church on Sunday, but I don't see how I can with the security problem. I'm a hazard to others. I hope God realizes how much I feel that I'm in a temple when I'm out in his beautiful forest & countryside, as we were this morning." In 1984, the year following the terrorist bombing of American Marines in Beirut, he wrote, "We have always been churchgoers and would be now if it were not for the terrorist threats. We could handle the usual kind of kooky threat directed against me. But the situation has changed, as we saw in Beirut. Our intelligence now indicates the possibility of attack, which could endanger a great many people." He added that he sometimes received the Lord's Supper in the White House and attended church services "with no advance warning and without creating a regular pattern." Five months later, he said, "I miss going to church, but I think the Lord understands." In 1988 his son Michael found him literally counting the months "until I will be out of office and . . . able to attend church again." Indeed, he returned to the small country church near his ranch that he had attended prior to the presidency, where he then worshipped regularly until felled by Alzheimer's.[81]

As a child, George H. W. Bush attended Episcopalian services at Christ Church in Greenwich, Connecticut. As an adult, he served as an elder in the First Presbyterian Church of Midland, Texas. He later attended Episcopalian services at St. Martin's Church in Houston, where he served as a vestryman and as an usher. While in Washington, he attended services at National Cathedral and St. John's Church but continued to call his pastor in Houston, Tom Bagsby, every Sunday to inquire about the church and its members. While serving as the United States' unofficial envoy to China in 1974 and 1975, he attended services at Chongmenwen Christian Church in Beijing. Later, as president, he recalled, "Our daughter was christened in a church service where there were maybe 10 or 12 Westerners and 5 or 6 faithful Chinese who were permitted in what used to be the YMCA to have this Sunday service, mainly for diplomats." By the time he returned in 1989, the church possessed almost one thousand members and had moved to a much larger building. Bush said, "I was all choked up. They welcomed me back, and they said, 'How is our sister, Dorothy?'—that's our daughter who was baptized in that church." He told the congregants there,

> Our family has always felt that church is the place to seek guidance and seek strength and peace. And when you are far away from home, you realize how much that means. This church, in a sense, was our home away from home. It's a little different, though. Today we came up with 20 motorcars in a motorcade, and I used to come to church on my bicycle, my Flying Pigeon. But it doesn't matter how you come to church; the important thing is that the feeling is the same, the feeling of being in the spirit of Jesus Christ. And, yes, our daughter, Dorothy, now the mother of two children, was baptized in this church, and that gives us a special feeling of identity and warmth.

Three of the church's ministers later visited Bush in the White House. After he retired, Bush returned to his old church, St. Martin's in Houston. When he and Barbara were given a service award by the church, he broke down and wept while attempting to speak. Finally, he said, "This church just means so much to us."[82]

George W. Bush attended services at First Presbyterian Church in Midland with his parents as a child. He later attended Episcopalian services in Houston and Kennebunkport. He went on to attend services at First United Methodist Church in Midland with his wife, Laura, and his two daughters in the late 1970s; Highland Park United Methodist Church in Dallas, after he moved there in 1989; and Tarrytown United Methodist Church in Austin while he was governor of Texas. Like his father, he attended services in Beijing while president, using the opportunity to call for religious freedom in China.[83]

Though raised by an irreligious mother and grandparents, Barack Obama attended Trinity United Church of Christ in the South Side of Chicago for over twenty years. In fact, he borrowed the title of his second memoir, *The Audacity of Hope*, from one of Reverend Jeremiah Wright's sermons. As Obama explained in his first memoir, *Dreams from My Father*, the sermon was "a meditation on a fallen world" and the hope that nonetheless survives it. Obama wrote,

> At the foot of that cross, inside the thousands of churches across the city, I imagined the stories of ordinary black people merging with the stories of David and Goliath, Moses and Pharaoh, the Christians [sic] in the lion's den, Ezekiel's field of dry bones. These stories—of survival, and freedom, and hope—became our story, my story; the blood that had spilled was our blood, the tears our tears; until this black church, on this bright day, seemed once more a vessel carrying the story of a people into future generations and into a larger world. Our trials and triumphs became at once unique and universal, black and more than black.

He found himself weeping. Regarding Reverend Wright, Obama later recalled, "His sermons were full of pop references, slang, humor, and genuine religious insight that not only prompted cheers and shouts from his members but burnished his reputation as one of the best preachers in the country." But Obama added, "There were times when I found Reverend Wright's sermons over the top," as they were laden with critiques of America that were tangential to the sermon topic and filled with conspiracy theories. Obama mused, "It was as if this erudite, middle-aged, light-skinned Black man were straining for street cred, trying to 'keep it real.'" Although the Obamas were sporadic churchgoers, they found the experience "meaningful" when they did go. In fact, Wright performed the marriage ceremony for Obama and his wife, Michelle. Nevertheless, while campaigning for the presidency in 2008, Obama broke with Wright following the national publicity given to the pastor's 2001 "chickens coming home to roost" sermon, in which he attributed the September 11 attacks to divine wrath against the United States because of the nation's past support for apartheid in South Africa and current support for alleged Israeli mistreatment of Palestinians. Other sermons that contained anti-Semitic statements, wild conspiracy theories, and deep bitterness ("God damn America!") soon surfaced.[84]

The second Catholic ever to hold the presidency, Joe Biden regularly attended Mass at St. Joseph on the Brandywine in Greenville, Delaware, for decades. As vice president and president, he attended Holy Trinity Church in Washington.[85]

Through their publication, the sermons of popular preachers sometimes outlived not only the preaching but the preachers themselves. Sermons were one of the most popular forms of literature in eighteenth- and nineteenth-century America. Published sermons played a key role in fomenting the American Revolution. Some presidents were avid readers of sermon collections. From 1809, when he boarded the ship taking him to his duties as the United States' first minister to Russia, until 1814, John Quincy Adams read a large number of sermons by Jean Baptiste Massillon, the Catholic bishop of Clermont (1663–1742). Adams appreciated the fact that Massillon was not one of those popularity-seeking clerics who would "make the preacher pleasing to the sinner, but not the sinner displeasing to himself." Adams also admired the sermons of John Tillotson, the archbishop of Canterbury from 1691 to 1694, and declared in a lecture to Harvard students, "To an ingenious youth, anxious to learn the extent of his duties for the purpose of performing them; to an ambitious youth, eager to possess the keys to the understanding and the heart; finally, to every parent who feels the happiness and comfort of his life to be bound up in the fortunes and the virtues of his children, I know not where I could look for a work more deserving of being recommended to their notice and meditation" than Tillotson's sermons. James Buchanan was fond of the sermons of John Wesley, the founder of Methodism, reading them "over & over again with great interest."[86]

Society

American presidents were raised in a profoundly Christian society. Some received biblical names like John, Thomas, James, Abraham, and Benjamin from parents who bore such names as Hannah, Jesse, Peter, and Sarah. Some married women with biblical names such as Martha, Abigail, and Elizabeth. Granted, most of these names had become so common that they often occasioned little thought about their biblical origins, but that is precisely the point: American presidents lived in a culture so steeped in Christianity that many of its biblical elements had begun to operate at a subconscious level.

These presidents were surrounded by communities with names derived from the Bible, such as Abilene, Ararat, Bethel, Bethesda, Bethlehem, Ebenezer, Eden, Eleazer, Elisha, Ephrata, Gaza, Goshen, Hebron, Jericho, Joppa, Los Angeles, Mizpah, Mt. Carmel, Mt. Gilboa, Mt. Hermon, Mt. Horeb, Mt. Moriah, Mt. Nebo, Mt. Olive, Mt. Tabor, Naomi, New Canaan, Newark, Pisgah, Rehoboth, Salem, San Jose, Sharon, Shiloh, Siloam, St.

Louis, St. Paul, Zarephath, and Zion. Providence was, of course, named after an important biblical concept, and Philadelphia derived its name from Revelation 3:7–10, in which Jesus praises the church located in a city of that name in Asia Minor.[87]

Presidents lived in a society that was filled with biblical expressions, including "My brother's keeper . . . (Genesis 4:9)"; "Man does not live by bread alone (Deuteronomy 8:3)"; "The apple of his eye . . . (Deuteronomy 32:10)"; "A voice crying in the wilderness . . . (Isaiah 40:3)"; "Nothing new under the sun . . . (Ecclesiastes 1:9)"; "Sparing the rod . . . (Proverbs 13:24)"; "Pride goes before destruction (Proverbs 16:18)"; "My cup overflows (Psalms 23:5)"; A man after his own heart . . . (1 Samuel 13:14)"; "How the mighty have fallen (2 Samuel 1:19)"; "The handwriting on the wall . . . (Daniel 5:5)"; "Into the lion's den . . . (Daniel 6:16)"; "Sowing the wind and reaping the whirlwind . . . (Hosea 8:7)"; "The meek shall inherit the earth (Matthew 5:5)"; "Blessed are the peacemakers (Matthew 5:9)"; "The salt of the earth . . . (Matthew 5:13)"; "A city on a hill . . . (Matthew 5:14)"; "Don't hide your lamp under a bushel (Matthew 5:15)"; "Turn the other cheek (Matthew 5:39)"; "One hand does not know what the other is doing (Matthew 6:3)"; "You cannot serve two masters (Matthew 6:24)"; "Casting your pearls before swine . . . (Matthew 7:6)"; The blind leading the blind . . . (Matthew 15:14)"; "Render unto Caesar what is Caesar's (Matthew 22:21)"; "Better for him if he had never been born (Matthew 26:24)"; "The spirit is willing but the flesh is weak (Matthew 26:41)"; "Those who live by the sword die by the sword (Matthew 26:52)"; "Washing one's hands of the whole affair . . . (Matthew 27:24)"; "A prophet is honored everywhere except in his own country (Mark 6:4)"; "Walking on water . . . (Mark 6:48)"; "Lambs among wolves . . . (Luke 10:3)"; "Casting the first stone . . . (John 8:7)"; "A doubting Thomas . . . (John 20:25)"; "Being all things to all people . . . (1 Corinthians 9:22)"; "The love of money is the root of all sorts of evil (1 Timothy 6:10)"; and "Fighting the good fight . . . (1 Timothy 6:12)."

Throughout American history, a series of revivals served to reenergize Christianity and magnify biblical influence. In the 1730s and 1740s, the colonies were rocked by a religious revival that later became known as the Great Awakening. Jonathan Edwards launched what became known as the Little Awakening in 1734 and 1735 in Northampton, Massachusetts. Inspired by Edwards's account of the revival, George Whitefield sought to save souls by preaching the gospel throughout Britain and the American colonies. Replacing the predominant logical and theological style with a more direct and dramatic simplicity, he attracted large audiences. His grand tour of the American colonies in 1739 and 1740 was a triumph in which his outdoor sermons attracted and inspired unprecedented crowds numbering in the thousands. His host in Philadelphia, Benjamin Franklin, later recalled, "From being thoughtless or indifferent about religion, it seemed as if all the world were growing religious, so that one could not walk thro' the town in an evening without hearing psalms sung in different families of every street."[88]

The Great Awakening helped cause the American Revolution in three ways. First, as we have seen, it led to the establishment of a host of colleges. These colleges, which taught Whig principles alongside Protestant Christianity, trained most of the founders. Second, as the first intercolonial movement, the Great Awakening united Americans by reminding them of a shared biblical tradition, thereby dissolving denominational and regional walls. The resultant formation of a national consciousness was crucial not only to the success of the Revolution but also to its very undertaking. No colony would have rebelled against the greatest power on earth without the assurance of assistance from the other colonies. The American Revolution's leaders would never have undertaken it had they not possessed a strong sense that it was a collective movement. Third, the Great Awakening revived two biblical themes, the danger of corruption and the concept of a divine mission, that had been central to American Puritanism and thus were deeply rooted in native soil.

When the parliamentary acts of the 1760s reawakened among the descendants of those who had fled religious persecution the belief that Britain was hopelessly corrupt, it was plain to many Americans that they must resist not merely to defend their natural rights of life, liberty, and property but also to save their very souls as well. In 1772 Samuel Adams, who has justly been called "the Father of the American Revolution" for his able leadership of the Boston patriots, asked, "Is it not High Time for the People of this Country explicitly to declare whether they will be Freemen or Slaves? . . . The Salvation of our Souls is interested in the Event. For whenever Tyranny is establish'd, Immorality of every Kind comes in like a Torrent. It is in the Interest of Tyrants to reduce the People to Ignorance and Vice." A year later, Benjamin Franklin maintained that the British government's claim to unlimited power over the colonists amounted to the contention that it could not only kill the colonist's bodies but even "damn their souls to all Eternity by compelling them, if it pleases, to worship the Devil." This was a reference to Matthew 10:28, in which Jesus warns, "Do not fear those who kill the body but are unable to kill the soul, but rather fear Him [God] who is able to destroy both soul and body in hell." The British government, in claiming unbounded powers, was claiming what rightly belonged to God alone. As such, it was a false idol that could be worshipped only at the peril of the colonists' souls. In 1776 John Witherspoon, soon to be a signer of the Declaration of Independence, preached a sermon in which he declared, "There is not a single instance in history in which civil liberty was lost and religious liberty preserved entire. If therefore we yield up our temporal property, we at the same time deliver the conscience into bondage."[89]

While Old Light opponents of revivalism (including most Anglican ministers, two-thirds of whom returned to England during the Revolutionary War) often remained loyal to Britain, New Light revivalist clergymen were among the first, the most ardent, and the most influential of patriots. Dubbed the "black regiment" by Boston loyalist Peter Oliver in reference to their clerical garb, these ministers were crucial to preparing the American public for independence in an age in which rebellion was considered the darkest act of villainy and rebels were summarily hanged, which they achieved by convincing Americans that God favored the Revolution. In 1774 the loyalist Daniel Leonard observed, "When the clergy engage in political warfare, they become a most powerful engine, either to support or overthrow the state. What effect must it have had upon the audience to hear the same sentiments and principles which they had before read in a newspaper delivered on Sundays from the sacred desk, with a religious awe, and the most solemn appeals to heaven from lips which they had been taught from their cradles to believe could utter nothing but eternal truths." John Adams reported to Abigail from Philadelphia, where he was serving in the Continental Congress: "The Clergy of all Denominations here Preach Politicks and War.... They are a Flame of Fire." Thomas Jefferson noted approvingly that sermons advocating resistance to British tyranny ran through Virginia "like a shock of electricity." A British colonial official reported that clergymen were so deeply involved in the conflict that it had become, "at the Bottom[,] very much a Religious war." John Adams later recalled, "The Revolution was in the minds and hearts of the people, a change in their religious sentiments of their duties and obligations."[90]

The revival of the Puritan fear of corruption was accompanied by the revival of the Puritan sense of divine mission. The religious mission of the Puritans to turn New England into the world's incubator for a purer form of Protestantism—into what John Winthrop called "a city upon a hill," based on Jesus' statement in Matthew 5:14 ("You are the light of the world; a city that is set on a hill cannot be hidden")—was gradually transformed into the political mission of all Americans to convert the United States into a model of republicanism. Rarely was this conception ever stated as baldly as when, in 1780, John Adams wrote, "America is the City set upon a Hill," but the idea was in the air everywhere. The transition to this secularized version of the

Puritan mission was greatly smoothed by the theological and moralistic tone of political rhetoric, which conflated tyranny with sin, liberty with virtue, and military victories on behalf of the latter with salvation.[91]

Before the founders even left the political stage, the country was rocked by a Second Great Awakening, which transformed American society. Beginning in 1795 and reaching a climax from 1800 to 1801, James McGready and four Presbyterian colleagues, joined by a Methodist preacher, spearheaded a series of summer revivals in central Kentucky. McGready's revival soon spread throughout the South and into Ohio, western Pennsylvania, and New York. Within a few decades, the entire nation had felt the reverberations of the Second Great Awakening.[92]

The Second Great Awakening spread postmillennialism, the belief that Jesus would return only after humans had created the Millennium, the utopia prophesied in the Bible, through their own efforts in combination with the Holy Spirit. Revivalist preachers like Lyman Beecher and Charles Finney suggested that the triumph of American-style democracy and freedom of thought and expression around the world would bring on the Millennium, a hope later destroyed by the Civil War. Postmillennialism spurred a plethora of social reform movements, including efforts on behalf of public education, temperance, aid for the poor and the mentally ill, prison reform, and women's rights.[93]

One of the most important reform efforts produced by the Second Great Awakening was the abolitionist movement. As late as 1830, most American emancipation societies were conservative, gradualist institutions located in the slave states of the South. But in the 1830s, the movement shifted to the North and became much more evangelical and, therefore, much more radical. On January 1, 1831, twenty-six-year-old William Lloyd Garrison established the first antislavery newspaper in America, the *Liberator*. Garrison declared that the Bible was opposed to slavery. In 1833 he joined with New York merchants Arthur and Lewis Tappan to form the American Antislavery Society, which called for the immediate emancipation of slaves without compensation to slaveholders. With the financial backing of the Tappans, the society filled the mails with 750,000 samples of abolitionist literature within five years. By that time the organization possessed 250,000 members. Garrison's passionately moralistic rhetorical style and his themes of sin, damnation, and salvation were as evangelical as those of the revivalists. In 1839 he wrote, "Genuine abolitionism . . . is of heaven, not of men."[94]

Most of the other abolitionists were also evangelical Christians. The western part of New York, which had become known as the "burned-over district" because of its fiery revivalists, became one of the strongholds of antislavery agitation. Abolitionists there were led by Theodore Weld, a man who had attended Lane Theological Seminary and whose father and older brother were ministers. Often beaten and pelted with rocks, eggs, and vegetables by angry mobs, Weld toured New England, New York, Pennsylvania, and Ohio on behalf of abolitionism. Harriet Beecher Stowe, the author of *Uncle Tom's Cabin*, the most popular and effective antislavery novel, was the daughter of one of the most famous preachers of the period, Lyman Beecher. Gradually, the antislavery movement absorbed most of the reformers and the zeal of the other movements.[95]

Persevering amidst persecution, the antebellum abolitionists gradually secured enough sympathy for their cause in the North that Abraham Lincoln, though fighting the Civil War primarily to save the Union, was able to envision the Emancipation Proclamation as a measure that would bring support rather than dissension to the Union war effort. Thus did the abolitionists bring to a successful conclusion the effort begun by the founders in their abolition of slavery throughout the North, applying the biblical principle of spiritual equality to the issue of servitude.

Of course, the influence of the Bible on American society and politics did not end with the Second Great Awakening. In the late nineteenth and early twentieth centuries, followers of the Social Gospel movement sought to mandate social reform by interpreting biblical passages regarding the individual's duty to aid his fellow humans. They played influential roles in the adoption of workman's compensation, safer working conditions, the abolition of child labor, the eight-hour workday, conservationism, public works programs, and women's suffrage. By the mid-twentieth century, a Christian clergyman named Martin Luther King Jr. was combining an appeal to the biblical principle of spiritual equality with the New Testament technique of nonviolent resistance to secure civil and political rights for African Americans. Like their fellow citizens, American presidents were products of these forces.[96]

CHAPTER 2

An Invaluable Guide

Given most presidents' immersion in Scripture as children due to its ubiquity in their homes, schools, churches, and society, it is not surprising that many of them have considered the Bible an invaluable guide, an incomparable source of spiritual and moral wisdom. The fact that presidents have referred to this source of wisdom in private diaries and letters and that they have continued to refer to it long after their political careers ended testifies to the sincerity of their devotion to Scripture. Though they were socially and politically useful, their public references to the Bible were not generally mere formalities or exercises in political opportunism. In fact, many presidents have taken advantage of the greater leisure time afforded by retirement from political office to study the Bible. Furthermore, throughout their lives, many presidents have promoted the spread of biblical knowledge not only in foreign nations via missionaries but among their own children and grandchildren and in American society in general. This is because they have deemed Christian faith crucial not only to the salvation of souls but also to fostering the morality they have considered essential to the survival and success of the republic.

Lifelong Study

Many presidents have studied the Bible throughout their lives. George Washington was an active man who desired portable scripture that could accompany him anywhere. In 1771 he ordered a combination Anglican Book of Common Prayer and translation of the Psalms in metrical verse. He specified that it must be compact enough to carry in his pocket.[1]

Washington's favorite verse was Micah 4:4, a prophecy of the reign of the Messiah, a reign that Christians equated with the Millennium of Christ's rule. Micah prophesied, "Every man will sit under his vine and under his fig tree, and none shall make him afraid." The imagery of this verse reminded Washington of the natural pleasures of his beloved estate, Mount Vernon. He used the "vine and fig tree" reference nearly four dozen times during the latter half of his life. Like other Federalists, Washington often cited the millennial verse as something he hoped could be achieved through the Constitution. He claimed,

> When the people shall find themselves secure under an energetic government, when foreign nations shall be disposed to give us equal advantages in commerce free from the dread of retaliation, when the burdens of the war shall be in a manner done away with by the sale of western lands, when the seeds of happiness which are sown here shall begin to expand themselves, and when everyone (under his own vine and fig tree) shall begin to taste the fruits of freedom, then all these blessings (for all these blessings will come) will be referred to the fostering influence of the new government.

As president in 1790, Washington wrote to a Jewish congregation in Newport, Rhode Island: "May the Children of the Stock of Abraham [Acts 13:26] who dwell in this land continue to merit and enjoy the good will of the other Inhabitants, while every one shall sit in safety under his own vine and fig tree, and there shall be none to make him afraid." In 1797 alone, newly released from the rigors of the presidency and enjoying his retirement, Washington used the phrase "under my own Vine and Fig tree" or "seated in the shade of my Vine and Fig tree" in at least six different letters. The references continued almost until the time of his death, two years later. Washington was not prone to quoting literary works of any kind, so his repeated use of the phrase indicates that its imagery touched a strong cord within him. It reflected the peace, rest, and natural beauty that his home represented—blessings that his public service had denied him for so many years. To Washington, Mount Vernon was a foretaste of the Millennium.[2]

Shortly after graduating from Harvard, John Adams embraced the combination of Christian and classical study then considered most likely to improve the mind. He wrote in his diary:

> I am resolved not to neglect my Time as I did last year. I am resolved to rise with the Sun and to study the Scriptures on Thursday, Friday, Saturday,

and Sunday mornings and to study some Latin author the other three mornings. Noons and Nights I intend to read English Authors. This is my fixt Determination, and I will set down every neglect and every compliance with this Resolution. May I blush whenever I suffer one hour to pass unimproved. I will rouse up my mind and fix my Attention. I will stand collected within myself and think upon what I read and what I see. I will strive with all my soul to be something more than Persons who have had less Advantages than myself.

In 1761, while acting as an attorney for Daniel Prat, who was suing Thomas Colson for violating the terms of apprenticeship by failing to teach him to read, Adams summarized his Protestant argument on the importance of Bible reading: "No Priest or Pope has any Right to say what I shall believe, and I will not believe one Word they say if I think it is not founded in Reason and in Revelation. Now how can I judge what my Bible justifies unless I can read my Bible?" Adams added that Bible reading was as useful in the fulfillment of a person's civic obligation to vote wisely as it was necessary to the performance of his religious and moral duties: "A Man who can read will find in his Bible, in the common sermon Books that common People have by them, and even in the Almanack and the News Papers, Rules and observations that will enlarge his Range of Thought and enable him the better to judge who has and who has not that Integrity of Heart and that Compass of Knowledge and Understanding which form the Statesman." More than half a century later, on Christmas Day in 1813, Adams wrote to Thomas Jefferson, asking, "Do you know anything of the Prophecy of Enoch? Can you give me a comment on the 6th, the 9th, the 14th verses of the epistle of Jude?" The first two of these verses refer to fallen angels; the last quotes of Enoch regard the coming of the Messiah, which Jude identifies as the Second Coming of Christ. Three years later, Adams declared, "For fifty years I have neglected all Sciences but Government & Religion," adding that while he had, by that time, relinquished the former preoccupation, "the latter still occupies my thoughts." Study of the Bible and sermon literature occupied much of the quarter century of his retirement.[3]

Jefferson was another lifelong student of the Bible. In 1787 he ordered a copy of the Septuagint, the Greek translation of the Old Testament, and a Greek New Testament. Thereafter, he ordered many different Greek, Latin, and English New Testaments, including the first Greek New Testament printed in America. In 1800, while awaiting the final outcome of his own presidential election, he ordered Scotcherd's pocket Bible, calling it "an edition which I have long been wishing to get to make part of a portable library which the course of my life has rendered convenient." While president, Jefferson often passed time in the evenings by studying the Bible. In 1813, after joining John Adams in praising Cleanthes's "Hymn to Jupiter," Jefferson added, "Yet in the contemplation of a being so superlative [as God], the hyperbolic flights of the Psalmist may often be followed with approbation, even with rapture; and I have no hesitation in giving him the palm over all the Hymnists of every language, and of every time." Jefferson then commented on the merits and flaws of numerous translations of the Psalms. Adams replied in full agreement, writing, "The Psalms of David, in Sublimity, beauty, pathos, and Originality, or, in one Word, poetry, are superior to all the Odes, Hymns, and Songs in any language. . . . Could David be translated as well [as some of the Greek and Latin authors] his superiority would be universally acknowledged."[4]

While serving as the United States' first minister to Russia in 1810, John Quincy Adams recorded in his diary: "I have made it a practice for several years to read the Bible through in the course of every year. I usually devote to this reading the first hour after I arise every morning." Because he knew that public duties, including travel, would prevent him from reading Scripture some days, he averaged about five chapters per morning on the days that he did read so as not to fall behind. This meant that some years, he finished early, in which case he would begin again. While he admitted that he found some parts of the holy book difficult to understand, he added, "At every perusal I do add something to my knowledge of the Scriptures, something to my veneration for them, and I would hope, something to the improvement which ought to result from this occupation and which is the great motive to it." In 1812 he read a German Bible and compared its translation to those of English and French Bibles. Five years later, he noted, "The New Testament I have repeatedly read in the original Greek, in the Latin, in the Genevan Protestant, and in Sacy's Catholic French translations, in Luther's German translation, in the common English Protestant, and in the Douay Catholic (Jesuitical) translations."[5]

Like Jefferson, Adams especially loved the Psalms. In 1812 he wrote,

I came in the course of my Scripture reading this morning to Psalm 37—'Fret not thyself because of evildoers' &c.—and was struck with its excellent and profound morality. The duty of reliance upon [the] redistributive justice of God, without being staggered either by the transient prosperities of the wicked or by the afflictions of the good, is inculcated with a force of sentiment and an energy of expression such as I have never met in any of the profane writers. Plutarch's Treatise on the Delays of Divine Justice and Juvenal's 13th Satire are not comparable to it. They contain, with more diffusion, a part of the same doctrine. But this Psalm was written centuries before Homer and a thousand years before Juvenal and Plutarch. There is not indeed in the Psalm any recurrence to the rewards and punishments of another life, and it leaves the argument entirely open for the sublime improvement of the Christian doctrine. But it is to be observed that one of its promises of blessedness (to the meek, for they shall inherit the earth) is expressly quoted and repeated by our Saviour in his Sermon on the Mount (Matt. 5 v. 5). There is so much prosperity to the wicked in this world, and the good, as far as human nature can be called good, are followed by such great and manifold afflictions, that some consolatory principle of trust upon divine justice is necessary to the comfort of existence. I know of none equal to that in this Psalm, with the addition of the Christian faith.

After reading both Joseph Addison's and J. B. Rousseau's translations of the nineteenth psalm, Adams praised the psalm's "sublime simplicity" and "elevating grandeur," and, regarding the heavens, added, "The Psalmist's idea that they declare the glory and handiwork of God was above the reach of Plato."[6]

In 1831 Adams devoted time every day to converting various psalms into stanzas of his own creation. Regarding the nineteenth psalm, he wrote, "This is one of the most beautiful, if not the most beautiful, of the whole collection of the Psalms. It contains two great associated ideas: first, that the firmament of heaven is a demonstration of an Omnipotent Creator; and, secondly, that His laws, statutes, and judgments are the demonstration of His moral perfection. The illustrations of these two ideas are very impressive." A couple of months later, he observed, "The Psalms appear to a person taking them in hand for translation a series of perpetual repetitions. Yet in every one of them there is some thought not expressed in any other." In 1840 he consoled himself about the depressing state of American politics with the remembrance of Psalm 42:5. He wrote, "Seeing, as I do from day to day the downward tendency of all moral principle in our politics, I am almost ready to sink into despondency and to believe that a judgment of heaven is impending over us. But 'why art thou cast down, O my soul? And why art thou disquieted within me? Trust in God!'" In 1845 he was thrilled when a church choir sang his verse translation of Psalms 65, writing, "Were it possible to compress into one pulsation of the heart the pleasure which, in the whole period of my life, I have enjoyed in praise from the lips of mortal man, it would not weigh a straw to balance the ecstasy of delight that streamed from my eyes as the organ pealed and the choir of voices sang the praise of Almighty God from the soul of David, adapted to my native language by me."[7]

In retirement, Andrew Jackson ended each day by reading a chapter from the Bible to his family, sometimes following it with a short commentary of his own, and then joined other family members in singing a hymn and kneeling in prayer. He also read biblical commentaries. On his deathbed, he told the members of his household that they must all "keep holy the Sabbath day and read the New Testament."[8]

When a Pittsburgh welcoming committee traveled to the boarding house where William Henry Harrison was staying before his inauguration, they found him reading the Bible. He explained that for the past twenty years, he had always read Scripture before retiring each evening, then added, "At first a matter of duty . . . it has now become a pleasure."[9]

Abraham Lincoln's scriptural quotations and references demonstrate a close familiarity with the Bible. His biographer and longtime friend, Isaac N. Arnold, recalled that Lincoln "knew the Bible by heart," adding, "There was not a clergyman to be found so familiar with it as he." In a famous speech at Springfield, Illinois, in 1858, Lincoln declared, "'A house divided against itself cannot stand.' I believe this government cannot endure permanently half slave and half free." Here Lincoln quoted Jesus in Matthew 12:25. Jesus had made the statement to refute the allegation that He was able to cast out demons because He was in league with them. The same year, while preparing a lecture on discoveries and inventions, Lincoln scoured the Old Testament for every reference to early clothing, iron working, transportation, and agriculture. His allusions to Adam and other biblical figures, as well as to the Bible in general, betrayed no hint of skepticism. The following year, he declared, "The good old maxims of the Bible are applicable, truly applicable, to human affairs."[10]

Lincoln's Gettysburg Address was composed in a biblical style and presented biblical themes. Lincoln employed the simplicity, archaic verbiage, cadence, and themes of the King James Bible to bestow on the oration an aura of authority and gravity. The first words of the speech, "Four score and seven years ago," harkened back to the reference in Psalms 90:10 to a human's "threescore and ten" years of earthly life. Lincoln then referred to the founders as "our fathers," a term often used for ancestors in the King James Bible. "Our fathers" was followed by "brought forth," a phrase that the

Bible employed in reference to God's creation of the universe (Genesis 1:12) and Mary's deliverance of the Christ child (Matthew 1:25). The pairing of "hallowed" with "ground" was reminiscent of the holy ground on which Moses encountered the burning bush (Exodus 3:5). Other biblical phrases in the address include "in vain," which appears over fifty times in the King James Bible, and "shall not perish," which echoes John 3:16. Like Jesus, the Union soldiers memorialized in Lincoln's oration "gave their lives" so that others "might live." The sacrifices of the war made possible "a new birth" for the nation, just as Jesus's death enabled believers to be "born again" (John 3:3). The sin of slavery produced national death in the form of a horrible civil war that ripped the nation apart, but the sacrifice of hallowed ones would enable the sin itself to be put to death. Thus, Lincoln highlighted the biblical themes of sin, death, redemption, and rebirth in the speech. He added the phrase "under God" to the address at the last minute to underscore its spiritual nature.[11]

Lincoln biographer David Donald noted regarding the president's years in office: "Often, when he could spare the time from his duties, he sought an answer to his questions in the well-thumbed pages of his Bible, reading most often the Old Testament prophets and the Psalms. He found comfort and reassurance in the Bible." In an 1864 letter made famous by the film *Saving Private Ryan*, Lincoln employed the biblical images of the sacrifice and the altar on which it was placed. Writing to Lydia Bixby, a mother who had reportedly lost five sons in battle (the actual number was two), he declared, "I feel how weak and fruitless must be any words of mine which should attempt to beguile you from the grief of a loss so overwhelming. But I cannot refrain from tendering you the consolation that may be found in the thanks of the Republic they died to save. I pray that our Heavenly Father may assuage the anguish of your bereavement and leave you only the cherished memory of the loved and lost and the solemn pride that must be yours, to have laid so costly a sacrifice upon the altar of Freedom."[12]

Lincoln often cited Genesis 3:19 with regard to slavery, albeit usually accompanying it with the admonition against judging others found in Matthew 7:1. In 1864 he immersed a group of Baptists (appropriately enough) in Scripture, writing,

> I can only thank you for thus adding to the effective and almost universal support which the Christian communities are so zealously giving to the country

and to liberty. Indeed, it is difficult to conceive how it could be otherwise with anyone professing Christianity or even having ordinary perceptions of right and wrong. To read in the Bible, as the word of God himself, that "In the sweat of thy face shalt thou eat bread," and to preach there from that, "In the sweat of other men's faces shalt thou eat bread" to my mind can scarcely be reconciled with honest sincerity. When brought to my final reckoning, may I have to answer for robbing no man of his goods, yet more tolerable even this than for robbing one of himself and all that was his. When a year or two ago, those professedly holy men of the South met in semblance of prayer and devotion, and, in the name of Him who said, "As ye would all men should do unto you, do ye even so unto them [Matthew 7:12]," appealed to the Christian world to aid them in doing to a whole race of men as they would have no man do unto themselves, to my way of thinking, they contemned and insulted God and His church far more than did Satan when he tempted the Saviour with the Kingdoms of the earth [Matthew 4:8–9]. The devil's attempt was no more false and far less hypocritical. But let me forbear, remembering it is also written, "Judge not, lest ye be judged."

Lincoln's phrase "the sweat of other men's faces" was a reference to Genesis 3:19, in which God condemns the human race, now expelled from the Garden of Eden, to toil for their food in punishment for sin. From this verse Lincoln concluded that anyone whose nourishment came from the forced sweat of others was defying the divine command. The same year he reported telling a Confederate woman, whose husband was a prisoner of war he had just released: "The religion that sets men to rebel and fight against their government because, as they think, that government does not sufficiently help some men to eat their bread in the sweat of other men's faces, is not the sort of religion upon which people can get to heaven." In his second inaugural address the following year, Lincoln repeated the scriptural sequence of his letter to the Baptists: "Both [northerners and southerners] read the same Bible and pray to the same God; and each invokes His aid against the other. It may seem strange that any man should dare to ask God's assistance in wringing their bread from the sweat of other men's faces; but let us judge not that we be not judged."[13]

Lincoln's second inaugural address represented the culmination of his biblically inspired oratory. In a brief speech consisting of a mere seven hundred words, Lincoln mentioned the Deity fourteen times, quoted the Bible four times, referenced prayer three times, and explicitly mentioned the Bible once. His phrase "bind up the nation's wounds" was taken from Psalms 147:3, and his reference to caring for the widow and the orphan derived from numerous biblical texts. The biblical themes of sin, judgment, atonement, redemption, and restoration pervade the speech. Frederick Douglass famously quipped that the president's "address sounded more like a sermon than a state paper." With the Union Army just one month away from capturing Richmond and forcing Robert E. Lee's surrender, the audience may well have expected to hear a victory speech, a bitter condemnation of the South, or a reconstruction plan. Instead, Lincoln delivered a brief but powerful sermon that combined an Old Testament rumination on the mysterious ways of Providence with a New Testament plea for mercy and forgiveness for the South.[14]

Ulysses Grant, the general who captured Richmond and Lee's army, was also a Bible reader. In 1876 he declared, "My advice to Sunday schools, no matter what their denomination, is: Hold fast to the Bible as the sheet-anchor of your liberties; write its precepts in your hearts, and practice them in your lives. To the influences of this book we are indebted to all the progress made in true civilization, and to this we must look as our guide in the future. 'Righteousness exalteth a nation, but sin is a reproach to any people [Proverbs 14:34].'" Grant so loved the Bible that he made it a point to visit the Holy Land the year after he left office, thereby becoming the first American president to do so. He was eager to see with his own eyes the places about which he'd frequently read in Scripture and heard mentioned from the pulpit. In his own words, he visited "Malta, where St. Paul was shipwrecked . . . Joppa—where Jonah was swallowed by the Whale . . . the garden of Gethsemane, the Mount of Olives . . . Bethlehem and the stable where Christ was born, and all the points of interest about Jerusalem." He also visited the ruins at Ephesus, the site of one of the early Christian churches that figures prominently in the Acts of the Apostles and the letters of Paul.[15]

Rutherford Hayes read the Bible in multiple languages. In 1844 he wrote in his diary, "Bought a German Testament; shall read it Sabbaths, and thus have the true doctrines of the Saviour at the same time that I add to my knowledge of the German language." He continued to read Scripture thereafter and, despite his skepticism regarding some biblical doctrines, always retained a great respect for the Bible. In 1853 he wrote, "Went to church this morning; have read half a dozen chapters in the Bible." Two months later, he claimed, "Have been reading Genesis several Sundays, not as a Christian reads for spiritual consolation, instruction, etc., not as an infidel reads to carp and quarrel and criticize, but as one who wishes to be informed and furnished in the earliest and most wonderful of all literary productions. The literature of the Bible should be studied as one studies Shakespeare, for illustration and language, for its true pictures of human nature, [and] for its early historical record." A temperance advocate, Hayes claimed that the story of Noah in

Genesis 9:20–27 was the earliest account of drunkenness. Additionally, he wrote regarding the story of Isaac and Rebecca: "Not many love tales have been told better than this, the first we have recorded in a book."[16]

While fighting with the Union Army in Tennessee in 1862, Benjamin Harrison took comfort in Romans 8:28. He wrote to his wife, Caroline: "I am enduring heavy trials in the army, but I believe that I was led to enter it by a high sense of Christian patriotism, and God has thus far strengthened me to bear all cheerfully. . . . It is a blessed promise that 'all things shall work together for good for those who love God.' Let us have faith to receive the promise in all its royal fullness."[17]

Theodore Roosevelt often cited the Ten Commandments. In 1895, as the New York City police commissioner, he responded to Comptroller Ashbel P. Fitch's letter to the *New York Tribune* criticizing him for his strict enforcement of a Sunday closing law, a law that Fitch considered archaic and outdated. In Fitch's epistle, he quoted several scriptures. According to Roosevelt, he also misreported a conversation between the two men. Roosevelt wrote sardonically, "Comptroller Fitch is fond of texts from the Bible. Let me cordially commend him to Exodus, chapter xx, verses 2 to 17, inclusive. They contain the recital of certain archaic rules known as the Ten Commandments. The sixteenth verse is especially worth Mr. Finch's attention." Exodus 20:16 states, "You shall not bear false witness against your neighbor." The following year, Roosevelt likened William Jennings Bryan's platform of inflation through the coinage of silver to a violation of the commandment regarding theft, as it robbed creditors. He confessed, "There is a certain difficulty in arguing the issue of the campaign, the question of free silver. It is always difficult to make an elaborate argument about the eighth commandment. When a man quotes, 'Thou shalt not steal,' and another promptly replies by asking, 'Why not?' really the best answer is to repeat the commandment again. If a man cannot at the first glance see that it is as immoral and vicious to repudiate debts as it is to steal, why, it becomes quite a hopeless task to try to convince him by the most elaborate arguments." In 1898, when urged to pursue the governorship of New York, Roosevelt confessed some trepidation. Although he would have to compromise with party leaders, in dealing "with anything touching the Eighth Commandment and general decency, I could not allow any consideration of party to come in." The following year, he stated his political philosophy in biblical terms: "I stand by the Ten Commandments; I stand by doing equal justice to the man of means and the man without means; I stand by saying that no man shall be stolen from and that no man shall steal from anyone else; I stand by saying that the corporations shall not be blackmailed on the one side and that the corporations shall not acquire any improper power by corruption on the other." In 1904, when Roosevelt was advised to emphasize his devotion to the Constitution in his presidential reelection campaign, he said he was happy to do so but added, "The only trouble is that I am ashamed to say it. It is a little like repeating my adherence to the Ten Commandments." Surely, American citizens should assume a president's adherence to both of these foundational documents.[18]

Roosevelt cited other scriptures as well. In 1903 he quoted Proverbs 31:28 in praise of good mothers. He declared, "The woman who has borne, and has reared as they should be reared, a family of children has in the most emphatic manner deserved well of the Republic. Her burden has been heavy, and she has been able to bear it worthily only by the possession of resolution, of good sense, of conscience, and of unselfishness. But if she has borne it well, then to her shall come the supreme blessing, for in the words of the oldest and greatest of all books, 'Her children shall rise up and call her blessed.'" The following month, in addressing a group of missionaries, he focused on two scriptures: "Thou shalt serve the Lord thy God with all thy heart and with all thy soul (Deuteronomy 10:12)," and "Be ye therefore wise as serpents and harmless as doves (Matthew 10:16)."[19]

The Bible was the first book Roosevelt listed as accompanying him on the African safari he took following his presidency. In 1913 he wrote that he felt sorry for anyone who could not "enjoy the Hebrew prophets."[20]

Roosevelt was especially fond of Micah 6:8, which listed God's chief requirement. In 1916 he told John J. Leary,

> I wonder if you recall one verse of Micah that I am very fond of—"to do justly and to love mercy and to walk humbly with thy Lord"—that to me is the essence of religion. To be just with all men, to be merciful to those to whom mercy should be shown, to realize that there are some things that must always remain a mystery to us, and when the time comes for us to enter the great blackness, to go smiling and unafraid. That is my religion, my faith. To me it sums up all religion; it is all the creed I need. It seems simple and easy, but there is more in that verse than in the involved rituals and confessions of faith of many creeds we know.[21]

William Howard Taft cited John 15:13 in a Memorial Day speech in 1907. He declared, "It is a beautiful custom to decorate the graves of those who died in war for their country. It is well for us to be brought to a contemplation of those crises in our history in which countrymen of ours, numbered by the hundreds of thousands, solely from a sense of duty, parted with all that the nation might live." He then quoted Jesus: "Greater love hath no man than this, that a man lay down his life for his friends [John 15:13]."²²

While a student at Princeton in 1876, Woodrow Wilson called the Bible "a treasury of poetry, history, philosophy, laws and morals which will never be equaled." He added, "Not in the whole range of literature can be found more sublime poetry than the Bible affords," especially in the Book of Psalms, in which were "to be found the truest descriptions of the human passions"; he then expounded that "in the free flow of his luxuriant imagination[,] Israel's bard pours forth the grandest images." Finally, Wilson concluded, "As a history, the Bible is one of the most valuable of ancient records. . . . As a philosophical work, this wonderful book is unsurpassed." While president of the same university in 1909, Wilson claimed, "The educational value of the Bible is that it both awakens the spirit to its finest and only true action and acquaints the student with the noblest body of literature in existence, a body of literature having in it more mental and imaginative stimulus than any other body of writings. A man has deprived himself of the best there is in the world who has deprived himself of this."²³

In 1911, while governor of New Jersey, Wilson declared that the Bible was "a mirror held up for men's hearts, and it is in this mirror that we marvel to see ourselves portrayed." He added, "[It] strips life of its disguises and its pretenses and elevates those standards by which alone true greatness and true strength and true valor are assessed." Five months later, he claimed,

> The reassuring thing about the Bible is that its biographies are not like any other biographies that you know of. Take up almost any biography outside of the Bible and the writer tries to make a hero of the man he is writing about. No writer in the Bible tries to make a hero out of mere human stuff. There isn't a character in the Bible—there isn't a character even amongst those who are picked out of the Bible itself by the special representatives and ambassadors of God—whose life is not displayed as full of faults and shortcomings and natural slips from the way of virtue. It were a matter of despair to those of us who have come after if the Bible had represented these persons as unimpeachable and unexceptionable in their conduct. . . . I am sorry for the men who do not read the Bible every day. I wonder why they deprive themselves of the strength and of the pleasure. It is one of the most singular books in the world, for every time you open it some old text that you have read a score of times suddenly beams with a new meaning. . . . There is no other book I know of of which this true; there is no other book that yields its meaning so personally; that seems to fit itself so intimately to the very spirit that is seeking its guidance. . . . It is very difficult, indeed, for a man or for a boy who knows the Scripture ever to get away from it. It haunts him like an old song. It follows him like the memory

of his mother. It reminds him like the word of an old and revered teacher. It forms part of the warp and woof of his life.

A few weeks later, when celebrating the tricentennial of the King James Version, Wilson contended that the Bible was the only universal book, claiming that despite its Judaic origin, "It does not seem to be a part of a national literature that is not our own, but to have the warp and woof of our own experiences, national and personal." He added, "The Bible is not something to turn aside to; the Bible is not something to which to resort for religious instruction and comfort; the Bible is not something to associate merely with churches and sermons. It stands right in the center, in the marketplace, of our life, and there bubbles with the water of life."[24]

Shortly before assuming the presidency, Warren Harding wrote, "While I have always been a great reader of the Bible, I have never read it so closely as in the last few weeks, when my mind has been bent upon the work I must shortly take up. I have obtained a good deal of inspiration from the Psalms of David and from many passages of the four gospels, and there's still wisdom in the sayings of old Solomon."[25]

Herbert Hoover revered the Bible. In 1929 he declared, "There is no other book so various as the Bible, nor one so full of wisdom. Whether it be of law, business, morals, or that vision which leads the imagination in the creation of constructive enterprises for the happiness of mankind, he who seeks for guidance in any of these things may look inside its covers and find illumination."[26]

In 1935 Franklin Roosevelt marked the quadricentennial of the first English Bible. He declared,

> It would be difficult to appraise the far-reaching influence of this work and subsequent translations upon the speech, literature, moral and religious character of our people and their institutions. It has done much to refine and enrich our language. To it may be traced the richest and best we have in our literature. Poetry, prose, painting, music, and oratory have had in it their guide and inspiration. In it Lincoln found the rounded euphonious phrases for his Gettysburg address. . . . Look where we will, even in periods that have been marked by apostasy and doubt, still men have found here in the sacred pages that which has refreshed and encouraged them as they prosecuted their pilgrimage and sought for higher levels of thinking and living. . . . This Book continues to hold its unchallenged place as the most loved, the most quoted, and the most universally read and pondered of all the volumes which our libraries contain.

Two years later, he declared that the Bible "ought to be read again and again." In 1938 he pledged, "I shall do whatever lies within my power to hasten the day foretold by Isaiah [2:4], when men 'shall beat their swords into plowshares and their spears into pruning hooks; nation shall not lift up arm against nation, neither shall they learn war anymore.'" The following year, with much of the world at war, Roosevelt quoted the Beatitudes in the Sermon on the Mount, which promise blessings for the meek, the righteous, the merciful, the pure, the persecuted, and the peacemakers. He added, "Those are the truths which are the eternal heritage of our civilization. I repeat them to give heart and comfort to all men and women everywhere who fight for freedom. . . . Today, through all the darkness that has descended upon our Nation and our world, those truths are a guiding light to all." He urged his audience to "pray that the nations which are at war may also read, learn, and inwardly digest these deathless words."[27]

Harry Truman read the Bible throughout his life. In 1941 he recalled his experience with it to his wife, Bess, saying, "At sixteen I had read all the books, including the encyclopedias, in the Independence Public Library and been through the Bible twice, and I thought—and still think—that you were Esther, Ruth, and Bathsheba, all combined." In 1952 he told an audience, "My mother owned a big deckle-edged Bible published in 1881, which contained the first revised version of the New Testament parallel to the King James version. I was raised on that book, and I want to say to you that my fondness for the King James version will never leave me." He later claimed,

> The Old Testament and the New will give you a way of life that will cause you to live happily. . . . Most of my own ideas on how the world runs I obtained very early in life from the Bible, the King James version of the Old and the New Testaments. The Bible is, among other things, one of the greatest documents of history. Every trouble that humanity is heir to is set out in the Bible. And the remedy is there, too, if you know where to find it. . . . The Bible must be read over and over again to get the full meaning of it.[28]

As a result of this training, Truman often cited Scripture. In 1945, while conferring with Winston Churchill and Joseph Stalin at Potsdam, he wrote in his diary, "We have discovered the most terrible bomb in the world. It may be the fire destruction prophesied in the Euphrates Valley." This was a reference to Revelation 9:14–18, in which the four angels unbound from the Euphrates River kill one-third of the world's population with fire and brimstone. In 1950, when laying the cornerstone of the new courts building for the District of Columbia, Truman quoted Amos 5:24: "In the words of the ancient Hebrew prophet, we should say, 'Let justice run down as waters, and righteousness as a mighty stream.'" Four months later, he signed the Bible of a distant relative and marked some passages for the young man to read: Psalms 149; Isaiah 40; Ecclesiastes 12; Matthew 5, 6, and 7; and Luke 6:26. The latter verse states, "Woe unto you when all men speak well of you, for so did their fathers to the false prophets."[29]

In 1951 Truman claimed, "We shall be strong as long as we keep that faith—the faith that can move mountains [1 Corinthians 13:2], the faith which, as St. Paul says [Hebrews 11:1], is the substance of things hoped for, the evidence of things not seen." (n.b., Paul's authorship of Hebrews is uncertain.) The following year, Truman wrote in his diary that the ideal president "believes in the Magna Carta and the Bill of Rights," adding, "But first he believes in the XX Chapter of Exodus, the Vth Chapter of Deuteronomy, and the V, VI, and VIIth chapters of the Gospel according to St. Matthew." This was a reference to the Ten Commandments and the Sermon on the Mount. Later, when asked by an interviewer about his favorite parts of the Bible, he responded excitedly,

> I think some of the passages in Jeremiah and Daniel are wonderful. I like the Proverbs and the Psalms—the 137th Psalm, 'By the rivers of Babylon,' of course, is the famous one, and the 96th, 'O, sing unto the Lord a new song.' They are wonderful; they are just like poetry. And read the passages in Deuteronomy that seldom are referred to. The Ten Commandments are repeated in Deuteronomy in sonorous language that really makes a tingle go down your spine to read them. Of course, the Sermon on the Mount is the greatest of all things in the Bible, a way of life, and maybe someday men will get to understand it as the real way of life.[30]

John F. Kennedy considered the Bible a source of wisdom. In his address to the Democratic National Convention that nominated him for president in 1960, he appealed "to all who respond to the scriptural call [Deuteronomy 31:6]: 'Be strong and of good courage; be not afraid, neither be dismayed.'" He then quoted Isaiah 40:31: "They that wait upon the Lord shall mount up with wings of eagles; they shall run, and not be weary." A few months later, he justified his strong rhetoric to a Miami audience by quoting 1 Corinthians 14:8: "Who will prepare for the battle if the trumpet sounds an uncertain note?" To a San Francisco audience, he claimed, "We can make this a time of greatness—a time of which history will truly say, when reciting our perils, that we lived by the scriptural injunction [Isaiah 41:6]: 'Everyone shall help his neighbor, and shall say to his brother: be of good courage.'" The following year, he declared,

It is an ironic fact that in this nuclear age, when the horizon of human knowledge and human experience has passed far beyond any that any age has ever known, we turn back at this time to the oldest source of wisdom and strength, to the words of the prophets and the saints, who tell us that faith is more powerful than doubt, that hope is more potent than despair, and that only through the love that is sometimes called charity can we conquer those forces within ourselves and throughout all the world that threaten the very existence of mankind.

He then quoted Proverbs 16:7: "When a man's ways please the Lord, He maketh even his enemies to be at peace with him." In a 1963 speech before the United Nations, Kennedy declared regarding peacekeeping missions: "Too often a project is undertaken in the excitement of a crisis and then it begins to lose its appeal as the problems drag on and the bills pile up. But we must have the steadfastness to see every project through. . . . As the Scripture tells us, 'No man who puts his hand to the plow and looks back is fit for the Kingdom of God [Luke 9:62].'"[31]

Lyndon Johnson's favorite verse was Isaiah 1:18, "Come now, let us reason together," a verse that appealed to his confidence in his considerable skills as a negotiator and to his sensibility as a longtime legislator. Johnson referenced the verse while criticizing the practice of separating men and women into different rooms at the presidential prayer breakfast, highlighting the need for negotiation with the Soviet Union in a nuclear age, and calling for negotiations between railroad titans and workers. He liked the Golden Rule (Matthew 7:12: "Do unto others as you would have them do unto you") so much that one year, he gave his wife and daughters watches with the verse engraved on them. In 1965, after Alabama state troopers had violently dispersed peaceful marchers journeying from Selma to Montgomery to protest disfranchisement, Johnson expressed his determination to guarantee voting rights but also pleaded for peace, quoting Abraham's statement to Lot in Genesis 13:8: "Let there be no strife between me and thee, for we be brethren." Two days later, regarding civil rights, he declared: "Should we defeat every enemy, should we double our wealth and conquer the stars and still be unequal to this issue, then we will have failed as a people and as a nation. For with a country as with a person, 'What is a man profited if he shall gain the whole world and lose his own soul? [Matthew 16:26].'" In 1966 he remarked, "So many of our pioneer ancestors often ventured into the wilderness with only three possessions—their rifle, their axe, and their Bible. And of the three, the Bible was by far their greatest personal treasure. For it contained the hope, and the promise, and the inspiration which gave them the necessary courage to keep going."[32]

Richard Nixon referred to the Book of Genesis when, after establishing the Environmental Protection Agency and signing the Clean Air Act, he proposed the creation of new national wilderness areas. He declared, "The first man created on earth, according to the ancient Scriptures [Genesis 2:15], was placed by his Creator in a huge natural garden and charged 'to dress it and keep it.' In the ages since, men have worked energetically at dressing and improving God's good earth—but their efforts at keeping and preserving it have been scant. Now, all around the world, people are awakening to the urgent need of protecting the fragile life-balance and of setting aside for the future such wildness and natural beauty as still remains to us."[33]

Gerald Ford often quoted the Bible. In 1956 he claimed, "I have always liked St. Paul's summation [Philippians 4:8]: 'Finally, brethren, whatsoever things are true, whatsoever things are honest, whatsoever things are just, whatsoever things are pure, whatsoever things are lovely, whatsoever things are of good report; if there be any virtue, and if there be any praise, think on these things.'" In 1971 he asked, "What is the most glorious book of all if not the Bible?" Ford then added, "There is in fact no literature more great nor music more glorious than the Psalms. And so it is that men 'make a joyful noise unto God [Psalms 66:1]' as they paint, sculpt, or write words and music in His honor." Three years later, he noted, "As usual, the Bible says it best—and I quote—'Where the spirit of the Lord is, there is liberty [2 Corinthians 3:17].'" Five months later, he said, "God speaks to us through the Bible and says that 'I have set before you life and death, blessing and cursing: therefore, choose life that both thou and thy seed may live [Deuteronomy 30:19].'" In 1976 Ford claimed, "In my own life and throughout my career in public service, I have found in the Bible a steady compass and a source of great strength and peace."[34]

Ford derived the title of his autobiography, *A Time to Heal*, from Ecclesiastes 3:1–4, which he quoted at the beginning of the volume: "To everything there is a season and a time to every purpose under heaven. A time to be born and a time to die; a time to plant and a time to pluck up that which is planted. A time to kill and a time to heal; a time to break down and a time to build up. A time to weep and a time to laugh; a time to mourn and a time to dance." Ford believed that his presidential term, which followed the Watergate scandal, was a time to heal Americans' distrust of their leaders.[35]

Indeed, in his inaugural address in 1977, Ford's successor, Jimmy Carter, thanked him for "all he has done to heal our land," a phrase borrowed from 2 Chronicles 7:14. Six months later, when hosting Israeli Prime Minister

Menachem Begin, Carter quoted Isaiah 32:17: "And the work of righteousness shall be peace, and the effects of righteousness will be quietness and assurance forever." Two days later, Carter said, "I believe that our planet must finally obey the Biblical injunction to 'follow after the things which make for peace [Romans 14:19].'" In 1978 Carter told a joint session of Congress regarding peace talks between Israel and Egypt: "The prayers at Camp David were the same as those of the shepherd King David, who prayed in the 85th Psalm [verses 6 and 8], 'Wilt thou not revive us again, that thy people may rejoice in thee? . . . I will hear what God the Lord will speak, for He will speak peace unto his people, and unto his saints, but let them not return again to folly.'" Regarding Begin and Egyptian President Anwar Sadat, he added, "And I would like to say as a Christian, to these friends of mine, the words of Jesus, 'Blessed are the peacemakers, for they shall be called the children of God [Matthew 5:9].'" Indeed, Carter brought his Bible with him to Camp David thinking—correctly as it turned out—that it would serve him well in the peace negotiations. Soon after, he claimed, "The Bible is not just a spiritual textbook, but it's an excellent and exciting story, a story about Jesus Christ, one of the most exciting stories of all time."[36]

In 1979 Carter related,

> Just before Christmas, we had Alec McCowen, a great British actor, come to the White House. And he stood there on a bare stage, and he quoted from memory the Book of Mark, I think about 16,000 verses, 2½ hours. He didn't use a modern translation; he used the King James Version. And there was a sense among those two or three hundred people that here came someone directly from the presence of Christ and told, almost like a newspaper, in the most vivid, moving terms, about the life of the Son of God. There was nothing stale about it. There was nothing ancient about it. There was nothing removed about it from the existence of those assembled in that room.

The following year, when urging energy conservation, Carter employed the theme of human stewardship over the earth, as presented in Genesis 1:26. Carter declared, "When God created the Earth and gave human beings dominion over it, it was with the understanding on the part of us, then and down through the generations, that we are indeed stewards under God's guidance, to protect not only those who are fortunate enough to grasp an advantage or a temporary material blessing or enjoyment but to husband these bases of enjoyment and for a quality of life for those less fortunate in our own generation and especially for those who will come after us." Eleven days later, he said,

Rosalynn and I read the Bible together every night, not as some sort of mystical guidebook, as some might think, to give us quick and simple answers to every problem of a nation or personal life, but because we find new insights and new inspirations in this present job in passages that we have read and known and loved ever since childhood. . . . I'm glad that the Bible does not tell us just about mighty warriors or great prophets or wise leaders. It also tells us about sinful men and women, men like the Disciples—sometimes stubborn, reluctant, selfish, weak, struggling with their own fears and failures and lack of faith. Yet with God's help, they were able to do great things. . . . Only when they realized their own personal limitations could God work fully in their lives.

When Rosalynn was anxious about her trip to Peru to represent the administration that year, Jimmy soothed her by reminding her that their previous night's reading included Jesus's words in John 14:1: "Let not your heart be troubled; ye believe in God, believe also in me." Jimmy's birthday present for her that year was "a beautiful little picture frame, within which I had written Ecclesiastes 9:9 in Spanish, translated from The Living Bible: 'Live happily with the woman you love through the fleeting days of life, for the wife God gives you is your best reward down here for all your earthly toil.'"[37]

Speaking as the student body president at his high school commencement ceremony in 1929, Ronald Reagan quoted one of his favorite Bible verses, John 10:10, in which Jesus says, "I have come that they may have life and that they may have it abundantly." Reagan claimed, "If one book had to be recommended or chosen for life of exile on the proverbial island, I think the Bible would be the unquestioned choice. I know of no other book that could be read and reread and continue to be a challenge as could the Old and New Testaments." In 1977 Reagan complained in a radio talk that some modern translations, such as the Good News Bible, served as poor substitutes for the King James Version. The man who would later be dubbed the Great Communicator offered a series of comparisons intended to demonstrate that the Good News Bible replaced the majestic words of the KJV with trite expressions—for instance, "In the New Testament—Matthew [3:3]—we read, 'The voice of the one crying in the wilderness. Prepare ye the way.' The Good News version translates that, 'Someone is shouting in the desert. Get the road ready.'" Reagan cracked, "It sounds like a straw boss announcing lunch hour is over." He added, "The sponsors of the Good News version boast that their bible is as readable as the daily paper—and so it is. But do readers of the daily news find themselves moved to wonder 'at the gracious words which proceeded out of his mouth [Luke 4:22]?'"[38]

In 1982 Reagan referred to his mother's favorite Bible verse. He said, "One of my favorite passages in the Bible is the promise God gave us in second Chronicles [7:14]: 'If my people, who are called by my name, shall humble themselves and pray and seek my face and turn from their wicked ways, then will I hear from heaven and will forgive their sin and will heal their land.'" He added, "That promise is the hope of America and of all our people." The following year, Reagan signed a proclamation marking 1983 as "the Year of the Bible." He said, "We're blessed to have its words of strength, comfort, and truth.... The Bible can touch our hearts, order our minds, and refresh our souls." He quoted Isaiah 40:8: "The grass withereth, the flower fadeth, but the word of our God shall stand forever." Two months later, he claimed,

> I believe that communism is another sad, bizarre chapter in human history whose last pages even now are being written. I believe this because the source of our strength in the quest for human freedom is not material but spiritual. And because it knows no limitation, it must terrify and ultimately triumph over those who would enslave their fellow man. For in the words of Isaiah [40:29, 31]: "He giveth power to the faint; and to them that have no might He increaseth strength.... They that wait upon the Lord shall renew their strength; they shall mount up with wings as eagles; they shall run and not be weary."

In a Mother's Day address two months later, Reagan quoted Proverbs 31:25–26 on the good mother: "Strength and dignity are her clothing, and she smiles at the future. She opens her mouth in wisdom, and the teaching of kindness is on her tongue." In 1984, noting that the national economy, which had languished for a decade, was now robust, Reagan referenced Psalms 30:5: "Weeping may endure for a night, but joy cometh in the morning." Perhaps it was no coincidence then that his most popular reelection campaign commercial that year was called "Morning in America." In 1988, when addressing the students and faculty of Moscow State University, he referred to Scripture in an attempt to counter the atheistic materialism of the Soviet regime: "Even as we explore the most advanced reaches of science, we're returning to the age-old wisdom of our culture, a wisdom contained in the Book of Genesis in the Bible: In the beginning was the spirit, and it was from this spirit that the material abundance of creation issued forth."[39]

Reagan was troubled by biblical prophecies regarding the end times, their possible correlation to unrest in the Middle East, and the advent of nuclear weapons. After reading an analysis of the Middle Eastern situation in 1979, he wrote, "It truly is frightening, and I found after I had read it that I couldn't keep from hearkening back to the Old Testament prophecies of the events that would foretell Armageddon." Four years later, he wrote about a futurist's predictions concerning nuclear war: "Lately I've been wondering about older prophecies—those having to do with Armageddon. Things that are news today sound an awful lot like what was predicted would take place just prior to 'A' day." In 1991 he noted, "If I mentioned Armageddon in my lifetime, it was accompanied by the Bible prophecy that no man would know [the day] of its coming, but certain signs and events would precede its coming. Many Bible students have called attention to those signs—wars fought to no conclusion, natural disasters, earthquakes, storms, volcanic eruptions, etc., that would increase." Reagan was probably referring to Jesus's statement about His return in Matthew 24:36: "But of that day and hour no one knows, not the angels of heaven, but my Father only." Reagan's list of omens match Jesus's, which are found in verse seven of that chapter, fairly closely: "Nation shall rise against nation, and kingdom against kingdom, and there shall be famines, pestilences, and earthquakes in various places."[40]

In a 1991 commencement address at the Federal Bureau of Investigation Academy, George H. W. Bush quoted Ezekiel 7:23: "The land is full of bloody crimes, and the city is full of violence." Bush added, "The battle between good and evil still rages." The following year, in expressing pride over the speech his grandson George P. Bush delivered at the Republican National Convention, he quoted Proverbs 17:6: "Grandchildren are the crown of the aged."[41]

The first post–Cold War president, Bill Clinton began his 1996 book *Between Hope and History* by quoting Proverbs 29:18. He wrote, "The Proverbs teach us that 'Where there is no vision, the people perish.' I ran for President in 1992 because I thought our nation lacked a unifying vision for our future and a strategy to achieve it, and that we were in danger of just drifting into the new era."[42]

For several consecutive years in the 1980s, George W. Bush's parents invited Reverend Billy Graham to lead the family in Bible studies at their home in Kennebunkport, Maine. After one such study in 1985, George W. took a long walk on the beach with the evangelist. Bush later recalled, "The Lord was so clearly reflected in his gentle and loving demeanor. . . . Billy Graham didn't make you feel guilty; he made you feel loved. . . . Over the course of that weekend, Reverend Graham planted a mustard seed in my soul [Matthew 13:31–32], a seed that grew over the next year. He led me to the path, and I began walking. . . . It was the beginning of a new walk where I would recommit my heart to Jesus

Christ." Bush began attending Bible studies at First Baptist Church in Midland, Texas, that helped him to overcome his drinking problem. He later recalled, "As I read the Bible, I was moved by the stories of Jesus's kindness to suffering strangers, His healing of the blind and crippled, and His ultimate act of sacrificial love when He was nailed to the cross." Bush also began to read the Bible every morning, "and I prayed to understand it more clearly." He added, "In time, my faith began to grow." It was then that he began the practice of reading from *The One Year Bible* (Tyndale, 1985), an edition that separates Scripture into brief daily readings, thus allowing the reader to peruse the whole Bible in a calendar year. Bush carried it with him on the presidential campaign trail and never fell behind in his reading. While governor of Texas, he hosted brown-bag Bible studies in the governor's mansion.[43]

In the days after the September 11 attacks, Bush "found solace in the Bible." At that time he often referenced Romans 12:21, in which Paul instructs Christians to "overcome evil with good," and claimed that Americans were doing just that. At the memorial service three days after the attacks, he quoted Romans 8:38–39: "As we have been assured, 'neither death nor life, nor angels nor principalities, nor things present nor things to come, nor height nor depth, can separate us from God's love.'" In 2004 he claimed, "God's word can humble the mighty, can lift up the meek, and can bring comfort and strength to all those who yearn for justice and freedom." Five months later, on the sixtieth anniversary of the D-Day invasion, he mentioned the Normandy beaches after the battle: "There were Bibles, many Bibles, mixed with the wreckage of war. Our boys had carried in their pockets the book that brought into the world this message: 'Greater love has no man than this, that a man lay down his life for his friends [John 15:13].'" In 2008, at a groundbreaking ceremony for the Walter Reed National Military Medical Center in Bethesda, Maryland, he declared, "It is fitting that this new facility be built in a place called 'Bethesda,' which draws its name from the Biblical pool of healing. It is there that a lame man was made to walk and was dispatched with the words: 'Behold, thou art made whole [John 5:2–9].'" As president, Bush continued to encourage Bible study groups in the workplace. At least seven such groups, comprised of two hundred staffers, met regularly in the White House and adjacent buildings.[44]

Barack Obama began his first memoir, *Dreams from My Father* (1995), with 1 Chronicles 29:15, in which David tells God, "For we are strangers before thee, and sojourners, as were all our fathers." We know David was referring to the fleeting lives of all humans, who are mere sojourners through this world, for the verse continues, "Our days on the earth are as a shadow, and there is none abiding." But Obama clearly believed that the verse had a special meaning for himself and his father, both wanderers, and for African Americans in general, who are descendants of those forcibly transplanted from the mother continent. While a US senator, Obama regularly attended a Wednesday-morning prayer breakfast that was open to senators of both parties; there, the senators took turns selecting a passage from Scripture and leading a group discussion about it. Obama was impressed by "the sincerity, openness, humility, and good humor with which even the most overtly religious senators" shared "their personal faith journeys."[45]

In his inaugural address in 2009, Obama declared, "We remain a young nation, but in the words of the Scripture [1 Corinthians 13:11], the time has come to set aside childish things." The following year, he remarked concerning a mining accident: "As we pray for the souls of those that we've lost and the safe return of those who are missing, we are also sustained by the words of the Psalm that are particularly poignant now. Those words read: 'You, O Lord, keep my lamp burning; my God turns my darkness into light [Psalms 18:28].'" In 2011 he said, "Nothing beats Scripture and the reminder of the Eternal." Five months later, he read the forty-sixth psalm at a tenth-anniversary memorial of the September 11 attacks. The psalm begins: "God is our refuge and strength, a very present help in trouble. Therefore, we will not fear, even though the earth be removed, and though the mountains be carried into the midst of the sea." The following year, he quoted Romans 5:3–4, "Tribulation produces perseverance, perseverance character, and character hope," regarding the Great Recession. He added, "This country has fought through some very tough years together, and while we still have a lot of work ahead, we've come as far as we have mainly because of the perseverance and character of ordinary Americans." In 2013 he revealed that for the past four years, he had begun each day with a daily meditation on a scripture verse sent to him by Reverend Joshua DuBois, the head of the White House's Faith-Based Office. Obama claimed, "It has meant the world to me." Regarding his second inauguration, he added,

> A few weeks ago, I was blessed to place my hand on the Bibles of two great Americans, two men whose faith still echoes today. One was the Bible owned by President Abraham Lincoln, and the other the Bible owned by Dr. Martin Luther King Jr. As I prepared to take the second oath, I thought about these two men, and I thought of how, in times of joy and pain and uncertainty, they turned to their Bibles to seek the wisdom of God's words and thought of how, for as long as we've been a nation, so many of our leaders—our Presidents and our preachers, our legislators and our jurists—have done the same. Each one faced their own challenges, each one finding in Scripture their own lessons

from the Lord. . . . Sometimes I search Scripture to determine how best to balance life as a President and as a husband and as a father. I often search Scripture to figure out how I can be a better man as well as a better President.

Seven months later, on the anniversary of the September 11 attacks, he began his address at a wreath-laying ceremony at the Pentagon with Psalms 71:20–21, a passage concerning "the miracle of restoration": "You who have made me see many troubles and calamities will revive me again. From the depths of the Earth you will bring me up again. You will increase my greatness and comfort me again." In a 2015 address commemorating the golden anniversary of the voting-rights march from Selma to Montgomery, he said regarding the marchers: "They did as Scripture instructed [Romans 12:12]: 'Rejoice in hope, be patient in tribulation, be constant in prayer.'"[46]

Promoting the Biblical Education of Future Generations

Most presidents have supported efforts to disseminate biblical knowledge among Native Americans and those in other nations. While cynics have characterized these missionary efforts as a means of controlling other peoples, it is important to note that the same presidents undertook even greater efforts to disseminate the same knowledge to their own children and grandchildren, as well as to other Americans. They have considered the Bible an invaluable guide not only to the salvation of souls but also to the identification and promotion of those virtues necessary for the preservation of the American republic. They have taken seriously Jesus's command in Matthew 28:19: "Go teach all nations, baptizing them in the name of the Father, and of the Son, and of the Holy Spirit."

George Washington supported the preaching of the gospel to Native Americans both for their own good and to increase their friendship with the United States. As early as 1779, Washington declared to the Delaware chiefs, "You do well to wish to learn our arts and ways of life, and above all, the religion of Jesus Christ. These will make you a greater and happier people than you are." Nine years later, Washington called an effort to preach the gospel to Native American tribes a "laudable" undertaking and made reference to "an event so long and so earnestly desired as that of converting the Indians to Christianity and consequently to civilization." While president in 1789, he instructed his commissioners to the southern tribes: "You will also endeavour to obtain a stipulation for certain missionaries to reside in the nation, provided the General Government should think proper to adopt the measure—these men to be precluded from trade or attempting to purchase any lands. . . . The object of this establishment will be the happiness of the Indians, teaching them great duties of religion and morality, and to inculcate a friendship and attachment to the United States." The same year, he wrote to the Moravian Society for Propagating the Gospel: "Be assured of my patronage in your laudable undertakings"; namely, "the disinterested endeavours of your society to civilize and Christianize the Savages of the Wilderness." He then added, "I pray Almighty God to have you always in his holy keeping." Four years later, Washington permitted a group of Moravians and Quakers to accompany his commissioners to the northwestern tribes.[47]

An incorrigible Indian fighter, Andrew Jackson nevertheless agreed with Washington that the gospel should be preached to Native Americans. Shocked by a letter from his old friend Sam Houston, who had gone to live among the Cherokees, Jackson replied that this course of action made sense only if Houston's intention was "to study theology and become a missionary amongst them." He added, "Thus you might apply your talents beneficially by teaching them the road to happiness beyond the grave. This might produce a benefit to the heathen and might be gratifying to your aged and pious mother."[48]

Martin Van Buren held a similar view. In his autobiography Van Buren recalled regarding his own administration: "As the Christian religion had been the greatest agent of civilization throughout the world, the Government could not, in attempting to extend its blessings to the Indians, omit to invoke the cooperation of the Christian ministry. Clerical missionaries were accordingly sent among them, and the Country from time to time heard of the great success which had attended their labours of love."[49]

In his Annual Message to Congress in 1863, Abraham Lincoln endorsed the preaching of the gospel to Native Americans. He declared, "Sound policy and our imperative duty to these wards of the government demand our anxious and conscious attention to their material well-being, to their progress in the arts of civilization, and, above all, to that moral training which, under the blessing of Divine Providence, will confer upon them the elevated and sanctifying influences, the hopes, and consolation of the Christian faith."[50]

Ulysses Grant believed so strongly in the benefits of evangelizing Native Americans that, as president in 1870, he declared in a message to Congress his decision to commission as federal Indian agents members of "such religious denominations as had hitherto established Missionaries among the Indians, and perhaps to some other denominations who would undertake to work on the same terms, i.e., as . . . Missionary work." He added, "The societies selected are allowed to name their own agents and are expected to watch over them, and aid them, as missionaries, to Christianize and Civilize the Indian, and to train him in the arts of peace." Grant had begun this policy the previous year with the Quakers, who'd had exceptionally good relations with Native American tribes reaching back to the seventeenth century. Regarding Native Americans, Grant declared, "It is highly desirable that they become self-sustaining, self-relying, Christianized, and Civilized." In 1871 he told a *New York Herald* reporter, "The Quakers are doing well, have done well, and will do more. Other denominations of Christians are also laboring with effect among the Indians. They are all laboring for the same end, and I will give them all the support I can." The following year, he wrote, "If any change is made [to Indian policy] it must be on the side of Civilization & Christianization of the Indian."[51]

Many presidents have also supported Christian missionary efforts outside the boundaries of the United States. James Buchanan endorsed such efforts in Hawaii when it was still a half century away from becoming an American territory. While secretary of state, in 1848, he praised the efforts of evangelists there in "raising the natives from barbarism by teaching them the truths of Christianity, by making their language a written one, and by translating into it the holy scriptures and such works, religious, moral, and political, as were adapted to their capacity and calculated to enable them to discharge their duties here as to have reason to hope for a higher destiny hereafter." The following year, he lauded "the zealous and disinterested labors" of these missionaries and noted their resultant influence on the people and government of Hawaii. He instructed an American trade representative, saying, "You will consequently by all honorable means cultivate the most friendly relations with the missionaries."[52]

John Tyler and Abraham Lincoln hoped that the emancipation and recolonization of American slaves in Africa might serve as a means of spreading the gospel to that continent. In 1838 Tyler expressed the belief that the return of Christian freedmen to Africa would provide more spiritual and moral uplift than "all the foreign missionary societies combined." In his eulogy for Henry Clay fourteen years later, Abraham Lincoln quoted Clay's statement about the benefits that the emancipation of slaves and their recolonization in Africa would bring to that continent, including the introduction of the gospel. Lincoln quoted Clay:

> There is a moral fitness to the idea of returning to Africa her children, whose ancestors have been torn from her by the ruthless hand of fraud and violence.

Transplanted in a foreign land, they will carry back to their native soil the rich fruits of *religion*, civilization, law, and liberty [emphasis added]. May it not be one of the great designs of the Ruler of the universe (whose ways are inscrutable to short-sighted mortals) thus to transform an original crime into a signal blessing to that most unfortunate portion of the globe? . . . This suggestion of the possible ultimate redemption of the African race and African continent was made twenty-five years ago. Every succeeding year has added to the hope of its realization. May it indeed be realized![53]

As president in 1900, William McKinley addressed the Ecumenical Council on Foreign Missions, a meeting presided over by former President Benjamin Harrison. McKinley delivered a glowing tribute to missionaries "for uplifting the races of men, teaching them the truth of the common fatherhood of God and the brotherhood of man and showing that, if we are not our brothers' keepers [Genesis 4:9], we can be our brothers' helpers." He added,

The story of the Christian missions is one of thrilling interest and marvelous results. The sacrifices of the missionaries for their fellow men constitute one of the most glorious pages of the world's history. The missionary, of whatever church or ecclesiastical body, who devotes his life to the service of the Master and of man, carrying the torch of truth and enlightenment, deserves the gratitude and homage of mankind. . . . Wielding the sword of the Spirit [Ephesians 6:17], they have conquered ignorance and prejudice. They have been the pioneers of civilization. They have illumined the darkness of idolatry and superstition with the light of intelligence and truth. They have been the messengers of righteousness and love. They have braved disease and danger and death, and in their exile have suffered unspeakable hardships, but their noble spirits have never wavered. . . . May this great meeting rekindle the spirit of missionary ardor and enthusiasm to 'go teach all nations [Matthew 28:19]'; may the field never lack a succession of heralds who will carry on the task—the continuous proclamation of His gospel to the end of time.[54]

In 1908 Theodore Roosevelt wrote a letter that later served as the introduction to John Raleigh Mott's *The Claims and Opportunities of the Christian Ministry* (1913). In this epistle Roosevelt argued, "We have a vast missionary responsibility not only in the Philippines but in Asia and Africa as well." From 1909 to 1910, Roosevelt visited many missions while on safari in Africa. He applauded the World Missionary Conference, an ecumenical gathering of Christian missionaries in Edinburgh, writing, "Surely every man imbued, as every man should be, with the ethical teachings of Christianity must rejoice in such an effort to combine the strength of all the churches in the endeavor to Christianize humanity, and to Christianize it not merely in name but in very fact.... Unity in a spirit of Christian brotherhood for such broad Christian work will tend, not to do away with differences of doctrine, but to prevent us from laying too much stress on these differences."[55]

As president in 1913, Woodrow Wilson lauded American missionaries in India and China. On the centennial of the first American mission in India, Wilson noted, "I should not let the occasion pass without a word of recognition of the great educational, Christianizing, and civilizing benefits which have occurred to that part of the world through the devotion of those self-sacrificing and self-forgetting men and women who, for the sake of a righteous cause and the good of humanity, exiled themselves from home and friends and country." Two years later, in a speech to Presbyterian ministers, he declared regarding Christian missionary work in China: "This is the most amazing and inspiring vision that can be offered you, this mission of that great sleeping nation suddenly cried awake by the voice of Christ. Could there be anything more tremendous than that? And could there be any greater contribution to the future momentum of the moral forces of the world than could be made by quickening this force which is being set afoot in China?" In a 1916 speech commemorating the centennial of the American Bible Society, a speech delivered in the midst of World War I, Wilson emphasized how the gospel spreads unity and peace: "Those who spread the Scriptures are engaged, as it were, in drawing the world together under the spell of one body of literature which belongs to no one race, to no one civilization, to no one time in the history of the world, but whose appeal is universal, which searches and illuminates all hearts alike. In proportion as men yield themselves to the kindly light of the Gospel, they are bound together in the bonds of mutual understanding and assured peace."[56]

In his inaugural address in 1925, Calvin Coolidge listed "the advancement of religion" as one of the priorities of his administration. He contrasted America's dispatching of missionaries around the world with the dispatching of soldiers by imperialistic nations: "The legions which she sends forth are armed, not with the sword, but with the cross. The higher state to which she seeks the allegiance of all mankind is not of human but of divine origin. She has no purpose save to merit the favor of Almighty God."[57]

Dwight Eisenhower thought of "Christian religious education" as "the hope of the world." In 1953 he served as the honorary chairman of the American Bible Society's annual worldwide drive to promote Bible reading during the holiday season.[58]

In 1961 John F. Kennedy also endorsed the American Bible Society's effort to encourage the reading of Scripture throughout the world. He wrote,

"It is not enough that the Bible be translated, published, and distributed; it must also be read." Four months later, he applauded the Pocket Testament League for distributing twenty million scripture portions in Asia, Africa, and South America. He declared, "The Bible is the common heritage of all men. It is the foundation upon which the great democratic traditions and institutions of our country stand. Recognizing what it has meant to the development of our American way of life, we can hope that other nations and societies will also find light and guidance in this book."[59]

As a boy in the 1930s, Jimmy Carter donated pennies and nickels for years to support Baptist missionaries in China, whom he regarded as "the ultimate heroes." He later recalled, "I was taught to look upon the Chinese as friends in urgent need of hospitals, food, schools, and the knowledge of Jesus Christ as their Savior." As president, he convinced Chinese Communist leader Deng Xiaoping to permit the distribution of Bibles in his country and to relax restrictions on the freedom of worship, though Deng still refused to allow the readmission of Christian missionaries. In 1997 Carter wrote, "In 1976 two unprecedented things happened in the small congregation of the Baptist Church in the village of Plains, Georgia. One family was chosen to go to the White House, and another family was assigned to be missionaries in West Africa. One has become famous, but the other is, justifiably, more honored in our church. For as long as I can remember, our most exalted heroes have been missionaries who go to foreign lands to serve Christ."[60]

In 1991 George H. W. Bush congratulated the Southern Baptist Convention on its missionary efforts in Africa, Asia, and Latin America, as well as among American servicemen and -women during Operation Desert Storm. He declared, "Southern Baptists have been doing quiet but crucial work, engaging in countless acts of kindness and compassion, spreading the word of God, demonstrating the profound power of religious freedom." The following year, he applauded other missionary efforts, saying to the National Association of Evangelicals: "Many of you bravely brought Bibles behind the Iron Curtain, sharing the Word of God with people who longed for it. . . . And now in the free countries of the former Communist bloc, your work continues to ensure that the vacuum left by communism's demise is filled by faith."[61]

Those American presidents who endorsed biblical training for Native Americans and other peoples were generally sincere, which is evident from those presidents' advocacy for the same training for their own children and grandchildren, as well as for Americans in general. Thomas Jefferson encouraged adult Bible reading because of its moral effects. As early as 1767 and often thereafter, he recommended the study of the New Testament to the young men seeking his educational advice. In 1809, he wrote regarding Americans, "We all agree in the obligation of the moral precepts of Jesus, & nowhere will they be found delivered in greater purity than in his discourses." In 1814 he contributed the then hefty sum of fifty dollars to the Bible Society of Virginia, writing, "There never was a more pure and sublime system of morality delivered to man than is to be found in the four evangelists." However, Jefferson objected to various Bible societies' missions to China. Not only did he fear that they would disturb the peace of an alien culture, but he also believed that American missionaries' obligation to provide biblical instruction in the United States took precedence over any duty to do so in other nations. He asked, "While we have so many around us, within the same social pale, who need instruction and assistance, why carry to a distance and to strangers what our neighbors need?" For this reason, Jefferson also contributed what were then considered substantial sums to the construction of Episcopalian, Presbyterian, Baptist, and Catholic churches.[62]

It is true that Jefferson famously argued against children's Bible reading in *Notes on the State of Virginia* (1782). Jefferson wrote, "Instead, therefore, of putting the Bible and Testament into the hands of children at an age when their judgments are not sufficiently matured for religious inquiries, their memories may be stored with the most useful facts from Grecian, Roman, European, and American history." But Jefferson applied this prohibition only to children. Furthermore, ever the moralist, Jefferson immediately added, "The first elements of morality too may be instilled in their minds." While Jefferson believed that children's rational capacities were too weak to engage successfully in religious inquiry, he believed that their moral senses were formed at an early age. Thus, he advocated for teaching moral principles to children via Bible stories and select scriptural passages.[63]

In fact, Jefferson himself engaged in just such a practice. In 1825, a year before his death, he was asked by a friend to write a letter of advice as a memorial for a baby boy he had named after Jefferson. Jefferson concluded this touching letter with his favorite translation of his favorite psalm, Nahum Tate's and Nicholas Brady's translation of the fifteenth psalm (1696), under the heading "The portrait of a good man by the most sublime of poets, for your imitation":

Lord, who's the happy man that may to Thy blest courts repair,
Not stranger-like to visit them, but to inhabit there?
'Tis he whose every thought and deed by rules of virtue moves,
Whose generous tongue disdains to speak the thing his heart disapproves.

Who never did a slander forge, his neighbor's fame to wound,
Nor hearken to a false report by malice whispered round.
Who vice, in all its pomp and power, can treat with just neglect;
And piety, though clothed in rags, religiously respect.
Who to his plighted vows and trust has ever firmly stood,
And though he promise to his loss, he makes his promise good.
Whose soul in usury disdains his treasure to employ.
Whom no rewards can ever bribe the guiltless to destroy.
The man who, by his steady course, has happiness insur'd,
When earth's foundations shake, shall stand, by Providence secur'd.

A year earlier, when asked by an editor for an essay on ethics, Jefferson simply replied, "Nothing is more moral, more sublime, than David's description of the good man in his 15th Psalm." The fact that even so biblically unorthodox a founder as Thomas Jefferson not only possessed a deep affection for portions of the Bible but was willing to contribute a large sum toward its dissemination is compelling evidence of the almost universal reverence that the Bible commanded in American society in the eighteenth and nineteenth centuries.[64]

In 1811, while serving as US minister to Russia, John Quincy Adams wrote from St. Petersburg to his ten-year-old son George to encourage him to read the Bible, which he called "the best of all Books." The following month, he claimed, "So great is my veneration for the Bible, and so strong my belief that when duly read and meditated upon it is of all the books in the world that which contributes most to make men good, wise, and happy, that the earlier my children begin to read it, the more lively and confident will be my hopes that they will prove useful citizens to their country, respectable members of society, and a real blessing to their parents." He added, "You know some of your duties, and the obligation you are under of becoming acquainted with them all. It is in the Bible that you must learn them, and from the Bible how to practice them."[65]

Andrew Jackson joined with several other men to finance the construction of a church near the Hermitage in Nashville. He asked his wife, Rachel, to convey the message to Colonel Edward Ward that it must be completed, even if it meant that the two men must bear the cost alone. Likewise, Jackson's protégé and eventual successor, James K. Polk, contributed to the establishment of a Lutheran church in Washington, though he was not a Lutheran.[66]

Zachary Taylor urged his children, Betty and Richard, to conclude each day by reading a chapter in the Bible. He became a lifetime member of the

American Sunday School Union, as well as an honorary member of the American Board of Commissioners for Foreign Missions.[67]

In 1856 James Buchanan urged Americans to "cherish the Constitution and the Union to your hearts, next to your belief in the Christian religion—the Bible for Heaven and the Constitution of your country for earth." Twelve years later, he wrote to a mother: "I sincerely and ardently pray for your [son's] long life, happiness, and prosperity; and that he may become a wise and useful man, under the blessing of Providence, in his day and generation." He emphasized that "much will depend on his early & Christian training." Buchanan's nephew and ward, James Buchanan Henry, later recalled, "I have known him to give a thousand dollars at a time in aid of building funds for churches of all denominations."[68]

In 1865 Ulysses S. Grant donated the hefty sum of $600 to the Spring Garden Street Methodist Episcopal Church in Philadelphia. The following year, he praised the Lincoln Institute, an orphanage for the sons of dead soldiers aged eleven to twenty-one, for its biblical training, declaring, "I especially approve of surrounding them with home comforts and Christian influences during that period of life when a boy is, for the first time, exposed to the temptations of the world—when he first attempts to make a living for himself." In an 1879 speech to the Protestant Orphan Asylum, he emphasized the advantages of religious endeavors funded by private charity, such as the orphanage, over secular efforts to help orphans that are funded by taxes. The former fostered love, morality, and gratitude, while the latter did not:

> Where it is a matter of law simply to provide by taxation a home for the destitute, and they are looked to by officials appointed with a salary, it is true [that] starvation is kept from overtaking them and that they are furnished homes. But their morals and their education are neglected, and their condition more resembles that of prisoners than of children being brought up to become suitable members of society. This institution, like others of its kind in the country, will serve to bring these little children up as useful members of society, and for that they will be ever grateful in their future lives to you and to the charitable people who support you without an enaction of law to compel support by taxation.

The following year, when Grant visited the Wesley Chapel, a Black Methodist church in New Orleans, he was pleased to hear of the church's ministrations throughout the South, declaring, "I hope the work which has been commenced to secure the Gospel and the spelling-book to every class will be continued, so all denominations and individuals, white and black, may have these blessings."[69]

Like many other presidents, Rutherford Hayes supervised the biblical instruction of his children. The Hayes family read a chapter of the Bible after breakfast every morning, each member taking turns reading a verse, which was followed by the whole family kneeling and repeating the Lord's Prayer.[70]

While in retirement in the 1880s and early 1890s, Hayes served as the vice president of a county Bible society and as president of the Slater Fund for Negro Education. The general object of the fund, established by industrialist John Slater, was, in Slater's own words, "the uplifting of the lately emancipated population of the Southern states and their posterity by conferring upon them the blessings of a Christian education." While some officials of the Slater Fund worried that critics might find fault with the religious component of the fund's work, Hayes was adamant that students aided by the fund be required to attend religious services and Sunday schools. In 1893 one of the fund's beneficiaries, W. E. B. Du Bois, wrote to express his gratitude for a Slater scholarship, which had made it possible for him to study in Berlin. He emphasized his gratitude to Hayes, who had since passed away: "I am especially grateful to the memory of him, your late head, through whose initiative my case was brought before you and whose tireless energy and singleheartedness for the interests of my Race God has at last crowned. I shall, believe me, ever strive that these efforts shall not be wholly without results."[71]

As the trustee of a Methodist church, Hayes supported holding revivals there. He pledged to pay one-fourth of the cost of constructing a new church. When it burned a few years later, he pledged the same share of the replacement cost.[72]

James Garfield took an even more direct approach to disseminating the Gospel. As a young man in the 1850s, he preached to various congregations within his Disciples of Christ denomination concerning a large array of biblical subjects, including Providence, the Pentateuch, "the design and effect of prayer," "the evidences of Christianity," forgiveness of sin, the hope of immortality, the Second Coming, the way of salvation, "the need of Faithfulness to all the trust that God has committed to us," the necessity of obedience to God, Christian duty, the life and character of the apostle Paul, and the great flood. He was also a member of a group that chartered the Christian Publishing Association in 1866 for the purpose of publishing a religious weekly. Garfield contributed pieces to this publication, the *Christian Standard*, which became the leading journal of the Disciples of Christ.[73]

Benjamin Harrison served as a Sunday school teacher. In 1861 he wrote to his young brother-in-law, Henry Scott, who was a soldier in the Union Army: "Avoid with more care the vices of the camp than you would the enemy's bullets.... They are more deadly.... By your priceless and immortal soul, let not the ribaldry of companions keep you from Scripture reading and prayers."[74]

Theodore Roosevelt also served as a Sunday school teacher. While studying at Harvard, he taught a Sunday school class at an Episcopalian church. He took a serious interest in his young pupils, many of whom came from poor neighborhoods. Even though it was a great inconvenience to ride to Cambridge early on Sunday mornings after staying out late with friends on Saturday nights, young Roosevelt missed only two classes in three years, and both times, he arranged for a friend to teach the class. When he stopped teaching, it was because the church decided that only Episcopalians should teach Sunday school classes there. Although he doubted his own effectiveness as a young teacher, he was later delighted when one of his former pupils, now a New York cabdriver, remembered his instruction fondly and related that he was now "an ardent Bull Mooser." Roosevelt also supported the efforts of the Young Men's Christian Association (YMCA) to minister to the American canal builders in Panama. In 1906 he wrote, "Nothing better could befall us on the Isthmus than to have these Y.M.C.A. organizations flourish as they have flourished on the railroad systems in the United States as well as in the army and navy." He added that the YMCA in Panama should have "an attractive, wholesome, decent club to which men won't have to be urged to go, but to which they will actually go of their own accord, probably with the purpose of getting amusement, but with the result also of their own moral and physical betterment." He concluded, "I hope that all that the Government can do to help along with this work will be done." In 1911 he urged, "I enter a most earnest plea that in our hurried and rather bustling life of today we do not lose the hold that our forefathers had on the Bible. I wish to see Bible study as much a matter of course in the secular college as in the seminary." Of the $45,482.83 Roosevelt was awarded with the Nobel Peace Prize for negotiating peace between Russia and Japan, he contributed $9,000 to the YMCA; $4,000 to the Young Women's Christian Association (YWCA); $4,000 to the Knights of Columbus; $4,000 to the Jewish Welfare Board; and $1,000 to Armenian and Assyrian Christians devastated by World War I. In other words, he contributed roughly half of the award money to religious organizations.[75]

William Howard Taft served as the chairman of the editorial board of the YMCA. In this capacity, he coauthored a lengthy, laudatory account of the organization's efforts to render both spiritual and material aid to millions of soldiers around the world during World War I.[76]

As a new father in 1886, Woodrow Wilson looked forward to fulfilling his obligation to teach his daughter Margaret about God. Wilson wrote to his wife Ellen, "My heart has been full to overflowing with thanksgiving to our heavenly Father for his unspeakable goodness to us! How gracious and loving He has been! What a sweet duty it will be to teach our little daughter to love Him!"[77]

While a professor at Princeton and later as president of the university, Wilson often taught Bible studies in Marquand Chapel, as well as in meetings of the Philadelphian Society, a student group. The topics of his sermons, which were peppered with scriptures, included righteousness, wisdom, public service, and love.[78]

As governor of New Jersey in 1911, Wilson addressed a large gathering of Sunday school advocates. He declared,

> I am interested in Sunday School work only as a study of the Scriptures. The only significant book, the only book that can have any possible significance as a textbook in the Sunday School is the Bible itself, and as we must train our children in the rest of the thought of the world, we must if we are to make progress as a nation ground each generation as it comes along in the established and tested moral judgments of the world. . . . Every Sunday School should be a place where this great book is not only opened, is not only studied, is not only revered, but is drunk of as if it were a fountain of life, is used as if it were the only source of inspiration and of guidance.[79]

In 1917, after the United States entered World War I, President Wilson urged American soldiers and sailors to read the Bible. He wrote,

> The Bible is the word of life. I beg that you will read it and find out for yourself—read, not little snatches here and there, but long passages that will really be the road to the heart of it. You will find it full of real men and women not only but also of the things you have wondered about and been troubled about all your life, as men have been always; and the more you read the more it will become plain to you what things are worthwhile and what are not, what things make men happy—loyalty, right dealing, speaking the truth, readiness to give everything for what they think their duty, and, most of all, the wish that they may have the approval of Christ, who gave everything for them—and the things that are guaranteed to make men unhappy—selfishness, cowardice, greed, and everything that is low and mean.

Wilson endorsed the effort of the American Bible Society to raise $400,000 to provide one million Bibles for members of the armed services, writing,

"They will need the support of the only book from which they can get it." The following year, he issued this statement:

> No study is more important to the child than the study of the Bible and of the truths which it teaches, and there is no more effective agency for such study than the Sunday school. It certainly is one of the greatest factors in our lives in the building of character and the development of moral fiber, for its influence begins almost as soon as the child is able to talk and continues throughout life. The Sunday school lesson of today is the code of morals of tomorrow. Too much attention cannot be paid the work which the Sunday School is doing.

In 1920 Wilson endorsed the "Christian Education Movement" of southern Methodists, writing, "I hope that it will meet with the greatest success. Every man who understands and loves the country must wish education brought to the highest point of development and efficiency and to be shot through at every point with Christian principles."[80]

In 1949 Harry Truman contributed more than $20,000 toward the construction of Grandview Baptist Church in Missouri and even brought the pastor and one of the deacons to the White House to discuss the building plans. Truman also bought the church's previous building and sold it to a Pentecostal church to assure that it remained a place of worship. The following year, he dedicated his new church as "a monument to the worship of God." In 1952, regarding the Bible, he declared, "If people understood the contents of this book from cover to cover, and we could get a complete understanding of it behind the Iron Curtain, there would be but one thing in this world: peace for all mankind."[81]

In 1956, after reading in the *New York Times* that a stenographer had paid a hefty $400 for a monthlong subway advertisement on the Brooklyn-Manhattan Transit System featuring the Ten Commandments, Dwight Eisenhower was so moved that he wrote to her. In the letter Eisenhower noted, "The newspaper account reported you as saying that a small thing can change the world. How right you are. The world can well use an accumulation of good thoughts and good deeds, such as yours, which can call forth what Lincoln described as 'the better angels of our nature.' . . . It is better to try to light a light than to bewail the darkness. For what you did, a personal 'thank you.'"[82]

Gerald Ford advocated the biblical instruction of youth. In 1970 he endorsed the evangelism of children because "it gives them the great guidance that flows from the truths of Christianity and the wisdom of its founder, Jesus Christ," thereby undercutting the allure of drug abuse and criminal activity. The following year, he declared, "If we need anything in America today, we need the private Christian college and the truths that it teaches, the basic wisdom it imparts to young minds, and the muscle it provides to the national character." As vice president in 1974, he expressed pride in his son Mike, a divinity student. He added, "He is making up for his father's sins." Two years later, he declared, "It remains our duty to remember our religious heritage, teach it to our children, and to order our own lives with courage, with justice and kindness and in the love of God."[83]

Beginning at age eighteen, Jimmy Carter served as a Sunday school teacher for virtually his entire adult life. He first served at Plains Baptist Church, then at the Naval Academy, then again at Plains Baptist, then at Northside Baptist Church in Atlanta while governor of Georgia, then at the First Baptist Church of Washington while president of the United States, and finally, at Maranatha Baptist Church in Plains while retired. In fact, in 1997, he published a compilation of his favorite Bible lessons entitled *Sources of Strength*. The compilation included fifty-two brief lessons, one for each week of the year. Carter wrote,

> For me, and for many of those in the classes, there is a surprising element of interest and even excitement in exploring Scripture together. . . . Since the Scripture selections and comments are so brief, my hope is that you will supplement what I have presented with further study of the Bible and associated commentaries. . . . For me, the ancient texts always come alive when I explore them with a searching heart. I hope they will be for you, as they have been for me, sources of strength. . . . The Scriptures are full of interesting, shocking, helpful, and inspiring stories. . . . The Bible offers concrete guidance for overcoming our weaknesses and striving toward the transcendent life for which we were created.[84]

As a teen, Ronald Reagan taught a Sunday school class for younger boys in his Disciples of Christ Church in Dixon, Illinois. He was so dedicated to the class that even after he moved away to Eureka College, he returned on weekends to teach it. In an address to governors in 1987, he endorsed the teaching of "the Judeo-Christian ethic," including the Ten Commandments and the call to "love thy neighbor as thyself," in public schools. He explained, "Standards of right and wrong are essential to any life that is lived well and should be a part of education. . . . The Judeo-Christian ethic is a prescription for a happy and productive community, city, state, or nation."[85]

George H. W. Bush served as a Sunday school teacher at the First Presbyterian Church of Midland, Texas. He was a large financial contributor to various programs at St. Martin's Church in Houston, funding outreach to the city's poor and the homeless.[86]

In addition to supervising the biblical training of their own children, a surprising number of presidents have served as Sunday school teachers at some point in their lives. Many have contributed to the construction of churches, sometimes even those belonging to other denominations. Most have lauded the work of missionaries. They have sincerely believed that the Bible is an invaluable guide to human happiness both here and in the hereafter.

CHAPTER 3

Heroes and Villains

The Bible has furnished presidents with a rich source from which to draw moral and political lessons that they have then applied to contemporary problems, both personal and political. Their political rhetoric has been suffused with biblical allusions to persuade their fellow citizens to pursue their favored courses of action.

Presidents have employed biblical references to impress and persuade. The Bible has facilitated communication by furnishing a standard set of stories, knowledge, and ideas, providing a literature select enough to provide common ground yet rich enough to address a wide range of human problems from a variety of perspectives. Biblical stories and the lessons they impart have proved a vital source of unity in a nation whose people are separated from one another by vast stretches of terrain as well as by an ever-increasing number of ethnicities and religious denominations. Scriptural references have also allowed presidents to impress audiences with their own piety and virtue and to appropriate the support of divine authority for their arguments and causes.

Presidents' recognition of the political utility of the Bible does not prove insincerity in their professions of admiration for it, because, in most cases, these presidents' private letters and diary entries reveal the same admiration as their public pronouncements, and, as we have seen, some continued to read and comment on the revered text in their retirement years, long after they ceased to derive any political benefit from it. Even those presidents who have rejected fundamental biblical doctrines have tended to view the Bible as a source of wisdom and to value the moral and political lessons they learned from its rich collection of stories.

The Importance of Biblical Heroes

Most presidents have turned to the vivid stories of the Bible for heroes who personify such virtues as charity, love, self-sacrifice, endurance, forgiveness, piety, righteousness, faith, humility, wisdom, courage, loyalty, truthfulness, and industriousness. Although many of these virtues are not directly related to politics, nearly all serve important civic ends. It is no wonder that most presidents have considered the Bible an invaluable resource for fostering the virtue necessary to all republics.

Jesus, the Chief Role Model

Raised in a profoundly Christian culture, most presidents naturally viewed Jesus as the chief role model. In 1865 James Garfield wrote to his wife, Lucretia, "The Bible is chiefly valuable to me for the example it gives me of a perfect life in the life of Christ." In 1876 a young Woodrow Wilson noted regarding Jesus: "His holiness shone forth in every act of His life, in every word that proceeded from His mouth. He did not wait for Sabbath or the weekly appointments for prayer and thanksgiving, but every day and hour was spent in the service of His father. Surely this is the way in which He would have us live! . . . By keeping our duty to our Creator and Savior before our eyes at all times, we are molding ourselves more and more after the perfect image of Christ." Twenty-seven years later, Wilson declared, "Jesus Christ presents the only perfect example of service for love's sake."[1]

In 1918 Calvin Coolidge presented Jesus as the greatest model of self-sacrifice. He argued, "The law of progress and civilization is not the law of the jungle. It is not an earthly law; it is a divine law. It does not mean the survival of the fittest; it means the sacrifice of the fittest. Any mother will give her life for her child. Men put women and children in the lifeboats before they themselves will leave the sinking ship. John Hampden and Nathan Hale did not survive, nor did Lincoln, but Benedict Arnold did." Coolidge then alluded to Jesus, saying, "The example above all others takes us back to Jerusalem some nineteen hundred years ago." Twenty years later, Herbert Hoover called Jesus "the greatest Leader humanity has ever known." In 1940 he referred to Jesus as "the greatest Teacher of mankind." Harry Truman also called Jesus "the world's greatest teacher." In 1952 he declared regarding Jesus: "He bore in His heart no hate and no malice—nothing but love for all mankind. We should try as nearly as we can to follow His example." In 1978 Jimmy Carter claimed, "Christ was a person who was alive, dynamic, vigorous, strong, with a great sense of humor." Nineteen years later, he wrote,

"Jesus is the supreme example of social courage. He gave his teaching, acceptance, and love to those generally considered least worthy of it: Gentiles, sinners, the sick, the outcast, and the despised. And He paid the ultimate price for his courage." In 1992 George H. W. Bush said, "We celebrate the birth of Jesus Christ, whose life offers us a model of dignity, compassion, and justice." Twelve years later, Bush's son, George W., declared, "Through His ministry and sacrifice, Jesus demonstrated God's unconditional love for us. He taught us the importance of helping others and loving our neighbors. His selfless devotion and mercy provide a remarkable example for all of us." In 2013 Barack Obama claimed concerning Jesus, "Through a life of humility and ultimate sacrifice, a life guided by faith and kindness towards others, Christ assumed a mighty voice, teaching us lessons of compassion and charity that have lasted more than two millennia. He ministered to the poor. He embraced the outcast. He healed the sick. And in Him we see a living example of scripture that we ought to love others not only through our words but also through our deeds."[2]

Old Testament Heroes

Presidents have also admired the heroes of the Old Testament. The first human mentioned in it, Adam, is both a hero and a villain, the progenitor of the human race and the cause of its fall. In 1854 Andrew Johnson, a former tailor, wrote that he was not ashamed of his past occupation because "Adam, our great father and head, the lord of the world, was a tailor by trade, for in the history of Adam and Eve as given by Moses, we get the original idea of sewing." This was a reference to Genesis 3:7, in which the first couple make a garment out of fig leafs to cover their nakedness following the Fall.[3]

Presidents have applauded Noah as the savior of the human race and as a man of uncommon faith. In 1891 Grover Cleveland claimed, "The construction of the ark was the turning-point in the scheme for the perpetuation of the human race. The builder's work in that emergency saved mankind from a watery grave." In 1976 Jimmy Carter emphasized Noah's faith: "Only Noah knew that the world was going to be destroyed. His neighbors did not know anything. You can imagine what Noah went through living back in the mountains building his ship. You can imagine what the neighbors said to him. The ridicule must have been unbearable, but his faith let him survive."[4]

Job exemplifies endurance. In 1999, when Bill Clinton was presenting Congressional Gold Medals to the nine African Americans who, more than forty years earlier, had persevered in the face of an angry mob to integrate Little Rock High School, he noted, "The Book of Job [23:10–12] says,

'My foot has held fast. I have not turned aside. And when tried, I shall come forth as gold.'" Clinton added, "For holding fast to their steps, for not turning aside, we now ask these nine humble children, grown into strong adults, to come forward for their gold."[5]

Clinton also applauded Abraham for his peaceable nature. In a 1995 address at the signing ceremony for the Israeli-Palestinian West Bank Accord, Clinton noted that Abraham had allowed his nephew Lot to select the best part of the land in order to keep the peace between their households. Clinton declared, "You, the children of Abraham, have made a peace worthy of your great forebear. Abraham, patriarch of both Arabs and Jews, sacrificed power for peace when he said to his nephew Lot, 'Let there be no strife between thee and me. If thou wilt take the left hand, then I will go to the right [Genesis 13:9].'" Clinton added, "Patience and persistence, courage and sacrifice: these are the virtues, then as now, that set peacemakers apart."[6]

Joseph personifies moral courage and wisdom. In 1997 Jimmy Carter referred to Genesis 39:7–20 when he stated regarding Joseph, "As a trusted slave in the house of Potiphar, an official of the pharaoh, he had the audacity to reject the sexual advances of Potiphar's wife. She was a beautiful woman who promised Joseph physical pleasure; political, social, and economic security; and personal advancement, if only he would betray his master. Yet he remained true to his principles and suffered imprisonment as a result." Bill Clinton was referring to Genesis 41:48–49 when he asked, "Remember Joseph? What did he do in a time of plenty? He did not rest. When people thought he was too farsighted and too burdensome, he instructed them to stockpile rich bounties of grain like sand of the sea. He knew that times of plenty had to be the busiest, the most productive, the most determined times of all." Likewise, Clinton asserted that the time to shore up Social Security was during the economic boom of the late 1990s.[7]

Early presidents often compared their leaders and nation to Moses and the Israelites at the time of the Exodus. This trope can be traced back to the Puritans, who saw themselves as latter-day Hebrews crossing a great sea to escape Egyptian-style persecution at the hands of an English pharaoh. In 1776, just a few weeks before his impassioned oratory helped secure the passage of an independence resolution by the Continental Congress, John Adams was deeply affected by a sermon that compared America to Israel and Britain to Egypt, a sermon that "indicated strongly the Design of Providence that We should be separated from G. Britain." Adams wrote to his wife, Abigail: "Is it not a saying of Moses, who am I that I should go in and out before this great People [Exodus 3:11]? When I consider the great Events which are passed, and those greater which are rapidly advancing, and that

I may have been instrumental in touching some Springs and turning some small Wheels which have had and will have such Effects, I feel an Awe upon my Mind which is not easily described." Adams regarded himself as a Moses, an unlikely man exalted by God for a crucial mission, leading his people to freedom and independence. Such a self-image must have provided tremendous motivation in the face of hardship during the long war.[8]

Soon after independence, Benjamin Franklin and Thomas Jefferson expressed similar views on the commonality of the United States and post-Exodus Israel in their proposals for the national seal. Benjamin Franklin described his proposed seal, which was based on Exodus 14:27–28: "Moses standing on the Shore, and extending his Hand over the Sea, thereby causing the same to overwhelm Pharaoh, who is sitting in an open Chariot, a Crown on his Head and a Sword in his Hand. Rays from a Pillar of Fire in the Clouds, reaching to Moses, to express that he acts by Command of the Deity. Motto: Rebellion to Tyrants is Obedience to God." Jefferson's proposal was virtually identical.[9]

The identification of America with post-Exodus Israel became even more frequent after the Revolution. In 1817 Jefferson wrote regarding European immigration to America: "This refuge, once known, will produce [a] reaction on the happiness even of those who remain there, by warning their task-masters that when the evils of Egyptian oppression become heavier than those of the abandonment of the country, another Canaan is open where their subjects will be received as brothers and secured against like oppressors by a participation in the right of self-government."[10]

During his time, George Washington was widely hailed as both the nation's Moses and its Joshua. In the ten weeks after Washington's death in 1799, countless eulogies compared him to many past heroes, but none more than to Moses. Among the most frequently cited texts in the Washington eulogies was Deuteronomy 34, which relates the death of Moses and the mourning of the Israelites. Eulogists claimed that God caused the ancestors of both Washington and Moses to move to the most fertile region of another continent to escape the scarcity of the former continent. Both were humble and patriotic men. Both relinquished luxuries for their people: Moses parted with the grandeur of the Egyptian court, and Washington, the bliss of Mount Vernon. Both were passionate men who learned to govern their passions. Both were tested and hardened in the wilderness. Both showed courage when others faltered—Moses, when cornered at the Red Sea, and Washington, during the most hopeless parts of the Revolutionary War—because both trusted God. Their trust was clearly merited because God saved both men repeatedly from certain death. God placed both in the seemingly hopeless situation of attempting to defeat the greatest empire of their day in order to make God's own power clear to the world. Just as Moses led the Israelites to safety and freedom through a red sea, so Washington led his people to the same blessings through a sea of blood. Just as Moses was compelled to confront those who rebelled against his authority, so Washington had to overcome a conspiracy against his command by lesser men. Each left a farewell address to guide his grief-stricken nation (Moses's was called the Book of Deuteronomy). The only differences were that Washington displayed more genuine faith than Moses, which is made evident by God speaking directly to Moses and not to Washington, and that Washington was even more successful than Moses, who died outside the Promised Land, in contrast to Washington, who conducted his people to it. While Moses died on a mount of hope (Nebo), Washington died on a mount of possession (Vernon). Because of the latter difference, some, like William Henry Hill of South Carolina, contended that Washington was not only a Moses who rescued his people from the hands of their enslavers, but also a Joshua who, as president, established them firmly in their promised land.[11]

In 1850 Andrew Johnson claimed that Moses was one of the greatest proponents of natural law, a universal code of ethics. Eight years later, Johnson referred to Moses as "the first law-writer—and I think one of the best, for we are informed that he wrote by inspiration."[12]

James Garfield contended that Moses was second only to Jesus. He wrote in his diary, "Except Jesus, no foot ever trod the earth and sustained the weight of so mighty a man as he—Historian, Lawgiver, Poet, and Man of God."[13]

Harry Truman applauded Moses's determination to do what was right, regardless of its unpopularity. In 1954 he wrote, "I wonder how far Moses would have gone if he'd taken a poll in Egypt?" Truman added for good measure, "What would Jesus Christ have preached if he'd taken a poll in Israel?"[14]

As the oldest president in American history at his time, Ronald Reagan found Moses's longevity encouraging. In 1981 Reagan told another geriatric leader, Israeli Prime Minister Menachem Begin, "Lately, I've been heartened to remember that Moses was 80 when God commissioned him for public service [Exodus 7:7], and he lived to be 120 [Deuteronomy 34:7]. And Abraham was 100 and his wife, Sarah, 90, when they did something truly amazing [Genesis 17:17]. He survived to be 175 [Genesis 25:7]. So, Mr. Prime Minister, we haven't even hit our full stride yet."[15]

Like John Adams, George W. Bush interpreted a sermon as connecting his own mission to that of Moses. In 1999, on the morning of his second inauguration as governor of Texas, when Bush was deciding whether to run for president the following year, he attended a service at First United Methodist Church in Austin. The sermon was delivered by Mark Craig, Bush's former pastor in Dallas. Bush later recalled regarding Craig,

> In his sermon he spoke about the Book of Exodus, when God calls Moses to action. Moses's first response was disbelief: "Who am I that I should go to Pharaoh and bring the Israelites out of Egypt?" He had every excuse in the book. He hadn't led a perfect life; he wasn't sure if people would follow him; he couldn't even speak that clearly. That sounded a little familiar. Mark described God's reassurance that Moses would have the power to perform the task he had been called to do. Then Mark summoned the congregation to action. He declared that the country was starving for moral and ethical leadership. Like Moses, he concluded, "We have the opportunity, each and every one of us, to do the right thing, and for the right reason." I wondered if this was the answer to my question. There were no mysterious voices whispering in my ears, just Mark Craig's high-pitched Texas twang coming from the pulpit. Then Mother leaned forward from her seat at the other end of the pew. She caught my eye and mouthed, "He is talking to you."

Bush was sworn in as president two years later.[16]

Barack Obama referred to the previous generation of civil rights leaders as "the Moses generation"—those who had secured the passage of landmark legislation, such as the Civil Rights Act of 1964 and the Voting Rights Act of 1965, thus opening the way to the "promised land." Continuing the analogy, Obama referred to his own generation as "the Joshua generation," those tasked with the struggle to occupy, defend, and enlarge that territory. He later recalled how much it meant to him that when he ran for president, former colleagues of Martin Luther King Jr. "lay their proverbial hands on me, vouching for me as an extension of their historic work." Obama derived the image of the laying on of hands from Numbers 27:22–23, in which Moses lays hands on Joshua before all the people as a symbol of the transfer of leadership.[17]

Moses's brother, Aaron, has been honored as a gifted speaker. In a lecture on rhetoric at Harvard, John Quincy Adams highlighted the importance of Aaron's oratorical gifts. Because Moses was a poor speaker, "another favored servant of the Most High was united in the exalted trust of deliverance and specially appointed for the purpose of declaring the divine will to the oppressor and the oppressed; to the monarch of Egypt and the children of Israel. 'Is not Aaron, the Levite, thy brother? I know that he can speak well. And he shall be thy spokesman unto the people [Exodus 4:14–16].'" Adams added,

It was not sufficient for the beneficent purposes of divine Providence that the shepherd of his flock be invested with the power of performing signs and wonders to authenticate his mission and to command obedience to his words. The appropriate instrument to appall the heart of the tyrant upon his throne, and to control the wayward dispositions of the people, was an eloquent speaker; and the importance of the duty is apparent in the distinction which separated it from all the other transcendent gifts with which the inspired leader was endowed, and committed it, as a special charge, to his associate. Nor will it escape your observation that, when the first great object of their joint mission was accomplished, and the sacred system of laws and polity for the emancipated nation was delivered by the voice of heaven from the holy mountain, the same Eloquent Speaker was separated from among the children of Israel to minister in the priest's office, to bear the iniquity of their holy things, [and] to offer up to God, their creator and preserver, the public tribute of their social adoration.[18]

Jimmy Carter appreciated Aaron's loyalty to his brother. In 1978 Carter told a group of supporters the story of the battle in which the Israelites prevailed only when Moses's arms were raised. When he grew tired, Aaron and Hur supported his arms (Exodus 17:11–13) so that the Israelites might be victorious. Carter told his supporters, "I'm depending on you that if my arm gets heavy and starts to sag, I'm going to depend on you to help me prop it up."[19]

Deborah has been honored as one of ancient Israel's greatest judges, who were the nation's judicial and political leaders during the premonarchical period of the nation. In 1969 Richard Nixon likened Israeli Prime Minister Golda Meir to Deborah and expressed the hope that Meir's leadership would lead to forty years of peace for Israel, as Deborah's had (Judges 5:31).[20]

Ruth exemplifies loyalty. In an 1858 senate speech, Andrew Johnson declared his love for Tennessee in the language of Ruth (1:16): "I will speak in strong language and upon high authority that 'Whither thou goest, I will go; and where thou lodgest, I will lodge; thy people shall be my people, and thy God my God." Ironically, three years later, Johnson chose not to go where Tennessee went; he was the only US senator from a seceded state who remained in the Senate. Lincoln rewarded him for his overriding loyalty to the Union, first, by appointing him military governor of Tennessee and, later, by selecting him as his running mate in his reelection bid, whereby Johnson became president after Lincoln's assassination. More than half a century later, the widower-president Woodrow Wilson wrote to his new love, Edith, "We will make a pledge to one another as old and sacred and sweet as love itself: 'Entreat me not leave thee or to return from following after thee: for whither thou goest I will go; and where thou lodgest, I will lodge; thy people shall be my people, and thy God my God.'" Wilson added, "Naught but death shall part thee and me."[21]

David has exemplified many noble qualities. In 1856 Abraham Lincoln called John C. Fremont, the first Republican nominee for president, "the man to right the ship of State, and, like the stripling of Israel, to slay the boasting Goliaths of slaveocracy that have beset the national capitol and defiled the sanctums of liberty, erected and consecrated by the old prophets and fathers of the republic." Lincoln utilized Fremont's relative youth and military exploits during the Mexican War to liken him to the young shepherd who slew the fierce Philistine giant.[22]

Jimmy Carter regarded David as a model of loyalty and humility. David remained loyal to Saul despite the king's implacable hatred and efforts to kill him. Furthermore, his willingness to confess his sins displayed an uncommon humility. Carter wrote, "How can this man, who violated almost every one of God's commandments, become a mighty leader of the Israelites? Through confession. Again and again, he repented and turned to God, freely admitting his wrongdoing and seeking forgiveness and new life. And each time, God granted him that gift."[23]

Solomon has personified wisdom. While a student at Princeton considering a ministerial career in the early 1770s, James Madison chose to copy extracts from the ninth through the twentieth chapters of Solomon's Book of Proverbs into his commonplace book. In 1828 John Quincy Adams wrote, "In the Proverbs of Solomon there is a great fund of worldly wisdom, the foundation of which is laid in the wisdom which is from above, in piety to God. There is no other genuine wisdom; all else is self-deception, the folly of fools." In 1854 Andrew Johnson instructed his son Robert: "Nothing great can be accomplished without effort and application. Solomon's remarks on the conduct of the sluggard and that lethargy which hangs about too many young men like the night mare [Proverbs 6:6–11] should be read by all young men at least once a week."[24]

Other presidents have also admired the wisdom of Solomon. Herbert Hoover cited Proverbs 31:25 in praise of women. In 1938 he declared, "It is not flattery but just a commonplace fact that the moral instincts of women are upon average higher than [those of] men. Solomon discovered that 'strength and honor are her clothing.'" Lyndon Johnson ended his inaugural address in 1965 as follows: "For myself, I ask only in the words of an ancient leader: 'Give me now wisdom and knowledge, that I may go out and come in before this people, for who can judge this thy people that is so great?'" This was a reference to Solomon's famous request for wisdom from God in 2 Chronicles 1:10, after he became king of Israel. Three years later, Gerald

Ford told graduates of the College of William and Mary that the Book of Proverbs contained "page after page of good advice."[25]

Presidents have also admired the prophets and other faithful Jews of the prophetic era. In 1809, upon retiring from political life at the end of his presidential administration, Thomas Jefferson cited the prophet Samuel's questions at the time of his own retirement (1 Samuel 12:3) in response to a message from the inhabitants of his Virginia county welcoming him home: "Of you, then, my neighbors, I may ask, in the face of the world, 'Whose ox have I taken, or whom have I defrauded? Whom have I oppressed, or of whose hand have I received a bribe to blind mine eyes therewith?'" Jefferson added, "On your verdict I rest with conscious security."[26]

During World War I, both President Woodrow Wilson and former President Theodore Roosevelt saw themselves as heirs to the prophets. In 1915, while arguing for military preparedness due to the war's outbreak in Europe, Wilson claimed that he often meditated on Ezekiel 33:7–8, in which God appoints Ezekiel as his proverbial watchman over Israel, warning the prophet that if he does not sound the alarm, he will be responsible for the nation's fate. Two years later, Roosevelt likened himself to another Old Testament prophet whose warnings were also ignored. Mixing classical and Christian metaphors, he noted, "An elderly male Cassandra has-been can do a little, a very little, towards waking the people now and then; but undue persistency in issuing Jeremiads does no real good and makes the Jeremiah an awful nuisance." While Cassandra was the Trojan prophetess who was cursed with the ability to issue accurate prophecies of calamity that were always disregarded, Jeremiah was the prophet whose prophecy of the Babylonian destruction of Jerusalem was likewise ignored. In 1918 Roosevelt wrote, "My whole concern at this time is practically the same concern that Amos and Micah and Isaiah had for Jerusalem nearly three thousand years ago! In those days a prophet was very apt to get himself stoned."[27]

Harry Truman often claimed that the world needed a new Isaiah. In 1941 he declared, "I pray to God to give the Dictators of Europe and Asia a change of heart. Oh, for an Isaiah to reawaken a sense of righteousness in the world's rulers. May we go back to the moral code which that most persecuted of peoples, the Hebrews, gave the world. May the nations of the world become so reformed in heart that right will rule instead of might, and then we can have eternal peace." Five years later, he repeated, "Oh, for an Isaiah or a Saint Paul to reawaken this sick world to its moral responsibilities!" In 1947, when dealing with the Arab-Israeli conflict, he claimed, "I surely wish God Almighty would give the children of Israel an Isaiah, the Christians a St. Paul, and the Sons of Ishmael a peep at the Golden Rule." A year later, he reiterated this desire in his diary: "May there be another awakening. We need an Isaiah, John the Baptist, Martin Luther—may he come soon." In 1949 Truman extolled the prophets: "The prophets were among the first of men who saw that the concept of the Fatherhood of God required men to do justice to one another. They called on people of their day, just as they call on us today, not only to recognize the humanity of others, but also to work unceasingly for the achievement of a greater justice in human relations." Similarly, he declared, "Amos was interested in the welfare of the average man. This is what the prophets were, they were the proponents of the common man. . . . Every one of these prophets was trying to help the underdog, and the greatest prophet was crucified because He was trying to help the underdog."[28]

Bill Clinton praised Isaiah's willingness to serve. In 1998, following al-Qaeda's bombing of two American embassies in Africa, Clinton declared, "In the book of Isaiah [6:8] it is written that the Lord called out, 'Whom shall I send, and who will go for us?' And Isaiah the prophet answered, 'Here am I, Lord; send me.'" Clinton added regarding the embassy workers, "These Americans, generous, adventurous, brave souls said, 'Send me. Send me in service. Send me to build a better tomorrow.' And on their journey they perished, together with proud sons and daughters of Kenya and Tanzania."[29]

Daniel was another revered prophet. In 1996, at a memorial service for victims of terrorism following a wave of suicide bombings in Israel, Bill Clinton told Israelis, "I remember the story of Daniel. Because his faith never wavered, even in the face of those who betrayed him and had him cast into the den of lions, God delivered Daniel [Daniel 6]. Have faith, and I believe God will deliver Israel from those powerful vipers who have the ability to turn young men into mad suicide bombers, those awful people who would slaughter young children to defeat those who only want those children to grow up in peace."[30]

New Testament Heroes

The New Testament has been as important to presidents as the Old Testament. First, as heirs to a Christian heritage, they have generally viewed the Old Testament through the prism of the New. Second, as we shall see later, they have derived from the New Testament beliefs regarding the nature of virtue, the afterlife, and other matters that have possessed not only great personal significance but also political implications.

Jesus is not the only New Testament figure presidents have admired. On his deathbed in 1826, Thomas Jefferson is reported to have murmured, "Lord, now lettest thy servant depart in peace." This was a reference to

Simeon, the elderly Jew who praised God after seeing the Christ child in the temple, saying, "Now let your servant depart in peace, according to your word, for my eyes have seen your salvation" (Luke 2:29–30). While not all reports of deathbed sayings can be taken seriously, this one has the ring of truth, for Christopher Gadsden made the same reference to Jefferson in a letter following the ratification of the Constitution. Indeed, it was a common biblical reference. During the War of 1812, John Quincy Adams wrote, "If I could by any act of mine contribute to the restoration of a just and honorable peace, I should be ready to say, 'Lord, now lettest thy servant depart in peace, for mine eyes have seen thy salvation.'" After the booming of cannons in Nashville conveyed the news of the presidential election of his protégé James K. Polk in 1844, Andrew Jackson wrote, "I thank my god that the Republic is safe & that he has permitted me to live to see it & rejoice, and I can say in the language of Simeon of old, 'Now let thy servant depart in peace.'" Following the Civil War, Andrew Johnson declared, "This Union being restored, the summit of my ambition has been reached, the measure of my ambition has been fulfilled, and I could now say, as Simeon did of old . . . 'Now let thy servant depart in peace!'"[31]

George Washington admired the poor widow Jesus praised for putting all the money she possessed (two mites, which were coins of extremely low value) into the collection plate (Mark 12:42–44). In 1783 Washington advised his nephew, "Let your heart feel for the affliction and distresses of everyone, and let your hand give in proportion to your purse; remember always the estimation of the Widow's mite."[32]

Jimmy Carter lauded the Samaritan woman at the well to whom Jesus spoke in John 4. Carter noted that the woman "takes her place alongside Mary Magdalene as one of the great female disciples of Jesus who rose from a despised social position to become an inspired witness." The woman's gender, ethnicity, and past all conspired to make her a social outcast, yet she became the means by which a whole village was saved.[33]

Presidents have found role models even in Jesus's parables. Thomas Jefferson considered the prodigal son's father an exemplar of forgiveness and the son a model of repentance. In writing to a friend who was estranged from his own son, Jefferson declared, "Persuaded that a reconciliation with your son would tend much to the quiet of your mind, it would give me particular pleasure to learn that he could see the duty he is under of 'arising and going unto his father and saying, father I have sinned' & c. and that you had fallen on his neck and kissed him" (Luke 15:18–20).[34]

The Good Samaritan has exemplified charity. In 1932 Franklin Roosevelt declared, "Charity is love of neighbor—the kind of love that was shown by the Good Samaritan. When we respond to its impulses, we are responding to the promptings of God." Four years later, Roosevelt addressed the students at Rollins College in Florida. After noting that Jesus told the parable of the good Samaritan in response to the question, "Who is my neighbor?" Roosevelt added, "When you return home, I wish you would read this parable of the Good Neighbor. You will find it in the tenth chapter of St. Luke's Gospel. This allegory should make a particular appeal to all of us today when a large portion of our country has been laid waste by the worst flood in our history."[35]

Abraham Lincoln considered the demoniac whom Jesus healed in Mark 5 an exemplar of effective advocacy. Lincoln argued that the best temperance advocates were not preachers but recovering alcoholics: "When one who has long been known as a victim of intemperance bursts the fetters that have bound him and appears before his neighbors 'clothed, and in his right mind' [Mark 5:15], a redeemed specimen of long lost humanity . . . there is a logic and an eloquence in it that few with human feelings can resist." The sufferers of alcoholism, "like the poor possessed [demoniac], who was redeemed from his long wanderings in the tombs [5:5], are publishing to the ends of the earth how great things have been done for them [5:20]."[36]

The apostle Paul has long been considered a hero of the Christian faith, as well as a model of endurance and love. In 1828 John Quincy Adams was moved by a sermon delivered at the US Capitol by Thomas Gallaudet, the pioneer for whom the famous university for the deaf was later named, in which Gallaudet emphasized his role as a religious instructor. Regarding the deaf students, Adams wrote, "He dwelt especially, and with power, upon the blessing imported to them in the ideas of a Supreme Creator, of their own immortality, and of the hopes and promises of the gospel." Adams then likened Gallaudet to Paul, another evangelist who carried the gospel to a new and overlooked group, the Gentiles. Additionally, Woodrow Wilson was "especially impressed by the fact that he [Paul] 'sang praises'" to God while imprisoned at Philippi (Acts 16:25), and Jimmy Carter extolled Paul as a model of steadfastness: "As he told the Corinthians [2 Corinthians 11:24–27], five times he had been given thirty-nine lashes by the Jews, three times he had been beaten by the Romans, he had been stoned, shipwrecked on three occasions, often cold and hungry, and imprisoned several times. He could very well have looked upon his life as a failure." Instead, his triumph was that of Christianity.[37]

The Significance of Biblical Villains

In addition to the numerous heroes presidents have encountered in the Bible, they have also discovered a rich collection of villains who have served as equally useful object lessons in their political discourse. The Bible highlights the dangers to society posed by their numerous vices.

Satan, the Chief Villain

The most despised figure in the Bible is, of course, Satan, a frightful figure in whose literal existence many presidents have believed. These presidents have considered him not only the chief opponent of goodness but also the principal enemy of freedom. In 1767 John Adams wrote regarding liberty: "The world, the flesh, and the devil have always maintained a confederacy against her, from the fall of Adam to this hour, and will probably continue so till the fall of the Antichrist." In 1796 John Quincy Adams condemned gleeful British newspaper articles about George Washington's decision to retire after two presidential terms as "the calumny of English spirits beholding the felicity of the Americans as Satan is represented beholding that of our first parents in the garden of Eden." During the Missouri Crisis in 1820, Adams complained that Rufus King was being slandered by slaveholders due to his opposition to slavery. The slaveholders claimed that King's position on that institution was based solely on political ambition. Adams added, "This imputation of bad motives is one of the most envenomed weapons of political and indeed of every sort of controversy. It came originally from the devil: 'Doth Job fear God for naught?'" Adams was referring to Satan's attempt to slander Job in Job 1:9. In the subsequent verse, the devil suggests that Job's loyalty to God is due solely to the blessings he has received. As a Greek scholar, Adams surely knew that the New Testament word *diabolos* (devil) literally means "slanderer."[38]

Allusions to Satan continued long after 1820. Near the end of his life, while composing a final statement of advice for his country, James Madison became concerned by the talk of disunion spawned by the Nullification Crisis in South Carolina. Madison mingled classical and Christian symbols of mayhem: "The advice nearest my heart and deepest in my convictions is that the Union of the States be cherished and perpetuated. Let the open enemy of it be regarded as a Pandora with her box opened, and the disguised one as the Serpent creeping with his deadly wiles into Paradise [Genesis 3:1–6]." In 1855 Andrew Johnson lambasted the anti-Catholic Know-Nothing Party, which had evolved from a secret society, declaring, "The Devil, his Satanic Majesty, the Prince of Darkness, who presides over the *secret conclave* [emphasis in original] held in Pandemonium, makes war upon all branches of Christ's church. The know-nothings advocate and defend none, but make war upon one of the churches, and thus far become the allies of the Prince of Darkness." During the Civil War, when denouncing Southern secessionists, Johnson often declared that the devil was the first secessionist, having seceded from heaven, that he then seduced Adam and Eve into secession, thus bringing misery on mankind, and that he was the force behind Southern secession. In 1864, having accepted the vice presidential nomination of the Union Party, a coalition of Republicans and War Democrats, Johnson scoffed at the proposal of George McClellan, the Northern Democratic presidential nominee, to negotiate an end to the war against the Confederacy: "When Beelzebub, His Satanic Majesty, made war with [the archangel] Michael when he rebelled against Heaven, would you have had Deity hold a parley and ask an armistice?" Johnson failed to note that the American founders he so revered had also been secessionists, having seceded from the British Empire.[39]

In one of the Lincoln-Douglas debates, Abraham Lincoln evoked laughter from the audience when he referred to his own House Divided Speech: "The sentiments expressed in it have been extremely offensive to Judge Douglas. He has warred upon them as Satan does upon the Bible." In 1872 Ulysses Grant, then in a heated presidential campaign against Horace Greeley, wrote regarding his opponents' efforts to convert Andrew Curtin, an influential Pennsylvania leader, to their side: "The Greeleyites will be as liberal in their offers to him as Satan was to our Savior, and with as little ability to pay." This was a reference to Satan's temptation of Jesus in the wilderness in Matthew 4. In 1920, while on his sickbed, Woodrow Wilson learned of the Senate's rejection of the Treaty of Versailles, a treaty for which he had campaigned across the country before suffering a stroke. His personal physician, Dr. Cary Grayson, later recalled that at 3:00 a.m., "He turned to me and said, 'Doctor, the devil is a busy man.' This is all he said."[40]

In 1938 Herbert Hoover claimed, "Science may have abolished the personal devil but invented new forms of devilment." However, the personal devil appears not to have been abolished in Hoover's own mind, because he finished the speech by quoting Ephesians 6:12–17, the apostle Paul's famous description of spiritual warfare between Christians and fallen angels that were led by Satan:

> For we wrestle not against flesh and blood, but against principalities, against powers, against the rulers of the darkness of this world, against spiritual wickedness in high places. Wherefore take unto you the whole armor of God, that ye may be able to withstand in the evil day, and having done all, to stand. Stand therefore, having your loins girt about with truth and having on the

breastplate of righteousness. And your feet shod with the preparation of the gospel of peace. Above all, taking the shield of faith, wherewith ye shall be able to quench all the fiery darts of the wicked. And take the helmet of salvation and the sword of the Spirit, which is the word of God.

Thirteen years later, Harry Truman expressed the same belief in a literal devil. After calling on Christians and Jews to issue a common affirmation of faith in God, the president added, "Such an affirmation would testify to the strength of our common faith and our confidence in its ultimate victory over the forces of Satan that oppose it." In 1981 Ronald Reagan identified Marxism as a diabolical religion: "The Marxist vision of man must eventually be seen as an empty and false faith—the second oldest in the world—first proclaimed in the Garden of Eden with whispered words of temptation: 'Ye shall be as gods.'" This is the devil's false promise to Eve in Genesis 3:5.[41]

Judas, the Runner-Up

The second most detested biblical figure has been Judas, the betrayer of Jesus. In 1825, after the House of Representatives was tasked with deciding the presidential election due to the failure of any candidate to secure a majority of the electoral votes, Andrew Jackson wrote, "I am informed this day by Colonel R. M. Johnston of the Senate that Mr. [Henry] Clay has been offered the office of Secretary of State and that he will accept it. So, you see, the Judas of the West has closed the contract and will receive the thirty pieces of silver. His end will be the same." As Speaker of the House, Clay's support for John Quincy Adams was crucial to that body's selection of Adams over Jackson. Adams's appointment of Clay as secretary of state, a traditional stepping stone to the presidency, shortly thereafter led to cries of a "corrupt bargain" by Jackson's followers, thereby crippling Adams's administration and contributing to the failure of Clay's numerous presidential bids. In writing, "His end will be the same," Jackson expressed the hope that Clay might suffer a death as ignominious as that of Judas, who hanged himself (Matthew 27:5). Likewise, in an 1861 speech denouncing secessionists, Andrew Johnson claimed, "Judas, after he had betrayed our Saviour for thirty pieces of silver, also seceded, and immediately put an end to his existence."[42]

Old Testament Villains

Adam and Eve, whose sin brought calamity to all of humankind, have personified the foolishness inherited by their descendants, who refuse to learn from their error. In 1787 John Adams referred to the first couple when writing to Thomas Jefferson regarding the human propensity to be ruled by passion rather than learning from the mistakes of others: "Lessons, my dear Sir, are never wanting. Life and History are full. The Loss of Paradise by eating a forbidden apple has been many Thousand years a Lesson to Mankind, but not much regarded." Others faulted the first man for his cowardly attempt to pass the buck when caught in sin (Genesis 3:12). In 1873 Ulysses Grant explained to George Childs that a miscommunication with Grant's wife, Julia, led to Grant's missing an invitation from Childs. Grant added slyly, "Like Adam of old, I must throw the blame on the woman."[43]

Cain, the assassin of his brother Abel, has been vilified as the first murderer. During the Mexican War, Congressman Abraham Lincoln harassed President James K. Polk with his Spot Resolutions, demanding that Polk show the American people the precise spot at which the Mexican army had allegedly shed American blood on American soil. Polk had ordered the US Army to move into disputed territory between the Nueces and Rio Grande Rivers, prompting a Mexican attack that Polk then utilized in calling for a declaration of war. Regarding his call for Polk to point out the spot on "American soil" that was violated, Lincoln declared, "If he can not, or will not, do this—if on any pretense, or no pretense, he shall refuse or omit it, then I shall be fully convinced of what I more than suspect already, that he is deeply conscious of being in the wrong—that he feels the blood of this war, like the blood of Abel, is crying to Heaven against him [Genesis 4:10]." Andrew Johnson used the same image regarding the radical abolitionist John Brown. Referring to the murders Brown committed while in Kansas, Johnson declared on the Senate floor: "The blood of these murdered men, not unlike that of the sacrificed Abel, cried even from the tongueless caverns of the earth to him for pity, and to Heaven for justice, but his iron heart, not soul, refused to yield; but Heaven, in the process of time, has meted out to him justice on the gallows." In 1960 John F. Kennedy noted ruefully, "We and the Russians now have the power to destroy with one blow one-quarter of the earth's population—a feat not accomplished since Cain slew Abel."[44]

Nimrod, the first king and first empire builder (Genesis 10:8–10), exemplifies tyranny and imperialism. In an 1828 speech, James Buchanan declared, "Since the days of Nimrod, the mighty hunter whose prey was man & who established the first empire over his fellow men, war has been waged between the lust of dominion & the love of liberty—between power & right—between the few & the many—the rulers & the ruled."[45]

The people of Sodom and Gomorrah have personified wickedness. In 1861 General Ulysses Grant complained about southeastern Missouri: "There is not a sufficiency of Union sentiment left in this portion of the state to save Sodom." He was referring to God's promise to Abraham to spare Sodom and Gomorrah if He could find ten righteous people there (Genesis 18:32). Unfortunately, only Lot, his wife, and their two daughters ultimately qualified, so God destroyed the cities after they evacuated. Later, when the young Theodore Roosevelt resigned from the Committee on Privileges and Elections in the New York State Assembly in protest over the Democratic majority's refusal to seat the duly elected Henry L. Sprague, he, too, referenced the ill-fated cities: "For the twelve or fourteen Democratic members who voted in favor of Mr. Sprague last night I have and shall always have a very sincere respect. They acted against the majority of their party; they acted as honest and manly men. But exactly as ten [righteous] men could have saved the 'cities of the plains' so these twelve men will not save the Sodom and Gomorrah of the Democracy." In 1904 Woodrow Wilson declared, "There are not enough men in politics who are there without ambition for offices or personal aggrandizement. . . . Such men make the professional politicians uneasy, but with a few such our modern Sodoms would be saved."[46]

Esau has been reviled for showing contempt for his birthright by selling it to his brother Jacob for a bowl of porridge (Genesis 25:29–34), a food that some Americans (following the King James Version) referred to as "pottage." In 1946, angry at the American people for rebelling against price controls, Truman wrote a speech, which was fortunately never delivered, in which he castigated them: "You've deserted your president for a mess of pottage, a piece of beef—a side of bacon. My fellow citizens, you are the government. This is a government of, by, and for the people. If you insist on following Mammon instead of Almighty God, your President can't stop you all by himself." The last sentence was a reference to Matthew 6:24, in which Jesus declares, "You cannot serve God and mammon," the last word referring to wealth.[47]

Similarly, Joseph's brothers, who sold him into slavery, have been likened to those who would betray their country for financial gain. In 1775 John Adams compared the Loyalists to the famous brothers, but he added a charitable line: "However, what the sons of Israel [Jacob's other name] intended for ruin to Joseph proved the salvation of his family; and I hope and believe that the whigs will have the magnanimity, like him, to suppress their resentment and the felicity of saving their ungrateful brothers." Here he was referencing Genesis 50:20, in which Joseph tells his brothers, "You intended evil for me, but God meant it for good," since Joseph's enslavement ultimately led to his premiership in Egypt, which, in turn, allowed him to feed his whole family during a time of famine.[48]

The Israelites of the Exodus epitomize idolatry. Benjamin Rush recalled that in 1777, John Adams told him, "I have been distressed to see some of our members [of Congress] disposed to idolize an image which their own hands have molten. I speak of the superstitious veneration which is paid to General Washington." This, of course, was a reference to those Israelites who formed and worshipped the golden calf in the wilderness (Exodus 32:4).[49]

Samson exemplifies the loss of power, seduction by a wicked woman, and self-destruction. In 1796 Thomas Jefferson wrote to Philip Mazzei regarding the infiltration of the federal government by men Jefferson regarded as supportive of monarchy and aristocracy: "It would give you a fever were I to name to you the apostates who have gone over to these heresies, men who were Samsons in the field and Solomons in the council, but who have had their heads shorn by the harlot England." In Jefferson's mind England was Delilah, seducing Federalist Samsons into "apostasy" and "heresy" against republicanism and thus destruction. The following year, this private letter was published without Jefferson's permission, thereby creating a scandal, for some considered George Washington as the chief Samson in the field to whom Jefferson referred.[50]

The welfare state was the Delilah that Herbert Hoover feared. In 1954 the former president warned regarding its corruption of young men into laziness: "The judgment of the Lord to Adam about sweat has not been repealed. When we flirt with the Delilah of security [without work] for our productive group, we had better watch out, lest in our blindness we pull down the pillars of the temple of free men." Hoover's first statement referred to Genesis 3:19: "By the sweat of your face will you eat bread."[51]

Saul, Israel's first king, has been regarded as one whose peace of mind was ruined by envy. Jimmy Carter wrote, "Saul's jealousy destroys joy in his own accomplishments. Saul is the undisputed leader, and the victories of his army, including the deeds of David, are ultimately to Saul's credit. Yet Saul is unable to celebrate them. His triumphs bring him no pleasure because he perceives David's as greater [1 Samuel 18:7–8]."[52]

Zedekiah, placed in power by the Babylonians following their conquest of Judah (2 Kings 24:17), personifies the weakness of a puppet king. In 1815 John Quincy Adams predicted that the conquerors of Napoleonic France would set up their own such king there: "The Bourbons will be set up like Zedekiah of Judah by Nebuchadnezzar."[53]

Haman, who died on the very gallows he had prepared for Mordecai, as related in Esther 7:10, exemplifies self-defeating evil. In 1848 Abraham Lincoln, despite having protested the Mexican War like many of his fellow Whigs, delighted in the party's nomination of General Zachary Taylor, one of the war's heroes. Lincoln noted regarding the Democrats, "It turns the war thunder against them. The war is now to them the gallows of Haman which they built for us and on which they are doomed to be hanged themselves." Seven years later, Lincoln noted that the Kansas legislature had passed "a law to hang men who shall venture to inform a negro of his legal rights." Lincoln added, "If, like Haman, they should hang themselves upon the gallows of their own building, I shall not be among the mourners for their fate."[54]

New Testament Villains

Presidents have encountered villains in the New Testament as well. The corrupt people who followed Jesus after His miracle of multiplying the loaves and fishes solely because they wanted free meals exemplify greed. To these Jesus said, "Very truly, I tell you, you seek me not because you saw the miracles but because you ate of the loaves and were filled [John 6:26]." In 1813 John Adams claimed, "The real terrors of both Parties have always been, and now are, the fear that they shall lose the Elections and consequently the Loaves and Fishes, and that their Antagonists will obtain them." James Buchanan, who was a Democrat, used the same analogy in a Senate speech after the election of the Whig William Henry Harrison, when addressing his colleagues of the opposite party regarding appointments to federal offices. According to the Congressional Record, Buchanan declared that "if any of his friends here should happen to be looking out for 'loaves and fishes,' all I can say is, I wish them God speed." Buchanan himself later received his own loaves and fishes during the Democratic administrations of Polk and Pierce. In a speech to his fellow Republicans the year before he himself was nominated for the presidency, Abraham Lincoln warned, "If we shall adopt a platform that fails to recognize or express our purpose, or elect a man that declares himself inimical to our purpose, we take nothing by our success, but we tacitly admit that we act upon no [other] principle but a desire to have 'the loaves and the fishes,' by which in the end our apparent success is really an injury to us."[55]

The money changers whom Jesus drove out of the Great Temple in Jerusalem (Matthew 21:12–13) have also served as villains. In 1832 John Tyler considered a recently passed tariff a form of robbery in which Northeastern manufacturers picked the pockets of Southern and Western farmers. In a speech to his fellow senators, Tyler presented the tariff as an example of the materialism then sweeping the nation. He preached, "Man cannot serve God and Mammon. If you would preserve the political temple pure and undefiled it can only be done by expelling the moneychangers and getting back to the worship of our fathers." In his first inaugural address a century later, Franklin Roosevelt applied the same appellation to his own nemeses, the bankers, adding that they had now been chased out of the temple. Roosevelt declared, "The moneychangers have fled from their high seats in the temple of our civilization. We may now restore the temple to the ancient truths."[56]

Ananias and Sapphira, who were struck down by God for claiming falsely that they had contributed the full proceeds from a property sale to the Church (Acts 5:1–10), personify prevarication. Whenever a reporter displeased Theodore Roosevelt by writing something he considered dishonest, Roosevelt designated the offender a member of "the Ananias Club" and thereafter refused him access.[57]

Just as presidents have encountered numerous virtues in the Bible's vivid and compelling stories, they have also encountered numerous vices there, including cruelty, dishonesty, greed, selfishness, folly, infidelity, pride, envy, idolatry, lust, and hypocrisy. However personal these vices are, many presidents believed that they would surely tear the nation's political fabric if practiced by a sufficient number of its citizens. Thus, these presidents have taken care to warn the public against their destructiveness through references to familiar biblical narratives.

CHAPTER 4

Providence

In addition to heroes and villains, most presidents derived from the Bible the concept of an omniscient, omnipotent, and caring God who not only created the universe but who also intervenes in it. Most have referred to this mysterious intervention as Providence. A few have believed that God carries out his will through natural causes alone, but many have been willing to speak of miracles. Presidents have found ways of reconciling their belief in such a God with the various misfortunes that have befallen them and their families, friends, and nation, sometimes attributing these hardships to divine judgment against sin and, at other times, emphasizing God's remarkable capacity to bring good out of evil.

Confidence in Providence

The Bible is one long record of divine intervention. Immediately after the sin of Adam and Eve in the Garden of Eden, God, rather than wash his hands of humanity, begins a program of damage control and repair that includes saving a righteous family from the judgment of the great flood, establishing a chosen people through the seed of Abraham, and finally, in the New Testament, assuming human form and dying for humanity's sin. This wise and loving form of divine intervention was as unknown to Greco-Roman religion, whose gods were interventionist but limited in knowledge and capacity (they could be fooled and manipulated), as well as selfish and capricious, as it was to most of classical philosophy, whose divine entities (the Platonic good, the Aristotelian prime mover, the Stoic world soul, the Epicurean gods, and the Neoplatonic One) were impersonal forces that did not concern themselves with individuals and their lives.[1]

Immersed in Scripture from their childhoods, most presidents have expressed confidence in Providence. No other president so continually espoused the biblical theme of divine intervention as George Washington. From the time that Washington's coat was riddled with bullet holes and he had two horses shot out from under him without being so much as scratched (serving under British General Edward Braddock at the Monongahela River during the French and Indian War), he possessed a firm conviction that God shielded him. Just a few days after Washington's narrow escape from death, he wrote that he had survived because of "the miraculous care of Providence that protected me beyond all human expectation." More surprisingly, this same belief concerning God's protection of Washington arose among his fellow citizens at precisely the same time. Tales of the Virginian's bravery and survival spread rapidly throughout the colonies, leading revivalist preacher Samuel Davies to refer to him in a sermon as "that heroic Youth, Colonel Washington, whom I cannot but hope Providence has hitherto preserved in so signal a Manner for some important Service to his Country," a hope that was later hailed as a prophecy. Washington was quite sincere when, in 1776, he wrote, "No Man has a more perfect Reliance on the all-wise and powerful dispensations of the Supreme Being than I have, nor thinks His aid more necessary." Two years later, his army having survived appalling conditions at Valley Forge, Washington wrote from there, "Providence has a . . . claim to my humble and grateful thanks for its protection and direction of me." In 1784, the year after the conclusion of the war, Washington claimed, "I feel now . . . as I conceive a wearied Traveler must do, who, after treading many a painful step, with a heavy burden on his shoulders, is eased of the latter, having reached the Goal to which all the former were directed, and from his House top is looking back, and tracing with a grateful eye the Meanders by which he escaped the quicksands and Mires which lay in his way, and into which none but the All-powerful guide and great disposer of human Events could have prevented his falling."[2]

Five years later, upon becoming the first president of the United States, Washington depended on Providence for support in the monumental task he took on of creating a federal government virtually from scratch. It was later alleged that Washington added the phrase "So help me, God" to the oath of office, a custom deeply embedded in the tradition of oath taking in Virginia and followed by many subsequent presidents. Whether or not Washington actually followed this custom at his inauguration, eyewitnesses attest that he did kiss the Bible, another long-standing tradition that denotes the oath taker's dependence on God. A few months later, Washington declared, "I know the delicate nature of the duties incident to the part which I am called to perform, and I feel my incompetence without the singular assistance of Providence to discharge them in a satisfactory manner." To the officials of Wilmington, Delaware, he wrote, "Heaven and my own heart are witnesses for me with how much reluctance I have yielded to that persuasion [to assume the presidency]. But a sense of duty, in my conception, ought to supersede every personal consideration, and the promises of support which I am daily receiving from my fellow citizens, together with a reliance upon that gracious Providence which sustained us through our struggle for Liberty, encourage me (notwithstanding a diffidence in my own abilities) to hope for a happy issue from my present arduous undertaking." A year before he died, after expressing concern about the admission of his grandson George Washington Custis into a cavalry unit because of his status as an only son, Washington added quickly, perhaps recalling his own improbable survival in battle, "But the same Providence that would watch over and protect him in domestic walks can extend the same protection to him in a Camp, or the field of battle, if he should ever be in one."[3]

In 1809, after John Quincy Adams was appointed the United States' first minister to Russia, he wrote in his diary, "On the integrity of my intention, and on the aid of that gracious Heaven which has never deserted me, I must rely. I pray for clearness of intellectual vision to see the right path, for the necessary courage to pursue it, and for the fortitude and temperance to bear with equanimity the vicissitudes of fortune, whether adverse or propitious. Grant, O God, that I may do good to my country and to mankind, and deal with me and mine, if it be thy gracious will, in mercy." Two years later, he credited "the smile of Providence" with the favorable trade conditions the Russian government had conferred on the United States. In 1814, as Adams traveled to Ghent to help conclude the peace treaty that ended the War of 1812, he wrote in his diary: "Never have I had more urgent necessity to implore the aid of the Divine Spirit to enable me to discharge those duties with zeal, energy, and fidelity; never more need of the guiding hand of that Being whose inspiration is wisdom and virtue, and who disposes all events and controls the passions of men and the course of events." In 1817, returning to the United States after an eight-year absence spent serving the nation as a diplomat in Europe, Adams wrote that he was so anxious about his new duties as secretary of state that "nothing but a firm reliance upon Him who has ever been my preserver, and the dispenser of every blessing, supported me from despondency."[4]

In 1819 Adams thanked God that an embarrassing mistake in the map that formed the basis for the Adams-Onís Treaty was caught in an impromptu cabinet meeting. He wrote, "Chance, by which I always understand a superintending Providence, has redeemed the fault of my own carelessness." After the signing of the treaty, in which Spain ceded Florida to the United States, he wrote in his diary: "What the consequences may be of the compact this day signed with Spain is known only to the all-wise and all beneficent Disposer of events, who has brought it about in a manner utterly unexpected and by means the most extraordinary and unforeseen. . . . Let no idle and unfounded exaltation take possession of my mind, as if I could ascribe to my own foresight or exertions any portion of the event. It is the work of an intelligent and all-embracing Cause." In 1823 he wrote, "It has been for more than thirty years my prayer to God that this might be my lot upon earth, to render service to my country and to my species. For the specific object, the end, and the means, I have relied alike upon the goodness of God. For 'it is not in man that walketh to direct his steps [Jeremiah 10:23].'" Adams closed each year by taking stock of "the blessings of Providence" and praying for the continuance of these blessings for himself, his family, and his nation the following year. He began all four of his state of the union addresses by thanking God for the nation's peace, prosperity, and freedom. Adams ended his inaugural address in 1825 by saying, "Knowing that 'except the Lord keep the city the watchmen waketh in vain [Psalms 127:1],' with fervent supplications for His favor, to His overruling providence I commit with humble but fearless confidence my own fate and the future destinies of my country." The same year, he rejected the proposal of a depiction of Hercules for the pediment of the US Capitol, saying it was "too much of the heathen mythology for my taste," substituting instead "a figure of Hope with an anchor—a Scriptural image, indicating that this Hope relies upon a Supreme Disposer of events, 'which hope we have as an anchor to the soul, sure and steadfast [Hebrews 6:19].'" In 1845, having finally achieved victory over the proslavery forces' "gag rule," which sought to prevent antislavery petitions from being read in Congress, Adams attributed this achievement to the Almighty, writing in his diary, "Blessed, forever blessed, be the name of God!"[5]

Andrew Jackson expressed a similar confidence in Providence. In the days leading up to the Battle of New Orleans, he wrote to his wife, Rachel: "I pray you be calm and Trust to the superintending being who has protected and saved me in the midst of so many dangers." In 1824 he wrote, "I have long since prepared my mind to say with heartfelt submission, may the Lord's will be done. If it is intended by providence that I should fill the presidential chair, I will submit to it with all humility and endeavor to labour four years with an eye single to the public good, imploring the guidance of providence in all things." The following year, as he waited for the House of Representatives to select the president, he wrote, "Situated as I am, patience and fortitude must be exercised, and the will of providence cheerfully submitted to. You see, I am still in the habit of ascribing the lot of man to the will of an overruling providence, and should I be brought into the presidential chair it must be by His influence counteracting the intrigues of men and the union of interests here." In his first inaugural address (1829), Jackson included, "Above all, trusting to the smiles of that overruling Providence, in the hollow of whose hand is the destiny of nations, for that animation of common council and harmonizing effort which shall enable us to steer the Bark of Liberty through every difficulty." In 1831 he wrote privately, "My energy has hitherto been equal to every emergency that has occurred to me in my eventful life. I trust in providence it will be so now. I have always trusted Him, and He has hitherto not forsaken me." In 1833, regarding the controversial national bank issue, Jackson claimed, "I trust in a kind Providence to guide and direct me and in a virtuous people's support." This was no empty rhetoric. Jackson believed that he received divine guidance via his conscience. The next day, he wrote regarding his destruction of the bank: "My God told me the measure was right—that the Morals of the People and the perpetuity of our republican government required it—and, as excruciating as it was to my private friendships and feelings, my public duty required my prompt action." Two years later, the first would-be presidential assassin, the deranged Richard Lawrence, fired two pistols at Jackson at close range, but both pistols misfired despite being properly loaded, an extremely unlikely outcome (the odds against it have been estimated at around 125,000 to 1). John Tyler called the misfires "almost a miracle." Jackson removed the "almost" from his own analysis, claiming that "a kind providence" had acted "to shield me."[6]

In 1832, when James Buchanan was dispatched to Russia to negotiate a commercial treaty, he was unhappy to leave Washington, a place he loved, and "to leave the most free and happy country on earth for a despotism more severe than any [other] in Europe." But he added that "these gloomy thoughts" were displaced "by a sense of reliance on that good Providence which hitherto had blessed and sustained me and by a conviction that I was about to go upon an important mission in which I might be made the instrument in His hands of rendering important services to my country." Less than a year later, he was able to write, "I have had my difficulties to contend with and much serious opposition to encounter, but through the blessing of Providence I have been made the instrument of accomplishing a work in which all my predecessors had failed." In his inaugural address in 1857, Buchanan declared, "In entering upon this great office, I most humbly invoke the God of our fathers for wisdom and firmness to execute its high and responsible duties in such a manner as to restore harmony and ancient friendship among the people of the several States and to preserve our institutions though many generations." Five months later, he wrote: "Every day of my life I feel how inadequate I am to perform the duties of my high station without the continued support of Divine Providence; yet, placing my trust in Him, and in Him alone, I entertain a good hope that He will enable me to do equal justice to all portions of the Union, and thus render me an humble instrument in restoring peace and harmony among the people of the several States."[7]

When Abraham Lincoln departed Springfield, Illinois, for his inauguration in 1861, he faced a dire situation. Seven states had seceded from the Union. In an emotional speech, Lincoln told his townsmen,

> No one not in my situation can appreciate my feeling of sadness at this parting. To this place, and the kindness of these people, I owe everything. Here I have lived a quarter of a century and have passed from a young to an old man. Here my children have been born and one is buried. I now leave not knowing when, or whether ever, I may return, with a task before me greater than that which rested upon Washington. Without the assistance of that Divine Being who ever attended him I cannot succeed. With that assistance I cannot fail. Trusting in Him who can go with me and remain with you and be everywhere for good, let us confidently hope that all will yet be well. To His care commending you, as I hope in your prayers you will commend me, I bid you an affectionate farewell.

Along his journey he often reiterated his trust in God. To the Ohio legislature, he promised to "look to the American people and to the God who has never forsaken them." At Steubenville he said he must be "sustained by the great body of the people and by the Divine Power, without whose aid we can do nothing." At Newark he declared, "I cannot succeed without the sustenance of the Divine Providence and of this great, happy, and intelligent people." In his first inaugural address, he implored Southerners to trust that God would work His will through the ballot box: "If the Almighty Ruler of nations, with his eternal truth and justice, be on the side of the North or on yours of the South, that truth and that justice will surely prevail by the judgment of this great tribunal, the American people." To a special session of Congress four months later, Lincoln declared, "Let us renew our trust in God and go forward without fear and with manly hearts."[8]

This confidence in Providence sustained Lincoln throughout the Civil War. In 1863 he wrote, "From the beginning I saw that the issue of our great struggle depended on the Divine interposition and favor. If we had that, all would be well." Four months later, he recalled concerning the beginning of his presidency: "I was early brought to a living reflection that there was nothing in the arms of this man, however there might be in others, to rely upon for such difficulties and that without the direct assistance of the Almighty I was certain of failing." He confessed, "I sincerely wish that I was a more devoted [devout] man than I am. Sometimes in my difficulties I have been driven to the last resort to say God is still my only hope." While Garry Wills has discussed the remarkable similarities between the rhetorical methods employed in Pericles's Funeral Oration, as recounted by Thucydides, and Lincoln's Gettysburg Address, equally striking is the one great difference: whereas the Athenian leader made no mention of the gods, Lincoln famously declared his confidence "that this nation, under God, shall have a new birth of freedom." The following year, Lincoln declared, "When the war began three years ago, neither party, nor any man, expected it would last till now. Each looked for the end, in some way, long ere today. Nor did any anticipate that domestic slavery would be much affected by the war. But here we are; the war has not ended, and slavery has been much affected—how much needs not now be recounted. So true is it that man proposes, and God disposes." Later that year, he attributed his reelection to Providence, expressing gratitude "to Almighty God for having directed my countrymen to a right conclusion."[9]

Andrew Johnson expressed a similar confidence in Providence during the Civil War. In 1864 he declared, "In the various periods of the world's history there have been manifestations of a power incomprehensible to us, and I believe that there is a direct and important connection between the moral and physical world." He cited biblical examples of divine retribution against the pharaoh of Exodus, the Babylonians, and Herod Agrippa. He added, "There are many ways in which the Almighty manifests his power." The next year, he claimed that "the foundation of his creed" was "that all things should be done with the approval of Him who controls the events and destinies of the world."[10]

Ulysses Grant was equally vociferous in expressing a belief in Providence. In 1864, when promoted to lieutenant general and appointed general in chief of the US Army, he wrote to President Lincoln, "I feel the full weight of the responsibilities now devolving on me; and I know that if they are met, it will be due to those armies [of the Union] and, above all, to the favor of that Providence which leads both nations and men." Fifteen years later, after returning from a two-year global tour, Grant claimed, "During the years of my absence, I have not known a single day's sickness, although I have been in every latitude." He concluded, "An invisible Power protected me on my journey." His widely acclaimed memoirs, written shortly before he died of cancer, begin with this statement: "Man proposes and God disposes. There are but few important events in the affairs of men brought about by their own choice." He argued that if Union forces had acted swiftly after the capture of Fort Donelson, they could have seized Chattanooga, Memphis, and Vicksburg, thereby shortening the war considerably. But, he asserted, "Providence ruled differently." In 1885 Grant's former pastor, John P. Newman, recalled, "He had a wonderful faith in divine Providence and believed in the special interpositions of Providence in the affairs of men and nations. I have heard him talk by the hour on that subject, giving illustrations drawn from his own life." For instance, Newman claimed, Grant saw God's hand in his own decision to resign from the army in 1854, which led to historically significant postings after his voluntary reenlistment at the outbreak of the Civil War—postings that differed from those he would have received had he remained in the army.[11]

Rutherford Hayes appears to have come to a belief in Providence later in life. In 1845 he scoffed at the notion that the Protestant Reformation "was the immediate work of the Divine hand," writing in his diary,

> It seems to me that Providence interferes no more in the greatest affairs of men than in the smallest and that neither individuals nor nations are any more the objects of a special interposition of the Divine Ruler than the inanimate things of the world. The Creator gave to every creature of his hand its laws at the time of its creation and whatever can happen in accordance with these laws He doubtless foresaw, and it cannot be supposed that his laws are so imperfect that special interpositions are necessary to render them capable of fulfilling their design nor that it is possible for them to be violated. The Reformation, like other revolutions, was agreeable to principles which have existed since the world began.

Yet seven years later, Hayes wrote to his uncle, "'Whom the Lord loveth He chasteneth [Hebrews 12:6].' Very consolatory text that is." Divine chastening is, of course, a form of intervention. Hayes was even clearer in 1882, writing, "There is a Divine Providence. In the hollow of his hand are all our interests." Seven years later, he wrote in his diary that while he remained a skeptic about some religious matters, "The true infidel, in the offensive or objectionable sense, is not the honest skeptic but the man who opposes all religion . . . [the] one who rejects and scoffs at all thought of a wise and benevolent Providence." Despite the grief produced by the death of his wife, Lucy, he declared, "I believe in the moral government of the universe. I trust and have faith in the power, wisdom, and goodness of the Divine Eternal."

He was grateful to God for giving him his beloved wife in the first place. In 1890 he recalled, "More than forty years ago I met at Sulphur Spring in Delaware one who was permitted while she lived, by a gracious Providence, to be the good angel of my life."[12]

Unlike Hayes, James Garfield possessed a faith in Providence from his youth. At the age of nineteen in 1850, he wrote in his diary, "Sickness and death are abroad in the land, but I rest myself in the hands of the Almighty." He began 1852 by writing, "Circumstances are controlled by the Great Disposer of all human events, and to Him I entrust my interests temporal and eternal. May He keep me as in the hollow of His hand during the coming year!" The following New Year's Day, he noted regarding his aspirations: "I trust it all to the hand that has brought me thus far on the journey of life and believe that God is preserving me for some wise purpose." In 1863 he wrote to his commander in the Union Army, General William S. Rosencrans, "No man can predict with certainty the result of any battle, however great the disparity in numbers. Such results are in the hand of God."[13]

Grover Cleveland believed that God granted him his wife, Frances. In 1890 he wrote, "As I look back upon the years that have passed since God, in His infinite goodness, bestowed upon me the best of all His gifts—a loving and affectionate wife—all else, honors, the opportunity of usefulness, and the esteem of my fellow countrymen, are subordinate in every aspiration of gratitude and thoughtfulness." Cleveland referred to "the sanctification which comes to man when Heaven-directed love leads the way to marriage."[14]

Benjamin Harrison believed that God had protected him during the Civil War. After being praised for his bravery in the capture of a well-defended Confederate battery at Resaca, Georgia, Harrison wrote to his wife Caroline: "We must not, however, think too much of the praises of the newspapers, nor forget that to God who sustains me belongs all the honor."[15]

William McKinley modeled his faith in Providence on George Washington's. On Washington's birthday in 1898, McKinley noted,

> At the very height of his success and reward, as he emerged from the Revolution, receiving by unanimous acclaim the plaudits of the people, and commanding the respect and admiration of the civilized world, he did not forget that his first official act as President should be fervent supplication to the Almighty Being who rules the universe. It is He who presides in the councils of nations, and whose providential aid can supply every human defect. It is His benediction which we most want, and which can and will consecrate the liberties and happiness of the people of the United States. With His help the

instrument of the citizens employed to carry out their purposes will succeed in the functions allotted to public life.[16]

William Howard Taft also expressed a belief in Providence. In 1914 the former president was discouraged by what he regarded as the poor quality of the potential Republican candidates for the presidency in 1916. However, he went on to claim, "But the Lord works these things out better than we poor mortals."[17]

Woodrow Wilson credited God with bringing him together with both of his wives. In 1883 he wrote to his then fiancée, Ellen, "God has been merciful to us, in giving us each the other's perfect love." Two years later, he even credited God with his initial feelings for her, writing, "What a happy God-sent inspiration it was that made me love you at first acquaintance!" Wilson carried this same view into his second marriage. As a widower-president in 1915, he wrote to Edith: "God comes to a man, I think, through the trust and love of a sweet, pure woman. Certainly, God seems very near when I am with you." A month later, he wrote, "I love to think how you walked out of the great world into my little circle here, almost as if by chance, but really by gracious beckoning of Providence." Two months later, he suggested that God had provided her love to shelter him from the debilitating effects of presiding over a nation during a world war: "My Darling came to me as a gift from Heaven. I would have grown old in these few weeks without her."[18]

Wilson did not confine his belief in Providence to his love life. In 1902 he claimed, "A man who has sought out the mysteries of life, who sees the truth of things . . . [will] know that an overruling Providence is above all things." A few weeks later, he declared,

> One of the most impressive things that was ever said, though when repeated in cold blood it sounds rhetorical, was what Mr. [James] Garfield said when Mr. Lincoln was assassinated. I am told that at that time Mr. Garfield was at the Fifth Avenue Hotel in New York, and that when the news reached New York[,] an excited crowd gathered in the square in front of the hotel ready for almost any outburst of frenzied excitement; that Mr. Garfield was asked to step up to the portico of the hotel and say something to quiet the crowd, and that this is what he said: "My friends, the President is dead; but the government lives and God omnipotent reigneth [Revelation 19:6]." And, as you may readily believe, the crowd was quieted.

At the time that Garfield made that statement, he could scarcely have guessed that not only would he succeed Lincoln in the presidency sixteen years later but that he would also become the second president assassinated shortly after; neither did Wilson know that he would succeed both men in the presidency just a little more than a decade after recounting this anecdote.[19]

World War I only increased Wilson's reliance on Providence. When the war erupted in 1914, Wilson wrote to his closest advisor, Colonel Edward House: "I know how deep a sorrow must have come to you out of this dreadful European conflict in view of what we had hoped the European world was going to turn to, but we must face the situation in the confidence that Providence has deeper plans than we could possibly have laid ourselves." In 1916 he observed, "It is one of the fine points of Providence that Providence so often makes damn fools of crooks; they haven't got sense enough to be successful. I praise God for that." In 1918 he declared, "I think one would go crazy if he did not believe in Providence. It would be a maze without a clue. Unless there were some supreme guidance, we would despair of the results of human counsel."[20]

In 1919, while in France to negotiate the global issues connected to the Treaty of Versailles, Wilson claimed, "I believe in divine Providence. If I did not, I would go crazy. If I thought the direction of the disordered affairs of this world depended upon our finite endeavor, I should not know how to reason my way to sanity." The same year, when contemplating the political betrayals he was suffering in his attempt to secure ratification of the Treaty of Versailles, he claimed, "When I reflect on these things, I do not know what I would do if I did not have God to fall back upon." Having suffered a devastating stroke while traveling the country on behalf of the treaty's ratification, he witnessed its rejection by the Senate from his sickbed the following year. He asked his physician to read 2 Corinthians 4:8–9: "We are troubled on every side, yet not distressed; we are perplexed, but not in despair; persecuted, but not forsaken; cast down, but not destroyed." Wilson then commented, "If I were not a Christian, I think I should go mad, but my faith in God holds me to the belief that He is in some way working out His plans through human perversities and mistakes."[21]

Calvin Coolidge expressed the same belief in Providence. In 1921 he declared in a speech regarding Theodore Roosevelt, "Great men are the ambassadors of Providence, sent to reveal to their fellow men their unknown selves." In an interview in 1926, Coolidge claimed, "It would be difficult for me to conceive of anyone being able to administer the duties of a great office like the Presidency without a belief in the guidance of a divine providence. Unless the President is sustained by an abiding faith in a divine power which is working for the good of humanity, I cannot understand how he would have the courage to attempt to meet the various problems that constantly pour in upon him from all parts of the earth." In his memoirs, Coolidge wrote,

"Any man who has been placed in the White House cannot feel that it is the result of his own exertions or his own merit. Some power outside and beyond him becomes manifest through him. As he contemplates the workings of his office, he comes to realize with an increasing sense of humility that he is but an instrument in the hands of God."[22]

Franklin Roosevelt expressed confidence in Providence during World War II. In his famous "date which will live in infamy" speech, Roosevelt called for a congressional declaration of war on Japan following the Japanese attack on Pearl Harbor, invoking biblical language to appeal for divine aid: "The American people in their righteous might will win through to absolute victory. . . . We will gain the inevitable triumph—so help us, God." Two years later, he assured the people of the Philippines that "the great day of your liberation will come, as surely as there is a God in heaven."[23]

Harry Truman believed that God had saved him from death when he served as a captain in an artillery unit during World War I. In 1918 he wrote to his girlfriend, Bess, regarding his destruction of German batteries: "I brought my Battery forward under fire and never lost a horse nor a man. Had shells fell on all sides, and I am as sure as I am sitting here that the Lord was and is with me." After Germany's surrender at the end of World War II (1945), he wrote in his diary, "No one was ever luckier than I've been since becoming the Chief Executive and Commander-in-Chief. Things have gone so well that I can't understand it—except to attribute it to God. He guides me, I think." Two years later, Truman wrote to Pope Pius XII emphasizing the necessity of divine aid in achieving world peace: "An enduring peace can be built only upon Christian principles. To such a consummation we dedicate all our resources, both spiritual and material, remembering always that except the Lord build the house, they labor in vain who build it [Psalms 127:1]." In 1952, when urged to run for a third term, Truman wrote in his diary, "What the hell am I to do? I'll know when the time comes because I'm sure God Almighty will guide me." He decided not to run.[24]

Dwight Eisenhower also relied on God. In 1943, on the first anniversary of American landings in North Africa, he declared, "The God of Justice fights on our side." A decade later, in his inaugural address, he claimed that inaugurations were a time of "conscious renewal of faith in our country and in the watchfulness of a Divine Providence." In 1957 he remarked that the presidency involved "occupying the desk to which come possibly more messengers of fear, more stories of probable disaster and risk, more people who want more things that can't be given." He added, as though channeling Woodrow Wilson, "Anyone sitting there who did not believe that there was a Power that after all does govern the affairs of men, in my opinion, would soon be in St Elizabeth's instead of in the White House." (St. Elizabeth's was a psychiatric hospital.)[25]

John F. Kennedy expressed a similar belief in Providence. In 1961 he noted,

> No man who enters upon the office to which I have succeeded can fail to recognize how every President of the United States has placed special reliance upon his faith in God. Every President has taken comfort and courage when told, as we are told today, that the Lord "will be with thee. He will not fail thee nor forsake thee. Fear not—neither be thou dismayed [1 Chronicles 28:20]." While they came from a wide variety of religious backgrounds and held a wide variety of religious beliefs, each of our Presidents in his own way has placed a special trust in God. Those who were strongest intellectually were also strongest spiritually. . . . The guiding principle and prayer of this Nation has been, is now, and shall ever be "In God We Trust."

A month later, he wrote to one of the men who had rescued him and his comrades after the Japanese sank their PT boat during World War II: "Like you, I am eternally grateful for the act of Divine Providence which brought me and my companions together with you and your friends who so valorously effected our rescue during time of war. Needless to say, I am deeply moved by your expressions, and I hope that the new responsibilities which are mine may be exercised for the benefit of my own countrymen and the welfare of all our brothers in Christ." The following year, Kennedy quoted Abraham Lincoln: "I believe there is a God. I see the storm coming, and I believe He has a hand in it. If He has a part and a place for me, I believe that I am ready." Kennedy added, "We see the storm coming, and we believe He has a hand in it, and if He has a place and a part for us, I believe that we are ready." Eight months later, he quoted the poem of an old British soldier:

God and the soldier all men adore
In time of danger and not before.
When the danger is passed and all things righted,
God is forgotten and the soldier slighted.

Kennedy added, "This country does not forget God or the soldier. Upon both we now depend."[26]

At the nation's bicentennial celebration in Philadelphia in 1976, Gerald Ford emphasized Americans' continual reliance on Providence. He declared, "The American adventure began here with a firm reliance on the protection of Divine Providence. It continues in a common conviction that the source of our blessings is a loving God, in whom we trust."[27]

Jimmy Carter agreed. In 1979 he said, "We accept our responsibilities and make our choices with all the will and determination at our command, but always in the full knowledge that we are finally in the hands of God. In the words of the prophet Zechariah [4:6], 'Not by might, nor by power, but by my spirit, saith the Lord of Hosts.'"[28]

Ronald Reagan believed that God had saved his life after he was wounded by John Hinckley. In his memoirs Reagan wrote, "After I left the hospital and was back in the White House, I wrote a few words about the shooting in my diary that concluded: 'Whatever happens now I owe my life to God and will try to serve Him in every way I can.'" In 1982, a year after penning that diary entry, he declared in a speech, "I've always believed that we were, each of us, put here for a reason, that there is a plan, somehow a divine plan for all of us. I know now that whatever days are left to me belong to Him." Three months later, Reagan declared, "When really needed, God provides a man. And I think in Pope John Paul II he did just that." Both men survived assassination attempts in 1981, collaborated to end the Cold War, and perceived God's hand in both facts.[29]

George W. Bush also expressed a belief in divine intervention. In 2003 he declared, "We can also be confident in the ways of providence, even when they are far from our understanding. Events aren't moved by blind change and chance. Behind all of life and all of history there's a dedication and a purpose set by the hand of a just and faithful God." He believed that Providence led him to his wife, Laura. Although the couple had grown up near each other in Midland, Texas, and had even lived in the same apartment complex in Houston later, they did not meet until 1977. Bush recalled, "While I couldn't pinpoint it at the time, I believe there is a reason Laura and I never met all those years before. God brought her into my life at just the right time, when I was ready to settle down and was open to having a partner at my side."[30]

Barack Obama also perceived the hand of God in his life. In 2014 Obama declared,

> He directed my path to Chicago and my work with churches who were intent on breaking the cycle of poverty in hard-hit communities there. And I'm grateful not only because I was broke and the church fed me, but because it led to everything else. It led me to embrace Jesus Christ as my Lord and Savior. It led me to Michelle—the love of my life—and it blessed us with two extraordinary daughters. It led me to public service. And the longer I serve, especially in moments of trial or doubt, the more thankful I am for God's guiding hand.[31]

Confidence in divine intervention did not lead presidents to laziness but to greater zeal in the fulfillment of their duties due to the hope it inspired. Thus, presidents' expressions of faith in Providence have often taken the form of admonitions to do one's duty and leave the rest to God. In 1794 George Washington wrote to John Jay in preparation for Jay's peace mission to Britain: "To deserve success, by employing the means with which we are possessed to the best advantage and trusting the rest to the all wise disposer, is all that an enlightened public and the virtuous and well-disposed part of the community can reasonably expect." Similarly, in 1798, Washington wrote to reassure his presidential successor, John Adams, who was struggling to avoid war with France: "Satisfied, therefore, that you have sincerely wished and endeavoured to avert war, and exhausted to the last drop the cup of reconciliation, we can with pure hearts appeal to Heaven for the justice of our cause, and may confidently trust the final result to the kind Providence which has heretofore, and so often, signally favoured the people of these United States."[32]

In 1810, while serving as the United States minister in Russia, John Quincy Adams provided his brother detailed instructions on the education of his son George and then reflected, "The best of all possible educations, I know, is but a lottery, and without a corresponding disposition in the child, all that you can do for him is but labor lost. Let us do, however, all that we can and leave the result to Providence." In 1813 Thomas Jefferson claimed, "My principle is to do whatever is right, and leave consequences to him who has the disposal of them." As an expression of his faith in the American people, Andrew Jackson added "and to the country" in his admonition to do one's best and leave the rest to God, a formulation that James K. Polk sometimes repeated.[33]

During the Civil War, Abraham Lincoln urged, "Let us diligently supply the means, never doubting that a just God, in His own good time, will give us the rightful result." In 1910 Woodrow Wilson declared, "That Cromwellian motto, 'Trust in God and keep your powder dry,' was just as important in one clause as in the other. . . . We are all instruments in the hands of Providence, but there is no quarrel against Providence if we are improvident of our resources and of the things that have been put at our disposal." In 1955 Dwight Eisenhower told a West Point graduating class, "All of us gratefully acknowledge, as our fathers before us, our dependence on the guidance of Divine Providence. But this dependence must not tempt us to evade our personal responsibility to use every one of our individual and collective talents for the better discharge of our lifetime missions." In 1968, Lyndon Johnson denied that the reality of Providence removed individual responsibility: "Belief in divine providence is not an escape or a tranquilizer. It is rather a compelling challenge to men to attain the ideals of liberty, justice, peace, and compassion." In 1979 Jimmy Carter repeated the maxim "We must pray as if everything depends on God, and we must act as if everything depends on ourselves." Although these presidents considered their own efforts insignificant when compared to God's, they also considered those efforts essential to securing God's invaluable aid.[34]

Misfortune

It is a testimony to the sincerity and power of the presidents' faith in Providence that their faith has endured over all misfortune. Presidents sometimes have considered hardship a form of divine judgment against sin, but they mostly have regarded it as intended for the good of its recipients.

As early as 1756, John Adams interpreted a devastating Lisbon earthquake and the Seven Years' War (or the French and Indian War) as products of God's wrath against human arrogance. The young man wrote in his diary:

> God Almighty has exerted the Strength of his tremendous Arm which shook one of the finest, richest, and most populous Cities in Europe into Ruin and Desolation by an Earthquake. The greatest Part of Europe and the greatest Part of America have been in violent Convulsions, and [God has] admonished the Inhabitants of both, that neither Riches nor Honours, nor the solid Globe itself, is a proper Basis on which to build our hopes of Security. . . . Is it not then the highest Frenzy and Distraction to neglect these Expostulations of Providence and continue a Rebellion against that Potentate who alone has Wisdom enough to perceive, and Power enough to procure for us, the only certain means of Happiness, and goodness enough to prompt him to both?

In 1774, when British troops occupied Massachusetts in the wake of the Coercive Acts, Adams was informed of a sermon that alleged "that the Judgments of God upon the Land were in consequence of the Mobs and Riots which had prevailed in the Country." He agreed with this assessment but also suggested that additional rampant sins, such as bribery, corruption, and theft, as possible "other Causes" of divine displeasure.[35]

In 1815 John Quincy Adams saw the hand of God in the conquest of Napoleonic France by its enemies. He wrote, "France, after having been twenty years the terror and oppressor of Europe, has now become the victim of oppression in her turn. As she has treated others, she is now treated herself. In this, whatever may be our opinion of the means or of the instruments on either side, we can at least perceive the distributive justice of providence." In 1837 Adams saw divine justice in the fates of Aaron Burr and Alexander Hamilton. He wrote in his diary: "The failure of my father's re-election in 1801 was the joint work of Burr and Alexander Hamilton; and it is among the most remarkable examples of Divine retributive justice that the result to them was the murder of one of them in a duel and the irretrievable ruin of the murderer by the very accomplishment of his intrigues."[36]

In 1846 James K. Polk attributed the sudden death of Senator Alexander Barrow of Louisiana, who died shortly after serving as a second in a duel, to God's judgment against that abominable practice. Polk wrote, "It was in the prosecution of this unchristian object that Mr. Barrow was suddenly seized with disease and cut off in the prime & vigour of life. I am a firm believer that it was a judgment of Heaven upon the immoral, unchristian, and savage practice of dueling."[37]

However, presidents generally have not attributed most misfortunes to divine wrath. More often, they have contended that God uses hardship to promote the greater good of the afflicted.

Some presidents have argued that misfortune teaches wisdom. George Washington believed that God intended the misfortunes of the Revolutionary War to achieve necessary ends. In 1778, when some Americans were angered by the failure of their new French ally to achieve any success against the British navy, Washington responded philosophically, writing to Jonathan Trumbull: "The violent gale which dissipated the two fleets when on the point of engaging and the withdrawing of the Count D'Estaing may appear to us as real misfortunes, but with you I consider storms and victory under the direction of a wise providence which no doubt directs them for the best of purposes and to bring round the greatest degree of happiness to the greatest number of his people." Soon after, he claimed, "Ours is a kind of struggle designed, dare I say, by Providence to try the patience, fortitude, and virtue of Man; none therefore that are engaged in it will suffer themselves, I trust, to sink under difficulties or be discouraged by hardships." Regarding disunity and profiteering in a time of war, he wrote, "Alas! We are not to expect that the path is to be strewed with flowers. That great and good Being who rules the Universe has disposed matters otherwise and for wise purposes, I am persuaded." A year later, Washington wrote regarding crop failure: "I look upon every dispensation of Providence as designed to answer some valuable purpose and hope I shall possess a sufficient degree of fortitude to bear without murmuring any stroke which may happen either to my person or estate from that quarter." In 1781 Washington declared, "Our affairs are brought to an awful crisis that the hand of Providence, I trust, may be more conspicuous in our deliverance."[38]

Washington believed that God was always ready to care for and console those who suffered hardship. He wrote to Jonathan Trumbull following the death of the latter's wife: "Although calamities of this kind are what we should be prepared to expect, yet few, upon their arrival, are able to bear them with a becoming fortitude. Your determination, however, to seek assistance from the great disposer of all human events is highly laudable and is the source from whence the truest consolation is to be drawn." He also wrote to Henry Knox on the death of his son: "I sincerely condole with Mrs. Knox on the loss you have sustained. In determining to submit patiently to the decrees of the Allwise disposer of Human events, you will find the only true and substantial comfort under the greatest of calamities." Washington wrote to the future architect of the nation's capital, Pierre Charles L'Enfant: "While I sincerely condole with you on the loss of your good father, you will permit me to remind you, as an inexhaustible source of consolation, that there is a good Providence which will never fail to take care of his children."[39]

Washington considered submission to Providence an essential duty, even when God's ways were mysterious. In 1797 he wrote to the courageous but failed Polish freedom fighter Thaddeus Kosciuszko: "I beg you to be assured that no one has a higher respect and veneration for your character than I have, or one who more sincerely wished, during your arduous struggle in the cause of liberty and your country, that it might be crowned with success. But the ways of Providence are inscrutable, and Mortals must submit." The following year, he wrote to his second cousin William Augustine Washington regarding the death of William's wife: "These are the decrees of an Allwise [sic] Providence, against whose dictates the skill or foresight of man can be of no avail; it is incumbent upon him, therefore, to submit with as little repining as the sensibility of his nature will admit." In 1799, just six months before his own death, Washington noted regarding the death of Patrick Henry: "At any time I should have received the account of this Gentleman's death with sorrow. In the present crisis of our public affairs, I have heard it with deep regret. But the ways of Providence are inscrutable and not to be scanned by short-sighted man, whose duty is submission, without repining at its decrees." Washington's repeated references to the inscrutable nature of Providence demonstrate that he was no Deist—not only because he believed in an intervening God, contrary to Deism, but also because he lacked the Deists' supreme confidence in the ability of human reason to comprehend fully the ways of an omniscient deity, a confidence that led them to declare with complete assurance which parts of the Bible were "rational" and which were not.[40]

In 1800 Thomas Jefferson noted that God often brought about good through misfortune. He claimed, "When great evils happen, I am in the habit of looking out for what good may arise from them as consolations to us, and Providence has in fact so established the order of things as that most evils are the means of producing some good." He later argued that the grief produced by life's hardships, such as the loss of loved ones and the ailments of the aging body, "prepares us to loose ourselves [from this life] without repugnance."[41]

James Madison concluded that the rarity of suicide proved that the blessings God bestowed on life outweighed the hardships. In 1821 he argued, "Afflictions of every kind are the onerous conditions charged on the tenure of life, and [yet] it is a silencing [of criticism of], if not a satisfactory vindication of, the ways of Heaven to Man that there are but few who do not prefer an acquiescence to them to a surrender of the tenure itself."[42]

John Quincy Adams was philosophical in the face of misfortune. In 1818, after losing his dear mother, Abigail, he quoted Jesus [Matthew 26:39]: "Not my will, heavenly Father, but thine be done."[43]

Within a single year, 1828–1829, Adams lost both the presidency and his eldest son, George. On New Year's Day in 1829, he wrote, "The year begins in gloom. . . . But, in good or in evil fortune, 'It is not in man that walketh to direct his steps [Jeremiah 10:23].' Let him look to the Fountain of all good; let him consult the oracles of God. I began the year with prayer, and then, turning to my Bible, read the first Psalm." The psalm undoubtedly encouraged Adams, for it states regarding the godly man (verses 2–3): "He shall be like a tree planted by a river that brings forth fruit in season. His leaf shall not wither, and whatever he does will prosper." The next month, Adams wrote, "I must take the dispensations of Providence as they come—thankful to Heaven for the good, resigned and submissive to the severe." Later that year, after George committed suicide, John Quincy characterized himself and his wife, Louisa, as "relying on him who chastiseth in Mercy." The couple read comforting passages from the Bible to each other. John Quincy walked alone through the same woods that he and George had trod together two months earlier, praying, "May we humble ourselves in the dust and be conscious that thy chastisements have been deserved." He interpreted the sight of a rainbow immediately after this prayer as a sign of God's goodness and mercy. At the end of 1829, he wrote,

> At the close of the year the only sentiment that I feel to be proper is humble gratitude to God for the blessings with which it has been favored. Its

chastisements have been most afflictive, but I have experienced mercy with judgment. The loss of power and of popular favor I could have endured with fortitude, and relief from the slavery of public office as more than a compensation for all the privations incident to the loss of place. Its vanities I despised, and its flatteries never gave me a moment of enjoyment. But my beloved son! Mysteries of Heaven! Let me bow in submission to thy will. Let me no longer yield to a desponding or distressful spirit. Grant me fortitude, patience, perseverance, and active energy, and let thy will be done!"

Three years later, Adams claimed regarding the cholera epidemic then sweeping most American cities, "The destroying angel is hovering over us. . . . I cannot reconcile it to my theory of divine benevolence that this visitation is without some great reforming and redeeming purpose."[44]

In 1841 Adams looked upon the death of William Henry Harrison, the first American president to die while in office (only one month after his inauguration), along with the accession to the presidency of John Tyler, a man "never thought of for it by anybody," as a disaster for both the Whig Party and the country. But he added, "To the benign and healing hand of Providence I trust, in humble hope of the good which it always brings forth out of evil." Four months later, though he had many political differences with Tyler, Adams was still convinced that "a special Providence placed John Tyler in the Presidential chair." The following month, he wrote, "The thunderbolt of heaven has fallen upon the Whigs. . . . We have no hope but in the redeeming power of heaven to overrule for good the seemingly most calamitous events."[45]

Adams retained this attitude for the rest of his life. In one of his last diary entries in 1846, Adams wrote regarding God, "May I never cease to be grateful for the numberless blessings received through life at His hands, never repine at what He has denied, never murmur at the dispensations of Providence, and implore His forgiveness for all the errors and delinquencies of my life!"[46]

Andrew Jackson frequently sought to comfort close friends and family members who lost loved ones. In 1833 he wrote to Mary Coffee, the daughter of one of his best friends who had just passed away: "It is religion alone that can support us in our declining years, when our relish is lost for all sublunary enjoyments and all things are seen in their true light, as mere vanity and vexation of spirit." Jackson continued regarding his own prayers: "They will be constantly offered up at the throne of grace for you all, and our dear Saviour has spoken it—'that he will be a father to the fatherless and a husband to the widow [Psalms 68:5].' Rely on his promises; they are faithful and true. . . .

Rely and trust on his goodness and mercies, and prepare your minds, in the language of your dear father, always to be ready to say with heartfelt resignation, 'May the Lord's will be done.'" Two years later, when his nephew's small son died, Jackson wrote, "This charming babe was only given you by your great creator and benefactor. . . . It is to him we owe all things; it is he that giveth, and he has a right to take away, and we ought humbly to submit to his will, and be always ready to say, 'Blessed be his name.'" In 1836, after both he and his nephew's wife appeared to have recovered from illnesses, he wrote to her: "My dear Emily, this chastisement by our Maker we ought to receive as a rebuke from him and thank him for the mildness of it, which was to bring to our view, and that it may be always before us, that we are mere tenants at will here. And we ought to live daily so as to be prepared to die; for we know not when we may be called home. Then let us receive our chastisement as blessings from God." Unfortunately, Emily died soon after, prompting Jackson to write to his nephew: "She has changed a world of woe for a world of eternal happiness, and we ought to prepare, as we too must soon follow. It becomes our duty to submit to this heavy bereavement with due submission and control our human passions, submit to the will of God, who holds our lives in His hand, and say with humble and contrite hearts, 'The Lord's will be done on earth as it is in heaven [Matthew 6:10].'"[47]

Jackson applied the lesson to his own hardships. In 1834, when he learned of a devastating fire at the Hermitage, he wrote, "The Lord's will be done. It was he that gave me the means to build it, and He has the right to destroy it, and blessed be his name." He often quoted Hebrews 12:6: "Whom the Lord loveth he chasteneth."[48]

In 1843 Franklin Pierce interpreted the death of his little son Frank of typhoid fever as a divine admonition to focus on eternal, spiritual matters rather than on temporal, material affairs. He wrote that unless we recognize that we are "placed here, as the blessed word of God teaches, to prepare for another and more exalted state of being, we are destined to waste our energies on things that are insubstantial, fleeting, passing away, and that bring no permanent peace—can give no calm hope that is an anchor of the soul."[49]

James Buchanan had the same attitude. In 1832, when his brother George lay on his deathbed, Buchanan wrote to another brother: "Such seems to be the inscrutable decree of an all wise Providence. May our dear mother & may we all be enabled to say, 'Father, thy will be done.'" Not only did Buchanan's brother die, but so did his mother the following year, prompting him to write, "It has been the will of the Almighty to take her to himself & we must bow in humble reverence."[50]

Abraham Lincoln's grief over the horrors of the Civil War, the worst war in American history, was assuaged by a firm belief in Providence. After a terrible Union defeat at the Second Battle of Bull Run, Lincoln wrote these notes of private meditation, intended for his eyes only:

> The will of God prevails. In great contests each party claims to act in accordance with the will of God. Both may be, and one must be, wrong. God cannot be for and against the same thing at the same time. In the present civil war it is quite possible that God's purpose is something different from the purpose of either party—and yet human instrumentalities, working just as they do, are of the best adaptation to serve His purpose. I am almost ready to say this is probably true—that God wills this contest and wills that it shall not end yet. By his mere quiet power on the minds of the now contestants He could either have saved or destroyed the Union without a human contest. Yet the contest began. And having begun He could give the final victory to either side any day. Yet the contest proceeds.

A month later, Lincoln wrote in a similar vein: "If I had had my way, this war would never have been commenced; and if I had been allowed my way, this war would have been ended before this, but we find it still continues; and we must believe that He permits it for some wise purpose of His own, mysterious and unknown to us; and though with our limited understandings we may not be able to comprehend it, yet we cannot but believe that He who made the world still governs it."[51]

Even as a young man in 1850, James Garfield saw the hand of God in an illness that caused him to lose his job as a canal boatman. Later, as a college student, he wrote in his diary,

> When I consider the sequel of my history thus far, I can see the providence of God in a striking manner. Two years ago I [was] ripe for ruin. On the Canal—my wages to be raised to $20.00 per month—ready to drink in every species of vice—and with the ultimate design of going on the ocean. See the facts. I was taken sick, unable to labor, went to school two terms, thus cultivating my moral and intellectual faculties, took a school in the winter, and greatest of all, obeyed the gospel. . . . Thus by the providence of God I am what I am, and not a sailor. I Thank Him.

In 1862 he wrote to a friend, "It may be a part of God's plan to lengthen out this war till our whole army has been sufficiently outraged by the haughty tyranny of proslavery officers and the spirit of slavery and slaveholders with whom they come in contact that they can bring back into civil life a healthy and vigorous sentiment that shall make itself felt at the ballot box and in social life for the glory of humanity and the honor of the country." A month later, he noted, "I try to see God's hand through this darkness and believe that the issue will redound to His glory." The following year, he wrote to his wife, "Nations less powerful and far less wealthy than we have waged fierce wars for 30 years continuously and still not gone to ruin. If this war lasts seven years yet I do not, cannot, would not, doubt in the final success of God's immutable justice and the terrible and complete overthrow of the rebellion."[52]

William McKinley accepted the rule of Providence even in his own death. Just before the operation to remove the assassin's bullet, McKinley quoted from the Lord's Prayer: "Thy kingdom come; thy will be done [Matthew 6:10]." Afterward, he added, "It is God's way. His will, not ours, be done." The latter sentence was a paraphrase of Jesus's words in the Garden of Gethsemane the night before His crucifixion, as recorded in Luke 22:42. McKinley then murmured his favorite hymn, "Nearer, My God, to Thee," and passed away. This prompted his successor, the young Theodore Roosevelt, to praise his "Christian fortitude." McKinley's pastor, Frank Bristol, testified, "No man ever believed more firmly the truth that God reigns than William McKinley, and no silly jest of scoffing unbeliever, no sneer of petty politician, ever made him hesitate to acknowledge God in all his ways and declare his faith in the providential control of human affairs."[53]

Although Woodrow Wilson's faith in Providence was tested by the unexpected passing of his first wife, Ellen, it prevailed. He even found some comfort in the conjunction between his own personal catastrophe and that of the world, which was now engulfed in war. He explained, "In God's gracious arrangement of things I have little time to think about myself. The day's work and responsibilities exhaust all the vitality I have and there is none left to spend on pity for myself." The following year, he vehemently disagreed with a friend of his daughter Margaret when she asserted that life would still be worth living even without a belief in Providence. Wilson told her, "My life would not be worth living if it were not for the divine power of religion, for faith, pure and simple. I have seen all my life arguments against it without ever being moved by them. . . . Never for a moment have I had one doubt about my religious beliefs. There are people who believe only insofar as they understand—that seems to me presumptuous and sets their understanding as the standard of the universe." Late in life, when suffering from the aftereffects of a severe stroke, he confessed, "I am sometimes discouraged at the exceedingly slow progress of my recovery, but I am ashamed of myself when I do because God has been so manifestly merciful to me, and I ought to feel much profound gratitude. I believe that it will turn out well, and that whether well or ill it will turn out right." Wilson came to accept even the failure of his most ardent campaign, his advocacy of the League of Nations, as a wise act of Providence. On his deathbed in 1924, he startled Margaret by saying, "Perhaps it is as well that the League failed." He responded to her gasp with this explanation: "You think I'm wandering, but I'm not. I meant what I said. If the Treaty had been ratified, it would have been a great personal triumph for me. But the American people were not ready for it, and so in the end it would have failed. God did not will it that way. Someday, when the people are prepared, it will come about in the right way."[54]

As governor of New York in 1931, Franklin Roosevelt even saw a silver lining in the Great Depression. It presented an opportunity for Americans to reassess their values and to exercise charity toward others. He began his Thanksgiving Day address with an archaic use of the word "meet," which was clearly intended to evoke the King James Bible: "In time of stress and trouble it is meet that we suffer not our faith in God to fail." He continued,

> Let us not forget that a time of material hardship and loss may well be a period of spiritual gain. We can be thankful for the opportunity of needful readjustment. In this world's goods we may be poorer, but at the same time we can be better men and women for the lessons we have learned. . . . For the restoring of relative values; for a reborn sense of fraternity with which to enrich our liberty; for the opportunity of giving and of sharing as well as of getting; for the high purpose of living more abundantly [John 10:10]—for these gifts and mercies let us give thanks to Almighty God.

The following year, he declared,

> I like to think, especially in times like these, that the Almighty is close to us, that He is watching over us to console, to strengthen, to inspire, that He is stirring the hearts of men to great deeds and to great sacrifices for those who are pressed down by worry, want, and suffering. Throughout our history these impulses from On High have seemed to dot our land with agencies and institutions dedicated to the service of our fellow men. They have inspired thousands of men and women to devote their lives to such service without hope of earthly reward. God is just as near to us today, and His guidance will lead us out of these troublous times.[55]

Harry Truman saw a different silver lining in the hardships caused by World War II: the restoration of Americans' reliance on God. In 1943 he declared,

The hard necessities of war may do us this good turn. They may draw us back to our national faith and to the spirit which alone can see us through the trials ahead. . . . We can still choose to be true to our destiny, to our national faith, to the American Idea. We can make "In God We Trust" not only an inscription on our coinage but the hallmark of our lives. . . . Above all, we can announce to the world that whatever any other nation or ideology may do, every town and every state—and every division of the United States Government—is going to be run according to the Declaration of Independence: "With a firm reliance on the protection of Divine Providence, we mutually pledge to each other our lives, our fortunes, and our sacred honor."[56]

Lyndon Johnson believed that God produced the same benefit from the tragedy of John F. Kennedy's assassination. The month after the assassination, Johnson told the members of an Austin synagogue, "Out of the evil visited upon us just recently, blessings can come and have come, for Americans have found strength to bear their sorrows in the only place that real strength is to be found—close to God and the works that He would have us do."[57]

In 1980 Jimmy Carter claimed that prayer should include thanks to God even for hardships, for they produce spiritual growth. Whenever his wife, Rosalynn, expressed anguish over the defeat of his reelection bid that year, he would tell her, "It's hard for us to accept the fact that our priorities are not the same as God's. We attach too much importance to things like popularity, wealth, and political success. To Him, problems that often seem most important to us at the time are really not very significant. But God trusts us to make the best use of the time we have, to try to live like Jesus, and to make our lives meaningful and beneficial to others no matter where we are." Indeed, the Carters exemplified postpresidential community service, contributing their fame and even their manual labor to worthwhile charities, such as Habitat for Humanity.[58]

Ronald Reagan agreed that hardship produced spiritual growth. In 1950, three years after he had lost a baby girl in premature birth and two years after his first wife had divorced him against his will, he said, "God intends us all to grow up. . . . Sometimes it takes a tragedy to help us grow up. I don't think we can always analyze why things happen, perhaps because we don't see all the results immediately. But there will usually come a day when we can understand the purpose behind some misfortunes." On another occasion, he cited Psalms 27:1 ("If the Lord is my light, my strength, and my salvation, whom shall I fear? Of whom shall I be afraid?"), adding, "We have a promise that can make all the difference, a promise from Jesus to soothe our sorrows, heal our hearts, and drive away our fears. He promised that there will never be a dark night that does not end. Our weeping may endure for a night, but joy cometh in the morning [Psalms 30:5]." As governor of California, Reagan wrote to a California Secret Service agent who had lost a leg to cancer: "I'm sure you must have some low moments when you wonder the why of things. I don't know that I have any particular answers to questions of the kind, and yet from the vantage-point of thirty-one years farther on, I have discovered that I believe very deeply in something I was raised to believe in by my mother. I now seem to have her faith that there is a divine plan." After hosting American prisoners of war returning from Vietnam in 1973, he wrote, "These men without exception have become stronger, kinder, gentler, and more sensitive men because of their experiences. Many who had no particular faith before are today deeply religious. Man after man told us very simply [that] he lived to come home only because of faith in God." In 1979 he wrote that his mother had "convinced me that when things happen that we can't understand or that seem as terrible setbacks, we must try to believe that everything happens for a reason and for the best and if we simply deal with it and trust in God, there will come a time when we will understand why that particular thing happened, and we will discover that because of it, something better resulted."[59]

George H. W. Bush and his wife, Barbara, learned to depend on God through the death of their three-year-old daughter, Robin, of leukemia. Bush claimed, "The pain of that experience taught us how dependent on God we really are, and how important our faith is. In a moment like that, all you have is God."[60]

Bill Clinton argued that God could turn evil to good. In 1997, regarding the effort by white Christians to help rebuild African American churches that had been burned by arsonists, he declared, "I am reminded what Joseph said in Genesis [50:20] when he met up with the brothers who sold him into slavery: 'You meant evil against me, but God meant it for good.'"[61]

At a worship service three days after the September 11 attacks, George W. Bush sought to comfort the American people. He said regarding God:

> This world He created is of moral design. Grief and tragedy and hatred are only for a time. Goodness, remembrance, and love have no end. And the Lord of life holds all who die and all who mourn. It is said that adversity introduces us to ourselves. This is true of a nation as well. In this trial, we have been reminded, and the world has seen, that Americans are generous and kind, resourceful and brave. We see our national character in rescuers working past exhaustion, in long lines of blood donors, in thousands of citizens who have

asked to work and serve in any way possible. . . . As we have been assured, "Neither death nor life, nor angels nor principalities nor powers, nor things present nor things to come, nor height nor depth, can separate us from God's love [Romans 8:38–39]."

The following year, he said, "Tragedy has brought forth the courage and the generosity of our people. None of us would ever wish on anyone what happened that day. Yet, as with each life, sorrows we would not choose can bring wisdom and strength gained in no other way. This insight is central to many faiths and certainly to the faith that finds hope and comfort in a cross."[62]

In the wake of a mining accident that left twenty-nine dead in 2010, Barack Obama declared, "If any comfort can be found, it can perhaps be found by seeking the face of God [2 Chronicles 7:14], who quiets our troubled minds, a God who mends our broken hearts, a God who eases our mourning souls."[63]

The presidents' supreme confidence in the goodness and wisdom of an omnipotent, interventionist God has been crucial to their success. It has given them the fortitude to endure deaths and disasters with a sense of optimism and purpose. The assurance that their individual efforts on behalf of the nation would be blessed has given them the confidence to overcome immense hardships and, in some cases, even to succeed in endeavors that even the most objective observers considered impossible.

CHAPTER 5

Prayer

An inevitable result of the presidents' belief in a caring, intervening God of infinite power has been their confidence in the efficacy of prayer. In turn, this confidence has led them to call for both public and private prayer.

Prayer in the Bible

The Bible is filled with stories about the power of prayer and with admonitions to pray. Hannah prays, and God gives her a son, the prophet Samuel (1 Samuel 1:10–20). Elijah prays, and God sends fire to confound the false prophets (1 Kings 18:36–38). Elisha prays, and God raises a child from the dead (2 Kings 4:32–35). Hezekiah prays, and God spares Israel from Assyrian conquest (2 Kings: 19:19, 35–37). Jesus often goes off alone to secluded spots to pray (e.g., Matthew 14:23). He even teaches his apostles a model prayer (Matthew 6:9–13). The early Christians pray, and God delivers Peter from prison (Acts 12:5–10). In Philippians 4:6 Paul advises, "Do not worry about anything, but in everything by prayer and supplication with thanksgiving let your requests be made known to God." In 1 Thessalonians 5:17 he urges, "Pray without ceasing." In 1 Timothy 2:1–2 he implores, "I urge, then, first of all, that requests, prayers, intercession, and thanksgiving be made for everyone," adding that believers should pray for all political leaders, "that we may live peaceful and quiet lives in all godliness and honesty." Regarding prayer, Hebrews 4:16 exults, "Let us therefore come boldly to the throne of grace." In 1 Peter 3:12, Bible readers are told that "the eyes of the Lord are on the righteous, and His ears are open to their prayers." James 5:16–17 commands, "Pray for one another that you may be healed. The fervent prayer of a righteous man avails much."

Belief in the Efficacy of Prayer

In 1775 John Adams applauded the Second Continental Congress's decision to call for a day of fasting and prayer on the grounds that "millions will be upon their Knees at once before their great Creator, imploring his Forgiveness and Blessing, his Smiles on American Councils and Arms." Adams expected a divine response to so great an upwelling of prayer. The following year, George Washington declared, "I, in behalf of the Noble cause we are Engaged in and of myself, thank with a grateful Heart all those who supplicate the throne of grace for success to the one & preservation of the other. That being from whom nothing can be hid will, I doubt not, listen to our Prayers and protect our Cause and the supporters of it, as far as we merit His favour and Assistance." In 1783 Washington concluded his final statement to his soldiers by promising to pray to "the God of Armies" that "the choicest of heaven's favours, both here and hereafter, attend those who, under the divine auspices, have secured innumerable blessings for others."[1]

Thomas Jefferson often closed his letters with promises to pray for the recipient and his nation. In 1791 Jefferson wrote to the Marquis de Lafayette, expressing his concern for the success of the French Revolution: "God bless you, my dear friend, and prosper those endeavors about which I never wrote to you because it would interrupt them, but for the success of which, and for your own happiness, nobody prays more sincerely than Your affectionate friend & servt. Th. Jefferson." A decade later, Jefferson wrote to the directors of the new Dutch republic, "We pray God to keep you, Citizen Directors, under his Holy protection." In 1809 he replied to a group of Democratic-Republicans from New London, Connecticut, who had written to applaud his administration, which was soon to conclude: "I thank you, fellow citizens, for your kind expressions of regard for myself and prayers for my future happiness, and I join in supplications to that Almighty Being who has heretofore guarded our councils, still to continue his gracious benefactions towards our country and that yourselves may be under the protection of his divine favor." Since such an end to letters was far from obligatory, there is no reason to suspect any insincerity on Jefferson's part.[2]

The same year, after James Madison's inauguration, he received letters from a host of people ranging from Benjamin Rush to the Ursuline nuns in New Orleans, all promising to pray for him. Rather than merely thanking his correspondents, which would have sufficed, he offered his own prayers for them in return. Given the nation's crisis with Great Britain, whose navy was seizing American ships and impressing American sailors, Madison also informed the Republican Committee of New York that he was "devoutly praying" for "the divine blessing . . . of preserving to our Country the advantages of peace without relinquishing its rights or its honor."[3]

John Quincy Adams closed each year by taking stock of the blessings of Providence that he had received in the past year and praying for the continuance of such blessings. At the beginning of 1797, he wrote regarding his father, the newly elected president, and a brewing crisis with France: "A profound anxiety has taken possession of my mind. The situation of two objects the nearest to my heart, my country and my father, press continually upon my reflections. . . . For my father and my country, my supplications to Eternal wisdom and goodness comprehend the issue and result of action and pray for their welfare and prosperity no less than for the means that tend to procure them." At the end of 1807, he prayed, "I implore the Spirit from whom every good and perfect gift descends to enable me to render essential service to my country and that I may never be governed in my public conduct by any consideration other than that of my duty." Two years later, on embarking for Russia to serve as the United States' first ambassador to that nation, he wrote, "At the commencement of this enterprise, perhaps the most important of any that I have ever in the course of my life been engaged in, it becomes me to close the day by imploring the blessing of Providence upon it—that its result may prove beneficial to my country, prosperous to my family and myself, and advantageous to all who are concerned in the voyage." On the morning of his presidential inauguration in 1825, he wrote in his diary, "After two successive sleepless nights, I entered upon this day with a supplication to Heaven, first, for my country, secondly, for myself and for those connected with my name and good fortunes, that the last results of its events may be auspicious and blessed." In the evening he added, "I closed this day as it had begun, with thanksgiving to God for all his mercies and favors passed, and with prayers for the continuance of them to my country, and to myself and mine." In between these two prayers was an inaugural address that closed with a prayer. Drawing from Psalms 127:1, the new president said, "Knowing that 'except the Lord keep the city the watchman waketh but in vain,' with fervent supplications for His favor, to His overruling providence I commit with humble but fearless confidence my own fate and the future destinies of my country." Two years later, he characterized as "sensible" a sermon that presented fervor as prayer's "most essential property" and dealt severely with "those who neglected this duty by a cold and careless performance of it." Adams added, "Jesus himself has composed in the short prayer which he prescribed to his disciples all that man can need to ask of Heaven."[4]

Andrew Jackson sometimes closed letters to his beloved wife, Rachel, with a prayer. In 1796 he wrote, "May the great 'I am' bless and protect you until that happy and wished for moment arrives when I am restored to your sweet embrace, which is the Nightly prayer of your affectionate husband." This was a reference to Exodus 3:14, in which God responds to Moses's question about His name with the reply, "I am" (Yahweh in Hebrew), which denotes God's status as the only being that has always existed and is the source of all other existence. In 1823 Jackson wrote, "I have only to add my prayers for your health and composure of mind during my absence, and believe me to be your affectionate Husband. P.S. Tell the two little Andrews [Jackson's son and nephew] I pray God to bless them, and I hope they will be good boys." A month later, he wrote, "I trust that the God of Isaac and Jacob will protect you and give you health in my absence. In Him alone we ought to trust. He alone can preserve and guide us through this troublesome world, and I am sure He will hear your prayers. We are told that the prayers of the righteous availeth much [James 5:16], and I add mine for your health and preservation until we again meet."[5]

Millard Fillmore often offered prayers for his friend Dorothea Dix, whose lifelong mission was to ease the plight of the mentally ill. In 1850 he wrote:, "It must be a source of unalloyed pleasure to sit as you do now and see the misery you have averted and contemplate the happiness you have produced. That you may long enjoy it is the prayer of your friend, Millard Fillmore." In 1854 he noted, "God has blessed your good work and sustained you in all trials. My sincere prayer is that He may continue to do so."[6]

Abraham Lincoln was encouraged by the fact that many Americans were praying for him during the Civil War. In 1863 a group of Iowa Quakers wrote to him to praise the Emancipation Proclamation and to promise prayer on his behalf. Delighted by the offer, Lincoln replied, "It is most cheering and encouraging for me to know that in the efforts which I have made and am making for the restoration of a righteous peace to our country, I am upheld and sustained by the good wishes and prayers of God's people. No one is more deeply than myself aware that without His favor our highest wisdom is but as foolishness [a paraphrase of 1 Corinthians 3:19] and that our most strenuous efforts would avail nothing in the shadow of His displeasure."[7]

According to Ulysses Grant's pastor and friend John P. Newman, "at all times, in the White House at Washington or at his cottage in Long Branch, he always had family prayer." In fact, Newman related that during Grant's last night in the White House, "at the general's request we knelt in prayer." While dying of cancer in 1885, Grant replied to the letter of a Catholic priest, Edmund Didier, who promised the prayers of his church:

I feel very grateful to the Christian people of the land for their prayers on my behalf. There is no sect or religion, as shown in the Old or the New Testament, to which this does not apply. Catholics, Protestants, Jews, and all the good people of the Nation, of all politics as well as religions, and all nationalities seem to have united in wishing or praying for my improvement. I am a great sufferer all the time, but the facts I have related are compensation for much of it. All I can do is to pray that the prayers of all those good people may be answered so far as to have us all meet in another and a better world.[8]

Rutherford Hayes prayed for divine guidance when his election as president remained undecided due to voting irregularities in three states. He wrote in his diary, "If the great trust shall devolve upon me, I fervently pray that the Divine Being who holds the destinies of the nations in his hands will give me Wisdom to perform its duties so as to promote the trust and best interests of the whole country." Fourteen years later, he wrote, "The efficacy of sincere prayer is this: it does not always procure the thing prayed for, but it does better—it brings what is best for you." God often substituted what was truly best for a person from an eternal perspective for the shortsighted thing he requested.[9]

Even at the age of nineteen in 1850, James Garfield loved to attend prayer meetings. Two years later, he recorded in his diary regarding a church service: "An invitation was given and 9 responded to the call of mercy. I thank God that my earnest prayer for these young persons has been answered." Regarding his New Year's resolution for 1854, Garfield wrote, "Most important of all I must more constantly read God's divine word and hold communion with Him in secret prayer and thanksgiving." In 1861 he was deeply impressed with the prayers of Methodist soldiers from Ironton, Ohio, who were newly mustered in Columbus. The following year, in the midst of a fierce battle in Kentucky, he "prayed to God for the reinforcements to appear." They did, in the nick of time. Eleven months later, when a close friend married, he wrote to him, "I ask from our Good Heavenly Father in this opening year and this beginning of your wedded life His blessings of love and joy upon you and your dear Libbie. I know you will kneel together and pray with a timidity and longing that you have never known before that you may live in His sight and in the sight of each other with mutual acceptance and blessing."[10]

Morning prayer was as regular as breakfast in Benjamin Harrison's home. On the eve of his first great battle, near Chattanooga, in 1864, Harrison wrote to his wife, Caroline, to inform her of his fervent prayer. He prayed, "Should you lose a husband and they [our children] a father in the fight, that in His grace you may find abundant consolation and in His providence abundant temporal comfort and support." He added that, in such a case, "Let your grief be tempered by the consolation that I died for my country and in Christ."[11]

No meal in Woodrow Wilson's household ever proceeded until grace was spoken. Even after his stroke, when he was so weak that he could not stand and his voice was barely audible, Wilson steadied himself on his chair and whispered a plea for divine blessing.[12]

Warren Harding acclaimed the power of prayer. Shortly before he took office in 1921, he wrote that, while he would never present himself "as the finest exemplar of what ought to be," he rejoiced "in the inheritance of a religious belief," and continued, "I don't mind saying that I gladly go to God Almighty for guidance and strength in the responsibilities that are coming to me." In his inaugural address a few weeks later, he declared, "I accept my part with single-mindedness of purpose and humility of spirit, and implore the favor and guidance of God in His Heaven. With these I am unafraid and confidently face the future." Later that year, he concluded an Armistice Day address by reciting the Lord's Prayer.[13]

Calvin Coolidge relied heavily on prayer when he was thrust into the presidency upon Harding's death in 1923. Coolidge later recalled his actions when he learned of Harding's demise while at his father's home in Plymouth, Vermont: "I knelt down, and with the same prayer with which I have since approached the altar of the church, asked God to bless the American people and give me power to serve them."[14]

Hebert Hoover expressed a similar confidence in the power of prayer. In 1950, after China fell to communism and the Korean War began, the former president ended a speech with the words "The truth is ugly. We face it with prayer and courage."[15]

In 1940 Franklin Roosevelt claimed, "Day and night I pray for restoration of peace in this mad world of ours." In a radio address two years later, he read a prayer addressed to "God of the free" in which he asked for faith, brotherhood, courage, wisdom, security, patience, compassion, and justice. As part of a Thanksgiving Day service broadcast from the East Room of the White House later that year, a service that featured hymns selected by the president himself, including "Onward Christian Soldiers" and the "Battle Hymn of the Republic," Roosevelt declared, "It is fitting that we recall the reverent words of George Washington, 'Almighty God, we make our earnest prayer that Thou wilt keep the United States in Thy holy Protection,' and that every American in his own way lift his voice to Heaven." Roosevelt then read the twenty-third psalm.[16]

But Roosevelt's most moving prayer was the one he read in a radio address on D-Day, in 1944. With the fate of the world hanging in the balance, Roosevelt pleaded,

> Almighty God, our sons, pride of our nation, this day have set upon a mighty endeavor, a struggle to preserve our Republic, our religion, and our civilization, and to set free a suffering humanity. Lead them straight and true; give strength to their arms, stoutness to their hearts, steadfastness to their faith.
>
> They will need Thy blessings. Their road will be long and hard. The enemy is strong. He may hurl back our forces. Success may not come with rushing speed, but we shall return again and again; and we know that by Thy grace, and the righteousness of our cause, our sons will triumph.
>
> They will be sore tried, by night and by day, without rest—till the victory be won. The darkness will be rent by noise and flame. Men's souls will be shaken with the violences of war.
>
> These are men lately drawn from the ways of peace. They fight not for the lust of conquest. They fight to end conquest. They fight to liberate. They fight to let justice arise, and tolerance and good will among all Thy people. They yearn but for the end of battle, for their return to the haven of home.
>
> Some will never return. Embrace these, Father, and receive them, Thy heroic servants, into Thy kingdom. . . .
>
> And, O Lord, give us faith. Give us Faith in Thee; Faith in our sons; Faith in each other; Faith in our united crusade. . . .
>
> With Thy blessings, we shall prevail over the unholy forces of our enemy. Help us to conquer the apostles of greed and racial arrogances. Lead us to the saving of our country, and with our sister nations to a world unity that will spell a pure peace—a peace invulnerable to the schemings of unworthy men. And a peace that will let all men live in freedom, reaping the just rewards of their honest toil. Thy will be done, Almighty God.

Roosevelt sent a bound copy of the prayer to Winston Churchill.[17]

After Roosevelt's sudden death in 1945, Harry Truman ended his first address to Congress: "At this moment, I have in my heart a prayer. As I have assumed my heavy duties, I humbly pray to Almighty God, in the words of King Solomon: 'Give therefore thy servant an understanding heart to judge thy people, that I may discern between good and bad; for who is able to judge so great a people?' I ask only to be a good and faithful servant of my Lord and my people." In 1952 Truman wrote in his diary, "Any man can tell the Almighty and Most Merciful God his troubles and directly ask for guidance. He will get it." Of his favorite prayer, he claimed, "[It] has been said by me—Harry S. Truman—from high school days, as a window washer, bottle duster, floor scrubber in an Independence, Missouri drugstore, as a timekeeper on a railroad contract gang, as an employee of a newspaper, as a bank clerk, as a farmer riding a gang plow behind four horses and mules, as a fraternity official learning to say nothing at all if good could not be said of a man, as a public official judging the weaknesses and shortcomings of constituents, and as President of the United States of America." He then shared the prayer: "Almighty and Everlasting God, Creator of Heaven, Earth, and the Universe: Help me to be, to think, to act what is right because it is right; make me truthful, honest, and honorable in all things; make me intellectually honest for the sake of right and honor and without thought of reward to me. Give me the ability to be charitable, forgiving, and patient with my fellow men—help me to understand their motives and their shortcomings—even as thou understandest mine! Amen, Amen, Amen."[18]

Dwight Eisenhower also believed in prayer. In 1943 he replied to a request for a prayer to be included in a collection entitled *Soldiers' and Sailors' Prayer Book*:

> A prayer that I once heard a company commander repeating to his men on a wet, cold night, just before starting a march to the front line, struck me more forcibly than almost any other I have heard. Possibly the drama of the occasion had something to do with my reaction, but in any event, it was a better prayer than I could compose. While I cannot repeat it verbatim, I am sending it to you, in response to your letter of December 3, in words that approximate the original: "Almighty God, we are about to be committed to a task from which some of us will not return. We go willingly to this hazardous adventure because we believe that those concepts of human dignity, rights, and justice that Your Son expounded to the world, and which are respected in the government of our beloved country, are in peril of extinction from the earth. We are ready to sacrifice ourselves for our country and our God. We do not ask, individually, for our safe return. But we earnestly pray that You will help each of us to do his full duty. Permit none of us to fail a comrade in the fight. Above all, sustain us in our conviction in the justice and righteousness of our cause so that we may rise above all the terror of the enemy and come to You, if called, in the humble pride of the good soldier and in the certainty of Your infinite mercy. Amen."

After the war, Eisenhower asked a reporter, "Do you think I could have fought my way through the war, ordered thousands of fellows to their deaths, if I couldn't have got down on my knees and talked to God and begged him to support me?"[19]

Eisenhower began and ended his presidential administration with prayer. He began his first inaugural address with one prayer and ended his farewell address with another. Prayer marked the intervening years as well.

He directed that cabinet meetings begin with prayer and instituted the presidential prayer breakfast. In 1953 he declared, "My grateful thanks go out to each of you for your prayers because your prayers for divine guidance on my behalf are the greatest gift you could possibly bring to me." Ten months later, he noted regarding George Washington: "In the bitter and critical winter at Valley Forge, when the cause of liberty was so near defeat, his recourse was sincere and earnest prayer. From it he received new hope and new strength of purpose, out of which grew the freedom in which we celebrate this Christmas season. As religious faith is the foundation of free government, so prayer is an indispensable part of that faith." In 1954 Eisenhower prayed five times over the question of war and peace as various military advisors urged him to go to war with China over its aid to North Korea and North Vietnam. Each time, he decided to remain at peace.[20]

John F. Kennedy frequently wrote letters to thank people for their prayers. He was particularly touched by the prayers of children. In 1961 he wrote to the children of Mr. and Mrs. Ralph Chambers of East Point, Georgia: "Many thanks for the special Novenas you have offered in my behalf. To know that I am being remembered in prayer, and especially in the prayers of children, is indeed an inspiration to me." Two months later, he wrote, "In these days of crises and repeated threats of war it is a source of great strength and inspiration to know that people throughout the country are remembering me in their prayers." In 1963, he declared,

> All of us believe in and need prayer. Of all the thousands of letters that are received in the office of the President of the United States, letters of good will and wishes, none, I am sure, have moved any of the incumbents half so much as those that write that those of us here who work in behalf of the country are remembered in their prayers. . . . The problems we face are complex; the pressures are immense, and both the perils and the opportunities are greater than any nation ever faced. In such a time, the limits of mere human endeavor become more apparent than ever. We cannot depend solely on our material wealth, on our military might, or on our intellectual skill or physical courage to see us safely through the seas that we must sail in the months and years to come.

He quoted Psalms 127:1: "Except the Lord build the house, they labour in vain that build it."[21]

Lyndon B. Johnson relied on prayer following Kennedy's assassination. After landing at Andrews Air Force Base following the assassination, Johnson ended his first statement with the words "I ask for your help—and God's." Three months later, he declared, "No man could live in the house where I live now or work at the desk where I work without needing and without seeking the strength and the support of earnest and frequent prayer. . . . In these last 70 days, prayer has helped me to bear the burdens of this first office which are too great to be borne by anyone alone." The following month, he said, "The occupant of the world's most powerful office, like the most private citizen, has nowhere to go for help but up, up to the secret place of the most high, where faith and spiritual power are abundantly available." In 1968, in the midst of the Vietnam War, he said, "In these long nights your President prays." He added, "America never stands taller than when her people go to their knees." During Johnson's final visit as president to National City Church in Washington in 1969, Reverend George Davis read a prayer that Johnson had written. It included the lines "In season and out [2 Timothy 4:2], help us to hold to the purposes Thou has taught us, feeding the hungry, healing the sick, caring for the needy, trusting our young, training them in the way they should go [Psalms 32:8]. . . . Blind our eyes to the colors of men's skins, close our hearts against hate and violence, and fill our souls with a love of justice and compassion. . . . Guard this Republic and guide us in its service."[22]

In the late 1960s and early 1970s, Gerald Ford participated in Wednesday-morning prayer sessions with his House colleagues. While vice president and president, he spent time reading the Bible and praying with Billy Zeoli, the president of Gospel Films, who sent him weekly devotionals that he cherished. Shocked to learn of President Nixon's imminent resignation in 1974, Ford instinctively turned to prayer. In his memoirs, he recalled his response and that of his wife, Betty: "As we lay there in the darkness, our hands reached out and touched simultaneously without either of us having said a word. Then we began to pray: 'God, give us strength, give us wisdom, give us guidance as the possibility of a new life confronts us. We promise to do our very best, whatever may take place. You have sustained us in the past. We have faith in Your guiding hand in the difficult and challenging days ahead. In Jesus's name we pray.'" Ford added, "I concluded with a prayer from the fifth and sixth verses of chapter three in the Book of Proverbs: 'Trust in the Lord with all thine heart and lean not unto thine own understanding. In all thy ways acknowledge Him, and He shall direct thy paths.'" He explained, "Fifty years before, I had learned that prayer as a child in Sunday school. I can remember saying it the night I discovered that my stepfather was not my real father. I had repeated it often at sea during World War II. It was something I said whenever a crisis arose." In fact, Ford made certain that the Bible was open to these verses when he was inaugurated as president. Shortly thereafter, Ford attended a service at St. John's Episcopal

Church in Washington to "pray for guidance and understanding" in deciding whether to pardon Nixon. He ultimately decided to do so to spare the nation a prolonged trial, a decision that may have cost him reelection.[23]

Like many of his predecessors, Ford was comforted by the prayers of others. In 1975 he spoke at the National Prayer Breakfast regarding what he had learned about the power of prayer after his accession to the presidency:

> Since we last met, I have discovered another aspect of the power of prayer: I have learned how important it is to have people pray for me. It is often said that the Presidency is the loneliest job in the world. Yes, in a certain sense, I suppose it is. Yet, in all honesty, I cannot say that I have suffered from loneliness these past 6 months. The reason, I am certain, has been that everywhere I go, among old friends or among strangers, people call out from the crowd or will say quietly to me, "We're praying for you," or "You are in my prayers," and I read the same sentiments in my mail . . . Believe me, having counted the votes and knowing that you have them is a great satisfaction, but the satisfaction of knowing that uncounted numbers of good people are praying for you is infinitely more rewarding.

He recalled,

> On the day that I suddenly became President of the United States, after all the guests had gone, I walked through some of the empty rooms on the first floor of the White House and stopped by that marble mantle in the dining room to read the words carved in it—words that were a prayer of the first President who ever occupied the White House: "I pray to heaven to bestow the best of blessings on this house and all that shall hereafter inhabit it," John Adams wrote. "May none but honest and wise men ever rule under this roof." I am grateful to President Adams for leaving that message and to all who have said amen to it for nearly two centuries.

Adams's words came from a letter to his wife, Abigail, in 1800, the day after becoming the first president to inhabit the White House in the newly constructed capital of Washington; it was Franklin Roosevelt who had them engraved on the mantel in 1945.[24]

Jimmy Carter increased his prayer time as his responsibilities grew. In 1976 he said, "I spent more time on my knees the four years I was governor [of Georgia] in the seclusion of a little private room off the governor's office than I did in all the rest of my life put together because I felt so heavily on my shoulders [that] the decisions I made might very well affect many, many people." He prayed frequently during the day, "almost like breathing . . . not often in a structured way but asking God for wisdom or sound judgment."[25]

After Carter became president, he would walk every morning to the Oval Office through the Rose Garden and repeat the prayer of Psalms 19:14: "Let the words of my mouth and the meditation of my heart be acceptable in thy sight, O Lord, my strength and my redeemer." At a special early morning service held at the First Baptist Church of Washington on behalf of Anwar Sadat's historic trip to Jerusalem that same day in 1977, Carter prayed publicly for peace. In 1980 Carter claimed, "Since I've been in Washington, I've come to learn much more clearly what Paul meant when he said that we should pray without ceasing. I do pray a lot every day, as I move from one event to another, as I wait for a new foreign leader or a national leader to come in my office, as I decide issues that might affect the life of one person or a small community or, perhaps, sometimes even the entire world." In 1997 Carter wrote, "Never give up on God, who always answers our prayers. Sometimes the answer is 'Wait' or 'No,' or perhaps, as our pastor Dan Ariail says, 'You've got to be kidding!' Then we must reassess what we are seeking. Continuing to pray hopefully in the face of profound disappointment seems contrary to human nature. Why should we do it? Because we invariably learn and grow in the process." He further explained, "We often find that our prayers bring about a change, at least in ourselves, as God opens our eyes to a better future than we could have envisioned for ourselves." He added,

> Like Isaiah, we need to maintain our confidence in God's steadfastness, even in times of loneliness and apparent rejection, and constant prayer is one of the best ways to both express and nurture this confidence. Communicating our questions, hopes, and fears in prayer makes them—even to ourselves—more open and clear; and the stronger the ties that bind us to God the more likely we are to live, react, and believe in harmony with exalted standards—and with greater joy, peace, and happiness. . . . We need to accept Jesus as our partner in setting priorities. Prayer can help us do that. When making our needs and desires known to God, we are most often praying in the transmitting mode—speaking and not listening to God. Yet if we're sincere, we can't help but sense God's response and reaction to the desires we express; we shift, almost automatically, into the receiving mode. It's one of the benefits of habitual, daily prayer.[26]

As a football player at Eureka College, Ronald Reagan prayed before every kickoff. He later recalled, "I didn't pray to win—I didn't expect God to take sides—but I prayed no one would be injured, we'd all do our best and have no regrets no matter how the game came out." In 1950 he said, "There hasn't been a crisis in my life when I haven't prayed and when prayer hasn't helped me." As governor of California in 1973, he claimed that he would be "lost and helpless" without prayer, adding, "During my first months in office, when day after day there were decisions that had to be made, I had an almost irresistible urge—really a physical urge—to look over my shoulder for someone I could pass the problem on to. Then, without my quite knowing how it happened, I realized I was looking in the wrong direction. I started looking up instead and have been doing so quite a while now." Prayer gave him "a peace beyond description." He thanked a couple for informing him that their church was praying for him, writing, "I believe very much in His promise that 'where two or more are gathered in My name, there will I be [Matthew 18:20].' I think I have known and felt the power and help of those prayers."[27]

In 1980, when campaigning for president, Reagan wrote, "I could not have faced the responsibilities I did as governor, nor would I have the courage to seek the office of the presidency, if I didn't think I could call on and have the help of God." On the day of his inauguration the following year, Reagan later remembered, "I peeked into the Oval Office as its official occupant for the first time. I felt a weight come down on my shoulders, and I said a prayer asking God's help in my new job." After he was shot by John Hinckley, Reagan said, "It's a remarkable feeling to know that people are praying for you and your strength. I know firsthand. I felt those prayers when I was recovering from that bullet." He also declared, "We are blessed with the special gift of prayer, the happiness and solace to be gained by talking to the Lord. It is our hopes and our aspirations, our sorrows and fears, our deep remorse and renewed resolve, our thanks and joyful praise, and most especially our love, all turned towards a loving God." In thanking those praying for him in 1983, he mentioned his mother: "Thanks to Nelle Reagan, I believe in intercessory prayer. And I know that those prayers are giving me a strength that I would not otherwise possess."[28]

Reagan loved his ranch, Rancho del Cielo (Ranch in the Sky), because it provided him with a quiet sanctuary, filled with God's creation, where he could commune with the Creator. His daughter Patti recalled that he often spoke to her about prayer while they were on horseback: "He simply described his own spiritual relationship in such a way that I was left with the impression that God was his friend and they had unstructured dialogues." In addition to these unstructured prayers, he liked to recite the Prayer of St. Francis:

Lord, make me an instrument of your peace.
Where there is hatred, let me sow love;
Where there is injury, pardon;
Where there is doubt, faith;

Where there is despair, hope;
Where there is darkness, light;
Where there is sadness, joy.
O Divine Master, grant that I may not so much seek
To be consoled as to console;
To be understood as to understand;
To be loved as to love.
For it is in giving that we receive;
It is in pardoning that we are pardoned;
It is in dying that we are born to eternal life.

Regarding his ranch, Reagan once said, "I suppose it's the scriptural line, 'I look to the hills whence cometh my strength.' I understand it a little better when I'm up here." Reagan was paraphrasing Psalms 121:1. The next verse states, "My help comes from the Lord, who made heaven and earth." One of Reagan's favorite hymns was "What a Friend We Have in Jesus," which begins as follows:

What a friend we have in Jesus,
All our sins and griefs to bear.
What a privilege to carry
Everything to God in prayer.[29]

In 1989 George H. W. Bush began his inaugural address with a prayer. The following month, he said, "There is no greater peace than that which comes from prayer and no greater fellowship than to join in prayer with others." He added that we should remember "with all that we have to be grateful for, to pause each day to offer a prayer of thanksgiving." On a day of thanksgiving for the successful outcome of the Persian Gulf War in 1991, Bush read a prayer:

> Dear God, we humbly give you our heartfelt thanks. We thank you for bringing the war to a quick end. We thank you for sparing the lives of so many of our men and women who went to the Gulf. We ask you to bring comfort to the families of those who gave their lives for their country. We also ask you to protect those innocents who this very day are suffering in Iraq and elsewhere. We give thanks for the bravery and steadfast support of our coalition partners, and yes, we pray for our enemies, that a just peace may come to their troubled land. . . . On this special day, this grateful nation says, "Thank you, God."

Two months later, he confessed to the Southern Baptist Convention that his Episcopalian background generally left him uncomfortable with displays of emotion during prayer. But the Persian Gulf War had changed that. He continued, "But as Barbara and I prayed at Camp David before the air war began, we were thinking about those young men and women overseas. And I had the tears start down the cheeks, and our minister smiled back. And I no longer worried how it looked to others.... Like a lot of others who had positions or responsibility in sending someone else's kid to war, we realized that what mattered is how it might have seemed to God." On the fiftieth anniversary of the Japanese attack on Pearl Harbor, Bush read another prayer: "Lord, give our rising generations the wisdom to cherish their freedom and security as hard-won treasures. Lord, give them the same courage that pulsed in the blood of their fathers."[30]

Prayer helped Bush's son, future president George W. Bush, give up drinking in 1986, at the age of forty. George W. later recalled, "For months I had been praying that God would show me how to better reflect His will. My Scripture readings had clarified the nature of temptation and the reality that the love of earthly pleasures could replace the love of God.... Faith showed me a way out. I knew I could count on the grace of God to help me change." It was far from easy: "My body craved alcohol." But Bush "prayed for the strength to fight off my desires," broke his addiction, and reached the point at which "prayer was the nourishment that sustained me." Three years later, at a service to commemorate his father's first day as president-elect, George W. read a prayer he'd composed for the occasion. In 2000, during his own campaign for the presidency, he said, "I don't pray for votes, and I don't pray for the stock market to go up. I pray for strength and patience and love and understanding."[31]

Before taking the presidential oath in 2001, Bush spent a half hour alone in personal prayer in St. John's Episcopal Church. He began cabinet meetings with a prayer. He made it clear that regardless of visitors' beliefs, he wanted grace to be spoken before every meal at the White House, at Camp David, and at his ranch in Crawford, Texas. A couple of weeks after his inauguration, he declared, "I believe in the power of prayer. It's been said, 'I would rather stand against the cannons of the wicked than against the prayers of the righteous.' The prayers of a friend are one of life's most gracious gifts. My family and I are blessed by the prayers of countless Americans." Three months later, he said, "Throughout our history, in danger and division, we have always turned to prayer. And our country has been delivered from many serious evils and wrongs because of that prayer." He added that the purpose of prayer was not simply to request things: "We pray for God's help, but as we do so, we find that God has changed our deepest selves. We learn humility before His will and acceptance of things beyond our understanding.

We discover that the most sincere of all prayers can be the simple words, 'Thy will be done.' And that is a comfort more powerful than all our plans." The following year, he said, "Prayer for others is a generous act. It sweeps away bitterness and heals old wounds. Prayer leads to greater humility and a more grateful spirit. It strengthens our commitment to things that last and things that matter. It deepens our love for one another. Prayer also deepens faith, reminding us of great truths: Evil and suffering are only for a time; love and hope endure. Even in the world's most bitter conflicts, prayer reminds us of God's love and grace, His mercy and faithfulness, the hope He provides and the peace He promises." Two weeks later, he said, "I work the ropelines a lot, and people say, 'Mr. President, I pray for you and your family.' I turn to them, look them in the eye and say, 'That's the greatest gift you can give.'" In 2003 he said, "I pray daily, and I pray in all kinds of places. I mean, I pray in bed, I pray in the Oval Office. I pray a lot . . . as the Spirit moves me." At the National Prayer Breakfast in 2004, Bush spoke to the assembled politicians of both parties: "When we come together every year, we leave aside the debates of the working day. We recognize our dependence on God and pray with one voice for His blessings on our country. We're in the capital of the most powerful nation on Earth, yet we recognize the limits of earthly power." Two years later, he declared, "In prayer, we're reminded that we're never alone in our personal trials or individual suffering. In prayer, we offer our thanksgiving and praise, recognizing our lives, our talents, and all we that we own ultimately flow from the Creator. And in these moments of our deepest gratitude, the Almighty reminds us that for those to whom much has been given, much is required [Luke 12:48]." In 2008 he claimed, "I believe in the power of prayer because I have felt it in my own life. Prayer has strengthened me in times of personal challenge. It has helped me meet the challenges of the Presidency."[32]

In that same year, Bush's successor, Barack Obama, had the powerful experience of inserting a prayer into a crevice of the Western Wall in Jerusalem. The prayer read, "Lord, protect my family and me. Forgive me my sins, and help me guard against pride and despair. Give me the wisdom to do what is right and just. And make me an instrument of your will." Unfortunately, the reason he was able to repeat the precise wording of this prayer in his presidential memoirs is that a bystander dug it out of the wall and gave it to a newspaper, which promptly published it. He later recalled the time just before his inauguration, sharing, "I closed my eyes and summoned the prayer that had carried me here, one I would continue to repeat every night I was president. A prayer of thanks for all I'd been given. A prayer that my sins be forgiven. A prayer that my family and the American people be kept safe from harm. A prayer for guidance."[33]

In 2010 Obama declared, "There is, of course, a need for prayer even in times of joy and peace and prosperity. Perhaps especially in such times, prayer is needed to guard against pride and to guard against complacency. But rightly or wrongly, most of us are inclined to seek out the divine not in the moments when the Lord makes his face shine upon us [Numbers 6:25], but in moments when God's grace can seem farthest away." He continued, "While prayer can buck us up when we are down, keep us calm in the storm, [and] stiffen our spines to surmount an obstacle—and I assure you, I'm praying a lot these days—prayer can also do something else. It can touch our hearts with humility. It can fill us with a spirit of brotherhood. It can remind us that each of us are children of an awesome and loving God." That year Obama began the tradition of an Easter prayer breakfast. The following year, he expressed gratitude that "pastor friends like Joel Hunter and T. D. Jakes come over to the Oval Office every once in a while to pray with me and pray for the Nation." He concluded, "When I wake up in the morning, I wait on the Lord, and I ask Him to give me the strength to do rightly by my country and its people. And when I go to bed at night, I wait on the Lord, and I ask Him to forgive me my sins and look after my family and the American people and make me an instrument of His will."[34]

In 2012 Obama recalled the moving experience of praying with Reverend Billy Graham in Graham's North Carolina home. Obama related:

> Before I left, Reverend Graham started praying for me, as he had prayed for so many Presidents before me. And when he finished praying, I felt the urge to pray for him. I didn't really know what to say. What do you pray for when it comes to the man who has prayed for so many? But like that verse in Romans [8:26], the Holy Spirit interceded when I didn't know quite what to say. And so I prayed—briefly, but I prayed from the heart. . . . And we ended with an embrace and a warm goodbye. . . . Growing up in a household that wasn't particularly religious, going through my own period of doubt and confusion, finding Christ when I wasn't even looking for him so many years ago, possessing so many shortcomings that have been overcome by the simple grace of God. And the fact that I would ever be on the top of a mountain saying a prayer for Billy Graham, a man whose faith had changed the world and that had sustained him through triumphs and tragedies and movements and milestones, that simple fact humbled me to my core. I have fallen on my knees regularly since that moment, asking God for guidance not just in my personal life and

my Christian walk, but in the life of the Nation and in the values that hold us together and keep us strong.[35]

Calls for Prayer

Given the presidents' belief in the efficacy of prayer, it is not surprising that they have often called for both collective and individual prayer. While a call for prayer could be politically advantageous, used as a means for a leader to display his piety, there is no reason to doubt the sincerity of most of the callers, whose own private papers reveal a personal belief in the efficacy of prayer.

The Continental Congress issued numerous calls for days of prayer and fasting or thanksgiving throughout the Revolutionary War, as did the states. Governors like Samuel Adams, John Jay, and John Hancock continued the practice during the Confederation period. In his first year as president (1789), George Washington designated a national day of prayer and thanksgiving to commemorate the adoption of the US Constitution. In 1795 he called for another such day to commemorate the suppression of the Whiskey Rebellion, a frontier revolt against the whiskey tax. In 1798 his successor, John Adams, designated a day of prayer and fasting as the nation faced the prospect of war with France. As president, James Madison called for days of prayer four times during the War of 1812, just as he had called for such a day while he was a Virginia legislator in 1785, though he later decided that such proclamations violated the First Amendment. In 1849 Zachary Taylor called for a day of prayer and fasting to combat a cholera epidemic that was sweeping the nation. In the 1850s, while governor of Tennessee, Andrew Johnson called for days of prayer and thanksgiving.[36]

In 1861, the first year of the Civil War, Abraham Lincoln issued a proclamation calling for a national day of prayer and fasting. The preamble to the proclamation stated,

> Whereas it is fit and becoming in all people at all times to acknowledge and revere the Supreme Government of God; to bow in humble submission to His chastisements; to confess and deplore their sins and transgressions in the full conviction that the fear of the Lord is the beginning of wisdom [Proverbs 1:7]; and to pray, with all fervency and contrition, for the pardon of past offences, and for a blessing upon their present and prospective action: And whereas, when our own beloved Country, once, by the blessing of God, united, prosperous, and happy, is now afflicted with faction and civil war; it is peculiarly fit for us to recognize the hand of God in this terrible visitation, and in sorrowful

remembrances of our own faults and crimes as a nation and as individuals, to humble ourselves before Him, and to pray for His mercy—to pray that we may be spared further punishment, though most justly deserved; that our arms may be blessed and made effectual for the reestablishment of law, order, and peace throughout the wide extent of our country; and that the inestimable boon of civil and religious liberty, earned under His guidance and blessing by the labors of our fathers, may be restored in all its original excellence.

After the Union victory at Shiloh the following year, Lincoln called for a day of prayer and thanksgiving.[37]

In 1863 Lincoln called for another day of prayer and fasting. He declared in the preamble to the proclamation, "Insomuch as we know that, by His divine law, nations like individuals are subjected to punishments and chastisements in this world, may we not justly fear that the awful calamity of civil war which now desolates the land may be but a punishment inflicted upon us for our presumptuous sins to the needful end of our national reformation as a whole People?" The proper response to national calamity was national prayer. In the same year, Lincoln called for a national day of prayer and thanksgiving for the Union victories at Gettysburg and Vicksburg and for a second one for the general blessings of bountiful harvests, peace with other nations, and population increases despite the war. Lincoln declared, "No human counsel hath devised nor hath any mortal hand worked out these great things. They are the generous gifts of the Most High God, who, while dealing with us in anger for our sins, hath nevertheless remembered mercy." The following year, Lincoln called for both another day of prayer and fasting and, later, following the capture of Atlanta, another day of prayer and thanksgiving. Indeed, it was Lincoln, who, in 1864, established the last Thursday in November as an annual holiday focusing on prayer and thanksgiving. In his final speech the following year, he promised that a call for a national day of prayer and thanksgiving was being prepared to celebrate the Confederate surrender at Appomattox.[38]

Ten days after Lincoln's death, Andrew Johnson appointed a national day of prayer and mourning. The proclamation began, "Whereas our country has become one great house of mourning, where the head of the family has been taken away," a day of prayer should be appointed "in order to mitigate that grief on earth which can only be assuaged by communion with the Father in Heaven."[39]

In 1876 Ulysses Grant called for a day of prayer and thanksgiving to mark the nation's centennial. He noted, "The founders of the Government at its birth and in its feebleness invoked the blessings and the protection of a

Divine Providence, and the thirteen colonies and three millions of people have expanded into a nation of strength and numbers commanding the position which then was asserted and for which fervent prayers were then offered." He continued, "It seems fitting that on the occurrence of the hundredth anniversary of our existence as a Nation a grateful acknowledgement should be made to Almighty God for the protection and the bounties which He has vouchsafed to our beloved country." Therefore, Grant called on the American people to mark Independence Day with "some public religious and devout thanksgiving to Almighty God for the blessings which have been bestowed upon us as a Nation during the century of our existence, and humbly to invoke a continuance of His favor and of His protection."[40]

In 1881 Chester Arthur called for a day of prayer and fasting to commemorate the assassination of his predecessor, James Garfield. Grover Cleveland also issued thanksgiving proclamations while governor of New York.[41]

Upon the eruption of World War I in 1914, Woodrow Wilson called for a national day of prayer for peace. Four years later, with the nation then at war, he called for a national day of prayer and fasting. Six months later, he called for a day of prayer and thanksgiving to celebrate the armistice. Conversely, in 1923, Calvin Coolidge called for a day of prayer and mourning after the death of his predecessor, Warren Harding.[42]

Franklin Roosevelt considered this centuries-old tradition of crisis response insufficient to the existential crisis of World War II. In 1944 he noted that many people had urged him to follow tradition by calling for a national day of prayer, but he had decided that such a proclamation would send the wrong message. Rather than assigning a specific day for prayer, Roosevelt deemed it absolutely essential that the American people pray every day. He explained, "Because the road is long and the desire great, I ask that our people devote themselves in continuance in prayer." He then instructed, "As we rise to each new day, and again when each day is spent, let words of prayer be on our lips," invoking God's help.[43]

Harry Truman called for prayer as well. In 1945, in a Passover service near the end of World War II, he declared, "All people should reverently pray for a lasting peace for the ultimate benefit of all humanity." The following month, in a speech in Providence, Rhode Island, he declared, "Here in this historic city, named in eternal gratitude for Divine guidance during the difficult days of the past, may we all join in asking Divine Providence again to guide us to that safe harbor, lasting peace on earth." Truman called for two different national days of prayer and thanksgiving to celebrate the victories in Europe and the Pacific, crediting God with the victory in both campaigns. In 1950, after the Korean War erupted, he declared, "All of us—at home, at war, wherever we may be—are within reach of God's love and power. We all can pray. We all should pray. We should ask the fulfillment of God's will. We should ask for courage, wisdom, for the quietness of soul which comes alone to them who place their lives in His hands. We should pray for peace, which is the fruit of righteousness." In that same year, he declared, "Again I ask all my countrymen to appeal to the most High, that the God of our fathers, who has blessed this land beyond all others, will in his infinite mercy grant to all nations that peace which the world cannot give. I entreat them in church, chapel, and synagogue, in their homes and in the busy walks of life, every day and everywhere to pray for peace."[44]

As the Supreme Commander of the Allied Expeditionary Forces during World War II, Dwight Eisenhower closed his order to Allied soldiers, sailors, and airmen on D-Day with this statement: "Let us all beseech the blessing of Almighty God upon this great and noble undertaking." In 1953, Eisenhower's first year as president, he issued a proclamation declaring July 4 a national day of prayer and penance. Two years later, he urged, "The path we travel is narrow and long, beset with many dangers. Every day we must ask that Almighty God will set and keep His protecting hand over us so that we may pass on to those who come after us the heritage of a free people, secure in their God-given rights and in full control of a Government dedicated to the preservation of those rights."[45]

John F. Kennedy responded to the Supreme Court's prohibition of the recitation of formal prayers in public schools in 1963 by reminding Americans of the importance of prayer in the home. Regardless of whether one agreed with the court's decision, Kennedy claimed, it was "a reminder to every American family that we can pray a good deal more at home, we can attend our churches with a good deal more fidelity, and we can make the true meaning of prayer much more important in the lives of all our children."[46]

The day after Kennedy's assassination in 1963, his successor, Lyndon Johnson, proclaimed the day of Kennedy's funeral a national day of prayer and mourning. Five days later, Johnson addressed the nation: "Tonight, on this Thanksgiving, I come before you to ask your help, to ask your strength, to ask your prayers that God may guard this Republic and guide my every labor. . . . I ask that you remember your country and remember me each day in your prayers." Seven years later, Richard Nixon called for a day of prayer for the safe return of the Apollo 13 astronauts.[47]

Having unexpectedly become president following Nixon's resignation, Gerald Ford requested prayer. The only president in American history who was elected neither as president nor as vice president, Ford declared, "I am acutely aware that you have not elected me your President by your ballots, and so I ask you to confirm me as your President with your prayers. And I hope that such prayers will be the first of many."[48]

In 1977 and again in 1978, Jimmy Carter designated Memorial Day as a day of prayer for peace. At his instigation in the latter year, Menachem Begin and Anwar Sadat joined Carter in calling "for the world to join us in prayer for the success of our efforts at Camp David." The ensuing Camp David Accords represented the first major step toward peace in the Middle East, as Egypt became the first Arab nation to recognize Israel's right to exist. Indeed, in 1979, in a new call for prayer, the three leaders referred to the earlier call, saying, "Our trust in God was well placed." Eight months later, Carter urged Americans to pray for the safe return of American embassy workers held hostage in Iran. Fourteen months later, Ronald Reagan designated a national day of prayer and thanksgiving to celebrate the Iranian government's release of the hostages on the day of his inauguration.[49]

George H. W. Bush designated a national day of prayer prior to the beginning of Operation Desert Storm. Bush added, "God is our rock and our salvation [Psalms 95:1], and we must trust Him and keep faith in Him. And so, we ask His blessings upon us and upon every member not just of our Armed Forces but of our coalition armed forces." After the war was completed swiftly and with relatively few coalition casualties, Bush designated a day of prayer and thanksgiving.[50]

On the evening of the September 11 attacks, George W. Bush asked Americans to pray. He declared, "Tonight I ask for your prayers for all those who grieve, for the children whose worlds have been shattered, for all those whose sense of safety and security has been threatened. And I pray they will be comforted by a power greater than any of us, spoken through the ages in Psalm 23 [verse 4]: 'Even though I walk through the valley of the shadow of death, I will fear no evil, for You are with me.'"[51]

In addition to their public calls for prayer, presidents have often urged their loved ones, family members, and others in their lives to pray. In 1847, while serving in the Mexican War, Ulysses Grant wrote to his fiancée, Julia: "Pray that the time may not be far distant when we may take our walks again up and down the banks of the Gravois." In 1851 James Buchanan urged his niece and ward Harriet, "Be constant in your devotions to your God. He is a friend who will never desert you. . . . Ask wisdom & direction from above." Two years later, he advised her regarding the choice of a husband: "Ask the guidance of Heaven." In 1943 Dwight Eisenhower implored his wife, Mamie, to pray that he would do his duty well: "When you remember me in your prayers, that's the special thing I want—always to do my duty to the extreme limit of my ability." Two years later, after becoming president due to Franklin Roosevelt's unexpected death amidst a global war, Harry Truman told reporters, "Boys, if you ever pray, pray for me now. I don't know whether you fellows ever had a load of hay fall on you, but when they told me yesterday what had happened, I felt like the moon, the stars, and all the planets had fallen on me. I've got the most terribly responsible job a man ever had." The last item in George H. W. Bush's advice to young people in 2003 was "Say your prayers!"[52]

The presidents' continual calls for public and private prayer have reflected their fervent belief in the efficacy of prayer. This conviction, in turn, has resulted from a belief in the biblical concept of a loving, caring God who intervenes on behalf of his people.

CHAPTER 6

God-Given Rights and Equality

While most presidents have believed that God is fully prepared to intervene in human affairs, they have also been convinced that he, as the author and enforcer of natural rights, is most eager to grant liberty equally to all people and to defend it. Both the belief in the existence of such rights and the belief that they are shared equally by all people is rooted in the narrative of the Book of Genesis, which states that God created humans in his own image, bestowing each individual with high value and dignity, and asserts that all human beings derive from the same parents. Presidents' belief in God-given rights and equality has been crucial, furnishing them the courage to struggle against both domestic and global opponents of these concepts. Their victories in the Civil War, in World War II, and in civil rights contests would not have been possible otherwise.

Belief in God-Given Rights

Thomas Jefferson's famous summary of patriot sentiment at the time of the American Revolution, "We hold these truths to be self-evident, that all men are created equal, that they are endowed by their Creator with certain inalienable Rights, that among these are Life, Liberty, and the pursuit of Happiness," was a product of the intermingling of biblical, classical, and Whig traditions. While the doctrine of natural rights was a modern Whig formulation of the classical theory of natural law, the concept of individual rights (coupled with duties) received valuable support from the biblical doctrine of individual accountability before God, and the theory of natural law received equally crucial support from the biblical concept of a universal moral order. Even more importantly, the biblical concept of an omniscient and omnipotent God who was both willing and able to endow and enforce rights was essential to the viability of this theory.[1]

Based on some intimations from the Pythagoreans, in the fourth century BC, philosophers Plato (*Meno*, 77c–78b; *Phaedo*, 63c–68b) and Aristotle (*Rhetoric*, 1.1375a.25–b.1–8) advanced the theory of natural law, the belief in a universal code of ethics inherent in nature and comprehensible to humans either through a form of intuition (knowledge arising from the preexistence of the soul in Plato's formulation) or through reason acting on experience (Aristotle's version). Epicurus (Diogenes Laertius, *Lives of the Eminent Philosophers*, 10.122–135) supported Aristotle's position on this issue. Both Cicero and the Stoics assumed a middle ground, believing that while an understanding of natural law was embedded in human nature through a sort of intuition, humans could access it only with the help of moral training (reason acting on sensory information).[2]

Although the writers of the Old Testament, the apostle Paul, and other early Christians embraced the concept of a universal moral order wholeheartedly, their belief in original sin left them far more pessimistic than the classical philosophers about humans' ability to understand this order fully, either through reason or intuition ("conscience" in Judeo-Christian terminology). Paul and Augustine maintained that while both reason and conscience still acted as guides to ethics, both had been so badly damaged by the fall of Adam as to become insufficient for the task. Humans were unable to lead ethical lives without the Bible to teach them true morality and without the infusion of God's grace via the Holy Spirit to help them adhere to it. Furthermore, the classical association of the universal moral order with nature rather than with the perfect and unchanging Creator was problematic for both Jews and Christians, for they believed that nature, due to the fall of Adam, had been corrupted from its original, perfect form into a scene of chaos and violence.[3]

Nevertheless, the theory of natural law persisted through both the Middle Ages and the Protestant Reformation, though it continued to be subordinated to the revealed law. While the Protestant reformers restricted the category of revealed law to scripture alone, opposing the inclusion of church teachings by Thomas Aquinas and other Catholic theologians, they agreed with these theologians that original sin rendered revealed law superior to natural law as a guide to ethics. Martin Luther concluded that while revelation did not contradict reason, it certainly transcended it. Without the aid of revelation, sinful humans could not formulate correct moral tenets, and without the aid of the Holy Spirit, they could not follow them. John Calvin agreed. He considered the Bible essential since reason alone would not necessarily have been able to deduce all of the Ten Commandments from nature. Furthermore, Calvin claimed that Plato had been naïve in assuming that to know the good was to do the good—that virtue required only wisdom. That simplistic formulation overlooked the importance of willpower, which only the Holy Spirit could supply.[4]

In the seventeenth century, British Whigs contributed a revolutionary emphasis on the natural rights of individuals, a deduction from natural law rarely pursued by the ancients. John Locke, the most influential of the Whigs, argued that men did not surrender their natural rights to the government when forming the social contract; rather, they only relinquished their prerogative of enforcing natural law. If a government threatened natural rights, its citizens were morally obligated to uphold natural law by opposing the government that violated it. Since such citizens resisted tyranny on behalf of law, they were in no sense rebels.[5]

Like other Christians before them, the founders added to the classical concept of a universal moral order, which is comprehensible to humans through reason and intuition, the biblical concept of an omniscient and omnipotent God who is not only the author but also the judge and enforcer of this moral code. The inclusion of an omniscient and omnipotent judge and enforcer was essential to the success of the theory of natural rights. Without such a being, the theory was largely meaningless, as there would be no penalty for even the most outrageous violations of these rights.

During the American Revolution, John Adams and Thomas Jefferson were among the many founders who emphasized the role of the Creator in granting and defending natural rights. In his "Dissertation on the Canon and the Feudal Law" (1765), Adams contended, "Liberty must at all hazards be supported. We have a right to it, derived from our Maker. . . . Consenting to slavery is a sacrilegious breach of trust, as offensive in the sight of God as it is derogatory to our own honor or interest or happiness." In his "Declaration of the Causes and Necessity of Taking Up Arms," approved by the Continental Congress in 1775, Jefferson wrote, "We do then most solemnly before God and the world declare that, regardless of every consequence, at the risk of every distress, the arms we have been compelled to assume we will use with perseverance, exerting to the utmost energies all those powers which our creator hath given us to preserve that liberty which he committed to us in sacred deposit."[6]

The belief in God-given rights continued long after the American Revolution. In 1795 Jefferson wrote regarding the success of Dutch republicans, with the help of the French, in driving out the stadtholder William IV and establishing a more democratic system in the Netherlands: "It proves there is a god in heaven, and he will not slumber without end on the iniquities of [such] tyrants, or would-be tyrants, as their Stadtholder. This ball of liberty, I believe most piously, is now so well in motion that it will roll around the globe. At least the enlightened part of it, for light and liberty go together. It is our glory that we first put it into motion."[7]

Andrew Jackson was one of many Americans who considered the British seizure of American ships and impressment of American sailors to be grievous enough violations of natural rights to justify the War of 1812. Shortly before the beginning of the war, a conflict that would make Jackson a national hero, he contended that if war came, it would be the case of "a free people compelled to reclaim by the power of their arms the rights which God has bestowed upon them and which an infatuated King has said they shall not enjoy."[8]

Some presidents considered slavery a gross violation of rights that are made sacred by the Creator. In 1820 John Quincy Adams called the Northwest Ordinance of 1787, which prohibited slavery in the Northwest Territory, "a compact laying the foundation of security to the most *sacred* rights of human nature against the most odious of oppressions [emphasis added]." While campaigning for president in 1860, Abraham Lincoln emphasized God's interest in freedom, declaring regarding slavery, "We think that a respect for ourselves, a regard for future generations and for the God that made us require that we put down this wrong where our votes will properly reach it."[9]

In 1840, in the days before the secret ballot, James Buchanan decried factory owners' efforts to force their workers to vote as they wished on pain of losing their jobs as a flagrant violation of the God-given right to an independent vote, which Buchanan likened to the right of conscience in religious matters: "The right of suffrage is the most sacred political right which the citizens of a free Government can enjoy. Like the right of conscience, it ought ever to be regarded as a question between the individual man and his Maker, with which no human power ought to interfere unless convincing the reason."[10]

Woodrow Wilson believed that God supported the efforts of those who sought to free others. In 1911 he declared, "Liberty is a spiritual conception, and when men take up arms to set other men free, there is something sacred and holy in the warfare."[11]

In 1921 Warren Harding lectured foreign delegates at the Washington Conference on the Limitation of Armaments concerning the divine origin of natural rights. He asserted, "Inherent rights are of God, and the tragedies of the world originate in their attempted denial."[12]

In 1934 former President Herbert Hoover wrote regarding the "great philosophy" of classical liberalism:

> The high tenet of the philosophy is that Liberty is an endowment from the Creator of every individual man and woman upon which no power, whether economic or political, can encroach, and that not even the government may deny. And herein it challenges all other philosophies of society and government; for all others, both and before and since, insist that the individual has no such unalienable rights, that he is but the servant of the state. Liberalism holds that man is the master of the state, not the servant; that the sole purpose of government is to nurture and assure these liberties.

Six years later, at the Republican National Convention, Hoover contrasted the traditional view of natural rights, rooted in the Bible, with Nazism, communism, and the New Deal. He asked, "Was man created a little lower than the angels [Psalms 8:5], a being for which the abundance of life consists of justice, liberty, and opportunity? Does he possess the right from the Creator to plan his own life, to dare his own adventure, to earn his own reward, so long as he does no harm to his fellows? Or must he submerge his life, his liberties, and his independent personality in an omnipotent government?" Hoover added, "If man is merely one of the herd, running with the pack, Stalin is right, Hitler is right, and, God help us for our follies and our greed, the New Deal is right. But if man is an inviolable human soul, possessed of dignity, endowed with unalienable rights, America is right. And this is a war that Americans dare not lose." In 1948, at the height of the Cold War, Hoover again contrasted Americans' biblical understanding of natural rights with the atheistic philosophy of communism: "At the time our ancestors were proclaiming that the Creator had endowed all mankind with rights of freedom as the children of God, with a free will, there was being proclaimed by Hegel, and later by Karl Marx, a satanic philosophy of agnosticism . . . [that said] the rights of men came from the State. The greatness of America today comes from one philosophy, the despair of Europe from the other."[13]

In his annual message to Congress in 1941, Franklin Roosevelt famously broadened the definition of rights. Among "the four freedoms" he hoped the whole world would adopt, two (the freedom of speech and the freedom of worship) were contained in the Bill of Rights, but two others ("the freedom from want" and "the freedom from fear") were novel. Roosevelt considered the Nazis the greatest violators of all rights. In his first wartime State of the Union address the following year, he declared, "Our enemies are guided by brutal cynicism, by unholy contempt of the human race. We are inspired by a faith that goes back through all the years to the first chapter of the Book of Genesis [1:27]: 'God created man in His own image.' We on our side are striving to be true to that divine heritage. . . . Those on the other side are striving to destroy this deep belief and to create a world in their own image—a world of tyranny and cruelty and serfdom."[14]

Harry Truman appreciated the American tradition of espousing and promoting God-given rights. In 1943 he wrote, "Man's inalienable rights, says the Declaration of Independence, are 'endowed by God.' That was the faith of Lincoln, who preserved the union. . . . We have often departed from that faith. We have never adequately lived up to it. But we have no other." Three years later, he declared regarding dictatorships: "These forces of evil have long realized that both religion and democracy are founded on one basic principle, the worth and dignity of the individual man and woman. Dictatorship, on the other hand, has always rejected that principle. Dictatorship, by whatever name, is founded on the doctrine that the individual amounts to nothing; that the State is the only thing that counts; and that men and women and children were put on earth solely for the purpose of serving the State." In 1948, in his State of the Union Address, Truman declared, "The basic source of our strength is spiritual. For we are a people with a faith. We believe in the dignity of man. We believe that he was created in the image of the Father of us all. We do not believe that men exist merely to strengthen the state or to be cogs in the economic machine. We do believe that governments are created to serve the people and that economic systems exist to minister to their wants. We have a profound devotion to the welfare and rights of the individual as a human being."[15]

In 1950, at a conference of state attorneys general, Truman told the attendees, "The fundamental basis of our Bill of Rights comes from the teachings which we get from Exodus and St. Matthew, from Isaiah and St. Paul. I don't think we emphasize that enough these days." Nine months later, when dedicating a Liberty Bell replica in his hometown of Independence, Missouri, Truman declared, "Written around the crown of this bell are the words, 'Proclaim liberty throughout the land and to all the inhabitants thereof [Leviticus 25:10].' Those words are 2,500 years old. I learned the first line over there in that Presbyterian Church. They come from the Bible. They reflect a deep belief in freedom under God and justice among men—a belief which is at the very heart of what the Bible teaches us. Our concept of freedom has deep religious roots." The following year, he emphasized that true freedom was based in morality: "Freedom for the human soul is, indeed, the most important principle of our civilization. We must always remember, however, that the freedom we are talking about is freedom based on moral principles. Without a firm moral foundation, freedom degenerates into selfishness and license. Unless men exercise their freedom in a just and honest way, within moral restraints, a free society can degenerate into anarchy. Then there will be freedom only for the rapacious and those who are stronger and more unscrupulous than the rank and file of the people." Two months later, he claimed, "We believe that there is something sacred about every human soul that God has put on this earth. We believe in the rights of the individual. We acknowledge his supremacy. This is the great mark of distinction between our democracy and totalitarian dictatorships. In the totalitarian countries little value is placed on human life. People are herded into slave labor camps by the millions and are allowed to die like flies from starvation, disease, or hardship."[16]

Dwight Eisenhower referred to God-given rights in his inaugural address in 1953. After noting the American belief "in the deathless dignity of man, governed by eternal moral and natural laws," he added, "This faith defines our full view of life. It establishes beyond debate those gifts of the Creator that are man's inalienable rights and that will make all men equal in His sight." The following month, he declared regarding "the right to worship as we please, to speak and to think, and to earn and to save": "One reason that we cherish these rights so sincerely is because they are God-given. They belong to the people, who have been created in His image." In 1954 he asserted in a radio and television address: "Our nation had a spiritual foundation, so announced by the men who wrote the Declaration of Independence. You remember what they said? 'We hold that all men are endowed by their Creator with certain rights.' That is very definitely a spiritual conception. It is the explanation of our form of government that our Founding Fathers decided upon." In his State of the Union Address in 1955, Eisenhower claimed regarding the Cold War, "It is not a struggle merely of economic theories, or of forms of government, or of military power. At issue is the true nature of man. Either man is the creature whom the Psalmist described as 'a little lower than the angels,' crowned with glory and honor, holding 'dominion over the works' of his Creator [Psalms 8:5–6]; or man is a soulless, animated machine to be enslaved, used, and consumed by the state for its own glorification."[17]

John F. Kennedy also referred to God-given rights in his inaugural address. Kennedy declared, "I have sworn before you and Almighty God the same solemn oath our forebears prescribed nearly a century and three quarters ago. The world is very different now. For man holds in his mortal hands the power to abolish all forms of human poverty and all forms of human life. And yet the same revolutionary beliefs for which our forebears fought are still at issue around the globe—the belief that the rights of man come not from the generosity of the state but from the hand of God." Ten months later, Kennedy noted regarding the speech: "I said that the basic issue was that the rights the citizen enjoyed did not come from the state but rather came from the hand of God. . . . It is written in the Old and New Testaments." The following year, Kennedy contended, "I do not suggest that religion is an instrument of the cold war. Rather, it is the basis of the issue which separates us from those who make themselves our adversary. And at the heart of the matter, of course, is the position of the individual—his importance, his *sanctity*, his relationship to his fellow men, his relationship to his country and his state [emphasis added]."[18]

At a bicentennial celebration in 1976, Gerald Ford declared, "From the moment we have a life of our own, we have a liberty of our own, and we receive both in equal shares. We are all born free in the eyes of God." The following month, he said, "The supreme value of every person to whom life is given by God is a belief that comes to us from the Holy Scriptures, confirmed by all the great leaders of the church." Two months later, he connected the nation's belief in God-given rights to its freedom from genocide: "When I think of the terrible atrocities of World War II, and when I recall the grim and moving day when I visited Auschwitz, when I think of the 6 million Jewish martyrs and others so brutally murdered, I reflect on how fortunate we are to be citizens of a country which exalts trust in God and God-given rights of every person to life, liberty, and the pursuit of happiness."[19]

Although Jimmy Carter employed the term "human rights" rather than the more traditional "natural rights," he based the concept on the same biblical principles that had undergirded it for centuries. In 1977 he claimed,

> In large measure the beginnings of the modern concept of human rights go back to the laws and the prophets of the Judeo-Christian tradition. I've been steeped in the Bible since early childhood, and I believe that anyone who reads the ancient words of the Old Testament with both sensitivity and care will find there the idea of government as something based on a voluntary covenant rather than force—the idea of equality before the law and the supremacy of the law over the whims of any ruler; the idea of the dignity of the individual human being and also of the individual conscience.

Carter possessed an expansive view of rights that included "the right of someone to have a place to work and a place to live and an education and an absence of disease and an alleviation of hunger." As a former president and the head of the Carter Center, which promoted human rights, he often wrote letters to foreign leaders, urging them to correct abuses of rights.[20]

Ronald Reagan also connected freedom to spirituality. In 1982 he declared, "Liberty has never meant license to Americans. We treasure it precisely because it protects the human and spiritual values that we hold most dear: the right to worship as we choose, the right to elect democratic leaders, the right to choose the type of education we want for our children, and freedom from fear, want, and oppression. These are God-given freedoms, not the contrivances of man." It is significant that the former Democrat included Franklin Roosevelt's innovations, "freedom from fear" and "freedom from want," in his list of natural rights. Three years later, Reagan quoted Jesus in Matthew 22:21: "Render, therefore, unto Caesar the things which are Caesar's, and unto God the things that are God's." He then claimed that this idea provided the basis for rights: "What this injunction teaches us is that the individual cannot be entirely subordinate to the state, that there exists a whole other realm, an almost mysterious realm of individual thought and action which is sacred and which is totally beyond and outside of state control. This idea has been central to the development of human rights."[21]

In the wake of the *Roe v. Wade* decision (1973), Reagan contended that abortion was the latest and greatest violation of natural rights. Although he had signed a law as governor of California permitting abortions when they were necessary to protect the life or the health of the mother, he came to regret the health exemption, as he believed that psychiatrists were exploiting this loophole cynically. In 1979 he claimed, "Interrupting a pregnancy means the taking of a human life. In our Judeo-Christian tradition, that can only be done in self-defense. Therefore, I will agree to an abortion only to protect the life of the prospective mother." He added that he supported the Hyde Amendment, a federal law that limited the use of Medicaid funds for abortion. In 1984 he declared,

> God's most blessed gift is the gift of life. He sent us the Prince of Peace as a babe in a manger.... This nation fought a terrible war so that black Americans would be guaranteed their God-given rights. Abraham Lincoln recognized that we could not survive as a free land when some could decide whether others should be free or slaves. Well, today another question begs to be asked: How can we survive as a free nation when some decide that others are not fit to live and should be done away with? I believe no challenge is more important to the character of America than restoring the right to life to all human beings. Without that right, no other rights have meaning. "Suffer the little children

to come to me, and forbid them not, for such is the kingdom of God [Matthew 19:14]."

In 1986 he contended that the fight against abortion was based on "our belief in a just and loving God, a God who created humankind in his image." The following year, he said, "There is no love like a mother's—she who carries the child that God knits in the womb." This was a reference to Psalms 139:13: "You have knitted me together in my mother's womb."²²

Reagan did not believe that the right to life extended to convicted murderers. As governor of California, he wrote, "I believe we must retain capital punishment, and I believe there is backing for this in Scripture." Reagan was perhaps referring to Genesis 9:6, in which God says, "Whoever sheds a man's blood, by man shall his own blood be shed, for in His own image God made mankind." Reagan believed that capital punishment prevented more loss of life than it caused, noting that even murderers ostensibly serving life sentences were often released to kill again. He wrote, "On my desk is a list of 12 murderers who were sentenced to prison and subsequently, having served their sentences, were released. They went on to murder 22 victims." He concluded, "If our system of justice, including all the courts of appeal, decree a man must die for a crime, I can only reverse that decision if evidence is presented later which indicates he is entitled to clemency. Believe me, no part of a governor's job is approached more prayerfully than this one."²³

Like his predecessors, Reagan viewed the Cold War through the prism of natural rights. He famously referred to the Soviet Union as "the evil empire," a designation he based on its systematic violation of God-given rights. In 1984 he claimed regarding the Soviets: "When men try to live in a world without God, it's only too easy for them to forget the rights that God bestows—too easy to suppress freedom of speech, to build walls to keep their countrymen in, to jail dissidents, and to put great thinkers in mental wards." In 1988 he complained, "For years, especially in the seventies, the cognoscenti spoke of the so-called superpower conflict in value-neutral terms, as if there was no essential difference between Western democracies and Soviet communism. Any suggestion that a system that denies its people God-given liberties was fundamentally evil was met with ridicule. Well, I challenge those people to go to Berlin and look upon that wall, look upon the works of tyranny." The following year, the wall fell.²⁴

In 1990 George H. W. Bush promised, "I will endorse policies that reflect the rights of the individual, a concept as old as the scriptures." Celebrating the victory of the West in the Cold War, he added, "The last year has been a victory for the freedoms with which God has blessed the United States of

America. We've seen [that] the rights of men move mountains or, as in East Berlin, even move a wall." Bush's allusion to the ability of rights to "move mountains" was based on Paul's reference to "faith that can move mountains" in 1 Corinthians 13:2.[25]

Bush's son, George W., promoted a "freedom agenda" as part of the Bush Doctrine, declaring, "Freedom is a universal gift from Almighty God." Nine days after the September 11 attacks, he claimed regarding the War on Terror: "The course of this conflict is not known, yet its outcome is certain. Freedom and fear, justice and cruelty have always been at war, and we know that God is not neutral between them." He often referred to terrorists as "evildoers" not only because they murdered innocent people but because the sharia law they championed trampled on the God-given rights of individuals, especially women. Regarding "universal, God-given values" of freedom, he declared, "We believe in the demands of human dignity that apply in every culture, in every nation. Human beings should have the right to free speech. Women deserve respect and opportunity. All people deserve equal justice, religious tolerance. This is true in America. This is true in Afghanistan. These rights are true everywhere." With her husband's full support, Laura, Bush's wife, made Afghan women's rights one of her chief concerns. Bush labeled North Korea, Iran, and Iraq "the axis of evil" because they trampled on God-given rights, though the axis part of the phrase made little sense, given that the leaders of Iran and Iraq loathed one another. In 2005 Bush declared, "In Iraq the terrorists used bombings and beheadings and torture to try to prevent people from exercising their God-given right [to vote], but they couldn't stop the march of freedom. Millions went to the polls in defiance of the terrorists."[26]

Like Reagan, Bush was an ardent foe of abortion. In 2001 he argued that the nation's goal should be "to build a culture of life, affirming that every person, at every stage and season of life, is created equal in God's image." For this reason, he reinstated Reagan's Mexico City policy, which included a ban on federal funding for groups that performed or actively promoted abortion in other nations. Seven months later, Bush's pro-life sympathies led him to oppose federal funding for research on any new stem cell lines derived from embryos while approving funding for research on the sixty existing cell lines and on adult stem cells. He said, "I believe human life is a sacred gift from our Creator. I worry about a culture that devalues life and believe as your President I have an important obligation to foster and encourage respect for life in America and throughout the world." Regarding his administration's pro-life policies, Bush later recalled, "My faith and conscience led me to conclude that human life is sacred. God created man in His image, and therefore every person has value in His eyes. It seemed to me that an unborn child, while dependent on its mother, is a separate and independent being worthy of protection in its own right. When I saw Barbara and Jenna [his daughters] on the sonogram for the first time, there was no doubt in my mind they were distinct and alive. The fact that they could not speak for themselves only enhanced society's duty to defend them." He also signed bills that banned partial-birth abortions, increased funding for crisis pregnancy centers, and provided tax credits for adoption. In 2006, after noting that he had recently signed a bill supporting research using stem cells from umbilical cord blood, he reiterated his opposition to the destruction of life involved in embryonic stem cell research, saying, "Because human life is a gift from our Creator and should never be used as a means to an end, we will not sanction the creation of life only to destroy it."[27]

While recent Democratic presidents have alluded to the existence of rights to abortion and same-sex marriage, they have not referred to these as God-given rights and have rarely attempted to cite scriptures in their defense; they have only referred to them as constitutional rights. While Jimmy Carter claimed that "abortions are wrong" (without doing anything to restrict them) and Bill Clinton spoke of the need to keep them "rare" (without doing anything to make them so), Barack Obama and Joe Biden have been more forceful in declaring abortion a constitutional right. Both issued similar statements in response to the Supreme Court's overturning of *Roe v. Wade* in the *Dobbs vs. Jackson Women's Health Organization* decision (2022). While Obama contended that the decision violated the right to privacy "enshrined in the Fourteenth Amendment of the Constitution," Biden claimed that it "blatantly violates the constitutional right established under *Roe v. Wade*." Similarly, in 2011, when Obama instructed the US Department of Justice to stop defending the Defense of Marriage Act in court, he was declaring a reversal of his previous position on the law, which banned federal recognition of same-sex marriage, for he now considered it unconstitutional. The following year, he became the first president to endorse same-sex marriage shortly after his vice president, Joe Biden, announced his own support. Except for Obama's fleeting reference to the Golden Rule, neither he nor Biden made any reference to the Bible in defense of these positions. In 2013 Clinton published an op-ed in the *Washington Post* calling for the Supreme Court to overturn the Defense of Marriage Act that he himself had signed, claiming it was "incompatible with the Constitution." Dodging the question of biblical authority was more challenging for Jimmy Carter than for the other Democratic presidents, given his long-standing reputation as an evangelical Christian. In a 2015 interview with the *Huffington*

Post, Carter was asked what Jesus would have thought of same-sex marriage. Carter responded that he thought "Jesus would approve gay marriage" but conceded that this was "just my own personal belief" and that he knew of no scriptures to support this hypothesis. He made no attempt to reconcile this belief with the numerous scriptures that condemn homosexuality (Genesis 19:4–24; Leviticus 20:13; Romans 1:26–27; 1 Corinthians 6:9–10; 1 Timothy 1:9–10; Jude 7).[28]

Nevertheless, Obama's reticence in identifying certain rights as God-given did not signify a general disbelief in the existence of such rights. In an address to the British Parliament in 2011, he declared, "As two of the most powerful nations in the history of the world, we must always remember that the true source of our influence hasn't been the size of our economies or the reach of our militaries or the land that we've claimed. It has been the values that we must never waver in defending around the world, the idea that all beings are endowed by their Creator with certain rights that cannot be denied."[29]

Belief in Spiritual Equality

In addition to their belief in God-given rights, most presidents have shared a crucial belief in spiritual equality, one of the chief principles of the Bible. This principle has provided them with a basic confidence in the majority that is essential to a republican government. By assuring presidents that African Americans possessed equal rights, the belief also led some to support the abolition of slavery and to promote civil rights.

The concept of spiritual equality, the principle that all people are equal in God's eyes, whatever their intellectual and physical attributes, is suggested in the first book of the Bible, where all of humanity is traced to a common pair of ancestors. The Old Testament is filled with prophets of low birth admonishing the Jews to care for widows and orphans, the poorest and most powerless people in ancient society. Jesus comes into the world as a poor carpenter's son, born in a stable (Luke 2:7). Shepherds are the first to hear the news of his birth (Luke 2:8–11) and women, of his resurrection (Matthew 28:1–6), from angels. Jesus's brother James admonishes Christians to treat the poor the same as the rich at church gatherings (James 2:1–4). The apostle Paul declares (Galatians 3:28), "There is neither Jew nor Greek, there is neither slave nor free, there is neither male nor female, for you are all one in Christ Jesus." Peter is quoted in Acts of the Apostles 10:34–35: "God is no respecter of persons. But in every nation he that fears Him and works righteousness is acceptable to Him."

The Christian emphasis on spiritual equality increased the religion's appeal to women of the Roman Empire, who constituted a solid majority of early church members. They gladly introduced the religion to their husbands since it taught the revolutionary doctrines that husbands should love their wives "as Christ loved the Church and gave Himself for it" (Ephesians 5:25) and that adultery was as serious a sin in a husband as in a wife (Exodus 20:14; Proverbs 5:15–21; Matthew 5:27–28; 1 Corinthians 6:9–10). In sharp contrast to classical biographers, who focused almost exclusively on political and military affairs, areas of life from which women were excluded, Christian authors included numerous female saints in their hagiography.[30]

The treasuries of Christian churches were often used to finance the manumission of slaves. Several freedmen became bishops. The Church contradicted Roman law in recognizing marriages between free and slave. While Paul instructed slaves to obey their masters, he also commanded masters to treat their slaves well, "remembering that you have a Master in heaven" (Ephesians 6:5–9). Although Aelius Aristides's accusation that Christians "show their impiety as you would expect them to, by having no respect for their betters" was more than a bit exaggerated, it expressed the outrage of aristocratic pagans at the much greater degree of egalitarianism among early Christians than in pagan society. Although the biblical concept of spiritual equality did not bring an end to slavery in the United States until the nineteenth century (due to a civil war caused by the agitation of an abolitionist movement led by evangelical Christians) and it did not lead to the enfranchisement of women on a large scale until the twentieth century (due to a suffrage movement also led by Christians), it did represent a huge advancement for the powerless even in Roman times, one that was pregnant with potential for the future.[31]

Far from being a uniquely American phenomenon, slavery was an ancient and ubiquitous institution. Near Eastern Muslims began the sub-Saharan African slave trade in the seventh century, a full millennium before Europeans became involved in it, and they imported as many as fourteen million African slaves over the next thirteen centuries, a number roughly equal to those removed by the Europeans. Both Near Eastern and European slave traders were actively assisted by African tribal leaders who were eager to profit from the trade. These tribal leaders undertook nearly all of the actual capturing of slaves, generally through wars against opposing tribes. Only 6 percent of the African slaves whom Europeans carried to the New World were brought to what is now the United States. What was remarkable about eighteenth- and nineteenth-century American Christians was not that they participated in an ancient, global institution but that they began a movement that restricted and eventually abolished that institution in their nation, just as British evangelicals led by William Wilberforce ended it in British possessions in 1833. At the heart of that movement was the biblical concept of spiritual equality.[32]

The American colonists' belief in spiritual equality combined with the fact that very few European aristocrats had any reason to settle in America resulted in the colonies beginning their existence as radically egalitarian societies, at least by the standards of the age. A European-style aristocracy of birth never developed in America. Although an aristocracy of wealth did arise, as a considerable amount of property was passed from one generation to the next, wealth in the relatively free market economy of colonial America was much more fluid than birth, so the absence of formal hereditary distinctions provided far greater opportunity for the industrious and ingenious poor (e.g., Benjamin Franklin) than the European caste system. As James Monroe noted in 1801, "The principles on which our ancestors colonized here, by precluding hereditary distinctions, placed man on the elevated ground he was destined to hold by his Creator." Indeed, the founders based the American Revolution largely on the belief that their own equality with the citizens of Britain entitled them to the same right to be taxed only with their consent. The Revolution also ended American submission to the British monarch, thereby abolishing what had long been the sole element of hereditary government in America.[33]

The biblical concept of spiritual equality undergirds the United States' republican form of government, as numerous presidents have insisted. For instance, when celebrating the sesquicentennial of the Declaration of Independence in 1926, Calvin Coolidge traced American democracy to the Bible: "It does not assume that all are equal in degree but all are equal in kind. On that precept rests a foundation for democracy that cannot be shaken. It justifies faith in the people."[34]

Yet for the most of the nation's history, legal and political equality among whites contrasted starkly with inequality between the races. Early American presidents were acutely aware that the institution of slavery stood as a most glaring contradiction to their self-image as the world's leading advocates of both human equality and natural rights. The unprecedented degree of equality among whites in the United States only served to highlight the aberration.

In the founders' day, belief in spiritual equality led not only to the abolition of slavery throughout the northern United States by 1804 and of the foreign slave trade by 1808 but also to the manumission of large numbers of slaves throughout the South. In the years following the

Revolution, more slaves were freed voluntarily in the South than by law in the North. This belief also prompted some real soul-searching even among those who were unwilling to support immediate emancipation in the South. The very questioning by numerous American leaders of an institution that had been a ubiquitous and unquestioned way of life throughout most of the world for millennia is far more remarkable than their inability to abolish it in the section of the nation where it was most socially and economically entrenched. There can be little doubt that the biblical concept of spiritual equality, with which their habits of studying Scripture and hearing biblically inspired sermons made them intimately familiar, played a crucial role in their willingness to overturn centuries of contradictory practice. The end result, the abolition of slavery throughout the North, established a balance of power between free and slave states, which ultimately led to the Civil War eradicating slavery throughout the United States.[35]

Although Thomas Jefferson denigrated the intellectual capacities of African Americans in *Notes on the State of Virginia* (1782), he never doubted their spiritual equality and, thus, their natural right to freedom. Indeed, he went out of his way to affirm their moral equality, writing, "The disposition to theft with which they have been branded must be ascribed to their situation and not to any depravity of the moral sense. The man in whose favour no laws of property exist probably feels himself less bound to respect those made in favour of others." On the other hand, he noted how slavery degraded the morality of whites: "There must doubtless be an unhappy influence on the manners of our people produced by the existence of slaves among us. The whole commerce between master and slave is a perpetual exercise of the most boisterous passions, the most unrelenting despotism on the one part and degrading submission on the other. Our children see this and learn to imitate it." Jefferson went out of his way to embrace the biblical concept of a single creation, as well as the spiritual equality among all the descendants of Adam and Eve that it entailed, preferring it over the racist and unbiblical doctrine, espoused by some European intellectuals, of separate creations of different species of humanity on different continents. Jefferson called God "the common Creator of man" and "the Father of all the members of the human family."[36]

While wavering on the question of the intellectual equality of African Americans, Jefferson always insisted on the issue's irrelevance to the slavery issue. When presented with evidence of black intellectual achievement in 1809, he responded,

> Be assured that no person living wishes more sincerely than I do to see a complete refutation of the doubts I have myself entertained and expressed on the grade of understanding allotted to them by nature and to find that in this respect they are on a par with ourselves. My doubts were the result of personal observation in the limited sphere of my State, where the opportunities for the development of their genius were not favorable and those of exercising it still less so. I expressed them therefore with great hesitation; but whatever be their degree of talent, it is no measure of their rights. Because Sir Isaac Newton was superior to others in understanding, he was not therefore lord of the person or property of others.

For this reason, Jefferson successfully pushed for the exclusion of slavery in the Ohio River valley under the Northwest Ordinance of 1787 and, while president, helped influence Congress to abolish the foreign slave trade.[37]

George Washington stopped buying slaves of his own in 1786, thirteen years before his death. In his will, he not only freed those previously purchased but also bequeathed funds for those too young or old to care for themselves.[38]

In 1841 John Quincy Adams successfully defended before the Supreme Court thirty-five Africans who had commandeered a slave ship called the *Amistad*. He observed in his diary:

> The world, the flesh, and all the devils in hell are arrayed against any man who now in this North American Union shall dare to join the standard of the Almighty God to put down the African slave trade; and what can I, upon the verge of my seventy-fourth birthday, with a shaking hand, a darkening eye, a drowsy brain, and with all my faculties dropping from me one by one, as the teeth are dropping from my head—what can I do for the cause of God and man, for the progress of human emancipation, for the suppression of the African slave trade? Yet my conscience presses me on; let me but die in the breach.

Adams's clients presented him a signed Bible in gratitude for their acquittal.[39]

In an Independence Day speech two years later, Adams declared, "The extinction of slavery from the face of the earth is a problem, moral, political, religious, which this moment rocks the foundation of human society throughout the regions of civilized man. It is indeed nothing more nor less than the consummation of the Christian religion." He explained,

> It is only as immortal beings that all men can in any sense be said to be born equal; and when the Declaration of Independence affirms as a self-evident truth that all men are born equal, it is precisely the same as if the affirmation

had been that all men are born with immortal souls; for, take away from man his soul, the immortal spirit that is within him, and he would be a mere tamable beast of the field, and, like others of his kind, would become the property of his tamer. Hence it is too that, by the laws of nature and God, man can never be the property of man.[40]

Abraham Lincoln envisioned equality as an ideal that, like all other ideals, was impossible to attain fully but that it was one for which God intended His creatures to strive. In 1858 he noted, "The Savior, I suppose, did not expect that any human creature could be perfect as the Father in Heaven, but He said, 'As your Father in Heaven is perfect, be ye also perfect [Matthew 5:48].' He set that up as a standard, and he who did most towards reaching that standard attained the highest degree of moral perfection. So, I say in relation to the principle that all men are created equal, let it be as nearly reached as we can." A month later, after quoting from the Declaration of Independence, Lincoln declared concerning the founders: "This was their majestic interpretation of the economy of the Universe. This was their lofty, and wise, and noble understanding of the justice of the Creator to His creatures. Yes, gentlemen, to *all* His creatures, to the whole great family of man [emphasis in original]. In their enlightened belief, nothing stamped with the Divine image and likeness was sent into the world to be trodden on, and degraded, and imbruted by its fellows."[41]

Lincoln's favorite general and eventual successor, Ulysses Grant, was equally appalled by slavery and equally apt to ridicule the notion that it was sanctioned by God. In his postbellum memoirs, he wrote, "There were people who believed in the divinity of human slavery, as there are now people who believe Mormonism and Polygamy to be ordained by the Most High. We forgive them for entertaining such notions but forbid their practice." Against those who sought to recolonize freedmen in Africa, Grant claimed that the African American "was brought to our shores by compulsion, and he should now be considered as having as good a right to remain here as any other class of our citizens." As president, Grant suspended habeas corpus in part of South Carolina to combat the Ku Klux Klan, whose violence against African Americans and their white allies threatened to nullify the "rights, privileges, immunities, and protections named in the Constitution of the United States." Grant was the first president to appoint African Americans as duly accredited representatives of the United States to embassies and consulates abroad. This policy earned him praise from the Colored Citizens' Association of New York and Brooklyn. He signed the Civil Rights Act of 1875, which prohibited segregation in public accommodations, schools, transportation, and juries. Unfortunately, the Supreme Court declared it unconstitutional in 1883.[42]

Grant's successors, Rutherford Hayes and James Garfield, also supported civil rights for spiritual reasons. Prior to the Civil War, Hayes worked as an attorney in Cincinnati, where he defended fugitive slaves against extradition. During the Civil War, he rose to the rank of general in the Union Army and was wounded in battle. In 1880 he defined "God's country" as a place where "equal rights—a fair start and an equal chance in the race of life—are everywhere secured to all." A decade later, he wrote in his diary, "Jefferson, the father of the Democracy, Lincoln, the embodiment of Republicanism, and the Divine author of the religion on which true civilization rests all proclaim the equal rights of all men." His consistent and passionate insistence on universal education and his tireless work for the Slater Fund for Negro Education demonstrated a faith in the ability of all to learn and a belief in their right to an opportunity to do so. Meanwhile, in 1855, Garfield abandoned his previous conviction that Christians had no business playing any role in politics, even that of voter, because he became incensed by "this giant evil" of slavery and convinced that "the religion of Christ" demanded that he oppose it.[43]

In his first year as president, Theodore Roosevelt was surprised by the outcry against his invitation to African American leader Booker T. Washington to dine with him at the White House. Roosevelt wrote,

> When I asked Booker T. Washington to dinner, I did not devote very much thought to the matter one way or the other. I respect him greatly and believe in the work he has done. I have consulted so much with him it seemed to me that it was natural to ask him to dinner to talk over this work. . . . As things have turned out, I am very glad that I asked him, for the clamor aroused by the act makes me feel as if the act was necessary. . . . The only wise and honorable and Christian thing to do is to treat each black man and each white man strictly on his merits as a man. . . . I know that we see through a glass dimly [1 Corinthians 13:12], and, after all, it may be that I am wrong; but if I am, then all my thoughts and beliefs are wrong, and my whole way of looking at life is wrong. . . . I do not intend to offend the prejudices of anyone else, but neither do I intend to allow their prejudices to make me false to my principles.[44]

During World War II, Franklin Roosevelt contended that Western civilization was under assault by a Nazi ideology that substituted a belief in racial hierarchy for the Christian doctrine of spiritual equality. In 1939 he wrote to Pope Pius XII, "The civilization handed down to us by our fathers was built by men and women who knew in their hearts that all were brothers because they were children of God." The following year, he claimed, "Our modern democratic way of life has its deepest roots in our great common religious tradition, which for ages past has taught to civilized mankind the dignity of the human being, his equality before God, and his responsibility in the making of a better and fairer world." In 1942 he contended, "We are fighting, as our fathers have fought, to uphold the doctrine that all men are equal in the sight of God."[45]

Harry Truman, the first modern civil rights president, addressed Congress concerning the issue in 1948. He declared, "We believe that all men are created equal and that they have the right to equal justice under the law." He called this proposition "our American faith." Eight months later, he argued, "Real prosperity is based on justice. Real prosperity depends on fair treatment for all groups of our society. That's a rule as old as the Bible. That's what the Bible means when it says, and I quote: 'We are . . . every one members, one of another. [Romans 12:5].'" Regarding Jesus, he told the National Negro Baptist Convention:

> He was born in a manger. He grew up as the son of a carpenter and was one Himself. He told the people who believed they were better than the poor where they stood. He called attention to the widow's mite as much more welcome to God the Father than was the gold contribution of the Pharisees. . . . He reminded them of the Good Samaritan who had helped his neighbor—and Samaritans were, in that day in Jerusalem, regarded as people of your color have been in some parts of the United States. . . . What is in the heart and mind is what counts with Almighty God—not the color of the skin.

Truman not only issued an executive order that fully integrated the military, leading "Dixiecrats" to defect from his reelection campaign, but he also asked Congress for a federal anti-lynching law, for the revival of the Fair Employment Practices Committee that had been disbanded after World War II, for an end to discrimination in interstate transportation, and for the protection of voting rights.[46]

Dwight Eisenhower also believed in spiritual equality. During World War II, when the Australian ambassador to the United States protested the dispatching of black troops to his country, Eisenhower responded that he would send no troops at all in that case. The Australian government backed down. Eisenhower also integrated Red Cross and United Service Organization (USO) clubs, and near the end of the war, he sent black replacements to white units, thereby integrating those units for the first time. He persisted in this policy despite criticism. In 1953 he declared, "The equality of man . . . is a completely false pretense unless we recognize the Supreme Being in front of whom we are all equal." He added, "Man is a person and an entity of dignity in front of his God, regardless of his religion or his race, or any other such things of inconsequential character." That same year, he ordered the integration of all public facilities in the District of Columbia. Immediately after the Supreme Court's decision in *Brown vs. the Board of Education of Topeka, Kansas*, which declared segregation in public schools unconstitutional in 1954, Eisenhower called the District of Columbia's commissioners to the Oval Office and urged them "to take the lead in desegregating its schools as an example to the entire country." They did so, and there was no violence. Later that year, he said, "It is only in that kind of government that America can continue to grow and be great—the kind of government that respects the human, respects him as an equal before the law and before God." In 1955 he reaffirmed, "Every individual among us has been created in the image of his Maker. He has equal rights."[47]

Throughout the remainder of his presidency, Eisenhower continued to apply the principle of spiritual equality to the civil rights movement. In 1956 he suggested to Reverend Billy Graham, "You might express some admiration for the Catholic Archbishop, Joseph Francis Rummel, in Louisiana, who had the courage to desegregate his parochial schools. . . . Likewise, there could be approval expressed concerning the progress made in certain areas in the border states and in all other areas of the South where any type of advance at all has been effected." Graham termed these suggestions "excellent" and followed through with them. The following year, Eisenhower signed the Civil Rights Act of 1957, the first act of its kind since Reconstruction, and federalized the Arkansas National Guard so they could protect the new African American students at Little Rock High School from a segregationist mob, the first time since Reconstruction that federal troops were employed to enforce the civil rights guaranteed by the Fourteenth Amendment. In justifying the order, Eisenhower declared, "I believe that all forms of free government are based either knowingly or unknowingly on [the] deeply held religious conviction . . . that all men are the sons of a Creator, a common Creator." In his final Christmas message in 1960, Eisenhower declared, "As we look into the mirror of conscience, we see blots and blemishes that mar the picture of a nation of people who devoutly believe that they were created in the image of their Maker." One of these blemishes was that "through bitter prejudice and because of differences in skin pigmentation, individuals can not enjoy equality of political and economic opportunity."[48]

John F. Kennedy proposed what would become the landmark Civil Rights Act of 1964. In an address to Congress in 1963, Kennedy declared that civil rights must be advanced both by the government and by individuals, including "religious leaders who recognize the conflict between racial bigotry and the Holy Word." The following month, he claimed, "We are trying to erase for all time the injustices and inequalities of race and color in order to assure all Americans a fair chance to fulfill their lives and their opportunity as Americans and as equal children of God."[49]

Lyndon Johnson oversaw the passage of the Civil Rights Act and the Voting Rights Act of 1965. In 1963 he urged, "Let us pray for divine wisdom in banishing from our land any injustice or intolerance or oppression to any of our fellow Americans whatever their opinion, whatever the color of their skin—for God made all of us, not just some of us, in His image. All of us, not just some of us, are His children." The following year, after signing the Civil Rights Act, Johnson noted proudly, "It does say that those who are equal before God shall also be equal in the polling booths, in the classrooms, in the factories, and in hotels, restaurants, movie theaters, and other places that provide service to the public."[50]

Jimmy Carter also believed in equality. Andrew Young, who served as the United States ambassador to the United Nations under Carter, recalled that when the Congressional Black Caucus met with various presidential candidates in 1976, all of the other candidates had replied to the question, "How many blacks are on your staff?" with either "One" or "None." Young continued, "Jimmy Carter didn't know how many he had on his staff, and he started listing names of people. Soon we realized there were more than twenty blacks involved at all levels of his campaign." More significantly, he added, "It was also clear to us that Carter hadn't even thought about it in those terms, but that he was practicing what the others were only preaching."[51]

Barack Obama, the first African American president, noted the spiritual basis of equality in his inaugural address in 2009. He referred to "the God-given promise that all are equal, all are free, and all deserve a chance to pursue their full measure of happiness."[52]

Unfortunately, American presidents have not been at the forefront of the women's rights movement. They were late to endorse women's suffrage and timid in advancing other rights for women. But, ultimately, they did begin appointing women to top cabinet posts, ambassadorships, and judgeships, then even to the position of running mate, leading Kamala Harris to become the nation's first female vice president. In touting his own appointment of women to high positions in 1964, Lyndon Johnson declared, "I am not one who believes that all intelligence and skill is for some obscure reason confined entirely to the male population. Providence has distributed brains and skills pretty evenly over our people."[53]

Jimmy Carter led a successful effort to persuade his own church to ordain female deacons. In 1979 he acknowledged that the Bible could be interpreted in different ways regarding the status of women but added, "I have a feeling that Christ meant for all of us to be treated equally, and He demonstrated this in many ways." He later explained, "As we see in the Gospels, Jesus challenged the prevailing suppression of women. Many of His most faithful and prominent followers were women, and, throughout Jesus's travels, He lived and spoke with women in terms of virtual equality. After his death, women were the first witnesses of the resurrection, and they were the ones who proclaimed the good news of His rising." The apostle Paul mentioned various female deacons and other women, such as Phoebe, Junia, and Priscilla, who served as important coworkers. Carter concluded, "To me, all of this is clear evidence that Christ intended women to play a major—even equal—role in His church. An increasing number of Christians believe, as I do, that no position, including deacon, pastor, or priest, should be withheld from women." Carter felt so strongly about the issue that he left the Southern Baptist Convention over it in 2000, saying, "I personally feel that the Bible says all people are equal in the eyes of God. I personally feel that women should play an absolutely equal role in the service of Christ in the church." With his encouragement, his own Maranatha Baptist Church joined the Cooperative Baptist Fellowship, an association of two thousand churches that ordains women.[54]

While many presidents have possessed a sincere belief in spiritual equality, their ability to act fully on this belief has been restrained by the political reality that large numbers of their fellow citizens did not really share it. Conversely, others have behaved as though they did not believe in spiritual equality at all. Andrew Jackson not only played a crucial role in the brutal expulsion of the so-called Five Civilized Tribes from the southeastern United States, but was also the first unapologetically proslavery president, even offering a fifty-dollar reward for the return of a runaway slave, adding the promise of "ten dollars extra for every hundred lashes any person will give him, to the amount of three hundred." Jackson's fellow Southern Democrats Andrew Johnson and Woodrow Wilson joined him in promoting democracy based on the equal rights of poor whites while justifying the enslavement of African Americans. Johnson vetoed the Civil Rights Act of 1866 and urged Southern states to reject the Fourteenth Amendment. Wilson expressed horror at the idea of racial intermarriage and, as president, allowed his Southern cabinet members to segregate the federal workers in their departments on the dubious grounds of preventing racial conflict (there had been little such conflict over the previous decades in which they had been integrated). Wilson's Republican successor, Warren Harding, declined to overturn this policy and endorsed segregation, saying, "Racial amalgamation there cannot be."[55]

Despite the poor records of some American presidents concerning slavery and civil rights, there is no question that the ultimate destruction of slavery and legalized segregation, a destruction aided and abetted by other presidents at great political risk, owed much to the biblical principle of spiritual equality. As the Christian minister Martin Luther King Jr. understood, the most effective means of undermining racial inequality was to highlight the stark contrast between the principles enshrined in the book the vast majority of Americans regarded as the Word of God and the actual practices of American society and government.

CHAPTER 7

Israels

Old, New, and Restored

Most presidents, reaching back to the very beginning of the nation, have shared the conviction that the United States is a new Israel, a nation chosen by God to accomplish a sacred purpose. Just as God selected Israel as his chosen vessel to advance ethical monotheism, so He destined the United States to play the chief role in spreading freedom around the globe. He did this by erecting the nation as a republican city on a hill, a model of liberty that would also serve as a safe haven for the world's oppressed. These presidents have believed that the United States' divine mission entails both blessings and responsibilities. This belief in a divine mission has given the presidents a sense of identity and purpose as well as the courage to face the challenges of their time. Nevertheless, some presidents have been troubled by the possibility of divine judgment on the United States for slavery or for other serious violations of the nation's covenant with God. Finally, since the early twentieth century, presidents have supported the restoration and defense of the nation of Israel itself, at least in part for biblical reasons, while, at the same time, retaining the traditional conception of the United States as a new Israel.

The Divine Mission

In 1789, when George Washington was inaugurated as the first president of the United States, he placed his hand on a Bible that was opened to Genesis 49, a passage that concerns Jacob's prophesy regarding the twelve tribes founded by his sons, the tribes that formed the nation of Israel. In this way Washington designated the United States the new Israel. In a 1790 letter to the Jewish community in Savannah, Washington explicitly connected the American mission to that of Israel, both operating under the same God: "May the same wonder-working Deity who long since delivering the Hebrews from their Egyptian Oppressors, planted them in the promised land—whose providential agency has lately been conspicuous in establishing these United States as an independent nation—continue to water them with the dews of Heaven and to make the inhabitants of every denomination participate in the temporal and spiritual blessings of that people whose God is Jehovah."[1]

This conception of Americans as God's latest chosen people was not new. A century and a half earlier, the Puritans had seen themselves as an elect group chosen by God to construct a Christian "city upon a hill" in the New World, a purer society that the English would wish to emulate. John Winthrop borrowed this term from the Sermon on the Mount. In Matthew 5:14 Jesus tells his followers, "You are the light of the world. A city that is set on a hill cannot be hidden." In other words, Christians were supposed to serve as a model to humanity. During the American Revolution, the Puritan mission to serve as a spiritual city on a hill transformed into a national mission to serve as a republican city on a hill. In "A Dissertation on the Feudal and Canon Law" (1765), John Adams, a descendant of the Puritans, declared that the settlement of America was "the opening of a grand scene and design in Providence for the illumination of the ignorant and the emancipation of the slavish part of mankind all over the earth." The same year, he claimed, "America was designed by Providence for the Theatre on which Man was to make his true figure, on which science, Virtue, Liberty, Happiness, and Glory were to exist in peace."[2]

James Buchanan agreed. In 1840 he contended, "We are a spectacle for all other nations—a rainbow of promise—a chosen people, to whose hands Providence has entrusted, in a great degree, the destinies of mankind. Should we fail in our grand experiment of free Government, a long night of Despotism will cover the nations. The hopes of the friends of liberty throughout the world are fixed upon us. They and we fondly believe in the steady advancement of mankind in the love of liberty and in the virtue and knowledge necessary to sustain free institutions." Seventeen years later, he declared in his inaugural address, "I feel an humble confidence that the kind Providence which inspired our fathers with wisdom to frame the most perfect form of Government and Union ever devised by man will not suffer it to perish until it shall have been peacefully instrumental, by its example, in the extension of civil and religious liberty throughout the world."[3]

In 1861 Abraham Lincoln referred to Americans as God's "almost chosen people." While the phrase "chosen people" clearly connected the United

States to biblical Israel, the qualifier "almost" displayed Lincoln's usual reticence in expressing the will of the Almighty.[4]

Andrew Johnson's belief in the divine mission of the United States to expand human freedom comforted him during the trying years of the Civil War and Reconstruction. In a flag ceremony held on a Sunday in 1864, he claimed that the flag's "every hue was sent from heaven; it was the symbol of a cause as holy as the day." Regarding the Union, he added, "It was ordained by God that it should never go down in dishonor. Therefore, was it not the fittest day of the week to fling out the banner that was the emblem of liberty?" The following year, having unexpectedly become president due to Lincoln's assassination, Johnson stated, "As I have often said, I believe that God sent this people on a mission among the nations of the earth and that when He founded our nation, He founded it in perpetuity. That faith sustains me now that new duties are devolved upon me and new dangers threaten us. I feel that whatever the means He uses, the Almighty is determined to preserve us as a people."[5]

Grover Cleveland agreed. In his fourth annual message to Congress in 1888, he declared, "Our mission among the nations of the earth, and our success in accomplishing the work God has given the American people to do, require of those entrusted with the making and execution of our laws perfect devotion, above all other things, to the public good."[6]

In 1912 Woodrow Wilson claimed, "I believe that God presided over the inception of this nation; I believe that God implanted in us the visions of liberty; I believe that men are emancipated in proportion as they lift themselves to the conception of Providence and of divine destiny; and therefore I cannot be deprived of the hope that is in me—in the hope not only that concerns myself, but the confident hope that concerns the nation—that we are chosen and prominently chosen to show the way to the nations of the world how they shall walk in the paths of liberty." As a new president celebrating the golden anniversary of the Battle of Gettysburg the following year, Wilson called the United States "the nation God has builded."[7]

Warren Harding agreed that it was the divine destiny of the United States to expand liberty by example. In 1904 he said, "God must have destined that the old world should learn of the new and of its possibilities, of its availability for the setting of new lights and the liberties that lead to real accomplishment." In 1918 he declared, "We do not proclaim ours the perfect republic nor . . . the ideal popular government, but we do maintain it is the best and the freest that the world has ever known, and under it mankind has advanced and achieved as under none other since civilization dawned, and in good conscience and consecrated citizenship and abiding faith and hope we mean, with God's good guidance, to go on to the fulfillment of the highest American destiny." In his inaugural address in 1921, Harding asserted, "There is reassurance in belief in the God-given destiny of our Republic."[8]

Both Herbert Hoover and Franklin Roosevelt believed in a divine national mission to serve as both a model and a promoter of freedom. Hoover called the United States "the greatest gift of God to freedom." On the golden anniversary of the Statue of Liberty in 1936, Roosevelt suggested, "Perhaps Providence did prepare this American continent to be a place of the second chance. Certainly, millions of men and women have made it that. They adopted this homeland because in this land they found a home in which the things they most desired could be theirs—freedom of opportunity, freedom of thought, freedom to worship God. Here they found life because here there was freedom to live."[9]

The transformation of the United States' mission from spreading liberty by serving as a model republic to spreading it by force of arms began during the world wars and increased during the Cold War. This was not an entirely new concept: the conquest of the continent in order to establish an "empire for liberty" as the "manifest destiny" God intended for the nation had involved waging wars against Native American tribes and Mexico. Indeed, the very establishment of the nation had involved a long war against Great Britain. But the notion that the nation's divine mission involved projecting military power on a global scale was certainly a new concept, one generated by the unprecedented threat to world freedom posed, first, by Nazi Germany and, later, by the Communist bloc.

Harry Truman believed in a national mission to fight for freedom. On Independence Day in 1945, the last year of World War II, he declared, "We have confidence that, under Providence, we soon may crush the enemy in the Pacific. We have humility for the guidance that has been given us of God in serving His will as a leader of freedom for the world." In 1948 he contended, "You know, in 1920 Almighty God intended this country to assume the leadership of the world, which it would not assume—which it shirked. This brought on another cataclysm." Truman suggested that World War III lay in store for the world if the United States continued to shirk its God-given responsibilities. In 1949 he claimed, "I have confidence in our ability to master the international problems which confront us and to achieve world peace. . . . Above all, I am confident because I believe that Almighty God has set before this Nation the greatest task in the history of mankind, and that He will give us the wisdom and the strength to carry it out." Two years later, he declared, "I do not think that anyone can study the history of this Nation of ours—study it deeply and earnestly—without becoming convinced that divine providence has played a great part of it. I have the feeling that God has created us and brought us to our present position of power and strength for some great purpose. And up to now we have been shirking it. Now we are assuming it, and now we must carry it through."[10]

Dwight Eisenhower possessed a similar view of the nation's divine mission. In 1954 he declared, "We carry the torch of freedom as a sacred trust for all mankind. We do not believe that God intended the light that He created to be put out by men."[11]

Lyndon Johnson often employed the term "city upon a hill" to refer to the nation's divine mission. In 1964 he declared, "America tonight is a city upon a hill, and those who watch us look not to our tall buildings or our prosperous streets or to our mighty arms. They look uncertainly and hopefully to see burning in the midst of the city a light of freedom, a flame of the spirit, the brightness of the nobility which is in man, and the arms of the Statue of Liberty awaiting them."[12]

Jimmy Carter also associated the nation's divine mission with freedom. In 1980 he told a group of African American ministers, "I think the United States was created by God with a purpose. We're beginning to set an example for the rest of the world with human rights, with basic decency, with equality of opportunity."[13]

Ronald Reagan often referred to the United States as "a shining city on a hill." In the 1979 announcement of his presidential candidacy, he declared, "We who are privileged to be Americans have had a rendezvous with destiny since the moment when John Winthrop, standing on the deck of the tiny *Arabella* off the coast of Massachusetts, told the little band of Pilgrims, 'We shall be a city on a hill.'" Reagan saw the nation as "a new civilization based on freedom unlike any other before it." In his acceptance speech at the Republican National Convention in 1980, he asked, "Can we doubt that Divine Providence placed this land, this island of freedom, here as a refuge for all those people in the world who yearn to breathe freely?" In 1982 he told a group of newly naturalized citizens, "It's long been my belief that America is a chosen land, placed by some Divine Providence between the two oceans to be sought out and found only by those with a special yearning for freedom. The nation is a refuge for all those people on Earth who long to breathe free." Ten days later, he called the United States an "anointed land . . . set apart in an uncommon way." In 1983 he maintained, "I've always believed that this blessed land was set apart in a special way, that some divine plan placed this great continent here between the two oceans to be found by people from every corner of the Earth—people who had a special love for freedom and the courage to uproot themselves, leave their homeland and friends to come to a strange land. And when coming here, they created something new in all the history of mankind—a country where man is not beholden to government, government is beholden to man." Six years later, in his farewell address, Reagan said, "I have spoken of the shining city all my political life, but I don't know if I've ever quite communicated what I saw when I said it. But in my mind, it was a tall, proud city built on rocks stronger than oceans, wind-swept, God-blessed, and teeming with people of all kinds living in harmony and peace, a city that hummed with commerce and creativity. And if there had to be city walls, the wall had doors and the doors were open to anyone with the will and the heart to get here. That's how I saw it, and still see it."[14]

Divine Blessings

Most of the presidents have been convinced that the United States' unique mission entails particular blessings. In his resignation message to the state governors immediately following the successful conclusion of the Revolutionary War in 1783, George Washington marveled at "the glorious events which Heaven has been pleased to produce in our favour." He counted among God's blessings "a vast tract of continent . . . the free cultivation of letters, the unbounded extension of commerce, the progressive refinement of manners, the growing liberality of sentiment, and above all, the pure and benign light of Revelation."[15]

Thomas Jefferson and James Monroe agreed. In his first inaugural address in 1801, Jefferson listed the benefits that a generous God had bestowed on the United States, noting that the Almighty had caused Americans to be "enlightened by a benign religion, professed indeed and practiced in various forms, yet all of them inculcating honesty, truth, temperance, gratitude, and the love of man, acknowledging and adoring an overruling providence, which by all its dispensations proves that it delights in the happiness of man here and his greater happiness thereafter." Four years later, in his second inaugural address, Jefferson connected divine blessings with the nation's status as the new Israel:

> I shall need the favor of that Being in whose hands we are, who led our forefathers, as Israel of old, from their native land and planted them in a land flowing with all the necessaries and comforts of life, who has covered our infancy with His providence and our riper years with His wisdom and power, and to whose goodness I ask you to join me in supplications that He will so enlighten the

minds of your servants, guide their councils and prosper their measures that whatsoever they shall do shall result in your good and secure the peace, friendship, and approbation of all nations.

For his part, Monroe declared that Americans had "much cause for grateful acknowledgments to the supreme Author of all things for the manifold blessings which he has been pleased to confer on this *highly favored* and very happy country [emphasis added]."[16]

In 1826 Andrew Jackson wrote to James Buchanan: "We ought to view ourselves as the chosen people of God, who has given us a happy government of laws and placed us in such a climate and fertile soil. We ought not only to be thankful, but we ought to cherish and foster this heavenly boon with vestal vigilance." In his first annual message to Congress in 1829, Jackson wrote, "I offer up to the almighty ruler of the universe my fervent thanks for the peace and prosperity He has been pleased to bestow upon our *favored country* and implore Him at the throne of grace for a continuation of these blessings and that He may endow by his spirit the councils of the nation with wisdom to discern, and united harmony to enact, all laws that may tend to promote the prosperity of His Kingdom and the best interests of the union [emphasis added]."[17]

In his third annual address to Congress in 1859, James Buchanan claimed, "Notwithstanding our demerits, we have much reason to believe, from the past events in our history, that we have enjoyed the special protection of Divine Providence ever since our origin as a nation. We have been exposed to many threatening and alarming difficulties in our progress, but on each successive occasion the impending cloud has been dissipated at the moment it appeared ready to burst upon our head, and the danger to our institutions has passed away. May we ever be under the Divine guidance and protection!" Unfortunately, the storm of secession burst the following year. When he returned home in 1861, Buchanan declared, "May God preserve the Constitution and the Union, and in His good providence dispel the shadows, clouds, and darkness which have now cast a gloom over the land! Under that benign influence we have advanced more rapidly in prosperity, greatness, and glory than any other nation in the tide of time."[18]

Abraham Lincoln also detected divine favor behind the many benefits the United States enjoyed. Lincoln's appeal to Southerners in his first inaugural address emphasized the nation's unique, divine status: "[Even] if it were admitted that you who are dissatisfied hold the right side in the dispute, there is still no single good reason for precipitate action. Intelligence, patriotism, Christianity, and a firm reliance on Him who has never yet forsaken this *favored land* are still competent to adjust, in the best way, all our present difficulty [emphasis added]." In his annual message to Congress in 1864, Lincoln recognized immigration as a divine blessing: "I regard our emigrants as one of the principal replenishing streams which are appointed by Providence to repair the ravages of internal war and its wastes of national strength and health."[19]

William McKinley agreed that the United States was a nation uniquely favored by God. In 1892 he declared, "Here in the New World on the North American continent, in the United States of America, the Almighty has permitted man the full development of his God-given rights and faculties, and opened up to him the widest possibilities and the attainment of the highest destiny. Here as nowhere else has been wrought out the great problems of a free and self-governed people and the advantages and blessings springing therefrom." In 1898, in the wake of the Spanish-American War, McKinley claimed, "Providence has been extremely kind to the American people—kind not only in the recent conflict of arms, but in every step and stage of our history from its very beginning until now. We have been singularly blessed and favored."[20]

In 1905 Theodore Roosevelt gave credit to God for the nation's unprecedented prosperity, declaring, "My fellow citizens, no people on earth have more cause to be thankful than ours, and this is said reverently, in no spirit of boastfulness in our own strength, but with gratitude to the Giver of Good, who has blessed us with the conditions which have enabled us to achieve so large a measure of well-being and of happiness."[21]

Like Lincoln, Woodrow Wilson believed that God blessed the United States by sending the nation hardworking and ingenious immigrants from all over the world. In a Thanksgiving Day address that he gave while governor of New Jersey in 1910, Wilson noted the cultural enrichment provided to the country by past immigration and maintained that the process was far from complete. He claimed, "God is sifting the nations yet to plant seed in America."[22]

Warren Harding believed that the nation's landscape indicated unprecedented divine favor. He told the Builders Exchange in Cleveland, "A recent trip to the Pacific coast has magnified my belief that ours is a land physically incomparable, the prodigal gift of the Creator. With our mountains and plains, rivers and lakes, fertile valleys and golden stretches, north, south, east, or west, it is a seemingly measureless expanse, unmatchable. There are everlasting wonders in the mountainous West, where one breathes a new reverence for God and feels a new love of country."[23]

Franklin Roosevelt saw divine blessing in the qualities of the American people. As World War II neared its conclusion in 1945, Roosevelt declared in his fourth and final inaugural address, "The Almighty God has blessed our land in many ways. He has given our people stout hearts and strong arms with which to strike mighty blows for freedom and truth. He has given to our country a faith which has become the hope of all people in an anguished world."[24]

Harry Truman believed that God had exercised vigilance over the United States throughout its history. In 1946 he referred to "Almighty God, who has watched over this Republic as it grew from weakness to strength." Four years later, he claimed that "the God of our fathers" had "blessed this land beyond all others." In 1951 he noted, "Our Founding Fathers believed that God created this Nation. And I believe it too. They believed that God was our strength in time of peril and the source of all our blessings."[25]

Dwight Eisenhower agreed that the nation was the recipient of a unique degree of divine favor. In 1956 he credited God "for the wisdom, the skills, the industry, and the resources that has made them the most fortunate people on earth."[26]

Lyndon Johnson associated the divine blessing of prosperity with the blessing of opportunity. In 1963 he declared, "We live in the one land where opportunity really exists, and we ought to get down on our knees and thank the good Lord Almighty for the providence and for the blessings that are ours." The following year, he claimed, "The Good Lord Almighty has blessed us with a bounty that excels that of any other nation in the world."[27]

Gerald Ford attributed the many divine blessings to the piety of the American people as well as to their exertions on behalf of freedom. In 1976 he claimed, "I believe it is no accident of history, no coincidence, that this Nation, which declared its dependence on God even while declaring its independence from foreign domination, has become the greatest nation in the history of the world. We are taught in the Psalms [33:12] that blessed is the nation whose God is the Lord. I believe that very, very deeply." He added, "Looking back over 200 years, we can see that America has always been a uniquely blessed nation, that we have had a very special role to play in the affairs of mankind. . . . We have demonstrated time and time again that the cause of freedom in the world has no better friend, no stronger ally, than the United States of America." Five months later, Ford noted that the reverse of the Great Seal included a Latin motto that translates, "God has favored our undertaking." Ford added, "Two hundred years later, we know God has."[28]

Jimmy Carter often referred to the unique blessings that God bestowed on the United States. In 1977 he declared, "No nation in the history of humankind has been more deeply blessed than we have." The following month, he emphasized the economic blessings: "God has blessed us with unequaled resources." In 1978 he declared, "God's blessed us beyond all reasonable expectation, compared to all other people on Earth," referring specifically to military, economic, and political blessings. In 1979 Carter contended, "We are a nation which has indeed been blessed by God with blessings which exceed those of any other people on Earth. We're a nation of freedom. We're a nation of strength, of courage, of vitality. We're a nation which has always been able and eager to meet any challenge, no matter how difficult it might have been, to solve any problem, no matter how complex it might be, or to answer any question which confronts the people of the United States of America."[29]

Like Ford, Ronald Reagan connected the nation's blessings to its devotion to God. In 1981 he claimed, "Throughout our history Americans have put their faith in God and no one can doubt that we have been blessed for it." The following year, he said, "Above all other nations of the world, America has been especially blessed and should give special thanks. We have bountiful harvests, abundant freedoms, and a strong, compassionate people."[30]

Bill Clinton and George W. Bush agreed that the United States was uniquely blessed by God. In 1996 Clinton declared, "For all the problems of this country, we have been given more from God than any nation in history." Five years later, Bush stated regarding the nation's founding, "We give thanks to the God who watched over our country then and who watches to this very day."[31]

Divine Assistance During the Revolutionary War

One of the most commonly shared beliefs among the founders and, indeed, among Americans generally, both during and after the Revolutionary War, was that the United States' startling triumph over Great Britain, the most powerful nation in the world in the eighteenth century, was the result of divine assistance. In 1776 George Washington, who commanded the army that drove the British from Boston, issued a statement to the Massachusetts legislature: "That the metropolis of your Colony is now released from the cruel and oppressive invasion of those who were sent to erect the Standard of lawless domination & to trample on the rights of humanity and is again open & free for its rightful possessors must give pleasure to every virtuous and Sympathetic heart—and, being effected without the blood of our Soldiers and fellow Citizens, must be ascribed to the Interposition of that providence which has manifestly appeared in our behalf thro' the whole of this important struggle." The following year, he announced to his soldiers regarding the turning point of the war, the British surrender at Saratoga: "On the 14th instant, General [John] Burgoyne and his whole Army surrendered themselves [as] prisoners of war. Let every face brighten and every heart expand with grateful Joy and praise to the supreme disposer of all events, who has granted us this signal success."[32]

In 1778, after thanking a friend, Washington claimed, "Providence has a joint claim to my humble and grateful thanks, for its protection and direction of me through the many difficult and intricate scenes which this contest hath produced and for the constant interposition on our behalf when the clouds were heaviest and seemed ready to burst upon us." He wrote to his brother regarding General Charles Lee's unexpected retreat at the Battle of Monmouth: "The disorder arising from it would have proved fatal to the Army had not that bountiful Providence which has never failed us in the hour of distress enabled me to form a Regiment or two of those that were retreating in the face of the Enemy." He wrote to one of his generals regarding the war: "The hand of Providence has been so conspicuous in all this that he must be worse than an infidel that lacks faith, and more than wicked, that has not gratitude enough to acknowledge his obligations."[33]

In 1780, a couple of weeks after Benedict Arnold's attempt to hand over West Point to the British had failed, Washington wrote privately, "In no instance since the commencement of the War has the interposition of Providence appeared more conspicuous than in the rescue of the Post and Garrison of West Point from Arnold's villainous perfidy. . . . An unaccountable deprivation of presence of Mind in a man of the first abilities and the virtuous conduct of three Militia men threw the Adjutant General of the British forces in America (with full proofs of Arnold's treachery) into our hands." Note that Washington attributed to the Almighty both Arnold's uncharacteristic blunders and the quick-wittedness of American militiamen in the timely capture of Major John Andre. Washington continued to attribute patriot success to Providence in countless letters throughout the rest of the war. In fact, in one epistle, he claimed, "It has at times been my only dependence, for all other resources have failed us."[34]

When the Treaty of Paris that ended the war was finally signed, Washington wrote to the inhabitants of Princeton, New Jersey:

> If in the execution of an arduous Office I have been so happy as to discharge my duty to the Public with fidelity and success and to obtain the good opinion of my fellow Soldiers and fellow Citizens, I attribute all glory to that Supreme Being who hath caused the several parts which have been employed in the

production of the wonderful Events we now contemplate to harmonize in the most perfect manner and who was able by the humblest instruments as well as by the most powerful means to establish and secure the liberty and happiness of these United States.

To the Comte de Rochambeau, his partner in the capture of Cornwallis's army at Yorktown, he wrote privately: "I shall . . . look back on our past toils with a grateful admiration of that beneficent Providence which has raised up so many instruments to accomplish so great a revolution as the one you have had a share in bringing about." In his final statement to his soldiers, Washington declared,

> A contemplation of the complete attainment (at a period earlier than could have been expected) of the object for which we contended against so formidable a power cannot but inspire us with astonishment and gratitude. The disadvantageous circumstances on our part under which the war was undertaken can never be forgotten. The singular interpositions of Providence in our feeble condition were such as could scarcely escape the attention of the most unobserving, while the unparalleled perseverance of the Armies of the United States through almost every possible suffering and discouragement for the space of eight long years was little short of a standing miracle.[35]

In Washington's resignation message to Congress in 1783, he recalled that he had accepted Congress's commission as commander of the Continental Army with "a diffidence in my abilities to accomplish so arduous a task, which however was superseded by a confidence in the rectitude of our Cause, the support of the Supreme Power of the Union, and the patronage of Heaven." Of these three, Washington clearly considered the last the most important, for he concluded the speech: "I consider it an indispensable duty to close this last solemn act of my Official life by commending the Interests of our dearest Country to the protection of Almighty God and those who have the superintendence of them to his holy keeping." According to James McHenry, at this point, Washington's "voice faltered and sunk, and the whole house felt his agitation." Nine years later, Washington claimed, "There never was a people who had more reason to acknowledge a divine interposition in their affairs than those of the United States, and I should be pained to believe that they have forgotten that agency which was so often manifested during our Revolution or that they failed to consider the omnipotence of that God who is alone able to protect them." Then, in 1795, Washington contended, "To the Great ruler of events, not to any exertions of mine, is to be ascribed the favorable termination of our late contest for liberty. I never considered the fortunate issue of any measure adopted by me in the progress of the Revolution in any other light than as the ordering of kind Providence."[36]

Other presidents have shared Washington's belief that God aided the United States during the Revolutionary War. In 1786 Thomas Jefferson attributed the success of the American Revolution to divine intervention, writing, "We put our existence to hazard, when the hazard seemed against us, and we saved our country, justifying at the same time the ways of Providence, whose precept is to do what is right, and leave the issue to him." In 1790 he wrote in a similar vein: "It is an animating thought that while we are securing the rights of ourselves and our posterity, we are pointing out the way to struggling nations who wish, like us, to emerge from their tyrannies also. Heaven help their struggles and lead them, as it has done us, triumphantly thro' them." In 1811 John Adams contended regarding the American Revolution, "God prospered our labors." In 1847 James K. Polk declared, "No country has been so much favored by, or should acknowledge with deeper reverence the manifestations of, the Divine protection. An all-wise Creator directed and guarded us in our infant struggle for freedom, and has constantly watched over our surprising progress, until we have become one of the greatest nations of the earth." In 1854 Martin Van Buren referred to the Revolutionary War as a "struggle which, by the blessing of God, resulted in the establishment of national independence." He added that Providence had directed all of George Washington's actions not only during the war but throughout "his most useful and brilliant life." In 1904 Warren Harding called the American Revolution "a miracle," adding, "The people were not trained for war, they were not equipped in any sense for the days of strife that fell to them, they were betrayed at home and abroad, but they won."[37]

The Constitution as a Divine Gift

It is sometimes suggested that the absence of any mention of God in the US Constitution constitutes evidence of a lack of piety on the part of its framers. Although the framers did indeed omit such a reference—perhaps because, as historian Paul Boller noted, they were "eager to avoid embroiling the new government in religious controversies" (another manifestation of the risk aversion that led them to omit a bill of rights from the original text)—most of them viewed God as the ultimate force behind the document. Anticipating its ratification, George Washington, the president of the Constitutional Convention, wrote to the Marquis de Lafayette:

Should everything proceed with harmony and consent according to our actual wishes and expectations, I will confess to you sincerely, my dear Marquis, it will be so much beyond anything we had a right to imagine or expect eighteen months ago that it will demonstrate as visibly the finger of Providence as any possible event in the course of human affairs can ever designate it. It is impracticable for you or anyone who has not been on the spot to realize the change in men's minds and the progress towards rectitude in thinking and acting which will then have been made.

Washington conveyed to another of his former generals, Benjamin Lincoln, the same belief that the Constitution was a divine gift, calling its ratification "the road to which the finger of Providence has so manifestly pointed." Regarding the failure of ratification, he added, "I cannot believe it will ever come to pass! The Author of all good has not conducted us so far on the Road to happiness and glory to withdraw from us, in the hour of need, His beneficial support." He wrote to Jonathan Trumbull Jr., "We may, with a kind of grateful and pious exultation, trace the finger of Providence through those dark and mysterious events which first induced the States to appoint a general Convention and then led them one after one another (by steps as were best calculated to effect the object) into an adoption of the system recommended by that general Convention—thereby, in all human probability, laying a lasting foundation for tranquility and happiness, when we had but too much reason to fear that confusion and misery were coming rapidly upon us." In another letter he marveled at how God had used the distresses caused by the Articles of Confederation, the nation's first constitution, to bring about a more perfect union: "A multiplication of circumstances, scarcely yet investigated, appears to have cooperated in bringing about that great, and I trust happy, revolution that is on the eve of being accomplished. It will not be uncommon that those things which were considered at the moment as real ills should have been no inconsiderable causes in producing positive and permanent national felicity. For it is thus that Providence works in the mysterious course of events 'from seeming evil still educing good.'" Washington borrowed the latter phrase from James Thomson's "A Hymn" (1730), the underlying concept from the Bible.[38]

In his first year as president, Washington often referred to the crucial role of Providence not only in securing American independence but also in leading the nation to a sound constitution. He wrote to the officials of Philadelphia: "When I contemplate the Interposition of Providence, as it was visibly Manifested in guiding us thro' the Revolution, in preparing us for the Reception of a General Government, and in conciliating the Good will of the People of America towards one another after its Adoption, I feel myself oppressed and almost overwhelmed with a sense of the Divine Munificence. I feel that nothing is due to my personal agency in all these complicated and wonderful Events except what can simply be attributed to the exertions of an honest Zeal for the Good of my Country."[39]

Ten days later, Washington returned to this theme in his first inaugural address. He declared,

> No People can be bound to acknowledge and adore the invisible hand which conducts the Affairs of men more than the people of the United States. Every step by which they have advanced to the character of an independent nation seems to have been distinguished by some token of providential agency. And in the important revolution just accomplished in the system of their United Government the tranquil deliberations and voluntary consent of so many distinct communities from which the event has resulted cannot be compared with the means by which most Governments have been established without some return of pious gratitude, along with an humble anticipation of the future blessings which the past seem to presage. These reflections, arising out of the present crisis, have forced themselves too strongly on my mind to be suppressed.

Six months later, Washington called for a national day of prayer and thanksgiving to thank God not only for intervening on behalf of the United States in the Revolutionary War and for the prosperity and freedom since enjoyed but also "for the peaceable and rational manner in which we have been enabled to establish constitutions of government for our safety and happiness, particularly the national One now lately instituted."[40]

Washington was not the only founder who considered the Constitution a divine gift. In *Federalist* No. 37, James Madison wrote regarding the Constitutional Convention: "The real wonder is that so many difficulties should have been surmounted, and surmounted with an unanimity almost as unprecedented as it must have been unexpected. It is impossible for any man of candour to reflect on this circumstance without partaking of astonishment. It is impossible for the man of pious reflection not to perceive in it a finger of that Almighty Hand which has been so frequently and signally extended to our relief in the critical stages of the revolution."[41]

This was not a judgment that Madison reserved for public consumption. Indeed, perhaps the most startling statement of belief in divine intervention on behalf of the Constitution came in a private letter that the Virginian, who was later dubbed the Father of the Constitution, penned to Thomas Jefferson. Just one month after the close of the Constitutional Convention, Madison wrote to his friend and political ally, saying that balancing all of the interests and concerns presented there "formed a task more difficult than can well be conceived by those who were not concerned in the execution of it." Yet despite the fact that Madison was generally reticent about expressing his religious beliefs and despite the fact that he was writing to a man he knew did not believe in miracles (however much he believed in the working of Providence through natural causes), Madison seemed compelled to add a sentence that must have startled its reader: "Adding to these considerations the natural diversity of human opinions on all new and complicated subjects, it is impossible to consider the degree of concord which ultimately prevailed as less than a miracle." That was as close to a sermon as the one-time divinity student ever preached.[42]

The numerous founders who considered the Constitution a divine gift were well aware that it possessed opponents in every state. But they were genuinely amazed that a collection of such diverse and proud men, each a leader in his own state, had managed to set aside their ideological differences, their pride, and their competing interests in order to produce so complex and impressive a document in a few months' time. They were even more astounded that every state ratified it, however close the vote and however heated the debate in some states.

Subsequent presidents also considered the Constitution a divine gift. In his second message to Congress in 1838, after thanking God for the nation's peace, prosperity, and unity, Martin Van Buren also expressed gratitude to the deity for the Constitution. He noted that the system it established had survived a half century of trials. Four years later, James Buchanan declared that the Constitution was "formed by as wise men and as pure patriots as the sun of heaven ever shone upon." He added, "We have every reason to believe that Providence smiled upon their labors and predestined them to bless mankind. Immediately after the adoption of the Constitution, order arose out of confusion; and a settled Government capable of performing all its duties to its constituents with energy and effect succeeded to the chaos and disorder which had previously existed under the Articles of Confederation. For more than half a century under this Constitution, we have enjoyed a greater degree of liberty and happiness than has ever fallen to the lot of any other nation on earth."[43]

Andrew Johnson was so fond of the Constitution that he arranged to have a copy of it serve as the pillow of his casket. In calling it "the Bible of our political faith" and adding that "it is our cloud by day and our pillar of fire by night [Exodus 13:21]" in 1841, he intimated that it was divinely inspired. Twenty-one years later, he called the government created by the Constitution "the best Government that God ever spoke into existence!"

On the Fourth of July that year, he asserted, "I hold that this Government is of divine birth, that it is a gift of God himself."[44]

Grover Cleveland also hailed the Constitution as a divine gift. At the centennial celebration of the drafting of the document in 1887, he called it the "rising sun," declaring,

> Clouds have sometimes obscured its rays, and dreadful storms have made us fear; but God has held it in its course and through its life-giving warmth has performed His latest miracle in the creation of this wondrous land and people. As we look down the past century to the origin of our Constitution, as we contemplate its trials and triumphs, as we realize how completely the principles on which it is based have met every national peril and every national need, how devoutly should we confess with [Benjamin] Franklin, "God governs in the affairs of men," and how solemn should be the reflection that to our hands is committed the ark of the people's covenant, and that ours is the duty to shield it from impious hands. We received it sealed with the tests of a century. It has been found sufficient in the past; and in all the future years it will be found sufficient, if the American people are true to their sacred trust. Another centennial day will come, and millions yet unborn will inquire concerning our stewardship and the safety of the Constitution. God grant that they may find it unimpaired; and as we rejoice in the patriotism and devotion of those who lived a hundred years ago, so may others who follow us rejoice in our fidelity and in our jealous love for constitutional liberty.

Three years later, at a celebration of the centennial of the inauguration of the Supreme Court under the Constitution, Cleveland contended,

> In the creation of the world, the earth was without form and void, and darkness was upon the face of the deep until God said, 'Let there be light, and there was light [Genesis 1:3].' In the creation of our new nation, our free institutions were without form and symmetry of strength, and the darkness of hopelessness brooded over the aspirations of our people, until a light in the temple of Justice and Law, gathered from the Divine fountain of light, illumined the work of the fathers of our republic. On this centennial day we will devoutly thank Heaven for the revelation, to those who formed our government, of this source of strength and light, and for the inspiration of disinterested patriotism and consecrated devotion which established the tribunal which we today commemorate.[45]

In 1908 William Howard Taft suggested that Providence had favored the United States in providing both victory in the Revolutionary War and the Constitution. He claimed,

When we consider the galaxy of great statesmen and patriots that waited upon the conception and birth of our Nation and made them possible, it is very difficult to avoid a conviction that there was Providential interference to secure to the life of our Nation a successful growth. Consider the wonderful adaptability of the character of Washington to the crises that were presented from time to time in the Revolutionary War, and then after the war was over, to the still greater crises in the life of the Nation when he was called to use his power of composing difficulties in the Constitutional Convention, whose work made the thirteen quarreling states a united country.[46]

A few weeks before assuming office in 1921, Warren Harding wrote regarding the framers of the Constitution: "The hand of destiny must have directed them; and the supreme accomplishment was wrought because God Himself had a purpose to serve in the making of the new Republic." In his inaugural address, Harding reiterated his contention that the founders had been divinely inspired. Speaking in the aftermath of a world war, he declared,

Standing in this presence, mindful of the solemnity of the occasion, feeling the emotions which no one may know until he senses the great weight of responsibility for himself, I must utter my belief in the divine inspiration of the founding fathers. Surely there must have been God's intent in the making of this new-world republic. Ours is an organic law which had but one ambiguity, and we saw that effaced in a baptism of sacrifice and blood, with union maintained, the Nation supreme, and its concord inspiring. We have seen the world rivet its hopeful gaze on the great truths which the founders wrought. We have seen civil, human, and religious liberty verified and glorified. In the beginning the Old World scoffed at our experiment; today our foundation of political and social belief stands unshaken, a precious inheritance to ourselves, an inspiring example of freedom and civilization to all mankind. Let us express renewed and strengthened devotion, in grateful reverence for the immortal beginning and utter our confidence in the supreme fulfillment.[47]

In 1924 Calvin Coolidge referred to Providence as one of the sources of the Constitution. Regarding politics, he wrote,

That there could have been gathered together a body of men so learned in that science, so experienced in its application, so talented and so wise in its statement and demonstration, as those who proposed, formulated, and secured the adoption of the American Constitution will never cease to be the wonder and admiration of the profoundest students of government. After making every allowance for a fortunate culmination of circumstances and the accomplishments of human ingenuity, they have been nearly all forced to come to the belief that it can be accounted for only by the addition of another element, which we must recognize as the guiding hand of Providence.[48]

Harry Truman often implied that God had exerted a powerful influence over the drafters of the Constitution. In many different speeches, he used some iteration of the same phrase: "It has been well said that what we fight for is a pattern of democracy designed by God and worked by everyone."[49]

Other Developments Considered Divinely Ordained

Presidents have considered other historical developments that favored the United States to be divinely ordained. John Quincy Adams considered the nation's acquisition of Florida and Louisiana as two such developments. In 1821, two years after the ratification of the Adams-Onís Treaty that he had negotiated with Spain, a treaty in which Spain ceded Florida to the United States, Adams wrote in his diary,

> Let my sons, if they ever consult the record of their father's life, turn back to the reflections of the journal of that day. Let them meditate upon all the vicissitudes which have befallen the treaty, and of which this diary bears witness, in the interval between that day and this. Let them remark the workings of private interests, of perfidious fraud, of sordid intrigues, of royal treachery, of malignant rivalry, and of envy masked with patriotism, playing to and fro across the Atlantic into each other's hands, all combined to destroy the treaty between the signature and the ratification, and let them learn to put their trust in the overruling providence of God.

In 1837, on reading Robert Livingston's memoirs, Adams was struck by the equally unlikely sequence of events that led to the Louisiana Purchase. He wrote, "The finger of Heaven appears in all this. . . . We can but contemplate with wonder the ways of God to men."[50]

Andrew Jackson considered his own victory in the Battle of New Orleans an act of God. Ten days after the event, he wrote, "If there ever was an occasion on which Providence interfered immediately in the affairs of men it seems to have been on this. What but such an interposition could have saved this Country? Let us mingle our joys and our thanksgivings together." Jackson requested that Abbe Guillaume Dubourg preside over a special thanksgiving Mass in New Orleans to celebrate "the signal interposition of heaven in giving success to our arms against the Enemy, who so lately landed on our Shores." Jackson was especially amazed by the small number of American casualties compared with the enemy's, writing, "It appears that the unerring hand of providence shielded my men from the showers of Balls, bombs, and Rockets, when every Ball and Bomb from our guns carried with it the mission of death." Secretary of State James Monroe agreed, writing to Jackson, "It is particularly gratifying to find that, in so signal a success, attended with the slaughter and captivity of so many of the invading foe, it has pleased Providence to extend a protecting arm over our fellow citizens."[51]

In 1826 President John Quincy Adams joined most Americans in considering the death of his father and Thomas Jefferson on the same day—namely, the golden anniversary of the Declaration of Independence—a sign of God's favor for the nation. He wrote in his diary, "The time, the manner, the coincidence in the decease of Jefferson [and John Adams], are visible and palpable marks of Divine favor, for which I would humble myself in grateful and silent adoration before the Ruler of the Universe. For myself, all that I dare to ask is that I may live the remnant of my days in a manner worthy of him from whom I came, and, at the appointed hour of my Maker, die as my father has died, in peace with God and man, sped to the regions of futurity with the blessings of my fellow men."[52]

American forces were so uniformly successful in the Mexican War that some presidents attributed this success to divine favor. Andrew Johnson declared, "Our country must have been in the right, or the God of Battles would sometimes have been against us." Although Rutherford Hayes was a critic of the war at the time, he expressed the same view four decades later, claiming, "The hand of God was in the work of adding a number of grand, rich states to our country, with every acre of American soil better as a result."[53]

Numerous presidents considered Union victory in the Civil War another manifestation of Providence. Andrew Johnson began the first presidential message to Congress following the war with this statement: "To express gratitude to God in the name of the people for the preservation of the United States is my first duty in addressing you." In 1908 William Howard Taft declared, "It is difficult not to yield to the conviction that the same Providence [that protected the United States previously] presided over the fate of this country when the terrible struggle caused by the cancer of slavery made necessary such a convulsion as that of the War of Rebellion and was manifested in the presence of Lincoln and Grant to meet the exigencies of that crisis." After the United States' entrance into World War I, Woodrow Wilson told a group of Confederate veterans that he believed God had saved the Union in order to preserve its effectiveness as a champion of liberty in such contests as the Great War. He claimed, "The wisest heart never questions the dealings of Providence because the great long plan, as it unfolds, has a majesty about it and a definiteness of purpose, an elevation of ideal, which we were incapable of conceiving as we tried to work things out with our own short sight and weak strength. . . . We did not know that God was working out in His own way the method by which we should best serve human freedom—by making this nation a great, united, indivisible, indestructible instrument in His hands for the accomplishment of these great things." Two years later, Calvin Coolidge employed Abraham's Lincoln's own biblical style and some biblical imagery to eulogize Lincoln as the divinely appointed savior of the nation: "Five score and ten years ago that Divine Providence which infinite repetition has made only the more a miracle sent into the world a new life, destined to save a nation. No star, no sign, foretold his coming. About his cradle all was poor and mean save only the source of all great men, the love of a wonderful mother." In 1931 Herbert Hoover asserted, "Lincoln was a builder in an epoch of destruction. It was his assignment by Providence to restore the national edifice, so badly shattered in its social and economic structure that it had well-nigh failed. His undying idealism and inflexible resolve builded a new temple of the national soul in which our succeeding generations have since dwelt secure and free and of a richer life." Hoover often employed the archaic word "builded," derived from the King James Bible, when referring to matters he regarded as sacred.[54]

William McKinley considered the emancipation of millions of slaves in the Civil War to be the work of Providence. In 1889 he contended, "[Emancipation was] not the outcome looked for in the beginning. That was not the expectation of the early volunteers. That was not the expectation of the Congress or the President and his Cabinet. Man's purposes were overruled, but not from man came the issue. From Him who is the Sovereign of soul and life came our ordeal of battle, that He might be God and that man might be free."[55]

McKinley also considered the United States' swift and complete victory in the Spanish-American War, a contest over which he presided, an act of Providence. In 1898 he declared, "The faith of a Christian nation recognizes the hand of Almighty God in the ordeal through which we have passed. Divine favor seemed manifest everywhere." Two months later, he claimed,

> How much, indeed, has this nation to be thankful for at this hour! With what reverent gratitude we should express our thankfulness to a divine Providence that has so tenderly cared for the American people! We have been at war with a foreign power. That war ended after one hundred and thirteen days of conflict in the West and East Indies, twelve thousand miles apart; with fifty

thousand of our own soldiers on distant shores, and with twenty thousand sailors and marines afloat; with a loss in army and navy of less than two thousand, and without the loss of a ship or sailor or soldier by capture.

The following year, McKinley added that God had also used the war to reunite the nation in the aftermath of the Civil War. Southerners had contributed as much as Northerners to the United States' military effort and had expressed as fervent a patriotism.[56]

Both Franklin Roosevelt and his successor, Harry Truman, considered the victory of the United States and its allies in World War II to be the product of divine intervention. In 1944, when writing to British Prime Minister Winston Churchill in support of an Allied invasion of Southern France that would supplement the Normandy landings, Roosevelt claimed, "I honestly believe that God will be with us as he has in [Operation] Overlord and in Italy and in North Africa." Five months later, in another message to Churchill, Roosevelt cited an earthquake and tsunami in Japan, which occurred on the third anniversary of the Japanese attack on Pearl Harbor, as further evidence of divine assistance: "Even the Almighty is helping. This magnificent earthquake and tidal wave is a proof." The following year, in his announcement of the dropping of the atomic bomb on Hiroshima, Truman noted, "We may be grateful to Providence that the Germans got the V-1s and V-2s late and in limited quantities and even more grateful that they did not get the atomic bomb at all." Three days later, after ordering the dropping of an atomic bomb on Nagasaki, Truman again expressed his gratitude to God that it was the Allies and not the Axis powers who developed the bomb: "It is an awful responsibility which has come to us. We thank God that it has come to us instead of to our enemies." A week later, following Japan's announcement of surrender, he declared, "[Victory] has come with the help of God, who was with us in the early days of adversity and disaster, and who has now brought us up to this glorious day of triumph." In 1946 he told a group of newspaper editors regarding the recent war: "God blessed us with the greatest set of military leaders that any country in the world ever had in this instance and also gave us 2 years in which to get ready."[57]

George H. W. Bush credited God with the United States' victory in the Cold War. In 1992 he noted, "Tonight our children and our grandchildren will go to their beds untroubled by the fears of nuclear holocaust that haunted two generations of Americans. In our prayers we asked for God's help. I know our family did, and I expect all of you did. We asked for God's help. And now in this shining outcome, in this magnificent triumph of good over evil, we should thank God." Five months later, he said, "In Berlin, like Jericho [Joshua 6:20], the wall came tumbling down. . . . Over the past 3½ years, bayonets have been no match for the righteousness of God. . . . By God's providence, the cold war is over, and America's views prevailed."[58]

The Nation's Accountability to God

Many presidents have believed that while the nation's divine mission to advance the cause of liberty has produced unique blessings, it also has entailed a unique responsibility, and they have thus recognized that failing to carry out this duty properly could result in a severe national punishment. In 1787 John Adams wrote, "The people in America have now the best opportunity and the greatest trust in their hands that Providence ever committed to so small a number since the transgression of the first pair; if they betray their trust, their guilt will merit even greater punishment than other nations have suffered in the indignation of Heaven."[59]

While it was unusual that Adams bypassed biblical Israel as the favorite American precursor and instead traveled all the way back to the Garden of Eden, his fear of divine judgment was not out of the ordinary. Many of the early presidents warned that God might punish the United States for its institution of slavery, which they regarded as a direct violation of the covenant of liberty between the Almighty and the New Israel. If it were true, as these presidents believed, that God had blessed the United States to a unique degree because of its divine mission to advance freedom, it might also be true that in the future. He would judge the nation severely for its gross violation of that very principle, much as God had blessed the original chosen people because of their divine mission to advance ethical monotheism yet had also sent them into captivity when they fell into forms of immorality and idolatry that violated its defining principles.

In *Notes on the State of Virginia* (1782), Thomas Jefferson expressed anxiety that slavery would bring down God's wrath on the United States. In a famous passage later engraved on a panel at the Jefferson Memorial, he asked,

> Can the liberties of a nation be thought secure when we have removed their only firm basis, a conviction in the minds of the people that these liberties are the gift of God? That they are not to be violated but with His wrath? Indeed, I tremble for my country when I reflect that God is just; that His justice cannot sleep forever; that considering numbers, nature, and natural means only, a revolution of the wheel of fortune, an exchange of situation is among possible events; that it may become probable by supernatural interference! The Almighty has no attribute which can take side with us in such a contest.

Note that Jefferson's anxiety was not for himself as a slaveholder but for the nation as a whole and that he fully expected divine retribution to come through natural means. Not generally known for dispensing jeremiads, Jefferson did add a hopeful postscript more in line with his optimistic disposition: "The spirit of the master is abating, that of the slave rising from the dust, his condition mollifying, the way I hope preparing, under the auspices of heaven, for a total emancipation, and that this is disposed, in the order of events, to be with the consent of the masters rather than by their extirpation." Jefferson envisioned "total emancipation" as the inevitable result of the divine will. The only question was whether it would come through peaceful means or by slaughter. A few years later, he marveled,

> What a stupendous, what an incomprehensible machine is man! Who can endure toil, famine, stripes, imprisonment, and death itself in vindication of his own liberty and the next moment be deaf to all those motives whose power supported him through his trial, and inflict on his fellow men a bondage one hour of which is fraught with more misery than ages of that which he rose in rebellion to oppose. But we must await, with patience, the workings of an overruling Providence and hope that it is preparing the deliverance of these, our suffering brethren. When the measure of their tears shall be full, when their groans shall have involved heaven itself in darkness, doubtless, a God of justice will awaken to their distress, and by suffusing light and liberality among their oppressors, or, at length, by His exterminating thunder, manifest His attention to the things of this world, and they are not left to the guidance of a blind fatality.

Jefferson again presented the possibility that divine intervention might take the form of enlightenment rather than destruction, though he believed the latter was still possible.[60]

Abraham Lincoln and James Garfield also feared divine judgment on the nation due to slavery. In 1852 Lincoln declared, "Pharaoh's country was cursed with plagues, and his hosts were drowned in the Red Sea for striving to retain a captive people who had already served them more than four hundred years. May like disasters never befall us!" Three years later, Garfield quoted from Samuel R. Phillips's "Nebraska," a poem that called for a modern-day Daniel to interpret the writing on the wall in Washington, DC, regarding the destruction that slavery was sure to bring upon the nation. In 1859 Garfield declared that, while he did not condone John Brown's violent actions in seeking to bring an end to slavery, he respected "his love of freedom drawn from God's word," adding, "It seems as though God's warning angel would sound through that infatuated assembly [at Brown's hanging] the words of a patriot of other and better days, the words 'I tremble for my country when I reflect that God is just, and his Justice will not always slumber.'" The same year Lincoln warned, "Those who deny freedom to others deserve it not for themselves and, under a just God, cannot long retain it." Five months later, like Garfield, he quoted Jefferson's statement, "I tremble for my country when I remember that God is just," expressing approval regarding the Virginian: "He supposed there was a question of God's eternal justice wrapped up in the enslaving of any race of men, or any man, and that those who did so braved the arm of Jehovah—that when a nation thus dared the Almighty, every friend of that nation had cause to dread His wrath." Lincoln contrasted the alarm of Thomas Jefferson, the founder of the Democratic Party, over the possibility of divine wrath with the indifference of contemporary Democrats, such as his own nemesis, Stephen Douglas. Regarding slavery, Lincoln declared, "Choose ye between Jefferson and Douglas as to what is the true view of this element among us." Lincoln's use of the biblical language "Choose ye" (e.g., Joshua 24:15; "Choose ye this day whom ye will serve") suited his argument regarding divine judgment. His own choice was clear.[61]

Lincoln was one of many Americans who considered the bloody Civil War, which remains by far the costliest war in terms of American lives in the nation's history, the long-feared product of divine wrath produced by slavery. In 1864 he wrote to a Kentucky newspaper editor, "I claim not to have controlled events, but confess plainly that events have controlled me. Now, at the end of three years struggle, the nation's condition is not what either party or any man devised or expected. God alone can claim it. Where it is tending seems plain. If God now wills the removal of a great wrong and wills also that we of the North as well as you of the South shall pay fairly for our complicity in that wrong, impartial history will find therein new cause to attest and revere the justice and goodness of God." The following year, in a famous passage of his second inaugural address, Lincoln reiterated this belief:

> The Almighty has His own purposes. "Woe unto the world because of offences! For it must needs be that offences come, but woe to that man by whom the offence cometh' [Matthew 18:7]!" If we shall suppose that American Slavery is one of those offences which, in the providence of God, must needs come, but which, having continued through His appointed time, He now wills to remove and that He gives to both North and South this terrible war as the woe due to those by whom the offence came, shall we discern therein any departure from those divine attributes which the believers in a Living God always ascribe to Him? Fondly do we hope—fervently do we pray—that this mighty scourge of

war may speedily pass away. Yet, if God wills that it continues until all the wealth piled by the bondsman's two hundred and fifty years of unrequited toil shall be sunk, and until every drop of blood drawn with the lash shall be paid by another drawn with the sword, as was said three thousand years ago, so still it must be said, "The judgments of the Lord are true and righteous altogether [Psalms 19:9]."[62]

Fourteen years after the conclusion of the Civil War, Ulysses Grant implied that the conflict was God's punishment for slavery. He claimed, "I have always believed, and now believe, that nations as well as individuals that act on other principles than those of right and justice receive punishment. The great conflict which we have gone through . . . was a punishment for national sins that had to come sooner or later in some shape, and probably in blood."[63]

The belief in the United States' accountability before God continued long after the Civil War. In his inaugural address in 1889, Benjamin Harrison declared, "God has placed on our head a diadem and has laid at our feet power and wealth beyond definition or calculation. But we must not forget that we take these gifts upon the condition that justice and mercy shall hold the reins of power and that the upward avenues of hope shall be free to all people." The following year, in protest against the disfranchisement of African Americans in the South, William McKinley contended, "God puts no nation in supreme place which will not do supreme duty. God keeps no nation in supreme place which will not perform the supreme duty of the hour, and He will not long prosper that nation which will not protect and defend its weakest citizens." In 1905 Theodore Roosevelt claimed, "Much has been given us, and much will rightfully be expected from us." This was a paraphrase of Jesus's statement in Luke 12:48: "To whom much is given, of him much shall be required." In his inaugural address in 1965, Lyndon Johnson declared, "Under this covenant of justice, liberty, and union, we have become a nation prosperous, great, and mighty. But we have no promise from God that our greatness will endure. . . . If we fail now, then we will have forgotten in abundance what we learned in hardship: that democracy rests on faith, that freedom asks more than it gives, and the judgment of God is harshest on those who are most favored."[64]

As late as 1990, George H. W. Bush reaffirmed the connection between blessing and accountability. He said, "America is not only divinely blessed; America is divinely accountable." Two years later, he claimed, "America will always have a special place in God's heart," but he added the qualifier "as long as He has a special place in ours."[65]

The Restoration of Israel

Beginning in the early twentieth century, American presidents have supported the restoration and survival of the nation of Israel. Much of this support has been based on the belief that this restoration and survival, like the establishment, survival, and prosperity of the new Israel, the United States, is the work of God.

After the British seized Jerusalem from the Turks during World War I (1917), the restoration of an independent Jewish state in the Holy Land became a real prospect for the first time in nearly two millennia. The same year, Woodrow Wilson applauded the Balfour Declaration, which announced the British government's support for the establishment of a Jewish national homeland in the Holy Land. The following year, former president Theodore Roosevelt declared that "the Jews [must be] given Palestine." He then penned two letters in support of the proposal.[66]

Herbert Hoover agreed with Wilson and Roosevelt. In 1929 he called the establishment of a Jewish homeland in Palestine "an inspiring enterprise." Three years later, he wrote to the American Palestine Committee that he would like "to add my expression to the sentiment among our people in favor of the realization of the age-old aspirations of the Jewish people for the restoration of their national homeland." Ten months later, he wrote to the Zionist Organization of America: "I have watched with genuine admiration the steady and unmistakable progress made in the rehabilitation of Palestine, which, desolate for centuries, is now renewing its youth and vitality through the enthusiasm, hard work, and self-sacrifice of the Jewish pioneers who toil there in a spirit of peace and social justice. It is very gratifying to note that many American Jews, Zionists and non-Zionists, have rendered such splendid service to the cause, which merits the sympathy and moral encouragement of everyone." Shortly after the conclusion of World War II in 1945, Hoover proposed the resettlement of "the Arabs from Palestine" in Iraq, noting, "This would clear Palestine completely for a large Jewish emigration and colonization."[67]

In 1939, at a time of Nazi persecution of Jews in Europe, Franklin Roosevelt protested the British decision to limit Jewish immigration to Palestine to a mere seventy-five thousand people over the next five years. Roosevelt considered the decision a violation of the Palestine Mandate that the Allies had given Britain after World War I on the assurance that Palestine would become a Jewish homeland.[68]

Harry Truman was a crucial supporter of the nation of Israel. Two months after the end of World War II, he asked British Prime Minister Clement

Atlee to admit 100,000 Jewish refugees into Palestine, at a time when the British were willing to admit only 1,500 per month. Not coincidentally, 100,000 was approximately the number of Jews in postwar refugee camps in Germany and Austria. The following year, Truman offered "to assume technical and financial responsibility for the transportation of these immigrants from Europe to Palestine." Three months later, Truman wrote to the king of Saudi Arabia, stating that it remained the position of the United States government "that a national home for the Jewish people should be established in Palestine." He added, "It is only natural, therefore, that this Government should favor at this time the entry into Palestine of considerable numbers of displaced Jews in Europe, not only that they may find shelter there, but also that they may contribute their talents and energies to the upbuilding of the Jewish National Home." He wrote to Eleanor Roosevelt, "My sympathy has always been on their side." Truman's chief aide, Clark Clifford, later recalled, "His own reading of ancient history and the Bible made him a supporter of the idea of a Jewish homeland in Palestine, even when others who were sympathetic to the plight of the Jews were talking of sending them to places like Brazil. He did not need to be convinced by Zionists."[69]

Truman played a leading role in the United Nations' decision to partition Palestine and create the nation of Israel in 1947. On May 14, 1948—ironically, the same day of the year that Jamestown, the first permanent English colony in America, was settled in 1607—Israel proclaimed itself a state. A mere eleven minutes later, Truman's press secretary, Charlie Ross, announced the United States' recognition of the new nation. The announcement constituted a stunning rejection by Truman of the advice of the State Department, whose diplomats had been arguing vociferously that the United States should not make such a move due to the danger that the Arabs, who controlled vital oil supplies, might move into the Soviet camp. When the Ashkenazi chief rabbi of Israel, Isaac Halevi Herzog, visited the White House and told Truman, "God put you in your mother's womb so you would be the instrument to bring about the rebirth of Israel after two thousand years," Truman wept. Five months later, he declared, "It is my desire to help build in Palestine a strong, prosperous, free, and independent state. It must be large enough, free enough, and strong enough to make its people self-supporting and secure. . . . What we need now is to help the people of Israel—and they have proved themselves worthy of the best traditions of hardy pioneers. They have created out of the barren desert a modern and efficient state, with the highest standards of Western civilization. They have demonstrated that Israel deserves to take its place in the family of nations." In 1952 he noted, "The growth and progress of the new state of Israel are a source of great satisfaction to me. I had faith in Israel even before it was established. I knew it was based on the love of freedom, which has been the guiding star of the Jewish people since the days of Moses." After noting with pleasure the naming of the village of Kfar Truman in the Holy Land, he prophesied, "Israel can be made the country of milk and honey as it was in the time of Joshua [Joshua 5:6]." Truman repeated this claim in his farewell address the following year.[70]

Truman was only one of many Americans who considered the restoration of Israel a miracle brought about by God in fulfillment of biblical prophecy. Some noted that the Jews were the only people in all of history to be dispersed throughout the world yet still somehow manage not only to retain their identity as a people for nineteen centuries but also to return to their homeland after so extensive a period and restore their nation. Furthermore, it appeared to these Americans that God had prophesied this seemingly miraculous development some 2,500 years ago. In Ezekiel 36:24, 34–35, God says to the Jewish people, "I will take you from the nations, and gather you from all the countries, and bring you into your own land.... The land that was desolate shall be tilled, instead of being the desolation that it was in the sight of all who passed by. And they will say, 'This land that was desolate has become like the garden of Eden; and the waste and desolate and ruined towns are now inhabited and fortified.'" The reference to "all the countries" appears to demonstrate that the prophecy did not refer to the Jews' return from the Babylonian Exile in the sixth century BC but to their return from all over the globe after the 1,900-year diaspora, which began with the Roman destruction of the Great Temple in 70 AD. Furthermore, Ezekiel's prophecy of the transformation of a desert into a paradise was believed to have been fulfilled only recently by modern irrigation. Before the Jewish return to Israel, travel accounts, such as one written by Mark Twain, were unanimous in describing the Holy Land as a wasteland. But after irrigation, even the Negev Desert was producing large quantities of vegetables. Other prophecies were allegedly fulfilled, including Ezekiel 37, which portrays Israel as a field of dry bones supernaturally restored to life by God; Isaiah's prophecy (35:1,7; 43:6; 60:8–10), that Jews from every nation would return, "flying like a cloud," to a blossoming Israel aided by foreign powers; and Jeremiah's prophecy (16:14–15) that Jews would return from "the land of the north," which, in the 1990s, was interpreted as referring to the planeloads of Jews immigrating to Israel from Russia.[71]

Dwight Eisenhower's support for Israel was influenced by his visits to Nazi concentration camps. In 1952 he wrote,

As Commander of the Allied Army during the last war I had the fullest opportunity to observe closely the tragic conditions of the war-ravaged and Nazi-decimated Jewish communities of Europe. It will be one of the enduring satisfactions of my life that I was privileged to lead the forces of the free world which finally crushed the brutal regime of Hitler with its responsibilities for all those unspeakable atrocities. . . . Those forces of the free world saved the remnant of the Jewish people of Europe for a new life and a new hope in the reborn land of Israel. Along with all men of good will, I salute the young state and all who wish it well. I know what great things it has accomplished. I admire the hardiness of its pioneers and the vision and quality of the work of resettlement and reclamation which they are so energetically processing.

Eisenhower's use of the biblical term "remnant," a term used by the prophets to refer to those Jews who returned to a reconstructed Israel after the period of the Babylonian Exile, and his employment of the word "reborn" in reference to Israel are highly significant.[72]

John F. Kennedy also connected modern Israel to the biblical nation. In 1939, after returning from a trip to what was then Palestine, he noted in a letter to his father that Jews viewed Jerusalem "as the capital of their new land of milk and honey." In 1960, following the partial realization of the Zionist dream, he wrote, "It is time that all nations of the world, in the Middle East and elsewhere, realized that Israel is here to stay. Surrounded on every side by violent hate and prejudice, living each day in an atmosphere of constant tension and fear, Israel is certain to survive the present crises and all future crises, and all negotiations between the United States and Arab nations should accept that fact." He added, "Israel is the bright light now shining in the Middle East." He recalled that when he had first visited Palestine, it was "a barren land," but when he returned in 1951, "the transformation that had taken place was hard to believe. For in those twelve years, a nation had been born, a desert had been reclaimed, and the most tragic victims of World War II—the survivors of concentration camps and ghettos—had found a home." He concluded, "The survival and success of Israel and its peaceful acceptance by the other nations of the Middle East is essential. . . . I think it would be the greatest mistake to attempt to appease the Arabs by joining the Soviet Union in the denunciation of Israel."[73]

Lyndon Johnson emphasized the common biblical heritage of the United States and Israel. In 1966 he told Zalman Shazar, the president of Israel, "Our Republic, like yours, was nurtured by the philosophy of the ancient Hebrew teachers who taught mankind the principles of morality, social justice, and universal peace. . . . God has showered our land with abundance.

The sharing of our blessings with others is a value we hold in common with Israel."[74]

The following year, Johnson acted to protect Israel from a possible Soviet invasion. Angry that Israel was not only defeating their Arab allies in the Six-Day War but also refusing to heed Soviet calls for a cease-fire, the Soviets threatened military action against the nation. In response Johnson ordered the Sixth Fleet to position itself within fifty miles of the Mediterranean coast. Johnson's move ended any Russian consideration of war against Israel.[75]

In a speech to the B'nai B'rith in 1968, Johnson alluded to biblical prophecies that foretold the restoration of Israel. He quoted Isaiah 11:12: "And He shall set up an ensign for the nations and shall assemble the outcasts of Israel and gather together the dispersed of Judah from all the four corners of the earth." He added, "Most, if not all of you, have very deep ties with the land and with the people of Israel, as do I, for my Christian faith sprang from yours. The Bible stories are woven into my childhood memories as the gallant struggle of modern Jews to be free of persecution is also woven into our souls."[76]

Like other American presidents, Johnson often heard about the need to support Israel from devout Christian relatives. One month after he had assumed the presidency, his Aunt Jessie, a plainspoken Texan, said to his brother Sam, "I want you to tell Lyndon something else for me, Sam Houston. Tell him to stick with the Jews and never do anything against them. Now, they're God's chosen people, you know. Says so right in the Bible, and don't you ever doubt it. The best thing Harry Truman ever did was create the state of Israel. . . . So, you tell Lyndon never to let the Jews down. They're the best people to have on your side. In politics or anything else."[77]

In 1970, when Syrian tanks poured into Jordan as a possible prelude to an invasion of Israel, Johnson's successor, Richard Nixon, again sent the Sixth Fleet into the eastern Mediterranean. There was no invasion. Three years later, during the Yom Kippur War, Nixon airlifted crucial arms to Israel, assuring congressional leaders, "We will not let Israel go down the tubes." Fearing the Arab reaction, the Defense Department wanted to dispatch only three planeloads of arms, but Nixon told Secretary of State Henry Kissinger, "Use every one we have. Tell them to send everything that can fly." Consisting of thirty planes, the ensuing operation exceeded the Berlin Airlift of 1948–1949 and proved crucial to Israeli victory in the war. Immediately after the war, Nixon requested that Congress provide Israel with $2.2 billion in military aid to replace its combat losses. The following year, he became the first American president to visit Israel while in office.[78]

The recipient of numerous awards from Jewish organizations for his staunch support of Israel, Gerald Ford noted in 1971, "I for one am proud of the part our countrymen played in the realization of the Zionist dream and of all the United States has done to strengthen the State of Israel and ensure its progress." Two years later, he denounced Soviet efforts to halt the immigration of Russian Jews to Israel, saying, "Every Jew who wishes to immigrate to Israel should be free to do so. The words of Genesis are just as meaningful today as they were 4,000 years ago when the Lord God said to Abraham [12:1–2]: 'Go forth from your country . . . to the land that I will show you. And I will make of you a great nation.'" Six months later, as vice president, Ford quoted Isaiah 58:6–8, claiming that the mission of Israel was "to loose the bands of wickedness, to undo the heavy burdens, and to let the oppressed go free . . . to deal thy bread to the hungry and . . . bring the poor that are cast out to thy house. . . . Then shall thy light break forth as the morning." Ford continued, "As you are well aware, the historical parallels between our age and the age of Isaiah are striking. Then, as now, for example, the Jewish people were returning to Zion to rebuild their nation." Ford then compared Isaiah's words to the famous poem on the pedestal of the Statue of Liberty, "The New Colossus" by Emma Lazarus, a Jewish woman who organized relief efforts for Jewish refugees from Russia in the nineteenth century. The poem begins, "Give me your tired, your poor." Ford concluded, "I think those words on the Statue of Liberty capture the essential spirit of both America and Israel—almost uniquely among the nations of the world—havens for the persecuted, the oppressed. And it is because of this unique common tradition, I believe, that the bonds between America and Israel are so very close." In 1974, as President Nixon and Secretary of State Kissinger journeyed to the Middle East to negotiate peace, Vice President Ford connected their mission to past events recorded in the Bible: "I feel it appropriate to observe that our president and his secretary of state are on a sacred mission in that region where the Son of God offered the Sermon on the Mount. It is an area where those kindred peoples, the Jews and Arabs, have suffered the torment of relentless wars and where the superpowers of the world have come to the brink of Armageddon. If peace can now be brought forth from the cruel carnage of so many years, who is to say that a divine presence is not again involved?"[79]

Jimmy Carter was excited to visit Israel with his wife, Rosalynn, while governor of Georgia in 1973, noting that this was "the land of the Bible, which we had studied since early childhood." The couple walked the streets of Old Jerusalem before dawn and visited Bethlehem, Nazareth, the Sea of Galilee, Cana, Capernaum, the Mount of Olives, the Garden Tomb, Jericho,

Mount Carmel, the Mount of the Beatitudes, and other biblical sites. Carter even startled Israeli Prime Minister Golda Meir by expressing concern about Israel's spiritual health, noting that he had seen only two worshippers at a synagogue service he had attended. Carter noted pointedly, "During biblical times, the Israelites triumphed when they were close to God and were defeated when unfaithful." In 1978 he declared, "Out of the ashes of the Holocaust was born the State of Israel, a promise of refuge and security and of return, at last, to the Biblical land from which the Jews were driven so many hundreds of years ago." He added significantly, "The establishment of the nation of Israel is a fulfillment of biblical prophecy." The following year, he addressed the Israeli Knesset, saying, "We share the heritage of the Bible, the worship of God." In 1982 he recalled, "The Judeo-Christian ethic and study of the Bible were bonds between Jews and Christians which had always been part of my life. I also believed very deeply that the Jews who had survived the Holocaust deserved their own nation and that they had a right to live in peace among their neighbors. I considered this homeland for the Jews to be compatible with the teachings of the Bible, hence ordained by God. These moral and religious beliefs made my commitment to the security of Israel unshakable." Three years later, he wrote, "For me there is no way to approach or enter Israel without thinking first about the Bible and the history of the land and its people. The names and images have long been an integral part of my life as a Christian. . . . It is rare indeed to find the past so intertwined with the immediate present, not just for historians and theologians in their classrooms and studies but for statesmen in the halls of government and military commanders on the field of battle." In a book called *The Blood of Abraham*, which is about the Middle East peace process, Carter noted that both the Jews and the Arabs were descended from Abraham, the former from Isaac, the latter from Ishmael. He concluded the book with the observation that too much of the blood of Abraham "has been spilled in grasping for the inheritance of the revered patriarch of the Middle East." Like the blood of Abel (Genesis 4:10), "the spilled blood in the Holy Land still cries out to God—an anguished cry for peace."[80]

In 1979 Ronald Reagan referred to the restoration of Israel as "carrying out a centuries old Bible prophecy." Two years later, he again referred to biblical prophecies regarding the restoration when speaking to Israeli Prime Minister Menachem Begin: "The prophet Ezekiel [36:35] spoke of a new age—'when land that was desolate has become like the Garden of Eden and the waste and ruined cities are now inhabited.' We see how miraculously you transformed and made the desert bloom." In 1985 Reagan called the restoration of Israel "the dream of generations, the sure sign of God's hand in history." Regarding the immigration of Ethiopian Jews to Israel, he said, "This was truly God's work." Thus, it is hardly surprising that in 1990, Reagan wrote, "No conviction I've ever held has been stronger than my belief that the United States must ensure the survival of Israel."[81]

As vice president in 1985, George H. W. Bush helped lead the effort, entitled Operation Joshua, to rescue eight hundred Ethiopian Jews stranded in Sudan and transport them to Israel. Five years later, as president, he applauded the sudden success of a decades' long effort made by a series of American presidents to persuade the Soviet government to allow Russian Jews to immigrate to Israel, tying the occasion to biblical precedent. Bush noted,

> "Let my people go [Exodus 5:1]." Those were the words of Moses nearly 4,000 years ago, when the Israelites took the first step on the march from captivity to freedom.... The modern exodus is a great event for all who delight in human freedom. The United States has worked hard to open up this lifeline, and we will continue to do everything necessary to make it possible for Soviet Jews to get to Israel, including continuing to press for direct and indirect flights. We are glad that so many will celebrate Seder in Israel, and we're going to keep working so that many more can join them.

In 1991 he facilitated the sudden departure of another fourteen thousand Ethiopian Jews from their civil war–torn nation to Israel, an airlift called Operation Solomon.[82]

Bill Clinton often connected the peace agreements between Israel and its adversaries that he brokered to the Old Testament. In a 1994 address to the Parliament of Jordan, he quoted Deuteronomy 30:19 from "Moses' farewell address to the children of Israel": "I have set before you life and death, blessings and curses. Choose life so that you and your descendants may live." He added, "Today the people of Jordan and the people of Israel have reached across the Jordan River. They have chosen life." Jordan had just become the second Arab nation to recognize the nation of Israel. The next day, in an address to the Israeli Knesset, Clinton recalled a trip to Israel he had made with his pastor, Worley Oscar Vaught of Immanuel Baptist Church of Little Rock, fourteen years earlier: "I relived the history of the Bible, of your scriptures and mine, and I formed a bond with my pastor. Later, when he became desperately ill, he said he thought I might one day become President." Vaught, who was dying of bone cancer, told Clinton, "If you abandon Israel, God will never forgive you," and "It is God's will that Israel, the biblical home of the people of Israel, continue forever and ever." The following year, during the funeral of Prime Minister Yitzhak Rabin, who was assassinated by a zealot for signing a peace agreement with the Palestinian Liberation Organization, Clinton noted, "This week, Jews all around the world are studying the Torah portion in which God tests the faith of Abraham, patriarch of the Jews and the Arabs [Genesis 22]. He commands Abraham to sacrifice Yitzhak [Isaac in English]. 'Take your son, the one you love, Yitzhak.' As we all know, as Abraham in loyalty to God was about to kill his son, God spared Yitzhak." Clinton continued, "Now, God tests our faith even more terribly, for he has taken our Yitzhak. But Israel's covenant with God for freedom, for tolerance, for security, for peace, that covenant must hold. That covenant was Prime Minister Rabin's life's work. Now we must make it his lasting legacy. His spirit must live on in us." In 1996 Clinton told a group of Tel Aviv students, "Israel is proof of your extraordinary resilience. Here in modern times, an ancient people have performed a miracle, forged a great and prosperous democracy, caused the desert to bloom, and given rise to great cities." The use of the word "miracle," combined with the reference to the blooming of the desert, clearly harkened back to Old Testament prophecies regarding the restoration of Israel. Two years later, at a reception celebrating the golden anniversary of Israel, Clinton declared regarding the biblical nation's restoration in 1948:

> The children of Abraham and Sarah, survivors of 2,000 years of exile and persecution, were home at last and free at last. For its founders, the Israeli State was, however, about even more than securing a haven for the Jewish people after centuries of suffering and wandering. Isaiah prophesied that Israel would become "a light unto the nations [49:6]," and David Ben-Gurion and his allies set out to make that prophecy come true by establishing a society of light, embracing what Ben-Gurion called the higher virtues of truth, justice, and compassion. . . . Hebrew, once the language only of sacred text, [is] now the voice of an Israeli renaissance.[83]

George W. Bush also saw God's hand in the success of Israel. In 2001 he stated, "I believe with the Psalmist that the Lord God of Israel neither slumbers nor sleeps [Psalms 121:4]." For this reason, Bush claimed, "At my first meeting of my National Security Council, I told them that a top foreign policy priority of my administration is the safety and security of Israel." In commemorating the sixtieth anniversary of Israel in 2008, Bush told the Knesset, "You've raised a modern society in the promised land, a light unto the nations that preserves the legacy of Abraham and Isaac and Jacob."[84]

Although, like some other presidents, Barack Obama could be critical of Israeli actions, in 2008, he faulted his former pastor, Jeremiah Wright, for viewing "the conflicts in the Middle East as rooted primarily in the actions of stalwart allies like Israel instead of emanating from the perverse and hateful ideologies of radical Islam." Obama also connected the biblical past to the Israeli present. In 2013, in a speech at Tel Aviv, he declared,

> More than 3,000 years ago, the Jewish people lived here, tended the land here, prayed to God here. And after centuries of exile and persecution, unparalleled in the history of man, the founding of the Jewish State of Israel was a rebirth, a redemption unlike any in history. Today, the sons of Abraham and the daughters of Sarah are fulfilling the dream of the ages to be masters of their own fate in their own sovereign state. And just as we have for these past 65 years, the United States is proud to stand with you as your strongest ally and your greatest friend.

Sixteen days later, still marveling at his visit to the Holy Land, Obama claimed at the Easter Prayer Breakfast, "There are few experiences more powerful or more humbling than visiting that sacred earth. It brings Scripture to life." Regarding Jesus, he added, "For Christians to walk where He walked and see what He saw are blessed moments."[85]

In 2018, on Israel's seventieth anniversary, Donald Trump became the first president to follow through on the continually broken promise to move the American embassy from Tel Aviv to Jerusalem. Trump based the decision on Israeli sovereignty, declaring, "Israel is a sovereign nation with the right like every other sovereign nation to determine its own capital." But it is significant that in the same statement, he referred to Jerusalem as "the capital the Jewish people established in ancient times." While Trump admitted two years later that he had made the decision "for the evangelicals," he may well have shared their sense that Israel had an ancient claim on the city based on the Bible. Trump's son-in-law and trusted advisor, Jared Kushner, is Jewish, his daughter Ivanka is a Jewish convert, and their children are being raised Jewish. In 2020 Trump was instrumental in bringing about the Abraham Accords between Israel and the United Arab Emirates (UAE), rewarding the UAE for becoming the third Arab nation to recognize Israel with a $23 billion arms deal.[86]

As we have seen, the restoration of Israel did not cause modern American presidents to abandon the deeply ingrained habit of referring to the United States' special status as the new Israel. Rather than interpreting the restoration of Israel as marking the end of the American mission—a returning of God's baton to the original chosen people—American presidents pivoted to embrace the view that both the United States and Israel were chosen nations with varying but interlocking missions and destinies.

CHAPTER 8

Faith, Morality, and the Survival of the Republic

In addition to believing in a God who intervenes in earthly affairs, especially to advance the cause of liberty through the United States, most presidents have believed in the excellence of Christian morality and in the necessity of faith and morality (defined largely in Judeo-Christian terms) to the survival and success of any republic. Not only have they considered piety essential to the nation's retention of God's favor, but they have also believed that popular virtue, which is vital to the survival and success of all republics, depends on a widespread belief in an omniscient God who rewards virtue and punishes vice.

The Excellence of Christian Ethics

Most presidents have praised Christian ethics, with some even going so far as to claim it is superior to all other moral codes. What these presidents have valued most about Christianity is its emphasis on humility, charity, and forgiveness.

Most presidents have placed a high value on the Christian virtue of humility. While classical heroes like Achilles and Odysseus were an exceedingly vain lot, constantly boasting about their exploits, Christians considered pride the greatest sin, constituting a form of blasphemy. It was the primordial sin, the sin of the devil, who aimed at equality with God (Isaiah 14:13–14), and the sin of Adam and Eve, who believed that by eating the forbidden fruit, they would become equal to God (Genesis 3:5). The New Testament taught that God had not only lowered Himself to become a man but had been born in a stable as a poor carpenter's son. What right to vanity had any mere human? In the Sermon on the Mount, Jesus declared, "Blessed are the meek, for they will inherit the earth [Matthew 5:5]." Paul commanded, "Do not become proud but stand in awe [Romans 11:20]."

Steeped in a Christian culture that emphasized humility, the early presidents' modesty led them to regard the egotism of their own Greek and Roman heroes with embarrassment. Hence, John Adams was at pains to defend his hero Cicero against the charge of vanity, a quality that few Romans would have considered a vice. Adams's need to Christianize Cicero by attributing modesty to him was based on a combination of reverence for the Roman icon and Christian discomfort with his vanity.[1]

Thomas Jefferson valued Christian humility as well. Although Jefferson approved Epicurus's four cardinal virtues—prudence, temperance, fortitude, and justice (a list Epicurus derived from Plato)—he also contrasted the Christian moral code of "humility, innocence, and simplicity of manners, neglect of riches, [and] absence of worldly ambition and honors" favorably with the more prideful classical code.[2]

John Quincy Adams shared Jefferson's emphasis on humility. In a letter to his son George in 1811, Adams identified it as one of the chief qualities that made Christianity superior to other ethical systems. He noted that "meekness and lowliness of Spirit" are "commanded in express terms by Jesus Christ," adding regarding Christian ethics, "As principles of morality, they are not only different from the maxims of every other known system of ethics but in direct opposition to them." Prideful classical virtues "only serve to shew forth in brighter evidence the unrivalled superiority of the moral code of the Bible."[3]

Jimmy Carter considered humility an essential Christian virtue. After rededicating his life to Christ in 1967, he "recognized much more clearly my own failures, fallibilities, and sinfulness," explaining, "I'm not better than other people but just have received the special blessing of God because He loves me through Jesus Christ." In 1976 he referred to John 13:4–17, saying, "One time when His disciples were arguing among themselves about who was the greatest, Christ got on his knees and said, 'I'm just a servant,' and He washed the disciple's feet." If Christ Himself was humble, what justified the arrogance of anyone else? (In ancient times the job of washing feet was reserved for the lowliest slave, and on this occasion, Jesus even washed the feet of Judas, whom he knew was about to betray him.) Four months later, Carter's confession that he had "lusted after women in my heart" created a stir, with most people missing his point, which is that he did not consider himself morally superior to anyone else. Carter said, "What Christ taught about most was pride, that one person should never think he was any better than anybody else."[4]

Ronald Reagan was famous for his humility, a value he had learned from his mother, Nelle. In 1981 he took the oath of office on her Bible, on the inside front cover of which she had penned the claim that pride disqualified one for divine service: "You can be too big for God to use, but you cannot be too small." Furthermore, Reagan kept on his desk in the Oval Office a sign that read, "There is no limit to what a man can do or where he can go if he doesn't mind who gets the credit."[5]

George H. W. Bush's pious mother taught him humility. She often admonished him, "Don't be talking about yourself," or "There are two many 'Is' in that sentence." Thus, more than half of the ten pieces of advice that Bush dispensed to young people in 2003 concerned humility. These items included: "2. Don't blame others for your setbacks. 3. When things go well, always give credit to others. 4. Don't talk all the time. Listen to your friends and mentors and learn from them. 5. Don't brag about yourself. Let others point out your virtues, your strong points. . . . 7. Nobody likes an overbearing big shot. 8. As you succeed, be kind to people. Thank those who helped you along the way." So great was Bush's humility that it sometimes reached absurd heights. To his daughter Dorothy, he expressed the concern that the biography of him that she was writing would be "too much about me."[6]

Some presidents' humility was the product of another biblical influence: their belief in Providence. Brissot de Warville wrote regarding George Washington, "His modesty is astonishing to a Frenchman. He speaks of the American War and of his victories as of things in which he had no direction." Washington's humility was the product of his self-conception as a Moses or a David, whose victories were really the work of God. Abraham Lincoln possessed a similar self-conception. When he entered Richmond two days after its capture by Union forces, he was followed by a throng of rapturous former slaves who viewed him as the Messiah. One elderly man exclaimed, "Glory, hallelujah!" and knelt at his feet. Lincoln admonished him gently, "Don't kneel to me. That is not right. You must kneel to God only and thank Him for the liberty you will hereafter enjoy. I am but God's humble instrument."[7]

Most presidents have also praised Christianity for its promotion of charity. It was largely on this basis that Thomas Jefferson considered Jesus the greatest ethical philosopher in history. In Jefferson's famous dialogue between the head and heart, the Christian heart informs the Epicurean head that happiness is not "the mere absence of pain" and that the warmth of friendship is a necessary comfort in life. After reminding his head of the numerous times in which it has chosen safety over aiding those in need, his heart concludes, "In short, my friend, as far as my recollection serves me, I do not know that I ever did a good thing on your suggestion, or a dirty one without it." Here we catch a glimpse of why Jefferson's Christian morality, with its emphasis on loving others, was more essential to his emotional health than Greek philosophy, which merely taught the avoidance of self-injury and injury to others. Jefferson called Jesus's ethical teachings "the most sublime and benevolent code of morals which has ever been offered to man." In 1803 he claimed regarding Jesus: "His natural endowments [were] great, his life correct and innocent. He was meek, benevolent, patient, firm, disinterested, and of the sublimest eloquence." Jefferson referred to "the peculiar superiority of the system of Jesus above all others," especially "in inculcating universal philanthropy, not only to kindred and friends, to neighbors and countrymen, but to all mankind, gathering all into one family under the bonds of love, charity, peace, common wants, and common aids." In 1816 Jefferson wrote of his own compilation of Jesus's ethical teachings, taken from the Gospels: "A more beautiful or precious morsel of ethics I have never seen; it is a document in proof that I am a real Christian, that is to say, a disciple of the doctrines of Jesus." He approved Jesus's teaching "to love our neighbors as ourselves and to do good to all men." Then he added, "It is the innocence of His character, the purity and sublimity of His moral precepts, the eloquence of His inculcations, the beauty of the apologues in which He conveys them that I so much admire." Jefferson's friend and ally James Madison, normally reticent in expressing his religious beliefs, was probably also thinking of Christianity's emphasis on charity when he called it "the best and purest religion" in 1833.[8]

John Adams claimed, "The Christian Religion as I understand it is the best," teaching the Golden Rule and love of neighbor. He declared, "We must come to the Principles of Jesus. But when will all Men and all nations do as they would be done by? Forgive all injuries and love their Enemies as themselves?" After praising *The Golden Verses of Pythagoras*, with its maxims on the sanctity of oaths, the respect due to parents, affection for friends, and connection to mankind, Adams nevertheless added, "How dark, mean, and meagre are these Golden Verses, however celebrated and really curious, in comparison with the Sermon on the Mount and the Psalms of David or the Decalogue!" He agreed with Jefferson that Christianity was "the most sublime and benevolent" system known to man. He concluded, "The Ten Commandments and The Sermon on the Mount contain my Religion."[9]

John Adams's son, John Quincy, was an even greater classical scholar than his father, yet he was just as emphatic in declaring the superiority of

Christian morality to Greco-Roman paganism and philosophy. In 1811 he listed benevolence, along with piety and humility, as a distinctive Christian virtue: "The love of our neighbors is very forcibly taught in the Old Testament, but to teach it more effectually was the special object of Christ's mission upon Earth." Adams then quoted Romans 13:10 and John 13:34 in support of the "new commandment" of sacrificial love. In 1813 he wrote that, although the philosophies of Plato and Cicero were laudable in many respects, "Nothing can stand in comparison with the genuine doctrines of Christianity in their application to the pursuit of happiness." For instance, in the person of Jesus, Christianity provided a perfect ethical model that was absent from the classics. In an 1816 speech to the Society of Friends of Foreigners in Distress in London, he declared, "The object of your labors is the first and noblest of moral and Christian virtues—charity; charity in its most extensive sense; charity not confined to one language, one religion, or one country, but expansive as the globe and universal as the blessings of Providence."[10]

Andrew Jackson also considered charity a distinctive Christian duty. In 1828, when Jackson was running for president, a stranger dying of tuberculosis arrived at the Hermitage unexpectedly and for no apparent reason other than that he knew Jackson's name. Rather than turn the man away, Jackson saw to it that the man was cared for at his home until he passed peacefully. Jackson explained, "Humanity compelled me to take him in & tend to the distressed, all that a good Samaritan could do." Five years later, Jackson wrote to his son regarding need: "When you have the means, relieve it, and providence will smile upon the act, provided it is done in the way pointed out by our saviour in his sermon on the mount, which I beg you to read. You will find it recorded in the fifth and sixth chapters of Matthew." In 1835 he wrote to his nephew, "I rejoice at your temporal prosperity. May it continue, but remember all these temporal blessings ought to make us more and more thankful to that kind providence from whom they all flow and ought to induce us to use them as blessings, and where charity presents itself, never to withhold relief from it. This is what is required of us by Him who gives and bestows wealth upon us."[11]

Jackson's protégé James K. Polk agreed. Although appalled by the numbers of people who came to the executive mansion to beg for money after word got out that Polk had helped a destitute man, he remained charitable, for he considered it "a Christian duty to relieve the wants of the needy." For this same reason, he contributed to a Presbyterian orphanage in 1847.[12]

Abraham Lincoln argued that slavery was the antithesis of Christian charity. In 1858 he attacked slaveholders at what they considered their strongest point, their claim that Africans were intellectually inferior. Lincoln reasoned, "Suppose it is true that the negro is inferior to the white in the gifts of nature; is it not the exact reverse [of] justice that the white should, for that reason, take from the negro any part of the little which has been given him? 'Give to him that is needy [Ephesians 4:28]' is the Christian rule of charity, but 'Take from him that is needy' is the rule of slavery."[13]

In addressing his fellow congregants at the consecration of Grace Memorial Reformed Church in Washington in 1903, Theodore Roosevelt emphasized the Christian duty of charity. He declared, "This church is consecrated to the service of the Lord, and we can serve Him by the way we serve our fellow men. This church is consecrated to service and duty. It was written of old that 'By their fruits ye shall know them [Matthew 7:16]'; and we can show the faith that is in us, we can show the sincerity of our devotion, by the fruits we bring forth." Roosevelt stressed the obligation of charity toward immigrants: "I feel that we should be peculiarly watchful over them because of our own history, because we or our fathers came here under like conditions. Now that we have established ourselves, let us see to it that we stretch out the hand of help, the hand of brotherhood, toward the new-comers. . . . No more important work can be done by our people: important to the cause of Christianity; important to the cause of true national life and greatness here in our own land." Eight years later, he declared, "Our success in striving to help our fellow men, and therefore to help ourselves, depends largely upon our success as we strive, with whatever shortcomings, with whatever failures, to lead our lives in accordance with the great ethical principles laid down in the life of Christ and in the New Testament writings which seek to expound and apply His teachings."[14]

Woodrow Wilson agreed that Christianity's emphasis on charity was one of the chief reasons for its superiority over other religions. In 1898 he claimed, "It is the most tender and unselfish of all religions, for no one who is a true lover of Christ thinks first of himself." Two years later, he contended that Christianity "has brought to the world through the Bible humanity, justice, higher civilization, and love." In 1923 he emphasized that Christianity extended beyond what most people called justice: "By justice the lawyer generally means the prompt, fair, and open application of impartial rules; but we call ours a Christian civilization, and a Christian conception of justice must be higher. It must include sympathy and helpfulness and a willingness to forego self-interests in order to promote the welfare, happiness, and contentment of others and of the community as a whole. This is what our age is blindly feeling after in its reaction against what it deems the too great selfishness of the capitalist system."[15]

Herbert Hoover also urged charity as a Christian obligation. Near the height of the Great Depression, in 1931, he contended, "This civilization and this great complex which we call American life is builded and can alone survive upon the translation into individual action of that fundamental philosophy announced by the Savior 19 centuries ago. Part of our national suffering today is from failure to observe these primary yet inexorable laws of human relationship." The following day, he claimed, "We are coming to our national thanksgiving festival, but we cannot fitly give thanks to the Father of us all if we close our eyes to our brother whom we see to be in need. Hearts that are grateful toward God must not be hard toward their fellow men. We are all of us His children and must now bear ourselves toward our brothers as His children should. Thus only may we look for His 'Well done [Matthew 25:21]!'" In 1938 Hoover warned that Nazism "represents the extinction of pity and mercy, which Christianity gave the world."[16]

Hoover contended that the Bible mandated voluntary private charity, not government confiscation and redistribution of wealth. In 1931 he declared, "Modern society cannot survive with the defense of Cain, 'Am I my brother's keeper [Genesis 4:9]?' No governmental action, no economic doctrine, no economic plan or project can replace that God-imposed responsibility of the individual man and woman to their neighbors. That is a vital part of the very soul of a people." Eighteen years later, the former president noted regarding the good Samaritan, "He did not enter into governmental or philosophical discussion. It is said when he saw the helpless man, 'He had compassion on him. . . . He bound his wounds . . . and took care of him [Luke 10:33–34].' That is your mission." Hoover contrasted the spiritual benefits of voluntary private charity, which produced a feeling of generosity in the giver and of gratitude in the recipient, with government redistribution of wealth, which generated resentment in those whose wealth was confiscated and an entitlement mentality in the recipients. He declared, "Those who serve secure in return untold spiritual benefits. The day when we decide that the Government is our brother's keeper, that is the day that personal responsibility for our brother has been lost."[17]

During and after both world wars, Hoover was tireless in leading global relief efforts, campaigns he consistently promoted by appealing to Christian charity. In 1940, when helping to organize a relief effort for Poland, a victim of Nazi aggression, he claimed that even amidst a Great Depression, "the American people earnestly wish that we as a Christian people and as a free people should not stand with a surplus of food and see other people in the world die for the want of it." Eight months later, when attempting to rally aid for the devastated populations of Europe, he declared,

One of the major distinctions of the Christian faith is mercy and compassion. The parable of the Samaritan has played a large part in the moral foundations of all these nations and has a live hold upon the hearts of their people and our people. . . . We cannot as a Christian nation dismiss our concern that some solution is found by which they may be saved. And the parable of the Samaritan has pungent implications other than the compassion of the Samaritan alone. Perhaps some will remember the condemnation, which has echoed over the centuries, of the priest and the Levite who passed by on the other side [Luke 10:31–32].

In 1948 Hoover expressed great pride in the United States' leadership in global aid: "We could point to an advancement of the spirit of Christian compassion such as the world has never seen, and prove it by the tons of food and clothes and billions of dollars we have made as gifts in saving hundreds of millions from famine and governments from collapse." The following year, he contended, "The world is in the grip of a death struggle between the philosophy of Christ and that of Hegel and Marx. The philosophy of Christ is the philosophy of compassion. The outstanding spiritual distinction of our civilization from all others is compassion." Then in 1954 he declared, "The Sermon on the Mount established the transcendent concept of compassion and good will among men. There was profound confirmation of the validity of religious faith when compassion defeated the scourges of famine and pestilence which were inevitable after the two great world wars, even to the extent of famine relief to the Communists."[18]

Hoover practiced what he preached. After starting as a lowly mining engineer and becoming a wealthy global investor, he left behind the prospect of untold riches in the private sector to head international relief efforts during World War I, subsequently serving in various public offices. In these capacities Hoover paid his own expenses and never accepted any payment for personal use for his services. His salaries as secretary of commerce and as president were deposited in a fund that was disbursed to charities, to aides who needed additional pay, and to expert personnel whose services were not covered by official budgets. Likewise, he donated all the money he earned from books and speeches to charity.[19]

Although Hoover's successor, Franklin Roosevelt, disagreed with him about the nature and extent of the government's proper role in American life, he also asserted the Christian duty of private charity. In his acceptance speech for nomination by the Democratic Party in 1936, he cited 1 Corinthians 13:13 on the duties of "faith, hope, and charity." He added, "Charity literally translated from the original [Greek] means love, the love that understands, that does not merely share the wealth of the giver, but in true sympathy and wisdom helps men to help themselves." Four years later, he declared, "The spirit of unselfish service personified by the life and the teachings of Christ makes appeal to the inner conscience and hope of every man and every woman in every part of the earth. It transcends in the ultimate all lines of race, of habitat, or nation. It lives in the midst of war, of slavery, of conquest. It survives prohibitions and decrees and force. It is an unquenchable Spring of Promise to humanity. . . . We still believe in the Golden Rule for all mankind."[20]

Harry Truman touted Christian benevolence as it is illustrated in the Sermon on the Mount. In promoting a charitable campaign in 1947, he declared, "In our generous impulses we should follow the admonition of St. Matthew's Gospel. Our Lord, bidding us to aid and comfort our stricken neighbor, whoever he may be, spoke words as true today as when he uttered them more than nineteen hundred years ago: 'Inasmuch as ye have done it unto one of the least of my brethren, ye have done it unto me [Matthew 25:40].'" Three months later, Truman told the American people that just as Jesus was born in a stable, "for many of our brethren in Europe and Asia this too will be a homeless Christmas." He added, "At this point in the world's history, the words of St. Paul have greater significance than ever before. He said [1 Corinthians 13:13]: 'And now abideth faith, hope, charity, these three; but the greatest of these is charity.' We believe this. We accept it as a basic principle of our lives. The great heart of the American people has been moved to compassion by the needs of those in other lands who are cold and hungry. We have supplied a part of their needs, and we shall do more. In this, we are maintaining the American tradition." In 1960 the Judeo-Christian principle of charity prompted Truman to claim, "The moral code that is in the Old and New Testaments is needed by all mankind. . . . The moral code set forth in the Bible is unequalled."[21]

Dwight Eisenhower agreed. In a 1960 dinner for the National Conference of Catholic Charities, he declared regarding charity: "This responsibility is not laid upon us by any constitutional or legal mandate. Our belief that men are brothers in divine origin and destiny is a part of our religious heritage that reaches back to the hills of Galilee and imposes upon each of us a spiritually rooted obligation."[22]

John F. Kennedy continued the practice, begun by Franklin Roosevelt and others, of partially redefining the individual duty of charity emphasized in the Bible as a collective obligation to aid the poor through government redistribution of wealth. In 1963 Kennedy called for a federal program to provide medical insurance for the elderly, which was the genesis of Medicare.

He declared, "'Cast me not off in the time of old age,' says the Psalmist [Psalms 71:9], and we intend to see to it that in modern times no American is forgotten or ill-treated or cast off by his country in his time of old age."[23]

As the chief architect of the greatest expansion of government in American history, Kennedy's successor, Lyndon Johnson, highlighted this reinterpretation of Christian duty. In advocating the Great Society programs in 1964, he declared,

> From our Jewish and Christian heritage, we draw the image of the God of all mankind, who will judge His children not by their prayers and by their pretensions but by their mercy to the poor and their understanding of the weak. We cannot cancel that strain and then claim to speak as a Christian society. To visit the widow and the fatherless in their affliction is still pure religion and undefiled [James 1:27]. I tremble for this Nation. I tremble for our people if at the time of greatest prosperity, we turn our back on the moral obligations of our deepest faith.

Two years later, when defending Social Security and Medicare, Johnson contended, "The Bible tells us to 'honor thy father and thy mother [Exodus 20:12].' It enjoins us to 'honor the face of the old man [Leviticus 19:32].' We have not always been true to that trust. Too often we have ignored our older Americans—too often we have condemned them to live out their lives in want." Nevertheless, like his Democratic predecessors, Johnson did not believe that government action obviated the individual duty of charity, both at home and abroad. At a commencement address in 1965, Johnson declared, "When the time of judgment comes, it will be no excuse to say that they were far away, or their language was strange, or their color was different, or I did not know their names. . . . You must give the hours of your life, and the fruits of your learning, and the courage of your spirit, and the substance of your home to those in need in every continent of the earth. You might, in the words of the Bible, 'Let your light so shine before men that they may see your good works [Matthew 5:16].'"[24]

Gerald Ford agreed that charity was a fundamental Christian obligation. As early as 1950, Congressman Ford declared, "The parables of the Bible, with their lessons of humanity and generosity, have been taught us with a very definite purpose in view. These implement 'conscience'—Christian conscience if you will." In a different speech that year, Ford argued that Americans' willingness to support the federal government's increased expenditures on foreign aid directly stemmed from a century of experience with private donations to foreign lands via Christian missionaries: "It was the churches which showed us how, and led us to see that this kind of thing, like all good and generous Christian giving, brings back a blessing on the giver too, sometimes a blessing so pronounced that a cynic would call the whole procedure selfish!"[25]

Jimmy Carter continued his Democratic predecessors' practice of conflating private charity and government programs under the heading of Christian obligation. In 1980 he claimed, "We are also fighting to care for the poor and the elderly and the afflicted. We cannot lose sight of our fundamental obligation to share what God has given us with those less fortunate than we are, even if it means sacrifice on the part of all. This is the reason I'm determined to maintain and to strengthen existing programs in the Federal Government."[26]

Yet, also like his Democratic predecessors, Carter urged private charity as well. Indeed, he practiced it in impressive fashion. After he joined Habitat for Humanity in 1984, he worked twelve-to-fourteen-hour days building houses for the poor. He was once seen down on his hands and knees, laying tile, at one o'clock in the morning so that a house would be finished on time. He and his wife, Rosalynn, slept in a tent while helping to build homes in Tijuana.[27]

Ronald Reagan steadfastly opposed the conflation of private charity and public spending. In 1982, after citing 1 Corinthians 13:13 on the obligation of faith, hope, and charity, he employed the same biblical example as Hoover had used to illustrate that the last of these three duties was a personal obligation, not one that could be delegated to the government. He declared, "[The good Samaritan] crossed to the other side of the road where the beaten pilgrim lay, bound up his wounds, and carried him to the nearest town. He didn't hurry on by and then when he got to town tell a caseworker that there was someone out there back aways that needed help." Three months later, after again invoking the good Samaritan, Reagan claimed, "Today, we've become so used to turning to government rather than taking the personal time and effort required to help those in need. Some even confuse charity as being the money that is given for lobbying to get more social programs passed."[28]

Reagan practiced the charity he preached. He often sent checks ranging from $50 to $1,000 to various individuals who were down on their luck, as well as to various charities. In fact, his staff members considered him a soft touch. As president, he established a task force on private-sector charities, which he considered a crucial replacement for big government. He sent fifty dollars to a thirteen-year-old Girl Scout troop president who was raising money for a European trip, writing, "After all, we presidents have to stick together." In addition to cash, Reagan often relinquished personal belongings. When a poor man who had decided that he was the same size as Reagan requested a suit for his wedding, Reagan sent him one of his own. When two sisters asked for a rocking chair for their intellectually disabled brother, he sent them his own rocker.[29]

George H. W. Bush also emphasized the good that private charitable organizations could do. In his acceptance speech at the Republican National Convention in 1988, he called such groups "a thousand points of light." Two years later, Bush retold Reverend Martin Luther King Jr.'s account of journeying along the same road from Jerusalem to Jericho that the good Samaritan had traveled. After following the "twisting road, full of blind curves," King realized that what had prevented the priest and the Levite from helping the battered victim was not apathy but the fear of ambush by robbers—just as fear prevented modern Americans from doing charitable deeds in inner-city neighborhoods. Christian charity required courage as well as kindness, and courage was the product of a selfless love. As Bush put it, "The priest and Levite asked, 'If I stop to help this man, what will happen to me?' whereas the Good Samaritan asked, 'If I don't stop to help this man, what will happen to him?'" In 1992 Bush declared, "Every day we face the question posed in the New Testament [1 John 3:17]: 'If anyone has the world's goods and sees his brother in need, yet closes his heart against him, how does God's love abide in him?'" In addition to sizable contributions to his church's charitable programs, Bush practiced charity on a personal level as well. One unusually cold Sunday morning at Bush's church in Houston, when he spotted an usher greeting visitors outside without a coat, he removed his own, wrapped it around the usher, and walked inside to find a seat.[30]

Following twelve years of Republican presidents, Bill Clinton returned to the practice of reinterpreting biblical admonitions to engage in private charity as mandates for government programs. In 1998, at a speech at the New Psalmist Baptist Church in Baltimore, he declared, "One thing the Bible tells us hundreds of times—hundreds and hundreds of times *about politics* [emphasis added]—the only thing it tells hundreds and hundreds of times is to care for the poor, the weak, the needy. In Matthew, Jesus says, 'Verily, I say unto you, even as you have done this unto the least of my brethren, you have also done it unto me.'" Clinton continued, "So I say to you, we believe that *our politics* [emphasis added] should be guided by what our Lord said." Clinton concluded that the way to do the Lord's will in the upcoming congressional elections was to vote for Democratic candidates who supported increased public spending on health care, education, and Social Security.[31]

Like the Democrats, George W. Bush advocated for both private and public funding of charity on religious grounds. In his inaugural address in 2001, he alluded to the priest and Levite in the parable of the good Samaritan: "And I can pledge our nation to a goal: when we see that wounded traveler on the road to Jericho, we will not pass to the other side." In 2003 he declared, "The voice first heard 20 centuries ago in Bethlehem stirs churches and communities to open homeless shelters and food pantries and job training centers to help those in need." He interpreted the scripture "To whom much is given, much is required [Luke 12:48]" as a challenge for the United States government to place itself at the forefront of the effort to fight AIDS in Africa. In 2003 he persuaded Congress to pass a $15 billion initiative to provide the continent with medication that combated HIV. Six months later, speaking at an AIDS clinic in Uganda, he said, "I believe God has called us into action. We have a responsibility to help a neighbor in need, a brother and sister in crisis." Elsewhere he said, "The Bible talks about love and compassion. . . . That's really behind my passion on the AIDS policy, for example." In five years the number of Africans who received this lifesustaining medication increased from fifty thousand to nearly three million. Maintaining the biblical theme, Africans dubbed the rejuvenation of the recipients of these medicines "the Lazarus Effect."[32]

Barack Obama often employed the biblical concept of being one's "brother's keeper" to promote government programs. In fact, he even established a federal program called My Brother's Keeper, which involved public-private partnerships to create mentorships for inner-city youth. In 2011 he declared, "Christian tradition teaches that one day the world will be turned right side up and everything will return as it should be. But until that day, we're called to work on behalf of a God that chose justice and mercy and compassion to the most vulnerable."[33]

Yet Obama often asserted that government alone was insufficient to carrying out this obligation. In 2012 he said regarding God:

> As a loving husband or a supportive parent or a good neighbor or a helpful colleague, in each of these roles, we help bring His kingdom to Earth. And as important as government policy may be in shaping our world, we are reminded that it's the cumulative acts of kindness and courage and love, it's the respect we show each other and the generosity which we share with each other that in our everyday lives will somehow sustain us during these challenging times. John tell us that, 'If anyone has material possessions and sees his brother in need but has no pity on him, how can the love of God be in him? Dear children, let us not love with words but with actions and in truth. [1 John 3:17–18].'"[34]

Forgiveness is another of the cardinal virtues presidents have believed constitute Christianity's excellence. John Adams forgave the nation's British enemies, writing to Benjamin Franklin during the Revolutionary War: "God forgive them and enable Americans to forget their Ungenerosity." He also forgave Joseph Priestley for allegedly financing libels against him during his presidency, writing to Thomas Jefferson that he prayed Priestley "may be pardoned for it all above."[35]

Thomas Jefferson preached both forgiveness and charity, two of the Christian traits he valued most, to his daughter Mary. In 1790 he wrote to her, "Never be angry with anybody nor speak harm of them; try to let everybody's faults be forgotten, as you would wish yours to be; take more pleasure in giving what is best to another than in having it for yourself, and then all the world will love you, and I more than all the world."[36]

In 1796, when comparing the writings of sixteenth-century Italian poet Torquato Tasso with the Greco-Roman classics, John Quincy Adams emphasized the role of Christianity in inculcating forgiveness. Adams wrote, "Achilles restored the body of Hector to Priam; but that was from a motive of generosity when he felt no resentment; at all other times he was unrelenting. The pious Aeneas is equally inflexible to the compunctious visitings of Nature; but Tancred and Rinaldo are both merciful and generous to their vanquished enemies. Their love is gentle, and their anger is humane. This is one of the benefits of Christianity [that is] the most clearly evident, as the revolution of manners is indisputable, and can be traced to no other source, while it naturally flows from that." Fourteen years later, when lecturing Harvard students concerning rhetoric, Adams noted that Aristotle and Quintilian had no problem recommending that speakers instill "envy, hatred, malice, and indignation" in their audiences, whereas "the Christian religion has commanded us to suppress the angry and turbulent passions in ourselves and forbids us to stimulate them in others." Christians "have been commanded to love their enemies; to return blessings for curses, prayers for persecution, and goodness for evil." In 1815, while in Ghent, negotiating the treaty that ended the War of 1812, Adams wrote to his wife, Louisa: "May it please God to forgive our enemies, and to turn their hearts!" In 1838 Adams heard Harriet Livermore preach a sermon on the Christian duty of forgiveness at the US Capitol. He predicted ruefully, "When Harriet Livermore preaches in the Representative Hall of the United States the forgiveness of injuries, alas, how few converts she will make." But he added, "Harriet Livermore, upon the close of her discourse on the absolute, unqualified, and irremissible command of Jesus Christ to His disciples to practice the duty of mutual forgiveness, said there was no portion of mankind upon whom that obligation was more imperiously binding than upon those who filled the seats in that hall. May some of those who heard her lay it to their hearts, and Harriet Livermore will have worthily fulfilled her destiny upon earth!"[37]

During the Civil War, former President Millard Fillmore urged the Christian virtue of forgiveness. In 1864 he declared that, following Union victory, "Let us show our magnanimity and generosity in winning back the deluded multitude [of the South] who have been seduced or coerced into this rebellion. This I conceive to be Christian forgiveness, the best policy, and [the] only one which can ever restore the Union."[38]

Abraham Lincoln agreed. In 1864 he objected to the wording of a loyalty oath requiring the citizens of seceded states who desired to serve in the Union Army to swear they had never served under any authority hostile to the United States. Lincoln wrote to Secretary of War Edwin Stanton: "On principle I dislike an oath which requires a man to swear he has not done wrong. It rejects the Christian principle of forgiveness on terms of repentance. I think it is enough if the man does no wrong hereafter." The famous conclusion of Lincoln's second inaugural address (1865) was a call for the implementation of the biblical virtues of forgiveness and charity: "With malice toward none, with charity for all, with firmness in the right, as God gives us to see the right, let us strive on to finish the work we are in, to bind up the nation's wounds, to care for him who shall have borne the battle, and for his widow and his orphan—to do all which may achieve and cherish a just and lasting peace among ourselves and with all nations." Here Lincoln even reproduced the Bible's emphasis on the care of widows and orphans, an especially timely reminder of Christian duty given the large numbers of those classes generated by the Civil War.[39]

Andrew Johnson, the first Reconstruction president and thus the one for whom the issue of political forgiveness loomed largest, was initially disinclined to offer the defeated rebels clemency, but he later softened. In 1865 he declared that justice demanded the punishment of the rebels. But six months later, he declared, "It should be the duty of every patriot and everyone who calls himself a Christian that with the termination of the war his resentments should cease, that angry feelings should subside, and that every man should be calm and tranquil." Indeed, Johnson signed thousands of individual pardons.[40]

Gerald Ford's mild manner rested, in part, on a willingness to forgive. In the notes he compiled for his memoirs, he claimed, "[Forgiveness] is a trait that I was brought up with under my Mother's guidance." He added, "Some of my friends, especially in the political area, believed I overdid it. I was taught that forgiveness is a good religious principle, and I believe it." Ford's pardon of Richard Nixon, issued even though Ford was angry that Nixon had personally lied to him about the Watergate scandal, may have cost him the election of 1976.[41]

Jimmy Carter considered forgiveness a Christian obligation. In 1980 he claimed regarding those who wronged him: "Every day I list them by name and say, 'God, I pray for that person or those people.'" This was the time of the Iranian hostage crisis, so he added, "Every day I pray for the Ayatollah Khomeini. Every day I pray for the kidnapers who hold our innocent Americans." In 1997 he wrote, "The point of Jesus' teaching is to make forgiveness a permanent attitude, a way of life. . . . The teachings of Jesus are predicated on the fact that we receive the unbounded love of God and absolute forgiveness of all our trespasses. Like the king in the parable [Matthew 18:23–35], God forgives our great debts and expects us to forgive the relatively insignificant grievances we may have against others." He added, "The Scriptures repeatedly state or imply that unless we are willing to forgive others, we ourselves will not be forgiven—not only by our fellow human beings but by God." Carter confessed that he had struggled to forgive a columnist who used a stolen debate briefing book to help Ronald Reagan prepare for a crucial debate against Carter, but ultimately, he forgave him.[42]

While lying in his own blood at George Washington University Hospital, Ronald Reagan forgave John Hinckley for the attempt on his life. Reagan later recalled, "I didn't feel I could ask God's help to heal Jim [Brady], the others, and myself and at the same time feel hatred for the man who had shot us, so I silently asked God to help him deal with whatever demons had led him to shoot us."[43]

Of course, presidents have not always lived up to the lofty biblical standard regarding forgiveness. John Adams refused to forgive Alexander Hamilton for destroying his presidency. His son, John Quincy, was unable to forgive his own nemesis, Andrew Jackson, whose supporters had slandered Adams during the election of 1828. Not one to turn the other cheek, Jackson himself frequently issued dueling challenges to those he believed had sullied his honor by their words, violating the Christian virtue of humility as well as forgiveness. On his deathbed, at a time when most people facing their own morality regret past acts of harshness, Jackson expressed regret that he had not executed his former vice president, John C. Calhoun, for treason for his role in fomenting the Nullification Crisis. Grover Cleveland refused to forgive Reverend George Ball of Hudson Street Baptist Church in Buffalo, Cleveland's hometown, as the reverend had led the dissemination of false and scandalous reports concerning Cleveland. Harry Truman refused to forgive reporters who had criticized him for taking a taxpayer-funded trip to Missouri to bury his mother. Ronald Reagan struggled to forgive Muammar Qaddafi, who was probably responsible for the assassination of Anwar Sadat, an assassination the Libyan leader celebrated publicly, as well as to forgive those who slandered his cabinet members based on allegations that were disproved in court. Richard Nixon even compiled an "enemies list," which does not appear to have been a catalog of individuals he planned to love in compliance with Jesus's command in Matthew 5:44. Donald Trump has been vindictive not only toward opponents but even toward supporters. While president, he often publicly attacked his own cabinet members in a bizarre manner that suggested someone else had appointed them. But, although the Christian concept of forgiveness has not always prevailed, it has undoubtedly produced a more wholesome political environment than would otherwise have been the case.[44]

Faith and Morality: Pillars of Republican Government

Most presidents have derived from the Bible and from their own experiences a fervent belief that faith and morality are crucial to the survival and success of republics. They have believed that in any system of government in which the majority holds most of the power, it is vital that most citizens be ethical, and they have considered religious belief essential to morality. By "religion," some presidents have meant orthodox Christianity, while others have meant only the belief in an omniscient, omnipotent God who rewards virtue and punishes vice either in this life or the next. While the latter definition does not entail an adherence to all biblical doctrines, it does involve, at a minimum, belief in a God who is very similar to the deity depicted in the Bible. In short, presidents have contended that religious belief is essential in two ways: supernaturally, by securing for the nation the favor of an omniscient, interventionist God, and naturally, by inclining individuals toward virtues necessary to society and against vices that endanger it.

George Washington expressed his confidence in the necessity of religious belief to republican government both at the beginning and end of his administration. Upon assuming the presidency in 1789, Washington spoke of "true religion," calling it "the best security of temporal peace and the sure means of attaining universal felicity." He added the promise, "It will be my endeavor (as far as human frailty can resolve) to inculcate the belief and practice of opinions which lead to the consummation of those desirable objects." In his Farewell Address (1796), Washington was famously emphatic concerning the need for religious belief in a republic:

Of all the dispositions and habits which lead to political prosperity, religion and morality are indispensable supports. In vain would that man claim the tribute of patriotism who should labor to subvert these great pillars of human happiness, these firmest props of the duties of men and citizens. The mere politician, equally with the pious man, ought to respect and to cherish them. A volume could not trace all their connections with private and public felicity. Let it simply be asked: Where is the security for property, for reputation, for life, if the sense of religious obligation desert the oaths which are the instruments of investigation in courts of justice? And let us with caution indulge the supposition that morality can be maintained without religion. Whatever may be conceded to the influence of refined education on minds of peculiar structure, reason and experience both forbid us to expect that national morality can prevail in exclusion of religious principle.

Far from being a conventional nod to piety, which one might expect from a politician of Washington's era, this was a full-throated assault on contemporary European irreligion, especially the famous claim of French revolutionaries that religious belief was unnecessary to virtue. Washington's final address to the American people constituted a heartfelt warning from an American who had witnessed the French Revolution unravel and who, like many Federalists, attributed the disastrous result to a barbarism that proceeded inevitably from atheism.[45]

Washington was far from alone in the conviction that faith was essential to morality and, thus, to republican government. In 1776 John Adams wrote to his cousin, a Congregationalist minister: "Statesmen, my dear Sir, may plan and speculate for liberty, but it is religion and morality alone which can establish the principles on which freedom can securely stand." He urged his cousin to pull "down the strong-holds of Satan," adding, "This is not cant, but the real sentiment of my heart." As the principal drafter of the Massachusetts Constitution of 1780, Adams approved the assertion that "the happiness of a people, and good order and preservation of civil government, essentially depend upon piety, religion, and morality." While president, Adams wrote in his diary, "One great advantage of the Christian religion is that it brings the great principles of the law of nature and nations—Love your neighbor as yourself and do to others as you would the others should do to you—to the knowledge, belief, and veneration of the whole people. . . . No other institution for education, no kind of political discipline, could diffuse this necessary information so universally among all ranks and descriptions of citizens. The duties and rights of the man and the citizen are thus taught from early infancy to every creature." In his copy of *A Letter to Dr. Waterland*, he wrote next to Conyer Middleton's assertion that Matthew Tindal wanted to abolish Christianity and establish reason as the basis for a national religion of Britain: "Abolish Christianity! Set up reason! The authority of reason is not stern enough to keep rebellious appetites and passions in subjection." Next to a reference to Tindal's contention that Christianity was unnecessary to good government, Adams retorted, "Deistical cant. Atheists are the most cruel persecutors."[46]

In 1811 Adams wrote to Benjamin Rush, "I agree with you in sentiment that religion and virtue are the only foundations not only of republicanism and of all free government but of social felicity under all governments and in all the combinations of human society." Six years later, Adams confessed that the contemplation of past crimes committed in the name of religion sometimes made him wonder if the world would be better off without it. But he added quickly that the truth was otherwise: "Without Religion this World would be Something not fit to be mentioned in polite Company, I mean Hell."[47]

While James Madison agreed with Adams that self-professed Christians had often violated biblical principles, he also agreed that the principles themselves were sound and essential. In 1787 Madison claimed that from the days of Constantine (fourth century) to modern times, religion "has been much oftener a motive to oppression than a restraint from it." But that was because so-called Christians had violated New Testament principles. Madison had no qualms about the positive social and political effects of a widespread belief in the biblical concept of an omniscient, omnipotent deity who judged humanity. On the contrary, in 1825, he contended, "The belief in a God All Powerful, wise, and good is so essential to the moral order of the world and to the happiness of man that arguments which enforce it cannot be drawn from too many sources nor adapted with too much solicitude to the different characters and capacities to be impressed with it."[48]

John Quincy Adams agreed. In an 1806 lecture to Harvard students, he declared regarding Christianity: "Its effects have been to soften the tempers and purify the morals of mankind; not in so high a degree as benevolence could wish, but enough to call forth our strains of warmest gratitude to that good being who provides us with the means of promoting our own felicity and gives us power to stand, though leaving us free to fall." Similarly, he claimed regarding the Christian command to restrain one's darker passions, "This precept, like so many others proceeding from the same source, is elevated so far above the ordinary level of human virtue that it is not always faithfully obeyed. But although perhaps not completely victorious over any one human heart, the command to abstain from malice and envy, and all the rancorous passions, has effected a general refinement of manners among men." In 1811 he wrote to his son George,

> There are three points of doctrine the belief of which forms the foundation of all human morality. The first is the existence of God; the second is the immortality of the human soul; and the third is a future state of rewards and punishments. Suppose it possible for a man to disbelieve either of these three articles of faith, and that man will have no conscience. He will have no other law than that of the tiger and the shark. The laws of man may bind him in chains, or may put him to death, but they never can make him wise, virtuous, or happy. . . . Human reason may be sufficient to get an obscure glimpse of these sacred and important truths, but it cannot discover them in all their clearness.

Thus, the Bible was essential.[49]

In 1823 Andrew Jackson asserted a strong connection between religious belief and republican government, claiming, "I have but one grand view, and that is to promote, as far as I have influence, a proper respect for character, religion, and morality, and thereby lay a solid foundation for the perpetuity of our happy form of Government." In 1844 he urged, "Let us look to the protection of religion and morals of our country and the perpetuation of our happy republican system, which is based upon the virtue of the people, and support none for office but good moral characters who will use their influence to put down vice and immorality and sustain true religion and virtue."[50]

Abraham Lincoln endorsed the widespread belief that assaults on religion injured morality and thus society. While campaigning for Congress in 1846, he responded to the charge that he was an enemy of faith:

> I do not think that I could myself be brought to support a man for office whom I knew to be an open enemy of, and scoffer at, religion. Leaving the higher matter of eternal consequences between him and his Maker, I still do not think any man has the right thus to insult the feelings and *injure the morals* of the community in which he may live [emphasis added]. If then, I was guilty of such conduct, I should blame no man who should condemn me for it, but I do blame those, whoever they may be, who falsely put such a charge in circulation against me.

In 1864 Lincoln drew an even clearer connection between faith and morality when he wrote regarding the Bible, "But for it we could not know right from wrong."[51]

Rutherford Hayes believed that biblical instruction promoted civilization and thus sound government. In 1884 he wrote in his diary, "The best religion the world has ever had is the religion of Christ. A man or a community adopting it is virtuous, prosperous, and happy." The following year, he reiterated, "The best religion the world has ever known is the religion of the Bible. It builds up all that is good. It suppresses or diminishes all that is bad. With it, men are happy, and nations are prosperous. Where it is not found vice and crime prevail."[52]

Grover Cleveland agreed. As mayor of Buffalo in 1882, when laying the cornerstone of the YMCA building there, he declared:

> When we consider the difference, as a member of the community, between the young man who, under the influence of such an association, has learned his duty to his fellows and to the State, and that one who, subject to no moral restraint, yields to temptation and thus becomes vicious and criminal, the importance of an institution among us which leads our youth and young men in the way of morality and good citizenship must be freely admitted. . . . Such earnest Christian endeavors . . . must make easier all our efforts to administer, safely and honestly, a good municipal government.

Two years later, Cleveland claimed, "Our churches, and the tolerant and almost universal observance of religious duties by every sect and creed, teach obedience to law and prepare our people for good citizenship." In 1887 he wrote,

> A wholesome religious faith thus inures to the perpetuity, the safety, and the prosperity of our Republic by exacting the due observance of civil law, the protection of public order, and a proper regard for the rights of all; and thus are its adherents better fitted for good citizenship and confirmed in a sure and steadfast patriotism. It seems to me that the conception of duty to the State which is derived from religious precept involves a sense of personal responsibility which is of the greatest value in the operation of a government by the people. It will be a fortunate day for our country when every citizen feels that he has an ever-present duty to perform to the State which he cannot escape from or neglect without being false to his religious as well as his civil allegiance.

Eleven months later, he declared,

> All must admit that the reception of the teachings of . . . Christianity results in the purest patriotism, in the most scrupulous fidelity to public trust, and in the best type of citizenship. Those who manage the affairs of government are by this means reminded that the law of God demands that they should be courageously true to the interests of the people and that the Ruler of the Universe will require of them a strict account of their stewardship. The people

too are thus taught that their happiness and welfare will be best promoted by a conscientious regard for the interest of a common brotherhood and that the success of a government by the people depends upon the morality, the justice, and the honesty of the people.[53]

William McKinley asserted the same connection between faith and the survival of the republic. In 1887 he claimed, "The hope of the Republic is in an educated and enlightened citizenship which fears God and walks uprightly." In 1892, in an address to the YMCA in Youngstown, Ohio, he highlighted the civic benefits of religious belief: "These Associations elevate and purify our citizenship and establish more firmly the foundations of our free institutions."[54]

Theodore Roosevelt agreed. In 1899 he told students at the Mount Pleasant Military Academy, "I urge you to have the widest toleration in matters of opinion but to have no toleration at all when it comes to matters of the Ten Commandments and the Golden Rule. These are fundamental, essential principles which must live in the heart of every American citizen and by which every man asking place or political power must be tested." A decade later, he declared, "Civilization can only be permanent and continue a blessing to any people if, in addition to promoting their material well-being, it also stands for an orderly individual liberty, for the growth of intelligence, and for equal justice in the administration of law. Christianity alone meets these fundamental requirements." In 1911 he claimed, "It would be a great misfortune for our people if they ever lost the Bible as one of their habitual standards and guides in morality." In 1914 he contended, "No democracy can afford to overlook the vital importance of the ethical and spiritual, the truly religious, element in life; and in practice the average good man grows clearly to understand this, and to express the need in concrete form by saying that no community can make much headway if it does not contain both a church and a school." Three years later, Roosevelt wrote,

> In this actual world a churchless community, a community where men have abandoned and scoffed at or ignored their religious needs, is a community on the rapid downgrade. It is perfectly true that occasional individuals or families may have nothing to do with church or with religious practices and observances and yet maintain the highest standard of spirituality and of ethical obligation. But this does not affect the case in the world as it now is, any more than that exceptional men and women under exceptional conditions have disregarded the marriage tie without moral harm to themselves interferes with the larger fact that such disregard if at all common means the complete moral disintegration of the body politic.

That same year, he claimed, "The most perfect machinery of government could not keep us as a nation from destruction if there is not within us a soul. No abounding material prosperity shall avail us if our spiritual senses atrophy. The foes of our own household shall surely prevail against us unless there be in our people an inner life which finds its outward expression in a morality not very widely different from that preached by the seers and prophets of Judea when the grandeur that was Greece and the glory that was Rome still lay in the future."[55]

When commemorating Princeton University's sesquicentennial in 1896, Woodrow Wilson noted the university's founding by Presbyterian ministers and its nondenominational Christian instruction. He contended, "There is nothing that gives such pith to public service as religion. A God of truth is no mean prompter to the enlightened service of mankind; and character formed, as if in His eye, has always a fiber and sanction such as you shall not easily obtain for the ordinary man from the mild promptings of philosophy.... It is noteworthy how often God-fearing men have been forward in those revolutions which have vindicated rights and how seldom in those which have wrought a work of destruction." A year later, he went so far as to declare, "Individual salvation is national salvation," as the former was essential to the latter. In 1911, while governor of New Jersey, Wilson claimed, "Religious principle is the one solid and remaining and abiding foundation. Find a man whose conscience is buttressed by that intimate principle, and you will find a man into whose hands you can safely entrust your affairs. For the man who steers by expediency, the man who trims his course by what he thinks will be the political consequence, the man who always has his eye upon the weather, is a man you cannot trust." A month later, he declared, "When a man is schooled by teachers who hold up to him the example of Christ and the history of the self-sacrifices of the church, these are no mean preparations for public life." Three months later, he wrote in a private letter to a friend, "The Bible (with its individual value of the human soul) is undoubtedly the book that has made democracy and been the source of all progress." Five months later, he declared, "No great nation can ever survive its own temptations and its own follies that does not indoctrinate its children in the Word of God." In 1923, while retired, Wilson wrote, "Our civilization cannot survive materially unless it be redeemed spiritually. It can be saved only by becoming permeated with the spirit of Christ and being made free and happy by the practices which spring out of that spirit."[56]

Warren Harding agreed. Shortly before taking office in 1921, he began his book, *Our Common Country*, thusly: "Sometimes I think the world has gone adrift from its moorings religiously, and I know it will help if we have a revival of religious faith. I want a government that is just, and I don't think a government can be just if it does not have somehow a contact with Omnipotent God." Regarding faith, he wrote, "We need more of it in our American life, more of it in government, the real spirit of it. I think there should be more of the 'Do unto others as you would be done by' spirit of service."[57]

Calvin Coolidge emphasized the importance of Christianity to the nation's past and future success. In 1923 he claimed that America "had its beginning, it found its inspiration, in the religious beliefs of the men who settled our country, made it an independent nation, and established and maintained its Constitution and its laws." He added, "If it is to endure, it will be through the support of men of like mind and like character. . . . Most of all, there is need of religion. From that source alone came freedom. Nothing else touches the soul of man. Nothing else justifies faith in the people." Two years later, he argued,

> The claim to the right of freedom, the claim to the right of equality, with the resultant right to self-government—the rule of the people—have no foundation other than the common brotherhood of man derived from the common fatherhood of God. . . . If this faith is set aside, the foundations of our institutions fail, the citizen is deposed from the high estate which he holds as amenable to a universal conscience, society reverts to a system of class and caste, and the Government instead of being imposed by reason from within is imposed by force from without. Freedom and democracy would give way to despotism and slavery. I do not know of any adequate support for our form of government except that which comes from religion.

The same year, at the laying of the cornerstone of the Jewish Center in Washington, Coolidge declared regarding future generations: "May they give due credit to the people among whom the Holy Scriptures came into being. And as they ponder the assertion that Hebraic mortar cemented the foundation of American democracy, they cannot escape the conclusion that if American democracy is to remain the greatest hope of humanity, it must continue abundantly in the faith of the Bible." Five months later, Coolidge expressed his views regarding religion: "Without its spirit either civilization will fall of its own weight, and that deep and abiding wisdom which supports society will cease to exist, or we shall have a type of mind keen in intelligence but greedy and cruel, which, armed with the power of modern science, in seeking to destroy others, will in the end accomplish its own destruction. Without the presence of a great directing moral force, intelligence either will not be developed or, if it be developed, it will prove self-destructive." In 1926, while celebrating the sesquicentennial of the Declaration of Independence, Coolidge declared regarding the American colonists, "While scantily provided with other literature, there was a wide acquaintance with the Scriptures. . . . They were a people who came under the influence of a great spiritual development and acquired a great moral power." He added, "If we are to maintain the great heritage which has been bequeathed to us, we must be like minded as the fathers who created it. We must not sink into pagan materialism. We must cultivate the reverence which they had for the things that are holy. We must follow the spiritual and moral leadership which they showed. We must keep replenished, that they may glow with a more compelling flame, the altar fires before which they worshipped."[58]

In 1929 Hebert Hoover declared, "As a nation we are indebted to the Book of Books for our national ideals and representative institutions. Their preservation rests in adhering to its principles." In 1938, with the Nazis on the move, he claimed, "Religious faith, morals, and democracy are indissolubly allied in the fate of the world." Four years later, during World War II, he contended,

> When our nation was founded, it drew its strength and being not only from great political and social truths, but from spiritual convictions—from a deep and abiding belief in Almighty God. From our religious faiths came the great inspiration that man should be free. Free in worship, free in conscience, free in speech. . . . These liberties cannot be sustained without religious faith. From that springs our spiritual guidance and our moral standards. These moral standards are sustained by faith alone. Without these supports Liberty degenerates into license and is lost. Just as our nation was founded by faith in God, so also can that faith sustain our nation in this time of dreadful trial. Our enemies have decried and sought to destroy our religious faiths. Theirs is the boast that cunning and brutality can rule. We refuse to believe this. We know that if civilization is to live it must be based upon religious faith and upon compassion that is part of faith.

In 1954 he applied the same lesson to the Cold War: "The great documents of that heritage [of freedom] are not from Karl Marx. They are the Bible, the Declaration of Independence, and the Constitution of the United States. Within them alone can the safeguards of freedom survive."[59]

Franklin Roosevelt agreed that faith was essential to democracy. In 1936 he declared,

> It is my very deep conviction that democracy cannot live without that true religion which gives a nation a sense of justice and of moral purpose. Above

our political forums, above our marketplaces, stand the altars of our faith—altars on which burn the fires of devotion that maintain all that is best in us and all that is best in our Nation. We have need of that devotion today. It is that which makes it possible for government to persuade those who are mentally prepared to fight each other to go on instead, to work for and sacrifice for each other. And that is why we need to say with the old Prophet: "What doth the Lord require of thee—but to do justly, to love mercy, and to walk humbly with Thy God [Micah 6:8]?"

Two years later, Roosevelt told Congress, "Storms from abroad directly challenge three institutions indispensable to Americans, now as always. The first is religion. It is the source of the other two—democracy and international good faith. Religion, by teaching man his relationship to God, gives the individual a sense of his own dignity and teaches him to respect himself by respecting his neighbors." In 1940, confronting a world at war, he contended, "We people of America know that man cannot live by bread alone [Matthew 4:4]. We know that we have a reservoir of religious strength which can withstand attacks from abroad and corruption from within. We the people of America will always cherish and preserve that strength. We will always cling to our religion, our devotion to God—to the faith which gives us comfort and the strength to face evil." The following month, he declared, "In teaching this democratic faith to American children we need the sustaining, buttressing aid of those great ethical and religious teachings which are the heritage of our modern civilization. For 'not upon strength, nor upon power, but upon the spirit of God [Zechariah 4:6]' shall our democracy be founded." In 1943 Roosevelt read the Beatitudes from Jesus's Sermon on the Mount in a radio address. He added, "Those are the truths which are the eternal heritage of our civilization. I repeat them to give heart and comfort to all men and women everywhere who fight for freedom. . . . Today, through all the darkness that has descended upon our nation and our world, those truths are a guiding light to all. We shall follow that light, as our forefathers did, to the fulfillment of our hopes for victory, for freedom, and for peace."[60]

Harry Truman shared Roosevelt's views concerning the connection between faith and democracy. In 1938 he claimed, "When a man believes in God and lives honorably with his neighbors, he can't help but be a good American citizen." In 1943 he quoted William Penn: "Men must be governed by God, or they will be ruled by tyrants." Then in 1950 he claimed, "Democracy's most powerful weapon is not a gun, tank, or bomb. It is faith—faith in the brotherhood and dignity of man under God." The following year, he contended, "We rely on the churches particularly to instill in our young people the moral ideals which are the basis of our free institutions." He added, "Our religion must live in our hearts not as a set of dull rules learned by rote, but as a burning faith. Only such a faith—only a living allegiance to such a faith—can carry this country through the trials which are ahead of it." In 1952 he declared, "I believe in the Sermon on the Mount. I think it is the fundamental basis of free government." The following month, he claimed,

> The fundamental basis of this Nation's ideals was given to Moses on Mount Sinai. The fundamental basis of the Bill of Rights comes from the teachings which we get from Exodus, St. Matthew, Isaiah, and St. Paul. The Sermon on the Mount gives a way of life, and maybe someday men will understand it as the real way of life. The basis of all great moral codes is "Do unto others as you would have others do unto you." Treat others as you would like to be treated. Some of you may think that such a philosophy has no place in politics and government. But it is the only philosophy on which you can base a lasting government. Governments built on that philosophy are built on a rock and will not fail.

Eight months later, he claimed, "It took faith in God to win our freedom. We will need that same faith today if we are to keep those freedoms in the face of the terrible menace of totalitarianism and war. If we do not hold to our faith in God, we cannot prevail against the dangers from abroad and the fears and distrust those dangers create among us here at home." The latter phrase was a reference to McCarthyism.[61]

Like James Madison, Truman maintained that while many people who called themselves Christians had engaged in bad behavior in the past, their actions violated the sacred text they purported to uphold. After contending that the Christian moral code was the best, Truman added, "This is not to say that Christianity has not had its difficulties throughout its history, but there are always difficulties in everything that pertains to man. There has been terrible bloodshed over Christianity, brought about by struggles between sects and denominations." Truman further argued, "[But] those who resorted to wars to inflict their kind of Christianity upon other faiths or denominations did not really understand Christianity."[62]

Dwight Eisenhower also connected Christianity to democracy. In 1943 he wrote, "The Allied soldier here in Africa is not often articulate in his profession of Christianity; but he is risking his life to uphold principles that are implicit alike in Democracy and Christianity, principles of justice, liberty, and right among men of all stations everywhere." Nine years later, he claimed, "Spiritual and religious stimulation throughout the entire free world is the first essential to the preservation of our liberties and rights. There is immediate and widespread need for it now. I firmly believe that free systems of government are based in a deeply felt religion." In 1953 he declared, "Every free government is imbedded soundly in a deeply felt religious faith or it makes no sense." Two months later, he told representatives of the Organization of American States, "We are Christian nations, deeply conscious that the foundation of all liberty is religious faith." Then in 1954 Eisenhower contended, "If there is no religious faith whatsoever, then there is little defense you can make of a free system. If men are only animals, why not try to dominate them?" Sixth months later, he declared, "Man is worthwhile because he was born in the image of God. . . . Democracy is nothing in the world but a spiritual conviction, a conviction that each of us is enormously valuable because of a certain standing before our own God." In 1958 he asserted, "The health of our society depends upon a deep and abiding respect for the basic commandments of the God of Israel." In 1960 he claimed, "For close to two centuries our nation has thrived under the bracing influence of belief in God and the dignity of the individual. Should this spiritual base of our democracy ever become dimmed, our faith in the destiny of America would disappear before a vain reliance on materialism and crass political maneuver."[63]

John F. Kennedy agreed. In 1961 he declared, "A democratic society is by its nature an ethical one, or its freedoms become fictitious." He added significantly, "We cannot have liberty ourselves, much less insure its success in the world, unless we also partake of the spirit of the Lord, which proclaims truth, justice, and charity of all men toward all men. . . . As long as men are able to perceive the reasons for their dignity in a higher destiny, they will strive to be free."[64]

Gerald Ford considered religious belief essential to democracy. As early as 1950, Congressman Ford had noted,

> Sometimes we talk and think of freedom as if it were merely a political device, without grasping the fact that fundamentally it is something spiritual and religious. . . . Both our ideas of right and wrong and our idea of the worth and rights and dignity of each individual derive from a growing comprehension of the Christian outlook of life and the world, which itself derives from the outlook of Moses and the prophets and the psalmists of Judaism. Although through the Christian centuries the truth has often been obscured, growingly there has been realized the human implications of the Gospel of Christ. Every man, says that Gospel, is of infinite worth, of such worth that Christ died for him.

Six years later, Ford declared, "Our form of government is predicated not only on a complete and total religious freedom, but on a deep and abiding faith in the Almighty. In fact, our fundamental form of government stems from the spiritual concept of the fatherhood of God."[65]

As president during the bicentennial celebrations of 1976, Ford identified a revival of the nation's religious heritage, then undermined by both the countercultural revolution of the 1960s and the political scandals of the 1970s, as essential to the survival of American democracy. He warned, "We stand in danger today of losing the soul of America to the seductions of material gain and moral apathy, to a new code of conduct which reviles the basic truths and mocks the basic beliefs on which this Nation and much of religion was founded. Forgiving hearts and tolerant attitudes are among the greatest lessons of Christianity, but at some point, we must take a stand and say, 'This is right, this is wrong; there is a difference.'" He added, "The American people have seen too much abuse of the moral imperatives of honesty and decency upon which religion and government and civilized society must rest. To remedy these abuses, we must look not only to government, but more importantly, to the Bible, the church, the human heart."[66]

Jimmy Carter maintained that the prevalence of faith within American society was crucial to the survival of its democracy. In 1973 he noted, "Our country was founded on a belief in God, on truth, integrity, patriotism, the worth of the individual human being, and those are the things that we will have to cling to." Five years later, he said, "I believe and hope that our Nation's deep belief in God will be a stabilizing factor in generations ahead." Six months later, he claimed, "Our Nation has an inherent strength, derived, to a major degree, from belief in God."[67]

Ronald Reagan agreed. In 1982 he contended, "To preserve our blessed land, we must look to God. . . . Do we really think that we can have it both ways, that God will protect us in a time of crisis even as we turn away from Him in our day-to-day life?" Three months later, he declared, "Our liberty springs from and depends upon an abiding faith in God." In 1984 he said, "I don't want us to be another great civilization that began its decline by forsaking its God." Five months later, he claimed, "Man was meant to flourish, was meant to be free. And that is why we were created. That's why it's been said that democracy is just a political reading of the Bible." The following month, he declared, "Politics and morality are inseparable. And as morality's foundation is religion, religion and politics are necessarily related. We need religion as a guide." He added, "We mandate no belief. But we poison our society when we remove its theological underpinnings. We court corruption when we leave it bereft of belief. . . . Without God, there is no virtue because there's no prompting of the conscience. Without God, we're mired in the material, that flat world that tells us only what the senses perceive. Without God, there is a coarsening of society. And without God, democracy will not and cannot long endure. If we ever forget that we're one nation under God, then we will be a nation gone under."[68]

In 1991 George H. W. Bush referred to faith and family as "the two fundamental pillars supporting our society." The following year, he declared, "Laws and budgets are not enough. We need a moral and, yes, a spiritual revival in our Nation so that families unite, fathers love mothers, stay together in spite of past pain and hard times because they love their children and look forward to another generation growing up tall and confident in the warmth of God's love." Three months later, he said, "It is our faith which will guarantee that the Sun never sets on our nation."[69]

Even those presidents who have been unwilling to assert that religious belief is essential to the attainment of virtue and, thus, to the survival of republics have considered faith a strong encouragement to virtue. In 1787 Thomas Jefferson wrote to his nephew Peter Carr regarding religious inquiry: "Do not be frightened from this enquiry by any fear of the consequences. If it ends in a belief that there is no god, you will find incitements to virtue in the comfort and pleasantness you feel in its exercise and the love of others which it will procure you." This was similar to what Jefferson wrote in 1814 regarding French atheists: "Diderot, d'Alembert, d'Holbach, Condorcet are known to have been among the most virtuous of men. Their virtue, then, must have had some other foundation than the love of God." Jefferson believed that this foundation was the moral sense, or conscience, which was itself a gift of God to every human being and which gave every person pleasure in doing good. Yet in the letter to his nephew, Jefferson also espoused the view that while religious belief might not be essential to virtue, it was a valuable aid to it: "If you find reason to believe there is a god, a consciousness that you are acting under his eye, and that he approves you, it will be a *vast* additional incitement [emphasis added]. If that there be a future state, the hope of a happy existence in that increases the appetite to deserve it; if that Jesus was also a god, you will be comforted by a belief in his aid and love." Similarly, in 1814, Jefferson listed belief in an afterlife characterized by rewards and punishments as one of the most powerful factors that motivated individuals to lead lives that benefited society. Thus, as we have seen, Jefferson donated the then large sum of fifty dollars to a Bible society and supported other missionary efforts in the United States based not only on a desire to spread the Christian system of ethics, which he considered the best, but also on the belief that some of the Bible's accompanying doctrines, including even the doctrine of Jesus's divinity that he himself rejected, led many people to virtue.[70]

George W. Bush seemed to take the same position. In 2001 he claimed, "Men and women can be good without faith, but faith is a force for goodness. Men and women can be compassionate without faith, but faith often inspires compassion. Human beings can love without faith, but faith is a great teacher of love." The following year, he reiterated, "Respect for the dignity of others can be found outside of religion, just as intolerance is sometimes found within it. Yet for millions of Americans, the practice of tolerance is a command of faith."[71]

Barack Obama agreed that faith, though not essential to virtue, was a strong incentive to it. In *The Audacity of Hope* (2006), he declared, "Organized religion doesn't have a monopoly of virtue, and one need not be religious to make moral claims or appeal to a common good." He presented his mother as an example: "Without the help of religious texts or outside authorities, she worked mightily to instill in me the values that many Americans learn in Sunday school: honesty, empathy, discipline, delayed gratification, and hard work." He credited her tutelage with his subsequent desire to serve as a community organizer and a public official. Nevertheless, he was acutely aware of the crucial role that churches played in the abolitionist and civil rights movements and of their continuing role in enhancing life. He wrote, "Faith can fortify a young woman's sense of self, a young man's sense of responsibility, and the sense of reverence all young people should have for the act of sexual intimacy." He added, "Secularists are wrong when they ask believers to leave their religion at the door before entering the public square; Frederick Douglass, Abraham Lincoln, William Jennings Bryan, Dorothy Day, Martin Luther King Jr.—indeed, the majority of great reformers in American history—not only were motivated by faith but repeatedly used religious language to argue their causes. To say that men and women should not inject their 'personal morality' into public policy debates is a practical absurdity; our law is by definition a codification of morality, much of it grounded in the Judeo-Christian tradition." Two years later, while a presidential candidate, Obama famously complained that working-class Pennsylvania voters "cling to their guns or religion." But he soon apologized for this choice of words and later explained in his presidential memoirs that he merely meant that working-class voters tended to "look to the traditions and way of life that have been constant in their lives," such as their faith, which explained why they had supported Republicans against their own economic interests: they became angry enough to do so when they felt that Democrats were denigrating these cherished traditions. Ironically, Obama's poor choice of words was itself considered a prime example of such a denigration, leading to his defeat in the Pennsylvania Democratic primary by nine points. In 2014 Obama claimed, "Religion strengthens America. Brave men and women have challenged our conscience and brought us closer to our founding ideals, from the abolition of slavery to civil rights, workers' rights."[72]

Even the few presidents who have stopped short of the contention that widespread faith in an omniscient, omnipotent, and intervening God is essential to the survival of republican government have argued that such faith is an invaluable aid to it. Like the other presidents, they have claimed that such faith inhibits behavior harmful to society and fosters a belief in the dignity and rights of all human beings, which is the bedrock of democracy.

CHAPTER 9

The Afterlife

Most presidents have derived from the Bible a belief in an afterlife characterized by rewards and punishments. This belief has comforted them in dealing with the deaths of loved ones and helped motivate their efforts and sacrifices on behalf of the nation.

There are some intimations of an afterlife in the Old Testament, though the doctrine is not emphasized there. The Book of Job, the oldest book in the Bible, suggests a resurrection (19:25–26): "For I know that my redeemer lives, and that he shall stand at the latter day upon the earth. And though worms destroy this body, yet in my flesh shall I see God." The Book of Daniel contains a similar reference to some sort of resurrection. In Daniel 12:2, the author states, "And many of them that sleep in the dust of the earth shall awaken, some to everlasting life, and some to shame and everlasting contempt." The famous twenty-third psalm that begins, "The Lord is my shepherd," concludes, "and I will dwell in the house of the Lord forever," suggesting an eternal afterlife. The death of Old Testament figures is often accompanied by the statement that they were "gathered to their ancestors" (e.g., Genesis 49:29; Judges 2:10; 2 Kings 22:20; 2 Chronicles 34:28), which makes no sense if they are considered to be moldering individually in widely separated graves. Indeed, in 2 Samuel 12:23, David says of his dead son, "I shall go to him." But it was in the New Testament that the existence of an eternal heaven and hell that awaited the deceased was emphasized since the chief importance of Jesus's death and resurrection was to enable believers to go to the former place and avoid the latter.

The Christian doctrine of the afterlife was one of the principal reasons that the faith overcame Roman persecution and defeated its pagan rivals. It was a great consolation during the late imperial period, when barbarian invasions, bloody civil wars, despotism, and recurrent epidemics severely limited life expectancy. Homer portrayed Hades, the Greek afterlife, as a dismal, shadowy realm of reduced consciousness for most and painful punishment for a few. Achilles, by then a resident of the place, informs the visiting Odysseus that it is better to be a slave on earth than the king of Hades (*Odyssey* 11.489–91). As a result, the Greek poets and playwrights often brooded over death. In Euripides's *Iphigenia in Aulis* (1218–19, 1251–52), Iphigenia pleads with her father, Agamemnon, who is about to sacrifice her to appease the gods: "Oh, my father, do not kill me. Life is so sweet, the grave is so black. . . . Death is nothingness. The most wretched life is better than the most glorious death." The Roman Catullus called Hades "a sad place from which no one returns," adding, "My hatred rises against your power, you that devours all things beautiful" (3.12–14). Even Virgil, who was not a brooder, referred to "Death's unpitying harness," which carried all away without exception. His Eurydice tells her husband, Orpheus, "Goodbye, forever. I am borne away, wrapped in endless night, stretching to you, no longer yours, these hands, these helpless hands" (*Georgics* 4.497–98). While the pagan Hades was not regarded as a place of extreme torture for most of its inhabitants, it was dismal enough that the New Testament writers felt comfortable employing it as their Greek name for hell.[1]

Thus deprived of the prospect of a pleasant existence in the afterlife, the Greek and Roman aristocratic classes sought immortality through fame. But fame as the ultimate reward for virtue possessed severe deficiencies. As the Roman emperor and Stoic philosopher Marcus Aurelius noted (*Meditations*, 4.19), sounding much like Solomon in the Book of Ecclesiastes, "Those who pursue posthumous fame do not take into account that posterity will be the same kind of men as those whom they now dislike. Posterity too will be mortal. What is it to you, anyway, what words they will utter about you or how they may think of you?" Even in the unlikely event that one attained posthumous fame, one would not be around to enjoy it. Many Romans of the Christian era decided that, like Woody Allen, they did not want to achieve immortality through their work but through not dying.

Although the Stoics and Neoplatonists did possess the concept of an afterlife, it centered on the soul's reintegration into a highly abstract world soul, which involved the loss of individuality. The deficiencies of this bland afterlife led their philosophers to a fatal emphasis on earthly happiness as the ultimate good—fatal because human life is prone to hardship. It was far easier for Christians to justify suffering by claiming that earthly existence was but a fleeting condition easily trumped by an eternal afterlife than for classical philosophers to justify it while locating the ultimate good in this life.[2]

George Washington believed in an afterlife. In 1788 he expressed the hope that a namesake "will have long enough to enjoy it [the name], long after I have taken my departure for the world of Spirits." In his Farewell Address (1796), Washington stated that he hoped his mistakes would be "consigned to oblivion, as [I] myself must soon be to the mansions of rest." This was a reference to Jesus's statement in John 14:2: "In my Father's house are many mansions. If it were not so, I would have told you. I go to prepare a place for you." Three years later, only nine months before his death, Washington wrote regarding the affairs of his estate: "My greatest anxiety is to leave all these concerns in such a clear and distinct form as that no reproach may attach itself to me when I have taken my departure for the land of Spirits." Washington's fellow Americans had no doubt about his place in "the mansions of rest," for after his death, the nation was flooded with various paintings titled *The Apotheosis of Washington*, which depicted him ascending into heaven flanked by angels.[3]

As a law student in the 1750s, John Adams argued on behalf of a "future State of Rewards and Punishments" against his mentor. In 1770 or 1771, John Adams wrote in his diary, "Virtue, by the constitution of nature, carries in general its own reward, and vice its own punishment, even in this world. But, as many exceptions to this rule take place upon earth, the joys of heaven are prepared, and the horrors of hell in a future state, to render the moral government of the universe perfect and complete." In 1796 he wrote to Thomas Jefferson regarding the French Revolution: "A Century must roll away before any permanent and quiet System will be established. An Amelioration of human affairs I hope and believe will be the result, but You and I must look down from the Battlements of Heaven if We ever have the Pleasure of Seeing it." In 1818 he declared, "I believe in God and in his Wisdom and Benevolence, and I cannot conceive that such a Being could make such a Species as the human merely to live and die on this Earth. If I did not believe [in] a future State, I should believe in no God. . . . And if there be a future State, why should the Almighty dissolve forever all the tender Ties which Unite Us so delightfully in this World and forbid Us to see each other in the next?" Less than six months before his death in 1826, Adams wrote,

> I am certainly very near the end of my life. I am far from trifling with the idea of Death, which is a great and solemn event. But I contemplate it without terror or dismay, "aut transit, aut finit" ["either it is a transformation or it is the end"]; if finit, which I cannot believe, and do not believe, there is then an end of all but I shall never know it, and why should I dread it, which I do

not; if transit, I shall ever be under the same constitution and administration of Government in the Universe, and I am not afraid to trust and confide in it.[4]

Thomas Jefferson espoused a belief in the afterlife throughout his life. As an adolescent, he copied into his literary commonplace book a few lines from Nicholas Row's popular play *Lady Jane Gray*:

Those who with Honest Hearts pursue the Right,
And follow faithfully Truth's sacred Light,
Tho' suffering here shall from their Sorrows cease,
Rest with the Saints & dwell in endless Peace.

Decades later Jefferson referred to the resurrection and divine judgment in a letter to Francis Willis. Jefferson claimed, "It is too soon for us as yet to despair of a rendezvous but in the valley of Jehoshaphat. I had rather flatter myself with seeing you here [at Monticello] or visiting you in Gloucester." The valley of Jehoshaphat in Israel is identified as the place of divine judgment in Joel 3:12. In 1804 Jefferson wrote to John Page to commiserate over the deaths of so many of their friends over the years. Jefferson claimed, "We have, however, the traveler's consolation. Every step shortens the distance we have to go; the end of our journey is in sight, the bed wherein we are to rest, and to rise in the midst of the friends we have lost. 'We sorrow not as others who have no hope.'" This last sentence was a quotation from 1 Thessalonians 4:13–14, in which the apostle Paul discusses the resurrection of the dead. Jefferson's quotation of Paul regarding the afterlife is striking considering his strong disagreement with some of the apostle's other doctrines, as we shall see later. Indeed, the famous Jefferson Bible, which excluded Paul's epistles and so much of the remainder of the actual Bible, included Jesus's parables concerning divine judgment and the coming of the Kingdom of God.[5]

In his later years, Jefferson often alluded to the afterlife in letters to Abigail and John Adams. In 1817 Jefferson wrote to Abigail regarding their deceased friends: "Our next meeting must then be in the country to which they have flown—a country for us not now very distant. For this journey we shall need neither gold nor silver in our purse, nor scrip, nor coats, nor staves [Matthew 10:9–10]." He added, "Perhaps, however, one of the elements of the future felicity is to be a constant and unimpassioned view of what is happening here." When Abigail died the following year, Jefferson wrote to John, "Nor, although mingling sincerely my tears with yours, will I say a word more where words are vain, but that it is of some comfort to us both that the term is not very distant at which we are to deposit in the same cerement our sorrows and suffering bodies and to ascend in essence to an ecstatic meeting with the friends we have loved and lost, and whom we shall still love and never lose again. God bless you and support you under your heavy affliction." The same year, he also wrote to John, "We shall be lookers on, from the clouds above, as now we look down on the labors, hurry, and bustle of the ants and bees." He added, "We may be amused with seeing the fallacy of our own guesses" about the future. In 1823 Jefferson wrote to John regarding heaven: "May we meet there again, in Congress, with our antient Colleagues, and receive with them the seal of approbation, 'Well done, good and faithful servants.'" This, of course, was a reference to the master's greeting of the good servant in Jesus's parable concerning Judgment Day (Matthew 25:21).[6]

In 1825, a year before his death, Jefferson wrote to a baby boy named Thomas Jefferson Smith:

> This letter will, to you, be as one from the dead. The writer will be in the grave before you can weigh its counsels. Your affectionate and excellent father has requested that I would address to you something which might possibly have a favorable influence on the course of life you have to run, and I too, as a namesake, feel an interest in that course. Few words will be necessary, with good dispositions on your part. Adore God. Reverence and cherish your parents. Love your neighbor as yourself, and your country more than yourself. Be just. Be true. Murmur not at the ways of Providence.

Just as Jefferson began with biblical advice, so he ended with a reference to the biblical reward for following that advice: "So shall the life into which you have entered be the portal to one of eternal and ineffable bliss. And if to the dead it be permitted to care for the things of this world, every action of your life will be under my regard. Farewell." Jefferson added his beloved fifteenth psalm as a postscript. Two days before his death, Jefferson penned a farewell poem for his daughter Martha that referred, in Old Testament style, to "going to my fathers" and to "welcoming the shore" at the end of life's voyage, where "two seraphs [his deceased wife and another daughter] await me."[7]

Jefferson derived considerable comfort from his belief in an afterlife. Upon the death of his wife, Martha, in 1782, he was plunged into an overwhelming, paralyzing grief that eventually subsided but never fully departed. After his own death, his family discovered small envelopes containing locks of hair from his wife and each of his deceased children, along with words of endearment about each written in his own hand, in a secret drawer of a private cabinet. The envelopes showed signs of frequent handling. Unlike Jefferson's other religious beliefs, each of which he attempted to justify rationally, he knew that it was impossible to prove the existence of an afterlife yet chose to believe in it unwaveringly throughout his life based on faith alone—the very trait he often decried in more orthodox Christians regarding other issues.[8]

A sickly youth, James Madison kept one eye on eternity. In 1772 he wrote to a close friend that it was acceptable to have earthly ambition "if we do not allow it to intercept our views towards a future State." He added, "A watchful eye must be kept on ourselves lest while we are building ideal monuments of Renown and Bliss here we neglect to have our names enrolled in the Annals of Heaven. . . . As to myself, I am too dull and infirm now to look out for any extraordinary things in this world, for I think my sensations for many months past have intimated to me not to expect a long or healthy life." He lived to be eighty-five, having played pivotal roles in the drafting and ratifying of the US Constitution and the Bill of Rights, in addition to serving as the fourth president.[9]

James Monroe appears to have possessed the same belief in an afterlife. In 1778 he wrote to Baron von Steuben's military secretary, Peter Duponceau, who was seriously ill: "The summit of the Christian fortitude [is] to prevail over the views of this transitory life and turn the mind on the more lasting happiness of that to come."[10]

John Quincy Adams called the immortality of the soul "a doctrine which constitutes the peculiar glory of Christianity, as that of an immaterial God did of the old testament . . . and vanquishes the heaviest of all human calamities." Adams maintained that an afterlife of rewards and punishments, such as that related in the Bible, was necessary to vindicate divine justice. Regarding Plutarch's essay, "On the Delay of Divine Justice," the Greek biographer-philosopher's attempt to explain why injustice often seemed to prevail in life, Adams wrote, "Plutarch reasons well, but leaves much of the mysterious veil over his subject which nothing but Christian doctrine can remove. If the existence of man was limited to this life, it would be impossible for me to believe the universe under any moral government. . . . It is not the affliction of the righteous, but the prosperity of the wicked, which would contribute most to stagger my faith in Divine Justice." An afterlife of rewards and punishments was crucial to divine justice since outcomes in this life were often clearly unfair. In 1822, after hearing a sermon on 1 Corinthians 15:26 ("The last enemy that shall be destroyed is death"), Adams wrote in his diary, "This is the chapter in which the immortality of the soul and the resurrection of the dead is argued to all the reason and urged to all the feelings of human nature and with the deepest logic and sublimest eloquence of St. Paul. I am always profoundly affected by the perusal of this chapter."

Adams particularly relished "that triumphant and transporting" fifty-fifth verse: "O Death, where is thy sting? O grave, where is thy victory?"[11]

In 1841 Adams concluded a lengthy oration before the Supreme Court in the *United States v. Amistad* case with a pointed reference to the afterlife, wishing that the justices would "be received at the portals of the next [life] with the approving sentence—'Well done, good and faithful servant; enter thou into the joy of the Lord.'" This was an unsubtle way of reminding the justices that they would soon stand before the bar of a far greater judge, who would hold them accountable for their own administration of justice.[12]

Andrew Jackson was devastated by the loss of his wife, Rachel, but took comfort in biblical promises regarding the afterlife. At a small gathering following Rachel's funeral, he said, "Friends and neighbors, I thank you for the honor you have done to the sainted one whose remains now repose in yonder grave. She is now in the bliss of heaven, and I know that she can suffer here no more on earth. That is enough for my consolation; my loss is her gain." The epitaph he wrote for her concluded, "Even death, when he tore her from the arms of her husband, could but transport her to the bosom of her God." A couple of weeks after her death, he wrote, "It pleased God to take her from this world on the night of 22d December and by this solemn dispensation of His Divine Providence to deprive me of my stay and solace whilst in it. I bow to the decree but feel its afflictive power; how weak are the sentiments of Philosophy without the aid of divine Grace—that grace which enables it to pierce the veil of futurity and find in the convulsions here an immortal birth in the hereafter, where the good unite again and the wicked disturb not." Four months later, he wrote, "Deprived of all hope of happiness this side of the grave, [I] often wish myself at the Hermitage, there to spend the remnant of my days and daily drop a tear on the tomb of my beloved wife, and be prepared, when providence wills it, to unite with her in the realms above." The next month, he wrote to Rachel's brother, who had just visited her grave,

> Yes, my friend, it is time that you should withdraw from the turmoils of this world and prepare for another. . . . I therefore join in the sentiments of my dear departed and beloved wife in admonishing you to withdraw from the busy cares of this world and put your house in order for the next by laying hold of "the one thing most needful." Go read the Scripture; the joyful promises it contains will be a balsam to all your troubles and create for you a kind of heaven here on earth, a consolation to your troubled mind that is not to be found in the hurry and bustle of this world.[13]

252 ~ Chapter 9

Jackson applied the same lesson to other deaths. Three months later, he wrote to his friend John Coffee, who had just lost his daughter Emily:

> We ought not to mourn for the dead but for the living. . . . You ought to be perfectly resigned to her death when you recollect the reply of our savior to his disciples, "Let little children come unto me, for such is the kingdom of heaven [Matthew 19:14]." She is a little angel, now with my Dear wife (her aunt) in the bosom of our savior enjoying that exquisite happiness bought by the death and sufferings of our dear redeemer on the cross, an atonement made for sinners that they might not perish but have everlasting life by repentance & belief in him. What a cheering thought to all the afflicted here below & the only that makes life supportable to me under my afflictions & arduous labours, that I am hastening to that bourn whence no traveler returns, with a hope that I shall unite again with my Dear Sainted wife in bliss in the mansions of the skies "where I will bathe my troubled soul in seas of heavenly rest & not a wave of trouble roll across my peaceful breast."

This last quote was from Isaac Watts's hymn "The Hopes of Heaven Our Support Under Trials on Earth." In 1835 Jackson wrote to his nephew regarding the death of that nephew's grandmother. He declared, "[She] was a long member of the church, and I have no doubt but she is in the regions of bliss enjoying the smiles of her dear redeemer and united with other saints gone before her, praising the one God for his undying love and redeeming grace." He added earnestly, "Remember, my dear Andrew, that we are all born to die, and we ought to live in such a manner as at all times to be prepared for death." In the last year of Jackson's own life, he wrote, "I am worn down with affliction, bad cough, pain in my side and great debility, and have written with great difficulty and pain, and am waiting with patience the summons of my precious Saviour for the call to my home."[14]

After losing his wife and his daughter within a few years, Millard Fillmore wrote in 1854: "I do not mean to grieve, much less complain. Heaven blessed me many years and has now withdrawn these precious jewels from my sight and taken them home to wean me from this world and tempt me to my celestial abode. I must, at any rate, follow soon, and I hope that I may be there again united to those who have gone before and who were so dear to me here." Three years later, as Fillmore watched his elderly father decline, he hoped that "my life may be spared to perform the last sad offices of filial affections to his mortal remains when his spirit shall seek its congenial resting place in the society of those who have gone before it."[15]

In 1839 James Buchanan thanked Andrew Jackson for a public declaration of faith precisely because Buchanan believed it would encourage Americans to prepare for their own afterlives. Buchanan wrote, "Although not a member of any church myself, yet I was gratified to learn, both for your own sake and that of the example, that you had borne a public testimony to the truth and power of religion. It alone can convert the inevitable ills attendant upon humanity into positive blessings and thus wean us from this world; and make death itself the portal to another and a better state of existence." In 1855 Buchanan wrote to his niece and ward Harriet following the death of her sister: "This sad event ought to teach you the vanity of all things human & transitory & cause you to fix your thoughts, desires, & affections on that Being with whom 'there is no variableness or shadow of turning [James 1:17].' ... At the last, all the proceedings of a mysterious Providence will be justified in another & a better world & it is our duty here to submit with humble resignation."[16]

In 1851 Abraham Lincoln wrote to John Johnston, a son of his stepmother by a different father:

> I sincerely hope Father may recover his health; but at all events tell him to remember to call upon and confide in our great, good, and merciful Maker, who will not turn away from him in any extremity. He notes the fall of a sparrow and numbers the hairs of our heads [Matthew 10:29–30]; and He will not forget the dying man who puts his trust in Him. . . . If it be his lot to go now, he will soon have a joyous [meeting] with many loved ones gone before, and where [the rest] of us, through the help of God, hope ere-long [to join] them.[17]

Andrew Johnson expressed a belief in the biblical afterlife. He declared, "The just and pure in heart are to be rewarded in heaven with crowns of glory, while the unjust and vile sinner is to be punished in a hell 'where the worm dieth not and the fire is never quenched [Mark 9:44].'"[18]

James Garfield agreed. In 1850 he contended, "Death is not an eternal sleep!" Two years later, he wrote regarding a revival meeting: "19 glorious souls were induced to obey the Lord. There was rejoicing [in heaven] and rejoicing on earth. These scenes stir the soul to its inmost depths and rouse the holiest joy e'er known to mortal man and gives him a foretaste of the celestial joys that await the righteous."[19]

While at Stanford to give a series of lectures in 1893, Benjamin Harrison attended a church service. To his astonishment, a lay speaker declared that heaven was "the myth of Savages." Harrison was so "outraged" and "so indignant that I could hardly sit still."[20]

William McKinley also believed in an afterlife. As a Union soldier in 1861, he wrote in his diary regarding his parents and siblings that if he should die "Let them be consoled with the solacing thought that if we never meet again on earth, we will meet around God's throne in Heaven." In 1889 he noted regarding Civil War veterans: "Our circle is narrowing with the passing years. Every annual roll call discloses one and another not present but accounted for. There is a muster roll over yonder as well as a muster roll here. The majority of that vast army are fast joining their old commanders who have preceded them on that other shore." Four years later, McKinley delivered a speech on the occasion of the departed Ulysses Grant's birthday, in which he mused, "Above him in his chamber of sickness and death hung the portraits of Washington and Lincoln, whose disembodied spirits in the Eternal City were watching and waiting for him who was to complete the immortal trio of America's first and best loved; and as the earthly scenes receded from his view and the celestial appeared, I can imagine these were the first to greet his sight and bid him welcome."[21]

William Howard Taft believed in an afterlife characterized by divine judgment. Even as a young lawyer, the future president and Supreme Court chief justice believed that, at their best, earthly courts foreshadowed the divine justice that awaited human souls in the afterlife. He claimed, "I love judges, and I love courts. They are my ideals that typify on earth what we shall meet hereafter in heaven under a just God."[22]

Woodrow Wilson believed in the biblical afterlife. In 1884 he wrote to his fiancée, Ellen: "Your dear father, however sad and tragic his death may have been, is happy now. His Saviour, we may be sure, did not desert his servant at the supreme moment; and it is a joy to think that he is now reunited to the sweet, noble mother who went before him."[23]

In an address at the Professional Athletes Prayer Brunch, Gerald Ford alluded to the afterlife, declaring,

> The ultimate reward is nothing less than a place in the kingdom of God. Each of you, famous, wealthy, and happy as you may be, knows that the things of this world are fleeting, that immortality is not something a sportswriter can bestow upon you, that all earthly things shall pass away. For this reason, you have made a commitment that will last beyond this mortal life into the true realm of immortality. You have made the great decision to live your lives in such a way that you would rejoice to serve your God through eternity. You are prepared to lay all your trophies at His feet. This is a worthy and wonderful goal for all of your lives. Let us strive always to achieve it so that we may say

with Paul at the end of our lives, "I have fought a good fight, I have finished my course, I have kept the faith [2 Timothy 4:7]."[24]

Jimmy Carter agreed. In 1971 he declared, "We Christians know that men live on, that mortal death need be no end." Six years later, he told his Sunday school class regarding death: "If we are Christians, that's the beginning of our promised life with Christ." Four months later, he said, "It is one of the crucial elements of Christian belief that life does not terminate at the time of physical death." In 1978 he said, "Christ's death and resurrection proved to us that there's life after death." Nineteen years later, Carter cited 1 Corinthians 15:42–44 to support the doctrine of a resurrection and afterlife. These verses state: "The body that is sown is perishable; it is raised imperishable. . . . It is sown a natural body; it is raised a spiritual body."[25]

In 1990 Ronald Reagan reflected on his duties during World War II: "As the adjutant of my Army Air Corps post during the war, I'd had the responsibility to call the parents of combat cameramen who had been killed in action and tell them their sons wouldn't be returning from the war. I learned then that there is not much you can say to comfort people in such a situation, but you have to try. All I could do was tell them how much they had to be proud of and that we had to believe God's promise that one day we will all be united with our loved ones." A few years after performing this duty, Reagan wrote in a fan magazine article, "I do think there's something beyond the grave, that we were given souls for a reason, that if we live as the Bible tells us to, a promise will be kept." Surprisingly, he added, "I don't believe in hell. I can't believe that an all wise and loving Father would condemn any of His children to eternal damnation." As president in 1985, however, Reagan was disinclined to make so sweeping a judgment while at the German cemetery at Bitburg, when he said regarding the soldiers buried there, "All these men have now met their supreme judge, and they have been judged by Him, as we shall all be judged." Judgment implies the possibility of a negative verdict and, thus, punishment of some sort. Seven months later, Reagan stated regarding Jesus: "He promised there will never be a long night that does not end. He promised to deliver us from the dark torment and tragedy into the warming sunlight of human happiness and, beyond that, into paradise. He's never been a half-way giver; His generosity is pure and perfect and sure." In 1986, at the memorial service for the crew of the space shuttle *Challenger*, Reagan declared, "We know in our hearts that you who flew so high and so proud now make your home beyond the stars, safe in God's promise of eternal life." The following year, at a memorial service for crew members of the USS *Stark*, which was attacked by an

Iraqi aircraft while patrolling the Persian Gulf, Reagan quoted Jesus in John 15:13: "Greater love than this has no man than to lay down his life for his friends." Reagan continued, "And because God is love [1 John 4:8], we know He was there with them when they died, and He is with them still. We know they live again, not just in our hearts but in His arms." Reagan concluded, "And as we submit to the will of Him who made us, we pray together in the words of scripture: 'Lord, now let thy servants go in peace. Thy word has been fulfilled [Luke 2:29].' . . . They have stepped through the door that God has promised all of us. They do live now in a world where there is no sorrow, no pain. And they await us, and we shall be together again." Reagan's son Michael later wrote, "The greatest gift my father ever gave me was the simple knowledge that I would see him in heaven one day."[26]

George H. W. Bush was comforted by his belief in heaven. He would often say about his daughter Robin, who died of leukemia when she was three years old, "She's in heaven now." He recalled his mother's death in 1992: "I knew for sure that she would go to heaven; I also knew that she looked upon death not with fear but with joy. She told me over and over again that she would be with my Dad in heaven. During that last visit, she was struggling for life; but I knelt by her bed and literally prayed that God would take her to heaven right then." Bush also recalled how appalled he had been by the funeral of Soviet General Secretary Leonid Brezhnev, which he attended as vice president in 1982. The funeral was lavish, but because it was a communist ceremony, "there was no mention of God. There was no hope, no joy, no life ever after, no mention of Christ and what His death has meant to many. So discouraging in a sense, so hopeless, so lonely."[27]

In 2001 George W. Bush declared, "We look beyond our lives to the hour when God will wipe away every tear [Revelation 21:4] and death will be swallowed up in victory [1 Corinthians 15:54]." He added, "Beyond the Gates of Time lie a life eternal and a love everlasting." Four years later, he stated, "In the end even death itself will be defeated. That is the promise of Easter morning." He ended his eulogy for his father in 2018: "Let us smile knowing that Dad is hugging Robin and holding Mom's hand again."[28]

In 2012 Barack Obama comforted the survivors of the Sandy Hook massacre by quoting 2 Corinthians 4:16–5:1: "Do not lose heart. Though outwardly we are wasting away, inwardly we are being renewed day by day. For our momentary troubles are achieving for us an eternal glory that far outweighs them. So, we fix our eyes not on what is seen, but on what is unseen, since what is seen is temporary, but what is unseen is eternal. For we know that if the earthly tent that we live in is destroyed, we have a building from God, an eternal house in heaven, not built by human hands." The author of this epistle, the apostle Paul, was a tentmaker by vocation, so the contrasting images of the earthly body as a tent and the heavenly body as a permanent structure came naturally to him. Obama preceded the reading of the names of the twenty-two children who had died in the massacre with Matthew 19:14: "'Let the little children come to me,' Jesus said, 'and do not hinder them—for to such belong the Kingdom of Heaven.'" Three years later, Obama noted, "Through God's mercy, Peter the Apostle said, we are 'given an inheritance that is imperishable, undefiled, and unfading, kept in heaven for you [1 Peter 1:4].'"[29]

Rutherford Hayes was alone among presidents in expressing uncertainty concerning the afterlife. In 1889, as his beloved wife, Lucy, lay dying, he was comforted by the fact that "without pain, without the usual suffering, she has been permitted to come to the gates of the great change which leads to the life where pain and suffering are unknown." His use of the word "life" rather than "state" suggests a belief in an afterlife. Indeed, after she died, he declared, "She is in Heaven. She is where all the best of earth have gone." Yet months later, he wrote that he could not state for certain that there was an afterlife, though he trusted in God regardless. Similarly, in the following year, he wrote, "I believe in the moral government of the universe. I trust and have faith in the power, wisdom, and goodness of the Divine Eternal." Therefore, he continued, "Death must be good for its victims." This statement stopped short of declaring a belief in heaven, and its comprehensiveness appeared to reject the biblical doctrine of hell. Indeed, in 1892, only a few months before his own death, Hayes dubbed as "monstrous" the biblical idea that "God, the Father of all, God, who is love, dooms millions of his creatures to eternal torment."[30]

The biblical doctrine of the afterlife has provided presidents with priceless comfort. While they have emulated the classical heroes in placing a high valuation on fame, which they have defined as the favorable "judgment of History," a valuation that has inspired them to perform great deeds in order to establish "a legacy," they have also been aware of posthumous fame's severe limitations. They have often claimed that true immortality rests on the judgment of an omniscient God and manifests itself in eternal bliss, rather than depending on the often conflicting judgments of subjective historians and manifesting itself in the fleeting praise of fellow mortals, a glory that cannot even be enjoyed by the deceased. While the Protestant denominations of most presidents have interpreted the Bible to assert that salvation comes through faith alone, not good deeds, they have also taught that good deeds are the inevitable product of a sincere faith and earn their doers greater rewards in heaven than those received by the slothful. This belief has likely played a larger role in motivating American presidents' sacrifices on behalf of the nation than their ambition for fame.

CHAPTER 10

The Orthodox and the Unorthodox

While many presidents have believed in the divine origin and authority of the Bible, a few have not. While nearly all have revered Jesus as the greatest ethical philosopher in history, a few have doubted or denied His divinity. While many have embraced the New Testament doctrine that faith in Jesus is essential to salvation, a few have rejected it.

The Divine Origin and Authority of Scripture

The biblical authors themselves refer to the divine origin and authority of Scripture. In Psalms 119:11 David declares to God regarding the Torah, the first five books of the Bible, "Your Word have I hidden in my heart that I might not sin against you." In 2 Timothy 3:16, the apostle Paul states, "All scripture is given by inspiration of God, and is profitable for doctrine, for reproof, for correction, and for instruction in righteousness." 2 Peter 1:20–21 claims, "No prophecy of the scripture is of any private interpretation. For the prophecy came in old time not by the will of man; but holy men of God spoke as they were moved by the Holy Spirit."

Most presidents have believed in the divine origin and authority of the Bible. Franklin Pierce referred to it as "the blessed Word of God." In 1831 James Buchanan called it "the fountain of all truth." A decade later, he called Christianity "the purest and best gift which ever descended from Heaven upon man."[1]

Abraham Lincoln was another believer in the Bible. Defending himself against what he regarded as slander hatched by his opponent in a congressional race in 1846, Lincoln declared, "That I am not a member of any Christian church is true, but I have never denied the truth of the Scriptures."

One evening in the terrible summer of 1864, when Union casualties were mounting at an alarming rate and Lincoln's prospects for reelection appeared dim, his old friend Joshua Speed found him intently reading the Bible. When Speed remarked that he remained skeptical about the book, Lincoln replied, "You are wrong, Speed. Take all of this book upon reason that you can, and the balance on faith, and you will live and die a happier man." A few months later, Lincoln wrote regarding the Bible: "In regard to this Great Book, I have but to say, it is the best gift God has given to man. All the good the Saviour gave to the world was communicated through this book. But for it we could not know right from wrong. All things most desirable for man's welfare, here and hereafter, are to be found portrayed in it."[2]

Andrew Johnson referred to the Bible as "the highest of all authority" in 1845. Seventeen years later, he declared, "I reverence the teachings of the Gospel," claiming that they "arched the circuit of the skies and rested on the ends of the Universe."[3]

Ulysses Grant agreed. His friend and pastor John P. Newman wrote, "Accepting the Bible as the word of God to man, he regarded Christianity as divine."[4]

James Garfield wrote in his diary in 1850, "I wish that men would let all human tradition alone and take the Bible alone for their guide." Twelve days later, he claimed,

> The Apostles spoke not their own experience, but they spoke as the Holy Spirit gave them utterance. Will then mortal man dare to dispute the teachings of God and supplant His own word? Let us rather meekly follow the precept and bright example of our savior and not attempt to spiritualize and explain away plain passages of Scripture to suit our views, but let us take the naked word, the truth as it is in Jesus, as our only rule of faith and practice. If the world would do this, how much less strife and contention would there be than at the present time.

Two years later, he wrote, "Truth is mighty, eternal, and the Bible firm as the Throne of God shall stand when kingdoms crumble and the planets crash. Its holy truths through ceaseless ages still shall send a blaze of heavenly light and drive the darkness from the nauseous tomb." Similarly, in 1903, Theodore Roosevelt referred to the Bible as not only "the oldest and greatest of books," but also as "the Word of God."[5]

As a Princeton student in 1876, Woodrow Wilson wrote that the Bible was filled with "divine inspiration and truth." He added, "The radical error among modern Christians is neglect of the Word of God. We are too apt to seek for real information and instruction from other sources. Christian people are too much in the habit of seeking for instruction and improvement from lesser streams of knowledge, in preference to going to the eternal fountainhead which is ever at hand." Regarding the Bible, he claimed, "With every perusal new rays of light burst upon the soul [of the reader] and give a new claim even to those portions with which he is most familiar. Let us value more this old and yet ever new volume." A decade later, he declared that the Bible "speaks of the human heart with a Maker's knowledge of the thing He had made" and contains "the deep things of daily life." In 1909 he referred to the Bible as "the book of rules for that great game" of life. Two years later, he declared regarding Scripture: "We know that there is a standard set for us in the heavens, a standard revealed to us in this book, which is the fixed and eternal standard by which we are to judge ourselves." In 1917, as a wartime president, he issued a statement to American soldiers and sailors in which he declared, "When you read the Bible, you will know that it is the Word of God because you will have found it the key to your own heart, your own happiness, and your own duty."[6]

In 1935 Franklin Roosevelt referred to the Bible as "these sacred pages." He added, "It has withstood assaults. It has resisted and survived the most searching microscopic examination. It has stood every test that could be applied to it. It continues to hold its supreme place as the Book of books."[7]

Other presidents have also believed in the divine origin and authority of Scripture. In 1949 Harry Truman referred to the Bible as "the word of God." Likewise, two years later, he referred to "the teaching that has come down to us from the days of the prophets and the life of Jesus" as "the word of God." John F. Kennedy also referred to the Bible as "the Word of God" and "the Holy Word," applauding its dissemination across the globe. Lyndon Johnson joined the chorus in terming the Bible "the Word of God." Additionally, Gerald Ford called the Bible "the Book of Truth," referred to the Ten Commandments as "truths that are not debatable," and declared that "God speaks to us through the Holy Bible."[8]

Jimmy Carter called the Bible "the operating manual for life on earth," "the inspired word of God," "the Holy Word of God," and "a foundation for everything we believe." In 1976 he complained to a newspaper editor: "The article in Monday's *Atlanta Constitution* states that I do not 'believe in such biblical accounts as Eve being created from Adam's rib and other such miracles.' I've never made such a statement and have no reason to disbelieve Genesis 2:21–22 or other biblical miracles." In 1997 he argued against the disregarding of troubling biblical passages: "If we begin eliminating verses that we consider outdated, we may find ourselves choosing just those verses that happen to suit our own temperaments, habits, and foibles. The Bible should help correct our personal tastes, not just reinforce them."⁹

Ronald Reagan referred to scripture as "the Holy Bible," "the inspired word of God," and "the infallible wellspring of our national goodness." In 1967 he wrote, "I believe the Bible is the result of Divine inspiration and is not just a history." In 1983 he declared, "Inside its pages lie all the answers to all the problems that man has ever known." George W. Bush also referred to the Bible as "the Word of God." In 2013 Barack Obama referred to scripture as "the words of God." He then added, "God has told us how He wishes for us to spend our days. His Commandments are there to be followed."¹⁰

A few presidents have believed that the Bible contains revelations from God but have not considered the book inerrant. In 1810 John Adams declared confidently that the attacks of skeptics "will never discredit Christianity, which will hold its ground in some degree as long as human nature shall have anything moral or intellectual left in it." He added, "The Christian religion, as I understand it, is the brightness of the glory and express portrait of the character of the eternal, self-existent, independent, benevolent, all powerful and all merciful creator, preserver, and father of the universe, the first good, first perfect, and first fair. It will last as long as the world. Neither savage nor civilized man, without a revelation, could ever have discovered or invented it." Three years later, he wrote, "The general principles of Christianity are as eternal and immutable as the Existence and Attributes of God."¹¹

Yet Adams's passionate defense of the Bible did not mean that he considered it inerrant. On the contrary, in 1813, he wondered if the Ten Commandments had been altered between the time of their promulgation and their recording in the Book of Exodus.¹²

Adams's son, John Quincy, shared both his father's reverence for the Bible and his doubts concerning its inerrancy. In an 1811 letter to his son George, John Quincy emphasized the unique truths contained in Scripture: "Almost all the Greek philosophers reasoned and meditated upon the nature of the gods, but scarcely any of them ever reflected enough even to imagine that there was but one God, and not one of them ever conceived of him as the Creator of the world." By contrast, Adams continued, "The first words of the Bible are, 'In the beginning God created the heaven and the earth.' This blessed and sublime God, the creator of the universe—the source of all human virtue and all human happiness, for which the sages and philosophers of Greece groped in darkness and never found, is revealed in the first verse of the Book of Genesis." Adams concluded, "To such a God [as is found in the Bible] the heart of man must yield with cheerfulness the tribute of homage, which it never could pay to the bleating gods of Egypt, to the dissolute debauchees of the Grecian mythology, nor even to the more elevated, but no less fantastical, imaginations of the Grecian philosophers and sages." A week later, he more clearly linked the unique benefits of the Bible to its divine status:

> The Bible contains the revelation of the will of God, it contains the history of the creation of the world and of mankind, and afterwards the history of one peculiar nation, certainly the most extraordinary nation that has ever appeared upon earth. It contains a system of religion and morality which we may examine upon its own merits, independent of the sanction it receives from being the word of God, and it contains a collection of books, written at different ages of the world by different authors, which we may survey as curious monuments of antiquity and as literary compositions. In what light soever we regard it, whether with reference to revelation, to history, to morality, or to literature, it is an invaluable and inexhaustible mine of knowledge and virtue.

A couple of weeks later, he wrote that the principal beliefs indispensable to happiness and virtue, belief in God and in the afterlife, were "disclosed in the Bible by special and distinct Revelations from God in a manner altogether different from the ordinary course of nature—and hence it follows that the Bible, considered as Divine Revelation, contains a series of direct Communications from the Creator of mankind to individual persons which have been by some of them committed to writing and which include a code of moral and religious Laws suitable for all mankind and binding upon all who are blest with the Knowledge of it."[13]

But this did not mean that Adams considered Scripture inerrant or that he never struggled with any doubts about biblical miracles. In one of the 1811 letters to his son, he wrote regarding the Bible: "I do not consider every part of it even in the original languages as having been written by preternatural inspiration from Heaven. I do not suppose it necessary to consider the Book as exempt from physical, geographical, and Chronological errors." In 1826 he wrote, "The miracles of the New Testament appear to have been performed as evidence of the divine mission of Christ; faith was to be founded on the mighty works by which it was authenticated. But now the order of proof is reversed: it is the doctrine of the Scriptures alone that can obtain credence for the miracles." Since the people of Jesus's day lacked the persuasive text of the New Testament propounding the glorious doctrines of Christianity, they required miracles to believe in the doctrines, whereas subsequent people lacked that direct experience of miracles and therefore required the powerful prose of the New Testament to believe in them. But even with the benefit of that text, Adams struggled to believe in some of the miracles. It was not that Adams doubted the ability of an omnipotent God to perform miracles, nor did he believe for a moment, like Thomas Jefferson and others, that God was somehow morally bound "to exclusive operation by general laws." On the contrary, Adams argued forcefully that the same being who created the laws that governed the universe had complete power and moral authority to make exceptions to them whenever he wished. It was the "fact of the miracles," rather than their mere possibility, that he considered inherently problematic for those who had not witnessed them. Adams wrote, "The miracles in the Bible furnish the most powerful of all the objections against authenticity, both historical and doctrinal; and were it possible to take its sublime morals, its unparalleled conception of the nature of God, and its irresistible power over the heart, with the simple narrative of the life and death of Jesus, stripped of all the supernatural agency and all the marvelous incidents connected with it, I should receive it without any of the misgivings of *unwilling* incredulity as to the miracles, which I find it impossible altogether to cast off [emphasis added]."[14]

Indeed, Adams tended to allegorize those passages with which he struggled the most. For instance, he wrote regarding Genesis 2 and 3: "The trees of knowledge and of life are personified abstractions, and the serpent is the fascinating and seductive spirit."[15]

Despite his ardor in disseminating Scripture while vice president of a county Bible society, Rutherford Hayes was skeptical about parts of it. Whereas, in 1844, he had claimed that the Bible contained "the true doctrines of the Saviour," by 1851, he was writing in the same diary, "Many of the notions—nay, most of the notions—which orthodox people have of the divinity of the Bible I disbelieve. I am so nearly an infidel in all my views, that too in spite of my wishes, that none but the most liberal doctrines can command my assent." The following year, he expressed agreement with the views of Theodore Parker: "The God of the Old Testament is partial, revengeful, hating and loving without just cause, unmerciful, etc. . . . The New Testament idea was juster, higher, but still imperfect. For it represents Him as not perfect in love, justice, goodness, or even power. For it makes Him the author of absolute and eternal evil, viz.: a Devil in Hell and endless punishment, and presents Him as compelled to resort to suffering to save his creatures." In 1862, when commanding a Union regiment in West Virginia, Hayes agonized over his own skepticism, writing regarding the Christian doctrine of immortality:

I have been and am an unbeliever of all these sacred verities. But will I not take refuge in the faith of my fathers at last? Are we not all impelled to this? The great abyss, the unknown future—are we not happier if we give ourselves up to some settled faith? Can we feel safe without it? Am I not more carried along, drifted, towards surrendering to the best religion the world has yet produced? It seems so. . . . [I] think of the closing years on the downhill side of life and picture myself a Christian, sincere, humble, devoted, as conscientious in that as I am now in this [war].[16]

While a student at Whittier College in California in the 1930s, Richard Nixon denied that the Bible was the infallible Word of God. He wrote, "My education has taught me that the Bible, like all other books, is the work of man and consequently has man-made mistakes."[17]

Thomas Jefferson was perhaps the most skeptical president concerning the Bible. He combined Christian ethics with elements of Epicureanism, a combination that could be sustained only by rejecting much of the Old Testament and by insisting that the New Testament was a corrupted record of Jesus's teachings.

When Jefferson was a young man in the 1760s, the largest single collection of passages that he had copied into his literary commonplace book, comprising almost 40 percent of it, consisted of excerpts from Bolingbroke's *Philosophical Works*, which attacked the Bible. Bolingbroke summarized his position on the matter: "There are gross defects and palpable falsehoods in almost every page of the scriptures, and the whole tenor of them is such as no man who acknowledges a supreme all-perfect being can believe [them] to be his word."[18]

Jefferson adopted Bolingbroke's skepticism regarding the integrity of Scripture. In 1814 he wrote concerning the Old Testament, "The whole history of these books is so defective and doubtful that it seems vain to attempt minute inquiry into it, and such tricks have been played with their text, and with the texts of other books relating to them, that we have a right, from that cause, to entertain much doubt what parts of them are genuine."[19]

Jefferson rejected Old Testament miracles. In 1786 he dismissed the great flood as the explanation for the discovery of seashells on mountaintops. He gave the biblical flood credence only as "a partial deluge in the country lying around the Mediterranean." The following year, Jefferson wrote to his nephew that he should read the Bible "as you would read Livy or Tacitus." He added,

For example, in the book of Joshua [10:12–14] we are told the sun stood still several hours. Were we to read that fact in Livy or Tacitus we should class it with their showers of blood, speaking of statues, beasts & c., but it is said that the writer of the book was inspired. The pretension is entitled to your inquiry because millions believe it. On the other hand, you are Astronomer enough to know how contrary it is to the law of nature that a body revolving on its axis, as the earth does, should have stopped, shall not by that sudden stoppage have prostrated animals, trees, buildings, and should after a certain time have resumed its revolution, and that without a second general prostration. Is this arrest of the earth's motion, or the evidence which affirms it, most within the law of probabilities?

Jefferson's own answer was clear.[20]

As the historian Daniel Boorstin has noted, Jefferson borrowed from the Bible the belief in an omniscient, omnipotent Creator but departed from it by denying that the Creator ever violated his own "natural laws" through miracles. While Jefferson never doubted the capacity of an omnipotent Creator to suspend His own laws and to circumvent the consequences that would otherwise result from such a suspension, he denied the rationality of his doing so. To Jefferson, God was the quintessential rationalist who could never act in any way that Jefferson deemed irrational. Jefferson never questioned whether humans, as limited beings, possessed the unlimited knowledge, experience, and wisdom that would logically be necessary to judge what was rational for an omniscient being to do. Part of Jefferson's abhorrence of the concept of a God who would violate His own "laws" derived from the traditional use of that term in reference to the causal sequences of the material world. It is one thing to state that God cannot violate His own moral laws without being both immoral and hypocritical; it is quite another to state that He cannot suspend causal sequences of His own creation on rare occasions in order to advance a good or to draw human attention to something important without betraying His character. (Indeed, the Greek New Testament word for miracle, *semeion*, means "sign," suggesting that its authors interpreted miracles as divine attempts to draw attention to something.) The former would constitute an ethical violation; the latter, a mere suspension of entirely amoral processes. For instance, to call the causal sequences associated with gravity "a law" is to endow them with a moral dimension they do not logically possess. Once the inherently ethical word "law" was attached to mere causal sequences, as it had been for a century by Jefferson's day, the crucial distinction between the moral and the amoral was fatally blurred.[21]

Furthermore, while Jefferson loved the Psalms and often referred to ethical models in the Old Testament, he was extremely critical of the Mosaic Law and other aspects of Old Testament morality. In 1803, after congratulating the Jews of the Old Testament for their belief in a single God, he added, "But their ideas of him and of his attributes were degrading and injurious. Their Ethics were not only imperfect but often irreconcilable with the sound dictates of reason and morality as they respect intercourse with those around us, and repulsive and anti-social as respecting other nations." In 1819 he declared, "I am not a Jew, and therefore do not adopt their theology, which supposes the God of infinite justice to punish the sins of the fathers upon their children unto the third and fourth generation (Exodus 20:5)."[22]

Jefferson identified Jesus as the great reformer of this corrupt ethical system. Jefferson wrote regarding the Old Testament Jews: "That sect had presented for the object of their worship a Being of terrific character, cruel, vindictive, capricious, and unjust. Jesus, taking for his type the best qualities of the human head and heart, wisdom, justice, [and] goodness, and adding to them power, ascribed all of these, but in infinite perfection, to the Supreme Being and formed him really worthy of their adoration." Here Jefferson inverts the biblical narrative: instead of a God who creates humans in His own image, Jefferson presents a God fashioned by Jesus in humanity's image. Jefferson continued, "Moses had bound the Jews to many idle ceremonies, mummeries, and observances of no effect towards producing the social utilities which constitute the essence of virtue; Jesus exposed their futility and insignificance. The one instilled into his people the most anti-social spirit towards other nations; the other preached philanthropy and universal charity and benevolence."[23]

Though an ardent champion of Christian ethics, Jefferson was as skeptical regarding the integrity of New Testament accounts as he was of the Old. In 1814 he contended, "In the New Testament there is internal evidence that parts of it have proceeded from an extraordinary man and that other parts are of the fabric of very inferior minds. It is as easy to separate those parts as to pick out diamonds from dunghills. The matter of the first was such as would be preserved in the memory of the hearers, and handed on by tradition for a long time; the latter such stuff as might be gathered up for embedding it anywhere at any time." He considered Jesus the victim of biographers who were "unlettered and ignorant men, who wrote too from memory, and not till long after the transactions had passed." Jefferson rejected the New Testament claim (John 14:26) that the Holy Spirit guided the memories of the Gospel writers. Rather he contended regarding Jesus that "fragments only of what he did deliver have come to us mutilated, misstated, and often unintelligible." Jefferson complained of "the follies, the falsehoods, and the charlatanisms" that Jesus's biographers foisted on him. This corruption was tragic, Jefferson lamented, because, "had the doctrines of Jesus been preached always as pure as they came from his lips, the whole civilized world would now have been Christian." Jefferson trusted, however, that "the dawn of reason and freedom of thought in the United States" would tear down "the artificial scaffolding" set up by these biographers. He concluded, "And the day will come when the mystical generation of Jesus by the supreme being as his father in the womb of a virgin will be classed with the fable of the generation of Minerva in the brain of Jupiter."[24]

By 1820 Jefferson was so displeased with the Bible that he literally cut and pasted passages from it to form his own. Shorn of the Old Testament, all miracles, all references to Jesus's divinity, and all apocalyptic prophecies, Jefferson's tiny volume, which he entitled *The Life and Morals of Jesus*, emphasized the ethical teachings of the Sermon on the Mount. The Jefferson Bible ended by saying, "There laid they Jesus, and rolled a great stone to the door of the sepulcher, and departed." While Jefferson believed in a general resurrection on Judgment Day, he did not believe that Jesus Himself had risen from the dead.[25]

How was Jefferson able to extract the true meaning of the doctrines of Jesus from their corrupt texts—to separate the diamonds from the dunghill, as he so colorfully put it? In 1813 Jefferson explained how one might compose an accurate account of the teachings of Jesus: "We must reduce our volume to the simple evangelists, select, even from them, the very words of Jesus, paring off the Amphibologisms into which they had been led by forgetting often, or not understanding, what had fallen from him, by giving their own misconceptions as his dicta, and expressing unintelligibly for others what they had not understood themselves. There will be found remaining the most sublime and benevolent code of morals which has ever been offered to man." In 1816 he claimed that a true biographer of Jesus should note only those incidents of his life "as are within the physical laws of nature, and offending none by a denial or even a mention of what is not." In 1820 Jefferson wrote concerning Jesus:

> Among the sayings and discourses imputed to him by his biographers I find many passages of fine imagination, correct morality, and the most lovely benevolence; and others again, of so much ignorance, so much absurdity, so much untruth, charlatanism, and imposture, as to pronounce it impossible that such contradictions should have proceeded from the same being. I separate, therefore, the gold from the dross, restore him the former, and leave the latter

to the stupidity of some and roguery of others of his disciples. Of this band of dupes and imposters, Paul was the great Coryphaeus [leader of the chorus] and first corruptor of the doctrines of Jesus. These palpable interpolations and falsifications of his doctrines led me to try to sift them apart. I found the work obvious and easy.

Thus, Jefferson excluded Paul's epistles from his Bible, though they constitute almost half of the New Testament. Jefferson declared regarding Jesus that he was trying to "rescue his character." He wrote regarding Jesus's perfect morals: "These could not be the invention of the groveling authors who relate them. They are far beyond the powers of their feeble minds." True, even after completing the distillation process, Jefferson was left with some objectionable passages, but he dismissed these as products of Jesus's need to escape the clutches of bloodthirsty priests.[26]

Despite Jefferson's repeated claims of rationality, his enterprise of cutting and pasting passages from the New Testament to create a Jesus whose opinions mirrored his own was far from rational. In fact, they represented a giant leap of faith by one of the leading figures of the "Age of Reason."

The Divinity of Jesus

The New Testament repeatedly proclaims the divinity of Jesus. This is made clearest in the Gospel of John, whose first verse declares that Jesus is the Logos (Word) that is God Himself and whose third verse proclaims that "all things were made through Him." In the same Gospel, Jesus declares, "I and my Father are one" (John 10:30) and "He who has seen me has seen the Father" (14:9). In John 8:58 Jesus calls Himself "I am," which was the Hebrew name for God (Yahweh; Exodus 3:13–14), a declaration that leads scandalized Jews to pick up stones with which to kill this man whom they regard as a blasphemer (8:59). He also calls Himself "the light of the world" (8:12) and "the truth" (14:6), then declares, "Apart from me you can do nothing" (15:5).

But John is far from being the only New Testament author who claims divinity for Jesus. Matthew 9:2–3 portrays him forgiving people's sins against the murmurs of the outraged scribes. In Matthew 22:41–45, Jesus presents a riddle to the Pharisees, asking why David calls the Messiah, his own descendant, "my Lord" in Psalms 110, when everyone knows that an ancestor is greater than his descendant. The implicit answer is that the Messiah, Jesus, is more than just a man. In Titus 2:13 Paul calls Jesus "the great God." In Colossians 1:15–16, he describes Jesus as "the image of the invisible God, the firstborn of every creature, for by Him were all things created that are in heaven and that are on earth, visible and invisible." To prove Jesus's divinity, Christians even referred to the Old Testament, where they noted that Isaiah 9:6 calls the Messiah "mighty God" and "everlasting Father" and that Daniel 7:13–14, which refers to the Messiah as "the Son of Man," depicts him descending from heaven to judge the nations and rule an "everlasting dominion."

Most presidents have believed in the divinity of Jesus. In the early 1770s, while a student at Princeton who was considering a career in ministry, James Madison noted in his commonplace book: "Christ's divinity appears by St. John, ch. XX, v. 28." Regarding Jesus, John 20:28 states, "And Thomas answered and said unto Him, 'My Lord and my God.'" Franklin Pierce referred to Jesus as "the Blessed Redeemer." In an 1836 speech in the Senate, James Buchanan referred to Jesus as "the Divine Author of our religion." Nearly three decades later, he referred to Jesus as "our Lord and Saviour" in a letter. Abraham Lincoln often referred to Jesus as "the Saviour" or "the Saviour of the world."[27]

In 1859 Andrew Johnson called the abolitionists' likening of John Brown and his gallows to Christ and his cross "blasphemy," then added, "[Brown] is not my god, and I shall not worship at his shrine." Johnson's characterization of the comparisons between Brown and Jesus as blasphemy suggests a belief in the divinity of Jesus; likewise, his statement implicitly contrasts Brown's false divinity with Jesus's true godhood. Similarly, Ulysses Grant referred to Jesus as "our Saviour."[28]

On Easter in 1852, James Garfield wrote in his diary: "It was on the blessed morning of the first day of the week that Jesus burst forth from the confinement to finish the work for which He left the shining abodes of beatitude on high . . . [and] stood forth as the prelude, the pattern, and the pledge of the resurrection of his followers to eternal life." The following year, Garfield responded to the claims of "infidels" who asserted that there were men among them who were morally superior to Jesus by exclaiming, "Blasphemy!" In similar fashion, in 1890, Grover Cleveland referred to Jesus as "the Redeemer of Mankind."[29]

In 1861 William McKinley referred to Jesus in his diary as "my blessed redeemer." More than three decades later, he referred to Jesus as the "Master who rules over all" and as "Him who came on earth to save fallen man and lead him to a higher plane." In 1899 he declared, "My belief embraces the Divinity of Christ and a recognition of Christianity as the mightiest factor in the world's civilization."[30]

In 1897 Woodrow Wilson referred to Jesus as "the Saviour of the world." A decade later, he called Jesus "our divine kinsman, for whom our spirits yearn whenever stirred by pain or hope," a "perfect individual" who epitomized wisdom and self-sacrifice. In 1910 he called Christ the embodiment "of divine sympathy, of that perfect justice which sees into the hearts of men and that sweet grace of love which takes the sting out of every judgment." He added that Jesus had "a sway over the hearts and lives of men which has not been broken or interrupted these nineteen hundred years" and that Jesus was "the embodiment of those things which, not seen, are eternal." In short, "He is God." The following year, Wilson declared, "He alone can rule over his own spirit who puts himself under the command of the spirit of God, revealed in His Son, Jesus Christ, our Savior. He is the captain of our souls; he is the man from whom suggestions and from whose life come the light that guideth every man that ever came into the world." Similarly, in 1936, Franklin Roosevelt referred to Easter as "the anniversary of the Resurrection of our Lord."[31]

Harry Truman believed in the divinity of Jesus. In 1949 he referred to Jesus as "the Savior." The next day, he noted that the prophet Isaiah had foretold the coming of Christ. Truman referred to this coming as "the Incarnation," a term that refers to the embodiment of God in earthly form. The following year, when referring to Jesus's birth, he declared, "We celebrate the hour in which God came to man." In 1951 Truman referred to Jesus as "the Redeemer of the World."[32]

In 1967 Lyndon Johnson called Jesus "His Holiness" and referred to the Resurrection. Johnson declared, "His death—so the Christian faith tells us—was not the end. For Him, and for millions of men and women ever since, it marked a time of triumph—when the spirit of life triumphed over death." Similarly, Gerald Ford called Jesus "the Son of God" and "the mediator between God and man (1 Timothy 2:5)."[33]

In 1976 Jimmy Carter told his Sunday school class, "In the Christian faith we believe that God came to earth as a human being in the person of Christ, that Christ was born of the virgin Mary.... He became a man, at the same time retaining His identity as God. This is a teaching crucial to the Christian faith because it helps us understand what God is." Twenty-one years later, Carter referred to Isaiah's prophecy of Jesus as the Messiah, to Jesus's Resurrection, to His "omnipotence," and to His "perfect life," claiming that He was "God as human." He elaborated that Jesus was "a man, yet God, who was there when the universe was created, knowing everything, totally powerful." He added, "Jesus's divine nature not only predates his life on earth but predates the very beginning of time itself." In his 2002 acceptance speech for the Nobel Peace Prize, Carter declared, "I worship Jesus Christ, whom we Christians consider to be the Prince of Peace."[34]

Ronald Reagan often affirmed Jesus's divinity. In 1978 he responded to an unorthodox minister who believed in Jesus's ethical teachings but not His divinity: "Is there really any ambiguity in his words: 'I am the way, the truth, and the life; no man cometh unto the Father but by me [John 14:6]'? When He said, 'In my Father's house are many mansions. If it were not so, I would have told you. I go to prepare a place for you [14:2].' In John 10 [verse 38] He says, 'I am in the Father and the Father is in me.' And He makes reference to being with God 'before the world was [John 17:5]' and sitting on the 'right hand of God [Luke 22:69].'" Reagan added,

> These and other statements He made about himself foreclose in my opinion any question as to his divinity. It doesn't seem to me that He gave us any choice; either He was what He said He was or He was the world's greatest liar. It is impossible for me to believe a liar or a charlatan could have had the effect on mankind that He has had for 2000 years. We could ask, would even the greatest of liars carry his lie through the crucifixion, when a simple confession would have saved Him? I could refer to the scores of prophecies in the Old Testament made several hundred years before His birth, all of which were realized in His life.

In 1981, when lighting the national Christmas tree, Reagan remarked, "There are some who celebrate this day, Christmas Day, as the birthday of a great teacher and philosopher. To others of us, He is more than that; He is also divine." Six days later, he repeated, "Some celebrate Christmas as the birthday of a great and good philosopher and teacher. Others of us believe in the divinity of the child born in Bethlehem, that He was and is the promised Prince of Peace. Yes, we've questioned why He who could perform miracles chose to come among us as a helpless baby, but maybe that was His first miracle, His first great lesson that we should learn to care for one another." The following day, Reagan said that the birth of Christ was "the fulfillment of age-old prophecies and the reaffirmation of God's great love for all of us." He added, "Through a generous Heavenly Father's gift of His son, hope and compassion entered a world weary with fear and despair and changed it for all time."[35]

George H. W. Bush called Jesus "our Savior." He referred to Jesus's birth as "the Incarnation." He further termed Jesus's birth "a miraculous event" that involved "God's gift of His Son."[36]

Bush's son, George W., called Jesus "our Savior" and "God's only Son" and referenced "Christ's miraculous Resurrection." He began his 2005 Christmas message by quoting Isaiah 7:14: "Behold, a virgin shall conceive and bear a son, and his name shall be called Emmanuel, which means, 'God with us.'" Bush continued, "More than 2,000 years ago, a virgin gave birth to a Son, and the God of heaven came to Earth. Mankind had received its Savior, and to those who had dwelled in darkness, the light of day had come. Each Christmas, we celebrate that first coming anew, and we rejoice in the knowledge that the God who came to Earth that night in Bethlehem is with us still and will remain with us forever." The following year, Bush began his Easter message with the angel's statement regarding Jesus in Matthew 28:6: "He is not here; for He is risen, as He said," and his Christmas message, with Isaiah 9:6: "For unto us a child is born . . . and His name will be called Wonderful Counselor, Mighty God, Everlasting Father, Prince of Peace." In 2007 Bush declared that Christmas was "the story of the Almighty, who entered history in the most vulnerable form possible, hidden in the weakness of a newborn child." He then added, "And we reflect on the call of our Creator, who by taking this form, reminds us of our duty to protect and care for the weak and the vulnerable among us." The following year, he began his Easter message with John 11:25: "I am the resurrection and the life. He who believes in me will live, even though he dies." Bush added, "The Resurrection of Jesus Christ reminds people around the world of the presence of a faithful God who offers a love more powerful than death."[37]

In 2013 Barack Obama referred to the Holy Trinity, claiming, "Jesus is there to guide us, the Holy Spirit to help us." Two months later he was even clearer concerning the divinity of Jesus, stating, "Our Savior, who suffered and died, was resurrected, both fully God and also a man."[38]

But some presidents denied Jesus's divinity. In 1813 John Adams rejected the related doctrine of the Holy Trinity, writing to Thomas Jefferson, "One is not three nor can three be one." Four years later, he claimed that the biblical doctrine stating that the creator of the universe had been crucified was blasphemous. In 1825 he ridiculed the idea that the God who "has produced this boundless Universe, Newton's Universe and Hershell's Universe, came down to this little Ball to be spit upon by Jews." The fact that Adams often contended that God aided the United States, which constituted only a small fraction of that "little Ball," demonstrates that his problem was not with the concept of divine intervention but with the doctrine of the Incarnation. By the time Adams died in 1826, he was a member of a Unitarian church in Quincy. Yet it is important to note that Adams had referred to Jesus in his presidential thanksgiving proclamations as "Redeemer of the World" and "the Great Mediator and Advocate." Rather than indicating either insincerity or a change in belief on Adams's part, this apparent contradiction was probably no contradiction at all; it may simply indicate that Adams, like his wife Abigail, had adopted an Arian position on the Trinity, one that recognized Jesus as the son of God and the redeemer of humankind but not as God himself.[39]

This differed from Thomas Jefferson's Socinian position that Jesus had been a mere man, albeit a great one. As early as 1788, Jefferson was claiming that his longtime doubts about the Trinity precluded his service as an Episcopalian godfather. He explained,

> The person who becomes sponsor for a child, according to the ritual of the church in which I was educated, makes a solemn profession before god and the world of faith in articles which I had never sense enough to comprehend, and it has always appeared to me that comprehension must precede assent. The difficulty of reconciling the ideas of Unity and Trinity have, from a very early part of my life, excluded me from the office of sponsorship, often proposed to me by my friends, who would have trusted, for the faithful discharge of it, to morality alone, instead of which the church requires faith.[40]

Jefferson's rejection of the doctrine of the Trinity, when combined with his judgment that Jesus was the greatest ethical philosopher in history, led him to either dismiss or reinterpret each of the various New Testament accounts of Jesus's claims to divinity. Surely, the greatest ethical philosopher in history would not lie; therefore, the New Testament authors must be, either wittingly or unwittingly, the real sources of the popular misconception regarding Jesus. In 1803 Jefferson declared, "I am a Christian in the only sense in which he wished any one to be: sincerely attached to his doctrines, in preference to all others; ascribing to himself every human excellence; and believing he never claimed any other." In some instances, rather than accuse the Gospel writers of deception, Jefferson attempted improbable interpretations of their statements. Thus, according to Jefferson, the Logos that had been with God from the beginning, as related in the first verse of the Gospel of John, did not refer to Jesus but to reason. To draw such an inference, Jefferson had to ignore verse 14 of the same chapter: "And the Word became flesh and dwelt among us," which is followed by a narrative of the life of Jesus. Jefferson used very little material from John's gospel, the one that most emphasizes Jesus's divinity, when compiling his own Bible. In 1820 Jefferson contended, "That Jesus did not mean to impose himself on mankind as the Son of God, physically speaking, I have been convinced by the writings of men more learned than myself in that lore. But that he might conscientiously believe himself inspired from above is very possible."[41]

Jefferson contended that the doctrine of the Trinity had been foisted on the Western world by Platonists, who, intent on establishing and maintaining power for a dissolute class of priests, had engrafted onto Christianity the sophisms of that pernicious philosopher. In 1814 Jefferson claimed, "The Christian priesthood, finding the doctrines of Jesus leveled to every understanding, and too plain to need explanation, saw in the mysticisms of Plato materials with which they might build an artificial system which might, from its indistinctiveness, admit everlasting controversy, give employment for their order, and introduce it to profit, power, and pre-eminence. The doctrines which flowed from the lips of Jesus himself are within the comprehension of a child; but thousands of volumes have not yet explained the Platonisms engrafted on them; and for the obvious reason that nonsense can never be explained." Influenced by the clergyman and chemist Joseph Priestley, Jefferson believed that conniving theologians, such as Augustine, had converted John's simple reference to reason into the Logos of the Platonists, a divinity begotten by the supreme deity ("the Good," in Plato's terminology, "the One" in Plotinus's) and through which the supreme deity created the universe. Jefferson's and Priestley's conspiracy theory ignored the many other references to Jesus's divinity contained in John's Gospel and in the other books of the New Testament as they endeavored to make the Trinity an invention of fourth-century priests.[42]

Jefferson maintained that this clerical conspiracy continued in his own day. American clergymen continued to appeal to mystical and absurd doctrines like that of the Trinity, as well as to slander those like Jefferson and Priestley who rejected them, as part of an effort to establish their individual sects as the state churches of the United States and Great Britain. Jefferson argued, "The mild and simple principles of the Christian religion would produce too much calm, too much regularity of good, to extract from its disciples a support for a numerous priesthood were they not to sophisticate it, ramify it, split it into hairs, and twist its texts till they cover the divine morality of its author with mysteries and require a priesthood to explain them." In 1820 he referred to "the metaphysical insanities of Athanasius," the leading advocate of the doctrine of the Trinity in ancient times, which Jefferson termed "mere relapses into polytheism, differing from paganism only in being more unintelligible." He added, "The religion of Jesus is founded in the Unity of God, and this principle chiefly gave it triumph over the rabble of heathen gods then acknowledged. Thinking men of all nations rallied readily to the doctrine of only one God and embraced it with the pure morals which Jesus inculcated." Then in 1822, Jefferson claimed, "Nor was the unity of the Supreme Being ousted from the Christian creed by the force of reason, but by the sword of the civil government, wielded at the will of the fanatic Athanasius. The hocus-pocus phantasm of a God like another Cerberus, with one body and three heads, had its birth and growth in the blood of thousands and thousands of martyrs." But Jefferson hoped that Christians would not, in the end, "give up morals for mysteries, and Jesus for Plato."[43]

Raised as a Unitarian, William Howard Taft also denied the divinity of Jesus. In 1899 he rejected Yale's offer of its presidency because he thought that many of the university's benefactors would withdraw their support from the institution due to the appointment of a Unitarian president. He wrote to his brother Henry: "I am a Unitarian. I believe in God. I do not believe in the Divinity of Christ." Many devout Christians opposed Taft's election as president of the United States in 1908 due to his Unitarianism.[44]

Despite his references to the Bible as "Holy Writ" and the "Book of Books," Richard Nixon tended to allegorize its references to Jesus. Like Jefferson, Nixon viewed Jesus as an ethical philosopher whose superlative qualities and philosophy made him a figurative rather than the literal son of God. While at Whittier College in California in the 1930s, Nixon strayed from the Quaker beliefs of his parents concerning the divinity of Jesus. Nixon wrote, "He reached the highest conception of God and of value that the world has ever seen. He lived a life which radiated those values. He taught a philosophy which revealed those values to men. I even go so far as to say Jesus and God are one because Jesus is the great example which is forever pulling men upward to the ideal life. His life was so perfect that he 'mingled' his soul with God's." Despite Nixon's use of the adjective "perfect," this allegorical conception of Jesus's divinity clearly departed from the literal claims of the New Testament. Nixon added, "It may be that the resurrection story is a myth, but symbolically it teaches the great lesson that men who achieve the highest values in their lives may gain immortality." Nixon's use of the word "symbolically" suggests that he was referring to immortality in the classical sense of fame. To this figurative conception of "immortality," he added a figurative conception of "resurrection": "I believe that the modern world will find a real resurrection in the teachings of Jesus." The fact that Nixon chose to insert his youthful writings about Jesus into his 1978 memoirs without comment suggests that he retained these views. In 1983 he told an interviewer that "one can be a good Christian without necessarily believing in the physical resurrection." In his 1990 memoirs, he repeated the passage about resurrection from his Whittier days, then added, "I adhere to those same beliefs today."[45]

Raised by Arian parents, John Quincy Adams engaged in a lifelong struggle to arrive at a definitive conclusion about the divinity of Jesus, but he ultimately failed to do so. In 1811 he wrote to his son George that the issue of Jesus' divinity was "one of those mysteries not intended to be unfolded to me during the present life," but he added quickly that, at a minimum, Jesus was "the only begotten Son of God, by whom he made the world and by whom he will judge the world in righteousness." In 1815 John Quincy wrote to his father: "The bias of my mind is towards the doctrine of the Trinitarians and Calvinists, but I do not approve of their intolerance. Most of the Boston Unitarians are my particular friends, but I never thought much of the eloquence or of the theology of Priestley. His *Socrates and Jesus Compared* is a wretched performance. Socrates and Jesus! A farthing candle and the Sun! I pray you to read Massillon's sermon upon the divinity of Jesus, and then the whole New Testament, after which be a Socinian if you can."[46]

A few months later, Adams wrote to his mother:

> That the Athanasian Trinity is clearly contained in the Scriptures I have not been able to convince my own mind beyond a question; but if I must choose between that and the belief that Christ was a mere man, to be compared with Socrates, and must mutilate the New Testament to suit the critical scruples of Dr. Priestley in order to maintain this creed, I have no hesitation in making my choice. I find in the New Testament Jesus Christ accosted in his own presence by one of his disciples as God without disclaiming the appellation. I see him emphatically declared by at least two of the other Apostles to be God, expressly and repeatedly announced not only as having existed before the worlds without beginning of days or end of years. I see him named in the great prophecy of Isaiah [9:6] concerning him "the mighty God"! . . . The texts are too numerous, they are from parts of the Scriptures too diversified, they are sometimes connected by too strong a claim of argument, and the inferences from them are to my mind too direct and irresistible to admit of the explanations which the Unitarians sometimes attempt to give them, or of the evasions by which at others they endeavor to escape from them.

Against the Unitarian argument, whose proponents included his father, that the doctrine stating three are one is incomprehensible, John Quincy retorted that the conception of a single God who was boundless was equally incomprehensible, as number implied boundary. He concluded, "It is therefore as difficult for me to conceive that God should be one as that he should be three, or three in one. . . . The question, therefore, is not whether the doctrine of the Trinity be incomprehensible, but whether it be contained in the Scriptures." The following month, he again wrote to his father about the matter, reiterating his disgruntlement with Unitarian arguments: "I have had many doubts about the Athanasian Creed, but if I read much more controversy about it, I shall finish by faithfully believing in it." He complained that the same Unitarians who claimed that they could not believe in the Trinity because they could not understand it had no such qualms when it came to the virgin birth or the other mysteries of the Bible.[47]

In 1817 John Quincy wrote to his father:

> My hopes of a future life are all founded on the Gospel of Christ, and I cannot cavil or quibble away, not single words and ambiguous expressions, but the whole tenor of his conduct, by which he sometimes positively asserted, and at others countenanced his disciples in asserting, that he was God. You think it blasphemous to believe that the omnipotent Creator could be crucified. God is a spirit. The spirit was not crucified. The body of Jesus of Nazareth was crucified. The Spirit, whether eternal or created, was beyond the reach of the cross. You see my orthodoxy grows upon me.[48]

But four years later, John Quincy again expressed uncertainty on the question. He wrote, "It appears to me that as a question upon the meaning of certain passages of Scripture, the disputants on each side have been more successful in combating the doctrines of their adversaries than in maintaining their own." In 1827 he claimed that the New Testament left the issue "on the whole in a debatable state, never to be either demonstrated or refuted till another revelation shall clear it up." After listening to a Trinitarian sermon, he wrote, "It was wheat sown by the wayside." Yet upon the death of his Unitarian pastor, Robert Little, Adams wrote, "I did not subscribe to many of his doctrines, particularly not to the fundamental one of his Unitarian creed. I believe in one God, but His nature is incomprehensible to me, and of the question between the Unitarians and Trinitarians I have no precise belief, because no definite understanding." In 1828, when asked about his opinion on the Trinity, he replied, "That I was neither a Trinitarian nor a Unitarian; that I believed the nature of Jesus Christ was superhuman; but whether he was God, or only the first of created beings, was not clearly related to me in the Scriptures." In 1835 he was impressed by an "admirable" sermon on "the manifestation of God in the person of Jesus Christ." Yet three years later, he complained about a Presbyterian preacher: "I have tried very hard and very sincerely to believe in the doctrine of the Trinity because there are passages in the New Testament which I cannot deny give countenance to it, but when a dogmatist gives me a text to which my naked reason furnishes an argument against it which I find it difficult to answer, and then threatens eternal damnation for not believing him—'incredulous odi'—my spirit revolts against the yoke and loses much of its reverence for him who would impose it."[49]

Adams never doubted Jesus's superhuman nature or his divine mission to redeem humanity. In 1843 he listed the "divine mission" of Jesus as one of the elements of his creed: "I have at all times been a sincere believer in the existence of a Supreme Creator of the world, of an immortal principle within myself, responsible to the Creator for my conduct upon earth, and of the divine mission of the crucified Saviour, proclaiming immortal life and preaching peace on earth, good will to men, and the natural equality of all mankind, and the law, 'Thou shalt love thy neighbor as thyself [Matthew 19:19].'" At this late date in his life, suffering from the ravages of old age and the loss of loved ones, Adams confessed that he sometimes entertained "involuntary and agonizing doubts, which I can neither silence nor expel," but he listed this as one of several reasons why it was important for him to attend worship services.[50]

Some presidents left no records (or very minimal ones) concerning their beliefs about Jesus. George Washington is one such president. In his resignation message to the state governors as commander of the Continental Army following the Revolutionary War, he referred to Jesus as "the Divine Author of our blessed Religion." But this is the only such reference to the divinity of Jesus in Washington's papers. It is true that this message, like many of the public statements Washington issued during the Revolutionary War, was probably written by a member of his staff, but it is also true that Washington read and edited such documents, especially addresses of this significance, carefully. Thus, at the very least, Washington declined to strike this reference to the divinity of Jesus from the document.[51]

Washington's reticence in discussing his beliefs concerning Jesus, even in letters to close friends, may simply reflect the man's intensely private nature, a quality so often noted (and admired) by his contemporaries, as well as his conviction that his religious beliefs were no one else's business. Nelly Custis, Washington's granddaughter, recalled, "He communed with his God in secret.... He was a silent, thoughtful man." By contrast, Thomas Jefferson often declared passionately that his own beliefs were no one else's business but then proceeded to detail them to intimate friends or, for that matter, to anyone he considered to be like-minded. Jefferson's reputation for reticence is actually a sham, which is precisely why we know so much about his religious views. Washington's similar reputation is far more genuine, which is why we know so little about his opinions. On the other hand, Washington never displayed any reticence in conveying publicly his strong beliefs in Providence and in the vital importance of religious belief to the survival and success of the republic, nor was he shy about alluding to his belief in an afterlife. Perhaps he considered his beliefs regarding Jesus more personal, or perhaps his views on the subject were less orthodox and, thus, less likely to be popular than his other beliefs. We simply do not know. Too often both Christians and secularists have sought to fill the vacuum of documentary evidence regarding Washington's religious beliefs with a depressing combination of dubious hearsay evidence and vast speculative leaps that reveal more about these authors' beliefs than their subject's.[52]

The later James Madison and James Monroe present similar puzzles. While he was at Princeton studying to be a clergyman and then for some time thereafter, Madison appears to have been a biblically orthodox Christian who led family worship in his father's house. There is no reason to question the sincerity of his expressions of belief in the divinity of Jesus and of his zeal for "the cause of Christ" at that time. But soon after he became engaged in law and politics, he grew silent about his religious opinions. He treated religion with respect, attended worship services, and invited ministers to his house to administer the Lord's Supper to his devout mother. There was some gossip about biblically unorthodox beliefs, and there were claims that he became orthodox again in later life, but there were no direct statements from the man himself. Monroe's beliefs, excepting his oft-expressed confidence in Providence, are an even greater mystery. The fact that Washington, Madison, and Monroe were all eighteenth- and early nineteenth-century Virginia Episcopalians may suggest that reticence in expressing religious opinions was a cultural tendency of this group, though by no means one shared by all its members.[53]

Salvation by Faith in Jesus

The New Testament states repeatedly that salvation comes solely through faith in Jesus. The most famous such verse is John 3:16: "For God so loved the world that He gave His only begotten Son, so that whoever believes in Him should not perish but have everlasting life." Two verses later, the doctrine is made even clearer: "Whoever believes in Him is not condemned, but whoever does not believe in Him is already condemned, because he has not believed in the name of the only begotten Son of God." In John 6:47 Jesus declares, "Very truly, I say to you, whoever believes in me has everlasting life." Although the thief on the cross beside Jesus has performed no good deeds—on the contrary, the Gospels of Matthew [27:38] and Mark [15:27] call him and his unrepentant colleague "plunderers" (the same Greek word Homer uses for pirates) and the Gospel of Luke [23:39], "evildoers"—his simple expression of faith, "Lord, remember me when you come into your kingdom," prompts Jesus to tell him, "Today you will be with me in paradise

(Luke 23:42–3)." In Romans 10:9 Paul declares, "If you confess with your mouth that Jesus is Lord and believe in your heart that God raised Him from the dead, you shall be saved." In Ephesians 2:8–9 Paul states, "For you are saved by grace through faith—and that not of yourselves, it is the gift of God—not of works, lest anyone should boast." While some Christian denominations have added works (good deeds) as a requirement for salvation, others, following the path of Martin Luther, have argued that such works are merely the by-products of a saving faith. But all biblically orthodox Christians have accepted the necessity of faith in Jesus for salvation since it is one of the clearest and most reiterated teachings of the New Testament. This belief in the efficacy of faith for salvation is grounded in the view, also repeatedly expressed in the New Testament, that Jesus's death on the cross constituted an atonement for the sins of humanity, a benefit received only by those who believe in and follow him. In John 1:29 John the Baptist sees Jesus and declares, "Behold, the Lamb of God who takes away the sins of the world." This refers to both the Passover lamb, an unblemished lamb whose smeared blood on the doorpost protected Israelites from the death of their firstborn sons (Exodus 12:3–13), and the spotless lamb whose blood was sprinkled on the Ark of the Covenant annually on Yom Kippur to cover the sins of the people.

Most presidents have believed that people could attain salvation through faith in Jesus's atonement for sin. In 1826, in response to a query about John Harris, a man whose execution Andrew Jackson had ordered for leading a mutiny during the War of 1812, Jackson noted that Harris himself had acknowledged "the Justice of his condemnation" and had stated "that he had no hope of pardon here but from his repentance and hoped for forgiveness hereafter." To this Jackson added, "which I hope he obtained through the atonement made by our blessed savior and his sincere repentance." In 1829 Jackson claimed that he considered his recently deceased wife, Rachel, to be "in the bosom of our saviour enjoying that exquisite happiness bought by the death and suffering of our dear redeemer on the cross, an atonement made for sinners that they might not perish but have eternal life by repentance & belief in him." In 1831 he wrote, "I am no sectarian, tho' a lover of the Christian religion. I do not believe that any who shall be so fortunate as to be received in heaven thro' the atonement of our blessed Saviour will be asked whether they belonged to the Presbyterian, Methodist, Episcopalian, Baptist, or Roman Catholic [Church]. All Christians are brethren, and all true Christians know they are such because they love one another."[54]

Jackson retained this view throughout his life. In the will he composed in 1843, he wrote, "First, I bequeath my body to the dust whence it comes, and my soul to God who gave it, hoping for a happy immortality through the atoning merits of our Lord Jesus Christ, the saviour of the world." Three months before he died in 1845, he refused, on republican grounds, the offer of an ancient sarcophagus that had once allegedly contained the corpse of a Roman emperor, adding,

> I have prepared an humble depository for my mortal body beside that wherein lies my beloved wife, where, without any pomp or parade, I have requested, when God calls me to sleep with my fathers [Deuteronomy 31:16], to be laid, for both of us there to remain until the last trumpet sounds to call the dead to judgment [1 Corinthians 15:52], when we, I hope, shall rise together, clothed with that heavenly body promised to all that believe in our glorious Redeemer [1 Corinthians 15:44], who died for us that we might live, and by whose atonement I hope for a blessed immortality.

On his deathbed, Jackson said regarding the Bible: "Upon that sacred volume, I rest my hope for eternal salvation through the merits and blood of our blessed Lord and Saviour, Jesus Christ." Jackson's last words were "We will meet in heaven."[55]

James Buchanan adhered to the doctrine of salvation by faith. In 1832 he wrote regarding his brother George, who was on his deathbed: "Still it is a great satisfaction to know that he does not feel alarmed at the prospect of death. I trust his philosophy may be of the genuine Christian character & that he may have disarmed death of its sting [1 Corinthians 15:55] by saving faith in the Redeemer of mankind."[56]

James Garfield also considered faith in Jesus a requirement for salvation. In 1851 he joyously noted in his diary, "A little girl 13 years old, Zelpha York, came forward, and with the mouth made confession unto salvation." This was a reference to Romans 10:9, which cites a confession of sincere faith as the only requirement for salvation.[57]

Theodore Roosevelt departed from the Dutch Reformed doctrine of salvation by faith alone for a belief in salvation by both faith and works. His father, Theodore Senior, though famed for his good deeds, had written that he could devote "all the time and much more than I was now doing to God's service and I would still fall far short of any hope of salvation except through His [God's] divine mercy." But his son disagreed. In 1908 the younger Theodore wrote, "I am mighty weak on the Lutheran and Calvinistic doctrines of salvation by faith [alone] myself, and, tho I have no patience with much of the Roman Catholic theory of church government, and the infallibility of the pope, the confessional, and a celibate clergy, I do believe in the gospel of works as put down by the Epistle of James." While Catholics believed that James 2:17 ("Faith without works is dead") implied salvation by both faith and works, most Protestants held it to mean that works were the inevitable product of a saving faith. Three years later, Roosevelt repeated, "I am a great believer in the doctrine of works." In 1915 Roosevelt quoted Micah 6:8: "What doth the Lord require of thee but to do justly and to love mercy and to walk humbly with thy God?" He added, "This verse has always been a favorite of mine because it embodies the Gospel of Works, with the necessary antidote in the last few words to that hard spiritual arrogance which is brought about by *mere* reliance on the Gospel of Works [emphasis in original]." Roosevelt believed that the first two parts of the verse ("to do justly and to love mercy") stated the necessity of works for salvation, while the reference to "walking humbly with thy God" expressed the necessity of faith, thereby counteracting any arrogance that might result from a person believing himself saved purely by his own good deeds.[58]

By contrast, as a staunch Presbyterian, Woodrow Wilson held tightly to the doctrine of salvation by faith alone. In 1895 he claimed that salvation "comes by belief . . . not by conduct, but by regeneration . . . [through] the blood of Christ." At an interdenominational conference a decade later, Wilson remarked, "I know I speak on controversial ground here, but before I got to this platform I spoke for a few moments with several gentlemen of those faiths which teach salvation by character. I regard such an enterprise as one of despair. Just how you may feel about your character I do not know, but I know how I feel about my own. I would not care to offer it as a certificate of my salvation." For Wilson, salvation came by faith, not by the demonstration of a good character through works.[59]

Jimmy Carter believed that faith in Jesus was necessary for salvation, while works were an essential byproduct of faith. In 1976 he said, "We're saved by grace through one required attitude. That is faith in Christ. We're saved by grace through faith in Christ." Twenty-one years later, he wrote regarding the doctrine of salvation by faith: "Some people may think that this path to salvation is too simple and easy—that something else must be required for us to receive God's mercy and everlasting life. After all, most of the achievements in life—education, a good family, a successful career—require hard work, persistence, and sacrifice. Yet God's forgiveness and blessings are given to us freely, by pure grace." He claimed, "We are reconciled to God through Jesus' love. . . . We are brought into a proper relationship with God, even though we have not merited his blessing because of our own character or good works. This seeming miracle is made possible by our faith, or trusting commitment to Christ and to God. Without this faith, we cannot be reconciled with God." Carter added, "Christ died for us and lived again, and, through faith in him, we too can enjoy a resurrected life." He elaborated,

> Some of us get so proud of our works that we think that's all there is, and neglect our own spiritual lives—prayer, worship, fellowship, and study. We sometimes seem to place our works above Christ's supreme sacrifice as our path to salvation—as though we can earn a place in heaven by being so good that God is actually in our debt. This attitude is obviously wrong; it devalues the grace of Jesus, which is given to us without being earned and which we can never deserve, because we all fall so far short of moral and spiritual perfection.

But Carter also warned against the neglect of works: "Yet, as James tries to show, the opposite attitude is equally wrong, when we place our faith so far above works as to imply that good deeds are unnecessary and unimportant." Carter interpreted the Book of James as saying, "If we have faith, let's show it! Prove it as Jesus did, by ministering not only to those like us, our friends and neighbors, but to the poor, the hungry, the lonely, and the despised." Carter concluded, "In the end James's message is a simple one. To be saved, we need faith surely; but self-satisfaction and self-glorification are not the end of faith. Rather, service to others, compassion, and justice exemplify the Christian life. When we emulate Christ by working to make these things real in our lives, we strengthen our faith as well."[60]

Ronald Reagan also believed in salvation by faith in Jesus. He declared, "Having accepted Jesus Christ as my Savior, I have God's promise of eternal life in heaven, as well as the abundant life here on earth that He promises to each of us in John 10:10." Reagan connected the requirement of faith to the Atonement and the Resurrection. In a 1981 Easter message, he said, "Christians will celebrate with their families the resurrection of Christ, His victory over death. We will remember that He gave His body and His blood—washing clean the faults and the shortcomings of the world. In our rejoicing we will renew the hope that is ours through the risen Lord."[61]

George W. Bush agreed. Once, in the 1980s, he argued with his mother about the need to be "born again"—the possession of a sincere faith in Christ leading to an indwelling of the Holy Spirit—as a requirement of salvation, basing his argument on Jesus's statement in John 3:3: "Very truly, I tell you, no one can see the kingdom of God without being born again." To settle the dispute, the Bushes called the evangelist Billy Graham, who sided with George.[62]

Barack Obama seems to have become more convinced of salvation by faith in Jesus over time. In *The Audacity of Hope* (2006), he recounted the story of his young daughter's question about "what happened when we die" and his own response, "You've got a long, long way before you have to worry about that," which seemed to satisfy her. He added, "I wondered whether I should have told her the truth, that I wasn't sure what happens when we die." While he hoped that his mother, an unbeliever who had died of cancer, would enjoy a blissful afterlife, he was uncertain about it. The question of faith did not enter his calculus at this point in his life. But in 2010 he declared regarding Jesus, "We are thankful for the sacrifice He gave for the sins of humanity. And we glory in the promise of redemption in the resurrection. . . . As Christians, we believe that redemption can be delivered by faith in Jesus Christ." In 2016 he said, "My faith tells me that I need not fear death, that the acceptance of Christ promises everlasting life and the washing away of sins."[63]

A few presidents have rejected the doctrine of salvation by faith. Thomas Jefferson rejected it because it conflicted with his conviction that beliefs were solely the products of reason operating on facts and, therefore, not subject to the will. His Bill for Establishing Religious Freedom (1779) began with a significant clause that, just as significantly, was deleted by the Virginia Senate: "Well aware that the opinions and belief of men depend not on their own will, but follow involuntarily the evidence proposed to their minds." Jefferson's complete severance of belief from the will stood in direct contradiction to the New Testament conception of faith as fundamentally an act of the will, a conception that made faith a legitimate criterion for salvation. Jefferson did not explain how the same facts could lead people of equal reasoning ability to different conclusions.[64]

In a 1783 letter to his daughter Martha, Jefferson suggested that salvation was the result of the avoidance of wrongdoing. He wrote,

> I hope you will have good sense enough to disregard those foolish predictions that the world is to be at an end soon. The almighty has never made known to anybody at what time he created it, nor will he tell anybody when he means to put an end to it, if ever he means to do it. As to preparations for that event, the best way is for you to be always prepared for it. The only way to be so is never to do nor say a bad thing. If ever you are about to say anything amiss or to do anything wrong, consider beforehand. You will feel something within you which will tell you it is wrong and ought not to be said or done: this is your conscience, and be sure to obey it. Our maker has given us all this faithful internal Monitor, and if you always obey it, you will always be prepared for the end of the world, or for a much more certain event, which is death. This must happen to all; it puts an end to the world as to us, and the way to be ready for it is never to do a wrong act.

The complete avoidance of wrongdoing is a very high, most would say impossible, standard.[65]

In 1801 Jefferson referred to his effort to "merit salvation," which was the terminology of salvation by works rather than faith. He wrote that rather than concern himself with the afterlife, "I have thought it better, by nourishing the good passions and controlling the bad, to merit an inheritance in a state of being of which I can know so little and to trust for the future to him who has been so good for the past." Neither Jefferson's mention of trusting in the deity for his salvation without regard to faith nor his comment on the attempt to merit it was biblical. In 1813 Jefferson claimed, "Of all the systems of morality, ancient or modern, which have come under my observation, none appear to me as pure as that of Jesus." He added, "He who follows this steadfastly [regardless of faith] need not, I think, be uneasy" about his salvation. Jefferson could not imagine that a person could be damned for coming to a wrong conclusion about Jesus any more than for coming to a wrong conclusion about a scientific question. This concept of belief as the mere product of reason operating on facts was very different from that of the apostle Paul, who maintained that unbelievers rejected the truth by an act of the will because its acceptance would force them to give up a life of sin they relished (Romans 1:20–25; Thessalonians 2:11–12). In 1819 Jefferson declared, "My fundamental principle would be the reverse of Calvin's, that we are to be saved by our good works, which are within our power, and not by faith, which is not within our power."[66]

In 1817 John Quincy Adams wrote, "My hopes of a future life are all founded on the Gospel of Jesus Christ." But it appears that, as time elapsed, "the Gospel of Jesus Christ" began to mean to Adams the ethical teachings and resurrection of Jesus, not the doctrine of His atonement for human sin on the cross. In 1811 he wrote to his son George, "The blood of the redeemer has washed out the pollution of our original Sin, and the certainty of eternal happiness in a future life is again secured to us on the primitive condition of obedience to the Will of God" through faith. This was a biblically orthodox statement, as was the one he made a week later: "The voluntary submission of Jesus Christ to his own Death, in the most excruciating and ignominious form, was to consummate the great plan of redemption." But by 1831, he was so disgusted by a Presbyterian sermon on the Atonement that he called it "solemn nonsense and inconceivable absurdity." Adams wrote, "That the execution, as a malefactor, of one person, the Creator of all worlds, eighteen hundred years ago, should have redeemed me, born nearly eighteen centuries after his death, from eternal damnation, is not only too shocking for my belief, but I ask myself what there can be above the level of the beasts which perish in the animated being that can believe it. A melancholy monument of mental aberration and impotence." In 1837 Adams claimed, "That man is a vicious, wicked animal is the fundamental doctrine of the Christian religion. That he cannot save himself from eternal punishment is the doctrine of the Catholic churches and of Calvin. If he cannot save himself, he is not a responsible being; that is the conclusion of justice, and a conclusion from which I could not escape if I would." Adams implied that humans were responsible for their own salvation but did not state the means. He added, "The mission of Christ was to teach all mankind the way to salvation. His death, an ignominious death, was necessary to the universal spread of his doctrine. He died for mankind, as Curtius died for his country, as Codrus died for his people. In this sense I can believe the doctrine of the atonement, and in no other. Christ died as a man, not as God." A week later, Adams wrote regarding God: "That He should suffer by His own decree to save man, His own creature, from the penalty of His own law, is as conceivable to me as that He should be His own Son. That such a bundle of absurdities as the abuse of human reason has drawn from the Gospel of John and the Epistles of Paul should, after nineteen centuries of Christianity, overspread the intellect of so large a portion of mankind is a mortifying and melancholy contemplation."[67]

In 1834 Adams identified the Resurrection, but not the Crucifixion, as crucial to Christ's mission. He wrote that, while Christmas is "the day of promise," "Easter is the day which consummated life and immortality." He added, "The resurrection of Christ was the accomplishment of the purposes for which He came into the world." Likewise, in 1840, he called the "resurrection of the dead the great and vital article of the Christian faith," and followed this reference with Jesus's statement of "I am the resurrection and the life (John 11:25)." Five years later, he praised a sermon by Reverend Stephen Olin, the president of Wesleyan University, whose message was that "belief in God is a barren and profitless creed unless subsidiary to it is the belief in a responsible hereafter to the existence of man; and to this belief in Christ is indispensable." To Adams, faith in Jesus's resurrection was necessary to salvation only because it led to belief in immortality, which was an essential motive to Christian virtue, the real means of salvation.[68]

Like Adams, Rutherford Hayes underwent a change in opinion regarding salvation by faith. In 1844 he held the orthodox position, which reconciled James's statement of "Faith without works is dead" with Paul's emphasis on salvation by faith alone. Hayes wrote in his diary, "If by faith is meant the internal disposition which will manifest itself in outward acts whenever opportunity occurs, this faith is essential to salvation. So that while Paul and James use different language, their doctrines are the same; they view the subject from different positions, but their views are the same. Paul looks to the origin of the act, James to the consummation of the disposition." Good deeds were the inevitable by-products of a sincere faith that saved. But by 1851, Hayes had converted to the position of Unitarian William Ellery Channing, who replaced the necessity of faith in Christ's sacrifice with the requirement of faith in God and the imitation of Jesus's behavior. Hayes wrote, "If a man feels the humility becoming [to] one prone to sinfulness, looks above for assistance, repents of what he does that is wrong, aspires to purity of intention and correctness of conduct in all the relations of life, such a man is a Christian, for he adopts the spirit of Christ's teaching and imitates His example; this too *in spite of his faith* [emphasis added]."[69]

While most presidents have professed beliefs regarding the origin and authority of the Bible, the divinity of Jesus, and the means of salvation that coincide with the teachings of the New Testament, a few have dissented, and some have expressed no opinion at all. While these differences between the presidents possess spiritual importance, their much larger areas of agreement have been far more significant to the nation's formation and development. The presidents' shared beliefs in Providence, the nation's divine mission, God-given individual rights and equality, the excellence of Christian ethics, the necessity of religion and morality to the survival and success of republican government, and the existence of an afterlife have provided their principal motivations for creating and shaping a republic.

CHAPTER 11

Human Nature and Balanced Government

In addition to their differences of opinion concerning the origin and authority of the Bible, the divinity of Jesus, and the means of salvation, presidents have also differed regarding human nature. While most of the early presidents possessed a pessimistic view of human nature that accords with the biblical doctrine of original sin, most modern presidents have possessed a more optimistic outlook. The pessimistic conception of human nature that prevailed in the early republican era had crucial consequences. It encouraged the founders to resist British claims to unchecked power and led them to establish numerous checks and balances in their national and state constitutions. Conversely, the optimistic view of human nature that has steadily increased in popularity since the Progressive Era has led to a dramatic increase in the power of the federal government.

The Biblical View

Contrary to the assertion of some historians, the doctrine of original sin was not the creation of Augustine four centuries after Christ; in fact, it is clearly present in both testaments of the Bible. It is no accident that, in the Book of Genesis, the fall of Adam and Eve (chapter 3) is followed immediately by the first murder (chapter 4), committed by their son Cain. The narrative clearly suggests that the propensity to sin was transmitted from one generation to the next. In 1 Kings 8:46, the author states, "There is no one who does not sin." The psalmist declares (Psalms 51:5), "I was born guilty, a sinner when my mother conceived me." Proverbs 20:9 asks, "Who can say, 'I have kept my heart pure; I am clean and without sin?'" Ecclesiastes 7:20 reiterates, "There is not a righteous man on earth who does what is right and never sins." Isaiah 64:6 proclaims, "We are all unclean, and all our righteous deeds are like filthy rags." Jeremiah 17:9 claims, "The heart is deceitful above all things and desperately wicked."[1]

The New Testament is even clearer in this regard. Paul explains (Romans 5:12, 19), "By one man sin entered into the world, and death through sin, and so death spread to all because all have sinned. . . . For just as by one man's disobedience many were made sinners, so by one man's obedience many will be made righteous." Just as sin and death came into world through Adam, redemption and life came into the world through Christ. Paul clearly ties the doctrine of original sin, humankind's inherited propensity to sin, to the doctrine of imputed righteousness, human salvation through faith in Jesus.

Checks and Balances

While none of the various governmental checks and balances contained in the US Constitution is biblical in origin, their inclusion in the document was, to a large extent, predicated on a pessimistic conception of human nature that was rooted in scripture, emphasized in Calvinist sermons, reiterated in political speeches, and transmitted from one generation to the next. It was Plato who, despite his optimistic conception of human nature, first suggested the theory of mixed government, the belief that governmental power should be balanced between the one, the few, and the many (the one leader, the few wellborn or wealthy, and the masses of ordinary folk). It was the French Enlightenment philosopher Montesquieu who popularized the separation of powers theory, the theory that the legislative, executive, and judicial functions of government—the power to make, execute, and interpret law, respectively—should be separated into different branches. Federalism, the belief that power should be balanced between national and state governments, was equally modern in formulation (though the Greeks possessed some confederacies). But the popularity of all of these systems of checks and balances in the modern world was based on the belief that innate human selfishness necessitated the dispersion of power, a conviction that was, in turn, based largely on the Bible, which was by far the most widely read work in the Western world, and the weekly diet of sermons based on it. While a person may derive a pessimistic view of human nature from a number of different sources—for instance, from the study of history, from reading newspapers, from observing toddlers (whose first spoken word is usually "Mine!"), or from honest introspection—the most prevalent source for such a view in the founders' day was the Bible.

John Adams, the most forceful advocate of mixed government in America, endorsed it on the basis of a conception of human nature that was thoroughly biblical. As early as 1763, he claimed in "An Essay on Man's Lust for Power": "No simple form of Government can possibly secure Men against the Violences of Power. Simple Monarchy will soon mould itself into Despotism, Aristocracy will commence on Oligarchy, and Democracy will soon degenerate into Anarchy, such an Anarchy that every Man will do what is right in his own Eyes, and no Man's life or Property or Reputation or Liberty will be safe." Thus, a mixed government that balanced the power of the three orders of society was absolutely essential. Adams's phrase "every Man will do what is right in his own Eyes" was a paraphrase of Judges 17:6. In a 1772 diary entry, Adams referred to the "mass of Corruption human Nature has been in general since the Fall of Adam." While far from deeming a nation's educational system irrelevant, Adams argued, in *A Defence of the Constitutions of Government of the United States of America* (1787–1788), his longest and most influential treatise on mixed government: "Millions must be brought up, whom no principles, no sentiments derived from education, can restrain from trampling on the laws. Orders of men, watching and balancing each other, are the only security; power must be opposed to power, and interest to interest. . . . Religion, superstition, oaths, education, laws, all give way before passions, interest, and power. . . . Although reason ought always to govern individuals, it certainly never did since the Fall, and never will till the Millennium." Adams believed that the Book of Genesis's portrayal of human nature was essentially accurate and that this nature necessitated a balance of governmental power between the three orders of society. Thus, the Constitution balanced power between a single president chosen by the Electoral College, an aristocratic, lengthy-termed Senate selected by the state legislatures, and a popularly elected "democratic branch" called the House of Representatives.[2]

Supporters of the separation of powers based their endorsement on the same pessimistic theory of human nature. At the Constitutional Convention, James Madison declared, "All men having power ought to be distrusted to a certain degree." In a letter that year, he wrote that, as a consequence of human nature, "Divide et impera [divide and rule], the reprobated maxim of tyranny, is, under certain qualifications, the only policy by which a republic can be administered on just principles." In *Federalist* No. 51, he contended, "The great security against a gradual concentration of the several powers in the same department consists of giving to those who administer each department the necessary constitutional means and personal motives to resist encroachments of the others. . . . Ambition must be made to counteract ambition.... It may be a reflection on human nature that such devices should be necessary to controul the abuses of government. But what is government itself but the greatest of all reflections on human nature? If men were angels, no government would be necessary." In *Federalist* No. 55, Madison claimed, "There is a degree of depravity in mankind which requires a certain degree of circumspection and distrust." Madison's selection of the word "depravity," the favored term of Calvinist preachers, is significant. The same year, Madison declared, "Wherever there is an interest and power to do wrong, wrong will generally be done, and not less readily by a powerful and interested party than by a powerful and interested prince." Thus, the Constitution balanced power between the legislative, executive, and judicial branches.[3]

The Federalist argument for a balance between national and state power was based on the same concept of human nature. George Washington adopted the view that human nature required a much closer balance between state and federal power than existed under the Articles of Confederation, which granted nearly all authority to the states. In 1786, the year before the Constitution was drafted, Washington wrote to John Jay:

> Your sentiments that our affairs are drawing rapidly to a crisis accord with my own.... We have probably had too good an opinion of human nature in forming our confederation. Experience has taught us that men will not adopt & carry into execution measures the best calculated for their own good without the intervention of a coercive power. I do not conceive we can exist long as a nation without having lodged somewhere a power which will pervade the whole Union in as energetic a manner as the authority of the different state governments extends over the several States.... We must take human nature as we find it. Perfection falls not to the share of mortals.

Thus, the Constitution balanced power between federal and state governments.[4]

Like Washington, Madison supported the Constitution because he considered the federal government under the Articles of Confederation too weak to balance the power of the states. But soon after the Constitution was ratified, Madison became alarmed by what he regarded as a rapid growth in federal power, a development he attempted to counter through claims of state authority. Later in life, frightened by South Carolina's attempt to nullify a federal law, he reverted to supporting federal power. However inconsistent his actions seemed to some contemporaries—and still appear to some historians—they were based on a consistent desire for balance that was, in turn, rooted in an equally consistent belief in a fundamentally selfish human nature.[5]

Indeed, the essay for which Madison is most famous reflected this conception of human nature. In *Federalist* No. 10, Madison claimed, "The latent causes of faction . . . are sown into the nature of man." Madison contended that human nature invariably produced differences in belief and in attachment to particular leaders, which, in turn, inevitably "divided mankind into parties, inflamed them with mutual animosity, and rendered them much more disposed to vex and oppress each other than to cooperate for their common good." Madison then famously argued that a stronger federal government was acceptable because the number of diverse interests in a large commercial republic like the United States was so large that majorities must be weak coalitions incapable of prolonged tyranny. But perhaps what is most intriguing about this essay is that Madison went beyond the commonplace assertion that humans were selfish to the biblical proposition that they were wicked—specifically, that they were creatures whose innate love of strife made them eager to fight about almost anything. Madison claimed, "So strong is this propensity of mankind to fall into mutual animosities that where no substantial occasion presents itself, the most frivolous and fanciful distinctions have been sufficient to kindle their unfriendly passions and excite their most violent conflicts."[6]

Continuing Pessimism in the Early Republic

Nothing these presidents experienced in the years after the ratification of the Constitution altered their opinion of human nature. In 1795 George Washington wrote that if men were honest and just, "Wars would cease and our swords would soon be converted into reaping-hooks." Instead, the earth was "moistened with human gore." Washington added, "The restless mind of man cannot be at peace; and when there is disorder within, it will appear without, and sooner or later will shew itself in acts. So it is with Nations, whose mind is only the aggregate of those of the individuals where the Government is Representative and the voice of a Despot where it is not."[7]

John Adams also remained pessimistic regarding human nature in his later years. In 1812 he wrote that politics had not improved, because human nature had not changed. He claimed regarding politics: "This is still the sport of passions and prejudices, of ambition, avarice, intrigue, faction, caprice, and gallantry as much as ever. Jealousy, envy, and revenge govern with as absolute a sway as ever." The following year, he preached his favorite theme: "Checks and balances, Jefferson, are our only Security for the progress of Mind, as well as the Security of Body. Every Species of these Christians would persecute Deists as [much as] either Sect would persecute one another if it had unchecked and unbalanced Power. Nay, the Deists would persecute Christians, and Atheists would persecute Deists, with as unrelenting Cruelty as any Christian would persecute them or one another. Know thyself, Human nature!" Although Adams considered piety and virtue vital to the survival of the republic, the sacred text of the very religion on which he relied for virtue, combined with his reading of history and his own experiences, taught him the folly of relying exclusively on these twin pillars. Human nature necessitated the erection of a third pillar: balanced government.[8]

James Madison retained a similar view. In 1825 he claimed, "All power in human hands is liable to be abused. . . . The superior recommendation of the federo-Republican system is that, whilst it provides more effectually against external danger, it involves a greater security to the minority against the hasty formation of oppressive minorities." At the Virginia Constitutional Convention of 1829, Madison took direct aim at the Scottish "common sense theory" of human nature, a theory that emphasized the goodness of human nature by focusing on the moral sense, or conscience, as the origin of humans' social nature. After observing that there were those who "would find a security [against tyranny] in our social feelings, in a respect for character, in the dictates of the monitor within," Madison declared, "But man is known to be a selfish as well as social being. . . . We all know that conscience is not a sufficient safeguard, and besides that, conscience itself may be deluded, may be misled . . . into acts which an enlightened conscience would forbid."[9]

Later Presidents Who Shared This View

Some later presidents shared the founders' biblical conception of human nature. In 1854, angered by the Supreme Court's usurpation of the power of judicial review, a power nowhere granted it in the Constitution, Martin van Buren argued that human nature necessitated the popular election of justices for a limited term. He contended, "The experience of ages proves that, with exceptions too few to impair the rule, men cannot be held to the performance of delegated political trust without a continued and practical responsibility to those for whose benefit it is conferred."[10]

James K. Polk possessed the same view of human nature. In 1824 none of the four presidential candidates succeeded in securing a majority of electoral votes. Therefore, for the second time in the nation's history, the House of Representatives was charged by the Constitution with selecting the president. The House selected John Quincy Adams, which infuriated James K. Polk, a Jacksonian Democrat. In his first speech to the House as a representative the following year, Polk cited the biblical concept of human nature as an argument for abolishing both the House's constitutional role in selecting presidents and for abolishing the Electoral College itself. He declared, "I have been taught to believe that, from the fall of our first great parent until the present hour, man has been depraved, frail, and impure." Thus, it was not safe to give corruptible electors and congressmen the power of selecting the president. The majority of the American people should elect the president. Polk did not acknowledge any danger that majorities of the people, acting according to the same human nature he identified, could also become corrupt and thus tyrannical, the very concern that had caused the framers of the Constitution to reject the idea of directly electing presidents by a majority vote.[11]

James Buchanan also cited the Bible for the human propensity to be corrupted by power. In 1828 he declared, "The very possession of power has a strong—a natural tendency, to corrupt the heart. The lust of dominion grows with its possession; and the man who in humble life was pure and innocent and just has often been transformed by the long possession of power into a monster. In the Sacred Book, which contains lessons in wisdom for the politician as well as for the Christian, we find a happy illustration of the corrupting influence of power upon the human heart." Buchanan then repeated the story of Hazael, a servant of the king of Syria, who was incredulous and indignant when the shuddering prophet Elisha informed him of the great atrocities he would one day commit, atrocities that were nowhere present in his thoughts at the time but that he did indeed commit later, after becoming king (2 Kings 8:12–13, 13:22). Buchanan concluded, "The nature of man is the same under Republics and under Monarchies. . . . Our rulers must be narrowly watched."[12]

Abraham Lincoln agreed that human nature was fundamentally selfish. While campaigning for president in 1860, he told an audience in Hartford, Connecticut, "The cash value of these slaves, at a moderate estimate, is $2,000,000,000. This amount of property value has a vast influence on the minds of its owners, very naturally. The same amount of property would have an equal influence upon us if owned in the North. Human nature is the same—people at the South are the same as those at the North, barring the difference in circumstances."[13]

Theodore Roosevelt distrusted human nature. After the Republicans nominated James G. Blaine, a candidate Roosevelt disliked, in 1884, Roosevelt wrote to his sister, "The voice of the people might be the voice of God in fifty-one cases out of one hundred, but in the remaining forty-nine it is quite as likely to be the voice of the devil, or what is still worse, the voice of a fool." In 1913 Roosevelt recalled that early in his political career, he had learned about demagogues and the flaws in human nature that won them popular support: "Human nature does not change; and that type of 'reformer' is as noxious now as he ever was. The loud-mouthed upholder of popular rights who attacks wickedness only when it is allied to wealth, and who never publicly assails any misdeed, no matter how flagrant, if committed nominally in the interest of labor, has either a warped mind or a tainted soul and should be trusted by no honest man." Regarding naïve reformers, he wrote, "The trouble is that the [corrupt city] boss does understand human nature, and that he fills a place which the reformer cannot fill unless he likewise understands human nature." The poor urban masses tolerated corrupt political bosses because they performed vital services for them that no one else did.[14]

Witnessing the Nazis on the move in 1938, Herbert Hoover disputed the view that advancements in science and technology necessarily produced progress. He claimed, "Science and technology have made us more interdependent, both individually and between nations. Cooperation is forced on us if we would live. But man is still by instinct a predatory animal given to devilish aggression." The mixture of Darwinism and Christianity in this last sentence, the combination of "predatory animal" and "devilish aggression," is intriguing. Hoover continued regarding the influence of human nature in thwarting progress: "We no longer burn witches, but we build bigger fires of intolerance and toss whole groups into them. . . While science is struggling to bring Heaven to earth, some men are using its materials in the construction of Hell."[15]

Having witnessed both Nazi concentration camps and the armed might it required to liberate them, Dwight Eisenhower was skeptical of peace proposals that were based on an optimistic conception of human nature. In 1954 he responded to the World Council of Churches' call for universal disarmament with a statement that both affirmed the need for Christianity in the world and cautioned against the unbiblical view of human nature that underlay this proposal. In the latter vein, he declared, "We must not forget that man isn't made up entirely of noble qualities and the ennobling virtues that send him doing his duty for his fellow men. He is also made up of a lot of selfish and greedy and ignoble qualities, and that we have got to prepare for, because we are of a dual nature. And if anybody thinks that the United States can be in better position in the pursuit of peace by being weak, I must say I disagree with him 100 percent." The following year, he contended, "We shall never be rid of strife in this world—international and, in some degree, among ourselves—so long as humans are human and the Millennium has not arrived."[16]

Confidence in Checks and Balances: Orthodox and Unorthodox

Although the popularity of various theories of checks and balances in the early republican era owed much to the pervasiveness of the biblical doctrine of original sin in American society, the supreme confidence expressed by their advocates in the ability of balanced political structures to overcome human depravity was not biblical at all. For instance, John Adams sometimes rested unbiblical, utopian hopes on his favorite form of balanced government. By contrast, James Madison and John Quincy Adams possessed more limited and, thus, more biblical expectations.

Having reviewed the horrors of the Peloponnesian War, the bloody conflict between Athens and Sparta that laid waste to all of Greece in the fifth century BC, John Adams concluded, "Such things ever will be, says Thucydides, so long as human nature remains the same. But if this nervous historian had known a balance of three powers, he would not have pronounced the distemper so incurable, but would have added—so long as parties in cities remain unbalanced." It is a testament to the powerful hold of Enlightenment optimism that Adams could write the latter sentence despite knowing that the most revered classical models of mixed government, Sparta and the Roman Republic, had fallen in spite of their vaunted balance and despite the fact that he himself had argued during the Revolution that the most revered modern model, Great Britain, had become corrupted. Enlightenment philosophers emphasized the power of reason to solve every sort of problem, and theories of checks and balances were products of reason intended to solve the problems caused by the less attractive attributes of human nature. Adams was simultaneously a man of the Bible who believed deeply in the darkness of human nature and a man of the Enlightenment who believed deeply in the power of reason to solve problems. The result was a fervent, almost obsessive, regard for mixed government as the answer to the problem posed by human nature. Thus, Adams even suggested that it was possible for a constitution to last forever, regardless of the qualities of the republic's citizens, if only it possessed a proper balance among the orders. Adding one piece of hyperbole to another, Adams added, "Perhaps it would be impossible to prove that a republic cannot exist even among highwaymen, by setting one rogue to watch another; and the knaves themselves may, in time, be made honest men by the struggle." Adams's euphoria over the power of mixed government to circumvent human nature resembled that of the more zealous advocates of laissez-faire economics, who also begin with the premise of a selfish human nature yet still somehow manage to sound utopian when expressing supreme confidence in the checks imposed by a free marketplace.[17]

Adams's giddy flight of optimism ended with a crash. By 1806 he was writing, "I once thought our Constitution was quasi or mixed government, but they have now made it, to all intents and purposes, in virtue, in spirit, and effect, a democracy. We are left without resources but in our prayers and tears, and having nothing that we can do or say, but the Lord have mercy upon us." It is crucial to note that Adams's renewed pessimism involved no loss of faith in the ability of mixed government to counter human nature but only the conviction that the American system had been democratized to a dangerous degree by such innovations as the rise of political parties and the elimination of property qualifications for voting. It does not appear to have occurred to Adams that part of the problem of human nature might lie in its propensity to destroy carefully constructed balances. Adams's unwillingness to face this truth is all the more startling given the long list of once-balanced republics that had fallen from a loss of balance that he himself presented in his work *A Defence of the Constitutions*.[18]

Both Madison's more nuanced understanding of human nature and his greater circumspection concerning the ability of checks and balances to thwart that nature were biblical. While conceding the general selfishness of human nature to Patrick Henry and George Mason at the Virginia Ratifying Convention, Madison noted that republican government was based on the assumption that some degree of popular virtue was not only possible but essential. Why were republican orators constantly calling for virtue if people were really incapable of it? Madison declared, "Is there no virtue among us? If there be not, we are in a wretched situation. No theoretical checks, no form of government, can render us secure. To suppose that any form of government will secure liberty or happiness without any virtue in the people is a chimerical idea." Madison was cautiously optimistic that a modicum of popular virtue, when combined with checks and balances, could preserve a republic for a long time, though by no means create a utopia. In this he reflected the teaching of his mentor, Reverend John Witherspoon, who claimed that although "man now comes into the world in a state of impurity or moral defilement," it was a mistake to conclude regarding human nature that "every act in every part of it is evil," and warned against going "to an extreme on the one hand or on the other in speaking of human nature." Witherspoon explained, "It is of consequence to have as much virtue among the particular members of a community as possible, but it is folly to expect that a state should be supported in integrity by all who have a share in managing it. They must be so balanced that when everyone draws to his own interest or inclination, there may be an even poise upon the whole."[19]

John Quincy Adams possessed a similar view. In 1806 he told Harvard students that, due to "the depravity of mankind," the powerful weapon of eloquence "often will be brandished for guilty purposes." Five years later, he confided to his son George, "Like the apostle Paul, I find a law in my members warring against the law of my mind [Romans 7:23]. But as I know that it is my nature to be imperfect, so I know it is my duty to aim at perfection; and feeling and deploring my own frailties, I can only pray Almighty God for the aid of his spirit to strengthen my good desires and to subdue my propensities to evil, for it is from him that every good and every perfect gift descends [James 1:17]." Two weeks later, he referred to "the original excellence and present fallen condition of man," as well as to "our original Sin." But in 1827 he wrote regarding human nature in a more nuanced way: "The Scripture says that the heart is deceitful and desperately wicked [Jeremiah 17:9]. This is certainly true and is a profound observation upon the human character. But the language is figurative. By the heart is meant in this passage the selfish passions of man. But there is also in man a spirit, and the inspiration of the Almighty giveth him understanding. It is the duty of man to discover the vicious propensities and deceits of the heart, to control them. This, with the grace of God, a large portion of the human race in Christian lands do accomplish."[20]

The Optimists

Some presidents have rejected the biblical doctrine of original sin for a more optimistic conception of human nature. In 1799 Thomas Jefferson wrote, "I am among those who think well of the human character generally. I consider man as formed for society, and endowed by nature with those dispositions which fit him for society. I believe also . . . that his mind is perfectible to a degree of which we cannot as yet form any conception."[21]

Jefferson's optimism led him to endorse a simpler and more democratic form of government than most of the other founders favored. After a brief flirtation with mixed government theory during the Revolution, Jefferson became an advocate of a simple representative democracy based on his conviction that the agricultural lifestyle of the vast majority of American voters rendered them capable of wielding supreme power. Influenced by classical poets and historians, Jefferson praised this lifestyle partly for the practical reason that it left the small farmer free from an overlord and, therefore, capable of thinking and acting independently. But Jefferson also suggested that it was the favored lifestyle of the Almighty:

> Those who labour in the earth are the chosen people of God, if ever He had a chosen people, whose breasts He has made His peculiar deposit for genuine and substantial virtue. He keeps alive that sacred fire which otherwise might escape from the face of the earth. Corruption of morals in the mass of cultivators is a phenomenon of which no age or nation has furnished an example. It is the mark set on those who, not looking up to heaven and to their own soil and industry as does the husbandman, for their subsistence, depend for it on the casualties and caprices of customers.

He also claimed, "Cultivators of the earth are the most valuable citizens. They are the most vigorous, the most independent, the most virtuous, and they are tied to their country, and wedded to its liberty and interests by the most lasting bonds." Hence, Jefferson predicted, "I think our governments will remain virtuous for many centuries; as long as they remain chiefly agricultural; and this will be as long as there will be vacant lands in any part of America." Jefferson rested his hope of a bright future for the new nation not on checks and balances, which were intended to thwart a corrupt human nature, but on the positive effects of a rural, agricultural lifestyle on a slate that was at worst blank, at best already inclined to goodness by the moral sense. For this reason, as president, Jefferson was willing to sacrifice one of his most cherished political principles, strict construction of the Constitution, in order to purchase Louisiana from France. When the absence of a constitutional provision allowing the president to buy foreign territory threatened the republic's future agricultural base and, thus, its virtue and longevity, he reluctantly sacrificed constitutional scruples in order to extend the life of the republic.[22]

Jefferson also rested his hopes on the power of education. Even the most pessimistic letter he ever wrote ended with a hint of the confidence he placed in education. In 1814 Jefferson wrote regarding "self-love": "It is the sole antagonist of virtue, leading us constantly by our propensities to self-gratification in violation of our moral duties to others. Accordingly, it is against this enemy that are erected the batteries of the moralists and religionists, as the only obstacle to the practice of morality. Take from man his selfish propensities, and he can have nothing to seduce him from the practice of virtue. Or subdue those propensities by education, instruction, or restraint, and virtue remains without a competitor." This passage begins in a seemingly Calvinist tone, albeit a peculiar one since it asserts that "the sole antagonist of virtue" and "the only obstacle to the practice of morality" is human nature itself, but it then reveals that this trait of self-love is actually so lightly rooted that it can be displaced by education, leaving virtue "without a competitor." Even this rather weak reference to the existence of an innate self-love in humanity is absent from most of Jefferson's other writings, which focus on the power of education to bring about progress. In 1816 he contended, "Enlighten the people generally, and tyranny and oppressions of body and mind will vanish like evil spirits at the dawn of day. Although I do not, with some enthusiasts, believe that the human condition will ever advance to such a state of perfection as that there shall no longer be pain or vice in the world, yet I believe it susceptible of much improvement, and most of all, in matters of government and religion; and that the diffusion of knowledge among the people is to be the instrument by which it is to be effected." Two years later, he helped draft a report concerning his beloved University of Virginia. The report declared that education "engrafts a new man on the native stock and improves what in his nature was vicious and perverse into qualities of virtue and social worth." The report continued, "And it cannot but be that each generation succeeding to the knowledge acquired by all those who preceded it, adding it to their own acquisitions and discoveries, and handing the mass down for successive and constant accumulation, must advance the knowledge and well-being of mankind not infinitely, as some have said, but indefinitely, and to a term no one can fix and foresee." The references to virtue and vice in this report make it clear that Jefferson and his coauthors were referring not merely to the certainty of scientific, technological, or economic progress, about which none of the founders expressed any significant doubt, but also to that of social and moral progress, about which there was considerable debate, with most coming down on the side of biblical pessimism.[23]

It is not surprising that Jefferson's heir to the leadership of American prodemocratic forces, Andrew Jackson, was another optimist regarding human nature. In fact, despite being a Presbyterian himself, he was once so offended by a Presbyterian sermon "on the depravity of the human heart" that he raised strenuous objections to it with the preacher. Jackson's passionate opposition to the sermon is remarkable given that, unlike Jefferson, he was a fairly orthodox Christian who never spoke ill of the Bible. Jackson often referred to his "faith in the people," by which he meant the majority, in the same breath as his faith in God. Like many Americans before and since, he glossed over the numerous biblical references to the universal effects of original sin, and he therefore considered it safe to give absolute power to the majority.[24]

Before the Civil War, Andrew Johnson was one of the many postmillennialist Christians influenced by the Second Great Awakening who believed that the world was on the verge of the utopian Millennium prophesied in the Bible. Yet, oddly enough, they thought that the Millennium would come about not in the way that scripture relates—as the result of the return of Christ to a world drowning in war, famine, pestilence, and tyranny—but by the progressive efforts of human beings aided by the Holy Spirit. Postmillennialism not only contradicted numerous prophecies regarding the end times, but it also contradicted the biblical theory that human nature was hopelessly corrupted by sin. In his first inaugural address as governor of Tennessee (1853), Johnson declared, "Man is not perfect, it is true, but we all hope he is approximating perfection and that he will, in the progress of time, reach this grand and most important end in all human affairs." Johnson believed that this perfection would arise from two sources: Christianity and democracy. He contended that democracy increased humans' likeness to their Maker by encouraging the use of their intellects for the purpose of self-government. Thus, he alleged,

> It is the business of Democracy to progress in the work of increasing this principle of Divinity and thereby elevate and make man more perfect. I hold that the Democratic party proper of the whole world, and especially of the United States, has undertaken the political redemption of man and, sooner or later, the great work will be accomplished. In the political world it corresponds to that of Christianity in the moral. They are going along, not in divergent, nor in parallel, but in converging lines—the one purifying and elevating man religiously, the other politically. Democracy progressive corresponds to the Church Militant: both fighting against error—one in the moral, the other in the political field. At what period of time they will have finished the work of progress and elevation is not now for me to determine; but when finished, these two lines will have approximated each other—man being perfected, both in a religious and in a political point of view. At this point the Church Militant will give way and cease to exist and the Church Triumphant begin.

In other words, the Millennium prophesied in the Bible will have arrived:

> The divinity of man being now fully developed, it may now be confidently and exultingly asserted that the voice of the people is the voice of God, and proclamation be made that the millennial morning has dawned, and that the time has come when the Lion and the Lamb shall lie down together . . . when "the sucking child shall play upon the hole of the asp and the weaned child shall put its hand upon the cockatrice's den [Isaiah 11:8]," and the glad tidings shall

be proclaimed throughout the land of men's political and religious redemption and that there is "on earth peace, good will toward men [Luke 2:14]."

Johnson then compared democracy to Jacob's ladder, a staircase to heaven (Genesis 28:11–12).[25]

Although postmillennialism bled to death on Civil War battlefields, an optimistic view of human nature revived in the Progressive Era. Indeed, the period's democratic reforms, such as the direct election of US senators (1913), were based on the view that human nature no longer stood in the way of a system of simple majority rule. Majority rule would not lead to majority tyranny, as the founders feared. The checks and balances of the Constitution were now viewed with impatience, as bugs that created gridlock rather than as features that protected rights. Thus, Woodrow Wilson, a devout Presbyterian but an even more devout Progressive, wrote in 1884, "I believe that there is a vast deal more good than evil in human nature," and he claimed the following year, "Both singly and collectively, man's nature draws him away from that which is brutish towards that which is human—away from his kinship with beasts towards a fuller realization of his kinship with God."[26]

Franklin Roosevelt, who served in Wilson's administration and later ushered in the New Deal, also believed that human nature was good. He told his labor secretary, Frances Perkins, "If you treat people right, they will treat you right—ninety percent of the time." Roosevelt often used that 90 percent figure, also claiming, for instance, that 90 percent of the people of the world wanted peace. He considered criminals victims of their environment, which he hoped to change through New Deal programs.[27]

This linkage between an optimistic assessment of human nature and a political agenda of increasing the size and power of the federal government on behalf of the majority became prominent during the administration of Lyndon Johnson. Johnson contended, "In any society, men of good will and moderation are in the majority. The cynics—and there are always some of them—are in the minority. Those in the majority are the proportions that God set out when He made us all. It is the task and the test of democracy to assure that the moderate and good-willed majority prevails and has its way." Like the founder of his political party, Thomas Jefferson, Johnson saw no need for limitations on the power of the majority, for his concept of human nature left him without fear of majority tyranny. For this reason, Johnson proposed a constitutional amendment to alter the Electoral College in favor of large states so that it would always reflect the results of the popular vote, an amendment that would have rendered the body superfluous and obstructed the founders' intent to protect the citizens of small states. However, Johnson differed from Jefferson in seeking to eliminate not only the framers' mixed government features on behalf of the majority but also their balance between federal and state governments. Unlike Jefferson, Johnson considered the federal government the best instrument for enacting the will of the majority. Thus, Johnson oversaw the greatest expansion of the federal government in American history. His Great Society agenda, which inaugurated Medicare, Medicaid, Head Start, and a plethora of other programs, was as based on a positive conception of human nature as his support for absolute majority rule. He possessed no fear of federal tyranny or majority tyranny. Thus, the balance between the federal and state governments carefully constructed by the framers of the Constitution was gradually undermined through a loose interpretation of the document. This interpretation was intended to increase the power of the federal government, which was increasingly considered the proper instrument for imposing the will of a majority that had a right to rule, for it was fundamentally good.[28]

Politicians of all stripes began to consider it inexpedient to include somber references to human selfishness in campaign speeches. It was much more politically beneficial to flatter voters with talk of their goodness than to tell them that they were depraved. Even those modern presidents who occasionally referred to the darker elements of human nature rarely drew any political inferences from them, and references to the fundamental goodness of humans often filled the addresses of even the advocates of a limited federal government. In fact, such optimism sometimes caused the same conservatives who opposed progressive domestic policies they considered utopian to propose utopian foreign policies of their own. Despite the opposition of key cabinet members and other advisors, Ronald Reagan returned again and again to his dream of abolishing nuclear weapons, apparently trusting that once the Communists were subdued, no other bad actors would arise to pursue these weapons. In Reagan's mind, abolishing handguns was unrealistic, but abolishing nuclear weapons was not. Similarly, George W. Bush often proclaimed his sincere belief that every person on the planet, regardless of culture, yearned for American-style individual freedom ("Etched in the soul of every person on the face of the Earth is the desire to be free"), a conviction that undergirded the Bush Doctrine.[29]

The biblical concept of human nature held by most of the founders, a concept they embedded in the very structure of the government they created, has been largely replaced by an optimistic one that has steadily increased in popularity since the Progressive Era, a concept that views all checks on majority rule as unnecessary and illegitimate. Which of these prevails in the long term will determine much about the future of the nation.

Epilogue

The degree of continuity in the biblical training, interests, beliefs, and themes of the forty-five distinct individuals who have served as American presidents, individuals who have belonged to a variety of different eras, geographical regions, religious denominations, and political parties, is truly startling. For three centuries American presidents—Northerners and Southerners, Easterners and Westerners, Episcopalians and Baptists, Presbyterians and Catholics, Federalists and Democratic-Republicans, Democrats and Republicans—have studied the same biblical texts, quoted the same Scriptures, and promoted the same biblical principles and themes. In the process presidents have both reflected and reinforced an American culture based largely on the Bible.

Since the 1960s, however, American culture has been transformed to such an extent that various observers, both Christian and secularist, have plausibly labeled it "post-Christian." Even many self-professed Christians now possess only a vague familiarity with the contents of the Bible and have come to reject its teachings concerning sexuality and other subjects.

This cultural transformation has not yet affected American presidential rhetoric on a fundamental level, because, thus far, all of the presidents except for Barack Obama were born in the 1940s or earlier and therefore were raised when biblical influences were far stronger than they are today. What the future holds for the nation when the presidency is held by generations that have not been raised on scriptural verities—what texts will be hailed as authorities and what unifying themes will be presented—remains to be seen.

APPENDIX I

Presidential Terms and Denominations

The denomination listed for each president refers to the church to which he possessed the strongest ties. It does not necessarily signify that he was an official member of that denomination, that he adhered to all of its doctrines, that he possessed no ties to any other church, or that he never attended the worship services of any other denomination.

1. George Washington, 1789–1797, Episcopalian
2. John Adams, 1797–1801, Unitarian
3. Thomas Jefferson, 1801–1809, Nondenominational Protestant[1]
4. James Madison, 1809–1817, Episcopalian
5. James Monroe, 1817–1825, Episcopalian
6. John Quincy Adams, 1825–1829, Unitarian
7. Andrew Jackson, 1829–1837, Presbyterian
8. Martin Van Buren, 1837–1841, Dutch Reformed
9. William Henry Harrison, 1841, Episcopalian
10. John Tyler, 1841–1845, Episcopalian
11. James K. Polk, 1845–1849, Methodist[2]
12. Zachary Taylor, 1849–1850, Episcopalian
13. Millard Fillmore, 1850–1853, Unitarian
14. Franklin Pierce, 1853–1857, Episcopalian
15. James Buchanan, 1857–1861, Presbyterian
16. Abraham Lincoln, 1861–1865, Nondenominational Protestant
17. Andrew Johnson, 1865–1869, Nondenominational Protestant
18. Ulysses S. Grant, 1869–1877, Methodist
19. Rutherford B. Hayes, 1877–1881, Methodist
20. James Garfield, 1881, Disciples of Christ

21. Chester Arthur, 1881–1885, Episcopalian
22. Grover Cleveland, 1885–1889, Presbyterian
23. Benjamin Harrison, 1889–1893, Presbyterian
24. Grover Cleveland, 1893–1897, Presbyterian
25. William McKinley, 1897–1901, Methodist
26. Theodore Roosevelt, 1901–1909, Dutch Reformed
27. William Howard Taft, 1909–1913, Unitarian
28. Woodrow Wilson, 1913–1921, Presbyterian
29. Warren G. Harding, 1921–1923, Northern Baptist
30. Calvin Coolidge, 1923–1929, Congregationalist
31. Herbert Hoover, 1929–1933, Quaker
32. Franklin D. Roosevelt, 1933–1945, Episcopalian
33. Harry S. Truman, 1945–1953, Southern Baptist
34. Dwight D. Eisenhower, 1953–1961, Presbyterian
35. John F. Kennedy, 1961–1963, Roman Catholic
36. Lyndon B. Johnson, 1963–1969, Disciples of Christ
37. Richard Nixon, 1969–1974, Quaker
38. Gerald Ford, 1974–1977, Episcopalian
39. Jimmy Carter, 1977–1981, Baptist[3]
40. Ronald Reagan, 1981–1989, Presbyterian[4]
41. George H. W. Bush, 1989–1993, Episcopalian
42. Bill Clinton, 1993–2001, Southern Baptist
43. George W. Bush, 2001–2009, Methodist
44. Barack Obama, 2009–2017, Nondenominational Protestant[5]
45. Donald Trump, 2017–2021, Nondenominational Protestant[6]
46. Joe Biden, 2021–2024, Roman Catholic
47. Donald Trump, anticipated term, 2025–2029, Nondenominational Protestant

APPENDIX II

Cherished Scriptures

George Washington—Micah 4:4: "Every man shall sit under his own vine and under his own fig tree, and none shall make him afraid." Washington referred to this verse dozens of times. Its imagery touched a strong cord within him, speaking of the peace, rest, and natural beauty that his home, Mount Vernon, represented, blessings that his public service denied him for many years.

John Adams—Exodus 3:11: "Moses said to God, 'Who am I that I should go to Pharaoh and bring the Israelites out of Egypt?'" After hearing a sermon based on this scripture in 1776, Adams envisioned himself as a second Moses, an unlikely man leading his people to freedom and independence.

Thomas Jefferson—Psalms 15, which begins, "O Lord, who may abide in your tent?" Jefferson copied his favorite translation of this, his favorite psalm, in a letter to a baby boy named after him, which was meant to be read when the boy was grown. Jefferson considered this psalm a perfect "description of the good man."

John Quincy Adams—1 Corinthians 15:55: "O death, where is thy sting? O grave, where is thy victory?" Adams believed this "triumphant and transporting" verse epitomized the excellence of Christianity, whose teachings concerning the immortality of the soul rescued humanity from the chronic fear of death.

Andrew Jackson—Hebrews 12:6: "He whom the Lord loves He chastens." Jackson often quoted this verse to console friends and family members who suffered misfortune.

James K. Polk—Acts 17:31: "He has appointed a day in which He will judge the world in righteousness by the man He has ordained." A sermon based on this scripture delivered on Polk's fiftieth birthday reminded him of his own mortality and of the need to "put my House in Order." He died less than four years later.

Abraham Lincoln—Genesis 3:19: "By the sweat of your face you shall eat bread." Lincoln often cited God's command to Adam following the Fall as an argument against slavery, claiming that anyone whose nourishment came from the forced sweat of others was defying the divine command.

James Garfield—Romans 6:4: "We have been buried with Him by baptism into death, so that, just as Christ was raised from the dead by the glory of the Father, so we too might walk in newness of life." Garfield referenced this verse in his diary the day he was baptized, at the age of eighteen, at a Disciples of Christ revival meeting.

William McKinley—Luke 22:42: "Not my will but yours be done." While dying from an assassin's bullet, McKinley repeated Jesus's words of submission to God's will in the Garden of Gethsemane the night before His crucifixion.

Theodore Roosevelt—Micah 6:8: "He has told you, O mortal, what is good; and what does the Lord require of you but to do justice, and to love kindness, and to walk humbly with your God?" Roosevelt claimed that this verse constituted "the essence of religion" and was "all the creed I need."

Woodrow Wilson—2 Corinthians 4:8–9: "We are troubled on every side, yet not distressed; we are perplexed, but not in despair; persecuted, but not forsaken; cast down, but not destroyed." When, following a devastating stroke, Wilson learned from his sickbed that the Senate had rejected the Treaty of Versailles, on which he had rested all his hopes for world peace, he asked his physician to read this scripture aloud.

Calvin Coolidge—John 1, which begins, "In the beginning was the Word, and the Word was with God, and the Word was God." This is the chapter that at six years old, Coolidge read to his grandfather, who was on his death-bed. Coolidge placed his hand on that chapter when taking the oath of office in 1925.

Herbert Hoover—Hebrews 13:5: "I will never leave you nor forsake you." Hoover kept on his wall this promise by God, a motto that had been given him by his beloved mother, who died of typhoid fever at thirty-five.

Franklin Roosevelt—Luke 10, the story of the Good Samaritan, Roosevelt believed captured the essence of Christianity, a generosity of spirit he considered essential to overcoming the Great Depression.

Harry Truman—Exodus 20:3–17 and Matthew 5:3–11, the Ten Commandments and the Beatitudes, respectively; these were the scriptures on which Truman rested his hands when he took the oath of office in 1945. He often claimed that these two foundational texts were crucial to human happiness. He called the Beatitudes "the greatest of all things in the Bible."

Dwight Eisenhower—Proverbs 16:32: "He who conquers his own soul is greater than he who takes a city." Eisenhower's mother recited this scripture to him as a child after he had a temper tantrum. He never forgot the verse. His subsequent self-control was crucial to his military and political success.

John F. Kennedy—Deuteronomy 31:6: "Be strong and of courage; be not afraid, neither be dismayed." Kennedy quoted this verse at the Democratic National Convention that nominated him for president in 1960.

Lyndon Johnson—Isaiah 1:18: "Come now, let us reason together." Johnson often quoted this scripture, which appealed to his considerable skills as a negotiator and to his sensibility as a longtime legislator.

Gerald Ford—Ecclesiastes 3:3: "[There is] a time to kill and a time to heal." Ford titled his autobiography *A Time to Heal* and began the volume with this scripture because he believed that his presidential term, which followed the Watergate scandal, was a time to heal Americans' distrust of their leaders.

Jimmy Carter—1 John 4:16: "God is love." This was the first Bible verse Carter's parents taught him, when he was only four years old.

Ronald Reagan—2 Chronicles 7:14: "If my people, who are called by my name, shall humble themselves and pray and seek my face and turn from their wicked ways, then will I hear from heaven and will forgive their sin and will heal their land." This was Reagan's mother's favorite verse, next to which she wrote, "A most wonderful verse for the healing of the nations." She wrote this in the Bible Reagan would later inherit from her. It became one of his own favorite verses.

Bill Clinton—Proverbs 29:18: "Where there is no vision the people perish." Clinton cited this verse to explain why he ran for president: he believed the nation lacked a unifying vision.

George W. Bush—Romans 12:21: "Do not be overcome by evil, but overcome evil with good." In the days following the September 11 attacks, Bush often quoted this scripture and claimed that Americans, by helping one another, were doing just that.

Barack Obama—Genesis 4:9: "Cain said, 'Am I my brother's keeper?'" Obama often used the phrase "being our brother's keeper" to support his policies and even named a federal program aimed at establishing public-private partnerships for mentoring inner-city youth My Brother's Keeper.

Notes

Chapter 1

1. Lawrence Cremin, *American Education: The Colonial Experience, 1607–1783* (Harper & Row, 1970), 129–30, 362.

2. Sheldon S. Cohen, *A History of Colonial Education, 1607–1776* (John Wiley & Sons, 1974), 47, 60; James Axtell, *The School upon a Hill: Education and Society in Colonial New England* (Yale University Press, 1974), 34–35, 174, 187–88; Robert Middlekauff, *Ancients and Axioms: Secondary Education in Eighteenth-Century New England* (Yale University Press, 1963), 14; John E. Rexine, "The Boston Latin School Curriculum in the Seventeenth and Eighteenth Centuries," *The Classical Journal* 72 (March 1977): 263–66.

3. Middlekauff, *Ancients and Axioms*, 76; Merrill D. Peterson, *James Madison: A Biography in His Own Words* (Harper & Row, 1974), 18; Cremin, *American Education*, 506–8; Marie B. Hecht, *John Quincy Adams: A Personal History of an Independent Man* (Macmillan, 1972), 32; Jack Shepherd, *Cannibals of the Heart: A Personal Biography of Louisa Catherine and John Quincy Adams* (McGraw-Hill, 1980), 33; Charles Grier Sellers Jr., *James K. Polk, Jacksonian, 1795–1843* (Princeton University Press, 1957), 41–42.

4. James MacGregor Burns, *Roosevelt: The Lion and the Fox* (Harcourt, Brace, 1956), 12, 16; Elliott Roosevelt, ed., *F.D.R.: His Personal Letters* (Duell, Sloan and Pearce, 1947–1950), 1:31–32; March 11, 1897, 1:73; May 3, 1897, 1:90; December 20, 1898, 1:247; October 15, 1899, 1:346; October 22, 1899, 1:349; Roosevelt to Reverend Endicott Peabody, November 29, 1904, 1:533; Dan Ariail and Cheryl Heckler-Feltz, *The Carpenter's Apprentice: The Spiritual Biography of Jimmy Carter* (Zondervan, 1996), 32.

5. Perry Miller, *The New England Mind* (Macmillan, 1939), 1:88, 448; Emory Elliott, *Power and the Pulpit in Puritan New England* (Princeton University Press, 1975), 47; Cremin, *American Education*, 175, 321; Cohen, *A History of Colonial Education*, 64, 98–99, 136–37.

6. Cohen, *A History of Colonial Education*, 167, 173–75; Paul K. Conkin, *The Uneasy Center: Reformed Christianity in Antebellum America* (University of North Carolina Press, 1995), 57; E. Digby Baltzell, *Puritan Boston and Quaker Philadelphia: Two Protestant Ethics and the Spirit of Class Authority and Leadership* (Free Press, 1979), 163; Leonard W. Labaree et al., eds., *The Papers of Benjamin Franklin* (Yale University Press, 1959), Franklin to Samuel Johnson, December 24, 1751, 4:222; Gottfried Achenwall, Observations on America from Oral Information Provided by Dr. Franklin, 1766, 13:363.

7. Cohen, *A History of Colonial Education*, 66; Gilbert Chinard, *Honest John Adams* (Little, Brown, 1933), 14; Labaree, *The Papers of Benjamin Franklin*, Franklin to Samuel Johnson, December 24, 1751, 4:222; Richard B. Morris, ed., *John Jay: The Making of a Revolutionary, Unpublished Papers, 1745–1780* (Harper & Row, 1975), Statutes of King's College, March 23, 1763, 1:56; King's College Commencement, May 22, 1764, vol. 1:62–63; May 19, 1767, 1:85; Sellers, *James K. Polk, Jacksonian*, 43–44; Roy F. Nichols, *Franklin Pierce: Young Hickory of the Granite Hills* (University of Pennsylvania Press, 1931), 15–17; Harry James Brown and Frederick D. Williams, ed., *The Diary of James A. Garfield* (Michigan University Press, 1967), October 1, 1853, 1:220; Arthur S. Link, ed., *The Papers of Woodrow Wilson* (Princeton University Press, 1966–1994), Four Items from a Wilson Notebook, September 1, 1873, 1:26–28.

8. C. Dewitt Hardy and Richard Hofstadter, *The Development and Scope of Higher Education in the United States* (Columbia University Press, 1952), 33–34; George M. Marsden, *The Soul of the American University: From Protestant Establishment to Established Nonbelief* (Oxford University Press, 1994), 148n34, 345; Mary Beth Brown, *Hand of Providence: The Strong and Quiet Faith of Ronald Reagan* (Thomas Nelson, 2004), 52.

9. David L. Holmes, *The Faiths of the Founding Fathers* (Oxford University Press, 2006), 80, 92–93; Robert A. Rutland et al., eds., *The Papers of James Madison* (University of Chicago Press, 1962–1977; repr. University Press of Virginia, 1977), Notes on Commentary on the Bible, 1770–1773, 1:51–56; Madison to William Bradford, September 25, 1773, 1:96; William Lee Miller, *The First Liberty: Religion and the American Republic* (Alfred A. Knopf, 1986), 89; Harry J. Brown and Margaret Leech, *The Garfield Orbit* (Harper & Row, 1978), 60, 67, 72.

10. Calvin Coolidge, *The Autobiography of Calvin Coolidge* (Cosmopolitan, 1929), 54–55.

11. Coolidge, *The Autobiography of Calvin Coolidge*, 68–70; Amity Shlaes, *Coolidge* (HarperCollins, 2013), 33; Donald R. McCoy, *Calvin Coolidge: The Quiet President* (Macmillan, 1967), 33.

12. Nichols, *Franklin Pierce*, 25; Harry J. Sievers, *Benjamin Harrison, Hoosier Warrior, 1833–1865* (Henry Regnery, 1952), 59–61; Charles W. Calhoun, *Benjamin Harrison* (Times Books, 2005), 13–14.

13. Hardy and Hofstadter, *The Development and Scope of Higher Education in the United States*, 5–6.

14. Holmes, *The Faiths of the Founding Fathers*, 114.

15. Edith B. Gelles, "The Way of Duty: Abigail Adams on Religion," in Daniel L. Dreisbach et al., eds., *The Forgotten Founders on Religion and Public Life* (University of Notre Dame Press, 2009), 26, 31–36; Charles Francis Adams, ed., *The Memoirs of John Quincy Adams, Comprising Portions of His Diary from 1795 to 1848* (Philadelphia, 1874–1877; repr., AMS, 1970), Introduction, 1:6; Holmes, *The Faiths of the Founding Fathers*, 118–20.

16. Adams, *The Memoirs of John Quincy Adams*, November 1, 1818, 4:155–58; Allan Nevins, ed., *The Diary of John Quincy Adams, 1794–1845: American Diplomacy, and Political, Social, and Intellectual Life from Washington to Polk* (Charles Scribner's Sons, 1951), August 1, 1843, 555.

17. Charles B. Sanford, *The Religious Life of Thomas Jefferson* (University Press of Virginia, 1984), 3, 7.

18. Harold D. Moser et al., eds., *The Papers of Andrew Jackson* (University of Tennessee Press, 1980), Rachel Jackson to Andrew Jackson Donelson, October 19, 1818, 4:244–45; Rachel Jackson to Ralph Earl, February 23, 1819, 4:272; Andrew Jackson to Mary Fogg, January 17, 1829, 7:14; Robert V. Remini, *Andrew Jackson and the Course of American Empire, 1767–1821* (Harper & Row, 1977), 7; John Spencer Bassett, ed., *Correspondence of Andrew Jackson* (Carnegie Institution, 1926–1935), Rachel Jackson to Elizabeth Watson, July 18, 1828, 3:416; Robert V. Remini, *Andrew Jackson and the Course of American Freedom, 1822–1832* (Harper & Row, 1981), 155; Robert V. Remini, *Andrew Jackson and the Course of American Democracy, 1833–1845* (Harper & Row, 1984), 433.

19. Sellers, *James K. Polk, Jacksonian*, 23; Wayne Cutler et al., eds., *Correspondence of James K. Polk* (Vanderbilt University Press, 1969–1989; repr. University of Tennessee Press, 1993), Jane Polk to James K. and Sarah Polk, January 5, 1828, 1:124; Benjamin Patton to Polk, May 26, 1845, 9:414.

20. Sellers, *James K. Polk, Jacksonian*, 211; Milo Milton Quaife, ed., *The Diary of James K. Polk During His Presidency, 1845 to 1849* (A. C. McClurg, 1910), September 21, 1845, 1:38.

21. Philip Shriver Klein, *President James Buchanan: A Biography* (Pennsylvania State University Press, 1962), 7, 93; John Bassett Moore, ed., *The Works of James Buchanan* (J. B. Lippincott, 1908–1911; repr., Antiquarian Press, 1960), Autobiographical Sketch, 12:290–91.

22. John Y. Simon, ed., *The Papers of Ulysses S. Grant* (Southern Illinois University Press, 1967–2012), *New York Times*, July 24, 1885, 31:212n; Ron Chernow, *Grant* (Penguin, 2017), 919; Ishbel Ross, *The General's Wife: The Life of Mrs. Ulysses S. Grant* (Dodd, Mead, 1959), 19.

23. Henry Barnard, *Rutherford B. Hayes and His America* (Bobbs-Merrill, 1954), 21, 23–24, 33, 74, 178–79; T. Harry Williams, ed., *Hayes: The Diary of a President, 1875–1881* (David McKay, 1964), Introduction, xxiv; December 30, 1877, 108; Louis D. Rubin Jr., ed., *Teach the Freeman: The Correspondence of Rutherford B. Hayes and the Slater Fund for Negro Education, 1881–1893* (Louisiana State University Press, 1959), Flora Mitchell to Hayes, April 23, 1890, 2:106n1; Charles Richard Williams, ed., *The Diary and Letters of Rutherford B. Hayes* (Ohio State Archaeological and Historical Society, 1922), Hayes to Guy M. Bryan, July 6, 1889, 4:483; Diary, July 7, 1889, 4:484; July 8, 1889, 4:485; July 19, 1889, 4:491.

24. John Shaw, ed., *Crete and James: Personal Letters of Lucretia and James Garfield* (East Lansing: Michigan State University, 1994), Lucretia Rudolph to James Garfield, March 3, 1854, 16; Lucretia to James Garfield, December 6, 1863, 193–94.

25. Allan Nevins, *Grover Cleveland, A Study in Courage* (Dodd, Mead, 1941), 12, 21–22; Allan Nevins, ed., *Letters of Grover Cleveland, 1850–1908* (Houghton Mifflin, 1933), Introduction, 1; George F. Parker, ed., *The Writings and Speeches of Grover Cleveland* (Cassell, 1892), Before the Northern and Southern Presbyterian Assemblies at Philadelphia, May 23, 1888, 187; At the Annual Meeting of the Actors' Fund of America, January 3, 1890, 193.

26. Sievers, *Benjamin Harrison, Hoosier Warrior*, 28–29.

27. H. Wayne Morgan, *William McKinley and His America* (Syracuse University Press, 1963), 5, 12, 246.

28. Wayne Andrews, ed., *The Autobiography of Theodore Roosevelt* (Charles Scribner's Sons, 1913; repr., Octagon, 1975), 9–10; Sylvia Jukes Morris, *Edith Kermit Roosevelt: Portrait of a First Lady* (Coward, McCann & Geoghegan, 1980), 47; Corinne Roosevelt Robinson, *My Brother, Theodore Roosevelt* (Charles Scribner's Sons, 1921), 5–6; Edmund Morris, *The Rise of Theodore Roosevelt* (Coward, McCann & Geoghegan, 1979), 58; Joshua David Hawley, *Theodore Roosevelt, Preacher of Righteousness* (Yale University Press, 2008), 59.

29. Arthur S. Link, *Woodrow Wilson: A Brief Biography* (World Publishing, 1963), 16–17; Link, *Papers of Woodrow Wilson*, Shorthand Diary, July 2, 1876, 1:148; July 9, 1876, 1:151; July 16, 1876, 1:154; July 23, 1876, 1:159; A News Item, *Princeton Press*, May 22, 1897, 10:242; A Religious Address, March 30, 1906, 16:350; Wilson to James Woodrow, May 25, 1914, 30:74; An Estimate of His Father, May 25, 1914, 30:75; An Interview, December 5, 1914, 31:395.

30. Link, *Papers of Woodrow Wilson*, Editorial Note, 2:333–334; Wilson to Ellen Louise Axson, November 4, 1883, 2:516; December 21, 1883, 2:595; February 10, 1884, 3:13; July 20, 1884, 3:254; January 29, 1885, 4:199; April 19, 1885, 4:501; April 17, 1886, 5:160; February 19, 1889, 6:106; Wilson to Sarah Caruthers Park Hughes, August 25, 1914, 30:452.

31. Frederick E. Schortemeier, ed., *Rededicating America: The Life and Recent Speeches of Warren G. Harding* (Bobbs-Merrill, 1920), Introduction, 12–13; Randolph C. Downes, *The Rise of Warren Gamaliel Harding, 1865–1920* (Ohio State

University Press, 1970), 10; Francis Russell, *The Shadow of Blooming Grove: Warren G. Harding in His Times* (McGraw-Hill, 1968), 46, 99, 386.

32. Coolidge, *The Autobiography of Calvin Coolidge*, 16–18, 30.

33. Eugene Lyons, *Herbert Hoover: A Biography* (Doubleday, 1948), 3–4; Herbert Hoover, *Memoirs of Herbert Hoover* (Macmillan, 1951–1952), 1:8; Herbert Hoover, *Addresses upon the American Road, 1955–1960* (Caxton, 1961); Herbert Hoover, "Thank You, Mrs. Gray," *Reader's Digest*, July 1959, 319; George H. Nash, *The Life of Herbert Hoover: The Engineer, 1874–1914* (W. W. Norton, 1983), 8–10, 15.

34. Roosevelt, *F.D.R.: His Personal Letters*, 2:196.

35. Harry S. Truman, *Mr. Citizen* (Random House, 1960), 86–87, 128.

36. Dwight D. Eisenhower, *At Ease: Stories I Tell to Friends* (Doubleday, 1967), 52, 60, 86–88.

37. Eisenhower, *At Ease: Stories I Tell*, 78, 82, 305; David L. Holmes, *The Faiths of the Postwar Presidents: From Truman to Obama* (University of Georgia Press, 2012), 27, 29; Alfred D. Chandler et al., eds., *The Papers of Dwight David Eisenhower* (Johns Hopkins University Press, 1970–2001), Eisenhower to Archibald F. Bennett, January 23, 1954, 15:845–46; Stephen E. Ambrose, *Eisenhower* (Simon & Schuster, 1983–1984), 1:16; Relman Morin, *Dwight D. Eisenhower: A Gauge of Greatness* (Associated Press, 1969), 13.

38. Eisenhower, *At Ease: Stories I Tell*, 51–52.

39. Eisenhower, *At Ease: Stories I Tell*, 305; Holmes, *The Faiths of the Postwar Presidents*, 31.

40. Doris Kearns Goodwin, *The Fitzgeralds and the Kennedys: An American Saga* (St. Martin's, 1987), 372, 800; Holmes, *The Faiths of the Postwar Presidents*, 47.

41. Robert A. Caro, *The Years of Lyndon Johnson: The Path to Power* (Alfred A. Knopf, 1982), 50–51, 67; Lyndon B. Johnson, *Public Papers of the Presidents of the United States, 1963–1964* (Government Printing Office, 1965), Remarks at the 12th Annual Presidential Prayer Breakfast, February 5, 1964, 262; Remarks to Members of the Southern Baptist Christian Leadership Seminar, March 25, 1964, 419–20; Lyndon B. Johnson, *Public Papers of the Presidents of the United States, 1965* (Government Printing Office, 1966), Remarks to Members of the Board of Directors of the International Association of Lions Clubs, September 23, 1965, 1016.

42. Gerald R. Ford, *A Time to Heal: The Autobiography of Gerald R. Ford* (Harper & Row, 1979), 44; Gerald R. Ford Presidential Library & Museum, "Notes for A Time to Heal, What Religion Means to Me," https://www.fordlibrarymuseum.gov/sites/default/files/pdf_documents/library/document/0065/atth-religion.pdf; Betty Ford Speech, Westminster Choir College Commencement, May 31, 1974; Holmes, *The Faiths of the Postwar Presidents*, 125–26, 135–36.

43. Ariail and Heckler-Feltz, *Carpenter's Apprentice*, 28, 91; Jimmy Carter, *Sources of Strength: Meditations on Scripture for a Living Faith* (Random House, 1997), 41, 192, 215; Jimmy Carter, *Public Papers of the Presidents of the United States, 1978* (Government Printing Office, 1979), Remarks at Mormon Church Ceremonies Honoring Family Unity, Salt Lake City, November 27, 1978, 2085; Wesley G. Pippert, ed.,

The Spiritual Journey of Jimmy Carter in His Own Words (Macmillan, 1978), Mens' Bible Class, Plains Baptist Church, July 18, 1976, 168; Jimmy Carter, *Public Papers of the Presidents of the United States, 1980–1981* (Government Printing Office, 1982), Remarks at a Democratic National Committee Fundraising Reception, Roswell, Georgia, September 15, 1980, 1748.

44. Ariail and Heckler-Feltz, *Carpenter's Apprentice*, 86–87, 91, 95, 107; Carter, *Sources of Strength*, xvi; Jimmy Carter and Rosalynn Carter, *Everything to Gain: Making the Most of the Rest of Your Life* (Random House, 1987), 22.

45. Ronald Reagan, *Public Papers of the Presidents of the United States, 1983* (Government Printing Office, 1984), Remarks at the Annual National Prayer Breakfast, February 3, 1983, 178–79; Radio Address to the Nation in Observance of Mother's Day, May 7, 1983, 666; Remarks at a Question and Answer Session with Female Leaders of Christian Organizations, October 13, 1983, 1450; Ronald Reagan, *Public Papers of the Presidents of the United States, 1986* (Government Printing Office, 1988), Remarks on Signing of the 1987 National Day of Prayer Proclamation, December 22, 1986, 1639; Ronald Reagan, *An American Life* (Simon & Schuster, 1990), 21–22, 45; Brown, *Hand of Providence*, 24, 27–28, 30, 32, 36, 68–69, 80.

46. George W. Bush, *Decision Points* (Crown Publishers, 2010), 10; Doro Bush Koch, *My Father, My President: A Personal Account of the Life of George H. W. Bush* (Warner Books, 2006), xix, 4, 245, 413; David Aikman, *A Man of Faith: The Spiritual Journey of George W. Bush* (Thomas Nelson, 2004), 23, 25.

47. Barbara Bush, *Barbara Bush: A Memoir* (Charles Scribner's Sons, 1994), 38, 215; Aikman, *A Man of Faith*, 32; Russell J. Levenson Jr., *Witness to Dignity: The Life and Faith of George H. W. and Barbara Bush* (Center Street, 2022), 180, 205, 288–90.

48. Roosevelt, *F.D.R.: His Personal Letters*, Editor's Note, 3:332; Eisenhower, *At Ease: Stories I Tell*, 56; Chandler, *Papers of Dwight David Eisenhower*, Eisenhower to Milton Eisenhower, January 13, 1947, 8:1438.

49. Axtell, *The School upon a Hill*, 49; Cremin, *American Education*, 451; Irving Brant, *James Madison: The Virginia Revolutionist, 1751–1780* (Bobbs-Merrill, 1941), 52.

50. Donald Jackson and Dorothy Twohig, eds., *The Diaries of George Washington* (University Press of Virginia, 1976–1979), September 25, 1774, 3:280; October 9, 1774, 3:285; May 27, 1787, 5:163; Editor's Note, 5:452; November 1, 1789, 5:488; July 3, 1791, 6:168.

51. Adrienne Koch and William Peden, eds., *The Selected Writings of John and John Quincy Adams* (Alfred A. Knopf, 1946), John Adams to Benjamin Rush, August 28, 1811, 161; L. H. Butterfield, ed., *The Adams Family Correspondence* (Harvard University Press, 1963), John to Abigail Adams, October 9, 1774, 1:167; Peter Shaw, *The Character of John Adams* (University of North Carolina Press, 1976), 308.

52. Marie Kimball, *Thomas Jefferson: The Road to Glory, 1743 to 1776* (Coward-McCann, 1943), 123; James H. Hutson, "Thomas Jefferson's Letter to the Danbury Baptists: A Controversy Rejoined," *William and Mary Quarterly* 56 (October 1999): 785–86, 788.

53. John Quincy Adams, *Lectures on Rhetoric and Oratory* (Hilliard and Metcalf, 1810; repr., Russell & Russell, 1962), 1:46–47.

54. Adams, *The Memoirs of John Quincy Adams*, September 29, 1799, 1:235; October 30, 1803, 1:268; November 19, 1809, 2:70; December 3, 1809, 2:73; April 27, 1810, 2:119; April 29, 1810, 2:121–22; September 11, 1810, 2:162–63; April 7, 1811, 2:248–49; April 12, 1811, 2:249–50; April 13, 1811, 2:250–54; January 7, 1820, 5:230–31; August 18, 1824, 6:407.

55. Adams, *The Memoirs of John Quincy Adams*, July 16, 1826, 7:131; December 9, 1827, 7:376.

56. Adams, *The Memoirs of John Quincy Adams*, May 29, 1836, 9:289; April 25, 1841, 10:466.

57. Adams, *The Memoirs of John Quincy Adams*, February 11, 1844, 11:508; November 27, 1844, 12:111.

58. Bassett, *Correspondence of Andrew Jackson*, Jackson to Rachel Jackson, December 21, 1823, 3:218; December 28, 3:220; January 5, 1824, 3:222; John Eaton to Rachel Jackson, February 8, 1824, 3:226; Jackson's Pew Rent, April 1, 1831, 4:255; Remini, *Andrew Jackson and the Course of American Democracy*, 447.

59. Freeman Cleaves, *Old Tippecanoe: William Henry Harrison and His Time* (Charles Scribner's Sons, 1939), 244, 341.

60. Sellers, *James K. Polk, Jacksonian*, 94, 111, 210; Quaife, *Diary of James K. Polk*, November 2, 1845, 1:86; January 4, 1846, 1:153; July 5, 1846, 2:12; August 2, 1846, 2:62; January 17, 1847, 2:335; March 21, 1847, 2:433; July 4, 1847, 3:72; October 1, 1848, 4:138; January 14, 1849, 4:280.

61. Klein, *President James Buchanan*, 7, 81, 429; Moore, *The Works of James Buchanan*, Autobiographical Sketch, 12:292.

62. Moore, *The Works of James Buchanan*, Diary, June 16, 1833, 2:356; September 8, 1853, 9:48; October 21, 1853, 9:73.

63. Simon, *The Papers of Ulysses S. Grant*, Grant to John H. Vincent, May 25, 1862, 5:133n; Grant to Hamilton Fish, March 1, 1873, 24:59n; *New York Times*, July 24, 1885, 31:212n.

64. Rubin, *Teach the Freeman*, Introduction, 1:xxxiii; Hayes to Atticus G. Haygood, October 2, 1887, 1:218n2.

65. Brown and Williams, *The Diary of James A. Garfield*, March 4, 1850, 1:36; March 7, 1850, 1:36; December 22, 1852, 1:165; February 6, 1853, 1:176; November 4, 1866, 1:363; August 4, 1867, 1:386–88; August 3, 1873, 2:208; Shaw, *Crete and James*, James to Lucretia Garfield, May 4, 1862, 138–39; Brown and Leech, *The Garfield Orbit*, 191.

66. Nevins, *Letters of Grover Cleveland*, Cleveland to Mrs. Henry Ward Beecher, May 22, 1887, 141; Nevins, *Grover Cleveland, A Study*, 25–26, 301.

67. Sievers, *Benjamin Harrison, Hoosier Warrior*, 240; Harry J. Sievers, *Benjamin Harrison, Hoosier President: The White House and After* (Bobbs-Merrill, 1968), 57.

68. William Carl Spielman, *William McKinley, Stalwart Republican: A Biographical Study* (Exposition, 1954), 17; Morgan, *William McKinley and His America*, 39, 89, 320.

69. Elting E. Morison, ed., *The Letters of Theodore Roosevelt* (Harvard University Press, 1951–1954), Roosevelt to Frederick Courteney Selous, February 7, 1900, 2:1175; Andrews, *The Autobiography of Theodore Roosevelt*, 188; Christian F. Reisner, *Roosevelt's Religion* (Abingdon, 1922), 347–49, 354–56; Herbert Ronald Ferleger and Albert Bushnell Hart, eds., *Theodore Roosevelt Cyclopedia* (Roosevelt Memorial Association, 1941), *Ladies' Home Journal*, October 1917, 77; Robinson, *My Brother, Theodore*, 335–36.

70. Link, *Papers of Woodrow Wilson*, Shorthand Diary, October 29, 1876, 1:218; Wilson To Ellen Axson Wilson, July 2, 1899, 11:143.

71. Link, *Papers of Woodrow Wilson*, Wilson to Mary Allen Hulbert, August 10, 1913, 28:135; September 7, 1913, 28:263–64; Remarks upon Laying the Cornerstone of the Central Presbyterian Church of Washington, December 19, 1913, 29:45; From the Diary of Dr. Grayson, May 18, 1919, 59:247–48; September 21, 1919, 63:423.

72. Claude M. Fuess, *Calvin Coolidge: The Man from Vermont* (Little, Brown, 1940), 315; McCoy, *Calvin Coolidge*, 396; Shlaes, *Coolidge*, 91.

73. Burns, *Roosevelt*, 237; Doris Kearns Goodwin, *No Ordinary Time: Franklin and Eleanor Roosevelt and the Home Front during World War II* (Simon & Schuster, 1994), 223; Frank Kingdon, *As F.D.R. Said: A Treasury of His Speeches, Conversations, and Writings* (Duell, Sloan and Pearce, 1950), 56, 147.

74. Robert H. Ferrell, ed., *Off the Record: The Private Papers of Harry S. Truman* (Harper & Row, 1980), Diary, April 13, 1952, 247; Harry S. Truman, *Public Papers of the Presidents of the United States, 1950* (Government Printing Office, 1965), Address in Independence at the Dedication of the Liberty Bell Replica, November 6, 1950, 704.

75. Truman, *Mr. Citizen*, 127, 130–31; Harry S. Truman, *Memoirs* (Doubleday, 1955–1956), 1:109.

76. Dorothy Brandon, *Mamie Doud Eisenhower: A Portrait of a First Lady* (Charles Scribner's Sons, 1954), 145; Dwight D. Eisenhower, *Mandate for Change, 1953–1956* (Doubleday, 1963), 100; Chandler, *Papers of Dwight David Eisenhower*, Eisenhower to Clifford Roberts, July 29, 1952, 13:1284; Diary, February 1, 1953, 14:16–17; Eisenhower to Milton Eisenhower, February 2, 1953, 14:20.

77. Goodwin, *The Fitzgeralds and the Kennedys*, 798.

78. Paul K. Conkin, *Big Daddy from the Pedernales: Lyndon Baines Johnson* (Twayne, 1986), 28, 196; Sam Houston Johnson, *My Brother Lyndon* (Cowles, 1969), 35; Lyndon B. Johnson, *Public Papers of the Presidents of the United States, 1966* (Government Printing Office, 1967), Remarks at a Columbus Day Dinner in Brooklyn, October 12, 1966, 1154; Holmes, *The Faiths of the Postwar Presidents*, 85.

79. Holmes, *The Faiths of the Postwar Presidents*, 130.

80. Carter and Carter, *Everything to Gain*, 22, 70; Carter, *Sources of Strength*, 149.

81. Holmes, *The Faiths of the Postwar Presidents*, 177, 181–82; Kiron K. Skinner et al., eds., *Reagan: A Life in Letters* (Free Press, 2003), Reagan to Jerry Mueller, May 31, 1984, 461; Ronald Reagan, *Public Papers of the Presidents of the United States, 1984* (Government Printing Office, 1986), Debate Between the President and Former Vice-President Walter Mondale, Louisville, October 7, 1984, 1447; Brown, *Hand of Providence*, 1–2, 199–200.

82. Levenson, *Witness to Dignity*, x, 18, 33, 36, 91–92; George H. W. Bush, *Public Papers of the Presidents of the United States, 1989* (Government Printing Office, 1990), Remarks at Chongmenwen Christian Church in Beijing, February 26, 1989, 141; Remarks at a Meeting with Amish and Mennonite Leaders in Lancaster, Pennsylvania, March 22, 1989, 290; Bush, *Barbara Bush*, 113–14.

83. Bush, *Decision Points*, 30; Aikman, *A Man of Faith*, 72, 88, 106–7; George W. Bush, *Public Papers of the Presidents of the United States, 2005* (Government Printing Office, 2009), Remarks Following a Church Service in Beijing, November 20, 2005, 1747; George W. Bush, *Public Papers of the Presidents of the United States, 2008–2009* (Government Printing Office, 2012), Remarks Following a Visit to the Beijing Kuanjie Protestant Christian Church, August 10, 2008, 1131.

84. Barack Obama, *The Audacity of Hope: Thoughts on Reclaiming the American Dream* (Crown Publishers, 2006), 202–4, 356; Barack Obama, *Dreams from My Father: A Story of Race and Inheritance* (Crown Publishers, 1995), 292–95, 440; Barack Obama, *A Promised Land* (Crown Publishers, 2020), 119–20; James T. Kloppenberg, *Reading Obama: Dreams, Hope, and the American Political Tradition* (Princeton University Press, 2011), 211; Clarence E. Walker, *The Preacher and the Politician: Jeremiah Wright, Barack Obama, and Race in America* (University of Virginia Press, 2009), 13–14, 27, 107–8.

85. Ruby Cramer, "'A Private Matter': Joe Biden's Very Public Clash with His Own Church," *Politico*, September 5, 2021, https://www.politico.com/news/magazine/2021/09/05/joe-biden-catholic-church-509396; Mike Menoli and Carol E. Lee, "Sunday Services: Biden's Faith on Display in Renewed Presidential Ritual," *NBC News*, January 24, 2021, https://www.nbcnews.com/politics/white-house/sunday-services-biden-s-faith-display-renewed-presidential-ritual-n1255460.

86. Adams, *Memoirs of John Quincy Adams*, August 13, 1809, 2:5–6; August 20, 1809, 2:7; September 3, 1809, 2:17; September 10, 1809, 2:18; October 15, 1809, 2:42; December 24, 1809, 2:81; January 28, 1810, 2:99; June 10, 1810, 2:133; December 30, 1810, 2:205; January 13, 1811, 2:212–13; February 24, 1811, 2:233; March 5, 1814, 2:581; March 20, 1814, 2:583; Adams, *Lectures on Rhetoric and Oratory*, 2:17–18; Moore, *Works of James Buchanan*, Buchanan to Reverend P. Coombe, May 2, 1865, 11:387.

87. Moshe Davis, *America and the Holy Land* (Praeger, 1995), 13–14, 137–41.

88. Patricia J. Tracy, *Jonathan Edwards, Pastor: Religion and Society in Eighteenth-Century Northampton* (Hill & Wang, 1979), 79–80, 113; John Frederick Woolverton, *Colonial Anglicanism in North America* (Wayne State University Press, 1984), 191,

198; L. Jesse Lemisch, ed., *Benjamin Franklin: The Autobiography and Other Writings* (Penguin, 1961), Autobiography, 93, 317.

89. Harry Alonzo Cushing, ed., *The Writings of Samuel Adams* (Octagon Books, 1968), Valerius Poplicola, October 5, 1772, 2:336; Labaree, *The Papers of Benjamin Franklin*, Rules by Which a Great Empire May Be Reduced to a Small One, *The Public Advertiser*, September 11, 1773, 20:395; Thomas Miller, ed., *The Selected Writings of John Witherspoon* (Southern Illinois University Press, 1990), The Dominion of Providence over the Passions of Men, May 17, 1776, 140–41.

90. Henry F. May, *The Enlightenment in America* (Oxford University Press, 1976), 91–93; Jon Butler, *Awash in a Sea of Faith: Christianizing the American People* (Harvard University Press, 1990), 201–4; Jon Butler, *Becoming America: The Revolution Before 1776* (Harvard University Press, 2000), 243; George William Pilcher, *Samuel Davies: Apostle of Dissent in Colonial Virginia* (University of Tennessee Press, 1971), 98; Cremin, *American Education*, 459; Butterfield, *The Adams Family Correspondence*, John to Abigail Adams, July 23, 1775, 1:254; William Wirt Henry, ed., *Patrick Henry: Life, Correspondence, and Speeches* (Scribner's Sons, 1891; repr., Burt Franklin, 1969), 1:189; Rhys Isaac, *The Transformation of Virginia, 1740–1790* (University of North Carolina Press, 1982), 170, 261; Mark A. Noll, *Christians in the American Revolution* (Christian University Press, 1977), 65; Jeffry H. Morrison, *John Witherspoon and the Founding of the American Republic* (University of Notre Dame Press, 2005), 71.

91. Charles Royster, *A Revolutionary People at War: The Continental Army and American Character, 1775–1783* (W. W. Norton, 1979), 158; Noll, *Christians in the American Revolution*, 59–61.

92. John B. Boles, *The Great Revival, 1787–1805* (University Press of Kentucky, 1972), 47, 70, 113–14, 124.

93. Conkin, *The Uneasy Center*, 45, 59, 82, 145, 277; Albert J. Raboteau, *Slave Religion: The "Invisible Institution" in the Antebellum South* (Oxford University Press, 1978), 133; Timothy L. Smith, *Revivalism and Social Reform: American Protestantism on the Eve of the Civil War*, 2nd. ed. (Johns Hopkins University Press, 1980), 19, 22, 36, 86, 114–15, 167; William G. McLoughlin, *Revivals, Awakening, and Reform: An Essay on Religion and Social Change in America, 1607–1977* (University of Chicago Press, 1978), 130, 134–35; Boles, *The Great Revival*, 41, 146–47; Whitney R. Cross, *The Burned-Over District: The Social and Intellectual History of Enthusiastic Religion in Western New York, 1800–1850* (Octagon, 1981), 40; Milton Rugoff, *The Beechers: An American Family in the Nineteenth Century* (Harper & Row, 1981), 21, 23; Daniel Walker Howe, *The Political Culture of the American Whigs* (University of Chicago Press, 1979), 157; Charles Capper and David A. Hollinger, eds., *The American Intellectual Tradition*, 3rd. ed. (Oxford University Press, 1997), Charles G. Finney, What a Revival of Religion Is, 1835, 1:194; Sarah Grimké, *Letters on the Equality of the Sexes and the Condition of Woman* (Isaac Knapp, 1838), 1:214–15, 218, 222, 225; Ronald G. Walters, *American Reformers, 1815–1860* (Hill & Wang, 1978), 108, 127, 129, 137, 174–75, 195–97, 200–202, 204, 207–9; Clifford S. Griffin, *Their Brothers' Keepers: Moral Stewardship in the United States, 1800–1865* (Rutgers University Press, 1981),

138; Helen E. Marshall, *Dorothea Dix: Forgotten Samaritan* (Russell & Russell, 1937), 65–66.

94. Walters, *American Reformers*, 78–80; John L. Thomas, *The Liberator: William Lloyd Garrison, a Biography* (Little, Brown, 1963), 98–99, 128, 203; William R. Merrill, *Against the Tide: A Biography of William Lloyd Garrison* (Harvard University Press, 1963), 54; Leon F. Litwack, *North of Slavery: The Negro in the Free States, 1790–1860* (University of Chicago Press, 1961), 70–71, 75–87, 97, 114.

95. Rugoff, *The Beechers*, 141, 146, 150; Griffin, *Their Brothers' Keepers*, 86–88; Cross, *The Burned-Over District*, 196.

96. McLoughlin, *Revivals, Awakenings, and Reform*, 170–71.

Chapter 2

1. W. W. Abbot, ed., *The Papers of George Washington: Colonial Series* (University Press of Virginia, 1983–1995), Washington to Robert Cary & Co., July 20, 1771, 8:509.

2. Daniel L. Dreisbach, "The Bible in the Political Rhetoric of the American Founding," *Politics and Religion* 4 (2011): 408; John C. Fitzpatrick, ed., The Writings of George Washington (Government Printing Office, 1931–1940), Washington to the Marquis de Lafayette, June 18, 1788, 18:184; W. W. Abbot, ed., *The Papers of George Washington: Presidential Series* (University Press of Virginia, 1987), To the Hebrew Congregation in Newport, Rhode Island, August 18, 1790, 6:285; W. W. Abbot, ed., *The Papers of George Washington: Retirement Series* (University Press of Virginia, 1998–1999), Washington to Oliver Walcott Jr., May 15, 1797, 1:142–43; Washington to Thomas Pinckney, May 28, 1797, 1:157; Washington to John Quincy Adams, June 25, 1797, 1:211; Washington to Rufus King, June 25, 1797, 1:213; Washington to David Humphreys, June 26, 1797, 1:218; Washington to Randnor, July 8, 1797, 1:291.

3. L. H. Butterfield, ed., *The Diary and Autobiography of John Adams* (Harvard University Press, 1962), Diary, July 21, 1756, 1:35; August 1, 1761, 1:220; Albert Ellery Bergh and Andrew A. Lipscomb, eds., *The Writings of Thomas Jefferson* (Thomas Jefferson Memorial Association, 1904), John Adams to Jefferson, December 25, 1813, 14:40; Edwin S. Gaustad, *Faith of Our Fathers: Religion and the New Nation* (Harper & Row, 1987), 88; Peter Shaw, *The Character of John Adams* (University of North Carolina Press, 1976), 308.

4. Julian P. Boyd, ed., *The Papers of Thomas Jefferson* (Princeton University Press, 1950), Jefferson to John Stockdale, July 1, 1787, 11:523; Jefferson to Van Damme, March 23, 1788, 12:688–89; January 25, 1789, 14:490; Caleb Alexander to Jefferson, February 20, 1793, 25:235n; Nicholas Gouin Dufief to Jefferson, December 23, 1800, 32:345n; Jefferson to Henry Remsen, December 31, 1800, 32:376; Charles B. Sanford, *The Religious Life of Thomas Jefferson* (University Press of Virginia, 1984), 102; Lester J. Cappon, ed., *The Adams-Jefferson Letters: The Complete Correspondence Between Thomas Jefferson and Abigail and John Adams* (University of North Carolina

Press, 1959), Jefferson to John Adams, October 12, 1813, 2:385–86; John Adams to Jefferson, November 14, 1813, 2:394.

5. Allan Nevins, ed., *The Diary of John Quincy Adams, 1794–1845: American Diplomacy and Political, Social, and Intellectual Life from Washington to Polk* (Charles Scribner's Sons, 1951), September 26, 1810, 74–75; March 13, 1812, 91; Adrienne Koch and William Peden, eds., *The Selected Writings of John and John Quincy Adams* (Alfred A. Knopf, 1946), John Quincy Adams to John Adams, January 3, 1817, 292.

6. Charles Francis Adams, ed., *Memoirs of John Quincy Adams, Containing Portions of His Diary from 1795 to 1848* (Philadelphia, 1874–1877; repr., AMS, 1970), June 24, 1812, 2:380–81; December 12, 1812, 2:432.

7. Adams, *Memoirs of John Quincy Adams*, March 30, 1831, 8:352; May 7, 1831, 8:362; July 20, 1831, 8:383; March 28, 1840, 10:248; June 29, 1845, 12:201.

8. Robert V. Remini, *Andrew Jackson and the Course of American Democracy, 1833–1845* (Harper & Row, 1984), 433, 447, 523.

9. Freeman Cleaves, *Old Tippecanoe: William Henry Harrison and His Time* (Charles Scribner's Sons, 1939), 332.

10. Isaac Newton Arnold, *The Life of Abraham Lincoln* (Jansen, McClurg, 1885), 45; Roy P. Basler, ed., *The Collected Works of Abraham Lincoln* (Rutgers University Press, 1953–1955), First Lecture on Discoveries and Inventions, April 6, 1858, 2:438–41; Speech at Springfield, Illinois, June 16, 1858, 2:461; Speech at Cincinnati, Ohio, September 17, 1859, 3:462.

11. Daniel L. Dreisbach, "Biblical Language and Themes in Lincoln's Gettysburg Address," *Perspectives on Political Science* (January 2015):44:34–38.

12. David Herbert Donald, *Lincoln* (Jonathan Cape, 1995), 514; Basler, *The Collected Works of Abraham Lincoln*, Lincoln to Lydia Bixby, November 21, 1864, 8:117.

13. Basler, *The Collected Works of Abraham Lincoln*, Lincoln to George B. Ide, James R. Doolittle, and A. Hubble, May 30, 1864, 7:368; Story Written for Noah Brooks, December 6, 1864, 8:155; Second Inaugural Address, March 4, 1865, 8:333.

14. Daniel L. Dreisbach, "Lincoln's 700 Words of Biblical Meditation," Law & Liberty, published March 4, 2015, https://lawliberty.org/lincolns-700-words-of-biblical-meditation/; Frederick Douglass, *Life and Times of Frederick Douglass* (Park Publishing, 1882), 441.

15. John Y. Simon, ed., *The Papers of Ulysses S. Grant* (Southern Illinois University Press, 1967–2012), Grant to the Editor of the *Sunday School Times*, June 6, 1876, 27:124; Grant to Elizabeth King, February 22, 1878, 28:350; Grant to Michael John Cramer, March 5, 1878, 28:353.

16. Charles Richard Williams, ed., *The Diary and Letters of Rutherford B. Hayes* (Ohio State Archaeological Historical Society, 1922), Diary, February 22, 1844, 1:145; Hayes to S. Birchard, February 26, 1853, 1:443; April 24, 1853, 1:449.

17. Harry J. Sievers, *Benjamin Harrison, Hoosier Warrior, 1833–1865* (Henry Regnery, 1952), 224.

18. Elting E. Morison, ed., *The Letters of Theodore Roosevelt* (Harvard University Press, 1951–1954), Roosevelt to Charles Anderson Dana, October 30, 1895,

11:494–95; Roosevelt to Francis Ellington Leupp, September 3, 1898, 2:871; Roosevelt to Nicholas Murray Butler, August 6, 1904, 4:884; Theodore Roosevelt, *The Works of Theodore Roosevelt* (Charles Scribner's Sons, 1925), Speech Before the Commercial Travelers' Sound-Money League, New York City, September 11, 1896, 16:384; Address at the Independent Club, May 15, 1899, 16:488–89.

19. Theodore Roosevelt, *Addresses and Presidential Messages of Theodore Roosevelt, 1902–1904* (G. P. Putnam's Sons, 1904; repr., Kraus, 1971), At the State Fair, Syracuse, New York, September 7, 1903, 242; At the Pan-American Missionary Service, Washington, October 25, 1903, 256.

20. Wayne Andrews, ed., *The Autobiography of Theodore Roosevelt* (Charles Scribner's Sons, 1913; repr., Octagon, 1975), 175, 303.

21. Herbert Ronald Ferleger and Albert Bushnell Hart, eds., *Theodore Roosevelt Cyclopedia* (Roosevelt Memorial Association, 1941), Talks with T. R., 1916, 517.

22. William Howard Taft, *Address of William H. Taft* (n.p., 1907), At the Miller's Convention in St. Louis, May 30, 1907, 18.

23. Arthur S. Link, ed., *The Papers of Woodrow Wilson* (Princeton University Press, 1966–1994), The Bible, August 25, 1876, 1:184–85; A Statement About the Bible, *Daily Princetonian*, October 8, 1909, 19:406.

24. Link, *The Papers of Woodrow Wilson*, An Address in Denver on the Bible, May 7, 1911, 23:16–17; A Religious Address in Trenton, October 1, 1911, 23:375–80; A Religious Address in Dallas, October 28, 1911, 23:497–99.

25. Warren G. Harding, *Our Common Country: Mutual Good Will in America* (Bobbs-Merrill, 1921), 15.

26. Herbert Hoover, *Public Papers of the Presidents of the United States, 1929* (Government Printing Office, 1974), Message to the National Federation of Men's Bible Classes, May 5, 1929, 136.

27. Frank Kingdon, *As F.D.R. Said: A Treasury of His Speeches, Conversations, and Writings* (Duell, Sloan and Pearce, 1950), 148–49; Franklin Access to the FDR Library's Digital Collection, "Fully Digitized Collections or Series," Franklin D. Roosevelt Presidential Library and Museum, updated 2011, http://www.fdrlibrary.marist.edu/archives/collections/franklin/, Radio Address, May 9, 1937; Christmas Tree Speech, December 24, 1938; Address at Christmas Lighting, December 24, 1939.

28. Harry S. Truman Library & Museum, "Welcome to the Harry S. Truman Presidential Library and Museum," National Archives, https://www.trumanlibrary.gov/, Truman to Bess Wallace, August 15, 1941; Harry S. Truman, *Public Papers of the Presidents of the United States, 1952–1953* (Government Printing Office, 1966), Remarks to Representatives of the National Council of Churches, September 26, 1952, 591; Harry S. Truman, *Mr. Citizen* (Random House, 1960), 141, 203.

29. Robert H. Ferrell, *Off the Record: The Private Papers of Harry S. Truman* (Harper & Row, 1980), Diary, July 25, 1945, 55; Truman to Ethel Noland, October 21, 1950, 197; Harry S. Truman, *Public Papers of the Presidents of the United States, 1950* (Government Printing Office, 1965), Address at the Laying of the Cornerstone of the New U.S. Courts Building for the District of Columbia, June 27, 1950, 496.

326 ~ Notes

30. Harry S. Truman, *Public Papers of the Presidents of the United States, 1951* (Government Printing Office, 1965), Address at the Lighting of the National Community Christmas Tree, December 24, 1951, 654; Ferrell, *Off the Record*, Diary, February 18, 1952, 239; William Hillman, ed., *Mr. President: The First Publication from the Personal Diaries, Private Letters, Papers, and Revealing Interviews of Harry S. Truman* (Farrar, Straus & Young, 1952), 105.

31. Lawrence H. Fuchs, *John F. Kennedy and American Catholicism* (Meredith Press, 1967), 216, 218–19; John F. Kennedy, *Public Papers of the Presidents of the United States, 1961* (Government Printing Office, 1962), Remarks at the Dedication Breakfast of the International Christian Leadership, February 9, 1961, 76; John F. Kennedy, *Public Papers of the Presidents of the United States, 1963* (Government Printing Office, 1964), Address Before the 18th General Assembly of the United Nations, September 22, 1963, 697.

32. Lyndon B. Johnson, *Public Papers of the Presidents of the United States, 1963–1964* (Government Printing Office, 1963–1964), Remarks at the 12th Annual Presidential Prayer Breakfast, February 5, 1964, 262; Remarks to the Legislative Conference of the Building and Construction Trades Department, AFL-CIO, March 24, 1964, 416; Remarks to New Participants in 'Plans for Progress' Equal Opportunity Agreements, April 9, 1964, 450; Remarks at a 'Salute to President Johnson' Dinner in Cleveland, October 8, 1964, 1261; Lyndon B. Johnson, *Public Papers of the Presidents of the United States, 1965* (Government Printing Office, 1966), President's News Conference, March 13, 1965, 275; Special Message to Congress, March 15, 1965, 281–82; Lyndon B. Johnson, *Public Papers of the Presidents of the United States, 1966* (Government Printing Office, 1967), Remarks at a Ceremony Marking 1966 as the Year of the Bible, January 19, 1966, 34; Lyndon B. Johnson, *Public Papers of the Presidents of the United States, 1967* (Government Printing Office, 1968), Television Interview, December 9, 1967, 1112.

33. Richard M. Nixon, *Public Papers of the Presidents of the United States, 1971* (Government Printing Office, 1972), Statement on Transmitting to Congress Proposals to Establish New National Wilderness Areas, April 28, 1971, 587–88.

34. Gerald R. Ford Presidential Library & Museum, "Museum and Library," National Archives, https://www.fordlibrarymuseum.gov/ - anchor-section, South High School Commencement Address, June 7, 1956; Remarks at the Dedication of the New Hope College Cultural Center, October 23, 1971; Speech, National Religious Broadcasters' Congressional Breakfast, January 29, 1974; Speech, Brotherhood Commission of the Southern Baptist Convention, June 15, 1974; Gerald R. Ford, *Public Papers of the Presidents of the United States, 1976–1977* (Government Printing Office, 1979), Remarks at the Southern Baptist Convention, June 15, 1976, 1880.

35. Gerald R. Ford, *A Time to Heal: The Autobiography of Gerald R. Ford* (Harper & Row, 1979), x.

36. Jimmy Carter, *Public Papers of the Presidents of the United States, 1977* (Government Printing Office, 1978), Inaugural Address, January 20, 1977, 1; Visit of Menachem Begin, July 19, 1977, 1282; Address at Southern Legislative Conference,

July 21, 1977, 1315; Jimmy Carter, *Public Papers of the Presidents of the United States, 1978* (Government Printing Office, 1979), Address Before a Joint Session of Congress, September 18, 1978, 1537; Remarks at White House Dinner in Observance of National Bible Week, November 22, 1978, 2070; Jimmy Carter, *Keeping Faith: Memoirs of a President* (Bantam, 1982), 322.

37. Jimmy Carter, *Public Papers of the Presidents of the United States, 1979* (Government Printing Office, 1980), Remarks at National Prayer Breakfast, January 18, 1979, 60–61; Jimmy Carter, *Public Papers of the Presidents of the United States, 1980–1981* (Government Printing Office, 1982), Remarks on Energy Conservation at a White House Briefing for Religious Leaders, January 10, 1980, 49; Remarks at the National Religious Broadcasters Association Convention, January 21, 1980, 181; Carter, *Keeping Faith*, 544, 554.

38. Mary Beth Brown, *Hand of Providence: The Strong and Quiet Faith of Ronald Reagan* (WND Books, 2004), 47, 52; Kiron K. Skinner et al., eds., *Reagan, in His Own Hand* (Free Press, 2001), The Bible, September 6, 1977, 410; Ronald Reagan, *Public Papers of the Presidents of the United States, 1981* (Government Printing Office, 1982), Remarks at the Welcoming Ceremony for King Juan Carlos I of Spain, October 13, 1981, 919.

39. Ronald Reagan, *Public Papers of the Presidents of the United States, 1982* (Government Printing Office, 1983), Remarks at a White House Ceremony in Observance of the National Day of Prayer, May 6, 1982, 574; Ronald Reagan, *Public Papers of the Presidents of the United States, 1983* (Government Printing Office, 1984), Remarks at the Annual Convention of the National Religious Broadcasters, January 31, 1983, 152; Proclamation 5018, February 3, 1983, 179; Remarks at the Annual Convention of the National Association of Evangelicals, March 8, 1983, 364; Radio Address to the Nation on the Observance of Mother's Day, May 7, 1983, 666; Ronald Reagan, *Public Papers of the Presidents of the United States, 1984* (Government Printing Office, 1986), Remarks at the Annual Convention of the National Religious Broadcasters, January 30, 1984, 121; Ronald Reagan, *Public Papers of the Presidents of the United States, 1988–1989* (Government Printing Office, 1990), Remarks and a Question-and-Answer Session with the Students and Faculty at Moscow State University, May 31, 1988, 683–84.

40. Kiron K. Skinner et al., eds., *Reagan: A Life in Letters* (Free Press, 2003), Reagan to Mrs. Peter D. Hannaford, February 10, 1983, 278; Reagan to Richard James Whalen, April 17, 1979, 452; Reagan to Lorraine Wagner, February 16, 1991, 821.

41. George H. W. Bush, *Public Papers of the Presidents of the United States, 1991* (Government Printing Office, 1992), Remarks at the Federal Bureau of Investigation Academy Commencement Ceremony, May 30, 1991, 583; George H. W. Bush, *Public Papers of the Presidents of the United States, 1992–1993* (Government Printing Office, 1993), Remarks at the National Affairs Briefing in Dallas, August 22, 1992, 1401.

42. William J. Clinton, *Between Hope and History: Meeting America's Challenges for the Twenty-First Century* (Random House, 1996), xi.

328 ~ Notes

43. David Aikman, *A Man of Faith: The Spiritual Journey of George W. Bush* (Thomas Nelson, 2004), 73–77, 132; George W. Bush, *Decision Points* (Crown Publishers, 2010), 32.

44. Bush, *Decision Points*, 140; George W. Bush, *Public Papers of the Presidents of the United States, 2001* (Government Printing Office, 2003), Remarks at the National Day of Prayer and Remembrance, September 14, 2001, 1109; George W. Bush, *Public Papers of the Presidents of the United States, 2002* (Government Printing Office, 2004), Radio Address, July 6, 2002, 1181; George W. Bush, *Public Papers of the Presidents of the United States, 2004* (Government Printing Office, 2007), Remarks to Faith-Based and Community Leaders in New Orleans, January 15, 2004, 61; Remarks on the Sixtieth Anniversary of D-Day, Colleville-sur-Mer, France, June 6, 2004, 1009; George W. Bush, *Public Papers of the Presidents of the United States, 2008–2009* (Government Printing Office, 2012), Remarks at a Groundbreaking Ceremony for the Walter Reed National Military Medical Center in Bethesda, Maryland, July 3, 2008, 975; Aikman, *A Man of Faith*, 139.

45. Barack Obama, *Dreams from My Father: A Story of Race and Inheritance* (Crown Publishers, 1995), v; Barack Obama, *The Audacity of Hope: Thoughts on Reclaiming the American Dream* (Crown Publishers, 2006), 208.

46. Barack Obama, *Public Papers of the Presidents of the United States, 2009* (Government Printing Office, 2013), Inaugural Address, January 20, 2009, 1; Barack Obama, *Papers of the Presidents of the United States, 2010* (Government Printing Office, 2013), Remarks on the Accident at the Upper Branch Mine in Montcoal, West Virginia, April 9, 2010, 478; Barack Obama, *Papers of the Presidents of the United States, 2011* (Government Printing Office, 2014), Remarks at the National Prayer Breakfast, February 3, 2011, 73; Remarks at an Easter Prayer Breakfast, April 19, 2011, 392; Reading at the National September 11 Memorial in New York City, September 11, 2011, 1049; Barack Obama, *Public Papers of the Presidents of the United States, 2012* (Government Printing Office, 2016), Remarks at the Alfred E. Smith Memorial Foundation Dinner, October 18, 2012, 1603; Barack Obama, *Public Papers of the Presidents of the United States, 2013* (Government Printing Office, 2018), Remarks at the National Prayer Breakfast, February 7, 2013, 83–85; Remarks at a Wreath-Laying Ceremony at the Pentagon Memorial in Arlington, Virginia, September 11, 2013, 1024; Barack Obama, *Public Papers of the Presidents of the United States, 2015* (Government Printing Office, 2020), Remarks Commemorating the Fiftieth Anniversary of the Selma to Montgomery March for Voting Rights, March 7, 2015, 278.

47. Fitzpatrick, *The Writings of George Washington*, Speech to the Delaware Chiefs, May 2, 1779, 15:55; Washington to Reverend John Etwein, May 2, 1788, 29:489; Abbot, *The Papers of George Washington: Presidential Series*, Washington to the Moravian Society for Propagating the Gospel, August 15, 1789, 3:466; John Elliott Jr. to Washington, August 18, 1789, 3:491n; Washington to the Commissioners to the Southern Indians, August 29, 1789, 3:557–58.

48. Harold D. Moser et al., eds., *The Papers of Andrew Jackson* (University of Tennessee, 1980), Jackson to Sam Houston, June 21, 1829, 7:294.

49. Martin Van Buren, *The Autobiography of Martin Van Buren* (American Historical Association, 1920; repr., Da Capo, 1973), 1:284.

50. Basler, *The Collected Works of Abraham Lincoln*, Annual Message to Congress, December 8, 1863, 7:48.

51. Simon, *The Papers of Ulysses S. Grant*, Draft of Annual Message, December 5, 1870, 21:41; To Congress, January 30, 1871, 21:152; Conversation with Ulysses Grant at West Point, June 7, 1871, 22:78; Grant to George H. Stuart, October 26, 1872, 23:270.

52. John Bassett Moore, ed., *The Works of James Buchanan* (J. B. Lippincott, 1908–1911; repr., Antiquarian Press, 1960), Buchanan to Anthony Ten Eyck, August 28, 1848, 8:188–89; Buchanan to Charles Eames, February 16, 1849, 8:336.

53. Robert Seager, *And Tyler Too: A Biography of John & Julia Gardiner Tyler* (McGraw-Hill, 1963), 109; Basler, *The Collected Works of Abraham Lincoln*, Eulogy on Henry Clay, July 6, 1852, 2:132.

54. William McKinley, *Speeches and Addresses of William McKinley from March 1, 1897, to May 30, 1900* (Doubleday & McClure, 1900), Address at the Ecumenical Conference on Foreign Missions, New York, April 21, 1900, 366–68.

55. Morison, *Letters of Theodore Roosevelt*, Roosevelt to John Raleigh Mott, October 12, 1908, 6:1284; Roosevelt to Robert Stewart McClenahan, March 19, 1910, 7:57–58; Roosevelt to Silas McBee, May 16, 1910, 7:84–85.

56. Link, *The Papers of Woodrow Wilson*, Wilson to James Levi Barton, July 25, 1913, 28:82; Remarks to Potomac Presbytery, April 21, 1915, 33:51; Remarks Celebrating the Centennial of the American Bible Society, May 7, 1916, 36:630.

57. Calvin Coolidge Presidential Foundation, "Inaugural Address," March 4, 1925," published April 24, 2014, Coolidge Foundation, https://coolidgefoundation.org/resources/inaugural-address/.

58. Dwight D. Eisenhower, *Public Papers of the Presidents of the United States, 1953* (Government Printing Office, 1960), Remarks at the Cornerstone-Laying Ceremony for the Anthony Wayne Library of American Study, Defiance College, Defiance, Ohio, October 15, 1953, 663; Alfred D. Chandler et al., eds., *The Papers of Dwight David Eisenhower* (Johns Hopkins University Press, 1970–2001), Eisenhower to Howell G. Crim, November 4, 1953, 14:642–43.

59. John F. Kennedy Library & Museum, "Presidential Library and Museum," National Archives, https://www.jfklibrary.org/, Kennedy to James Z. Nettings, July 19, 1961; Kennedy to Alfred A. Kuna, November 20, 1961.

60. Carter, *Keeping Faith*, 48, 186, 207; Jimmy Carter, *Sources of Strength: Meditations on Scripture for a Living Faith* (Random House, 1997), 137.

61. Bush, *Public Papers of the Presidents, 1991*, Remarks at the Annual Southern Baptist Convention, June 6, 1991, 614; Bush, *Public Papers of the Presidents, 1992–1993*, Remarks to the National Association of Evangelicals, March 3, 1992, 367.

62. Saul K. Padover, ed., *The Complete Jefferson: Containing His Major Writings, Published and Unpublished, Except His Letters* (Duell, Sloan and Pearce, 1943), Education for a Lawyer, 1767, 1043–44; J. Jefferson Looney, ed., *The Papers of Thomas Jefferson: Retirement Series* (Princeton University Press, 2004), Jefferson to James Fishback, September 27, 1809, 1:566; Bergh and Lipscomb, *Writings of Thomas Jefferson*, Jefferson to Samuel Greenhow, January 31, 1814, 14:81; Jefferson to Michael Megear, May 29, 1823, 15:434; Sanford, *The Religious Life*, 5, 25.

63. William Peden, ed., *Notes on the State of Virginia* (University of North Carolina Press, 1955), 147.

64. Bergh and Lipscomb, *Writings of Thomas Jefferson*, Jefferson to Isaac Englebrecht, February 25, 1824, 16:16; Jefferson to Thomas Jefferson Smith, February 21, 1825, 16:110.

65. The National Historical Publications and Records Commission, "Founders Online," National Archives, https://founders.archives.gov/, John Quincy Adams to George Washington Adams, August 15, 1811; Worthington Chauncey Ford, ed., *Writings of John Quincy Adams* (Macmillan, 1913–1916), Adams to George Washington Adams, September 8, 1811, 4:212, 216.

66. John Spencer Bassett, ed., *Correspondence of Andrew Jackson* (Carnegie Institution, 1926–1935), Jackson to Rachel Jackson, December 21, 1823, 3:219; Milo Milton Quaife, ed., *The Diary of James K. Polk During His Presidency, 1845 to 1849* (A. C. McClurg, 1910), October 12, 1848, 4:157.

67. Holman Hamilton, *Zachary Taylor, Soldier of the Republic* (Bobbs-Merrill, 1941), 114; Holman Hamilton, *Zachary Taylor, Soldier in the White House* (Bobbs-Merrill, 1951), 241.

68. Moore, *The Works of James Buchanan*, Speech at New York, April 24, 1856, 10:78; Buchanan to Mrs. Henry E. Johnston, January 1, 1868, 11:461; Biographical Sketch by James Buchanan Henry, 12:330.

69. Simon, *The Papers of Ulysses S. Grant*, Editor's Note, 15:529; Speech, November 18, 1879, 29:304; *New Orleans Picayune*, April 6, 1880, 29:376n; Grant to Morton McMichael, February 1866, 32:86–87.

70. Williams, *The Diary and Letters of Rutherford Hayes*, Diary, March 18, 1878, 3:469.

71. Louis D. Rubin, Jr., ed., *Teach the Freeman: The Correspondence of Rutherford B. Hayes and the Slater Fund for Negro Education, 1881–1893* (Louisiana State University Press, 1959), Introduction, 1:xiv, xx, xxxiii; Hayes to J. L. M. Curry, July 15, 1882, 1:50; W. E. B. Du Bois to Daniel Coit Gilman, 1893, 2:281.

72. Henry Barnard, *Rutherford B. Hayes and His America* (Bobbs-Merrill, 1954), 504.

73. Harry James Brown and Frederick D. Williams, eds., *The Diary of James A. Garfield* (Michigan State University Press, 1967), March 27, 1853, 1:183; May 1, 1853, 1:190; June 26, 1853, 1:201; July 24, 1853, 1:211; October 9, 1853, 1:221; October 30, 1853, 1:225; November 27, 1853, 1:228; October 11, 1857, 1:292; December 4, 1857, 1:306; December 5, 1857, 1:306; December 6, 1857, 1:307; December 13, 1857, 1:309;

February 3, 1858, 1:321; April 29, 1873, 2:174n78; Frederick D. Williams, ed., *The Wild Life of the Army: Civil War Letters of James A. Garfield* (Michigan State University Press, 1964), Garfield to J. Harrison Rhodes, September 17, 1862, 42.

74. Sievers, *Benjamin Harrison, Hoosier Warrior*, 113, 170.

75. Andrews, *The Autobiography of Theodore Roosevelt*, 10; Corinne Roosevelt Robinson, *My Brother, Theodore Roosevelt* (Charles Scribner's Sons, 1921), 98; Morison, *Letters of Theodore Roosevelt*, Roosevelt to John Frank Stevens, May 21, 1906, 5:281; Roosevelt to Anna Cabot Mills Lodge, September 20, 1907, 5:800; Roosevelt to James Ambrose Galliman, August 22, 1918, 8:1365; Ferleger and Hart, *Theodore Roosevelt Cyclopedia*, At the Pacific Theological Seminary, Spring 1911, 42.

76. William Howard Taft, *Service with the Fighting Men: An Account of the Work of the Young Men's Christian Associations in the World War* (Association Press, 1922).

77. Link, *The Papers of Woodrow Wilson*, Wilson to Ellen Axson Wilson, April 26, 1886, 5:174.

78. Link, *The Papers of Woodrow Wilson*, Notes for a Chapel Talk, April 5, 1891, 7:187–88; A News Report, *Daily Princetonian*, May 5, 1893, 8:207; Notes for a Chapel Talk, May 7, 1893, 8:208; A News Report of an Address, *Daily Princetonian*, April 13, 1894, 8:579; Notes for a Chapel Talk, November 8, 1896, 10:42; Notes for a Chapel Talk, March 13, 1898, 10:477; Notes for a Religious Talk, November 2, 1899, 11:273; A News Report of a Religious Talk, *Daily Princetonian*, February 21, 1902, 12:274; A News Report, *Daily Princetonian*, May 15, 1903, 14:458; Notes for a Talk at Vesper Service, September 21, 1902, 14:133; Baccalaureate Service, June 10, 1903, 14:484; An Address on Christian Education, October 13, 1904, 15:518; News Report on an Address in New York on Youth and Christian Progress, *New York Times*, November 20, 1905, 16:228; Baccalaureate Address, June 9, 1907, 17:187, 192.

79. Link, *The Papers of Woodrow Wilson*, A Religion Address in Trenton, October 1, 1911, 23:373, 377.

80. Link, *The Papers of Woodrow Wilson*, A Statement, July 23, 1917, 43:244; Wilson to John Fox, September 1, 1917, 44:118; A Statement, September 3, 1918, 49:422; Wilson to Elmer Talmage Clark, October 13, 1920, 66:229.

81. David L. Holmes, *The Faiths of the Postwar Presidents: Truman to Obama* (University of Georgia Press, 2012), 3; Ferrell, *Off the Record*, Diary, December 24, 1950, 206; Truman, *Public Papers of the Presidents, 1952–1953*, Remarks to Representatives of the National Council of Churches, September 26, 1952, 591.

82. Chandler, *The Papers of Dwight Eisenhower*, Eisenhower to Adelaide O'Mara, August 6, 1956, 17:2235.

83. Gerald R. Ford Presidential Library & Museum, "Museum and Library," National Archives, https://www.fordlibrarymuseum.gov/ - anchor-section, Speech, International Child Evangelism Fellowship Conference, May 25, 1970; Remarks at the Dedication of the New Hope College Cultural Center, October 23, 1971; Speech, Father of the Year Awards, May 22, 1974; Ford, *Public Papers of the Presidents, 1976–1977*, Remarks at the Combined Convention of the National Religious Broadcasters and the National Association of Evangelicals, February 22, 1976, 414.

84. Dan Ariail and Cheryl Heckler-Feltz, *The Carpenter's Apprentice: The Spiritual Biography of Jimmy Carter* (Zondervan, 1996), v–vii, xiv–xvi.

85. Brown, *Hand of Providence*, 45; Ronald Reagan, *Public Papers of the Presidents of the United States, 1987* (Government Printing Office, 1989), Remarks to the National Governors' Association, March 26, 1987, 292.

86. Russell J. Levenson Jr., *Witness to Dignity: The Life and Faith of George H. W. and Barbara Bush* (Center Street, 2022), x, 290.

Chapter 3

1. John Shaw, ed., *Crete and James: Personal Letters of Lucretia and James Garfield* (Michigan State University, 1994), Lucretia to James Garfield, November 22, 1865, 226; Arthur S. Link, *The Papers of Woodrow Wilson* (Princeton University Press, 1966–1994), Work-Day Religion, August 11, 1876, 1:176–77; A News Report of an Address to the Trenton Y.M.C.A., *Trenton Daily True American*, February 9, 1903, 14:355.

2. Calvin Coolidge Presidential Foundation, "Bunker Hill Day Address, June 17, 1918," Coolidge Foundation, https://coolidgefoundation.org/resources/bunker-hill-day/; Herbert Hoover, *Further Addresses upon the American Road, 1938–1940* (Charles Scribner's Sons, 1940), Morals in Government, September 28, 1938, 3; Relief for Poland, March 12, 1940, 249; Harry S. Truman, *Public Papers of the Presidents of the United States, 1946* (Government Printing Office, 1962), Address at the Lighting of the National Community Christmas Tree on the White House Grounds, December 24, 1946, 512; Harry S. Truman, *Public Papers of the Presidents of the United States, 1952–1953* (Government Printing Office, 1966), Remarks at the Lighting of the National Community Christmas Tree, December 24, 1952, 1097; Jimmy Carter, *Keeping Faith: Memoirs of a President* (Bantam, 1982), 48, 186, 207; Jimmy Carter, *Public Papers of the Presidents of the United States, 1978* (Government Printing Office, 1979), Remarks at the White House Dinner in Observance of National Bible Week, November 22, 1978, 2070; Jimmy Carter, *Sources of Strength: Meditations on Scripture for a Living Faith* (Random House, 1997), 190; George H. W. Bush, *Public Papers of the Presidents of the United States, 1992–1993* (Government Printing Office, 1993), Message on the Observance of Christmas, December 8, 1992, 2179; George W. Bush, *Public Papers of the Presidents of the United States, 2004* (Government Printing Office, 2007), Message on the Observance of Easter, April 9, 2004, 546; Barack Obama, *Public Papers of the Presidents of the United States, 2013* (Government Printing Office, 2018), Remarks on Lighting the National Christmas Tree, December 6, 2013, 1346.

3. Leroy P. Graf and Ralph W. Haskins, eds., *The Papers of Andrew Johnson* (University of Tennessee Press, 1967–2000), Johnson to William W. Pepper, July 17, 1854, 2:237.

4. George F. Parker, ed., *The Writings and Speeches of Grover Cleveland* (Cassell, 1892), At the Banquet of the National Association of Builders, February 12, 1891, 170–71; Wesley G. Pippert, ed., *The Spiritual Journey of Jimmy Carter in His Own Words* (Macmillan, 1978), Men's Bible Class, Plains Baptist Church, March 28, 1976, 155.

5. William J. Clinton, *Public Papers of the Presidents of the United States, 1999* (Government Printing Office, 2000), Remarks on Presenting Congressional Gold Medals to the Little Rock Nine, November 9, 1999, 2030.

6. William J. Clinton, *Public Papers of the Presidents of the United States, 1995* (Government Printing Office, 1996), Remarks at the Signing Ceremony for the Israeli–Palestinian West Bank Accord, September 28, 1995, 1510.

7. Carter, *Sources of Strength*, 190; William J. Clinton, *Public Papers of the Presidents of the United States, 1998* (Government Printing Office, 1999), Remarks at the Congressional Black Caucus, September 19, 1998, 1625.

8. Eran Shalev, *American Zion: The Old Testament as a Political Text from the Revolution to the Civil War* (Yale University Press, 2013), 19; L. H. Butterfield, ed., *The Adams Family Correspondence* (Harvard University Press, 1963), John to Abigail Adams, May 17, 1776, 1:410.

9. Julian P. Boyd, ed., *The Papers of Thomas Jefferson* (Princeton University Press, 1950), Report on a Seal for the United States, August 20, 1776, 1:494–95.

10. Albert Ellery Bergh and Andrew A. Lipscomb, eds., *The Writings of Thomas Jefferson* (Thomas Jefferson Memorial Association, 1904), Jefferson to George Flower, September 12, 1817, 15:141.

11. Robert P. Hay, "George Washington: American Moses," *American Quarterly* 21, no. 4 (Winter 1969): 782–88; Linda K. Kerber, *Federalists in Dissent: Imagery and Ideology in Jeffersonian America* (Cornell University Press, 1970), 6–8; Edwin S. Gaustad, *Faith of Our Fathers: Religion and the New Nation* (Harper & Row, 1987), 75.

12. Graf and Haskins, eds., *The Papers of Andrew Johnson*, Speech on the Homestead Bill, July 25, 1850, 1:564; Speech on the Homestead Bill, May 20, 1858, 3:133.

13. Harry James Brown and Frederick D. Williams, eds., *The Diary of James A. Garfield* (Michigan State University Press, 1967), October 5, 1857, 1:290.

14. Robert H Ferrell, ed., *Off the Record: The Private Papers of Harry S. Truman* (Harper & Row, 1980), Memorandum, 1954, 310.

15. Ronald Reagan, *Public Papers of the Presidents of the United States, 1981* (Government Printing Office, 1982), Toasts of the President and Prime Minister Menachem Begin at State Dinner, September 9, 1981, 769–70.

16. George W. Bush, *Decision Points* (Crown Publishers, 2010), 60–61.

17. Barack Obama, *Papers of the Presidents of the United States, 2010* (Government Printing Office, 2013), Statement on the 45th Anniversary of the 1965 Voting Rights March, March 7, 2010, 327; Barack Obama, *A Promised Land* (Crown Publishers, 2020), 122.

18. John Quincy Adams, *Lectures on Rhetoric and Oratory* (Hilliard and Metcalf, 1810; repr., Russell & Russell, 1962), 1:16–17.

19. Carter, *Public Papers of the Presidents, 1978*, Remarks at the Southern Salute to the President Dinner, January 20, 1978, 158.

20. Richard M. Nixon, *Public Papers of the Presidents of the United States, 1969* (Government Printing Office, 1971), Toasts of the President and Prime Minister Golda Meir of Israel, September 25, 1969, 745–46.

21. Graf and Haskins, *The Papers of Andrew Johnson*, Exchanges Concerning Volunteer Forces, February 18, 1858, 3:42; Link, *The Papers of Woodrow Wilson*, Wilson to Edith Bolling Galt, August 25, 1915, 34:323.

22. Roy P. Basler, ed., *The Collected Works of Abraham Lincoln* (Rutgers University Press, 1953–1955), Speech at Peoria, Illinois, October 9, 1856, 2:379.

23. Carter, *Sources of Strength*, 62–63, 178.

24. Robert A. Rutland et al., eds., *The Papers of James Madison* (University of Chicago Press, 1962–1977; repr., University Press of Virginia, 1977), Notes on Commentary of the Bible, 1770–1773, 1:57–58; Charles Francis Adams, ed., *Memoirs of John Quincy Adams, Comprising Portions of His Diary from 1795 to 1848* (n.p., 1874–1877; repr., AMS, 1970), July 27, 1828, 8:65; Graf and Haskins, *The Papers of Andrew Johnson*, Johnson to Robert Johnson, April 16, 1854, 2:230.

25. Herbert Hoover, *Addresses upon the American Road, 1933–1938* (Charles Scribner's Sons, 1938), Morals in Government, Fresno, April 26, 1938, 336; Lyndon B. Johnson, *Public Papers of the Presidents of the United States, 1965* (Government Printing Office, 1966), Inaugural Address, January 20, 1965, 74; Michael Doyle, ed., *Gerald R. Ford: Selected Speeches* (R. W. Beatty, 1973), Commencement Address at the College of William and Mary, June 9, 1968, 60.

26. J. Jefferson Looney, ed., *The Papers of Thomas Jefferson: Retirement Series* (Princeton University Press, 2004), Jefferson to the Inhabitants of Albemarle County, April 3, 1809, 1:103.

27. Link, *The Papers of Woodrow Wilson*, Wilson to Seth Low, November 8, 1915, 35:180–81; Elting E. Morison, ed., *The Letters of Theodore Roosevelt* (Harvard University Press, 1951–1954), Roosevelt to Quentin Roosevelt, September 1, 1917, 8:1234; Roosevelt to Edwin A. Van Valkenburg, April 23, 1918, 8:1312.

28. Harry S. Truman Library & Museum, "Welcome to the Harry S. Truman Presidential Library and Museum," National Archives, https://www.trumanlibrary.gov/, Speech at Welch, West Virginia, November 11, 1941; Truman, *Public Papers of the Presidents, 1946*, Address to the Federal Council of Churches, March 6, 1946, 142; Harry S. Truman, *Memoirs* (Doubleday, 1955–1956), 2:157; Ferrell, *Off the Record*, Diary, April 4, 1948, 129; Harry S. Truman, *Public Papers of the Presidents of the United States, 1949* (Government Printing Office, 1964), Address at a Luncheon of the National Conference of Christians and Jews, November 11, 1949, 562; William Hillman, ed., *Mr. President: The First Publication from the Personal Diaries, Private Letters, Papers, and Revealing Interviews of Harry S. Truman* (Farrar, Straus, and Young, 1952), 104.

29. Clinton, *Public Papers of the Presidents, 1998*, Remarks at a Memorial Service for the Victims of the Embassy Bombings in Kenya and Tanzania, September 11, 1998, 1566.

30. William J. Clinton, *Public Papers of the President of the United States, 1996* (Government Printing Office, 1997), Remarks at a Memorial Service for Victims of Terrorism, March 5, 1996, 374.

31. Charles B. Sanford, *The Religious Life of Thomas Jefferson* (University Press of Virginia, 1984), 172; John P. Kaminsky, et al., eds., *The Documentary History of the*

Ratification of the Constitution (State Historical Society of Wisconsin, 1976–2008), Christopher Gadsden to Thomas Jefferson, October 29, 1787, 13:508; Worthington Chauncey Ford, ed., *Writings of John Quincy Adams* (Macmillan, 1913–1916), Adams to Benjamin Waterhouse, October 24, 1813, 4:527; Charles Grier Sellers Jr., *James K. Polk, Continentalist, 1843–1846* (Princeton University Press, 1966), 157; Graf and Haskins, *The Papers of Andrew Johnson*, Remarks to Maryland Legislators, March 8, 1866, 10:230.

32. John C. Fitzpatrick, ed., *The Writings of George Washington* (Government Printing Office, 1931–1940), Washington to Bushrod Washington, January 15, 1783, 26:40.

33. Carter, *Sources of Strength*, 38.

34. Boyd, *The Papers of Thomas Jefferson*, Jefferson to Nicholas Davies, August 6, 1794, 28:110.

35. Franklin Access to the FDR Library's Digital Collection, "Fully Digitized Collections or Series," Franklin D. Roosevelt Presidential Library and Museum, updated 2011, http://www.fdrlibrary.marist.edu/archives/collections/franklin/, Catholic Charities Luncheon, April 9, 1932; Rollins College Speech, March 23, 1936.

36. Basler, *The Collected Works of Abraham Lincoln*, Temperance Address, February 22, 1842, 1:272, 276.

37. Adams, *Memoirs of John Quincy Adams*, February 17, 1828, 7:437–38; Link, *The Papers of Woodrow Wilson*, Wilson to Ellen Louise Axson, March 13, 1884, 3:85; Carter, *Sources of Strength*, 196–97.

38. Robert J. Taylor, ed., *The Papers of John Adams* (Harvard University Press, 1977), "Governor Winthrop to Governor Bradford," February 9, 1767, 1:200; Ford, *Writings of John Quincy Adams*, Adams to Johan Luzac, November 25, 1796, 2:49–51; Allan Nevins, ed., *The Diary of John Quincy Adams, 1794–1845: American Diplomacy and Political, Social, and Intellectual Life from Washington to Polk* (Charles Scribner's Sons, 1951), May 4, 1820, 232.

39. Richard B. Mattern, ed., *James Madison's "Advice to My Country"* (University Press of Virginia, 1997), 104–5; Graf and Haskins, *The Papers of Andrew Johnson*, Speech at Murfreesboro, May 1, 1855, 2:296; Speech in Reply to Senator Lane, March 2, 1861, 4:361; Speech at Elizabethton, May 15, 1861, 4:477; Speech at Newport, Kentucky, September 2, 1861, 5:3; Speech to Davidson County Citizens, March 22, 1862, 5:231; Speech at Philadelphia, March 11, 1863, 6:170; Speech on Restoration of State Government, January 21, 1864, 6:584; Speech near Gallatin, July 19, 1864, 7:41; Speech at Logansport, Indiana, October 4, 1864, 7:228.

40. Basler, *The Collected Works of Abraham Lincoln*, Seventh and Last Debate with Stephen A. Douglas at Alton, Illinois, October 15, 1858, 3:305; John Y. Simon, ed., *The Papers of Ulysses S. Grant* (Southern Illinois University Press, 1967–2012), Grant to Elihu B. Washburne, August 26, 1872, 23:237; Link, *The Papers of Woodrow Wilson*, Gilbert Monell Hitchcock to Wilson, March 20, 1920, 65:109n1.

41. Hoover, *Further Addresses upon the American Road, 1938–1940*, The Imperative Need for Moral Rearmament, November 22, 1938, 183, 190–91; Harry S.

Truman, *Public Papers of the Presidents of the United States, 1951* (Government Printing Office, 1965), Address to the Washington Pilgrimage of American Churchmen, September 28, 1951, 551; Reagan, *Public Papers of the Presidents, 1981*, Remarks at the Conservative Political Action Conference Dinner, March 20, 1981, 278.

42. John Spencer Bassett, ed., *Correspondence of Andrew Jackson* (Carnegie Institution, 1926–1935), Jackson to Major William Lewis, February 14, 1825, 3:276; Graf and Haskins, *The Papers of Andrew Johnson*, Speech at Elizabethton, May 15, 1861, 4:477.

43. Boyd, *The Papers of Thomas Jefferson*, John Adams to Jefferson, October 9, 1787, 12:220; Simon, *The Papers of Ulysses S. Grant*, Grant to George W. Childs, April 16, 1873, 24:110.

44. Basler, *The Collected Works of Abraham Lincoln*, Speech in the United States House of Representatives on the War with Mexico, January 12, 1848, 1:439; Graf and Haskins, *The Papers of Andrew Johnson*, Speech on Harper's Ferry Incident, December 12, 1859, 3:348; John F. Kennedy, *The Strategy of Peace* (Harper & Row, 1960), 164.

45. John Bassett Moore, ed., *The Works of James Buchanan* (J. B. Lippincott, 1908–1911; repr., Antiquarian Press, 1960), Address, June 1, 1828, 1:371.

46. Simon, *The Papers of Ulysses S. Grant*, Grant to Captain John C. Kelton, November 22, 1861, 3:212; Theodore Roosevelt, *The Works of Theodore Roosevelt* (Charles Scribner's Sons, 1925), Speech in the New York Assembly, March 9, 1883, 16:26; Link, *The Papers of Woodrow Wilson*, A News Report of an Address in Syracuse, New York, *Syracuse Herald*, February 17, 1904, 15:172.

47. Ferrell, *Off the Record*, Draft of Undelivered Speech, October 1946, 102.

48. Taylor, *The Papers of John Adams*, To the Inhabitants of the Colony of Massachusetts-Bay, February 13, 1775, 2:258.

49. Ellis Sandoz, *A Government of Laws: Political Theory, Religion, and the American Founding* (Louisiana State University Press, 1990), 107.

50. Boyd, *The Papers of Thomas Jefferson*, Jefferson to Philip Mazzei, April 24, 1796, 29:82.

51. Herbert Hoover, *Addresses upon the American Road, 1950–1955* (Stanford University Press, 1955), The Protection of Freedom, August 10, 1954, 81–82.

52. Carter, *Sources of Strength*, 63.

53. Ford, *Writings of John Quincy Adams*, Adams to John Adams, August 31, 1815, 5:364.

54. Basler, *The Collected Works of Abraham Lincoln*, Lincoln to William Herndon, June 12, 1848, 1:477; Joseph R. Fornierei, ed., *The Language of Liberty: The Political Speeches and Writings of Abraham Lincoln* (Regnery, 2009), Lincoln to Joshua F. Speed, August 24, 1855, 190.

55. Lester J. Cappon, ed., *The Adams-Jefferson Letters: The Complete Correspondence Between Thomas Jefferson and John and Abigail Adams* (University of North Carolina Press, 1959), John Adams to Jefferson, June 30, 1813, 2:347; Moore, *Works of James Buchanan*, Remarks on the Disposition of the Public Lands, January 20,

1841, 4:354; Basler, *The Collected Works of Abraham Lincoln*, Speech at Cincinnati Oho, September 17, 1859, 3:461.

56. Robert Seager, *And Tyler Too: A Biography of John & Julia Gardiner Tyler* (McGraw-Hill, 1963), 91–92; Franklin Access to the FDR Library's Digital Collection, "Fully Digitized Collections," http://www.fdrlibrary.marist.edu/archives/collections/franklin/, Inaugural Address, March 4, 1933.

57. Lewis L. Gould, *Theodore Roosevelt* (Oxford University Press, 2012), 29.

Chapter 4

1. For a much fuller discussion of the Greco-Roman gods and of the divine entities posited by classical philosophers, see Carl J. Richard, *Why We're All Romans: The Roman Contribution to the Western World* (Rowman & Littlefield, 2010), 135–63, 239–43, 260–68.

2. Paul K. Longmore, *The Invention of George Washington* (University of California Press, 1988), 29–30; John C. Fitzpatrick, ed., *The Writings of George Washington* (Government Printing Office, 1931–1940), Washington to Reverend William Gordon, May 3, 1776, 37:526; Paul F. Boller, *George Washington and Religion* (Southern Methodist University Press, 1963), 107–9.

3. Daniel L. Dreisbach, *Reading the Bible with the Founding Fathers* (Oxford University Press, 2017), 209; W. W. Abbot, ed., *The Papers of George Washington: Presidential Series* (University Press of Virginia, 1987), Washington to the Citizens of Baltimore, April 17, 1789, 2:62; Washington to the Officials of Wilmington, Delaware, April 19, 1789, 2:77; Fitzpatrick, *The Writings of George Washington*, Washington to David Stuart, December 30, 1798, 37:78.

4. Charles Francis Adams, ed., *Memoirs of John Quincy Adams, Comprising Portions of His Diary from 1795 to 1848* (n.p., 1874–1877; repr., AMS, 1970), July 11, 1809, 1:550; March 31, 1814, 2:590; August 6, 1817, 4:4; Worthington Chauncey Ford, ed., *Writings of John Quincy Adams* (Macmillan, 1913–1916), Adams to John Adams, June 25, 1811, 4:119–20.

5. Adams, *Memoirs of John Quincy Adams*, December 29, 1809, 2:92; December 30, 1810, 2:205; December 31, 1812, 2:436; December 31, 1814, 3:136; December 31, 1817, 4:33; December 30, 1818, 4:202; January 30, 1819, 4:236; February 22, 1819, 4:274; July 31, 1823, 6:167; December 31, 1827, 7:393–94; December 30, 1828, 8:159–60; December 31, 1831, 8:450; January 1, 1832, 8:450; Allan Nevins, ed., *The Diary of John Quincy Adams, 1794–1845: American Diplomacy and Political, Social, and Intellectual Life from Washington to Polk* (Scribner's Sons, 1951), May 31, 1825, 347; December 3, 1845, 573; James Linden, ed., *State of the Union Addresses of John Quincy Adams* (Project Gutenberg eBooks, 2004), https://www.gutenberg.org/ebooks/5015, December 6, 1825, December 5, 1826, December 4, 1827, December 2, 1828; The American Presidency Project, "Inaugural Address, March 4, 1825," UC Santa Barbara, https://www.presidency.ucsb.edu/.

6. John Spencer Bassett, ed., *Correspondence of Andrew Jackson* (Carnegie Institution, 1926–1935), Jackson to Rachel Jackson, August 28, 1814, 2:35; Jackson to John Donelson, February 9, 1824, 3:227; Jackson to General John Coffee, January 23, 1825, 3:274; Jackson to Andrew Jackson Donelson, May 5, 1831, 4:278; Harold D. Moser et al., eds., *The Papers of Andrew Jackson* (University of Tennessee Press, 1980), Inaugural Address, March 4, 1829, 7:75. For Jackson's 1833 letters regarding the bank, see Martin Van Buren, *The Autobiography of Martin Van Buren* (American Historical Association, 1920; repr., Da Capo, 1973), 2:604; Robert V. Remini, *Andrew Jackson and the Course of American Democracy, 1833–1845* (Harper & Row, 1984), 228; John William Ward, *Andrew Jackson: Symbol for an Age* (Oxford University Press, 1955), 114.

7. John Bassett Moore, ed., *The Works of James Buchanan* (J. B. Lippincott, 1908–1911; repr., Antiquarian Press, 1960), Diary, March 21, 1832, 2:182; Buchanan to Reverend Edward Buchanan, January 9, 1833, 2:312; Inaugural Address, March 4, 1857, 10:105; Reply to a Memorial of Citizens of Connecticut on Kansas, August 15, 1857, 10:122.

8. Roy P. Basler, ed., *The Collected Works of Abraham Lincoln* (Rutgers University Press, 1953–1955), Farewell Address at Springfield, Illinois, February 11, 1861, 4:190; Address to the Ohio Legislature, February 13, 1861, 4:204; Speech at Steubenville, Ohio, February 14, 1861, 4:207; Remarks at Newark, New Jersey, February 21, 1861, 4:234; First Inaugural Address, March 4, 1861, 4:270; Message to Congress in Special Session, July 4, 1861, 4:441.

9. Basler, *The Collected Works of Abraham Lincoln*, Reply to the Members of the Presbyterian General Assembly, June 2, 1863, 6:244; Remarks to the Baltimore Presbyterian Synod, October 24, 1863, 6:536; Gettysburg Address, November 19, 1863, 7:23; Address at Sanity Fair, Baltimore, April 18, 1864, 7:301; Response to a Serenade, November 10, 1864, 8:101; Garry Wills, *Lincoln at Gettysburg: The Words That Remade America* (Simon & Schuster, 1992), 41, 52–59, 249–54.

10. Leroy P. Graf and Ralph W. Haskins, eds., *The Papers of Andrew Johnson* (University of Tennessee Press, 1967–2000), Speech on Restoration of State Government, January 21, 1864, 6:585; Speech to Washington Sunday School Union, May 29, 1865, 8:139.

11. Ulysses S. Grant, *Personal Memoirs of U.S. Grant* (Charles L. Webster, 1885–1886), 1:7, 317–18; 2:215–16; John Y. Simon, ed., *The Papers of Ulysses S. Grant* (Southern Illinois University Press, 1967–2012), *New York Herald*, December 14, 1879, 29:326n; *New York Times*, July 24, 1885, 31:213n.

12. Charles Richard Williams, ed., *The Diary and Letters of Rutherford B. Hayes* (Ohio State Archaeological Historical Society, 1922), Diary, April 15, 1845, 1:163–64; Hayes to Sardis Birchard, November 3, 1852, 1:429; December 18, 1882, 4:99; August 18, 1889, 4:502; July 23, 1890, 4:589; Henry Barnard, *Rutherford B. Hayes and His America* (Bobbs-Merrill, 1954), 511.

13. Harry James Brown and Frederick D. Williams, ed., *The Diary of James A. Garfield* (Michigan University Press, 1967), August 30, 1850, 1:55; January 1, 1852,

1:112; January 1, 1853, 1:168; Frederick D. Williams, ed., *The Wild Life of the Army: Civil War Letters of James A. Garfield* (Michigan State University Press, 1964), Garfield to General William S. Rosencrans, June 12, 1863, 281.

14. Allan Nevins, ed., *Letters of Grover Cleveland, 1850–1908* (Houghton Mifflin, 1933), Cleveland to John Temple Graves, December 20, 1890, 240.

15. Charles W. Calhoun, *Benjamin Harrison* (Times Books, 2005), 23.

16. William McKinley, *Speeches and Addresses of William McKinley from March 1, 1897 to May 30, 1900* (Doubleday & McClure, 1900), Address to the Officers and Students of the University of Pennsylvania, February 22, 1898, 72.

17. Henry F. Pringle, *The Life and Times of William Howard Taft* (Farrar & Rinehart, 1939), 2:884.

18. Arthur S. Link, ed., *The Papers of Woodrow Wilson* (Princeton University Press, 1966–1994), Wilson to Ellen Louise Axson, November 20, 1883, 2:536; March 30, 1885, 4:435; Wilson to Edith Bolling Galt, May 7, 1915, 33:125; June 1, 1915, 33:301; August 19, 1915, 34:262.

19. Link, *The Papers of Woodrow Wilson*, A News Report of a Talk to the Philadelphian Society, *Daily Princetonian*, November 7, 1902, 14:201–2; An Address to the Commercial Club of Chicago, November 29, 1902, 14:238.

20. Link, *The Papers of Woodrow Wilson*, Wilson to Edward Mandell House, August 3, 1914, 30:336; Remarks at a Press Conference, September 29, 1916, 38:289; Remarks in London to Free Church Leaders, December 28, 1918, 53:530.

21. Link, *The Papers of Woodrow Wilson*, A Luncheon Address in San Francisco, September 18, 1919, 63:350; From the Papers of Cary Travers Grayson, 1919, 64:488; Gilbert Monell Hitchcock to Woodrow Wilson, March 20, 1920, 65:109–10n1.

22. Calvin Coolidge, *The Price of Freedom: Speeches and Addresses* (Charles Scribner's Sons, 1924), "Theodore Roosevelt," January 23, 1921, 17; Claude M. Fuess, *Calvin Coolidge: The Man from Vermont* (Little, Brown, 1940), 27; Calvin Coolidge, *The Autobiography of Calvin Coolidge* (Cosmopolitan, 1929), 234–35.

23. Franklin Access to the FDR Library's Digital Collection, "Fully Digitized Collections or Series," Franklin D. Roosevelt Presidential Library and Museum, updated 2011, http://www.fdrlibrary.marist.edu/archives/collections/franklin/, Address to Congress Declaring War on Japan, December 8, 1941; To the People of the Philippines, August 12, 1943.

24. Harry S. Truman Library & Museum, "Welcome to the Harry S. Truman Presidential Library and Museum," National Archives, https://www.trumanlibrary.gov/, Truman to Bess Wallace, October 6, 1918; Robert H. Ferrell, ed., *Off the Record: The Private Papers of Harry S. Truman* (Harper & Row, 1980), Diary, May 27, 1945, 38; March 4, 1952, 245; Harry S. Truman, *Public Papers of the Presidents of the United States, 1947* (Government Printing Office, 1963), Truman to Pope Pius XII, August 6, 1947, 424.

25. Alfred D. Chandler et al., eds., *The Papers of Dwight David Eisenhower* (Johns Hopkins University Press, 1970–2001), To American Forces, November 6, 1943, 3:1553; Dwight D. Eisenhower Presidential Library, Museum & Boyhood Home,

"Eisenhower Library," National Archives, https://www.eisenhowerlibrary.gov/, Inaugural Address, January 20, 1953; Dwight D. Eisenhower, *Public Papers of the Presidents of the United States, 1957* (Government Printing Office, 1958), Remarks at the Graduation Exercises of the FBI National Academy, November 8, 1957, 803.

26. John F. Kennedy, *Public Papers of the Presidents of the United States, 1961* (Government Printing Office, 1962), Remarks at the Dedication Breakfast of the International Christian Leadership, February 9, 1961, 76; John F. Kennedy Library & Museum, "Presidential Library and Museum," National Archives, https://www.jfklibrary.org/, Kennedy to Binku Gasa, March 11, 1961; John F. Kennedy, *Public Papers of the Presidents of the United States, 1962* (Government Printing Office, 1963), Remarks at the Tenth Annual Presidential Prayer Breakfast, March 1, 1962, 176; Remarks at Fort Stewart, Georgia, to Members of the First Armored Division, November 26, 1962, 840.

27. Gerald R. Ford, *Public Papers of the Presidents of the United States, 1976–1977* (Government Printing Office, 1979), Remarks in Philadelphia, July 4, 1976, 1970.

28. Jimmy Carter, *Public Papers of the Presidents of the United States, 1979* (Government Printing Office, 1980), National Day of Prayer, September 19, 1979, 1694.

29. Ronald Reagan, *An American Life* (Simon & Schuster, 1990), 263; Ronald Reagan, *Public Papers of the Presidents of the United States, 1982* (Government Printing Office, 1983), Remarks at Annual National Prayer Breakfast, February 4, 1982, 109; Interview with Representatives of Western European Publications, May 21, 1982, 698.

30. George W. Bush, *Public Papers of the Presidents of the United States, 2003* (Government Printing Office, 2006), Remarks at a National Prayer Breakfast, February 6, 2003, 131; George W. Bush, *Decision Points* (Crown Publishers, 2010), 26–27.

31. Barack Obama, *Public Papers of the Presidents of the United States, 2014* (Government Printing Office, 2019), Remarks at the National Prayer Breakfast, February 6, 2014, 103.

32. Boller, *George Washington and Religion*, 103–4.

33. Ford, *Writings of John Quincy Adams*, Adams to Thomas Boylston Adams, October 27, 1810, 3:530; Albert Ellery Bergh and Andrew A. Lipscomb, eds. *The Writings of Thomas Jefferson* (Thomas Jefferson Memorial Association, 1904), Jefferson to George Logan, October 3, 1813, 13:387; Wayne Cutler et al., eds., *Correspondence of James K. Polk* (Vanderbilt University Press, 1969–1989; repr., University of Tennessee Press, 1993), Polk to Silas Wright Jr., July 17, 1845, 10:73; Polk to Gideon J. Pillow, February 4, 1846, 11:69; Polk to Archibald Wright, September 1, 1846, 11:301; Polk to Hopkins L. Turney, May 15, 1847, 12:256; Milo Milton Quaife, ed., *The Diary of James K. Polk During His Presidency, 1845 to 1849* (A. C. McClurg, 1910), August 26, 1845, 1:5.

34. Basler, *The Collected Works of Abraham Lincoln*, Lincoln to James C. Conkling, August 26, 1863, 6:410; Link, *The Papers of Woodrow Wilson*, A Campaign Address in Passaic, New Jersey, November 1, 1910, 21:498; Dwight D. Eisenhower, *Public Papers of the Presidents of the United States, 1955* (Government Printing Office, 1959), Address at the Graduation Ceremonies of the United States Military Academy, June

7, 1955, 577; Lyndon B. Johnson, *Public Papers of the Presidents of the United States, 1968–9* (Government Printing Office, 1970), Remarks at the Presidential Prayer Breakfast, February 1, 1968, 122; Carter, *Public Papers of the Presidents, 1979*, Address Before the Knesset, March 12, 1979, 425.

35. L. H. Butterfield, ed., *The Diary and Autobiography of John Adams* (Harvard University Press, 1962), Diary, July 22, 1756, 1:36; L. H. Butterfield, ed., *The Adams Family Correspondence* (Harvard University Press, 1963), John to Abigail Adams, July 5, 1774, 1:124.

36. Ford, *Writings of John Quincy Adams*, Adams to William Plumer, October 5, 1815, 5:398; Nevins, *The Diary of John Quincy Adams*, December 6, 1837, 490.

37. Quaife, *The Diary of James K. Polk During His Presidency, 1845 to 1849*, December 29, 1846, 2:297.

38. Fitzpatrick, *The Writings of George Washington*, Washington to Jonathan Trumbull, September 6, 1778, 12:406; Washington to Andrew Lewis, October 15, 1778, 13:79; Washington to Joseph Reed, November 27, 1778, 13:348; Washington to Lund Washington, May 29, 1779, 15:180; Washington to General John Armstrong, March 26, 1781, 21:378.

39. Fitzpatrick, *The Writings of George Washington*, Washington to Jonathan Trumbull, June 11, 1780, 18:511; Washington to Henry Knox, September 12, 1782, 25:150n; Washington to Pierre Charles L'Enfant, April 28, 1788, 29:481.

40. Fitzpatrick, *The Writings of George Washington*, Washington to Thaddeus Kosciuszko, August 31, 1797, 36:22; Washington to William Augustine Washington, February 27, 1798, 36:171; Washington to Archibald Blair, June 24, 1799, 37:244.

41. Julian P. Boyd, ed., *The Papers of Thomas Jefferson* (Princeton University Press, 1950), Jefferson to Benjamin Rush, September 23, 1800, 32:167; Charles B. Sanford, *The Religious Life of Thomas Jefferson* (University Press of Virginia, 1984), 156.

42. David B. Mattern, ed., *James Madison's "Advice to My Country"* (University Press of Virginia, 1997), Madison to John G. Jackson, December 28, 1821, 10.

43. Ford, *The Writings of John Quincy Adams*, Adams to Abigail Adams, July 13, 1812, 4:366; Adams, *Memoirs of John Quincy Adams*, November 1, 1818, 4:155.

44. Adams, *Memoirs of John Quincy Adams*, February 28, 1829, 8:100; December 30, 1829, 8:159–60; Nevins, *The Diary of John Quincy Adams*, January 1, 1829, 386; Jack Shepherd, *Cannibals of the Heart: A Personal Biography of Louisa Catherine and John Quincy Adams* (McGraw-Hill, 1980), 319–20; Marie B. Hecht, *John Quincy Adams: A Personal History of an Independent Man* (Macmillan, 1972), 518.

45. Nevins, *The Diary of John Quincy Adams*, April 4, 1841, 520; Adams, *Memoirs of John Quincy Adams*, August 14, 1841, 10:531; September 16, 1841, 11:19.

46. Adrienne Koch and William Peden, eds., *The Selected Writings of John and John Quincy Adams* (Alfred A. Knopf, 1946), Diary, October 31, 1846, 410.

47. Bassett, *Correspondence of Andrew Jackson*, Jackson to Mary Coffee, August 15, 1833, 5:158; Jackson to Andrew J. Hutchings, January 25, 1835, 5:322; Jackson to Mrs. Andrew J. Donelson, November 27, 1836, 5:440; Jackson to Andrew J. Donelson, December 31, 1836, 5:443.

48. Remini, *Andrew Jackson and the Course of American Democracy*, 186, 448.

49. Roy F. Nichols, *Franklin Pierce: Young Hickory of the Granite Hills* (University of Pennsylvania Press, 1931), 124–25.

50. Moore, *The Works of James Buchanan*, Buchanan to Reverend Edward Buchanan, October 13, 1832, 2:242; July 20, 1833, 2:371.

51. Basler, *The Collected Works of Abraham Lincoln*, Meditation on the Divine Will, September 2, 1862, 5:403–4; Lincoln to Eliza P. Gurney, October 26, 1862, 5:478.

52. Brown and Williams, *The Diary of James A. Garfield*, October 1, 1850, 1:60; Williams, *The Wild Life of the Army*, Garfield to J. Harrison Rhodes, May 1, 1862, 90; Garfield to Mary Hopkins, June 9, 1862, 109; Garfield to Lucretia Garfield, March 14, 1863, 249.

53. William McKinley, *Bits of Wisdom of William McKinley* (H. M. Caldwell, 1901), 81–82, 86–87; H. Wayne Morgan, *William McKinley and His America* (Syracuse University Press, 1963), 524.

54. Link, *The Papers of Woodrow Wilson*, Wilson to Mary Allen Hulbert, September 6, 1914, 31:3; From the Diary of Nancy Saunders Toy, January 3, 1915, 32:8–9; Wilson to James Henry Taylor, June 1, 1923, 68:370; Alden Hatch, *Edith Bolling Wilson: First Lady Extraordinary* (Dodd, Mead, 1961), 264.

55. Franklin Roosevelt, *Public Papers of Franklin Roosevelt, Forty-Eighth Governor of the State of New York, 1931* (J. B. Lyon, 1937), Thanksgiving Day Address, November 1931, 32; Franklin Access to the FDR Library's Digital Collection, "Fully Digitized Collections or Series," http://www.fdrlibrary.marist.edu/archives/collections/franklin/, Catholic Charities Luncheon, April 9, 1932.

56. Harry S. Truman Library & Museum, "Welcome to the Harry S. Truman Presidential Library and Museum," https://www.trumanlibrary.gov/, Speech to the National Association of Secretaries of State, October 18, 1943.

57. Johnson, *Public Papers of the Presidents, 1963–1964*, Remarks in Austin at the Dedication of the Agudas Achim Synagogue, December 30, 1963, 101.

58. Jimmy Carter, *Public Papers of the Presidents of the United States, 1980–1981* (Government Printing Office, 1982), Remarks at the National Prayer Breakfast, February 7, 1980, 277; Jimmy Carter and Rosalynn Carter, *Everything to Gain: Making the Most of the Rest of Your Life* (Random House, 1987), 23.

59. Mary Beth Brown, *Hand of Providence: The Strong and Quiet Faith of Ronald Reagan* (WND Books, 2004), 106–8, 142; Kiron K. Skinner et al., eds., *Reagan: A Life in Letters* (Free Press, 2003), Reagan to Reverend B. H. Cleaver, May 24, 1973, 94; Reagan to Elena Kellner, July 20, 1979, 681.

60. David Aikman, *A Man of Faith: The Spiritual Journey of George W. Bush* (Thomas Nelson, 2004), 32.

61. William J. Clinton, *Public Papers of the Presidents of the United States, 1997* (Government Printing Office, 1998), Radio Address, January 18, 1997, 41.

62. George W. Bush, *Public Papers of the Presidents of the United States, 2001* (Government Printing Office, 2003), Remarks at the National Day of Prayer and

Notes 343

Remembrance Service, September 14, 2001, 1108–9; George W. Bush, *Public Papers of the Presidents of the United States, 2002* (Government Printing Office, 2004), Remarks at the National Prayer Breakfast, February 7, 2002, 187–88.

63. Barack Obama, *Papers of the Presidents of the United States, 2010* (Government Printing Office, 2013), Remarks at the Memorial Service for the Victims of the Upper Big Branch Mining Accident in Beckley, West Virginia, April 25, 2010, 538.

Chapter 5

1. L. H. Butterfield, ed., *The Adams Family Correspondence* (Harvard University Press, 1963), John to Abigail Adams, June 17, 1775, 1:216; W. W. Abbot, ed., *The Papers of George Washington: Revolutionary War Series* (University Press of Virginia, 1985), Washington to Lund Washington, August 26, 1776, 6:137; John C. Fitzpatrick, ed., *The Writings of George Washington* (Government Printing Office, 1931–1940), Farewell Order to the Armies of the United States, November 2, 1783, 27:227.

2. Julian P. Boyd, ed., *The Papers of Thomas Jefferson* (Princeton University Press, 1950), Jefferson to the Marquis de Lafayette, November 21, 1791, 22:313; Jefferson to the Executive Directory of the Batavian Republic, May 30, 1801, 34:209; Saul K. Padover, ed., *The Complete Jefferson: Containing His Major Writings, Published and Unpublished, Except His Letters* (Duell, Sloan and Pearce, 1943), Jefferson to the Republican Young Men of New London, February 24, 1809, 548.

3. J. C. A. Stagg, ed., *The Papers of James Madison: Presidential Series* (University Press of Virginia, 1992), Madison to the Chairman of the Republican Committee of Essex County, New Jersey, March 18, 1809, 1:66; Madison to Benjamin Rush, March 20, 1809, 1:88; Madison to the Mother Superior of the Ursuline Convent, April 24, 1809, 1:136; Madison to the Republican Committee of New York, September 24, 1809, 1:389.

4. Charles Francis Adams, ed., *Memoirs of John Quincy Adams, Comprising Portions of His Diary from 1795 to 1848* (n.p., 1874–1877; repr., AMS, 1970), December 31, 1796, 1:187; January 1, 1797, 1:188; December 31, 1803, 1:282; December 31, 1805, 1:379–80; December 29, 1809, 2:92; December 16, 1827, 7:381; December 31, 1827, 7:393–94; December 31, 1833, 9:63; December 31, 1836, 9:339–40; Allan Nevins, ed., *The Diary of John Quincy Adams, 1794–1845: American Diplomacy and Political, Social and Intellectual Life from Washington to Polk* (Charles Scribner's Sons, 1951), December 31, 1807, 50–51; August 5, 1809, 60–61; December 30, 1810, 78; December 31, 1812, 103; April 28, 1814, 119; March 4, 1825, 343–44; John Quincy Adams, "March 4, 1825: Inaugural Address," UVA Miller Center, https://millercenter.org/the-presidency/presidential-speeches/march-4-1825-inaugural-address.

5. Harold D. Moser et al., eds., *The Papers of Andrew Jackson* (Knoxville: University of Tennessee Press, 1980–), Jackson to Rachel Jackson, May 9, 1796, 1:92; John Spencer Bassett, ed., *Correspondence of Andrew Jackson* (Washington, D.C.: Carnegie Institution, 1926–1935), Jackson to Rachel Jackson, November 19, 1823, 3:215; December 21, 1823, 3:218.

6. Charles M. Snyder, ed., *The Lady and the President: The Letters of Dorothea Dix and Millard Fillmore* (University of Kentucky Press, 1975), Fillmore to Dix, October 20, 1850, 95–96; August 29, 1854, 215.

7. Roy P. Basler, ed., *The Collected Works of Abraham Lincoln* (Rutgers University Press, 1953–1955), Lincoln to Caleb Russell and Sallie A. Fenton, January 5, 1863, 6:39–40.

8. John Y. Simon, ed., *The Papers of Ulysses S. Grant* (Southern Illinois University Press, 1967–2012), *New York Times*, July 24, 1885, 31:212n; Grant to Reverend Edmund Didier, July 8, 1885, 31:414.

9. T. Harry Williams, ed., *Hayes: The Diary of a President, 1875–1881* (David McKay, 1964), February 25, 1877, 77–78; Charles Richard Williams, ed., *The Diary and Letters of Rutherford B. Hayes* (Ohio State Archeological and Historical Society, 1922), Diary, October 26, 1891, 4:609.

10. Harry James Brown and Frederick D. Williams, ed., *The Diary of James A. Garfield* (Michigan University Press, 1967), March 30, 1850, 1:38; December 27, 1852, 1:166; January 1, 1854, 1:238; Frederick D. Williams, ed., *The Wild Life of the Army: Civil War Letters of James A. Garfield* (Michigan State University Press, 1964), Garfield to Lucretia Garfield, April 28, 1861, 10–11; January 13, 1862, 60; Garfield to J. Harrison Rhodes, December 31, 1862, 205–6.

11. Harry J. Sievers, *Benjamin Harrison, Hoosier Statesman: From the Civil War to the White House, 1865–1888* (University Publishers, 1959), 105; Harry J. Sievers, *Benjamin Harrison, Hoosier Warrior, 1833–1865* (Henry Regnery, 1952), 245–46.

12. Arthur S. Link, ed., *The Papers of Woodrow Wilson* (Princeton University Press, 1966–1994), A News Report, September 26, 1921, 67:396.

13. Warren G. Harding, *Our Common Country: Mutual Good Will in America* (Bobbs-Merrill, 1921), 15; James D. Richardson, ed., *Supplements to the Messages and Papers of the Presidents, 1921–1925* (Bureau of National Literature, 1925), Inaugural Address of Warren Harding, 1921, 8929–30; Address, November 11, 1921, 9013.

14. Calvin Coolidge, *The Autobiography of Calvin Coolidge* (Cosmopolitan, 1929), 175.

15. Herbert Hoover, *Addresses upon the American Road, 1948–1950* (Stanford University Press, 1951), Our National Policies in this Crisis, December 20, 1950, 210.

16. Frank Kingdon, *As F.D.R. Said: A Treasury of His Speeches, Conversations, and Writings* (Duell, Sloan and Pearce, 1950), 226; Franklin Access to the FDR Library's Digital Collection, "Fully Digitized Collections or Series," Franklin D. Roosevelt Presidential Library and Museum, updated 2011, http://www.fdrlibrary.marist.edu/archives/collections/franklin/, United Nations Flag Day Address, June 14, 1942; Thanksgiving Day Proclamation, November 26, 1942.

17. Franklin Access to the FDR Library's Digital Collection, "Fully Digitized Collections or Series," http://www.fdrlibrary.marist.edu/archives/collections/franklin/, D-Day Prayer, June 6, 1944. For Churchill's acknowledgement of the bound copy of the prayer, see Warren F. Kimball, ed., *Churchill and Roosevelt: The Complete*

Correspondence (Princeton University Press, 1984), Winston Churchill to Franklin Roosevelt, January 11, 1945, 3:507.

18. Harry S. Truman, *Public Papers of the Presidents of the United States, 1945* (Government Printing Office, 1961), Address Before a Joint Session of Congress, April 16, 1945, 6; Robert H. Ferrell, ed., *Off the Record: The Private Papers of Harry S. Truman* (Harper & Row, 1980), Diary, June 1, 1952, 252; William Hillman, ed., *Mr. President: The First Publication from the Personal Diaries, Private Letters, Papers, and Revealing Interviews of Harry S. Truman* (Farrar, Straus & Young, 1952), iii.

19. Alfred D. Chandler et al., eds., *The Papers of Dwight David Eisenhower* (Johns Hopkins University Press, 1970–2001), Eisenhower to Gerald Mygatt, December 28, 1943, 3:1628–29; David L. Holmes, *The Faiths of the Postwar Presidents: Truman to Obama* (University of Georgia Press, 2012), 34.

20. Dwight D. Eisenhower Presidential Library, Museum & Boyhood Home, "Eisenhower Library," National Archives, https://www.eisenhowerlibrary.gov/, Inaugural Address, January 20, 1953; Farewell Address, January 17, 1961; Holmes, *The Faiths of the Postwar Presidents*, 38; Dwight D. Eisenhower, *Public Papers of the Presidents of the United States, 1953* (Government Printing Office, 1960), Remarks Recorded for the American Legion "Back to God" Program, February 1, 1953, 11; Remarks upon Lighting the National Community Christmas Tree, December 24, 1953, 858; Stephen E. Ambrose, *Eisenhower* (Simon & Schuster, 1983–1984), 2:229–30.

21. John F. Kennedy Library & Museum, "Presidential Library and Museum," National Archives, https://www.jfklibrary.org/, Kennedy to the Chambers Children, July 12, 1961; Kennedy to Reverend Cecil E. Berry, September 11, 1961; John F. Kennedy, *Public Papers of the Presidents of the United States, 1963* (Government Printing Office, 1964), Remarks at the 11th Presidential Prayer Breakfast, February 7, 1963, 138–39.

22. Lyndon B. Johnson, *Public Papers of the Presidents of the United States, 1963–1964* (Government Printing Office, 1963–1964), Remarks upon Arrival at Andrews Air Force Base, November 22, 1963, 1; Remarks at the 12th Annual Presidential Prayer Breakfast, February 5, 1964, 261; Remarks to Members of the Southern Baptist Christian Leadership Seminar, March 25, 1964, 420; Lyndon B. Johnson, *Public Papers of the Presidents of the United States, 1968–1969* (Government Printing Office, 1970), Remarks at the Presidential Prayer Breakfast, February 1, 1968, 121–22; Text of the President's Prayer Read at Church Services Attended by the First Family, January 19, 1969, 1368.

23. Holmes, *Faiths of the Postwar Presidents*, 130, 138; Gerald R. Ford, *A Time to Heal: The Autobiography of Gerald R. Ford* (Harper & Row, 1979), 10, 175; Gerald R. Ford, *Public Papers of the Presidents of the United States, 1975* (Government Printing Office, 1977), Remarks at the Annual Congressional Breakfast of the National Religious Broadcasters, January 28, 1975, 117; Gerald R. Ford, *Public Papers of the Presidents of the United States, 1976–1977* (Government Printing Office, 1979), Exchange with Reporters on Arrival at El Paso, April 10, 1976, 1077.

24. Ford, *Public Papers of the Presidents, 1975*, Remarks at the National Prayer Breakfast, January 30, 1975, 131–32; National Historical Publications & Records Commission, "Founders Online," National Archives, last updated July 2024, https://founders.archives.gov/, John Adams to Abigail Adams, November 2, 1800.

25. Wesley G. Pippert, ed., *The Spiritual Journey of Jimmy Carter in His Own Words* (Macmillan, 1978), 8, 10–11.

26. Dan Ariail and Cheryl Heckler-Feltz, *The Carpenter's Apprentice: The Spiritual Biography of Jimmy Carter* (Zondervan, 1996), 86; Jimmy Carter, *Public Papers of the Presidents of the United States, 1980–1981* (Government Printing Office, 1982), Remarks at the National Religious Broadcasters Association Convention, January 21, 1980, 183; Jimmy Carter, *Keeping Faith: Memoirs of a President* (Bantam, 1982), 297; Jimmy Carter, *Sources of Strength: Meditations on Scripture for a Living Faith* (Random House, 1997), 152–53, 232.

27. Ronald Reagan, *An American Life* (Simon & Schuster, 1990), 56; Mary Beth Brown, *Hand of Providence: The Strong and Quiet Faith of Ronald Reagan* (WND Books, 2004), 105, 142; Kiron K. Skinner et al., eds., *Reagan: A Life in Letters* (Free Press, 2003), Reagan to Reverend and Mrs. Ben Cleaver, January 4, 1973, 279.

28. Skinner, *Reagan: A Life*, Reagan to Tommy Thorson, January 15, 1980, 334; Reagan, *An American Life*, 229; Brown, *Hand of Providence*, 15, 28; Ronald Reagan, *Public Papers of the Presidents of the United States, 1983* (Government Printing Office, 1984), Remarks at a Question and Answer Session with Female Leaders of Christian Organizations, October 13, 1983, 1451.

29. Brown, *Hand of Providence*, 127, 146–51.

30. George H. W. Bush, *Public Papers of the Presidents of the United States, 1989* (Washington, DC: Government Printing Office, 1990), Inaugural Address, January 20, 1989, 1; Remarks at the Annual Prayer Breakfast, February 2, 1989, 40–41; George H. W. Bush, *Public Papers of the Presidents of the United States, 1991* (Washington, DC: Government Printing Office, 1992), Remarks at the National Prayer Breakfast, January 31, 1991, 86; Remarks Commemorating the National Day of Thanksgiving, April 7, 1991, 340–41; Remarks at the Annual Southern Baptist Convention, June 6, 1991, 614; Remarks to the Pearl Harbor Survivors Association, Honolulu, December 7, 1991, 1570.

31. George W. Bush, *Decision Points* (Crown Publishers, 2010), 2–3, 33; Barbara Bush, *Barbara Bush: A Memoir* (Charles Scribner's Sons, 1994), 248–49; David Aikman, *A Man of Faith: The Spiritual Journey of George W. Bush* (Thomas Nelson, 2004), 135.

32. Aikman, *A Man of Faith*, 136, 138, 149, 157; George W. Bush, *Public Papers of the Presidents of the United States, 2001* (Government Printing Office, 2003), Remarks at the National Prayer Breakfast, February 1, 2001, 43; Remarks at a National Day of Prayer, May 3, 2001, 485; George W. Bush, *Public Papers of the Presidents of the United States, 2002* (Government Printing Office, 2004), Remarks at a National Day of Prayer Reception, May 2, 2002, 709; Remarks at the National Hispanic Prayer Breakfast, May 16, 2002, 810; George W. Bush, *Public Papers of the Presidents of the*

United States, 2004 (Government Printing Office, 2007), Remarks at the National Prayer Breakfast, February 5, 2004, 183; George W. Bush, *Public Papers of the Presidents of the United States, 2006* (Government Printing Office, 2010), Remarks at the National Prayer Breakfast, February 2, 2006, 172; George W. Bush, *Public Papers of the Presidents of the United States, 2008–2009* (Government Printing Office, 2012), Remarks at the National Prayer Breakfast, February 7, 2008, 156.

33. Barack Obama, *A Promised Land* (Crown Publishers, 2020), 160, 230.

34. Barack Obama, *Papers of the Presidents of the United States, 2010* (Government Printing Office, 2013), Remarks at the National Prayer Breakfast, February 4, 2010, 161–62; Barack Obama, *Papers of the Presidents of the United States, 2011* (Government Printing Office, 2014), Remarks at the National Prayer Breakfast, February 3, 2011, 73, 75; Remarks at an Easter Prayer Breakfast, April 9, 2011, 392.

35. Barack Obama, *Public Papers of the Presidents of the United States, 2012* (Government Printing Office, 2016), Remarks at the National Prayer Breakfast, February 2, 2012, 120–21.

36. Carl E. Prince, ed., *The Papers of William Livingston* (New Jersey Historical Commission, 1979–1988), Proclamation in Congress, March 16, 1776, 1:43–44; Proclamation, January 17, 1777, 1:200; Jeffry H. Morrison, *John Witherspoon and the Founding of the American Republic* (University of Notre Dame Press, 2005), 21, 40; Fitzpatrick, *The Writings of George Washington*, General Orders, November 30, 1777, 10:123; Boyd, *The Papers of Thomas Jefferson*, Proclamation Appointing a Day of Thanksgiving and Prayer, November 11, 1779, 3:177–78; John P. Kaminsky et al., eds, *The Documentary History of the Ratification of the Constitution* (State Historical Society of Wisconsin, 1976–2008), Governor John Hancock: Proclamation for a Day of Public Thanksgiving, October 25, 1787, 4:147; Harry Alonzo Cushing, ed., *The Writings of Samuel Adams* (Octagon, 1968), Proclamation, February 19, 1794, 3:361–62; October 14, 1795, 4:383; Paul F. Boller, *George Washington and Religion* (Southern Methodist University Press, 1963), 62; Harold C. Syrett, ed., *The Papers of Alexander Hamilton* (Columbia University Press, 1961–1979), Draft of a Proclamation by George Washington, January 1, 1795, 18:2–3; Thomas Pickering to Hamilton, March 25, 1798, 21:370n1; Stagg, *Papers of James Madison: Presidential Series*, Presidential Proclamation, July 9, 1812, 4:581–82; Vincent Phillip Munoz, *God and the Founders: Madison, Washington, and Jefferson* (Cambridge University Press, 2009), 42; Marvin Meyers, ed., *The Mind of the Founder: Sources of the Political Thought of James Madison* (Bobbs-Merrill, 1973), Madison to Edward Livingston, July 10, 1822, 432; K. Jack Bauer, *Zachary Taylor: Soldier, Planter, and Statesman of the Old Southwest* (Louisiana State University Press, 1985), 268; Leroy P. Graf and Ralph W. Haskins, eds., *The Papers of Andrew Johnson* (University of Tennessee Press, 1967–2000), Thanksgiving Proclamation, November 7, 1853, 2:185–86.

37. Basler, *The Collected Works of Abraham Lincoln*, Proclamation of a National Fast Day, August 12, 1861, 4:482; Proclamation of Thanksgiving for Victories, April 10, 1862, 5:185.

38. Basler, *The Collected Works of Abraham Lincoln*, Proclamation Appointing a National Fast Day, March 30, 1863, 6:155–56; Proclamation of Thanksgiving, July 15, 1863, 6:332; Proclamation of Thanksgiving, October 3, 1863, 6:496–97; Proclamation of a Day of Prayer, July 7, 1864, 7:431–432; Proclamation of Thanksgiving and Prayer, September 3, 1864, 7:533–34; Proclamation of Thanksgiving, October 20, 1864, 8:55–56; Last Public Address, April 11, 1865, 8:400.

39. Graf and Haskins, *The Papers of Andrew Johnson*, Proclamation for Day of Humiliation and Mourning, April 25, 1865, 7:641.

40. Simon, *The Papers of Ulysses S. Grant*, Proclamation, June 26, 1876, 27:156.

41. Chester A. Arthur, *The State Papers of Chester A. Arthur* (Government Printing Office, 1885), Proclamation Concerning the Death of President Garfield, September 22, 1881, 15; George F. Parker, ed., *The Writings and Speeches of Grover Cleveland* (Cassell, 1892), Proclamation of the Governor of New York, October 29, 1883, 526; November 8, 1884, 527.

42. Link, *The Papers of Woodrow Wilson*, A Proclamation, September 8, 1914, 31:10–11; A Proclamation, May 11, 1918, 47:599; A Thanksgiving Proclamation, November 16, 1918, 53:95–96; Richardson, *Supplements to the Messages and Papers of the Presidents, 1921–1925*, A Proclamation, August 24, 1923, 9321.

43. Franklin Access to the FDR Library's Digital Collection, "Fully Digitized Collections or Series," http://www.fdrlibrary.marist.edu/archives/collections/franklin/, D-Day Prayer, June 6, 1944.

44. Harry S. Truman Library & Museum, "Welcome to the Harry S. Truman Presidential Library and Museum," National Archives, https://www.trumanlibrary.gov/, Annual Passover Service, March 26, 1945; Speech in Providence, April 15, 1945; Truman, *Public Papers of the Presidents of the United States, 1945*, News Conference on V-E Day, May 8, 1945, 49; Proclamation 2660: Victory in the East—Day of Prayer, August 16, 1945, 223; Harry S. Truman, *Public Papers of the Presidents of the United States, 1950* (Washington, DC: Government Printing Office, 1965), Address at the Lighting of the National Community Christmas Tree on the White House Grounds, December 24, 1950, 760; George S. Caldwell, ed., *The Wit and Wisdom of Harry S. Truman* (New York: Stein and Day, 1966), 94.

45. Dwight D. Eisenhower Presidential Library, Museum & Boyhood Home, "Eisenhower Library," National Archives, https://www.eisenhowerlibrary.gov/, Order of the Day, June 6, 1944; Chandler, *The Papers of Dwight David Eisenhower*, Eisenhower to Cardinal Francis Spellman, July 8, 1953, 14:376–77; Dwight D. Eisenhower, *Public Papers of the Presidents of the United States, 1955* (Government Printing Office, 1959), Remarks Recorded for the "Back to God" Program of the American Legion, February 20, 1955, 274.

46. Lawrence H. Fuchs, *John F. Kennedy and American Catholicism* (Meredith Press, 1967), 210.

47. Johnson, *Public Papers of the Presidents of the United States, 1963–1964*, Proclamation on National Day of Mourning for President Kennedy, November 23, 1963, 2; The President's Thanksgiving Address to the Nation, November 28, 1963, 11–12;

Richard M. Nixon, *Public Papers of the Presidents of the United States, 1970* (Washington, DC: Government Printing Office, 1971), Remarks at a Special Church Service in Honolulu, April 19, 1970, 370.

48. Gerald R. Ford, *Public Papers of the Presidents of the United States, 1974* (Government Printing Office, 1975), Remarks on Taking the Oath of Office, August 9, 1974, 1.

49. Jimmy Carter, *Public Papers of the Presidents of the United States, 1977* (Government Printing Office, 1978), Prayer for Peace, April 25, 1977, 716; Jimmy Carter, *Public Papers of the Presidents of the United States, 1978* (Government Printing Office, 1979), Prayer for Peace, May 19, 1978, 931; Carter, *Keeping Faith*, 331; Jimmy Carter, *Public Papers of the Presidents of the United States, 1979* (Government Printing Office, 1980), Joint Statement of Carter, Begin, and Sadat, March 25, 1979, 490–91; White House Statement on American Hostages in Iran, November 17, 1979, 2141; Ronald Reagan, *Public Papers of the Presidents of the United States, 1981* (Government Printing Office, 1982), Remarks on Signing a Resolution Proclaiming a Day of Thanksgiving for the Freed American Hostages, January 26, 1981, 39.

50. Bush, *Public Papers of the Presidents, 1991*, Remarks at the National Prayer Breakfast, January 31, 1991, 86; Address on the National Day of Thanksgiving, March 22, 1991, 298.

51. Bush, *Public Papers of the Presidents, 2001*, Address to the Nation on the Terrorist Attacks, September 11, 2001, 1100.

52. Simon, *The Papers of Ulysses S. Grant*, Grant to Julia Dent, September 1847, 1:148; John Bassett Moore, ed., *The Works of James Buchanan* (J. B. Lippincott, 1908–1911; repr., Antiquarian Press, 1960), Buchanan to Harriet Lane, November 4, 1851, 8:423; August 26, 1853, 9:38; J. Philipp Rosenberg, "Dwight D. Eisenhower and the Foreign Policymaking Process," in *Dwight D. Eisenhower: Soldier, President, Statesman*, ed. Joann P. Krieg (Greenwood, 1987), 119; Harry S. Truman, *Memoirs* (Doubleday, 1955–1956), 1:19; George H. W. Bush Presidential Library & Museum, "Archives and Research," National Archives, https://bush41library.tamu.edu/, Advice to Young People, April 23, 2003.

Chapter 6

1. Julian P. Boyd, ed., *The Papers of Thomas Jefferson* (Princeton University Press, 1950), Declaration of Independence, July 4, 1776, 1:429.

2. Maryanne Cline Horowitz, "The Stoic Synthesis of the Idea of Natural Law in Man: Four Themes," *Journal of the History of Ideas* 35 (January–March 1974): 6, 9–10, 12–15.

3. Augustine, *On Free Choice of the Will*, trans. Anna S. Benjamin and L. H. Hackstaff (Bobbs-Merrill, 1964), 49, 155.

4. Thomas Aquinas, *Summa Theologica*, trans. the Fathers of the English Dominican Province (Benziger Brothers, 1947), 1:398–99, 422–23, 851, 989; Alister McGrath, *The Intellectual Origins of the European Reformation* (Basil Blackwell, 1987),

140; John Dillenberger, ed., *Martin Luther: Selections from His Writings*, Preface to the Epistle of St. Paul to the Romans, 1522, 20; John Calvin, *Institutes of the Christian Religion*, trans. Henry Beveridge (Eerdmans, 1970), 1:64, 72; William J. Bouwsma, *John Calvin: A Sixteenth-Century Portrait* (Oxford University Press, 1988), 139, 142, 147–48, 155.

5. Paul K. Conkin, *Self-Evident Truths* (Indiana University Press, 1974), 92, 95; Paul A. Rahe, *Republics, Ancient and Modern: Classical Republicanism and the American Revolution* (University of North Carolina Press, 1992), 509.

6. Adrienne Koch and William Peden, eds., *The Selected Writings of John and John Quincy Adams* (Alfred A. Knopf, 1946), Dissertation on the Canon and the Feudal Law, 1765, 18, 22; Boyd, *The Papers of Thomas Jefferson*, Declaration of the Causes and Necessity for Taking Up Arms, June–July 1775, 1:202.

7. Boyd, *The Papers of Thomas Jefferson*, Jefferson to Tench Coxe, June 1, 1795, 28:373.

8. Harold D. Moser et al., eds., *The Papers of Andrew Jackson* (University of Tennessee Press, 1980), Jackson to the 2nd Division, March 7, 1812, 2:292.

9. Charles Francis Adams, ed., *Memoirs of John Quincy Adams, Comprising Portions of His Diary from 1795 to 1848* (n.p., 1874–1877; repr., AMS, 1970), March 3, 1820, 5:7; Roy P. Basler, ed., *The Collected Works of Abraham Lincoln* (Rutgers University Press, 1953–1955), Speech at New Haven, Connecticut, March 6, 1860, 4:16.

10. John Bassett Moore, ed., *The Works of James Buchanan* (J. B. Lippincott, 1908–1911; repr., Antiquarian Press, 1960), Remarks in Reply to Mr. Davis on the Independent Treasury Bill, March 3, 1840, 4:205.

11. Arthur S. Link, ed., *The Papers of Woodrow Wilson* (Princeton University Press, 1966–1994), An Address in Denver on the Bible, May 7, 1911, 23:15.

12. James D. Richardson, ed., *Supplements to the Messages and Papers of the Presidents, 1921–1925* (Bureau of National Literature, 1925) President Harding's Opening Address at the Conference on the Limitation of Armament, November 12, 1921, 9042.

13. Herbert Hoover, *The Challenge to Liberty* (Charles Scribner's Sons, 1934), 3–4, 205; Herbert Hoover, *Addresses upon the American Road, 1940–1941* (Charles Scribner's Sons, 1941), Republican National Convention, June 25, 1940, 223; Herbert Hoover, *Addresses upon the American Road, 1945–1948* (Van Nostrand, 1949), The Meaning of America, August 10, 1948, 79.

14. The U.S. National and Records Administration, "Declaration 250 National Archives," National Archives, https://www.archives.gov/, President Roosevelt's Annual Message to Congress, January 6, 1941; Franklin Access to the FDR Library's Digital Collection, "Fully Digitized Collections or Series," Franklin D. Roosevelt Presidential Library and Museum, updated 2011, http://www.fdrlibrary.marist.edu/archives/collections/franklin/, State of the Union Address, January 6, 1942.

15. Harry S. Truman, "America Has Enough of Everything—But Faith," Harry S. Truman Library & Museum, *Reader's Digest*, published November 1943, https://

www.trumanlibrary.gov/library/truman-papers/draft-file-1935-1945/november-1943 -america-has-enough-everything-faith-0?documentid=NA&pagenumber=1; Harry S. Truman, *Public Papers of the Presidents of the United States, 1946* (Government Printing Office, 1962), Address to the Federal Council of Churches, March 6, 1946, 141; Harry S. Truman, *Public Papers of the Presidents of the United States, 1948* (Government Printing Office, 1964), State of the Union Message, January 7, 1948, 2.

16. Harry S. Truman, *Public Papers of the Presidents of the United States, 1950* (Government Printing Office, 1965), Address Before the Attorney Generals' Conference on Law Enforcement Problems, February 15, 1950, 157; Address in Independence at the Dedication of the Liberty Bell Replica, November 6, 1950, 706; Harry S. Truman, *Public Papers of the Presidents of the United States, 1951* (Government Printing Office, 1965), Address at the Cornerstone Laying of the New York Avenue Presbyterian Church, April 3, 1951, 211; Address at the Dedication of the National Institutes of Health Clinical Center, June 22, 1951, 350.

17. Dwight D. Eisenhower Presidential Library, Museum & Boyhood Home, "Eisenhower Library," National Archives, https://www.eisenhowerlibrary.gov/, Inaugural Address, January 20, 1953; Dwight D. Eisenhower, *The Public Papers of the Presidents of the United States, 1953* (Washington, DC: Government Printing Office, 1960), Remarks for the American Legion "Back to God" Program, February 1, 1953, 11; Dwight D. Eisenhower, *Public Papers of the Presidents of the United States, 1954* (Washington, DC: Government Printing House, 1960), Radio and Television Address to the American People on the State of the Union, April 5, 1954, 373; Dwight D. Eisenhower, *Public Papers of the Presidents of the United States, 1955* (Washington, DC: Government Printing Office, 1959), Annual Message to the Congress on the State of the Union, January 6, 1955, 7–8.

18. John F. Kennedy, *Public Papers of the Presidents of the United States, 1961* (Government Printing Office, 1962), Inaugural Address, January 20, 1961, 1; Remarks to the Trustees of the Union of American Hebrew Congregations, November 13, 1961, 716; John F. Kennedy, *Public Papers of the Presidents of the United States, 1962* (Government Printing Office, 1963), Remarks at the Tenth Annual Presidential Prayer Breakfast, March 1, 1962, 175.

19. Gerald R. Ford, *Public Papers of the Presidents of the United States, 1976–1977* (Government Printing Office, 1979), Remarks at the Bicentennial Celebration at the National Archives, July 2, 1976, 1956; Remarks at the Conclusion of the International Eucharistic Conference, August 8, 1976, 2138; Remarks at the Yeshiva at Flatbush High School in Brooklyn, October 12, 1976, 2489.

20. Jimmy Carter, *Public Papers of the Presidents of the United States, 1977* (Government Printing Office, 1978), Remarks at the Meeting of the General Council of World Jewish Congress, November 2, 1977, 1953; Dan Ariail and Cheryl Heckler-Feltz, *The Carpenter's Apprentice: The Spiritual Biography of Jimmy Carter* (Zondervan, 1996), 73–74.

21. Ronald Reagan, *Public Papers of the Presidents of the United States, 1982* (Government Printing Office, 1983), Remarks Following a Meeting with Pope John Paul II

in Vatican City, June 7, 1982, 737; Ronald Reagan, *Public Papers of the Presidents of the United States, 1985* (Government Printing Office, 1988), Remarks at a Conference on Religious Liberty, April 16, 1985, 437–38.

22. Kiron K. Skinner et al., eds., *Reagan: A Life in Letters* (Free Press, 2003), Reagan to Robert L. Mauro, October 11, 1979, 198; Ronald Reagan, *Public Papers of the Presidents of the United States, 1984* (Government Printing Office, 1986), Remarks at the Annual Convention of the National Religious Broadcasters, January 30, 1984, 119; Ronald Reagan, *Public Papers of the Presidents of the United States, 1986* (Government Printing Office, 1988), Remarks by Telephone to the Annual Convention of the Knights of Columbus, August 5, 1986, 1056; Ronald Reagan, *Public Papers of the Presidents of the United States, 1987* (Government Printing Office, 1989), Mother's Day Proclamation, April 28, 1987, 422.

23. Skinner, *Reagan: A Life*, Reagan to Johnson [first name unknown], January 1967, 199–200.

24. Reagan, *Public Papers of the Presidents, 1984*, Remarks at the Annual Convention of the National Association of Evangelicals, March 6, 1984, 307; Ronald Reagan, *Public Papers of the Presidents of the United States, 1988–1989* (Government Printing Office, 1990), Remarks at the Annual Leadership Conference of the American Legion, February 29, 1988, 274.

25. George H. W. Bush, *Public Papers of the Presidents of the United States, 1990* (Government Printing Office, 1991), Remarks at the Annual Convention of the National Religious Broadcasters, January 29, 1990, 123.

26. George W. Bush, *Decision Points* (Crown Publishers, 2010), 397; George W. Bush, *Public Papers of the Presidents of the United States, 2001* (Government Printing Office, 2003), Address Before a Joint Session of Congress on the United States Response to the Terrorist Attacks of September 11, September 20, 2001, 1144; George W. Bush, *Public Papers of the Presidents of the United States, 2002* (Government Printing Office, 2004), Remarks to the Armed Forces at Elgin Air Force Base in Fort Walton Beach, Florida, February 4, 2002, 172; Remarks on Humanitarian Aid to Afghanistan, October 11, 2002, 1783; George W. Bush, *Public Papers of the Presidents of the United States, 2004* (Government Printing Office, 2007), Remarks on Efforts to Globally Promote Women's Human Rights, March 12, 2004, 375; George W. Bush, *Public Papers of the Presidents of the United States, 2005* (Government Printing Office, 2009), Remarks at the National Republican Congressional Committee Dinner, March 15, 2005, 439–40.

27. Bush, *Public Papers of the Presidents, 2001*, Statement to Participants in the March for Life, January 22, 2001, 9; Memorandum on the Restoration of the Mexican City Policy, January 22, 2001, 10; Address to the Nation on Stem Cell Research, August 9, 2001, 955–56; George W. Bush, *Public Papers of the Presidents of the United States, 2003* (Government Printing Office, 2006), Statement on the Senate Passage of Partial-Birth Abortion Legislation, October 22, 2003, 1380; Bush, *Decision Points*, 118; George W. Bush, *Public Papers of the Presidents of the United States, 2006*

(Government Printing Office, 2010), Telephone Remarks to the March for Life, January 23, 2006, 101.

28. Jimmy Carter, "Interview on NBC's 'Meet the Press' with Jimmy Carter," July 11, 1976, The American Presidency Project, https://www.presidency.ucsb.edu/documents/interview-nbcs-meet-the-press; Caitlyn Flanagan, "Losing the Rare in 'Safe, Legal, and Rare,'" *The Atlantic*, December 6, 2019, https://www.theatlantic.com/ideas/archive/2019/12/the-brilliance-of-safe-legal-and-rare/603151/; Sarakshi Rai, "Obama Denounces 'Devastating' Abortion Ruling," *The Hill*, June 24, 2022, https://thehill.com/blogs/blog-briefing-room/3535819-obama-denounces-devastating-abortion-ruling/; Ruby Cramer, "'A Private Matter': Joe Biden's Very Public Clash with His Own Church," *Politico*, September 5, 2021, https://www.politico.com/news/magazine/2021/09/05/joe-biden-catholic-church-509396; Kate Steinmetz, "See Obama's 20-Year Evolution on LGBT Rights," *Time*, April 10, 2015, https://time.com/3816952/obama-gay-lesbian-transgender-lgbt-rights/; "Robin Roberts ABC News Interview with President Obama," May 9, 2012, ABC News, https://abcnews.go.com/Politics/transcript-robin-roberts-abc-news-interview-president-obama/story?id=16316043; Maureen E. McCarty, "President Clinton Urges End to DOMA in WaPo Op-Ed," HCR, March 7, 2013, hrc.org; Ryan Buxton, "Jimmy Carter Says Jesus Would Approve of Gay Marriage," *Huffpost*, July 7, 2015, https://www.huffpost.com/entry/jimmy-carter-gay-marriage_n_7744390.

29. Barack Obama, *Papers of the Presidents of the United States, 2011* (Government Printing Office, 2014), Remarks to the British Parliament, May 25, 2011, 603.

30. Henry Chadwick, *The Early Church* (Penguin, 1969), 58–59.

31. Chadwick, *The Early Church*, 59–60.

32. David Brion Davis, *Challenging the Boundaries of Slavery* (Harvard University Press, 2003), 10, 25.

33. Stanislaus Murray Hamilton, ed., *The Writings of James Monroe* (AMS, 1969), To the Speakers of the House of Delegates and the Senate, December 7, 1801, 3:304.

34. Calvin Coolidge Presidential Foundation, "The Inspiration of the Declaration of Independence, July 5, 1926," Coolidge Foundation, published April 23, 2014, https://coolidgefoundation.org/resources/inspiration-of-the-declaration-of-independence/.

35. For reference to the manumission of slaves throughout the South, see Edmund S. Morgan, "The Puritan Ethic and the American Revolution," *William and Mary Quarterly* 24 (January 1967): 23.

36. William Peden, ed., *Notes on the State of Virginia* (University of North Carolina Press, 1955), 138–43, 162; Daniel Boorstin, *The Lost World of Thomas Jefferson* (Henry Holt, 1948), 73–74; Charles B. Sanford, *The Religious Life of Thomas Jefferson* (University Press of Virginia, 1984), 98.

37. Albert Ellery Bergh and Andrew A. Lipscomb, eds., *The Writings of Thomas Jefferson* (Thomas Jefferson Memorial Association, 1904), Jefferson to Henri Gregoire, February 25, 1809, 12:255; Sanford, *The Religious Life of Thomas Jefferson*, 70.

38. Gordon S. Wood, *Revolutionary Characters: What Made the Founders Different* (Penguin, 2006), 39–40.

39. Allan Nevins, ed., *The Diary of John Quincy Adams, 1794–1845: American Diplomacy and Political, Social, and Intellectual Life from Washington to Polk* (Charles Scribner's Sons, 1951), May 29, 1841, 519; Adams, *Memoirs of John Quincy Adams*, November 19, 1841, 11:29.

40. Koch and Peden, *The Selected Writings of John and John Quincy Adams*, To the Citizens of Bangor, Maine, July 4, 1843, 408.

41. Basler, *The Collected Works of Abraham Lincoln*, Speech at Chicago, July 10, 1858, 2:501; Speech at Lewistown, Illinois, August 17, 1858, 2:546–47.

42. Ulysses S. Grant, *Personal Memoirs of U.S. Grant* (Charles L. Webster, 1885–1886), 2:217–18, 550; John Y. Simon, ed., *The Papers of Ulysses S. Grant* (Southern Illinois University Press, 1967–2012), Proclamation, October 12, 1871, 22:162; Proclamation, October 17, 1871, 22:176–78; *New York Times*, January 15, 1880, 30:117n; Ron Chernow, *Grant* (Penguin, 2017), 795.

43. Louis D. Rubin, Jr., ed., *Teach the Freeman: The Correspondence of Rutherford B. Hayes and the Slater Fund for Negro Education, 1881–1893* (Louisiana State University Press, 1959), Introduction, 1:xiv, xxxii; T. Harry Williams, ed., *Hayes: The Diary of a President, 1875–1881* (David McKay, 1964), July 25, 1880, 289; Charles Richard Williams, ed., *The Diary and Letters of Rutherford B. Hayes* (Ohio State Archaeological Historical Society, 1922), December 15, 1890, 6:623; Harry James Brown and Frederick D. Williams, eds., *The Diary of James A. Garfield* (Michigan State University Press, 1967), November 2, 1855, 1:273.

44. Elting E. Morison, ed., *The Letters of Theodore Roosevelt* (Harvard University Press, 1951–1954), Roosevelt to Albion Winegar Tourgée, November 9, 1901, 3:190–91.

45. Pope Pius XII and Franklin D. Roosevelt, *Wartime Correspondence Between President Roosevelt and Pope Pius XII* (Macmillan, 1947), Roosevelt to Pope Pius XII, December 23, 1939, 18; Franklin Access to the FDR Library's Digital Collection, "Fully Digitized Collections or Series," http://www.fdrlibrary.marist.edu/archives/collections/franklin/, State of the Union Address, January 6, 1942; Frank Kingdon, *As F.D.R. Said: A Treasury of His Speeches, Conversations, and Writings* (Duell, Sloan and Pearce, 1950), 155.

46. Truman, *Public Papers of the Presidents, 1948*, Special Message to Congress on Civil Rights, February 2, 1948, 121; Address in Buffalo, October 8, 1948, 720; Harry S. Truman, *Mr. Citizen* (Random House, 1960), 140; Robert H. Ferrell, *Harry S. Truman: A Life* (University of Missouri Press, 1994), 295.

47. Michael S. Mayer, "Regardless of Station, Race, or Calling: Eisenhower and Race," in Joann P. Krieg, ed., *Dwight D. Eisenhower: Soldier, President, Statesman* (Greenwood, 1987), 34; Editor's Note, 13:1133n1; Eisenhower, *Public Papers of the Presidents of the United States, 1953*, Remarks at a Luncheon Meeting of the General Board of the National Council of Churches, November 18, 1953, 793; Dwight D. Eisenhower, *Waging Peace, 1956–1961* (Doubleday, 1965), 150; Eisenhower, *Public*

Papers of the Presidents, 1954, Remarks in Indianapolis at the Colombia Republican Club, October 15, 1954, 904; Eisenhower, *Public Papers of the Presidents, 1955*, Remarks at a Dinner Sponsored by the District of Columbia Republican Women's Finance Committee, May 23, 1955, 525; Stephen E. Ambrose, *Eisenhower* (Simon & Schuster, 1983–1984), 2:126.

48. Alfred D. Chandler et al., eds., *The Papers of Dwight David Eisenhower* (Johns Hopkins University Press, 1970–2001), Eisenhower to William Franklin Graham, March 22, 1956, 16:2086; March 30, 1956, 16:2105n2; Dwight D. Eisenhower, *Public Papers of the Presidents of the United States, 1957* (Government Printing Office, 1958), News Conference, October 3, 1957, 713; Dwight D. Eisenhower, *Public Papers of the Presidents of the United States, 1960–1961* (Government Printing Office, 1961), Remarks at the Pageant of Peace, December 23, 1960, 884.

49. John F. Kennedy, *Public Papers of the Presidents of the United States, 1963* (Government Printing Office, 1964), Special Message to the Congress on Civil Rights and Job Opportunities, June 19, 1963, 493; Remarks at Dinner Given in His Honor by President Segni, July 1, 1963, 549.

50. Lyndon B. Johnson, *Public Papers of the Presidents of the United States, 1963–1964* (Government Printing Office, 1965), The President's Thanksgiving Address to the Nation, November 28, 1963, 12; Radio and Television Remarks upon Signing the Civil Rights Bill, July 2, 1964, 843.

51. Ariail and Heckler-Feltz, *The Carpenter's Apprentice*, 65.

52. Barack Obama, *Public Papers of the Presidents of the United States, 2009* (Government Printing Office, 2013), Inaugural Address, January 20, 2009, 1.

53. Johnson, *Public Papers of the Presidents of the United States, 1963–1964*, Remarks at a Reception for Recently Appointed Women in Government, April 13, 1964, 460.

54. Jimmy Carter, *Public Papers of the Presidents of the United States, 1979* (Government Printing Office, 1980), Remarks at a Town Meeting in Elk City, Oklahoma, March 24, 1979, 473; Jimmy Carter, *Sources of Strength: Meditations on Scripture for a Living Faith* (Random House, 1997), 129; David L. Holmes, *The Faiths of the Postwar Presidents: Truman to Obama* (University of Georgia Press, 2012), 168–69.

55. Robert V. Remini, *Andrew Jackson and the Course of American Democracy, 1833–1845* (Harper & Row, 1984), 51; Leroy P. Graf and Ralph W. Haskins, eds., *The Papers of Andrew Johnson* (University of Tennessee Press, 1967–2000), Speech on the Gag Resolution, January 31, 1844, 1:136; Speech at Bristol, May 29, 1859, 3:277; Speech on Harper's Ferry Incident, December 12, 1859, 3:329; Veto of Civil Rights Bill, March 27, 1866, 10:312–22; Interview with Paschal B. Randolph, July 21, 1866, 10:711; Chernow, *Grant*, 550; Link, *The Papers of Woodrow Wilson*, Wilson to Ellen Louise Axson, December 11, 1884, 3:532; Remarks by Wilson and a Dialogue, November 12, 1914, 31:303; Andrew Sinclair, *The Available Man: The Life Behind the Masks of Warren Gamaliel Harding* (Macmillan, 1965), 230–32.

Chapter 7

1. Ellis Sandoz, *A Government of Laws: Political Theory, Religion, and the American Founding* (Louisiana State University Press, 1990), 113; W. W. Abbot, ed., *The Papers of George Washington: Presidential Series* (University Press of Virginia, 1987), To the Savannah Hebrew Congregation, May 1790, 5:448–49.

2. Gordon S. Wood, *The Radicalism of the American Revolution* (Alfred A. Knopf, 1992), 191; Gordon S. Wood, *Revolutionary Characters: What Made the Founders Great* (Penguin, 2006), 179.

3. John Bassett Moore, ed., *The Works of James Buchanan* (J. B. Lippincott, 1908–1911; repr., Antiquarian Press, 1960), Speech Before the Pennsylvania State Democratic Convention at Lancaster, August 5, 1840, 4:303–4; Inaugural Address, March 4, 1857, 10:109–10.

4. Roy P. Basler, ed., *The Collected Works of Abraham Lincoln* (Rutgers University Press, 1953–1955), Address to the New Jersey Senate, February 21, 1861, 4:236.

5. Leroy P. Graf and Ralph W. Haskins, eds., *The Papers of Andrew Johnson* (University of Tennessee Press, 1967–2000), Speech at Nashville Flag Ceremony, November 6, 1864, 7:269; Johnson to David Wills, July 3, 1865, 8:344.

6. George F. Parker, ed., *The Writings and Speeches of Grover Cleveland* (Cassell, 1892), Fourth Annual Message to Congress, December 1888, 97.

7. Arthur S. Link, ed., *The Papers of Woodrow Wilson* (Princeton University Press, 1966–1994), An Address in Jersey City, May 25, 1912, 24:443; An Address at the Gettysburg Battlefield, July 4, 1913, 28:26.

8. Francis Russell, *The Shadow of Blooming Grove: Warren G. Harding in His Times* (McGraw-Hill, 1968), 160–61; Frederick Schortemeier, ed., *Rededicating America: The Life and Recent Speeches of Warren G. Harding* (Bobbs-Merrill, 1920), Washington Day Address, February 22, 1918, 144; James D. Richardson, ed., *Supplements to the Messages and Papers of the Presidents, 1921–1925* (Bureau of National Literature, 1925), Inaugural Address of Warren Harding, 1921, 8929.

9. Herbert Hoover, *Addresses upon the American Road, 1950–1955* (Stanford University Press, 1955), Address at the Republican National Convention, July 8, 1952, 65; Maxwell Meyersohn, ed., *The Wit and Wisdom of Franklin D. Roosevelt* (Beacon Press, 1950), Address on the Fiftieth Anniversary of the Statue of Liberty, October 28, 1936, 127.

10. Harry S. Truman, *Public Papers of the Presidents of the United States, 1945* (Government Printing Office, 1961), Fourth of July Statement, July 4, 1945, 157; Harry S. Truman, *Public Papers of the Presidents of the United States, 1948* (Government Printing Office, 1964), Informal Remarks in Nebraska, June 5, 1948, 292; Harry S. Truman, *Public Papers of the Presidents of the United States, 1949* (Government Printing Office, 1964), Radio and Television Report to the American People on the State of the National Economy, July 13, 1949, 375; Harry S. Truman, *Public Papers of the Presidents of the United States, 1951* (Government Printing Office, 1965), Address

at the Cornerstone Laying at the New York Avenue Presbyterian Church, April 3, 1951, 212–13.

11. Dwight D. Eisenhower, *Public Papers of the Presidents of the United States, 1954* (Government Printing House, 1960), Remarks Recorded for Program Marking the 75th Anniversary of the Incandescent Lamp, October 24, 1954, 948.

12. Lyndon B. Johnson, *Public Papers of the Presidents of the United States, 1963–1964* (Government Printing Office, 1965), Remarks in Boston at Post Office Square, October 27, 1964, 1468.

13. Jimmy Carter, *Public Papers of the Presidents of the United States, 1980–1981* (Government Printing Office, 1982), Remarks at a White House Reception for Black Ministers, October 23, 1980, 2428.

14. Kiron K. Skinner et al., eds., *Reagan: A Life in Letters* (Free Press, 2003), Editor's Note, 256; Ronald Reagan, *An American Life* (Simon & Schuster, 1990), 299; Mary Beth Brown, *Hand of Providence: The Strong and Quiet Faith of Ronald Reagan* (WND Books, 2004), 167; Ronald Reagan, *Public Papers of the Presidents of the United States, 1982* (Government Printing Office, 1983), Remarks at a Swearing-In Ceremony for New United States Citizens, White House Station, New Jersey, September 17, 1982, 1178; Proclamation 4979, September 27, 1982, 1221; Ronald Reagan, *Public Papers of the Presidents of the United States, 1983* (Government Printing Office, 1984), Remarks at the Annual Convention of the National Religious Broadcasters, January 31, 1983, 152; Ronald Reagan, *Public Papers of the Presidents of the United States, 1988–1989* (Government Printing Office, 1990), Farewell Address, January 11, 1989, 1727.

15. John P. Kaminsky et al., eds., *The Documentary History of the Ratification of the Constitution* (The State Historical Society of Wisconsin, 1976–2008), George Washington to the Executives of the States, *United States Chronicle*, March 1783, 13:62–63.

16. Julian P. Boyd, ed., *The Papers of Thomas Jefferson* (Princeton University Press, 1950), First Inaugural Address, March 4, 1801, 33:150; Albert Ellery Bergh and Andrew A. Lipscomb, eds., *The Writings of Thomas Jefferson* (Thomas Jefferson Memorial Association, 1904), Second Inaugural Address, 1805, 17:iv; Stanislaus Murray Hamilton, ed., *The Writings of James Monroe* (AMS, 1969), To the Speakers of the House of Delegates and the Senate, December 7, 1801, 3:304.

17. John Spencer Bassett, ed., *Correspondence of Andrew Jackson* (Carnegie Institution, 1926–1935), Jackson to L. H. Coleman, April 26, 1824, 3:250; Moore, *The Works of James Buchanan*, Andrew Jackson to Buchanan, October 16, 1826, 1:218; Remarks on Duties on Coal, February 24, 1837, 3:227; Harold D. Moser et al., eds., *The Papers of Andrew Jackson* (University of Tennessee Press, 1980), First Annual Message to Congress, December 8, 1829, 7:601–2.

18. Moore, *The Works of James Buchanan*, Third Annual Message to Congress, December 19, 1859, 10:339; Mr. Buchanan's Return to Wheatland, March 6, 1861, 11:162.

19. Roy P. Basler, *The Collected Works of Abraham Lincoln: Supplement* (Greenwood Press, 1974), First Inaugural Address, March 4, 1861, 4:271; Annual Message to Congress, December 6, 1864, 8:141.

20. William McKinley, *Speeches and Addresses of William McKinley from His Election to Congress to the Present Time* (D. Appleton, 1893), Speech at the Columbian Celebration in Chicago, October 22, 1892, 631; William McKinley, *Speeches and Addresses of William McKinley from March 1, 1897 to May 30, 1900* (Doubleday & McClure, 1900), Speech at Carroll, Ohio, October 11, 1898, 96.

21. Theodore Roosevelt, *The Works of Theodore Roosevelt* (Charles Scribner's Sons, 1925), Inaugural Address, March 4, 1905, 17:311.

22. Link, *The Papers of Woodrow Wilson*, A Thanksgiving Day Address, November 24, 1910, 22:90.

23. Schortemeier, *Rededicating America*, Address to the Builders Exchange in Cleveland, no date given, 241.

24. Franklin Access to the FDR Library's Digital Collection, "Fully Digitized Collections or Series," Franklin D. Roosevelt Presidential Library and Museum, updated 2011, http://www.fdrlibrary.marist.edu/archives/collections/franklin/, Fourth Inaugural Address, January 20, 1945.

25. Harry S. Truman, *Public Papers of the Presidents of the United States, 1946* (Government Printing Office, 1962), Address at the Dedication of the Home of Franklin D. Roosevelt as a National Shrine, April 12, 1946, 199; George S. Caldwell, ed., *The Wit and Wisdom of Harry S. Truman* (Stein and Day, 1966), Thanksgiving Proclamation, October 20, 1950, 94; Truman, *Public Papers of the Presidents of the United States, 1951*, Address to the Washington Pilgrimage of American Churchmen, September 28, 1951, 547.

26. Dwight D. Eisenhower, *Public Papers of the Presidents of the United States, 1956* (Government Printing Office, 1958), Radio and Television Address Opening the President's Campaign for Reelection, September 19, 1956, 780.

27. Johnson, *Public Papers of the Presidents, 1963–1964*, Remarks in Austin at the Dedication of the Agudas Achim Synagogue, December 30, 1963, 102; Remarks to the National Congress of American Indians, January 20, 1964, 151.

28. Gerald R. Ford, *Public Papers of the Presidents of the United States, 1976–1977* (Government Printing Office, 1979), Remarks at the Combined Convention of the National Religious Broadcasters and the National Association of Evangelicals, February 22, 1976, 413; Remarks at the Centennial Safe Opening at the Capitol, July 1, 1776, 1942.

29. Jimmy Carter, *Public Papers of the Presidents of the United States, 1977* (Government Printing Office, 1978), Thanksgiving Address, November 23, 1977, 2049; Remarks at the Meeting of the Business Council, December 14, 1977, 2110; Jimmy Carter, *Public Papers of the Presidents of the United States, 1978* (Government Printing Office, 1979), Remarks at Dinner for Newly Elected Members of Congress, December 6, 1978, 2168; Jimmy Carter, *Public Papers of the Presidents of the United States, 1979*

(Government Printing Office, 1980), Remarks at Wabash, Minnesota, August 18, 1979, 1468.

30. Ronald Reagan, *Public Papers of the Presidents of the United States, 1981* (Government Printing Office, 1982), Proclamation, National Day of Prayer, March 19, 1981, 268; Reagan, *Public Papers of the Presidents of the United States, 1982*, Proclamation 4979, September 27, 1982, 1221.

31. William J. Clinton, *Public Papers of the Presidents of the United States, 1996* (Government Printing Office, 1997), Remarks at a Democratic Leadership Council Luncheon, December 11, 1996, 2191; George W. Bush, *Public Papers of the Presidents of the United States, 2001* (Government Printing Office, 2003), Remarks at an Independence Day Celebration in Philadelphia, July 4, 2001, 826.

32. W. W. Abbot, ed., *The Papers of George Washington: Revolutionary War Series* (University Press of Virginia, 1985), Address to the Massachusetts General Court, April 1, 1776, 4:9; John C. Fitzpatrick, ed., *The Writings of George Washington* (Government Printing Office, 1931–1940), General Orders, October 18, 1777, 9:391.

33. Fitzpatrick, *The Writings of George Washington*, Washington to Landon Carter, May 30, 1778, 11:492; Washington to John Augustine Washington, July 4, 1778, 12:156–57; Washington to General Thomas Nelson, August 20, 1778, 12:343.

34. Fitzpatrick, *The Writings of George Washington*, Washington to Henry Laurens, October 13, 1780, 20:173; Washington to Reverend William Gordon, March 9, 1781, 21:332.

35. Fitzpatrick, *The Writings of George Washington*, Washington to the Inhabitants of Princeton, August 25, 1783, 27:116; Washington to Comte de Rochambeau, October 15, 1783, 27:191; Farewell Orders to the Armies of the United States, November 2, 1783, 27:223.

36. Boyd, *The Papers of Thomas Jefferson*, George Washington's Resignation as Commander-in-Chief, December 23, 1783, 6:406, 411–12; Paul F. Boller, *George Washington and Religion* (Southern Methodist University Press, 1963), 107; Fitzpatrick, *The Writings of George Washington*, Washington to Jonathan Williams, March 2, 1795, 34:130.

37. Boyd, *The Papers of Thomas Jefferson*, Jefferson to Maria Cosway, October 12, 1786, 10:451; Response to the Address of Welcome, March 11, 1790, 16:225; Douglass Adair and John A. Schutz, eds., *The Spur of Fame: Dialogues of John Adams and Benjamin Rush, 1805–1813* (Huntington Library, 1966), Adams to Rush, August 28, 1811, 191; Moore, *The Works of James Buchanan*, President Polk's Annual Message, December 7, 1847, 7:466; Martin Van Buren, *The Autobiography of Martin Van Buren* (American Historical Association, 1920; repr., Da Capo, 1973), 1:132, 180; Russell, *The Shadow of Blooming Grove*, 161.

38. Boller, *George Washington and Religion*, 98, 147; Kaminsky, *Documentary History of the Ratification*, George Washington to the Marquis de Lafayette, May 28, 1788, 18:82–83; George Washington to Benjamin Lincoln, June 29, 1788, 18:208; George Washington to Jonathan Trumbull, Jr., July 20, 1788, 18:274–75.

39. Abbot, *The Papers of George Washington: Presidential Series*, To the Mayor, Recorder, Aldermen, and Common Council of Philadelphia, April 20, 1789, 2:83–84.

40. Abbot, *The Papers of George Washington: Presidential Series*, First Inaugural Address, April 30, 1789, 2:174; Thanksgiving Proclamation, October 3, 1789, 4:132.

41. George W. Carey and James McClellan, eds., *The Federalist* (Liberty Fund, 2001), Federalist No. 37, 184–85.

42. David B. Mattern, ed., *James Madison's "Advice to My Country"* (University Press of Virginia, 1997), Madison to Thomas Jefferson, October 24, 1787, 27.

43. Irving Sloan, ed., *Martin Van Buren, 1782–1862: Chronology, Documents, Bibliographical Aids* (Oceana, 1969), Second Annual Message, December 3, 1838, 69; Moore, *The Works of James Buchanan*, Speech on the Veto Power, February 2, 1842, 5:102.

44. Graf and Haskins, *The Papers of Andrew Johnson*, Speech in Defense of the Immortal Thirteen, October 27–28, 1841, 1:55; Speech in Nashville, March 13, 1862, 5:202; Speech in Nashville, July 4, 1862, 5:537.

45. Parker, *The Writings and Speeches of Grover Cleveland*, At the Constitutional Centennial, Philadelphia, September 17, 1887, 120–21; At the Celebration of the Origin of the Supreme Court, February 4, 1890, 126.

46. William Howard Taft, *Present Day Problems: A Collection of Addresses Delivered on Various Occasions* (Dodd, Mead, 1908), An Appreciation of General Grant, New York City, May 30, 1908, 65–66.

47. Warren G. Harding, *Our Common Country: Mutual Good Will in America* (Bobbs-Merrill, 1921), 275; Richardson, *Supplements to the Messages and Papers*, Inaugural Address of Warren Harding, 1921, 8923.

48. Calvin Coolidge, *America's Need for Education and Other Educational Addresses* (Houghton Mifflin, 1925), 7.

49. See, for instance, Harry S. Truman Library & Museum, "Welcome to the Harry S. Truman Presidential Library and Museum," National Archives, https://www.trumanlibrary.gov/, Speech to the National Association of Secretaries of State, October 18, 1943.

50. Allan Nevins, ed., *The Diary of John Quincy Adams, 1794–1845: American Diplomacy and Political, Social, and Intellectual Life from Washington to Polk* (Charles Scribner's Sons, 1951), February 22, 1821, 255; April 25, 1837, 480.

51. Bassett, *Correspondence of Andrew Jackson*, Jackson to Governor David Holmes, January 18, 1815, 2:145; Jackson to Abbe Guillaume Dubourg, January 19, 1815, 2:150; Jackson to Colonel Robert Hays, January 26, 1815, 2:153; James Monroe to Jackson, February 5, 1815, 2:158.

52. Nevins, *The Diary of John Quincy Adams*, July 9, 1826, 360.

53. Graf and Haskins, *The Papers of Andrew Johnson*, Speech on Veto Power and Responsibility for War with Mexico, August 2, 1848, 1:456; Henry Barnard, *Rutherford B. Hayes and His America* (Bobbs-Merrill, 1954), 150.

54. Graf and Haskins, *The Papers of Andrew Johnson*, Message to Congress, December 4, 1865, 9:466; Taft, *Present Day Problems*, An Appreciation of General Grant, New York City, May 30, 1908, 66; Link, *The Papers of Woodrow Wilson*, Remarks to Confederate Veterans in Washington, June 5, 1917, 42:352; Calvin Coolidge Presidential Foundation, "Lincoln Day Proclamation, January 30, 1919," Coolidge Foundation, published April 24, 2014, https://coolidgefoundation.org/resources/lincoln-day-proclamation/; Herbert Hoover, *Public Papers of the Presidents of the United States, 1931* (Government Printing Office, 1976), Radio Address on Lincoln's Birthday, February 12, 1931, 71.

55. McKinley, *Speeches and Addresses of William McKinley from His Election to Congress to the Present Time*, Address at the Metropolitan Opera House, May 30, 1889, 364.

56. McKinley, *Speeches and Addresses of William McKinley from March 1, 1897 to May 30, 1900*, Address at the Trans-Mississippi Exposition at Omaha, October 12, 1898, 105; Speech at Macon, Georgia, December 19, 1898, 178–79; Speech at Canton, Illinois, October 6, 1899, 229.

57. Warren F. Kimball, ed., *Churchill and Roosevelt: The Complete Correspondence* (Princeton University Press, 1984), Franklin Roosevelt to Winston Churchill, July 1, 1944, 3:232; December 9, 1944, 3:449; Harry S. Truman Library & Museum, "Welcome to the Harry S. Truman Presidential Library and Museum," National Archives, https://www.trumanlibrary.gov/, Press Release, August 6, 1945; Truman, *Public Papers of the Presidents, 1945*, Radio Report on the Potsdam Conference, August 9, 1945, 213; Proclamation 2660: Victory in the East—Day of Prayer, August 16, 1945, 223; Truman, *Public Papers of the Presidents, 1946*, Conference with the American Society of Newspaper Editors, April 18, 1946, 207.

58. George H. W. Bush, *Public Papers of the Presidents of the United States, 1992–1993* (Government Printing Office, 1993), Remarks to the National Association of Evangelicals, March 3, 1992, 367; Remarks at a Prayer Breakfast, Houston, August 20, 1992, 1378.

59. John Witte Jr., "'A Most Mild and Equitable Establishment of Religion': John Adams and the Massachusetts Experiment," in *Religion in the New Republic: Faith in the Founding of America*, ed. James H. Hutson (Rowman & Littlefield, 2000), 30.

60. William Peden, ed., *Notes on the State of Virginia* (University of North Carolina Press, 1955), 163; Bergh and Lipscomb, *The Writings of Thomas Jefferson*, Jefferson to Jean Nicholas Demeunier, January 24, 1786, 17:103.

61. Basler, *The Collected Works of Abraham Lincoln*, Eulogy on Henry Clay, July 6, 1852, 2:132; Speech at Columbus, Ohio, September 6, 1859, 3:410; Joseph R. Fornierei, ed., *The Language of Liberty: The Political Speeches and Writings of Abraham Lincoln* (Regnery, 2009), Lincoln to H. L. Pierce and Others, April 6, 1859, 750; Harry James Brown and Frederick D. Williams, eds., *The Diary of James A. Garfield* (Michigan State University Press, 1967), November 2, 1855, 1:274; December 2, 1859, 1:345.

62. Basler, *The Collected Works of Abraham Lincoln*, Lincoln to Albert G. Hodges, April 4, 1864, 7:282; Second Inaugural Address, March 4, 1865, 8:333.

63. John Y. Simon, ed., *The Papers of Ulysses S. Grant* (Southern Illinois University Press, 1967–2012), Speech, December 4, 1879, 29:37–318.

64. The American Presidency Project, "Inaugural Address of Benjamin Harrison, March 4, 1889," University of California, Santa Barbara, https://www.presidency.ucsb.edu/documents/inaugural-address-41; McKinley, *Speeches and Addresses of William McKinley from His Election of Congress to the Present Time*, Speech in the House of Representatives, July 2, 1890, 458; Roosevelt, *Works of Theodore Roosevelt*, Inaugural Address, 1905, 17:311; Lyndon B. Johnson, *Public Papers of the Presidents of the United States, 1965* (Government Printing Office, 1966), Inaugural Address, January 20, 1965, 73.

65. George H. W. Bush, *Public Papers of the Presidents of the United States, 1990* (Government Printing Office, 1991), Remarks at the Liberty University Commencement Ceremony, May 12, 1990, 656; Bush, *Public Papers of the Presidents of the United States, 1992–1993*, Remarks Accepting the Presidential Nomination at the Republican National Convention, August 20, 1992, 1386.

66. Link, *The Papers of Woodrow Wilson*, A Memorandum by Jacob de Haas, May 6, 1917, 42:235; Edmund Morris, *Colonel Roosevelt* (Random House, 2010), 531; Elting E. Morison, ed., *The Letters of Theodore Roosevelt* (Harvard University Press, 1951–1954), Roosevelt to James Bryce, August 7, 1918, 8:1359; Roosevelt to Julian H. Miller, September 16, 1918, 8:1372.

67. Herbert Hoover, *Public Papers of the Presidents of the United States, 1929* (Government Printing Office, 1974), Message for Jewish Organizations, August 29, 1929, 273; Herbert Hoover, *Public Papers of the Presidents of the United States, 1932–1933* (Government Printing Office, 1977), Message to the American Palestine Committee, January 17, 1932, 23; Message to the Zionist Organization of America, November 3, 1932, 695–96; Herbert Hoover, *Addresses upon the American Road, 1945–1948* (Van Nostrand, 1949), On the Palestine Question, *New York World-Telegram*, November 19, 1945, 16.

68. Elliott Roosevelt, ed., *F.D.R.: His Personal Letters* (Duell, Sloan and Pearce, 1947–1950), Roosevelt to Cordell Hull, May 17, 1939, 4:885–87.

69. Truman, *Public Papers of the Presidents, 1945*, News Conference, October 18, 1945, 402; Truman, *Public Papers of the Presidents, 1946*, Statement on the President's Meeting with Leaders of the Jewish Agency for Palestine, July 2, 1946, 335; Message to the King of Saudi Arabia Concerning Palestine, October 28, 1946, 467–68; Margaret Truman, *Harry S. Truman* (William Morrow, 1973), 298–99, 383, 385–86; David McCullough, *Truman* (Simon & Schuster, 1992), 597.

70. McCullough, *Truman*, 601–2, 620; Truman, *Public Papers of the Presidents, 1948*, Statement by the President Announcing Recognition of the State of Israel, May 14, 1948, 258; Address in Madison Square Garden, October 28, 1948, 913; Harry S. Truman, *Memoirs* (Doubleday, 1955–1956), 2:149, 164; Harry S. Truman, *Public Papers of the Presidents of the United States, 1952–1953* (Government Printing Office, 1966), Address at a Dinner of the Jewish National Fund, May 26, 1952, 374,

377; Caldwell, *The Wit and Wisdom of Harry S. Truman*, Farewell Address, January 15, 1953, 72, 74; Truman, *Harry S. Truman*, 389.

71. Mark Twain, *The Innocents Abroad* (American Publishing Company, 1875), 485, 607–8.

72. Alfred D. Chandler et al., eds., *The Papers of Dwight David Eisenhower* (Johns Hopkins University Press, 1970–2001), Eisenhower to Abba Hillel Silver, October 18, 1952, 13:1388.

73. John F. Kennedy Library & Museum, "Presidential Library and Museum," National Archives, https://www.jfklibrary.org/, Kennedy to Joseph P. Kennedy Sr., 1939; John F. Kennedy, *The Strategy of Peace* (Harper & Row, 1960), 112, 118, 218.

74. Lyndon B. Johnson, *Public Papers of the Presidents of the United States, 1966* (Government Printing Office, 1967), Toasts of the President and President Zalman Shazar, August 2, 1966, 796.

75. Lyndon B. Johnson, *The Vantage Point: Perspectives of the Presidency, 1963–1969* (Holt, Rinehart and Winston, 1971), 302.

76. Lyndon B. Johnson, *Public Papers of the Presidents of the United States, 1968–1969* (Government Printing Office, 1970), Remarks at the 125th Anniversary Meeting of B'nai B'rith, September 10, 1968, 947, 949.

77. Sam Houston Johnson, *My Brother Lyndon* (Cowles, 1969), 132.

78. Richard M. Nixon, *Public Papers of the Presidents of the United States, 1972* (Government Printing Office, 1974), Radio Address on Defense Policy, October 29, 1972, 1067; Richard M. Nixon, *RN: The Memoirs of Richard Nixon* (Grosset & Dunlap, 1978), 924; Richard M. Nixon, *Public Papers of the Presidents of the United States, 1973* (Government Printing Office, 1975), Special Message to Congress, October 19, 1973, 885; Richard M. Nixon, *In the Arena: A Memoir of Victory, Defeat, and Renewal* (Simon & Schuster, 1990), 336; Richard M. Nixon, *Public Papers of the Presidents of the United States, 1974* (Government Printing Office, 1975), Remarks on Arrival at Tel Aviv, June 16, 1974, 516.

79. Gerald R. Ford Presidential Library & Museum, "Museum and Library," National Archives, https://www.fordlibrarymuseum.gov/ - anchor-section, Address to the Zionist Organization of America, September 4, 1971; Award Received from Cleveland Region, Zionist Organization of America, March 19, 1972; Address to American-Israel Public Affairs Committee, May 8, 1973; Address to United Jewish Appeal, November 26, 1973; American-Israel Friendship Gold Medal Received, B'Nai Zion American-Israel Friendship Dinner, February 24, 1974; Address to Brotherhood Commission of the Southern Baptist Convention, June 14, 1974.

80. Carter, *Public Papers of the Presidents, 1978*, Remarks on the 30th Anniversary of the State of Israel, May 1, 1978, 812–13; Carter, *Public Papers of the Presidents of the United States, 1979*, Address Before the Knesset, March 12, 1979, 426; Jimmy Carter, *Keeping Faith: Memoirs of a President* (Bantam, 1982), 273–74; Jimmy Carter, *The Blood of Abraham* (Houghton-Mifflin, 1985), 5, 24, 29, 31, 208.

81. Kiron K. Skinner et al., eds., *Reagan, in His Own Hand* (Free Press, 2001), Palestine, March 27, 1979, 218; Reagan, *Public Papers of the Presidents, 1981*, Remarks

for the Welcoming Ceremony for Prime Minister Menachem Begin, September 9, 1981, 767; Ronald Reagan, *Public Papers of the Presidents of the United States, 1985* (Government Printing Office, 1988), Remarks on Presenting the Congressional Gold Medal to Elie Wiesel, April 19, 1985, 459; Reagan, *An American Life*, 410.

82. Doro Bush Koch, *My Father, My President: A Personal Account of the Life of George H. W. Bush* (Warner Books, 2006), 205–6; Bush, *Public Papers of the Presidents, 1990*, Remarks on Signing the Passover Message, April 4, 1990, 455; George H. W. Bush, *Public Papers of the Presidents of the United States, 1991* (Government Printing Office, 1992), Remarks at the Awards Presentation Ceremony for Emigration Assistance to Ethiopian Jews, June 4, 1991, 606.

83. William J. Clinton, *Public Papers of the Presidents of the United States, 1994* (Government Printing Office, 1995), Remarks to the Jordanian Parliament, October 26, 1994, 1881; Remarks at the Knesset, October 27, 1994, 1892; William J. Clinton, *Public Papers of the Presidents of the United States, 1995* (Government Printing Office, 1996), Remarks at the Funeral of Prime Minister Yitzhak Rabin, Jerusalem, November 6, 1995, 1724; Clinton, *Public Papers of the Presidents, 1996*, Remarks and a Question and Answer Session with Students in Tel Aviv, March 14, 1996, 452; William J. Clinton, *Public Papers of the Presidents of the United States, 1998* (Government Printing Office, 1999), Remarks at a Reception Celebrating Israel's 50th Anniversary, April 27, 1998, 628; David L. Holmes, *The Faiths of the Postwar Presidents: Truman to Obama* (University of Georgia Press, 2012), 227.

84. Bush, *Public Papers of the Presidents, 2001*, Remarks to the American Jewish Committee, May 3, 2001, 486–87; George W. Bush, *Public Papers of the Presidents of the United States, 2008–2009* (Government Printing Office, 2012), Remarks to Members of the Knesset, May 15, 2008, 687.

85. Clarence E. Walker, *The Preacher and the Politician: Jeremiah Wright, Barack Obama, and Race in America* (University of Virginia Press, 2009), 108; Barack Obama, *Public Papers of the Presidents of the United States, 2013* (Government Printing Office, 2018), Remarks at an Arrival Ceremony in Tel Aviv, March 20, 2013, 202; Remarks at an Easter Prayer Breakfast, April 5, 2013, 281.

86. U.S. Embassy in Israel, "Alerts and Messages," https://il.usembassy.gov/, Statement on Jerusalem, December 6, 2017; TOI Staff, "Trump Says He Moved U.S. Embassy to Jerusalem 'for the Evangelicals,'" *The Times of Israel*, August 18, 2020, https://www.timesofisrael.com/trump-says-he-moved-us-embassy-to-jerusalem-for-the-evangelicals/; newyorker.com, Ruth Margalit, "Trump's Legacy in Israel," *The New Yorker*, July 12, 2021, https://www.newyorker.com/news/dispatch/donald-trumps-legacy-in-israel.

Chapter 8

1. Zoltan Haraszti, *John Adams and the Prophets of Progress* (Harvard University Press, 1972), 60.

2. Julian P. Boyd, ed., *The Papers of Thomas Jefferson* (Princeton University Press, 1950), Notes on the Doctrine of Epicurus, 1799, 31:285; Albert Ellery Bergh and Andrew A. Lipscomb, eds., *The Writings of Thomas Jefferson* (Thomas Jefferson Memorial Association, 1904), Jefferson to William Short, August 4, 1820, 15:259.

3. National Historical Publications & Records Commission, "Founders Online," National Archives, last updated July 2024, https://founders.archives.gov/, John Quincy Adams to George Washington Adams, September 22, 1811.

4. Dan Ariail and Cheryl Heckler-Feltz, *The Carpenter's Apprentice: The Spiritual Biography of Jimmy Carter* (Zondervan, 1996), 48; Wesley G. Pippert, ed., *The Spiritual Journey of Jimmy Carter in His Own Words* (Macmillan, 1978), Introduction, 13; Men's Bible Class, Plains Baptist Church, July 18, 1976, 170.

5. Nancy Reagan, *My Turn: The Memoirs of Nancy Reagan* (Random House, 1989), 233; Mary Beth Brown, *Hand of Providence: The Strong and Quiet Faith of Ronald Reagan* (WND Books, 2004), 197.

6. Doro Bush Koch, *My Father, My President: A Personal Account of the Life of George H. W. Bush* (Warner Books, 2006), xviii, 12; George H. W. Bush Presidential Library & Museum, "Archives and Research," National Archives, https://bush41library.tamu.edu/, Advice to Young People, April 23, 2003.

7. Gordon S. Wood, *Revolutionary Characters: What Made the Founders Different* (Penguin, 2006), 37; Garry Wills, *Cincinnatus: George Washington and the Enlightenment* (Doubleday, 1984); Ron Chernow, *Grant* (Penguin, 2017), 495.

8. Boyd, *The Papers of Thomas Jefferson*, Jefferson to Maria Cosway, October 12, 1786, 10:451; Bergh and Lipscomb, *The Writings of Thomas Jefferson*, Jefferson to Benjamin Rush, April 21, 1803, 10:383, 385; Jefferson to Samuel Kercheval, January 19, 1810, 12:345; Jefferson to Charles Thomson, January 9, 1816, 14:385; Jefferson to Ezra Stiles, June 25, 1819, 15:203; Jefferson to William Short, October 31, 1819, 15:219, 223–24; April 13, 1820, 15:244; Lester J. Cappon, ed., *The Adams-Jefferson Letters: The Complete Correspondence Between Thomas Jefferson and Abigail and John Adams* (University of North Carolina Press, 1959), Jefferson to John Adams, October 12, 1813, 2:384; Merrill D. Peterson, *Thomas Jefferson and the New Nation: A Biography* (Oxford University Press, 1970), 53; Jeffry H. Morrison, *John Witherspoon and the Founding of the American Republic* (University of Notre Dame Press, 2005), 37.

9. Haraszti, *John Adams and the Prophets*, 302; Cappon, *The Adams–Jefferson Letters*, John Adams to Jefferson, July 16, 1813, 2:359; February 2, 1816, 2:462; November 4, 1816, 2:494; Bergh and Lipscomb, *The Writings of Thomas Jefferson*, John Adams to Jefferson, April 19, 1817, 15:106.

10. National Historical Publications & Records Commission, "Founders Online," https://founders.archives.gov/, John Quincy Adams to George Washington Adams, September 22, 1811; Charles Francis Adams, ed., *Memoirs of John Quincy Adams, Comprising Portions of His Diary from 1795 to 1848* (n.p., 1874–1877; repr., AMS Press, 1970), April 17, 1813, 2:462; June 5, 1816, 3:378.

11. Robert V. Remini, *Andrew Jackson and the Course of American Freedom, 1822–1832* (Harper & Row, 1981), 142; Harold D. Moser et al., eds., *The Papers of*

Andrew Jackson (University of Tennessee Press, 1980), Jackson to Andrew Jackson Jr., November 16, 1833, 5:226; Jackson to Andrew J. Hutchings, March 24, 1835, 5:332.

12. Milo Milton Quaife, ed., *The Diary of James K. Polk During His Presidency, 1845 to 1849* (A. C. McClurg, 1910), September 14, 1846, 2:138; February 21, 1847, 2:389.

13. Roy P. Basler, ed., *The Collected Works of Abraham Lincoln* (Rutgers University Press, 1953–1955), Fragment on Pro-Slavery Theology, October 1, 1858, 3:204.

14. Theodore Roosevelt, *Addresses and Presidential Messages of Theodore Roosevelt, 1902–1904* (G. P. Putnam's Sons, 1904; repr., Kraus, 1971), At the Consecration of Grace Memorial Reformed Church, Washington, June 7, 1903, 225–26; Herbert Ronald Ferleger and Albert Bushnell Hart, eds., *Theodore Roosevelt Cyclopedia* (Roosevelt Memorial Association, 1941), *Outlook*, May 27, 1911, 76.

15. Arthur S. Link, ed., *The Papers of Woodrow Wilson* (Princeton University Press, 1966–1994), A News Report of a Religious Talk, *Daily Princetonian*, May 20, 1898, 10:533; A Report of a Religious Address, *Daily Princetonian*, March 1, 1900, 11:453; A Draft of an Essay, April 8, 1923, 68:323.

16. Herbert Hoover, *Public Papers of the Presidents of the United States, 1931* (Government Printing Office, 1976), Radio Address to the Nation on Unemployment Relief, October 18, 1931, 490; Address on the 150th Anniversary of the Surrender of General Cornwallis at Yorktown, October 19, 1931, 496–97; Herbert Hoover, *Addresses upon the American Road, 1933–1938* (Charles Scribner's Sons, 1938), Challenge to Liberty, April 8, 1938, 327.

17. Hoover, *Public Papers of the Presidents, 1931*, Radio Address to the Nation on Unemployment Relief, October 18, 1931, 490; Herbert Hoover, *Addresses upon the American Road, 1948–1950* (Stanford University Press, 1951), The Government Cannot Do It All, April 25, 1949, 176.

18. Herbert Hoover, *Further Addresses upon the American Road, 1938–1940* (Charles Scribner's Sons, 1940), Relief for Poland, March 12, 1940, 249; Herbert Hoover, *Addresses upon the American Road, 1940–1941* (Charles Scribner's Sons, 1941), When Winter Comes to Europe, *Collier's Magazine*, November 23, 1940, 145–46; Hoover, *Addresses upon the American Road, 1948–1950*, The Miracle of America, *Woman's Home Companion*, November 1948, 4; The Government Cannot Do It All, April 25, 1949, 175–76; Herbert Hoover, *Addresses upon the American Road, 1950–1955* (Stanford University Press, 1955), Resistance to Communism, November 26, 1954, 98.

19. Eugene Lyons, *Herbert Hoover: A Biography* (Doubleday, 1948), 81–83.

20. Franklin Access to the FDR Library's Digital Collection, "Fully Digitized Collections or Series," Franklin D. Roosevelt Presidential Library and Museum, updated 2011, http://www.fdrlibrary.marist.edu/archives/collections/franklin/, Acceptance of Renomination, June 27, 1936; Christmas Tree Lighting, December 24, 1940.

21. Harry S. Truman, *Public Papers of the Presidents of the United States, 1947* (Government Printing Office, 1963), Radio Address Concerning the Community

Chest Campaign, September 26, 1947, 444; Address at the Lighting of the National Community Christmas Tree on the White House Grounds, December 24, 1947, 530; Harry S. Truman, *Mr. Citizen* (Random House, 1960), 203.

22. Dwight D. Eisenhower, *Public Papers of the Presidents of the United States, 1960–1961* (Government Printing Office, 1961), Address at the Golden Jubilee Dinner of the National Conference of Catholic Charities, September 26, 1960, 729.

23. John F. Kennedy, *Public Papers of the Presidents of the United States, 1963* (Government Printing Office, 1964), Remarks in Philadelphia at a Dinner Sponsored by the Democratic County Executive Committee, October 30, 1963, 823.

24. Lyndon B. Johnson, *Public Papers of the Presidents of the United States, 1963–1964* (Government Printing Office, 1965), Remarks at a Reception for Members of the American Society of Newspaper Editors, April 17, 1964, 485; Lyndon B. Johnson, *Public Papers of the Presidents of the United States, 1966* (Government Printing Office, 1967), Remarks at the Social Security Administration Headquarters in Baltimore, October 12, 1966, 1144–45; Lyndon B. Johnson, *Public Papers of the Presidents of the United States, 1965* (Government Printing Office, 1966), Remarks at the Commencement Exercises of the National Cathedral School, June 1, 1965, 601.

25. Gerald R. Ford Presidential Library & Museum, "Museum and Library," National Archives, https://www.fordlibrarymuseum.gov/ - anchor-section, The Christian Attitude in the Atomic Age, 1950; The Contribution of the Church to the Preservation of Freedom, September 6, 1950.

26. Jimmy Carter, *Public Papers of the Presidents of the United States, 1980–1981* (Government Printing Office, 1982), Remarks at the Annual Convention of the Opportunities Industrialization Centers of America, June 9, 1980, 1067.

27. Ariail and Heckler-Feltz, *The Carpenter's Apprentice*, 9, 17.

28. Ronald Reagan, *Public Papers of the Presidents of the United States, 1982* (Government Printing Office, 1983), Remarks at the New York Partnership Lunch, January 14, 1982, 30; Remarks on Private Sector Institutions at White House Luncheon for National Religious Leaders, April 13, 1982, 454.

29. Kiron K. Skinner et al., eds., *Reagan: A Life in Letters* (Free Press, 2003), 653, 655, 657; Brown, *Hand of Providence*, 140.

30. George H. W. Bush Presidential Library & Museum, "Archives and Research," National Archives, https://bush41library.tamu.edu/, Speech at Republican National Convention, August 18, 1988; George H. W. Bush, *Public Papers of the Presidents of the United States, 1990* (Government Printing Office, 1991), Remarks to the American Society of Association Executives, March 6, 1990, 326; George H. W. Bush, *Public Papers of the Presidents of the United States, 1992–1993* (Government Printing Office, 1993), Remarks at the Southern Methodist University Commencement Ceremony, May 16, 1992, 785; Russell J. Levenson Jr., *Witness to Dignity: The Life and Faith of George H. W. and Barbara Bush* (Center Street, 2022), ix, 52.

31. William J. Clinton, *Public Papers of the Presidents of the United States, 1998* (Government Printing Office, 1999), Remarks at the New Psalmist Baptist Church, Baltimore, November 1, 1998, 1946–1947.

32. George W. Bush, *Public Papers of the Presidents of the United States, 2001* (Government Printing Office, 2003), Inaugural Address, January 20, 2001, 2; George W. Bush, *Public Papers of the Presidents of the United States, 2003* (Government Printing Office, 2006), Radio Address, December 27, 2003, 1761; George W. Bush, *Decision Points* (Crown Publishers, 2010), 333–34; David Aikman, *A Man of Faith: The Spiritual Journey of George W. Bush* (Thomas Nelson, 2004), 171.

33. Barack Obama, *Public Papers of the Presidents of the United States, 2011* (Government Printing Office, 2014), Remarks at the National Prayer Breakfast, February 3, 2011, 74; Remarks at a Democratic National Committee Fundraiser, April 27, 2011, 462; Barack Obama, *Public Papers of the Presidents of the United States, 2015* (Government Printing Office, 2020), Remarks and a Question and Answer Session at a Town Hall Meeting at Ivy Tech Community College in Indianapolis, February 6, 2015, 155.

34. Barack Obama, *Public Papers of the Presidents of the United States, 2012* (Government Printing Office, 2016), Remarks at the National Prayer Breakfast, February 2, 2012, 120.

35. Leonard W. Labaree et al. eds, *The Papers of Benjamin Franklin* (Yale University Press, 1959), John Adams to Franklin, April 16, 1781, 34:552; Haraszti, *John Adams and the Prophets*, 284.

36. Jean M. Yarbrough, *American Virtues: Thomas Jefferson and the Character of a Free People* (University Press of Kansas, 1998), 52.

37. Adams, *Memoirs of John Quincy Adams*, August 25, 1796, 1:182; June 3, 1838, 10:7–8; John Quincy Adams, *Lectures on Rhetoric and Oratory* (Hilliard and Metcalf, 1810; repr., Russell & Russell, 1962), 1:373–74; Worthington Chauncey Ford, ed., *Writings of John Quincy Adams* (Macmillan, 1913–1916), Adams to Louisa Adams, October 14, 1814, 5:161.

38. Charles M. Snyder, ed., *The Lady and the President: The Letters of Dorothea Dix and Millard Fillmore* (University of Kentucky Press, 1975), Editor's Note, 358.

39. Basler, *The Collected Works of Abraham Lincoln*, Lincoln to Edwin M. Stanton, February 5, 1864, 7:169; Second Inaugural Address, March 4, 1865, 8:333.

40. Leroy P. Graf and Ralph W. Haskins, eds., *The Papers of Andrew Johnson* (University of Tennessee Press, 1967–2000), Remarks to Pennsylvania Citizens in Washington, April 28, 1865, 7:655; Speech to First Regiment, USCT, October 10, 1865, 9:220.

41. Gerald R. Ford Presidential Library & Museum, "Museum and Library," https://www.fordlibrarymuseum.gov/ - anchor-section, Notes for *A Time to Heal*, Revenge or Forgiveness.

42. Carter, *Public Papers of the Presidents, 1980–1981*, Remarks at the National Prayer Breakfast, February 7, 1980, 277; Jimmy Carter, *Sources of Strength: Meditations on Scripture for a Living Faith* (Random House, 1997), 22–23, 67–69.

43. Ronald Reagan, *An American Life* (Simon & Schuster, 1990), 261, 292.

44. L. H. Butterfield, ed., *The Diary and Autobiography of John Adams* (Harvard University Press, 1962), Autobiography, 3:434–35; Lynn Hudson Parsons, *John

Quincy Adams (Madison House, 1998), 215–16; John Spencer Bassett, ed., *Correspondence of Andrew Jackson* (Carnegie Institution, 1926–1935), Jackson to Andrew J. Donelson, 2:382; Jackson to General John Coffee, late 1827 or early 1828, 3:388; Robert V. Remini, *Andrew Jackson and the Course of American Democracy, 1833–1845* (Harper & Row, 1984), 14; Allan Nevins, ed., *Letters of Grover Cleveland, 1850–1908* (Hougton Mifflin, 1933), Cleveland to William S. Bissell, November 13, 1884, 48; Robert H. Ferrell, ed., *Off the Record: The Private Papers of Harry S. Truman* (Harper & Row, 1980), Diary, December 6, 1952, 279; Skinner, *Reagan*, Reagan to William Rusher, April 9, 1984, 560; Daniel G. Axtel, "The Complete, Annotated Nixon's Enemies List," EnemiesList.info, published 2024, https://www.enemieslist.info/; Jennifer Hansler, "Trump's Twitter Attacks on Sessions: An Annotated Timeline," *CNN Politics*, August 25, 2018, https://www.cnn.com/2018/08/25/politics/trump-sessions-twitter-timeline/index.html.

45. W. W. Abbot, ed., *The Papers of George Washington: Presidential Series* (University Press of Virginia, 1987), Washington to the Congregational Ministers of New Haven, October 17, 1789, 4:198; Washington to the Synod of the Dutch Reformed Church in North America, October 1789, 4:264; Saul K. Padover, ed., *The Washington Papers: Basic Selections from the Public and Private Writings of George Washington* (Grosset & Dunlap, 1967), Farewell Address, September 19, 1796, 318–19.

46. Edwin S. Gaustad, *Faith of Our Fathers: Religion and the New Nation* (Harper & Row, 1987), 79, 92; Linda K. Kerber, *Federalists in Dissent: Imagery and Ideology in Jeffersonian America* (Cornell University Press, 1970), 208; Daniel Boorstin, *The Lost World of Thomas Jefferson* (Henry Holt, 1948), 156; Haraszti, *John Adams and the Prophets*, 291.

47. Douglass Adair and John A. Schutz, eds., *The Spur of Fame: Dialogues of John Adams and Benjamin Rush, 1805–1813* (Huntington Library, 1966), Adams to Rush, August 28, 1811, 192; Cappon, *Adams-Jefferson Letters*, John Adams to Jefferson, April 19, 1817, 2:509.

48. John P. Kaminsky et al., eds., *The Documentary History of the Ratification of the Constitution* (The State Historical Society of Wisconsin, 1976–2008), James Madison to Thomas Jefferson, October 24, 1787, 13:448; Richard B. Mattern, ed., *James Madison's "Advice to My Country"* (University Press of Virginia, 1997), Madison to Frederick Beasley, November 29, 1825, 51.

49. Adams, *Lectures on Rhetoric and Oratory*, 1:24, 373; Adrienne Koch and William Peden, eds., *The Selected Writings of John and John Quincy Adams* (Alfred A. Knopf, 1946), John Quincy Adams to George Washington Adams, September 15, 1811, 278–79.

50. Bassett, *Correspondence of Andrew Jackson*, Jackson to John McNairy, September 6, 1823, 3:208; Jackson to D. G. Goodlett, March 12, 1844, 6:275.

51. Basler, *The Collected Works of Abraham Lincoln*, Handbill Replying to Charges of Infidelity, July 31, 1846, 1:382; Response to the Loyal Colored People of Baltimore upon Presentation of a Bible, September 7, 1864, 7:542.

52. Charles Richard Williams, ed., *The Diary and Letters of Rutherford B. Hayes* (Ohio State Archaeological Historical Society, 1922), Diary, October 15, 1884, 4:168; November 9, 1885, 4:248.

53. George F. Parker, ed., *The Writings and Speeches of Grover Cleveland* (Cassell, 1892), At the Semi-Centennial Celebration of Rochester, New York, June 10, 1884, 113; At the Laying of the Cornerstone of the YMCA Building in Buffalo, September 7, 1882, 182–83; To the Evangelical Alliance, December 9, 1887, 186; Nevins, *Letters of Grover Cleveland*, Cleveland to Colonel John I. Rogers, January 26, 1887, 129–30.

54. William McKinley, *Speeches and Addresses of William McKinley from His Election to Congress to the Present Time* (D. Appleton, 1893), Address at the Dedication of a Public School Building in Canal Fulton, Ohio, August 30, 1887, 219; Address at the Dedication of the YMCA Building in Youngstown, Ohio, September 6, 1892, 607.

55. Ferleger and Hart, *Theodore Roosevelt Cyclopedia*, Outlook, May 27, 1911, 42; At the Methodist Episcopal Church, Washington, January 18, 1909, 76; *Ladies' Home Journal*, October 1917, 77; Work unknown, 1917, 354; Work unknown, 1914, 517; At the Mount Pleasant Military Academy, Sing Sing, New York, June 3, 1899, 606.

56. Link, *The Papers of Woodrow Wilson*, A Commemorative Address, October 21, 1896, 10:21; Notes for a Religious Talk, March 28, 1897, 10:198; An Address in Jersey City, January 5, 1911, 22:305; A Tribute to Mark Anthony Sullivan, February 1, 1911, 22:401; Wilson to Mary Allen Hulbert Peck, May 7, 1911, 23:11; A Religious Address in Trenton, October 1, 1911, 23:377, 379; A Draft of an Essay, April 8, 1923, 68:324.

57. Warren G. Harding, *Our Common Country: Mutual Good Will in America* (Indianapolis, IN: Bobbs-Merrill, 1921), 13–15, 112.

58. Calvin Coolidge, *The Price of Freedom: Speeches and Addresses* (Charles Scribner's Sons, 1924), The Price of Freedom, January 21, 1923, 229, 244; Calvin Coolidge, *America's Need for Education and Other Educational Addresses* (Houghton Mifflin, 1925), 30; Calvin Coolidge Presidential Foundation, "*New York Times*, May 4, 1925," Coolidge Foundation, published, https://coolidgefoundation.org/resources/; "To the Annual Council of the Congregational Churches, October 20, 1925," published April 14, 2020, https://coolidgefoundation.org/resources/annual-council-of-the-congregational-churches/; "The Inspiration of the Declaration, July 5, 1926," published April 23, 2014, https://coolidgefoundation.org/resources/inspiration-of-the-declaration-of-independence/.

59. Herbert Hoover, *Public Papers of the Presidents of the United States, 1929* (Government Printing Office, 1974), Message to the National Federation of Men's Bible Classes, May 5, 1929, 136; Hoover, *Further Addresses upon the American Road, 1938–1940*, The Imperative Need for Moral Rearmament, November 22, 1938, 190; Herbert Hoover, *Addresses upon the American Road, 1941–1945* (Van Nostrand,

1946), United Church Canvass, November 1942, 378–79; Hoover, *Addresses upon the American Road, 1950–1955*, The Protection of Freedom, August 10, 1954, 83.

60. Franklin Access to the FDR Library's Digital Collection, "Fully Digitized Collections or Series," http://www.fdrlibrary.marist.edu/archives/collections/franklin/, Campaign Address, October 31, 1936; Election Eve Broadcast, November 4, 1940; Christmas Tree Lighting, December 24, 1940; Washington's Birthday Celebration, February 22, 1943; Frank Kingdon, *As F.D.R. Said: A Treasury of His Speeches, Conversations, and Writings* (Duell, Sloan and Pearce, 1950), Message to Congress, December 1938, 152.

61. Harry S. Truman Library & Museum, "Welcome to the Harry S. Truman Presidential Library and Museum," National Archives, https://www.trumanlibrary.gov/, Speech to National Postal Employees, October 2, 1938; Speech to the National Association of Secretaries of State, October 18, 1943; Harry S. Truman, *Public Papers of the Presidents of the United States, 1950* (Government Printing Office, 1965), Address at the Lighting of the National Community Christmas Tree on the White House Grounds, December 24, 1950, 760; Truman, *Public Papers of the Presidents of the United States, 1951*, Address at the Cornerstone Laying of the New York Avenue Presbyterian Church, April 3, 1951, 210–12; Truman, *Public Papers of the Presidents, 1952–1953*, Remarks at a Masonic Breakfast, February 21, 1952, 169; Address at the Convention of the Columbia Scholastic Press Association, March 15, 1952, 205; Remarks at the Laying of the Cornerstone of the New Temple of the Washington Hebrew Congregation, November 16, 1952, 1050–51.

62. Truman, *Mr. Citizen*, 131–32.

63. Alfred D. Chandler et al., eds., *The Papers of Dwight David Eisenhower* (Johns Hopkins University Press, 1970–2001), Eisenhower to Frederick J. Michel, July 5, 1943, 2:1242; Eisenhower to Merv Rosell, March 27, 1952, 13:1133; Dwight D. Eisenhower, *Public Papers of the Presidents of the United States, 1953* (Government Printing Office, 1960), Remarks at the Dedicatory Prayer Breakfast of the International Christian Leadership, February 5, 1953, 38; Address Before the Council of the Organization of American States, April 12, 1953, 175; Dwight D. Eisenhower, *Public Papers of the Presidents of the United States, 1954* (Government Printing House, 1960), Remarks to the Committee for Economic Development, May 20, 1954, 502; Remarks to the First National Conference on the Spiritual Foundations of American Democracy, November 9, 1954, 1031; Dwight D. Eisenhower, *Public Papers of the Presidents of the United States, 1958* (Government Printing Office, 1959), Statement by the President on the Jewish High Holidays, September 14, 1958, 703; Remarks to the National Committee for the White House Conference on Children and Youth, December 16, 1958, 863; Eisenhower, *Public Papers of the Presidents, 1960–1961*, Address at the Golden Jubilee Dinner of the National Conference of Catholic Charities, September 26, 1960, 731.

64. John F. Kennedy Library & Museum, "Presidential Library and Museum," National Archives, https://www.jfklibrary.org/, Kennedy to Rabbi Maurice N. Eisendrath, November 14, 1961.

65. Gerald R. Ford Presidential Library & Museum, "Museum and Library," https://www.fordlibrarymuseum.gov/ - anchor-section, The Contribution of the Church to the Preservation of Freedom, September 6, 1950; South High School Commencement Address, June 7, 1956.

66. Gerald R. Ford, *Public Papers of the Presidents of the United States, 1976–1977* (Government Printing Office, 1979), Remarks at the Southern Baptist Convention, June 15, 1976, 1879.

67. Frank Daniel, ed., *Addresses of Jimmy Carter, Governor of Georgia, 1971–1975* (Georgia Department of Archives and History, 1975), Clayton Junior College, December 3, 1973, 31–32; Jimmy Carter, *Public Papers of the Presidents of the United States, 1978* (Government Printing Office, 1979), Remarks at a Town Meeting in Nashua, New Hampshire, February 18, 1978, 370; Remarks at a Democratic Party Rally for John Ingram, Wilson, North Carolina, August 5, 1978, 1389.

68. Reagan, *Public Papers of the Presidents, 1982*, Remarks at the Annual Convention of National Religious Broadcasters, February 9, 1982, 157–58; Message to Congress Transmitting a Proposed Constitutional Amendment on Prayer in School, May 17, 1982, 647; Ronald Reagan, *Public Papers of the Presidents of the United States, 1984* (Government Printing Office, 1986), Interview with the Knight-Ridder News Service on Foreign and Domestic Issues, February 13, 1984, 207; Remarks at a Spirit of America Festival in Decatur, Alabama, July 4, 1984, 1001; Remarks at an Ecumenical Breakfast in Dallas, August 23, 1984, 1167–68.

69. George H. W. Bush, *Public Papers of the Presidents of the United States, 1991* (Government Printing Office, 1992), Remarks at the Annual Southern Baptist Convention, June 6, 1991, 614; Bush, *Public Papers of the Presidents, 1992–1993*, Remarks at a Town Hall Meeting in Los Angeles, May 29, 1992, 851; Remarks at the National Affairs Briefing, Dallas, August 22, 1992, 1403.

70. Boyd, *The Papers of Thomas Jefferson*, Jefferson to Peter Carr, August 10, 1787, 12:16–17; Eleanor Davis Berman, *Thomas Jefferson Among the Arts: An Essay in Early American Esthetics* (Philosophical Library, 1947), 24; Charles B. Sanford, *The Religious Life of Thomas Jefferson* (University Press of Virginia, 1984), 145.

71. Bush, *Public Papers of the Presidents, 2001*, Remarks at the National Prayer Breakfast, February 1, 2001, 42; George W. Bush, *Public Papers of the Presidents of the United States, 2002* (Government Printing Office, 2004), Remarks at the National Prayer Breakfast, February 7, 2002, 188.

72. Barack Obama, *The Audacity of Hope: Thoughts on Reclaiming the American Dream* (Crown Publishers, 2006), 37, 205–6, 214–15, 218; Katharine Q. Seelye and Jeff Zeleny, "On the Defensive, Obama Calls His Words Ill-Chosen," *New York Times*, April 13, 2008; Barack Obama, *A Promised Land* (Crown Publishers, 2020), 144–45; Barack Obama, *Public Papers of the Presidents of the United States, 2014* (Government Printing Office, 2019), Remarks at the National Prayer Breakfast, February 6, 2014, 103.

Chapter 9

1. For a lengthier discussion of the advantages that Christianity possessed in its contest against paganism, see Carl J. Richard, *Why We're All Romans: The Roman Contribution to the Western World* (Rowman & Littlefield, 2010), 260–69.

2. Richard, *Why We're All Romans*, 159, 241.

3. Paul F. Boller, *George Washington and Religion* (Southern Methodist University Press, 1963), 111–13; Harold C. Syrett, ed., *The Papers of Alexander Hamilton* (Columbia University Press, 1961–1979), Draft of Washington's Farewell Address, July 30, 1796, 20:287; Edwin S. Gaustad, *Faith of Our Fathers: Religion and the New Nation* (Harper & Row, 1987), 81–83.

4. L. H. Butterfield, ed., *The Diary and Autobiography of John Adams* (Harvard University Press, 1961), Autobiography, 3:265; Adrienne Koch and William Peden, eds., *The Selected Writings of John and John Quincy Adams* (Alfred A. Knopf, 1946), Diary of John Adams, 1770 or 1771, 30; Julian P. Boyd, ed., *The Papers of Thomas Jefferson* (Princeton University Press, 1950), John Adams to Jefferson, January 31, 1796, 28:600; Lester J. Cappon, ed., *The Adams-Jefferson Letters: The Complete Correspondence Between Thomas Jefferson and Abigail and John Adams* (University of North Carolina Press, 1959), John Adams to Jefferson, December 8, 1818, 2:530; January 14, 1826, 2:613.

5. Douglas L. Wilson, ed., *Jefferson's Literary Commonplace Book* (Princeton University Press, 1989), 123; Boyd, *Papers of Thomas Jefferson*, Jefferson to Francis Willis, July 15, 1796, 29:153; Albert Ellery Bergh and Andrew A. Lipscomb, eds., *The Writings of Thomas Jefferson* (Thomas Jefferson Memorial Association, 1904), Jefferson to John Page, June 25, 1804, 11:31; Charles B. Sanford, *The Religious Life of Thomas Jefferson* (University Press of Virginia, 1984), 146–47.

6. Bergh and Lipscomb, *The Writings of Thomas Jefferson*, Jefferson to Abigail Adams, January 11, 1817, 15:96–97; Jefferson to John Adams, November 13, 1818, 15:174; April 11, 1823, 15:430; Sanford, *The Religious Life of Thomas Jefferson*, 159.

7. Bergh and Lipscomb, *The Writings of Thomas Jefferson*, Jefferson to Thomas Jefferson Smith, February 21, 1825, 16:110–11; Sanford, *The Religious Life of Thomas Jefferson*, 159.

8. Sanford, *The Religious Life of Thomas Jefferson*, 154; Jean M. Yarbrough, *American Virtues: Thomas Jefferson and the Character of a Free People* (University Press of Kansas, 1998), 186.

9. Robert A. Rutland et al., eds., *The Papers of James Madison* (University of Chicago Press, 1962–1977; repr., University Press of Virginia, 1977), Madison to William Bradford, November 9, 1772, 1:75.

10. David L. Holmes, *The Faiths of the Founding Fathers* (Oxford University Press, 2006), 102.

11. John Quincy Adams, *Lectures on Rhetoric and Oratory* (Hilliard and Metcalf, 1810; repr., Russell & Russell, 1962), 2:261, 263; Charles Francis Adams, ed., *Memoirs of John Quincy Adams: Comprising Portions of His Diary from 1795 to 1848*

(Philadelphia, 1874–1877; repr., AMS, 1970), August 16, 1811, 2:297; October 13, 1822, 6:78.

12. John Quincy Adams, *Argument of John Quincy Adams Before the Supreme Court of the United States in the Case of the United States, Appellants, vs. Cinque and Other Africans Captured in the Schooner Amistad* (S. W. Benedict, 1841; repr., Negro University Press, 1969), 135.

13. Robert V. Remini, *Andrew Jackson and the Course of American Freedom, 1822–1832* (Harper & Row, 1981), 154–55; Harold D. Moser et al., eds., *The Papers of Andrew Jackson* (University of Tennessee Press, 1980), Jackson to Katherine Morgan, January 3, 1829, 7:5; John Spencer Bassett, ed., *Correspondence of Andrew Jackson* (Carnegie Institution, 1926–1935), Jackson to Reverend Hardy M. Cryer, May 16, 1829, 4:33; Jackson to Captain John Donelson, June 7, 1829, 4:41.

14. Moser, *The Papers of Andrew Jackson*, Jackson to John Coffee, September 21, 1829, 7:444; Bassett, *Correspondence of Andrew Jackson*, Jackson to Andrew J. Hutchings, May 24, 1835, 5:332; Jackson to Benjamin F. Butler, January 4, 1845, 6:358.

15. Charles M. Snyder, ed., *The Lady and the President: The Letters of Dorothea Dix and Millard Fillmore* (University of Kentucky Press, 1975), Fillmore to Dix, August 29, 1854, 215; May 11, 1857, 287.

16. John Bassett Moore, ed., *The Works of James Buchanan* (J. B. Lippincott, 1908–1911; repr., Antiquarian Press, 1960), Buchanan to Andrew Jackson, April 9, 1839, 4:117; Buchanan to Harriet Lane, December 21, 1855, 9:481.

17. Roy P. Basler, ed., *The Collected Works of Abraham Lincoln* (Rutgers University Press, 1953–1955), Lincoln to John D. Johnston, January 12, 1851, 2:97.

18. Leroy P. Graf and Ralph W. Haskins, eds., *The Papers of Andrew Johnson* (University of Tennessee Press, 1967–2000), To the Freemen of the First Congressional District of Tennessee, October 15, 1845, 1:240.

19. Harry James Brown and Frederick D. Williams, eds., *The Diary of James A. Garfield* (Michigan State University Press, 1967), August 22, 1850, 1:54; December 26, 1852, 1:165.

20. Charles W. Calhoun, *Benjamin Harrison* (Times Books, 2005), 158.

21. H. Wayne Morgan, *William McKinley and His America* (Syracuse University Press, 1963), 19; William McKinley, *Speeches and Addresses of William McKinley from His Election to Congress to the Present Time* (D. Appleton, 1893), Address at the Metropolitan Opera House, May 30, 1889, 367; Address at the Celebration of the Seventy-First Anniversary of Ulysses Grant's Birth in Galena, Illinois, April 27, 1893, 444.

22. Jonathan Lurie, *William Howard Taft: The Travails of a Progressive Conservative* (Cambridge University Press, 2012), 17.

23. Arthur S. Link, ed., *The Papers of Woodrow Wilson* (Princeton University Press, 1966–1994), Wilson to Ellen Louise Axson, June 1, 1884, 3:200.

24. Gerald R. Ford, *Public Papers of the Presidents of the United States, 1976–1977* (Government Printing Office, 1979), Remarks at the Professional Athletes Prayer Brunch, February 15, 1976, 337.

25. Frank Daniel, ed., *Addresses of Jimmy Carter, Governor of Georgia, 1971–1975* (Georgia Department of Archives and History, 1975), Honoring Senator Richard B. Russell, January 24, 1971, 24; Wesley G. Pippert, ed., *The Spiritual Journey of Jimmy Carter in His Own Words* (Macmillan, 1978), Couples' Class, First Baptist Church of Washington, August 28, 1977, 63; December 18, 1977, 207–8; January 29, 1978, 63; Jimmy Carter, *Sources of Strength: Meditations on Scripture for a Living Faith* (Random House, 1997), 146.

26. Ronald Reagan, *An American Life* (Simon & Schuster, 1990), 402; David L. Holmes, *The Faiths of the Postwar Presidents: Truman to Obama* (University of Georgia Press, 2012), 179; Ronald Reagan, *Public Papers of the Presidents of the United States, 1985* (Government Printing Office, 1988), Remarks at a Joint German-American Military Ceremony at Bitburg Air Base, May 5, 1985, 566; Remarks on Lighting the National Christmas Tree, December 12, 1985, 1474; Ronald Reagan, *Public Papers of the Presidents of the United States, 1986* (Government Printing Office, 1988), Remarks at the Memorial Service for the Crew of the Space Shuttle *Challenger*, Houston, January 31, 1986, 111; Ronald Reagan, *Public Papers of the Presidents of the United States, 1987* (Government Printing Office, 1989), Remarks at a Memorial Service for Crew Members of the U.S.S. *Stark*, Jacksonville, May 22, 1987, 555; Mary Beth Brown, *Hand of Providence: The Strong and Quiet Faith of Ronald Reagan* (WND Books, 2004), x.

27. Doro Bush Koch, *My Father, My President: A Personal Account of the Life of George H. W. Bush* (Warner Books, 2006), 5, 35, 182.

28. George W. Bush, *Public Papers of the Presidents of the United States, 2001* (Government Printing Office, 2003), Remarks at the Dedication of the National Memorial Center Museum in Oklahoma City, February 19, 2001, 101; George W. Bush, *Public Papers of the Presidents of the United States, 2005* (Government Printing Office, 2009), Radio Address, March 26, 2005, 522; Russell J. Levenson Jr., *Witness to Dignity: The Life and Faith of George H. W. and Barbara Bush* (Center Street, 2022), 255.

29. Barack Obama, *Public Papers of the Presidents of the United States, 2012* (Government Printing Office, 2016), Remarks at the Sandy Hook Interfaith Prayer Vigil in Newtown, Connecticut, December 16, 2012, 1857, 1859; Barack Obama, *Public Papers of the Presidents of the United States, 2015* (Government Printing Office, 2020), Remarks at an Easter Prayer Breakfast, April 7, 2015, 393.

30. Charles Richard Williams, ed., *The Diary and Letters of Rutherford B. Hayes* (Ohio State Archeological and Historical Society, 1922), Diary, June 24–25, 1889, 4:474; Hayes to Harriet C. Herron, December 5, 1889, 4:527; August 24, 1890, 4:595; September 4, 1892, 5:102; Henry Barnard, *Rutherford B. Hayes and His America* (Bobbs-Merrill, 1954), 511.

Chapter 10

1. Roy F. Nichols, *Franklin Pierce: Young Hickory of the Granite Hills* (University of Pennsylvania Press, 1931), 124; John Bassett Moore, ed., *The Works of James Buchanan* (J. B. Lippincott, 1908–1911; repr., Antiquarian Press, 1960), Argument

in the Senate for the Conviction of Judge Peck, January 28–29, 1831, 2:86; Remarks on Removals from Office, June 24, 1841, 4:458.

2. Roy P. Basler, ed., *The Collected Works of Abraham Lincoln* (Rutgers University Press, 1953–1955), Handbill Replying to Charges of Infidelity, July 31, 1846, 1:382; Response to the Loyal Colored People of Baltimore upon Presentation of a Bible, September 7, 1864, 7:542; David Herbert Donald, *Lincoln* (Jonathan Cape, 1995), 514.

3. Leroy P. Graf and Ralph W. Haskins, eds., *The Papers of Andrew Johnson* (University of Tennessee Press, 1967–2000), To the Freemen of the First Congressional District of Tennessee, October 15, 1845, 1:228; Speech at Nashville, July 4, 1862, 5:537.

4. John Y. Simon, ed., *The Papers of Ulysses S. Grant* (Southern Illinois University Press, 1967–2012), *New York Times*, July 24, 1885, 31:212n.

5. Harry James Brown and Frederick D. Williams, eds., *The Diary of James A. Garfield* (Michigan State University Press, 1967), May 19, 1850, 1:43; May 31, 1850, 1:44; May 20, 1852, 1:131; Theodore Roosevelt, *Addresses and Presidential Messages of Theodore Roosevelt, 1902–1904* (G. P. Putnam's Sons, 1904; repr., Kraus, 1971), At the Consecration of Grace Memorial Reformed Church, Washington, June 7, 1903, 225; At the State Fair, Syracuse, New York, September 7, 1903, 242.

6. Arthur S. Link, ed., *The Papers of Woodrow Wilson* (Princeton University Press, 1966–1994), The Bible, August 25, 1876, 1:185; Of the Study of Politics, November 25, 1886, 5:399; A Report of an Address at the Phillips Exeter Academy, *Exeter Exonian*, November 13, 1909, 19:499; An Address in Denver on the Bible, May 7, 1911, 23:13; A Statement, July 23, 1917, 43:244.

7. Frank Kingdon, *As F.D.R. Said: A Treasury of His Speeches, Conversations, and Writings* (Duell, Sloan and Pearce, 1950), 149.

8. Harry S. Truman, *Public Papers of the Presidents of the United States, 1949* (Government Printing Office, 1964), Address at the Unveiling of a Memorial Carillon in Arlington National Cemetery, December 21, 1949, 582; Harry S. Truman, *Public Papers of the Presidents of the United States, 1951* (Government Printing Office, 1965), Address to the Washington Pilgrimage of American Churchmen, September 28, 1951, 550; John F. Kennedy Library & Museum, "Presidential Library and Museum," National Archives, https://www.jfklibrary.org/, Kennedy to Alfred A. Kuna, November 20, 1961; John F. Kennedy, *Public Papers of the Presidents of the United States, 1963* (Government Printing Office, 1964), Special Message to the Congress on Civil Rights and Job Opportunities, June 19, 1963, 493; Lyndon B. Johnson, *Public Papers of the Presidents of the United States, 1966* (Government Printing Office, 1967), Remarks at a Ceremony Marking 1966 as the Year of the Bible, January 19, 1966, 34; Gerald R. Ford Presidential Library & Museum, "Museum and Library," National Archives, https://www.fordlibrarymuseum.gov/ - anchor-section, Lincoln Day Dinner Speech, February 8, 1969; Commencement Address, St. Michael's College, Winooski, Vermont, June 8, 1969; Speech, Brotherhood Commission of the Southern Baptist Convention, June 14, 1974.

9. Jimmy Carter, *Sources of Strength: Meditations on Scripture for a Living Faith* (Random House, 1997), xiv–xv, 128; Jimmy Carter, *Public Papers of the Presidents of the United States, 1980–1981* (Government Printing Office, 1982), Remarks at a White House Reception for Ministers and Religious Leaders, November 25, 1980, 2747; Wesley G. Pippert, ed., *The Spiritual Journey of Jimmy Carter in His Own Words* (Macmillan, 1978), Introduction, 17.

10. Kiron K. Skinner et al., eds., *Reagan: A Life in Letters* (Free Press, 2003), Reagan to Mrs. Warne, 1967, 276; Ronald Reagan, *Public Papers of the Presidents of the United States, 1983* (Government Printing Office, 1984), Remarks at the Annual Convention of the National Religious Broadcasters, January 31, 1983, 152; Remarks at the Annual National Prayer Breakfast, February 3, 1983, 178; Ronald Reagan, *Public Papers of the Presidents of the United States, 1988–1989* (Government Printing Office, 1990), Remarks at the Annual Convention of the National Religious Broadcasters Association, February 1, 1988, 156; George W. Bush, *Public Papers of the Presidents of the United States, 2005* (Government Printing Office, 2009), Interview with Reporters Aboard Air Force One, April 8, 2005, 573; Barack Obama, *Public Papers of the Presidents of the United States, 2013* (Government Printing Office, 2018), Remarks at the National Prayer Breakfast, February 7, 2013, 85.

11. Douglass Adair and John A. Schutz, eds., *The Spur of Fame: Dialogues of John Adams and Benjamin Rush, 1805–1813* (Huntington Library, 1966), Adams to Rush, January 21, 1810, 160; Lester J. Cappon, ed., *The Adams-Jefferson Letters: The Complete Correspondence Between Thomas Jefferson and Abigail and John Adams* (University of North Carolina Press, 1959), John Adams to Jefferson, June 28, 1813, 2:340.

12. Albert Ellery Bergh and Andrew A. Lipscomb, eds., *The Writings of Thomas Jefferson* (Thomas Jefferson Memorial Association, 1904), John Adams to Jefferson, November 15, 1813, 13:440.

13. Adrienne Koch and William Peden, eds., *The Selected Writings of John and John Quincy Adams* (Alfred A. Knopf, 1946), John Quincy Adams to George Washington Adams, September 1, 1811, 279–81; Worthington Chauncey Ford, ed., *Writings of John Quincy Adams* (Macmillan, 1913–1916), Adams to George Washington Adams, September 8, 1811, 4:216–17; National Historical Publications & Records Commission, "Founders Online," National Archives, last updated July 2024, https://founders.archives.gov/, Adams to George Washington Adams, September 22, 1811.

14. National Historical Publications & Records Commission, "Founders Online," https://founders.archives.gov/, John Quincy Adams to George Washington Adams, September 22, 1811; Charles Francis Adams, ed., *Memoirs of John Quincy Adams, Comprising Portions of His Diary from 1795 to 1848* (n.p., 1874–1877; repr., AMS Press, 1970), November 12, 1826, 7:177.

15. Adams, *Memoirs of John Quincy Adams*, December 23, 1838, 10:76.

16. Charles Richard Williams, ed., *The Diary and Letters of Rutherford B. Hayes* (Ohio State Archaeological Historical Society, 1922), Diary, February 22, 1844, 1:145; August 18, 1851, 1:385; Hayes to Fanny Platt, November 8, 1852, 1:431; October 29, 1861, 2:128.

17. David L. Holmes, *The Faiths of the Postwar Presidents: Truman to Obama* (University of Georgia Press, 2012), 104.
18. Douglas L. Wilson, ed., *Jefferson's Literary Commonplace Book* (Princeton University Press, 1989), 55, 156.
19. Cappon, *The Adams-Jefferson Letters*, Jefferson to John Adams, January 24, 1814, 2:421.
20. Julian P. Boyd, ed., *The Papers of Thomas Jefferson* (Princeton University Press, 1950), Jefferson to John Jay, January 25, 1786, 9:216; Jefferson to Peter Carr, August 10, 1787, 12:15–16; Linda K. Kerber, *Federalists in Dissent: Imagery and Ideology in Jeffersonian America* (Cornell University Press, 1970), 90.
21. Daniel Boorstin, *The Lost World of Thomas Jefferson* (Henry Holt, 1948), 41–42.
22. Bergh and Lipscomb, *The Writings of Thomas Jefferson*, Jefferson to Benjamin Rush, April 21, 1803, 10:382; Jefferson to Ezra Stiles, June 25, 1819, 15:203.
23. Bergh and Lipscomb, *The Writings of Thomas Jefferson*, Jefferson to William Short, August 4, 1820, 15:259.
24. Cappon, *The Adams-Jefferson Letters*, Jefferson to John Adams, January 24, 1814, 2:421; April 11, 1823, 2:594; Bergh and Lipscomb, *The Writings of Thomas Jefferson*, Jefferson to Benjamin Rush, April 21, 1803, 10:384; Jefferson to William Short, August 4, 1820, 15:257; Jefferson to Benjamin Waterhouse, June 26, 1822, 15:385.
25. Dickinson W. Adams, ed., *Jefferson's Extracts from the Gospels* (Princeton University Press, 1983), 37, 125, 297; Edwin S. Gaustad, *Faith of Our Fathers: Religion and the New Nation* (Harper & Row, 1987), 102–3.
26. Cappon, *The Adams-Jefferson Letters*, Jefferson to John Adams, October 12, 1813, 2:384; Bergh and Lipscomb, *The Writings of Thomas Jefferson*, Jefferson to F. A. Van der Kemp, April 25, 1816, 15:3; Jefferson to William Short, April 13, 1820, 15:244–45; August 4, 1820, 15:259–60.
27. Robert A. Rutland et al., eds., *The Papers of James Madison* (University of Chicago Press, 1962–1977; repr., University Press of Virginia, 1977), Notes on Commentary of the Bible, 1770–1773, 1:59; Nichols, *Franklin Pierce*, 124; Moore, *The Works of James Buchanan*, Remarks on a Petition for the Abolition of Slavery in the District of Columbia, March 2, 1836, 3:23; Buchanan to George G. Leiper, October 23, 1865, 11:405; Basler, *The Collected Works of Abraham Lincoln*, Speech on the Sub-Treasury, December 26, 1839, 1:167; Speech at Chicago, July 10, 1858, 2:501; Response to the Loyal Colored People of Baltimore upon Presentation of a Bible, September 7, 1864, 7:542.
28. Graf and Haskins, *The Papers of Andrew Johnson*, Speech on Harper's Ferry Incident, December 12, 1859, 3:342; Simon, *The Papers of Ulysses S. Grant*, Grant to Elihu B. Washburne, August 26, 1872, 23:237.
29. Brown and Williams, *Diary of James A. Garfield*, April 4, 1852, 1:124; July 6, 1853, 1:208; George F. Parker, ed., *The Writings and Speeches of Grover Cleveland*

(Cassell, 1892), Address to the Southern Society of New York on Washington's Birthday, February 22, 1890, 348.

30. H. Wayne Morgan, *William McKinley and His America* (Syracuse University Press, 1963), 19; William McKinley, *Speeches and Addresses of William McKinley from His Election to Congress to the Present Time* (D. Appleton, 1893), Address at the Dedication of the YMCA Building in Youngstown, Ohio, September 6, 1892, 607; William McKinley, *Bits of Wisdom of William McKinley* (H. M. Caldwell, 1901), 120.

31. Link, *The Papers of Woodrow Wilson*, Notes for a Religious Talk, March 28, 1897, 10:198; Baccalaureate Address, June 9, 1907, 17:195; A Baccalaureate Address, June 2, 1910, 20:526–27; A Religious Address in Trenton, October 1, 1911, 23:377; Franklin Access to the FDR Library's Digital Collection, "Fully Digitized Collections or Series," Franklin D. Roosevelt Presidential Library and Museum, updated 2011, http://www.fdrlibrary.marist.edu/archives/collections/franklin/, National Conference of Young Democrats, April 13, 1936.

32. Truman, *Public Papers of the Presidents, 1949*, Truman to Pope Pius XII, December 23, 1949, 587; Address at the Lighting of the National Community Christmas Tree, December 24, 1949, 589; Harry S. Truman, *Public Papers of the Presidents of the United States, 1950* (Government Printing Office, 1965), Address at the Lighting of the National Community Christmas Tree, December 24, 1950, 759; Truman, *Public Papers of the Presidents, 1951*, Address at the Lighting of the National Community Christmas Tree, December 24, 1951, 654.

33. Lyndon B. Johnson, *Public Papers of the Presidents of the United States, 1967* (Government Printing Office, 1968), Remarks at the Lighting of the Nation's Christmas Tree, December 15, 1967, 1147; Gerald R. Ford Presidential Library & Museum, "Museum and Library," https://www.fordlibrarymuseum.gov/ - anchorsection, Speech, Brotherhood Commission of the Southern Baptist Convention, June 14, 1974.

34. Pippert, *Spiritual Journey of Jimmy Carter*, Men's Bible Class, Plains Baptist Church, July 18, 1976, 164–65; Carter, *Sources of Strength*, 9–11, 13, 58; Holmes, *Faiths of the Postwar Presidents*, 172.

35. Skinner, *Reagan*, Reagan to Reverend Thomas H. Griffith, March 1, 1978, 277; Ronald Reagan, *Public Papers of the Presidents of the United States, 1981* (Government Printing Office, 1982), Remarks on Lighting the National Community Christmas Tree, December 17, 1981, 1172; Address to the Nation About Christmas and the Situation in Poland, December 23, 1981, 1185; Christmas Message, December 24, 1981, 1188.

36. George H. W. Bush, *Public Papers of the Presidents of the United States, 1989* (Government Printing Office, 1990), Message on the Observance of Christmas, December 18, 1989, 1716; George H. W. Bush, *Public Papers of the Presidents of the United States, 1990* (Government Printing Office, 1991), Message on the Observance of Christmas, December 18, 1990, 1803–4.

37. George W. Bush, *Public Papers of the Presidents of the United States, 2002* (Government Printing Office, 2004), Message on the Observance of Christmas, December

20, 2002, 2209; George W. Bush, *Public Papers of the Presidents of the United States, 2003* (Government Printing Office, 2006), Message on the Observance of Easter, April 17, 2003, 352; Bush, *Public Papers of the Presidents, 2005*, Message on the Observance of Christmas, December 19, 2005, 1889–90; George W. Bush, *Public Papers of the Presidents of the United States, 2006* (Government Printing Office, 2010), Message on the Observance of Easter, April 13, 2006, 730; Message on the Observance of Christmas, December 18, 2006, 2202; George W. Bush, *Public Papers of the Presidents of the United States, 2007* (Government Printing Office, 2011), Remarks on the Lighting of the National Christmas Tree, December 6, 2007, 1530; George W. Bush, *Public Papers of the Presidents of the United States, 2008–2009* (Government Printing Office, 2012), Message on the Observance of Easter, March 21, 2008, 409.

38. Obama, *Public Papers of the Presidents, 2013*, Remarks at the National Prayer Breakfast, February 7, 2013, 85; Remarks at an Easter Prayer Breakfast, April 5, 2013, 281.

39. Bergh and Lipscomb, *The Writings of Thomas Jefferson*, John Adams to Jefferson, September 14, 1813, 13:369; Koch and Peden, *The Selected Writings of John and John Quincy Adams*, John Quincy Adams to John Adams, January 3, 1817, 292; Matthew Stewart, *Nature's God: The Heretical Origins of the American Republic* (W. W. Norton, 2014), 112; David L. Holmes, *The Faiths of the Founding Fathers* (Oxford University Press, 2006) 77.

40. Paul K. Conkin, "The Religious Pilgrimage of Thomas Jefferson," in *Jeffersonian Legacies*, ed. Peter S. Onuf (University Press of Virginia, 1993), 41; Boyd, *The Papers of Thomas Jefferson*, Jefferson to J. P. P. Derieux, July 25, 1788, 13:418.

41. Bergh and Lipscomb, *The Writings of Thomas Jefferson*, Jefferson to Benjamin Rush, April 21, 1803, 10:380; Jefferson to William Short, August 4, 1820, 15:261; Conkin, "The Religious Pilgrimage of Thomas Jefferson," 40.

42. Cappon, *The Adams-Jefferson Letters*, Jefferson to John Adams, July 5, 1814, 2:432–33.

43. Boyd, *The Papers of Thomas Jefferson*, Jefferson to Joseph Priestley, March 21, 1801, 33:393; Jefferson to Elbridge Gerry, March 29, 1801, 33:491–92; Bergh and Lipscomb, *The Writings of Thomas Jefferson*, Jefferson to Jared Sparks, November 4, 1820, 15:288; Jefferson to James Smith, December 8, 1822, 15:408–9.

44. Henry F. Pringle, *The Life and Times of William Howard Taft* (Farrar & Rinehart, 1939), 1:44–45.

45. Richard M. Nixon, *Public Papers of the Presidents of the United States, 1969* (Government Printing Office, 1971), Statement About National Bible Week, October 22, 1969, 829–30; Richard M. Nixon, *RN: The Memoirs of Richard Nixon* (Grosset & Dunlap, 1978), 16; Holmes, *The Faiths of the Postwar Presidents*, 105; Richard M. Nixon, *In the Arena: A Memoir of Victory, Defeat, and Renewal* (Simon & Schuster, 1990), 89.

46. National Historical Publications & Records Commission, "Founders Online," https://founders.archives.gov/, John Quincy Adams to George Washington Adams,

September 22, 1811; Ford, *Writings of John Quincy Adams*, Adams to John Adams, August 31, 1815, 5:362.

47. Ford, *Writings of John Quincy Adams*, Adams to Abigail Adams, December 5, 1815, 5:432–33; Adams to John Adams, January 5, 1816, 5:459.

48. Koch and Peden, *The Selected Writings of John and John Quincy Adams*, John Quincy Adams to John Adams, January 3, 1817, 292.

49. Ford, *The Writings of John Quincy Adams*, Adams to George Sullivan, January 20, 1821, 7:90; Adams, *Memoirs of John Quincy Adams*, February 18, 1827, 7:229; May 13, 1827, 7:273; August 13, 1827, 7:324; March 17, 1828, 7:477; June 3, 1835, 9:240; March 11, 1838, 9:507.

50. Koch and Peden, *The Selected Writings of John and John Quincy Adams*, Diary, March 19, 1843, 397.

51. John P. Kaminsky et al., eds, *The Documentary History of the Ratification of the Constitution* (State Historical Society of Wisconsin, 1976–2008), George Washington to the Executives of the States, *United States Chronicle*, March 1783, 13:70; Paul F. Boller, *George Washington and Religion* (Southern Methodist University Press, 1963), 71–75.

52. For Nelly Custis's statement, see Holmes, *The Faiths of the Founding Fathers*, 70.

53. Holmes, *The Faiths of the Founding Fathers*, 91–92, 97; Rutland, *The Papers of James Madison*, Notes on Commentary of the Bible, 1770–1773, 1:59; Madison to William Bradford, September 25, 1773, 1:96–97n2.

54. John Spencer Bassett, ed., *Correspondence of Andrew Jackson* (Carnegie Institution, 1926–1935), Jackson to Ebenezer H. Cummins, August 31, 1826, 3:311–12; Jackson to William B. Conway, April 4, 1831, 4:256; Harold D. Moser et al., eds., *The Papers of Andrew Jackson* (University of Tennessee Press, 1980), Jackson to John Coffee, September 21, 1829, 7:444.

55. Bassett, *Correspondence of Andrew Jackson*, Jackson's Will, June 7, 1843, 6:220; Jackson to Jesse Duncan Elliott, March 27, 1845, 6:391–92; Robert V. Remini, *Andrew Jackson and the Course of American Democracy, 1833–1845* (Harper & Row, 1984), 519, 524.

56. Moore, *The Works of James Buchanan*, Buchanan to Reverend Edward Buchanan, September 18, 1832, 2:231.

57. Brown and Williams, *Diary of James A. Garfield*, June 8, 1851, 1:85.

58. Joshua David Hawley, *Theodore Roosevelt, Preacher of Righteousness* (Yale University Press, 2008), 14; Elting E. Morison, ed., *The Letters of Theodore Roosevelt* (Harvard University Press, 1951–1954), Roosevelt to William Howard Taft, August 28, 1908, 6:1200; Roosevelt to Maurice Francis Egan, January 19, 1911, 7:211; Roosevelt to Raymond Robins, June 3, 1915, 8:928.

59. Link, *The Papers of Woodrow Wilson*, Notes for a Chapel Talk, January 13, 1895, 9:121; News Report of an Address in New York on Youth and Christian Progress, *New York Times*, November 20, 1905, 16:228.

60. Dan Ariail and Cheryl Heckler-Feltz, *The Carpenter's Apprentice: The Spiritual Biography of Jimmy Carter* (Zondervan, 1996), 117; Carter, *Sources of Strength*, 6, 85–86, 89, 147, 235–37.

61. Mary Beth Brown, *Hand of Providence: The Strong and Quiet Faith of Ronald Reagan* (WND Books, 2004), xiv; Reagan, *Public Papers of the Presidents, 1981*, Statement on the Celebration of Passover and Easter, April 17, 1981, 361.

62. David Aikman, *A Man of Faith: The Spiritual Journey of George W. Bush* (Thomas Nelson, 2004), 127.

63. Barack Obama, *The Audacity of Hope: Thoughts on Reclaiming the American Dream* (Crown Publishers, 2006), 226; Barack Obama, *Papers of the Presidents of the United States, 2010* (Government Printing Office, 2013), Remarks at an Easter Prayer Breakfast, April 6, 2010, 464; Barack Obama, *Public Papers of the Presidents of the United States, 2016–2017* (Government Printing Office, 2021), Remarks at the National Prayer Breakfast, February 4, 2016, 96.

64. Boyd, *The Papers of Thomas Jefferson*, A Bill for Establishing Religious Freedom, 1779, 2:545.

65. Boyd, *The Papers of Thomas Jefferson*, Jefferson to Martha Jefferson, December 11, 1783, 6:380–81.

66. Boorstin, *The Lost World of Thomas Jefferson*, 263n24; Bergh and Lipscomb, *The Writings of Thomas Jefferson*, Jefferson to William Canby, September 18, 1813, 13:377–78; Adams, *Jefferson's Extracts from the Gospels*, Jefferson to Thomas B. Parker, May 15, 1819, 386.

67. National Historical Publications & Records Commission, "Founders Online," https://founders.archives.gov/, John Quincy Adams to George Washington Adams, September 22, 1811 and September 29, 1811; Adams, *Memoirs of John Quincy Adams*, April 3, 1831, 8:353; November 26, 1837, 9:435; December 3, 1837, 9:439.

68. Adams, *Memoirs of John Quincy Adams*, March 30, 1834, 9:117; June 21, 1840, 10:316; January 5, 1845, 12:139–40.

69. Williams, *The Diary and Letters of Rutherford B. Hayes*, Diary, May 26, 1844, 1:152; Hayes to Lucy Webb, August 21, 1851, 1:389.

Chapter 11

1. For the erroneous theory that Augustine was the originator of the doctrine of original sin, see, for instance, Elaine Pagels, *Adam, Eve, and the Serpent* (Random House, 1988).

2. Robert J. Taylor, ed., *The Papers of John Adams* (Harvard University Press, 1977), An Essay on Man's Lust for Power, August 29, 1763, 1:83; L. H. Butterfield, ed., *The Diary and Autobiography of John Adams* (Harvard University Press, 1962), Diary, December 31, 1772, 2:75; John Adams, *A Defence of the Constitutions of Government of the United States of America* (n.p., 1787–1788; repr., Da Capo, 1971), 1:322–24.

3. Richard B. Mattern, ed., *James Madison's "Advice to My Country"* (University Press of Virginia, 1997), Speech to the Constitutional Convention, July 11, 1787, 79; Edward M. Burns, "The Philosophy of History of the Founding Fathers," *The Historian* 16 (Spring 1954):168; Jeffry H. Morrison, *John Witherspoon and the Founding of the American Republic* (University of Notre Dame Press, 2005), 39; Julian P. Boyd, ed., *The Papers of Thomas Jefferson* (Princeton University Press, 1950), James Madison to Jefferson, October 17, 1788, 14:19; Harold C. Syrett, ed., *The Papers of Alexander Hamilton* (Columbia University Press, 1961–1979), *Federalist* No. 51, February 6, 1788, 4:498–99. Although Syrett provides the text of *Federalist* No. 51, he concludes that Madison, not Hamilton, was almost certainly the author.

4. W. W. Abbot, ed., *The Papers of George Washington: Confederation Series* (University Press of Virginia, 1992–1997), Washington to John Jay, August 15, 1786, 4:212.

5. For reference to Madison's alarm at and response to the Nullification Crisis, see Adrienne Koch, *Madison's "Advice to My Country"* (Princeton University Press, 1966), 128–32.

6. Alexander Hamilton, John Jay, and James Madison, *The Federalist: A Commentary on the Constitution of the United States* (Modern Library, 1941), No. 10, 58–59.

7. John C. Fitzpatrick, ed., *The Writings of George Washington* (Government Printing Office, 1931–1940), Washington to Dr. James Anderson, December 24, 1795, 34:407.

8. Zoltan Haraszti, *John Adams and the Prophets of Progress* (Harvard University Press, 1952), 218; John Witte Jr., "'A Most Mild and Equitable Establishment of Religion': John Adams and the Massachusetts Experiment," in *Religion and the New Republic: Faith in the Founding of America*, ed. James H. Hutson (Rowman & Littlefield, 2000), 4.

9. Mattern, *James Madison's "Advice to My Country,"* Madison to Thomas Ritchie, December 18, 1825, 80; Ralph Ketcham, *From Colony to Country: The Revolution in American Thought, 1750–1820* (Macmillan, 1974), 144.

10. Martin Van Buren, *The Autobiography of Martin Van Buren* (American Historical Association, 1920; repr., Da Capo, 1973), 1:184–85.

11. Charles Grier Sellers Jr., *James K. Polk, Jacksonian, 1795–1843* (Princeton University Press, 1957), 106–7.

12. John Bassett Moore, ed., *The Works of James Buchanan* (J. B. Lippincott, 1908–1911; repr., Antiquarian Press, 1960), Speech, February 4, 1828, 1:287–88.

13. Roy P. Basler, ed., *The Collected Works of Abraham Lincoln* (Rutgers University Press, 1953–1955), Speech at Hartford, Connecticut, March 5, 1860, 4:9.

14. Henry F. Pringle, *Theodore Roosevelt: A Biography* (Harcourt, Brace, 1931), 87; Wayne Andrews, ed., *The Autobiography of Theodore Roosevelt* (Charles Scribner's Sons, 1913; repr., Octagon, 1975), 51–52, 91.

15. Herbert Hoover, *Further Addresses upon the American Road, 1938–1940* (Charles Scribner's Sons, 1940), The Imperative Need for Moral Rearmament, November 22, 1938, 183–84.

16. Dwight D. Eisenhower, *Public Papers of the Presidents of the United States, 1954* (Government Printing House, 1960), President's News Conference, November 23, 1954, 1068; Dwight D. Eisenhower, *Public Papers of the Presidents of the United States, 1955* (Government Printing Office, 1959), Remarks for the Cornerstone Laying Ceremony of the American Federation of Labor, April 30, 1955, 444.

17. Adams, *A Defence of the Constitutions*, 1:vi, 99, 181–82; 3:505.

18. Douglass Adair and John A. Schutz, eds., *The Spur of Fame: Dialogues of John Adams and Benjamin Rush, 1805–1813* (Huntington Library, 1966), Adams to Rush, September 9, 1806, 66–67.

19. Bernard Bailyn, *The Ideological Origins of the American Revolution*, 2nd. ed. (Harvard University Press, 1992), 369; Morrison, *John Witherspoon and the Founding of the American Republic*, 39; James H. Smylie, "Madison and Witherspoon: Theological Roots of American Political Thought," *American Presbyterians* 73 (Fall 1995):157–58.

20. John Quincy Adams, *Lectures on Rhetoric and Oratory* (Hilliard and Metcalf, 1810; repr., Russell & Russell, 1962), 1:65; Worthington Chauncey Ford, ed., *Writings of John Quincy Adams* (Macmillan, 1913–1916), Adams to George Washington Adams, September 8, 1811, 4:212–13; National Historical Publications & Records Commission, "Founders Online," National Archives, https://founders.archives.gov/, John Quincy Adams to George Washington Adams, September 22, 1811; Charles Francis Adams, ed., *Memoirs of John Quincy Adams, Comprising Portions of His Diary from 1795 to 1848* (n.p., 1874–1877; repr., AMS Press, 1970), May 6, 1827, 7:269.

21. National Historical Publications & Records Commission, "Founders Online," https://founders.archives.gov/, Thomas Jefferson to William G. Munford, June 18, 1799.

22. Gordon S. Wood, *The Creation of the American Republic* (University of North Carolina Press, 1969), 201, 213, 215, 436; William Peden, ed., *Notes on the State of Virginia* (University of North Carolina Press, 1955), 165; Richard K. Matthews, *The Radical Politics of Thomas Jefferson: A Revisionist View* (University Press of Kansas, 1984), 43; A. Whitney Griswold, "Jefferson's Agrarian Democracy," in Henry C. Dethloff, ed., *Thomas Jefferson and American Democracy* (D. C. Heath, 1971), 46–47.

23. Eleanor Davidson Berman, *Thomas Jefferson Among the Arts: An Essay in Early American Esthetics* (Philosophical Library, 1947), 25; Albert Ellery Bergh and Andrew A. Lipscomb, eds., *The Writings of Thomas Jefferson* (Thomas Jefferson Memorial Association, 1904), Jefferson to DuPont de Nemours, April 24, 1816, vol. 14, 491–92; Wilson Smith, ed., *Theories on Education in Early America, 1655–1819* (Bobbs-Merrill, 1973), Report of the Commissioners Appointed to Fix the Site of the University of Virginia, 1818, 326.

24. Robert V. Remini, *Andrew Jackson and the Course of American Democracy, 1833–1845* (Harper & Row, 1984), 446.

25. Leroy P. Graf and Ralph W. Haskins, eds., *The Papers of Andrew Johnson* (University of Tennessee Press, 1967–2000), First Inaugural Address, October 17, 1853, 2:175–77.

26. Arthur S. Link, ed., *The Papers of Woodrow Wilson* (Princeton University Press, 1966–1994), Wilson to Ellen Louise Axson, December 22, 1884, 3:570; The Modern Democratic State, December 1–20, 1885, 5:90.

27. Thomas H. Greer, *What Roosevelt Thought: The Social and Political Ideas of Franklin D. Roosevelt* (Michigan State University Press, 1958), 9.

28. Lyndon B. Johnson, *Public Papers of the Presidents of the United States, 1968–1969* (Government Printing Office, 1970), Remarks of Welcome at the White House to Chancellor Josef Klaus of Austria, April 10, 1968, 503.

29. Paul Lettow, *Ronald Reagan and His Quest to Abolish Nuclear Weapons* (Random House, 2006); George W. Bush, *Public Papers of the Presidents of the United States, 2006* (Government Printing Office, 2010), News Conference in Chicago, July 7, 2006, 1347.

Appendix I

1. Jefferson was a vestryman at two different Anglican/Episcopalian churches for nearly twenty years, but later in life, he preferred to attend multidenominational Protestant services.

2. Polk had a conversion experience at a Methodist camp meeting and thereafter considered himself a Methodist, though he often attended Presbyterian services with his wife, who was a Presbyterian.

3. Most of his life, Carter was a Southern Baptist, but in 2000, he left the Southern Baptist Convention because it refused to ordain women. With his encouragement, his Maranatha Baptist Church in Plains, Georgia, joined the Cooperative Baptist Fellowship.

4. Reagan was raised in the Disciples of Christ Church and was a devoted member of the church for many years, but after 1963, he generally attended Presbyterian services, especially at Bel Air Presbyterian Church, of which he became a member after retiring from the presidency.

5. Obama was a member of Trinity United Church of Christ in Chicago for more than twenty years, but he broke with the church in 2008. He has attended the services of various other denominations.

6. For many years Trump's closest affiliation was with Lakeside Presbyterian Church in West Palm Beach, Florida, but in October 2020, he declared that he was no longer a Presbyterian and was now nondenominational.

Index

Aaron, 85–86
Abel, 95, 209, 219
abolitionist movement, 39–40, 104, 167–68, 243–44
abortion, 161–64
Abraham, 42, 56, 82, 84, 96, 101, 208–9, 211–12
Acts of the Apostles, 13, 24, 42, 49, 91, 99, 129, 165, 310
Adam, 46, 81, 93–95, 97, 101, 154, 168, 213, 261, 289–91, 310
Adams, Abigail, 6–7, 19, 38, 119, 139, 248–49, 274, 277
Adams, John, xv, 6–7, 21, 25, 38, 43, 82–84, 92, 95–97, 115–16, 130–31, 139, 146, 155, 178, 189, 196, 199, 214, 216, 226, 228, 230–31, 247–49, 262, 273–74, 277, 291, 293, 297–98, 307, 309
Adams, John Quincy, xv, 2, 6–8, 22–24, 35, 44–46, 71, 85–87, 90–92, 94, 97–98, 103–4, 116–17, 119–20, 131, 156, 169–70, 195–96, 214, 216–17, 226–28, 231–32, 250–51, 262–64, 276–79, 286–87, 294, 297, 299, 307, 309

Adams, Louisa, 119, 226
Adams, Samuel, 37, 146
Adams-Onis Treaty, 103–4, 195
Africa, 34, 66–67, 69, 89, 166, 169–70, 198, 210, 225
afterlife, belief in, xv–xvi, 7–9, 19–20, 23–24, 37, 45, 89, 91, 121, 182, 232, 242, 245–57, 263–64, 273, 278, 280–88, 309
American Bible Society, 68–69, 75–76
American Revolution, xi, xv, 1, 21, 35, 37–39, 116, 155, 167–68, 178
Amistad, 169, 251
Amos, Book of, 54, 88–89
angels, 54, 61–62, 93–94, 120, 127, 157, 159, 200, 292
Anglicans, 3, 21–22, 25, 30, 38
Aquinas, Thomas, 154
Aristotle, 101, 154, 226
Armageddon, 61, 208
Arthur, Chester, 148, 308
Articles of Confederation, 190, 192, 292
Assyrians, 74, 129
Athanasius, 275–78

Atlanta, Georgia, 31, 77, 147, 261
atomic bomb, 54, 56, 60–61, 95, 159, 198, 304
Augustine, 154, 275, 289
Austin, Texas, 33, 85, 125

Babylonians, 88, 97, 107, 205–06
baptism, 10, 18, 20, 26, 31, 33, 310
Baptists, 3, 13–14, 16–17, 22, 24–25, 30, 47–48, 62, 69–70, 76–77, 140, 142–43, 172, 175, 210, 281, 305, 308
Bathsheba, 54
Battle of New Orleans, 104, 195–96
Beatitudes, 54, 209, 238, 311
Beecher, Henry Ward, 26–27
Beecher, Lyman, 39–40
Begin, Menachem, 58, 84, 150, 209
Ben-Gurion, David, 211
Berlin, Germany, 73, 162–63, 198–99, 207
Bethlehem, 30, 35, 49, 208, 225, 272–73
Biden, Joseph (Joe), 34–35, 164, 308
Boston, Massachusetts, 37–38, 186, 277
Bowdoin College, 3, 5
Brezhnev, Leonid, 256
Brown, John, 95, 200–1, 270
Bryan, William Jennings, 50
Buchanan, Elizabeth, 9, 121
Buchanan, James, 9, 25, 35, 66, 72, 95, 98, 105–6, 121, 150, 156, 178, 183, 192, 253, 259, 270, 282, 295, 307
Buffalo, New York, 228, 233
Burr, Aaron, 117
Bush, Barbara, 19–20, 85, 126, 256, 284
Bush, Dorothy, 19, 33, 215, 256
Bush, George H. W., 19–20, 32–33, 61, 69, 77–78, 81, 126, 142–43, 150–51, 162–63, 198–99, 202, 210, 215, 224, 242, 256, 272, 308, 312
Bush, George W., 19, 33, 61–62, 81, 84, 114, 126–27, 143–44, 150, 163–64, 186, 211, 225, 242, 256, 262, 272–73, 284, 304, 308
Bush, Jeb, 20
Bush, Laura, 114, 163
Bush, Robin, 19, 126, 256

Cain, 95, 219, 289
Calhoun, John C., 228
Calvin, John, 154–55, 277, 282, 286–87, 290, 292
Camp David, 58, 143, 150
Carter, Earl, 17
Carter, James Earl (Jimmy), 2, 17–18, 31–32, 57–59, 69, 77, 80–82, 86–87, 90–91, 97, 114, 116, 125, 139–40, 150, 160–61, 164–65, 175, 181, 185–86, 208–9, 214, 222, 228, 241, 255, 261–262, 271–72, 283–84, 308, 311
Carter, Rosalynn, 17–18, 31–32, 59, 125, 208–9, 223
charity, 14, 16, 18, 21, 31, 56, 69, 72, 78, 81, 90–91, 124, 138, 213, 215–27
Chicago, Illinois, 13, 34, 114
China, 33, 68–70, 134, 137
Chronicles, 1 and 2, 18, 57, 60, 62–63, 87, 113, 127, 245, 312
Churchill, Winston, 30, 54, 135, 198
Cicero, Marcus Tullius, 154, 214, 217
Cincinnati, Ohio, 10, 24
city on a hill, concept of, xiv, 36, 38–39, 177–78, 181–82
civil rights movement, xi, xiv, 1, 56, 64, 81–82, 85, 153, 165–66, 170–74, 243–44
classics, Greco-Roman, 44–45, 70, 88, 104, 107, 153–54, 166, 213–17, 226, 246, 257, 262–63, 265–66, 268, 276, 297, 299
Clay, Henry, 66–67, 94
Cleaver, Ben, 32
Cleveland, Frances, 109
Cleveland, Grover, ix, 11, 27, 81, 109, 148, 179, 193, 228, 233–34, 270, 308
Cleveland, Richard, 11
Clinton, William Jefferson (Bill), 61–82, 89, 126, 164, 186, 224, 308, 312

Cold War, xiv, 54, 56, 60–61, 69, 76, 94–95, 114, 134, 157, 159–60, 162–63, 180, 198–99, 237, 304
College of William and Mary, 3, 88
Colossians, Book of, 269–70
Confederates, 48–49, 93, 108, 122–23, 147, 196–97, 227
Congregationalists, 21, 23, 25, 80, 230, 308
Continental Congress, 21, 38, 82, 97, 130, 146, 155, 249
Coolidge, Calvin, 4–5, 13, 29, 68, 111–12, 134, 148, 167, 194–95, 197, 236–37, 308, 310–11
Coolidge, Grace, 29
Coolidge, Sarah, 13
Corinthians, 1 and 2, 8, 20, 22, 36, 55, 57, 63, 91, 111, 132, 163, 165–66, 171, 220–21, 223, 250–51, 255–57, 282, 309
Craig, Mark, 85

D-Day, 62, 134, 149, 198
Dallas, Texas, 33, 85
Daniel, Book of, 36, 55, 89, 245, 270
David, 34, 44, 46, 53, 58, 62–63, 71, 87, 97, 215–16, 259, 269
Davies, Samuel, 102
Davis, Patti, 141
days of public prayer, officially designated, 146–50
Deborah, 86
Declaration of Independence, 38, 125, 153, 158–59, 167, 169–70, 196, 237
Deists, 7, 118–19, 293–94
Delilah, 97
democracy, xv, 39, 158–59, 167, 172, 195, 202, 234–42, 244, 298–99, 301–4
Democratic-Republicans, 130, 305
Democrats, 55, 96, 98, 161, 164–65, 175, 201, 220, 222–25, 243–44, 305, 311

Deng, Xioping, 69
Desert Storm, Operation, 69
Deuteronomy, Book of, 8, 36, 51, 55, 57, 83–84, 210, 282, 311
Disciples of Christ Church, 4, 18, 26–27, 31, 73, 77, 307–8, 310
divinity of Jesus, belief in, xv, 242–43, 268–80, 288–89
Dix, Dorothea, 132
Douglas, Stephen, 93, 201
Douglass, Frederick, 49, 243
DuBois, W. E. B., 73
Dutch Reformed Church, 3, 21, 28, 282, 307–8

Eastern Orthodox Church, 22
Ecclesiastes, Book of, 36, 55, 57, 59, 246, 289–90, 311
Eden, Garden of, 48, 57, 92, 94, 101, 199, 205, 209, 264
Edwards, Jonathan, 36
Egypt, 58, 82–85, 97, 150, 178, 200, 262, 309
Eisenhower, David, 14–15, 30–31
Eisenhower, Dwight, 14–15, 20, 68, 76, 112–13, 115, 136–37, 149–51, 159, 172–73, 181, 185, 205–6, 221, 239–40, 308, 311
Eisenhower, Ida, 14–15, 311
Eisenhower, Mamie, 30–31, 150–51
elections, presidential, 8–9, 22–23, 34, 43, 50, 55, 60–62, 86, 93–94, 104–5, 117, 125, 133, 141, 143, 156, 172, 276, 294–95, 311
Electoral College, 94, 291, 294, 303
Elijah, 129
Elisha, 129, 295
Emancipation Proclamation, 40, 132
Enoch, 43
Ephesians, Paul's letter to, 67, 93–94, 166, 218, 281
Ephesus, 49
Epicureans, 101, 154, 214–16, 265

Episcopalians, 2, 4, 14, 16, 21–24, 28–33, 70, 74, 138–39, 142–43, 274, 281, 305, 307
equality, belief in spiritual, xiii–xiv, 40, 165–76, 288
Esau, 96
Esther, 54, 97–98
Ethiopia, 210
Eureka College, 4, 77, 140
Eve, 81, 93–95, 101, 168, 213, 261, 289
Exodus, Book of, 47, 50, 55, 82–85, 96, 107, 132, 158, 166, 192, 210, 222, 239, 262, 267, 281, 309, 311
Ezekiel, Book of, 34, 61, 88, 205, 209

federalism, theory of, 290, 292, 294, 304
The Federalist, 191, 292–93
Federalists, 42, 97, 230, 305
Fillmore, Millard, 132, 227, 252, 307
Finney, Charles G., 39
Flood, belief in the Great, 73, 101, 265
Ford, Betty, 16–17, 138
Ford, Dorothy, 16, 227
Ford, Gerald R., 16, 31, 57, 76–77, 87–88, 113–14, 138–39, 149, 185–86, 208, 227, 240–41, 254–55, 261, 271, 308, 311
forgiveness, 16, 19, 73, 213, 216, 226–29, 241, 269
France, 6, 29, 97, 102, 111, 116–17, 130–31, 146, 198, 230, 242, 300
Franklin, Benjamin, 3, 37, 83, 167, 193, 226
French and Indian War (Seven Years' War), 102, 116
French Revolution, 130, 230, 247

Galatians, Paul's letter to, 165
Galilee, 208, 221
Gallaudet, Thomas, 91
Gamaliel, 13
Garfield, James, 3–4, 10–11, 26–27, 73, 80, 84, 109–11, 122–23, 133, 148, 171, 200–1, 253, 260, 270, 282, 307, 310

Garfield, Lucretia, 10, 26, 80
Garman, Charles E., 5
Garrison, William Lloyd, 39
Genesis, Book of, xiii, 6, 36, 47–50, 56–58, 60, 67, 81–82, 84, 92, 94–97, 126, 153, 158, 162, 165, 177, 193, 208–9, 211, 213, 219, 245, 261–62, 264, 289, 291, 303, 310, 312
Germany, 20, 44, 49, 73, 112, 204, 255
Gethsemane, Garden of, 49, 123, 310
Gettysburg Address, 46–47, 53, 107
Golden Rule, 10, 56, 88, 164, 216, 221, 230, 234, 236, 239
Goliath, 34, 87
Gomorrah, 95–96
Good Samaritan, 90–91, 172, 217, 219–20, 223–25, 311
Graham, Billy, 61, 145–46, 173, 284
Grant, Hannah, 10
Grant, Julia, 10, 25, 95, 150
Grant, Ulysses, 10, 25, 49, 65–66, 72, 93, 95–96, 107–8, 132–33, 147–48, 150, 170, 196, 202, 254, 260, 270, 307
Great Awakening, 3, 36–39
Great Britain, xiv–xv, 25–26, 28, 36–37, 67, 82–84, 92–93, 113, 115–17, 130, 156, 165, 167, 180, 186, 198, 203–4, 226, 231, 275, 289, 297
Great Depression, 18, 124, 219, 311
Great Society, 222, 304
Great Temple of Jerusalem, 98, 205
Greeley, Horace, 93

Habitat for Humanity, 125, 223
Haman, 97–98
Hamilton, Alexander, 117, 228
Hancock, John, 146
Hannah, 129
Harding, Phoebe, 12–13
Harding, Warren G., 12–13, 53, 134, 148, 156, 176, 179–80, 184, 189, 194, 235–36, 308
Harris, Kamala, 174

Harrison, Benjamin, 5, 11, 27, 50, 67, 73–74, 109, 133–34, 202, 253, 308
Harrison, Caroline, 27, 50, 109, 133–34
Harrison, Elizabeth, 11
Harrison, William Henry, 24, 46, 98, 120, 307
Harvard University, 2–3, 22, 42, 74, 85, 226, 231, 299
Hawaii, 66
Hayes, Lucy, 10, 26, 108–9, 257
Hayes, Rutherford, xv, 10, 49, 73, 108–9, 133, 171, 196, 232–33, 257, 264–65, 287–88, 307
Hayes, Sophia, 10
Hazael, 295
Hebrew (language), 4, 27, 132, 211
Hebrews, Book of, 11, 14, 23, 55, 88, 104, 108, 129, 269, 310–11
Henry, Patrick, 118, 298
Hermitage, 24, 71, 217, 251
Hezekiah, 129
Hinckley, John, 32, 114, 141, 228
Hitler, Adolf, 157, 206
Holocaust, 160, 205–6, 209
Holy Spirit, 17, 39, 64, 94, 144–45, 154–55, 260, 267, 273, 284, 299, 302
Holy Trinity, 7, 273–75
Homer, 3, 246, 280
Hoover, Herbert, 13–14, 53, 80, 87, 93–94, 97, 134, 157, 180, 197, 203, 219–20, 223, 237, 296, 308, 311
Hoover, Huldah, 13–14, 311
Hoover, Rebecca, 13
Hosea, Book of, 36
Houston, Sam, 16, 65, 224
Houston, Texas, 20, 33, 78, 114
human nature, xv–xvi, 289–304
humility, 11–12, 62, 80–81, 83, 87, 112, 144–45, 213–15, 228, 288

India, 68
Iranian Hostage Crisis, 150, 228
Iraq, 142, 163, 203, 256
Isaac, 50, 132, 209, 211

Isaiah, Book of, 6, 36, 54–56, 58, 60, 88–89, 140, 158, 205, 207–8, 211, 213, 239, 270–71, 273, 277, 290, 302, 311
Ishmael, 88, 209
Israel, modern, xiv, 34, 49, 57–58, 82, 84, 86, 89, 150, 177, 203–12

Jackson, Andrew, 8–9, 24, 65, 71, 90, 94, 104–5, 115, 120–21, 132, 156, 175, 183, 195–96, 228, 232, 251–53, 281–82, 301, 307, 310
Jackson, Elizabeth, 8
Jackson, Rachel, 8–9, 71, 104, 132, 251, 281
Jacob, 96, 132, 178, 211, 303
James, Book of, 129, 132, 165, 222, 253, 283–84, 287–88, 299
James, William, 5
Jamestown, Virginia, 204
Japan, 74, 112–13, 143, 198
Jay, John, 115, 146, 292
Jefferson, Jane, 8–9
Jefferson, Martha, 249
Jefferson, Thomas, xv, 7, 21–22, 38, 43–44, 69–70, 83, 88–90, 95, 97, 115, 119, 130, 153, 155–56, 168–69, 171, 182–83, 189, 191–92, 196, 199–201, 214–16, 226, 242–43, 247–250, 264–69, 273, 276, 279, 285–86, 293, 299–301, 303–4, 307, 309
Jehovah's Witnesses, 14–15
Jeremiah, Book of, 55, 88, 104, 119, 205, 289, 299
Jericho, 35, 199, 208, 224–25
Jerusalem, 49, 80, 98, 140, 144, 178, 206, 208, 224
Jesus, xv, 5, 7–12, 16, 20, 22–23, 25–26, 33, 37–39, 42–43, 45–49, 52, 54, 58–59, 61–62, 64, 69–70, 75–76, 80–81, 84, 89–90, 93, 96, 98, 101, 114, 119, 123, 125, 129, 131, 134, 136, 140, 142, 145, 161, 165–66, 170, 172, 175, 178, 202, 212–21, 226, 228,

233, 235, 238, 240, 242, 245, 247, 249, 252, 255–57, 259–61, 263–88, 290, 302, 310
Jews, 17, 42, 74, 82, 88, 91, 94, 133, 154, 165, 177–78, 203–12, 222, 236, 267, 269, 273
Job, 26, 245
Job, Book of, 8, 81–82, 92
Joel, Book of, 248
John, 1, 2, and 3, 17, 224–25, 256, 311
John, Gospel of, 3, 9, 13, 20, 36, 47, 52, 59, 62, 98, 124, 214, 217, 247, 256, 267, 269–70, 272–275, 280–81, 287, 310–11
John the Baptist, 89, 281
John Paul II, Pope, 114
Johnson, Andrew, 81, 84, 86–87, 90, 92–95, 107, 146–47, 175, 179, 192–93, 196, 206–7, 253, 260, 270–71, 302, 307
Johnson, Claudia (Lady Bird), 31
Johnson, Lyndon B., 16, 31, 56, 87, 115–16, 125, 137–38, 149, 174–75, 181, 185, 202, 222, 227, 261, 271, 303–4, 308, 311
Johnson, Rebekah, 16
Jonah, 49
Jordan, nation of, 207, 210
Joseph, son of Jacob, 82, 96, 126
Joshua, 83–85, 201, 205, 210
Joshua, Book of, 199, 205, 266
Judas, 94, 214
Jude, Book of, 43, 165
Judges, Book of, 86, 245, 291

Kennebunkport, Maine, 20, 33, 61
Kennedy, John F., 15–16, 31, 55–56, 68–69, 95, 113, 125, 137, 149, 159–60, 173–74, 206, 221–22, 240, 261, 308, 311
Kennedy, Rose, 15–16
Khomeini, Ayatollah, 228
King, Martin Luther Jr., xiv, 40, 85, 176, 224, 243

King James Version of the Bible, xii, 46–47, 53–54, 58–59, 63–64, 96, 124
Kings, 1 and 2, 97, 129, 245, 289, 295
Kissinger, Henry, 207–8
Korean War, 134, 148

labor reforms, 40, 244
Lafayette, Gilbert du Motier de, 130, 189
League of Nations, 124
Lee, Robert E., 49
Leviticus, Book of, 7, 31, 158, 165, 222
Lillie, William, 26
Lincoln, Abraham, xii, 40, 46–49, 53, 63–67, 80, 86–87, 91, 93, 95, 97–98, 106–7, 110–11, 113, 115, 122, 132, 146–47, 156, 158, 161, 170–71, 178–79, 183–84, 196–97, 200–1, 215, 217–18, 227, 232, 243, 253–54, 259–60, 270, 295, 307, 310
Little Rock, Arkansas, 81–82, 173
Livermore, Harriet, 226–27
Lloyd George, David, 29
Locke, John, 1, 155
Lord's Prayer, 2, 6–7, 73, 123, 129, 131, 134
Lord's Supper, 21–22, 32, 280
Los Angeles, California, 29
Lot, 56, 82, 96
Louisiana Purchase, 195, 300
Luke, Gospel of, 4, 16, 22, 36, 55–56, 59, 90–91, 123, 144, 165, 202, 219–20, 225, 256, 272, 280–81, 303, 310–11
Luther, Martin, 20, 44, 89, 154, 281
Lutherans, 25, 71

Madison, James, xv, 2, 4, 87, 92, 119, 130–31, 146, 191, 216, 231, 239, 250, 270, 280, 291–94, 297–98, 307
Magna Carta, 55
Mark, Gospel of, 36, 58, 90–91, 253, 280
Marxism, 94, 157, 220, 237

Mary, mother of Jesus, 47, 271
Mary Magdalene, 90
Mason, George, 298
Massillon, Jean-Baptiste, 35, 277
Matthew, Gospel of, 4–8, 11, 30–31, 36–38, 46–47, 51, 55–56, 58–59, 61, 64, 67, 93–94, 96, 98, 119, 121, 129, 141, 158, 161–62, 165–66, 170, 178, 201, 213–14, 217–19, 221–22, 224, 228–29, 238–39, 248–49, 252–53, 257, 269, 273, 279–80, 311
McClellan, George, 93
McGready, James, 39
McKinley, Allison, 11–12
McKinley, William, 11–12, 27, 29, 67, 108–9, 123, 184, 197–98, 202, 234, 254, 270, 308, 310
Medicaid, 161, 304
Medicare, 221–22, 304
Meir, Golda, 86, 209
Methodists, 10–12, 17, 22, 24–27, 29–30, 33, 35, 39, 72–73, 76, 133, 281, 307–8
Mexican War, xiv, 87, 95, 150, 180, 196
Micah, Book of, 42, 51, 88, 238, 283, 309–10
Millennium, biblical prophecy of the, 39, 42, 291, 296, 302–3
miracles, xiii, 101, 189, 192–93, 197, 263–66, 268, 283
missionaries, xii, 10, 41, 51, 64–69, 72, 78, 222–23
mixed government theory, 290–91, 297–99
Monroe, James, xv, 167, 182–83, 196, 250, 280, 307
Montesquieu, Charles de Secondat, 290
moral sense, theory of the, 168, 242, 294, 300
Mordecai, 97
Moses, 34, 81–86, 132, 205, 210, 215, 239–40, 267
Mount of Olives, 49, 208
Mount Vernon, 42, 83–84, 309

Native Americans, 3, 64–66, 69, 175, 180
natural law, 84, 154–55
natural rights, xiii–xiv, xvi, 153–65, 288
Nazareth, 208, 278
Nazis, 157–58, 171, 180, 198, 203, 205–6, 219, 237, 296
Nebuchadnezzar, 97
New Deal, 157, 303
New Orleans, Louisiana, 72, 104, 130, 195–96
New York City, New York, 12, 21, 28, 50, 74, 76, 110
Newman, John P., 25, 108, 132, 260
Newton, Isaac, 169, 273
Nimrod, 95
Nixon, Richard, xv, 57, 86, 138–39, 149, 207–8, 228–29, 265, 276, 308
Noah, 49–50, 81
Nobel Peace Prize, 74, 271–72
North Korea, 137, 163
Northwest Ordinance of 1787, 156, 169
Nullification Crisis, 92, 228, 292
Numbers, Book of, 7, 85, 145

Obama, Barack, 34, 62–64, 81, 85, 114, 127, 144–45, 164–65, 174, 211, 225–26, 243–44, 256–57, 262, 273, 284–85, 305, 308, 312
Obama, Michelle, 34, 114
Original sin, xv, 154, 286, 289–99, 301–2

Panama, 30, 74
Passover, 148, 210, 281
Paul, the apostle, 3, 13, 26, 49, 55, 57, 73, 88, 91, 93–94, 129, 140, 154, 158, 163, 165, 175, 214, 221, 239, 248, 250–51, 255–57, 259, 269, 281, 286–88, 290, 299
Peabody, Endicott, 2
Pearl Harbor, Japanese attack on, 112, 143, 198
Penn, William, 238

Persian Gulf War, 142–43, 150
Peter, 1 and 2, 16–17, 25, 129, 257, 259
Peter, the apostle, 129, 165
Philadelphia, Pennsylvania, 3, 21, 36–37, 72, 113, 190
Philippians, Paul's letter to, 8, 57, 129
Philippines, 67, 112
Philistines, 87
Pierce, Franklin, 3, 5, 98, 121, 259, 270, 307
Pius XII, Pope, 112, 171
Plains, Georgia, 2, 17, 31–32, 69, 77
Plato, 45, 101, 154–55, 214, 217, 275–76, 290
Plutarch, 45, 250–51
Polk, James K., 2–3, 9, 24–25, 71, 90, 95, 98, 115, 117, 189, 217, 294–95, 307, 310
Polk, Jane, 9
Polk, Sarah, 9, 24
postmillennialism, 39, 302–3
Potiphar, 82
prayer, xiii, xvii, 2–7, 11–19, 30, 46, 56, 63, 73, 119–20, 125, 129–51, 222, 226, 228, 284
Prayer of St. Francis, 17, 141–42
Presbyterians, 2–3, 5, 9, 11–12, 19, 21, 24–25, 27–33, 39, 68, 70, 158, 217, 278, 281, 283, 286, 301, 303, 305, 307–8
Priestley, Joseph, 226, 275, 277
Princeton University, 2–4, 52, 75, 87, 235, 280
Prodigal Son, 91
Progressive Era, xi, xv, 1, 289, 303–4
Promised Land, 84–85
Protestant Reformation, 108, 154
Proverbs, Book of, x, 7, 15–16, 36, 49, 51, 55–56, 60–61, 87–88, 138, 146, 166, 289, 311–12
Providence, divine, xiii, xvi, 6, 9, 18, 26, 65, 67, 72–73, 82, 86, 101–27, 131, 134, 148, 178–200, 215, 217, 251, 253, 279–80, 288

Providence, Rhode Island, 36, 148
Psalms, Book of, 1–2, 7, 14, 19, 21, 23, 29, 37, 41, 44–48, 52–53, 55, 57–58, 60, 63–64, 70–71, 104, 112, 119–20, 125–26, 131, 134, 137–38, 140, 142, 150, 157, 159, 162, 185, 202, 211, 216, 222, 240, 245, 249, 259, 267, 269, 289, 309
Puritans, 3, 13, 37–39, 82, 178, 181
Pythagoras, 154, 216

Qaddafi, Muamar, 229
Quakers, 13–14, 65–66, 132, 276, 308

Rabin, Yitzak, 210–11
Reagan, Maureen, 18–19
Reagan, Michael, 18–19, 32, 256
Reagan, Nelle, 18–19, 60, 126, 141, 215, 312
Reagan, Ronald, 4, 18–19, 32, 59–61, 77, 84, 94, 114, 125–26, 140–42, 150, 161–62, 181–82, 186, 209–10, 215, 223–24, 228–29, 241–42, 255–56, 262, 272, 284, 304, 308, 312
Rebecca, 50
Reconstruction Period, 173, 179, 227
Republicans, 61, 87, 93, 98, 110, 156, 176, 181, 224, 243, 295, 305
Revelation, Book of, 8, 23, 36, 54, 110, 256
Revolutionary War, xiv, 102, 117, 146, 182, 186–89, 191, 193–94, 226, 279
Richmond, Virginia, 49, 215
Roman Catholics, 15–16, 21–22, 25, 31, 34–35, 44, 70, 74, 92–93, 132, 281–83, 305, 308
Romans, Paul's letter to, 3, 25–26, 50, 58, 62–64, 127, 145, 165, 172, 214, 217, 281–82, 286, 290, 299, 312
Roosevelt, Eleanor, 204
Roosevelt, Franklin D., 2, 14, 20, 29–30, 53–54, 90–91, 99, 112, 124, 134–35, 139, 148, 151, 157–58, 161,

171–72, 180, 185, 198, 203, 220–21, 237–38, 261, 271, 303, 308, 311
Roosevelt, James, 14
Roosevelt, Theodore, 12, 28, 50–51, 67–68, 74, 88, 96, 99, 111, 123, 171, 184, 202–3, 218, 234–35, 260, 282–83, 295–96, 308, 310
Rummel, Joseph Francis, 173
Rush, Benjamin, 97, 130, 231
Russia, 22, 25, 35, 44, 71, 74, 103, 105, 115, 131, 205, 208, 210
Ruth, 54, 86

Sabbath, 3, 9, 13–14, 24, 27–28, 46, 49, 80, 179, 224
Sadat, Anwar, 58, 140, 150, 229
salvation by faith in Jesus, xv, 1, 23–24, 252, 255, 257, 280–88
same-sex marriage, 164–65
Samson, 97
Samuel, 1 and 2, 6, 36, 88, 97, 129, 245
Sarah, 84, 211–12
Satan, 48, 92–93, 213, 230, 264, 295–96
Saudi Arabia, 204
Saul, 87, 97
Schneider, Wunibald, 31
Second Coming of Christ, 43, 73
Second Great Awakening, 39–40, 302
separation of powers theory, 290–292
September 11 attacks, 34, 62–64, 126–127, 150, 163, 312
Septuagint, 43
Sermon on the Mount, 9, 45, 54–55, 178, 208, 213–14, 216, 220–21, 238–39, 268
Seventh Day Adventists, 12–13
Shakespeare, William, 49
Simeon, 89–90
slavery, 39, 47–49, 63, 66–67, 87, 92, 98, 104, 107, 122–23, 126, 156, 159, 161, 165–71, 175–176, 196–97, 199–202, 217–18, 221, 295, 310
Social Gospel movement, 40

Social Security, 82, 222, 224
Socrates, 5, 277
Sodom, 95–96
Solomon, 53, 87–88, 97, 135, 210, 246
Soviet Union, 56, 60, 95, 162, 206–8, 210, 256
Spain, 104, 195
Spanish-American War, xiv, 184, 197–98
Springfield, Illinois, 46, 106
Spurgeon, Charles, 26
Stalin, Joseph, 54, 157
Statue of Liberty, 180–81, 208
Stoics, 101, 154, 246
Stowe, Harriet Beecher, 40
Sunday school, xi, 2, 10, 12–13, 16–19, 30–32, 49, 72–78, 138, 243, 255, 271
Syria, 207, 295

Taft, William Howard, xv, 51–52, 74, 110, 193–94, 196, 254, 276, 308
Taylor, Zachary, 71–72, 97–98, 146, 307
Tel Aviv, Israel, 211–12
temperance movement, 39, 49, 91
Ten Commandments, 9, 50–51, 55, 77, 155, 216, 222, 234, 239, 261, 311
Thanksgiving Day, 124, 134, 147, 149, 184, 219
Thessalonians, 1 and 2, 8, 129, 248, 286
Thomas, the apostle, 270
Tillotson, John, 35
Timothy, 1 and 2, 36, 129, 138, 165, 255, 259, 271
Titus, Paul's letter to, 269
Treaty of Ghent, 103, 226
Treaty of Versailles, 29, 93, 111, 310
Truman, Elizabeth (Bess), 14, 30, 54, 112
Truman, Harry S., 7, 11–14, 30, 54–55, 76, 80, 84, 94, 96, 112, 124–25, 135–36, 148–49, 151, 158–59, 172, 180–81, 185, 195, 198, 203–4, 207, 221, 228–29, 238–39, 261, 271, 308, 311

Trump, Donald, 211–12, 229, 308
Twain, Mark, 205
Tyler, John, 66, 98–99, 105, 120, 307

Unitarians, 7, 21–22, 273, 276–78, 288, 307–8
United Nations, 56, 174, 204
University of Virginia, 301
U.S. Bill of Rights, 55, 146, 157–58, 239, 250
U.S. Civil War, xi, xiv, 1, 26–27, 39–40, 46–50, 73–74, 86, 90, 93, 95–96, 106–9, 115, 122–23, 132–33, 146–47, 153, 168, 171, 179, 196–98, 201–2, 226, 254, 260, 264, 302–3
U.S. Constitution, xiv–xvi, 42, 51, 55, 72, 90, 146, 157–58, 164, 170, 173, 175, 183, 189–95, 236–37, 250, 290–92, 294, 298, 303–4
U.S. Constitutional Convention, 21, 191–92, 194–95, 291, 300

Valley Forge, Pennsylvania, 102, 137
Van Buren, Martin, 65, 189, 192, 294, 307
Vietnam War, 126, 138

War of 1812, xiv, 90, 103–4, 146, 156, 195–96, 226, 281
Washington, Booker T., 171
Washington, D.C., 9, 20, 22, 24–31, 33, 35, 54, 71, 77, 105, 118, 138–140, 173, 200, 218, 236
Washington, George, xv, 21, 41–42, 64–65, 83–84, 90, 92, 97, 102–3, 109–110, 115, 117–19, 130, 134, 137, 146, 169, 177–78, 182, 186–89, 194, 215, 229–30, 247, 254, 279–80, 292–93, 307, 309
Washington, Martha, 6

Watergate scandal, 57, 228, 311
Weld, Theodore, 40
Wesley, John, 35
Whig Party, 97–98, 120
Whigs, British, 37, 153, 155
White House, 10, 20, 28, 30, 32, 69, 76, 112, 114, 132, 134, 139–41, 143–44, 173, 215
Whitefield, George, 36–37
Wilberforce, William, 167
Wilson, Edith, 86–87, 110
Wilson, Ellen, 12, 75, 110, 123, 254
Wilson, Joseph, 12, 28
Wilson, Woodrow, 3, 12, 28–29, 52–53, 68, 75–76, 80, 86–88, 91, 96, 110–12, 115, 123, 134, 148, 156, 175–76, 179, 184, 196–97, 203, 218, 235, 254, 260–61, 271, 283, 303, 308, 310
Winthrop, John, 38, 178, 181
Witherspoon, John, 4, 38, 298–99
women's rights, 39–40, 163, 166, 174–75
World War I, xiv, 28, 54, 62, 68, 74–75, 88, 110–12, 123, 148, 194, 196–97, 220, 261
World War II, xiv, 15, 112–13, 124–25, 134–35, 138, 148, 151, 153, 172, 180, 185, 198, 203, 205–6, 237–39, 255
Wright, Jeremiah, 34, 211–12

Yale University, 3, 276
Yom Kippur War, 207
Young Man's Christian Association (YMCA), 33, 74, 233–34
Young Woman's Christian Association (YWCA), 74

Zechariah, Book of, 114, 238
Zedekiah, 97